Nicknames of Places

# Nicknames
# of Places

*Origins and Meanings of the
Alternate and Secondary Names,
Sobriquets, Titles, Epithets and Slogans
for 4600 Places Worldwide*

### ADRIAN ROOM

McFarland & Company, Inc., Publishers
*Jefferson, North Carolina, and London*

LIBRARY OF CONGRESS CATALOGUING-IN-PUBLICATION DATA

Room, Adrian.
Nicknames of places : origins and meanings of
the alternate and secondary names, sobriquets, titles, epithets
and slogans for 4600 places worldwide /
Adrian Room.
p.     cm.
Includes bibliographical references and index.

**ISBN-13: 978-0-7864-2497-9**
**ISBN-10: 0-7864-2497-4**
(illustrated case binding : 50# alkaline paper) ∞

1. Names, Geographical.   I. Title.
G105.R65   2006        910.3 — dc22        2006018559

British Library cataloguing data are available

Cover images ©2006 PhotoSpin

Manufactured in the United States of America

*McFarland & Company, Inc., Publishers*
*Box 611, Jefferson, North Carolina 28640*
*www.mcfarlandpub.com*

For Lydia
Whose artistic postcards regularly lightened my daily labors
With love and thanks

# Table of Contents

Some names have a large retinue of sobriquets; Rome, e.g., may be the Eternal City, the City of the Seven Hills, the Papal City, the Scarlet Woman, the Scarlet Whore, the Empress of the Ancient World, the Western Babylon; [cricketer] Mr Warner may be Plum, or P.F., or the Middlesex Captain, or the Recoverer of the Ashes; & neither's list of sobriquets is half told.— H.W. Fowler, *A Dictionary of Modern English Usage*, 1926

# Introduction

Many places in the world, from the smallest settlement to the largest expanse of land or water, have a nickname or an alternative or secondary name. This new dictionary is devoted to about 4,600 such names.

What is a secondary placename? For the purposes of this book, it is a name, nickname, title, or slogan by which a place is known in addition to its formal or usual name. Such a name is rarely if ever found on maps or in gazetteers, although it features widely in travel guides, journalistic articles, and literature of all kinds, especially when used appositively in order to avoid repetition. (A biographer might thus write: "She had never been to New York and eagerly awaited her first sight of the Big Apple.") It can even occur in the franking of mail, as frequently found on letters from France. A Christmas card from Villard-de-Lans received in 2005 was franked "tout vert ou tout blanc" ("all green or all white") by way of promoting the little town as both a summer and a winter sports station.

The *Big Apple*, just mentioned, is a widely known secondary name, *New York City* being the primary name. This particular city is also known by a number of other secondary names, such as *Baghdad on the Hudson*, *City of Ambition*, *Empire City*, *Gateway of the USA*, *Gotham*, *Noo Yawk*, and simply *NYC*. These give a good representative sampling of the different types of secondary names that exist.

Let us look at these categories in a little more detail.

Secondary names fall into two distinct groups: those based on a past or present primary name, and those differing completely from the primary name, often as a descriptive phrase. (Most United States names are of the latter type. See the headnote to the Bibliography, p. 331, for comments on one work devoted exclusively to them.)

In the former group, a secondary name may be a simple abbreviation of the primary name. This can be formed either as an initialism (*LA* for Los Angeles, *SF* for San Francisco) or as a contraction (*Alex* for Alexandria, *Chi* for Chicago, *Nam* for Vietnam). Some abbreviations are not quite so straightforward, and are formed either from letters in the primary name (*Frisco* for San Francisco) or from its spoken form (*Soo* for Sault Sainte Marie, *Jax* for Jacksonville). A name consisting of more than one word may be reduced to just one of them, whether English or in some other language, such as *Addis* for Addis Abeba, *Alice* for Alice Springs, *Orleans* for New Orleans.

Abbreviations of English county names, such as *Hants* for Hampshire, also belong here. These are generally regarded as formal when written, as in a postal address, but colloquial when spoken. Hence the regular definition "semiofficial" in the entries for such names. (See also Appendix 6, p. 325.)

Some abbreviations are formed with a distinctive suffix, such as the Australian "-o" in *Darlo* for Darlington or *Flemo* for Flemington, while the English Oxford "-er," often with an appended "-s," is found in

*Honkers* for Hong Kong and *Singers* for Singapore.

A secondary name can also exist as a revival (or the continued use) of a former name. Old names of places often die hard, and linger in the mind. There is thus a natural reluctance to replace an old familiar name with a new and unfamiliar one, and the historic name can remain in everyday use, as China's *Canton* for Guangzhou or Vietnam's *Saigon* for Ho Chi Minh City. The Iran of today was long familiar as *Persia*, and Sri Lanka is better known to older generations as *Ceylon*. In similar fashion, *Constantinople* is a city name recognized by most, even by those who do not relate it to modern Istanbul. A special subcategory here is the Roman name, often resurrected for commercial or touristic use, as *Deva* for England's Chester or *Eblana* for Ireland's Dublin. (For a list of such names, see Appendix 5, p. 321.)

Many classical names of this kind become familiar from literature, especially poetry, and are similarly found in revived usage, as *Caledonia* for Scotland, *Cambria* for Wales, or *Lusitania* for Portugal. Old literary names such as *Afric* for Africa and *Ind* for India are found in verse as recently as the 19th century, and country names ending in -y (as *Araby* for Arabia) in fact follow the development of regular names such as Italy (from *Italia*), Sicily (from *Sicilia*), and Germany (from *Germania*).

Some places acquire a form of secondary name by way of a meaningful alteration of the original, in many cases punningly. The motive for such a creation may be promotional or commercial, as *Amazingstoke* for Basingstoke, *Hot Lanta* for Atlanta, or simply to make sense of a non–English name, as the British soldier's names for battle locations in World War I, as *Agony* for Agny in France, *Cherry Ripe* for Centuripe in Italy. The classic example of such a name is *Wipers* for Ypres (Ieper) in Belgium, representing not only a rationalized pronunciation of the written form but also a subconscious suggestion of a town (or force of men) at risk of being wiped out.

Many places have a standard adjective added to their regular name, so that they are fixed in a stock description. The placename itself is the current one, but the accompanying epithet gives the overall name a secondary status. Examples are *Auld Ayr* for the Scottish town, *Colorful Colorado* for the U.S. state, and *Glorious Devon* for the English county. *Australia Fair* and *America the Beautiful* also belong here. *Colorful Colorado* is just one of several alliterative names of this type. Others include *Beautiful Barmouth*, *Drukken Dunblane*, *Fashionable Frinton*, *Glorious Goodwood*, *Marvellous Melbourne*, *Proud Preston*, *Silly Suffolk* and *Wild Wales*.

Names differing completely from the primary name are more common than those formed from the present or past name. They typically form a descriptive phrase, which may itself be formally adopted by the place in question as a promotional slogan. Familiar examples of names of this type are those of U.S. states, such as the *Apache State* for Arizona, *Artesian State* for South Dakota, *Flickertail State* for North Dakota, *Keystone State* for Pennsylvania, and *Maple Sugar State* for Vermont. Such names are often displayed on automobile license plates, or on road signs at a state border. Cities can also have descriptive names, such as *Windy City* for Chicago, while elsewhere in the world one has *Diamond City* for Amsterdam, *Marmalade Country* for Scotland, and *Quaky Isles* for New Zealand.

The *Apache State* is named for the Apache Indians who live there. A similar type of secondary name is based on the nickname for a country's inhabitants, adding a generic word or element such as -*land*. Thus England is *Limeyland* or *Pommyland*, France is *Frogland*, Germany is *Bocheland*, *Hunland*, or *Krautland*, Ireland is *Paddyland* or *Patland*, New Zealand is *Kiwiland*, Russia is *Russkiland*, Wales is

*Taffyland*, and the United States of America is *Yankeeland*. A less common suffix is *-dom* or *-shire*, as *Yankeedom* for the U.S.A. or *Bimshire* for Barbados. A name of this kind may also be used for a smaller region. The English county of Yorkshire is thus *Tykedom*, while London and Liverpool are respectively *Cockneyshire* and *Scouseland*.

Several cities around the world have gained the sacred status of a *Holy City*, the religion itself varying. Familiar examples are Adelaide, Australia, as a Christian city, Allahabad, India, as a Hindu city, Mecca and Medina, Saudi Arabia, as holy cities of Islam, and Jerusalem, Israel, sacred to Christians, Jews, and Muslims.

Some cities gained a distinctive type of descriptive name incorporating the Greek element "-opolis" (from *polis*, "city"). The first part of such a name usually indicates the commodity for which the city is noted, as *Cottonopolis* for Manchester, England, *Coalopolis* for Newcastle, Australia, *Juteopolis* for Dundee, Scotland, *Linenopolis* for Belfast, Northern Ireland, and *Porkopolis* for both Chicago and Cincinnati. But some names of this type are more playful, so that Kansas City, Missouri, became known as *Mushroomopolis* not for its marketing of the edible fungus but for its rapid growth, while Beverly Hills was dubbed *Poshopolis* for its supposed superior social status.

A good number of such names are more elaborate, and do not always include the generic term (state, city) for the named place. Examples are *Arsenal of Democracy* for the United States, *Cradle of Liberty* for Boston, *Dark and Bloody Ground* for Kentucky, and *Northern Bear* for Russia. More frequently, however, names of this type include the generic term, *Capital*, *City*, and *Land* being especially common, as *Capital of Smoke* for Osaka, Japan, *City of Dreaming Spires* for Oxford, England, and *Land of the Free* for the United States. The generic term is sometimes less formal, as *Home of Mother Nature* for Ireland.

In several instances the generic term is semimetaphorical, as *Garden* for a place that is either naturally beautiful or agriculturally productive (or both) and *Gateway* for a place that occupies a key location (but usually not an actual gate) on a route to a larger area. Examples here are *Garden of the Sun* for Indonesia and *Gateway to the North* for Edmonton, Canada. Fully metaphorical are the many names with *Mother*, denoting a historical precedent or superior status. Names of this type include *Mother of Presidents* for Virginia and *Mother of Books* for Alexandria, Egypt. Similar to these are the many names crowning a place as *Queen*, such as *Queen of the Mountains* for Knoxville, Tennessee, and *Queen of Watering Places* for the English seaside resorts of Brighton, Eastbourne, Scarborough, and Torquay. Other common metaphorical denotators are *Gem*, as *Gem of the Mountains* for Idaho, *Jewel*, as *Jewel in the Crown* for India in its colonial days, and *Pearl*, as *Pearl of the Desert* for Timbuktu (Tombouctou) in Mali.

A descriptive of this kind, whether literal or metaphorical, may single out a place for a particular attribute. Thus Holguín is the *Granary of Castile*, Beauce is the *Granary of France*, Jalisco is the *Granary of Mexico*, and Andalusia is the *Granary of Spain*. All of these places are so named for their agricultural produce, here specifically their grain.

As a corollary, a large number of titles describe one place in terms of another, naming the designated place either with its national epithet, as *American Mediterranean* for the Caribbean Sea, or *English Naples* for Bournemouth, or with a possessive ("of") phrase stating its particular region, such as a country, continent, or quarter of the compass. Thus North Palmerston, New Zealand, is the *Chicago of New Zealand*, Baku, Azerbaijan, is the *Chicago of the Caspian*, Harbin, China, is the *Chicago of the East*, and Anchorage, Alaska, is the

*Chicago of the North*. If a place is seen as a smaller or miniature version of another place, it will often be described as *Little*. Miami, Florida, is thus *Little Cuba*, Barbados, in the West Indies, is *Little England*, Bucharest, capital of Romania, is *Little Paris*, and Liverpool, England, is *Little Rome*. (There are *Big* descriptive names, but almost always with a generic word. New York is thus not only the *Big Apple* but also the *Big Lady*, *Big Onion*, *Big Smear*, and *Big Town*.)

A particularly desirable comparison was (and in some cases still is) with *Paris*, the French capital, a city regarded as a paradigm of sophistication and panache. The present dictionary includes at least 20 such equations, from Annapolis as the *Paris of America* to Havana as the *Paris of the Western Hemisphere*.

In a few instances, a place may be referred to by its official title or generic status. Thus, in Britain, Wales is known as the *Principality*, and Lancashire as the *County Palatine*. Luxembourg, sinilarly, is the *Grand Duchy*. At a more local level, St. Louis County, Missouri, is known as the *County* for distinction from St. Louis, the *City*, while in England the *City* is invariably understood to mean London, as is *Town* (without "the").

London itself is divided into postal districts designated by a combination of one or more letters and numbers, and these designations are often used as a secondary name for the district itself. Thus *SW19* is Wimbledon, home of the lawn tennis championships, and *W2* denotes Paddington. Such names serve as shorthand in media reports. These codes are so well known that cryptic crossword setters use them as part of their vocabulary. "City" in a clue thus represents the letters EC, from the postal district *EC2* (east central 2), while "Westminster" denotes the three letters SWI, from the postal district *SW1* (southwest 1, with the figure 1 doubling as the letter I).

All of the secondary names in this dictionary were taken from printed or written sources, these being mainly either the titles listed in the Bibliography, p. 331, especially the reference works, or from literary texts such as novels and poems, touristic material such as travel ads and holiday brochures, and contemporary press reports. Some names can be traced to a specific originator. Thus Winston Churchill is said to have first described Uganda as the *Pearl of Africa*, and radio personality Gerry Anderson designated Belfast as *Stroke City*. Touristic literature is apt to be hyperbolic: visit our wonderful country, our beautiful city, our special county, with its memorable attractions, its unique history, its unforgettable sights! But in among all the overblown descriptions there are the less flattering descriptive names, given by disenchanted visitors or residents. The Persian Gulf was the *Arsehole of the World* to members of the British Royal Air Force posted there, and Daniel Webster hardly thought any higher of the District of Columbia, which for him was the *Great Dismal*. Las Vegas may be *America's Playground* to those in search of fast bucks, while others, speaking from rueful experience, regard it (punningly) as a land of *Lost Wages*.

Not all secondary names are still current, of course, and many are now disused or half-forgotten. But they are true enough to their type, and so find their place in this dictionary.

## Arrangement of the Dictionary

The dictionary entries to follow run alphabetically and comprise the following elements: (1) the secondary name or nickname; (2) the real name and its location by (present) country or geographical region; (3) an explanation of the secondary name. In many cases there then follow one or more quotations containing the secondary name, or a relevant reference to it.

A word about each of these components.

(1) Occasionally, the secondary name may have an alternate form or spelling, as **Glesca** or **Glesga** or **Glesgae** or **Glesgie** for Glasgow. In cases of more radical alternate forms, the first part of the name is not usually repeated. Thus "**Gibraltar of England** or **Wessex, the**" for the Isle of Portland means that the peninsula is known as both **the Gibraltar of England** and **the Gibraltar of Wessex**. In names of this type, the definite article ("the") follows the secondary name. In general, where the definite article is omitted, it is not normally used, as **Jeff City** (not "the Jeff City") for Jefferson City. (The definite article is not included in cross-references. The entry itself will of course indicate its presence or absence.) Alternate spellings, where noticeably different from the entered name, are usually cross-referenced to the relevant entry, as **Kasey** *see* **Casey**. The alternate forms for Glasgow cited above, however, are close enough to the main entry to be subsumed under it.

(2) The real name is given in its normally accepted form, and its location is the current one, even for historic secondary names. Thus Dubrovnik, Croatia, was known as the **South Slav Athens** in the days when it was the city-republic of Ragusa, but it is identified under its present name and present country. However, where a secondary name refers to the Soviet Union, rather than earlier or later Russia, it is identified as such. Moscow was known as the **Red Capital** in the Soviet period, and not before or after it. The real name is given as normally spelled or accepted in the English-speaking world, but with due observance of non-English requisites, as accents. British places named for saints usually omit the period, as St Albans and St Helens (not "St. Albans" or "St. Helens"), while elsewhere the period is the norm, as St.-Étienne in France, St. Louis in the U.S.A., and St. Petersburg in Russia.

In the United States and Canada, in order to avoid ambiguity, towns and cities, as well as certain other geographical entities, are identified by state, province, or territory, in addition to country. It is thus Allentown, Pennsylvania, that is known as **Mack City**, not Allentown, New Jersey, and Durham, North Carolina, that gained fame as **Tobacco City**, not Durham, New Hampshire. An exception is made in the case of New York City, which is not further identified as being in New York State but is simply located in the USA. (Note that where a name is that of a place in the United States, its country of location is given as the "USA," but where the name is actually used for the United States itself, the country is identified as such, not as the USA.) Where a political region is not given in this part of the entry, it will normally follow in the description, especially for English-speaking countries such as Britain, South Africa, and Australia. The description will also state the nature of the place. Thus the **Scarlet Town**, identified as Reading, England, is described as a Berkshire town, while Thursday Island, Australia, nicknamed **Thirsty Island**, is located in Queensland.

Places in the UK are located in the appropriate country (England, Scotland, Wales, or Northern Ireland), without the added general location of Britain for the first three of these. (Northern Ireland is politically not in Great Britain but the United Kingdom.)

Where a secondary name has been given to more than one place, these are given in alphabetical order. Thus both Bangkok, Thailand, and Los Angeles, USA, are known as the **City of Angels** and are named in this order, even though many will first associate the name with the American city. The description that follows usually (but not always) deals with the places in this order. The identity of a city district will normally name the city in question, so that Twickenham, nicknamed **Twickers**, is identified as being in London, England, and **Paddo** is Paddington, a district of Sydney, Australia. For ease of identification, cities that have recently adopted a local form of their name are given their former name in brackets, so that the **City of Dreadful Night** is identified as Kolkata (Calcutta), India.

(3) The description and explanation of the secondary name is generally straightforward, and may contain a cross-reference to a related name of the particular place, or to another place of identical or similar nickname. Thus **Paddy's Milestone**, as a name for the island of Ailsa Craig, between Scotland and Ireland, refers to **Paddyland** as a nickname of Ireland, and Harlem, New York City, as the **Rotten Apple**, is cross-referred to the **Big Apple** that is New York itself. Secondary names that are no longer current are stated to be as much by the wording of the text, as for Lyon, France, formerly known as the **Manchester of France**.

(4) The quotations below a name's description are often not simply illustrative but explanatory, and the main part of the entry will indicate this. An example is the quote for Shanghai, China, as the **Model Settlement**, or for Geelong, Australia, as the **Pivot City**. The quotes are thus not simply isolated usages but form an integral part of the entry as a whole. In some cases, a reference or allusion in a quotation is explained in the main text, as a sign of this. See, for example, the gloss on "total on*snort*" in the quote for **Snor City** as a nickname of Tshwane (Pretoria), South Africa. Some quotes are longer than others, notably where they contain important information regarding the origin of a secondary name. Thus the quotes for **Treeplanter State** and **Wonder State** cite the protocols assigning these titles to Nebraska and Arkansas respectively.

The quotations themselves, incorporated as a special feature of this dictionary, are supplied with their sources and dates. A quote from any of the titles listed in the Bibliography, identified by author only, will not normally give a date but will include a page number. Those from *The Times* are from the London paper, dated with day, month, and year. Quotations from the Bible, which are undated, are from the King James (Authorized) Version of 1611, while those from Shakespeare, for sake of consistency, are from the Oxford Standard Authors edition of 1905, edited by W.J. Craig. Quotations from one or other of the works by Hadfield are dated for purposes of distinction as Hadfield 1980 or Hadfield 1981, as are those by Wagner as Wagner 1892 or Wagner 1893. Where there is more than one quote, they run in chronological order, although the date of the quote may not be contemporary with that of the name, and a recently dated one may well refer to a former usage. This most obviously applies in a source of historic texts, such as the 1910 *Oxford Book of Ballads*, where some of the material comes from medieval writings. The progression of the seven quotations for **Merry England** shows how the meaning has changed over the years, while other successive citations, as for **Sin City**, show how a name gradually breaks out of its cautious caging in quotation marks to gain full independent assimilation. In a few cases, a quote is in a foreign language, as for **City of Light** (French) and **Mainhattan** (German), but it is then translated. Quotations from online (internet) sources are supplied with the site address and date of accession, i.e., the date when the text was actually read and transcribed.

Additions in square brackets are used in the quotations to give clarification where helpful, either in the form of extra words or as a gloss following the abbreviation "i.e." Thus "he" in the quote for the **Palmyra of the North** is identified as Peter the Great, and *Angela's Ashes* in the first quote for **Stab City** is identified as the title of a novel by Frank McCourt.

## The Appendices

This dictionary has seven appendices, relevant in their different way to the main subject. Each appendix has its own preamble, but it may help to indicate here that they are respectively devoted to: (1) nicknames of regions; (2) nicknames of roads and streets; (3) Romany names of places, as listed by George Borrow; (4) names of recently renamed countries (with former names often still in use as secondary names); (5) names of Roman cities in Europe (potentially revivable for modern use); (6) names of English counties with regard to their short forms; and (7) informal names of astronomical objects. All of the entries in Appendix 1 are cross-referenced in the main part of the dictionary, as it may be there that readers will first look for a particular name (e.g., **Alphabet City** or **Cocktail Isles**).

A bibliography then follows and finally an index with its own introduction to all of the entries in the main body of the dictionary.

Many readers will know of names that have not found a place in the book. But there are more than enough in this worldwide garnering, an unusual blend of information and entertainment, to give a valuable insight into a popular and important aspect of naming.

Adrian Room
July 2006

# The Dictionary

**Abbevillage** see in Appendix 1, p. 269.

**Aber** *Aberystwyth, Wales*. A handy shortening of the name of the university town and seaside resort, and one found for other places in Wales with names beginning Aber- ("river mouth"), as in quote (3) below. Quote (4) is a student-oriented American take on the old English equation in quote (1).

(1) The visitor expecting a "Welsh Brighton" (as the old guide-books styled it) may perhaps be disappointed; but anyone who has lived or studied at "Aber" comes away with a lasting affection for the place [Ruth Thomas, *South Wales*, 1977].

(2) The west coast town of Aberystwyth, 'Aber' to older generations who have memories of it as a popular resort [John Julius Norwich, ed., *Treasures of Britain*, 2002].

(3) Abergwyngregyn. Otherwise simply known as 'Aber' [Travel brochure *Snowdonia*, 2005].

(4) Aberystwyth is a compact and attractive seaside town, described as the "Welsh California" in the student-produced Alternative Prospectus [*The Times* (Student Guide Supplement), August 18, 2005].

**Aberbrothock** *Arbroath, Scotland*. The town's present name is a worn-down form of the fuller spelling, preserved in Southey's lines quoted below.

And then they knew the perilous rock,
And blessed the Abbot of Aberbrothock [Robert Southey, "The Inchcape Rock," 1802].

**Aberdeen of Ireland, the** *Ballymena, Northern Ireland*. The county town of Antrim derives its nickname from its supposed reputation for parsimony, referring to the alleged closefistedness of the Scots.

**Abode of the Little Tin Gods, the** *Shimla (Simla), India*. The former summer capital of British India was so dubbed by Rudyard Kipling, who is said to have coined the term "little tin god" to describe a petty autocrat or self-important person.

This is Shimla, the Indian hill station known to the Raj as Simla. The British may have gone, but Shimla's old-timers still harbour nostalgia for the days of "The Abode of the Little Tin Gods," as Rudyard Kipling called the summer home of the colonial government [*The Times*, April 9, 2005].

**About Turn** *Hébuterne, France*. A British soldiers' World War I army-inspired version of the name of the village near Arras.

**Abrahampstead** *Hampstead, London, England*. A punning elaboration of the name of the fashionable district, where a number of Jewish families reside.

**Abyla** *Jebel Musa, Ceuta, Morocco*. The original Greek name of the mountain has remained in latinized form for poetic use. Together with **Calpe** it formed the **Pillars of Hercules**.

**Abyss** see in Appendix 1, p. 269.

**Abyssinia** *Ethiopia*. A once familiar name for the African country, in use until at least the end of World War II, when the present name began to take over. Purists have objected to the equation, pointing out that in classical writings the name Ethiopia referred to the region of Africa extending south from Egypt as far as Zanzibar.

(1) Abyssinia is not mentioned in some books, but Ethiopia is. The two names stand for the same country [Johnson, p. 12].

(2) There are some who would insist that we call it Ethiopia. But Ethiopia is the name of a country known to the ancient world, and it did not lie within the same limits as modern Abyssinia [Aurousseau, p. 6].

**Acadia** *Nova Scotia, Canada*. The classical-style name, with its suggestion of "Arcadia" (*see* **Arcady**), was in use for the former French territory from the late 16th century, and is still on the map for Acadia National Park on the Maine coast, USA, established in 1919 (originally as Lafayette National Park but renamed in 1929).

List to a Tale of Love in Acadie, home of the happy [H.W. Longfellow, *Evangeline*, 1847].

**ACT, the** *Australian Capital Territory, Australia*. The common abbreviation denotes the territory that consists of two enclaves, the first around the capital city of Canberra, the second at Jervis Bay. Unless otherwise qualified, the first is usually implied, and often serves as a synonym for the capital itself.

(1) [I] asked her where she was from. 'ACT.' Seeing my mind whirring to little effect, she added:

'Australian Capital Territory. Canberra' [Bill Bryson, *Down Under*, 2000].

(2) On clear days, the panoramic view of Canberra and the ACT from the ... viewing platform ... is magnificent [*The Rough Guide to Australia*, 2001].

**Addis** *Addis Abeba, Ethiopia.* A colloquial abridgement of the capital city's name. (The name itself means "new flower," so to use the first word alone is to say simply "new.")

**Adria** *Adriatic Sea.* A poetic form of the sea's name, itself used by the Romans. For the reference in quote (1), *see* **Hesperia.**

(1) Fled over Adria to th' Hesperian fields [John Milton, *Paradise Lost*, 1667].

(2) Long quiet she reign'd; till thitherward steers A flight of bold eagles from Adria's strand [Robert Burns, "Caledonia," 1791].

(3) And the white sheep are free to come and go Where Adria's purple waters used to flow [Oscar Wilde, "Ravenna," 1878].

**Adrian Bell Country** see in Appendix 1, p. 269.

**Adrianople** *Edirne, Turkey.* A long familiar name for the Turkish city, whose present name evolved from it and was officially adopted by the Turks in 1922. The original classical form was *Adrianopolis*, "city of Hadrian," after the Roman emperor.

Adrianople. A town in north-west Turkey in Europe, sometimes called Edirneh [*sic*] [Johnson, p. 14].

**Adventure Capital of the World, the** *Queenstown, New Zealand.* The South Island town, on the shore of Lake Wakatipu, is a leading international resort and world center for adventure sports such as bungee jumping and skydiving. Hence its nickname.

(1) Disembarking in Milford Sound, there will be a two night stay in Queenstown, the 'adventure capital' [Travel ad, *The Times Magazine*, November 12, 2005].

(2) Queenstown, world capital of adrenaline adventure [*Sunday Times*, November 27, 2005].

**Afric** or **Africk** *Africa.* A regular poetic shortening of the continent's name.

(1) Methinks, our garments are now as fresh as when we put them on first in Afric [William Shakespeare, *The Tempest*, 1611].

(2) Thy eyes are seen in di'monds bright, Thy breath is Africk's spicy gale [John Gay, "Sweet William's Farewell to Black-Eyed Susan," 1720].

(3) So geographers, in Afric-maps, With savage-pictures fill their gaps [Jonathan Swift, "On Poetry," 1733].

(3) From Greenland's icy mountains, From India's coral strand, Where Afric's sunny fountains Roll down their golden sand [Bishop Reginald Heber, hymn, 1819].

(4) And sword in hand upon Afric's passes Her last republic cried to God [G.K. Chesterton, "A Song of Defeat," 1915].

**Africa in Exile** *Salvador da Bahia, Brazil.* The city's black population dates from the 16th century, when African slaves were imported to work in the sugar plantations. Hence the name.

The population is mostly black, earning Bahia the soubriquet, "Africa in Exile" [Dodd/Donald, p. 82].

**Africa's Last Great Wilderness** *Kaokoland, Namibia.* A touristic nickname designed to attract visitors to this isolated northwest corner of Namibia.

**Africk** *see* **Afric**

**Agincourt** *Achicourt, France.* A British soldiers' World War I substitution of a familiar French name for an unfamiliar one. Achicourt is a village just south of Arras.

**Agnes** *St Agnes, Scilly Isles, England.* A local name for an island community whose formal name wrongly implies a saintly connection, probably by association with the Cornish village of the same name.

Where the 'saint' in front of the name came from is anybody's guess; the islanders don't use the prefix when speaking of the island [Booth/Perrott, p. 150].

**Agony** *Agny, France.* A British soldiers' World War I poignant perversion of the name of the village near Arras.

**Aix-la-Chapelle** *Aachen, Germany.* The name of the German town is sometimes found in its French form, partly because of the city's location near the Belgian border, but more probably because of the better-known French name, familiar from Aix-en-Provence in the southeast of France and Aix-les-Bains in the east. Browning's classic poem "How They Brought the Good News From Ghent to Aix" (1845), although not based on any historical event, relates to the German town and further popularized the name.

**Akemanchester** *Bath, England.* A pseudohistorical name for the city, supposedly meaning "sick man's town" (literally "ache man's town"), referring to the famous Roman baths and thermal springs, visited by rheumatic sufferers. The Roman road from Bath to St Albans is known as Akeman Street. The true origin of the name is uncertain, but it may relate to Latin *aquae*, "waters," from the Roman name of Bath, *Aquae Sulis*, "waters of Sulis."

**Alabamy** or **Alabam'** *Alabama, USA.* A homely colloquial name for the southern state. *Cp.* **Bama.**

(1) "Down in Alabam'" [Bryant's Minstrels, song title, 1860s].

(2) "When the Midnight Choo Choo Leaves for Alabam'" [Irving Berlin, song title, 1912].

(3) "Alabamy Bound" [Ray Henderson, Bud Green and B.G. "Buddy" De Sylva, song title, 1925].

**Alamo City** *San Antonio, Texas, USA.* A name deriving from the city's historic fort, a symbol of heroic resistance following the siege of the Alamo in 1836, when a group of Texan warriors fought for the independence of their land from Mexico.

**Alba** *see* **Albion**

**Albania** *see* **Albion**

**Albany** *see* **Albion**

**Albertopolis** see in Appendix 1, p. 269.

**Albin** *see* **Albion**

**Albion** *(1) England or Britain; (2) Scotland.* The oldest name of Britain, used poetically for England and historically also for Scotland, is traditionally derived from Latin *albus*, "white," referring to the white cliffs of Dover, the first natural feature seen on the English coast as one crosses the English Channel by the shortest route from France. But the name is almost certainly Celtic, and related to *Alba*, the Gaelic name of Scotland. In the form Alban or Albania it is that of the ancient kingdom of the Picts and Scots, the historical source of present Scotland. The name has also been personified. According to the Welsh chronicler Geoffrey of Monmouth, writing in the 12th century, Albion was a giant who ruled on the island of Britain, while Raphael Holinshed, in *The Chronicles of England, Scotland, and Ireland* (1577), has Albina as a princess who arrives on the island with a band of 50 women banned for killing their husbands. Another form of the name, Albany, is familiar as an English aristocratic title held by members of the Scottish Stewart family. (The first duke of Albany was Robert Stewart, defeated by the English in 1402 in his plot to gain the Scottish throne.) The name is now generally held to mean "the land," "the world," a term used by Britain's early inhabitants for their own country, from a word related to Welsh *elfydd*, "world." The quotes below show the name in its various forms, with quote (1) deriving the name of Scotland from a mythical Albanact. (For other names in this quote, *see* **Loegria** for England and **Cambria** for Wales.) *See also* **Perfidious Albion**. In modern journalistic parlance, the name is fairly frequently used of England (Britain) by its European neighbors, and especially by France, its nearest neighbor, as in quote (12). Quote (3) has two forms of the name: Albion denoting Britain, with its three kingdoms of England, Wales, and Scotland, and Albany as the title of Lady Charlotte Stewart, duchess of Albany (1753–1789), the (originally illegitimate) daughter of Prince Charles Edward Stewart (the "Young Pretender" or "Bonnie Prince Charlie"). She was killed in a riding accident.

(1) *Locrine* was left the soueraine Lord of all;
But *Albanact* had all the Northrene part,
Which of [i.e. after] himself *Albania* he did call;
And *Camber* did possesse the Westerne quart,
Which *Seuerne* now from *Logris* doth depart [Edmund Spenser, *The Faerie Queene*, 1590].

(2) When usurers tell their gold i' the field;
And bawds and whores do churches build;
Then shall the realm of Albion
Come to great confusion [William Shakespeare, *King Lear*, 1608].

(3) This lovely maid's of royal blood
That rulèd Albion's kingdoms three,
But oh, alas! for her bonnie face,
They hae wrang'd the Lass of Albany [Robert Burns, "The Bonnie Lass of Albany," 1787].

(4) But woe to his kindred and woe to his cause, When Albin her claymore indignantly draws [Thomas Campbell, "Lochiel's Warning," 1802].

(5) All things begin and end in Albion's ancient Druid rocky shore [William Blake, *Jerusalem*, 1804].

(6) Don Juan now saw Albion's earliest beauties, Thy cliffs, *dear* Dover! harbour, and hotel [Lord Byron, *Don Juan*, 1823].

(7) The pure Culdees
Were Albyn's earliest priests of God,
Ere yet an island of her seas
By foot of Saxon monk was trod [Thomas Campbell, "Reullura," 1824].

(8) It's wonderful to come to England as a tourist ... I could write a sketch or even a series of sketches — real ones drawn from life with a good title: "On the Greenwich Meridian," or "British Changes," or, a bit more romantically and generally, "Foggy Albion Without the Fog" [Larisa Vasilieva, *Albion and the Secret of Time*, 1978].

(9) Dover and Folkestone cliffs, whose white bastions at the gateway into England gave us our name of Albion [Richard Church in Hadfield 1981, p. 132].

(10) The island of Albion, inhabited only by giants until Brutus renamed it Britain, is a storied land, but it is a fragile inheritance [Jennifer Westwood, *Albion*, 1986].

(11) Albion was the name of the primaeval giant who made his home upon the island of Britain ... His traces can be seen in the huge white horses which populated the primitive landscape, inscribed in the chalk of the hills. Today, like those fading memorials, Albion is not so much a name as the echo of a name [Peter Ackroyd, *Albion*, 2002].

(12) [The French magazine] *Le Point* ... proclaimed Britain the current winner of the historic duel between the rival neighbours. "Albion, for the moment, is causing us envy rather than pity," it said [*The Times*, May 18, 2005].

(13) The Russians still refer to "Foggy Albion" [*The Times*, November 23, 2005].

**Albyn** *see* **Albion**

**Alex** *Alexandria, Egypt.* A colloquial shortening and personalization of the name of the Egyptian city and port, itself named for Alexander the Great, king of Macedonia, who founded it in the 4th century AD.

(1) *Ice Cold in Alex* [Film title, 1958 (US title *Desert Attack*)].
(2) Today you must look at Alex out of the desert, and allow for a lot of noise [James Morris, *Places*, 1972].
(3) The [new] library is a symbol ... of Alexandria's determination to turn its past into the future, and to gainsay that school of nostalgists who would hold that the best of Alex is long gone [Dodd/Donald, p. 362].

**Alexandretta** *Iskenderun, Turkey.* A formerly familiar Italian name for the seaport city, which was at one time also known as *Scanderoon*, an English corruption of the Turkish original.

SCANDEROON, a port-town of Aleppo, in Asiatick Turky, situated on the coast of the Lesser Asia [*Encyclopædia Britannica*, 1771].

**Alice** or **the Alice** *Alice Springs, Australia.* A straight personalization of the name of the Northern Territory town, that of Lady Alice Todd, wife of Sir Charles Heavitree Todd (1826–1910), postmaster general of South Australia. (The town was founded as Stuart.) The prefixing of a placename (or its short or colloquial form) with "the" is an Australian peculiarity, as illustrated in quote (3) below.

(1) It's railhead, of course, for trucking cattle down to Adelaide — that's one thing. But it's a go-ahead place is Alice; all sorts of things go on there [Nevil Shute, *A Town Like Alice*, 1950].
(2) 'The Alice' is sometimes called 'the capital of the Centre' [A.W. Reed, *Place Names of Australia*, 1973].
(3) My friend said, 'At least you're not short of definite articles.' I knew what he meant. The Isa. The 'Loo. The Tennant. The Alice. The Elliott. The Kath-er-ine. The Daly. The 'Curry. Yet it's strange I've never heard The Darwin or The Batchelor or The Renner or The Pine Creek. Some names just seem to fit naturally with an article, others are awkward [Douglas Lockwood, *My Old Mates and I*, 1979].
(4) "The Alice," as it's affectionately known [*The Rough Guide to Australia*, 2001].

**Alligator Alley** or **State, the** *Florida, USA.* The name refers to the alligators formerly found in Florida's numerous swamps. They are now protected in the Everglades National Park.

**Alligatorland** *Queensland, Australia.* The nickname refers not to the crocodiles found in the state but to its horses, so colloquially dubbed for their toughness.

**Almaine** or **Almany** *Germany.* A poetic name for the country known in French as *Allemagne*.

(1) Forth he went into Speyne
And after into Almeyne [*Guy of Warwick, c.* 1314].
(2) White ivory skin and tress of gold,
Her shy and bashful comrade told
For daughter of Almaine [Sir Walter Scott, *The Bridal of Triermain*, 1813].

**Almesbury** *Amesbury, England.* This form of the Wiltshire town's name occurs in Sir William Malory's 15th-century account of the Arthurian romances as that of the site where Queen Guinevere took refuge after her adulterous affair with Lancelot of the Lake.

Queen Guinevere had fled the court, and sat
There in the holy house at Almesbury
Weeping, none with her save a little maid [Alfred, Lord Tennyson, *Idylls of the King*, "Guinevere," 1859].

**Aloha State, the** *Hawaii, USA.* The state nickname, officially adopted in 1959, derives from the Hawaiian word for "love," used on meeting or parting.

(1) Open cars passed ... The number plates proclaimed Hawaii the Aloha State [Jeremy Potter, *Going West*, 1972].
(2) There are many other things to do in America's Aloha State besides volcano-walking [*Sunday Times Magazine*, January 23, 2005].

**Alphabet City** see in Appendix 1, p. 269.

**Alphaville-on-Thames** *Oxford, England.* Alphaville is a name applicable to any city of excellence, from *alpha*, the first letter of the Greek alphabet, and French *ville*, "town." The river name distinguishes this one from others. The name was popularized by the 1965 Franco-Italian futuristic fantasy movie *Alphaville*.

Oxford is now a very large incubator for eggheads of both sexes and all classes: Alphaville-on-Thames [Godfrey Smith, *The English Companion*, 1996].

**Alps in Midocean, the** *South Georgia, South Atlantic.* The island, a dependency of the Falkland Islands, has a terrain of glaciers and high snow-covered mountains. Hence the nickname.

South Georgia is one of the world's natural wonders, the 'Alps in mid-ocean' [Travel ad, *The Times Magazine*, February 26, 2005].

**Alps of America, the** *Rocky Mountains, North America.* A former touristic name for the famous mountain chain.

The familiar tourist haunts — Niagara, the Mammoth Cave, the White Mountains, Colorado, the Grand Canyon, ... the Rockies ('the Alps of America') [Piers Brendon, *Thomas Cook: 150 Years of Popular Tourism*, 1991].

**Amazingstoke** *Basingstoke, England.* A former promotional pun based on the name of the Hampshire town.

Nottingham may have milked the Robin Hood legend for all its worth, but the city has not over-sold itself in the manner of Basingstoke, which once styled itself Amazingstoke [*The Times*, October 26, 2004].

**Amber Coast** see in Appendix 1, p. 269.

**American Mediterranean, the** *Caribbean Sea.* The nickname arose following the opening in 1914 of the Panama Canal, which paved the way for increased US interest in this strategically sited sea. More generally, the New World Caribbean and Old World Mediterranean can be equated for their touristic popularity and favorable climatic conditions. *Cp.* **Mediterranean of the New World.**

**American Nile, the** *St. John's River, Florida, USA.* The name refers to the reeds and tropical vegetation of the St. John's River banks, resembling those of the Nile.

**American Riviera, the** *San Diego, California, USA.* The seaport city, with its fine natural harbor, has a historic downtown and beaches to north and south. Hence the nickname, comparing it with the French Riviera.

> The old convents and churches ... and the yachting in the adjacent waters, furnish a great variety of interest for visitors to the American Riviera [Moses F. Sweetser, *The King's Handbook of the United States*, 1891].

**American Weimar, the** *Concord, Massachusetts, USA.* The town gained its nickname in the 19th century, when it was a noted cultural center, like the German city.

> Concord, the "American Weimar," was one of many settlements around Boston that housed its expectant intellectuals and fed its literary, reformist spirit [Malcolm Bradbury, ed., *The Atlas of Literature*, 1996].

**America's Casablanca** *Miami, Florida, USA.* The city and resort was so nicknamed in the 1980s for its drug dealers and for the vast sums of money that went with their product. As a direct result of this trade, many Savings & Loans (S&Ls) opened here. The Moroccan seaport city of Casablanca had a similar reputation.

> While *Newsweek* magazine called Miami 'America's Casablanca,' locals dubbed it the 'City with the S&L Skyline' [*Lonely Planet Miami*, 1999].

**America's Dairyland** *Wisconsin, USA.* The promotional name, displayed on automobile license plates, refers to the dairy farming that is the state's main agricultural activity.

> There's a definite dualism to the Dairy State [*Lonely Planet USA*, 2004].

**America's Fattest City** *Houston, Texas, USA.* The city was so named in 2003 for the third year running by *Men's Fitness* magazine. The cause of

the condition is attributed to Houston's humid climate, its poor air quality, and a dearth of outdoor recreation facilities. An inherent indulgence in junk food also plays its part. Second place that year was taken by Chicago, while Detroit was in third place.

**America's Finest City** *San Diego, California, USA.* A self-vaunting promotional name for the city.

> San Diegans are fiercely proud of their city and shamelessly, yet endearingly, promote it as 'America's Finest City.' After a few days of exploration, you may well agree [*Lonely Planet USA*, 2004].

**America's First Wilderness** *Catskill Mountains, New York, USA.* The nickname refers to the natural wilderness formed by the region's deep gorges and massive uplands, within which one can "lose" oneself not far from New York City.

> I grew up in the Catskill Mountains in upstate New York, where the landscape is full of forests, rivers, waterfalls, farms and lakes — it's often referred to as America's "first wilderness" [*Sunday Times Magazine*, July 10, 2005].

**America's Literary Emporium** *Boston, Massachusetts, USA.* The sobriquet relates to the city's many literary figures and publishing houses in the early 19th century. The term itself is said to have been coined by British actor Edmund Kean in a speech from the stage when touring America in 1820.

**America's Most Beautiful City** *(1) Kansas City, Missouri, USA; (2) Savannah, Georgia, USA; (3) Tulsa, Oklahoma, USA.* These are just three of the contenders for this desirable title. Georgia's oldest city was planned around a system of squares which were made into parks and planted with semitropical flora, while the Prayer Tower at Tulsa's Oral Roberts University overlooks a scene of attractively arranged walks and gardens. Kansas City's claim to the sobriquet is perhaps more aspirational than patently apparent (see the quote at **Heart of America**).

**America's Paris** *Cincinnati, Ohio, USA.* Better known as **Porkopolis** or **Queen of the West**, Cincinnati's claimed kinship with the French capital is mainly due to its high cultural profile, with a symphony orchestra, opera and ballet companies, and museums of art and natural history.

**America's Playground** *Las Vegas, Nevada, USA.* A nickname implying that the city known as the **Gambling Capital of the World** has much more to offer pleasure-bent Americans than the casinos for which it is famous. *Cp.* **Sin City.**

> To really love this city, sometimes you just have to ... get stuck into the shamelessly glitzy, unutter-

ably cheesy, high-fat, lowbrow side to America's Playground [*Sunday Times*, May 15, 2005].

**America's Walking City** *Boston, Massachusetts, USA*. The narrow, thronged streets of central Boston make walking a much more realistic option than driving. Hence the nickname, which also refers to the city's many jaywalkers.

You don't need a car in Boston, known as America's walking city [*Sunday Times*, November 21, 2004].

**America the Beautiful** *United States*. A eulogistic sobriquet for a land where all is (or should be) fair and good. The phrase quotes the title of a patriotic hymn by Katharine Lee Bates published in 1895 and set to music in 1913 by Samuel Augustus Ward. The poem was written while Bates was standing on Pikes Peak, Colorado. *Cp.* **Australia Fair**.

It isn't the early championship of America the Beautiful that people tend to remember about *The Modern Review* [Julie Burchill in *The Times*, June 22, 2005].

**Amerika** or **Amerikkka** *United States*. A name dating from the 1960s, and deriving from the initials of the Ku Klux Klan. It was devised by the revolutionaries of the time and viewed America as the embodiment of a right-wing, quasifascist government policy. The nickname also hints at *Amerika*, the German name of the country, thus also evoking Germany's own associations with fascism (Nazism).

(1) The oppressive contract canot be broken as long as any sort of hierarchy exists to perpetuate the sensitized relationships of tribalism (in Amerikkka?) [*Black Scholar*, June 1971].
(2) Exiled from Amerika (the spelling comes naturally) Beck ... lived a nomadic existence in Europe [*New Statesman*, September 27, 1985].

**'Ampstead** *Hampstead, London, England*. A typical Cockney "h"-less pronunciation of the name, referring primarily to Hampstead Heath, a favorite resort of Londoners on public holidays. "'Appy 'Ampstead" was the best-known song in Albert Ketelbey's popular "Cockney Suite" (1924).

Hampstead Heath — "'Appy 'Ampstead," scene of the traditional Bank Holiday fair [*Holiday Guide 1952: Area No. 5, South & South East England*].

**Ancient Dominion** *see* **Old Dominion**

**Andytown** *Andersonstown, Belfast, Northern Ireland*. A colloquial abbreviation and personalization of the city district's name.

Women from 'Andytown' singing on the train [*Irish Times*, December 21, 2000].

**Angel City** *Los Angeles, California, USA*. An obvious reference to the the city's regular name, as is the similar **City of Angels**.

**Anglesea** *Anglesey, Wales*. An informal spelling of the island's name, presumably from an association with *sea*. The name itself is popularly interpreted as "isle of the Angles," referring to the Germanic people who settled in Britain, but it probably means "Ongull's isle," with a Scandinavian personal name.

**Anglia** *England*. A classical and poetic name of England, preserved in the region of East Anglia (the counties of Norfolk and Suffolk), where it is implied in the names of various commercial organizations, such as Anglia Television and Anglian Water, based in that region.

**Angling Capital of the West, the** *Ballinrobe, Ireland*. The Co. Mayo town, in western Ireland, is so nicknamed for its proximity to Loughs Mask, Carra, and Corrib, where there is good fishing.

**Anna Liffey** *Liffey River, Ireland*. The personification of the river on which Dublin stands represents its Irish name, *Abhainn na Life*, "the river Liffey." It is also familiar in the Latinate form *Anna Livia*, adopted by James Joyce for Anna Livia Plurabelle, the riverine heroine of *Finnegans Wake* (1939).

(1) There is nothing about Anna Livia that outrages expectation. She is a woman and a river, and women have been identified with water before this ... She is named for Dublin's brown river, the Anna Liffey (Anna means "grace") that rises in the Wicklow hills and empties into the salt Dublin Bay at Island Bridge [Adaline Glasheen, *A Census of Finnegans Wake*, 1956].
(2) We walked back ... over the Ha'penny Bridge, pausing to look down into the freezing water of "Anna Livia Plurabelle" [Bel Mooney in *The Times*, December 10, 2005].

**Anster** *Anstruther, Scotland*. A local short name for the Fife resort and fishing port. It was popularized by William Tennant's mock-heroic poem *Anster Fair* (1812). *Cp.* **Auld Ainster**.

**Antelope State, the** *Nebraska, USA*. The state derived its former nickname, current in the 1870s, from the herds of antelope that roamed its plains.

**Anthrax Island** *Gruinard Island, Scotland*. The uninhabited island off the northwest coast of Scotland was so nicknamed because in World War II it was seeded with anthrax spores as an experiment in biological warfare. The Ministry of Defence, who owns the island, declared it free of anthrax in 1990.

Dubbed "Anthrax Island," Gruinard became a sinister presence [*Sunday Times Magazine*, June 26, 2005].

**Antipodes, the** *Australia and New Zealand*. The plural name derives from the identical Greek word meaning literally "with feet opposite." Australasia is on the opposite side of the earth to Europe. (South Island, New Zealand, is traversed by latitude 45°S, while France, Italy, and Romania are traversed by latitude 45°N.) *Cp.* **Down Under**.

(1) These are the Antipodes! "The world turned upside down!" [*Sydney Herald*, December 12, 1833].

(2) In Great Britain, Australia is regarded as the antipodes and there is no reason why Australia should not regard Great Britain as the antipodes [Johnson, p. 25].

(3) This was a time when Britain was offloading most of its undesirables on ships heading to the Antipodes, conveniently on the other side of the world [Dodd/Donald, p. 210].

**Antone** *see* **San Antone**

**Apache State, the** *Arizona, USA*. The Apache Indians live mainly in Arizona and New Mexico, with the Western Apaches on reservations in east central Arizona. Hence the nickname.

**Apostle's Grove, the** *St John's Wood, London, England*. A punning alteration of the district name, which properly derives from the Knights of St. John of Jerusalem, who were granted land here in the 14th century. *Cp.* **Grove of the Evangelist**.

**Apple Capital of the World, the** *Wenatchee, Washington, USA*. Wenatchee lies in a fertile fruit-growing valley famous for its apples, pears, and grain. Hence the pomological promotion.

**Apple Isle** or **Island, the** *Tasmania, Australia*. The island state is a noted apple-growing region. Hence the name.

(1) The apple isle still continues to *fête* Senator Keating and his bride [*Gadfly* (Adelaide), March 7, 1906].

(2) The apple island still continues to attract a few stragglers from our city [*Gadfly* (Adelaide), March 21, 1906].

**'Appy 'Ampstead** *see* **'Ampstead**

**Arabia Felix** *Yemen*. In Roman times, the Arabian Peninsula was divided into Arabia Petraea ("rocky Arabia") in the northwest, Arabia Deserta ("desert Arabia") in the north, and the much larger Arabia Felix ("fertile Arabia") as the rest of the peninsula, so called for the fecundity of its coastal regions. Some geographers applied the latter name to the former Yemen Arab Republic, or North Yemen, and by extension it passed to present-day Yemen when North Yemen united with South Yemen in 1990. *See also* **Araby**.

**Arabian Gulf, the** *Persian Gulf*. An alternate name that today makes more sense that one based on the outmoded **Persia**.

**Araby** *Arabia*. A poetic name for the Arabian Peninsula that seems to echo French *Arabie*, "Arabia." In quote (1) below, "Araby the Blest" is historic **Arabia Felix**, famed for its spices and herbs.

(1) Off at sea north-east winds blow
Sabean odours from the spicy shore
Of Araby the Blest [John Milton, *Paradise Lost*, 1667].

(2) Farewell — farewell to thee, Araby's daughter! [Thomas Moore, *Lalla Rookh*, 1817].

(3) I'll sing thee songs of Araby,
And tales of wild Cashmere [W.G. Wills, song from cantata *Lalla Rookh*, 1877, based on Moore's work, above].

(4) "The Sheik of Araby" [Ted Snyder, song title, 1921].

**Arcady** *Arcadia, Greece*. A poetic name for the ancient country, similar to that of **Araby** for Arabia. The name itself came to represent a paradise of nymphs and shepherds, as in the quotes below.

(1) Of famous Arcady ye are, and sprung
Of that renowned flood, so often sung [John Milton, "Arcades," 1645].

(2) And round us all the thicket rang
To many a flute of Arcady [Alfred, Lord Tennyson, *In Memoriam*, 1850].

(3) The woods of Arcady are dead,
And over is their antique joy [W.B. Yeats, "The Song of the Happy Shepherd," *Crossways*, 1889].

(4) "Arcady is Ever Young" [Lionel Monckton, Arthur Wimperis, Howard Talbot, song title in musical *The Arcadians*, 1909].

**Archangel** *Arkhangel'sk, Russia*. The traditional English form of the Russian name, itself deriving from the city's 12th-century monastery dedicated to St. Michael the Archangel.

From Land's End to Vladivostok, from Archangel to the Cape of Good Hope [Upton Sinclair, *World's End*, 1940].

**Archipelago, the** *Aegean Sea, Greece/Turkey*. The English word "archipelago," meaning a group of islands, represents a former alternate name for the Aegean (which is dotted with islands), by way of Italian *Arcipelago*, itself from *Egiopelagos*, its Medieval Latin name, in turn from Greek *Aigaion pelagos*, "Aegean Sea." The first part of the English word does not thus represent Greek *archi-*, "chief."

The line [of Euboean hills] is further prolonged by a series of islands in the Archipelago [George Grote, *A History of Greece*, 1846–56].

**Argentine, the** *Argentina*. A dated form of the country's name that evolved from the former Argentine Republic.

The Argentine is, roughly, the shape of an inverted triangle [Johnson, p. 27].

**Argier** *Algiers, Algeria*. A poetic form of the

capital city's name, close to its Spanish form of *Argel*.

> Where was she born? speak; tell me.
>   Sir, in Argier [William Shakespeare, *The Tempest*, 1611].

**Ark City** *Arkansas City, Arkansas, USA*. A neat abbreviation of the city's formal name.

**Armenteers** *Armentières, France*. A colloquial name for the French town near Lille, in vogue among British soldiers fighting in France in World War I. It became widely known from the song quoted below, and may well have suggested "armament" to the military. Less common variants were Arm-in-Tears (perhaps evoking an "army man in tears" or a wounded soldier) and Arminteers.

> A mademoiselle from Armenteers,
>   She hasn't been kissed for forty years [Edward Rowland, "Mademoiselle from Armenteers," song, *c*. 1915].

**Arm-in-Tears** *see* **Armenteers**
**Arminteers** *see* **Armenteers**
**Armorica** *Brittany, France*. The classical name survives in that of the Brittany department of Côtes-d'Armor.

> (1) In Armorik, that called is Britayne,
>   There was a knight that loved and dide his payne [i.e. took pains]
>   To serve a lady in his beste wyse [i.e. way] [Geoffrey Chaucer, "The Franklin's Tale," *Canterbury Tales, c*.1386].
> (2) From earliest times it [i.e. Brittany] has been known by its Celtic appellation of 'Armor' or 'Armorica'—the land of the sea [Young, p. 161].

**Arnham** *Arnhem, Netherlands*. A common British misspelling of the Dutch town's name, familiar in Britain from the First Airborne Division's heroic (but unsuccessful) attempt in 1944 to secure the Rhine bridges encircled by the Germans. In fact the *-hem* of the name etymologically equates to the common English *-ham*, both meaning "village."

> A question in the Fowlmere sports quiz some weeks ago was to name the town where the Allied airborne landings took place in 1944. In order to get a point, the spelling had to be precise. The answer was given as Arnham. Protests to the quizmaster were in vain ... This was the spelling, or so he claimed, that he had read in *The Times* [Letter to the Editor, *The Times*, November 23, 2004].

**Arsehole of the World, the** *Persian Gulf*. A name applicable to any unpleasant or dangerous place, but usually associated with The Gulf. The "old saying" in quote (2) below is said to have originated in the 1920s with the British Royal Air Force, who had a transit camp at Shaibah (Shu'aiba), southeastern Iraq.

> (1) The Persian Gulf is the arsehole of the world,

and Basra is eighty miles up it [Harry Hopkins to a British general, *c*.1941, quoted in John Masters, *The Road Past Mandalay*, 1961].
> (2) You know the old saying: the Persian Gulf's the arsehole of the world—and Shaiba's half-way up it [Eric Partridge, *A Dictionary of Catch Phrases*, 1977].

**Arsenal of Democracy, the** *United States*. The phrase was originally used by French diplomat Jean Monnet in conversation with US judge Felix Frankfurter, who is said to have asked Monnet not to use it any more but to let President Roosevelt use it. He duly did so, as in the quote below.

> We must be the great arsenal of democracy [Franklin D. Roosevelt, broadcast address to Forum on Current Problems, December 29, 1940].

**Arsenal of the Nation, the** *Connecticut, USA*. The name more narrowly refers to the Connecticut River valley, where various armories arose, such as the present Colt Industries in Hartford.

**Artesian State, the** *South Dakota, USA*. The name refers to the artesian wells used in the state for the irrigation of agricultural land.

**Artichoke Center of the World, the** *Castroville, California, USA*. The town is noted for its artichokes, and holds an annual Artichoke Festival.

**Asia Minor** *(1) Belgravia, London, England; (2) Cheltenham, England; (3) Kensington, London, England*. Of the two London districts, Belgravia was so nicknamed for its wealthy Jewish residents and Kensington for its retired Indian civil servants (although latterly for its actual immigrant Asian population). The Gloucestershire town formerly shared the second characteristic, as can be seen from the quote below. The name itself is an equivalent of "Little Asia," adopted from the historic name of the peninsula, now in Turkey, that forms the western extremity of Asia, between the Black Sea and the Mediterranean.

> (Cheltenham) Anglo-Indians form so large a part of its society, that the town has been called 'Asia Minor' [Karl Baedeker, *Handbook to Great Britain*, 1890].

**Asia West** *Richmond, British Columbia, Canada*. The island city is often so nicknamed for its almost exclusively Chinese population.

**Astrodome City** *Houston, Texas, USA*. The city, with its famed Johnson Space Center, founded in 1961 as the command post for flights by US astronauts, is also noted for its Astrodome, built in 1965. *Cp.* **Space City**.

**Athens of America, the** *(1) Annapolis, Maryland, USA; (2) Bogotá, Colombia; (3) Boston,*

*Massachusetts, USA; (4) Philadelphia, Pennsylvania, USA.* All four cities lay claim to the title as cultural centers, with Annapolis boasting its United States Naval Academy, Bogotá its universities, Boston its Museum of Fine Arts, Boston Symphony Orchestra, Boston Public Library, Boston University, and Harvard Medical School, and Philadelphia its renowned Philadelphia Orchestra. (The Athenaeum, Boston's private library, directly reflects the name.) Bogotá (*see* **Athens of South America**) was so dubbed in *c.*1800 by the German naturalist Alexander von Humboldt. Annapolis is also known as the **Paris of America**, while Boston is alternately known as the Athens of the New World.

(Philadelphia) In colonial days Philadelphia was known as the "Athens of America," and it retains a high place in the artistic achievement of the nation [*Britannica*, vol. 25, p. 534].

**Athens of Cuba, the** *Matanzas, Cuba.* The city earned its nickname from the many artists, musicians, and intellectuals living here in the second half of the 19th century.

**Athens of Dixie** *see* **Athens of the South**

**Athens of England, the** *(1) Oxford, England; (2) Warrington, England.* Oxford, with its university, was so named by the German traveler and jurist Paul Hentzner (1558–1629). The Cheshire town of Warrington earned the sobriquet by virtue of the short-lived Warrington Academy, established in 1757, with such noted names among its founders as chemist Joseph Priestley and mathematician George Walker. It closed in 1783.

(Oxford) Oxonium, Oxford, the famed Athens of England; that glorious seminary of wisdom and learning, whence religion, politeness, and letters, are abundantly dispersed into all parts of the kingdom [Paul Hentzner, *Travels in England during the Reign of Queen Elizabeth, c.* 1598].

**Athens of Germany, the** *Weimar, Germany.* As noted in the quote below, the city's residents included several poets, among them such famed figures as Goethe, Herder, and Schiller. In the 19th century, composers Liszt and Wagner worked here, and architect Walter Gropius founded the Bauhaus school here in 1919.

It is a very queer little place, although called the "Athens of Germany" on account of the great poets who have lived here [G.H. Lewes, letter to Charles and Thornton Lewes, September 27, 1854].

**Athens of Ireland, the** *(1) Belfast, Northern Ireland; (2) Cork, Ireland.* Although growing into a typical 19th-century industrial city, Belfast's earlier intellectual and cultural life had been encouraged by the Huguenots, who fled here in the 17th century to seek refuge from religious persecution in France. Cork has retained its tradition of learning. The University of Cork was founded in 1845, and became part of the University of Ireland in 1909. Writers resident in the early 19th century included poet Richard Millikin, humorist Francis Mahony ("Father Prout"), and folklorist Thomas Crofton Croker.

(1) (Belfast) In the eighteenth century the intellectual activities of the town, and not its commercialism, earned for it the name of the "Athens of Ireland," or the "Northern Athens," a term which, if not actually coined by John Lawless, the editor of "The Irishman," was much used by him, and must have originated in his time [D.J. Owen, *The History of Belfast*, 1921].

(2) (Cork) At this period [i.e. the early 19th century] Cork had so many literary men that the city became known as "the Athens of Ireland" [David and Mary Coakley, *Wit and Wine*, 1975].

**Athens of Scotland** *see* **Athens of the North**

**Athens of South America, the** *Bogotá, Colombia.* As implied in the quote below, the Colombian capital owed its literary and artistic prominence to the Spanish, who settled the city in 1538. It now boasts several universities and a wide range of other cultural institutions, including a number of modern art galleries. *See also* **Athens of America**.

Bogota has long had a reputation for artistic credibility; its *tertulias*, literary salons held in cafés, were admired throughout the Spanish-speaking world. "The Athens of South America," they called it [Dodd/Donald, p. 119].

**Athens of Switzerland, the** *Zürich, Switzerland.* Zürich owes its cultural reputation to the many religious scholars who settled here in the 16th century and turned the town into the center of the Swiss Protestant Reformation. Coverdale's Bible was printed here in 1535, Zwingli preached here, and Lavater, over a century later, was a pastor here and became prominent as a poet, mystic, and theologian. *Cp.* **Protestant Rome.**

**Athens of the New World** *see* **Athens of America**

**Athens of the North, the** *(1) Belfast, Northern Ireland; (2) Copenhagen, Denmark; (3) Edinburgh, Scotland; (4) Reims, France; (5) Valenciennes, France.* All five cities came to be so named as a northern equivalent of their classical Greek prototype. The name is particularly associated with Edinburgh, which was not only a flourishing cultural center in the 18th and 19th centuries but boasts some fine neoclassical buildings in the New Town and, on the Calton Hill, an unfinished war memorial that was intended to be a model of the Parthenon. Belfast became known more locally as the **Athens of Ireland**, while the Danish and French cities also have cultural associations, in the case of Valenciennes with the artists and sculptors who first favored the city in the 15th century. As an important Roman city, Reims is said to have been so named by the emperor Hadrian.

(1) (Belfast) After 30 years of violence it is hard to credit that Belfast was once known as the Athens of the North [*Irish Times*, June 14, 2000].

(2) (Edinburgh) It is possible that it is one of the hundred best places that may be called Athens of the North. That would be optional; what is obligatory is that it is one of the few places that absolutely may not be called the Venice of the North on any account [Theodora Benson and Betty Askwith, *Muddling Through, or Britain in a Nutshell,* 1936].

(3) (Edinburgh) The playwright Tom Stoppard said [in his 1972 play *Jumpers*] that rather than being the Athens of the North, Edinburgh is the 'Reykjavik of the South' [Sam Jordison and Dan Kieran, eds., *The Idler Book of Crap Towns II,* 2004].

(4) (Edinburgh) Old Town and New Town are the self-proclaiming divisions. It's "Auld Reekie" versus the "Athens of the North" [Dodd/Donald, p.35].

(5) (Edinburgh) With its magnificent Neo-Classical architecture, its renown as a centre for enlightened thinking and glowing literature, it is little surprise that Edinburgh is known as the Athens of the North [*The Times*, December 10, 2004].

**Athens of the South** or **of Dixie, the** *Nashville, Tennessee, USA.* The city's name, quoted in John Gunther's *Inside U.S.A.* (1947), is justified both from its numerous institutions of higher education and from its many buildings of classical design, including a replica of the Parthenon, built in 1897.

There is a strong manufacturing presence ... and an impressive academic tradition ... The latter earned Nashville the name "the Athens of the South" [Dodd/Donald, p. 161].

**Athens of the West, the** *Córdoba, Spain.* Córdoba justified its name as the intellectual center of Spain from the 8th to the 13th century.

**Athens of the Western World, the** *Texcoco, Mexico.* Texcoco was long a noted cultural center. Hence the name.

**Athens on the Spree** *Berlin, Germany.* The capital city, on the Spree River, gained its 19th-century nickname (in German, *Spree-Athen*) for its architecture and its eminence in the arts and sciences.

Berlin blossomed into a great cultural centre some even called 'Athens on the Spree' [*Lonely Planet Germany,* 2004].

**Atomic City, the** *Los Alamos, New Mexico,* *USA.* The city is so nicknamed for the Atomic Research Laboratory opened here by the US government in 1942 to develop the first atomic bomb (under the code name Manhattan Project). After World War II the laboratory developed the first hydrogen bomb.

**Augusta** *London, England.* The poetic name of London (meaning "venerable") was an honorific Roman title. It is said to have been conferred on the occasion of the visit of the emperor Constantius in the early 4th century. The title did not last long, and the city's more familiar Roman name is *Londinium.*

(1) Close to the Walls which fair *Augusta* bind,
(The fair *Augusta* much to fears inclin'd) [John Dryden, *Mac Flecknoe,* 1682].

(2) Behold! Augusta's glittering spires increase,
And temples rise, the beauteous works of Peace [Alexander Pope, *Windsor Forest,* 1713].

(3) Where full in view Augusta's spires are seen,
With flowery lawns and waving woods between [William Falconer, *The Shipwreck,* 1762].

**Auld Ainster** *Anstruther, Scotland.* The nickname reflects the local pronunciation of the name of the Fife port and resort.

'Auld Ainster' is a fishing town to its seaboot tips [Christopher Somerville, *Coast: A Celebration of Britain's Coastal Heritage,* 2005].

**Auld Ayr** *Ayr, Scotland.* The epithet refers both to the town's medieval origin and to the Auld Kirk ("old church") of Ayr and Auld Brig ("old bridge") of Ayr that are two of its most famous buildings.

Auld Ayr, wham ne'er a town surpasses
For honest men and bonnie lasses [Robert Burns, "Tam o' Shanter," 1791].

**Auld Grey Town, the** *Kendal, England.* The Cumbria town is so nicknamed for its many gray limestone buildings. (Kendal is far enough north to have Scottish "auld" for English "old.") *Cp.* **Grey Auld Toon.**

At Kendal, the Gateway to the Lakes, the Seven Stars Hotel and the Shakespeare Inn offer every comfort for visitors to the "Auld Grey Town" [*Holiday Haunts 1960: Area No. 2, North West England and North Wales*].

**Auld Reekie** *Edinburgh, Scotland.* The name is Scots for "old smoky" and dates from the 18th century. It originally applied to the smoking chimneys of Edinburgh's Old Town but later came to be used of the whole city. Today it is simply a term of affection, as atmospheric pollution in Edinburgh is negligible.

(1) Auld Reikie! wale [i.e. best] o' ilka [i.e. every] town
That Scotland kens beneath the moon [Robert Fergusson, "Auld Reikie, A Poem," 1773].

(2) Nae heathen name shall I prefix
Frae Pindus or Parnassus;
Auld Reekie dings [i.e. beats] them a' to sticks
For rhyme-inspiring lasses [Robert Burns, "To
Miss Ferrier," 1787].

(3) This designation reminds one, that the quarter of the city to which it particularly refers, presents, even to this day, the spectacle of the most flagrant violation of the most elementary rules for the preservation of public health and the maintenance of domestic decency [*London Review*, quoted in Wheeler, p. 29].

(4) By the beginning of the nineteenth century Edinburgh was still "Auld Reekie" ("Old Smokey," because housewives in Fife could tell when it was approaching dinner time across the Forth in Edinburgh by the pall of smoke that rose over the city when cooking commenced) but it was also the "Athens of the North" [David Daiches and John Flower, *Literary Landscapes of the British Isles*, 1979].

**Auld Sod** *see* **Old Sod**

**Auliana** *Dublin, Ireland.* The poetic name of the Irish capital is traditionally explained as in the quote below.

It obtained its present name from Alpinus, a lord or chief among the Irish, whose daughter, Auliana, having been drowned at the ford where now the Whitworth-bridge is built, he changed the name to Auliana [Joseph Haydn, *Dictionary of Dates*, 1847].

**Aunt Jane** *Tijuana, Mexico.* The nickname is a popular English equivalent of the town's name, as a translation of Spanish *tia Juana*. If applied to Mexico as a whole, it is possible the name is also seen as a sort of female equivalent to **Uncle Sam.**

**Auschwitz** *Oświęcim, Poland.* The German name of the town is invariably used by Westerners when referring to the Nazi concentration camp located there in World War II, when it was part of German territory. It is likely, however, that few could give the town's current Polish name and, as implied in quote (2) below, even the historic name appears to be fading from public awareness. Even so, it was the Polish name that figured in many contemporary press reports, as evident in quote (1).

(1) A State commission ... has completed its investigation into conditions at the concentration camp at Oswiecim, in Polish Silesia [*The Times*, May 8, 1945].

(2) Of the 4,000 adults surveyed by the BBC, 45 per cent said they had never heard of Auschwitz [*The Times*, January 15, 2005].

**Ausonia** *Italy.* The classical and poetic name ultimately derives from that of Auson, son of Ulysses, who is said to have settled there.

(1) I would not yet exchange thy [i.e. England's] sullen skies,

And fields without a flow'r, for warmer France
With all her vines; not for Ausonia's groves
Of golden fruitage, and her myrtle's bowers
[William Cowper, *The Task*, 1785].

(2) Romantic Spain,—
Gay lillied fields of France, or, more refined,
The soft Ausonia's monumental reign [Thomas Campbell, *Gertrude of Wyoming*, 1809].

**Aussie** or **Aussieland** *Australia.* A familiar shortening of the country's name, today more often used for the inhabitants (the Aussies), especially in a sporting (often cricketing) context. *Cp.* **Oz.**

(1) A farewell dance for the boys going home to 'Aussie' tomorrow [G.F. Moberly, *Experiences of a 'Dinki Di' R.R.C. Nurse*, 1915].

(2) The girl he left in Aussieland
Went nearly out her mind [*The Aussie* (Sydney), August 1920].

(3) People with complaints were so glad to be back in dear old Aussie that they forgot their troubles [Graham McInnes, *The Road to Gundagai*, 1965].

(4) Cries of "Aussie Aussie Aussie Oi Oi Oi" filled the air as Australia won its biggest pile of gold medals ever [*The Rough Guide to Australia*, 2001].

**Austral** *Australia.* An old poetic name for the island continent.

That we're sons of old England we ne'er shall forget,
And must think of our own native home with regret—
But, aye let us remember in Austral's bright strand
We live in a free,— perhaps a happier, land [*The Colonial Society* (Sydney), December 31, 1868].

**Australia Fair** *Australia.* The praiseworthy epithet comes from the Australian national anthem, as in the quote below. *Cp.* **America the Beautiful.**

Australians all, let us rejoice,
For we are young and free;
We've golden soil and wealth for toil,
Our home is girt by sea.
Our land abounds in Nature's gifts
Of beauty rich and rare;
In hist'ry's page let ev'ry stage
Advance Australia fair [Peter Dodds McCormick, "Advance Australia Fair," *c.* 1878].

**Austrian Leeds, the** *Brno, Czech Republic.* A name formerly used for Brünn when in the Austrian Empire. It alluded to the city's woolen manufactures, for which the English city of Leeds was famous.

**Auto Capital of the British Empire, the** *Windsor, Ontario, Canada.* The name arose in the early 20th century, when Ford, General Motors, Chrysler and other automobile companies built plants in the city (and when the British Empire was at its height).

**Auto Capital of the World, the** *Detroit, Michigan, USA.* Auto manufacturing began in Detroit in the closing years of the 19th century, when the early carriage industry helped Henry Ford and others make the city worthy of its nickname. The industry has since declined. *Cp.* **Motown.**

**Auto State, the** *Michigan, USA.* The state largely owes its nickname to the concentration of the auto industry in Detroit, the **Auto Capital of the World.**

**Avalon** *Glastonbury, England.* The Somerset town is popularly identified with the Isle of Avalon in the Arthurian legends, and Arthur himself is said to be buried here, together with his queen, Guinevere. The equation dates from 1191, when Arthur's tomb was supposedly discovered at the (now ruined) abbey here, as testified by Geoffrey of Monmouth: *"Hic iacet sepultus inclitus rex Arturius in insula Avalonia"* ("Here lies buried the celebrated king Arthur in the island of Avalon"). Today the town is more widely known for its annual music festival (*see* **Glasto**).

> [The road to] Glastonbury, or 'The Ancient Isle of Avalon,' is well-signposted [Charlie Godfrey-Faussett, *Footprint England*, 2004].

**Aviary of England, the** *Lincolnshire, England.* Lincolnshire is a fenland county (*see* **Fens** in Appendix 1, p. 269), so a home of water birds.

> Lincolnshire may be termed the aviary of England, for the wild fowl therein [Thomas Fuller, *The History of the Worthies of England*, 1662].

**Aviation City** *Dayton, Ohio, USA.* Dayton was the home of the aviation pioneers Wilbur and Orville Wright, who after their flight near Kitty Hawk, North Carolina, in 1903 established a research aircraft plant here. Today the city's Air Force Museum has the most diverse collection of aircraft in the world.

**Azania** *South Africa.* The indigenous name for South Africa was adopted from classical geography, where it was probably based on Arabic *zanj*, "dark-skinned African." The same word gave the name of Zanzibar. The name was adopted by Evelyn Waugh for the imaginary African kingdom in his novel *Black Mischief* (1932).

> (1) It has become pretty obvious to us that these are crucial years in the history of Azania [*New York Times*, September 18, 1977].
> (2) Azania has been adopted as a name for South Africa by some radicals. Originally, it was used by the mapmakers of ancient Egypt to describe all the unknown territories to their south [*Sunday Times*, May 27, 1979].

**Aztec State, the** *Arizona, USA.* The nickname arose because the remains of old Indian cultures in the state were at one time taken to be of Aztec origin. The Aztecs are now chiefly associated with neighboring Mexico.

**BA** *Buenos Aires, Argentina.* An initial-based abbreviation even briefer than **Baires.**

> BA is an erotic, sensuous place [Dodd/Donald, p. 95].

**Bab, the** *Bab-el-Mandeb, Red Sea.* A short form of the Arabic name of the strait, which translates as English **Gate of Tears.**

**Babylon** *(1) London, England; (2) New York City, USA; (3) Rome, Italy; (4) United States.* The name of the biblical city of Babylon, in what is now Iraq, became a symbol for the repressive power of Rome, as the center of the Roman Empire, against the Christians, as in quote (1) below. (The name is sometimes qualified as the Western Babylon, from Rome's geographical location in relation to the historic Babylon.) In modern times the name came to be used for any grand or multicultural city, as both London and New York are (*cp.* **Modern Babylon**). African Americans similarly applied the name to the USA with regard to its many races and languages. The biblical Babylon is identified with the Tower of Babel, where the one language spoken by all men is confused by God into many tongues (Genesis 11:1–9).

> (1) (Rome) And there followed another angel, saying, Babylon is fallen, is fallen, that great city [Revelation 14:8].
> (2) (London) Through this, and much, and more, is the approach
> Of travellers to mighty Babylon:
> Whether they come by horse, or chaise, or coach [Lord Byron, *Don Juan*, 1823].
> (3) (London) London is a modern Babylon [Benjamin Disraeli, *Tancred*, 1847].
> (4) (New York) New York, which Washingtonians contemptuously think of as Babylon-on-the-Hudson [Alistair Cooke, *Letter from America*, "Washington, DC," September 11, 1949 (2004)].

**Babylon of the West, the** *Dodge City, Kansas, USA.* The former nickname refers to the city's infamous lawlessness in the latter half of the 19th century. The historical city of Babylon was notorious for the constant disorders that accompanied its tribal occupation.

**Baby State, the** *Arizona, USA.* Arizona was long the youngest state in the Union, admitted in 1912. Hence the nickname.

**BAC** *Dublin, Ireland.* The abbreviation represents the initials of the city's official Irish name, Baile Átha Cliath, itself meaning "town of the hurdle ford." Mail from the Irish capital is franked with this name, not "Dublin," although that is also an Irish name (meaning "black pool").

There were things about the letter that I didn't understand. What did BAC mean, for instance? It was explained to me that BAC was short for Baile Átha Cliath, and was the Provo's [i.e. Provisional IRA's] way of referring to the Irish government [Fergus Finlay, *Snakes and Ladders*, 1998].

**Backbone of England, the** *Pennines, England.* "Backbone" is a standard metaphor for a lengthy mountain chain, especially one running down the middle of a country or region. As England's longest range, the Pennines extend southward in a succession of hills some 160 miles (257 km) from the Scottish border to the Peaks in Derbyshire. The description can also extend further south, as in quote (1) below.

(1) Right down the middle of England runs a long ridge of hills, beginning with the Cheviots in the far North, and ending in the tableland of Salisbury Plain. This ridge, which is sometimes called "the backbone of England," divides our country into two very different portions [E.S. Symes, *The Story of the East Country*, n.d. (*c.* 1910)].

(2) There, far below, is the knobbly backbone of England, the Pennine Range [J.B. Priestley, *The Good Companions*, 1929].

(3) Colloquially, the Pennines are often called the backbone, or spine, of England; if this were the case, then it would be a sadly dislocated system of vertebrae that they represented! [Hogg, p. 69].

(4) There is a choice of long-distance National Trails including the Cleveland Way through the North York Moors and the Pennine Way along England's great backbone [Yorkshire tourist brochure, 2005].

**Backbone of Italy, the** *Apennines, Italy.* A name on the same lines as that of the **Backbone of England**. Italy's Apennines, their name perhaps giving that of England's Pennines, extend the full length of the peninsula for some 838 miles (1,350 km) from the northwest to the south.

The Mount Appenine ... runnes all the length of Italy, in the forme of a fishes backe bone [Fynes Moryson, *An Itinerary*, 1617].

**Backbone of Kent, the** *North Downs, England.* A metaphor similar to that of the **Backbone of England**. The North Downs are a range of low hills running across Surrey and Kent for a distance of some 100 miles (161 km).

Beyond the river [Medway] are the chalk hills forming the 'backbone of Kent' [Karl Baedeker, *Handbook to Great Britain*, 1890].

**Backbone of North America, the** *Rocky Mountains, North America.* The Rockies are the main mountain system of North America, extending southward over 3,000 miles (4,800 km) from the Arctic to the Mexican frontier. (See quote at **Great Divide**.)

**Backbone of the Confederacy, the** *Mississippi River, USA.* A nickname arising in the Civil War, when supplies for the Confederate forces had to be shipped on the Mississippi through New Orleans after Union ships blockaded the east coast.

**Back o' Bourke** see in Appendix 1, p. 269.

**Badger State, the** *Wisconsin, USA.* The inhabitants of Wisconsin are nicknamed badgers because 19th-century lead miners lived in caves in the hillside that resembled badger burrows. The name has now lost its initial derogatory overtones, and the badger is the official state animal.

"Do you know why we're going to win on November 2?" asked Robin Kreibich, a Republican state representative at a party rally last week... "Because hunting, not windsurfing, is the hobby of choice in the Badger State" [*Financial Times*, October 4, 2004].

**Badingues, les** *Les Batignolles, Paris, France.* A popular perversion of the name of the northwestern district. It was probably suggested by *Badinguet*, the nickname of the French emperor Napoleon III, itself the name of the workman as whom he was disguised when escaping from the fortress of Ham, near Amiens, in 1846.

**Bad O** *Bad Oeynhausen, Germany.* A convenient abbreviation of the town's lengthy name, as used by members of the BAOR (British Army of the Rhine), whose base was here after World War II.

**Bag City** *Baltimore, Maryland, USA.* A mock deprecatory name for the city based loosely on its formal name and implying a presence of bag ladies.

**Baghdad by the Bay** *San Francisco, California, USA.* A name similar to that of **Baghdad on the Hudson**.

'Baghdad by the Bay' still earns its hedonistic, unconventional stripes every day [*Lonely Planet USA*, 2004].

**Baghdad on the Hudson** or **on the Subway** *New York City, USA.* The name was used by the writer O. Henry for his beloved New York, comparing it to Baghdad as a city of exotic excess, famed through the Arabian Nights stories. He also dubbed it Baghdad on the Subway. The former name has been applied more recently in a quite different context, comparing New York with the Iraqi capital as a city subject to violence and violation, as in the mammoth power grid failure of August 2003.

**Bahamaland** *Bahamas.* The alternate form of the name of the island state appears in the opening line of its national anthem, quoted below.

Written by Timothy Gibson (1903–1978), it was adopted in 1973.

> Lift up your head to the rising sun, Bahamaland.

**Baht 'At Country** see in Appendix 1, p. 269.

**Baires** *Buenos Aires, Argentina.* A contraction of the city's formal name that still sounds like a name.

**Baked Bean State, the** *Massachusetts, USA.* The nickname relates to the state capital, Boston, as **Bean Town**.

**Bal City** *Baltimore, Maryland, USA.* A conventional shortening of the city's name.

**Ballmer** *Baltimore, Maryland, USA.* A colloquial version of the city's name representing a frequently heard form of the original.

**Balloo** *Bailleul, France.* A British soldiers' World War I form of the name of the French town near the Belgian border, a region where there was heavy fighting. They also dubbed it Ballyhooly, a sort of cross between the real Irish placename and English (originally American) slang *ballyhoo.*

**Ballyhooly** *see* **Balloo**

**Balt** or **Balto** *Baltimore, Maryland, USA.* A colloquial truncation of the city's name.

> Senator Smoot is an institute
> Not to be bribed with pelf;
> He guards our homes from erotic tomes
> By reading them all himself.
> Smite, Smoot, Smite for Ut.
> They're smuggling smut from Balt. to Butte
> [Ogden Nash, "Invocation," in *The New Yorker*, January 1930].

**Baltics** see in Appendix 1, p. 269.

**Balti Triangle** see in Appendix 1, p. 269.

**Bama** or **'Bam** *Alabama, USA.* A shortening of the state name based on its stressed syllable. *Cp.* **Alabamy**.

> "'Bam 'Bam 'Bammy Shore" [Ray Henderson and Mort Dixon, song title, 1925].

**Banana** see in Appendix 1, p. 269.

**Banana Belt** see in Appendix 1, p. 269.

**Banana City, the** *(1) Brisbane, Australia; (2) Durban, South Africa.* The nickname of both cities derives from their banana crops. Brisbane is the capital of Queensland and Durban the largest city in KwaZulu-Natal, both known as **Bananaland**.

> (1) (Brisbane) He had, he flattered himself, ... been making rapid progress with the damsels of the Banana city [J.A. Barry, *Steve Brown's Bunyip and Other Stories*, 1893].
> (2) (Durban) Collecting beauty crowns comes sort of naturally with this peach from the Banana City. She is Miss Durban, Miss South Africa 1971, Miss Chamber of Commerce, Miss Natal and Miss Ambi Look [*Drum*, November 8, 1972].

**Bananaland** *(1) KwaZulu-Natal, South Africa; (2) Queensland, Australia.* The South African province (earlier Natal) and Australian state derive their nickname from their distinctive fruit crop. *Cp.* **Banana City**.

> (1) (Queensland) Notes from Banana Land (from our Brisbane Correspondent) [Headline, *The Bulletin* (Sydney), June 26, 1880].
> (2) (KwaZulu-Natal) Natal is jocularly referred to as 'Bananaland' [Eric Rosenthal, comp., *Encyclopaedia of Southern Africa*, 7th ed., 1978].

**Banba** *Ireland.* The early poetic name for Ireland derives from one of the three sister goddesses whose names contested to be chosen for the country. The winner was Eriu (*see* **Eire**). It is sometimes stated that the name of the Scottish town of Banff derives from Banba.

**Bandar** *Bandar Seri Begawan, Brunei.* A colloquial shortening of the capital city's name.

**Bandit Country** *South Armagh, Northern Ireland.* The nickname describes the region from the point of view of the British government and the British Army. It was first used in November 1975 by Merlyn Rees, British secretary of state for Northern Ireland, when he spoke of "the violence of the bandit country of South Armagh" in a comment on the shooting by the IRA of three British soldiers near Crossmaglen.

> The deeper you go into the Catholic counties, the more soporific the scenery becomes until you arrive in South Armagh, close by the Irish Republic's border... This is "Bandit Country" [P.J. O'Rourke, *Holidays in Hell*, 1988].

**Banffshire Riviera** see in Appendix 1, p. 269.

**Bangkok of Europe, the** *Budapest, Hungary.* As indicated in the quote below, the Hungarian capital gained a colorful reputation that was both exotic and erotic, as a sort of Western counterpart to oriental Bangkok.

> Budapest ... was the liveliest, brashest city in the Eastern bloc [but gained] a seedy reputation that drew the label "the Bangkok of Europe" [Dodd/Donald, p. 389].

**Bangla Town** see in Appendix 1, p. 269.

**Banker Chapel Ho** *Whitechapel, London, England.* A facetious nickname for the district, current in the early 20th century. It has been explained as in the quote below (although "Ho" may really represent the typical Italian ending *-o*).

> A ludicrous Italian translation—*Bianca*, white; *cappella*, chapel ... Anglicisation entering in, the first word got into "Banker" and the second back into "Chapel," with the addition of the rousing and cheery "oh!" [J. Redding Ware, *Passing English of the Victorian Era*, 1909].

**Bankfurt** *see* **Mainhattan**

**Bank Robbery Capital of the World, the** *Los Angeles, California, USA.* The city gained notoriety for this particular type of crime. Hence the descriptive nickname.

**Banner County, the** *(1) Clare, Ireland; (2) Madison, Mississippi, USA.* The Irish county's nickname, occurring mostly in sports commentaries, refers to the banners displayed in support of parliamentary candidate (later political leader) Daniel O'Connell at an election rally in the county in 1828. For the US county, the name denotes general excellence, as if the county merited a banner as a distinction. *Cp.* **Banner State.** As can be seen from the quote below, the title has been claimed by other US counties.

> The banner county. Designation is claimed by Worcester, Massachusetts [*Niles' National Register*, December 5, 1840].

**Banner State, the** *Texas, USA.* A nickname denoting excellence, as if the state were entitled to a banner as a distinction. The title was current before Texas was admitted to the Union in 1845.

> Which is the Banner State?— The Whigs ... proposed to designate whichever state should give the Harrison ticket the largest majority, as the banner state [*Niles' National Register*, December 5, 1840].

**Banyan City, the** *Fuzhou, China.* The city was at one time known by this name for the banyan trees that grew there.

**Barbary Coast** see in Appendix 1, p. 269.

**Barça** *Barcelona, Spain.* A shortening of the name that primarily relates to the city's famed football team but that later came to apply to the city itself. The cedilla is needed to reflect the pronunciation as "Barsa."

> (1) Barcelona is emerging as *the* place for Britons to buy second homes in Spain. A city that echoes to the sound of late-night salsa is getting used to a new sound — the Anglo-Saxon vowels of the new breed of "Barça Brits" [*Sunday Times*, July 11, 2004].
> (2) Barça had a disastrous start to the season and, by the Christmas break, were 18 points behind Real [Madrid]. [*The Times*, November 22, 2004].

**Barcelona of Britain, the** *Manchester, England.* As implied in the quote below, Manchester has undergone an urban facelift that invites comparison with the Spanish city.

> I am not sure I would go as far as George Ferguson, the president of the Royal Institute of British Architects. He claims that Manchester is now "spoken of as the Barcelona of Britain" (presumably by the same people who speak of Blackpool as "the new Las Vegas") [*The Times*, January 14, 2004].

**Barcino** *Barcelona, Spain.* A colloquial form of the city's name.

**Barkshire** *Ireland.* The former nickname, punning on the English county name Berkshire, derives from Bark as an old slang term for a rowdy Irishman, who "barks" like an angry dog.

> Bark, an Irish person of either sex. From this term, much in use among the London lower orders, but for which no etymology can be found, Ireland is now and then playfully called Barkshire [*The Slang Dictionary*, 1894].

**Barney** *Barnard Castle, England.* A friendly shortening and personalization of the Co. Durham town's name. The form occurs in a local wry saying, "Barney Cassel, the last place that God made."

> The locals call it Barney, which hardly describes this wonderful market town [*Lonely Planet Great Britain*, 2005].

**Barramundi Capital of Queensland, the** *Burketown, Australia.* The Queensland village and river port so styles itself for the prized game fish found locally.

**Barum** *Barnstaple, England.* The name of the Devon town and former port has been shortened thus, with an abbreviated form apparently on the lines of **Sarum.** Local residents are sometimes known as Barumites.

> (1) BARNSTAPLE, or BARUM [Samuel Lewis, *A Topographical Dictionary of England*, 1840].
> (2) They presented to "Barumites in London" one of the choicest production of the Royal Barum ware pottery [*Westminster Gazette*, March 6, 1899].

**Basin State, the** *Utah, USA.* The name refers to the region known as the Great Basin that includes the Great Salt Lake in northern Utah.

> The Judge has friends goin' to arrive from New Yawk for a trip across the Basin [Owen Wister, *The Virginian*, 1902].

**Bastaga, la** *La Bastille, Paris, France.* A colloquial name of the district centering on the site of the notorious fortress.

**Batavia** *(1) Holland; (2) Jakarta, Indonesia.* The poetic name of Holland, preserved in that of the region of Betuwe between the Rhine and Waal rivers in the central Netherlands, derives from the people known as the Batavi who inhabited it. In 1619 Dutch colonists gave the name to the present Indonesian city of Jakarta, which kept it until 1949. (The historic part of the city is still known as "Old Batavia.")

> (1) (Holland) Lo! where through flat Batavia's willowy groves,
> Or by the lazy Seine, the exile roves [William Wordsworth, "Taken During a Pedestrian Tour Among the Alps," *Descriptive Sketches*, 1793].
> (2) (Holland) Look east, and ask the Belgian why,
> Beneath Batavia's sultry sky,

He seeks not eager to inhale
The freshness of the mountain gale [Sir Walter Scott, *Marmion*, 1808].

**Bath** or **Baths, the** *Bath, England*. An 18th-century way of naming the famous city and spa (whose name means what it says).

I am going to the Bath, with more opinion of ... the change of air, than of the waters [Horace Walpole, *Letters to Sir Horace Mann*, September 25, 1759].

**Bath of Ireland, the** *Mallow, Ireland*. The comparison is valid to the extent that the Co. Cork town was a famous mineral-water spa in the 18th and 19th centuries, like its English counterpart, although lacking its Roman baths.

**Bath of the East, the** *Tunbridge Wells, England*. The Kent town and health resort (as its name implies) has been so nicknamed as a fashionable spa on the lines of Bath in the West of England.

Royal Tunbridge Wells has been called the Bath of the East. Because of its chalybeate waters ... and its long tradition as a magnet for the fashionable world, since the time of Charles II, the comparison can be allowed [*Holiday Guide 1952: Area No. 5, South and South East England*].

**Battle-Born State, the** *Nevada, USA*. Nevada was admitted to the Union on October 31, 1864, at the height of the Civil War. Hence its nickname.

**Battlebridge** *King's Cross, London, England*. The name of the district, current until the 1830s, is preserved in Battle Bridge Road, behind King's Cross station. The name has nothing to do with battles but is a corruption of Bradford Bridge, for a bridge (replacing a "broad ford") over the Holborn River. The name fell out of general use when a monument to King George IV was erected at the crossroads here in 1830.

**Battleground Coast** see in Appendix 1, p. 269.

**Battleground of Freedom, the** *Kansas, USA*. The nickname relates to the latter half of the 1850s, when following passage of the Kansas-Nebraska Act of 1854, Kansas became a battleground between proslavery and antislavery factions. (*Cp.* **Bleeding Kansas.**)

**BA without the LA** *Montevideo, Uruguay*. The Uruguayan capital has often been unfavorably compared with the Argentinian capital, Buenos Aires, to the west across the Río de la Plata. But not in this nickname, where the comparison is extended to Los Angeles.

(1) B.A. without the L.A. The unfortunate problem with the "Paris of the South" is that it's also the sprawling, traffic-clogged "L.A. of the South." For congestion-haters, there's Montevideo [Josh Schonwald, "The Full Montevideo," *Washington Post*, April 9, 2000].

(2) There's none of the traffic chaos of Buenos Aires—"BA without the LA," as it has been dubbed [Dodd/Donald, p. 92].

**Bawlamer** or **Bawl'more** *Baltimore, Maryland, USA*. Two representations of a local pronunciation of the city's name. *Cp.* **Ballmer.**

(1) Baltimore (pronounced by all natives Bawlamer) [Alistair Cooke, *Letter from America*, "HLM: RIP," February 3, 1956 (2004)].

(2) The [city's] revival was achieved, but without losing Bawl'more's charm [Dodd/Donald, p. 129].

**Bay, the** *(1) Bay of Biscay, France/Spain; (2) Botany Bay, Australia; (3) Glenelg, Australia; (4) Port Elizabeth, South Africa; (5) Port Phillip Bay, Australia*. A short name often used for a well-known bay, or for a city that has "Bay" in its name or that lies on a bay. Glenelg, a southern suburb of Adelaide, is on Gulf St. Vincent; Port Elizabeth is on the western side of Algoa Bay; Port Phillip Bay is the natural harbor of Melbourne. The abbreviated name is no longer current for Botany Bay.

(1) (Bay of Biscay) Leaking like a lobster-pot, steering like a dray—
Out we took the *Bolivar*, out across the Bay! [Rudyard Kipling, "The Ballad of the *Bolivar*," 1890].

(2) (Port Elizabeth) Only a day's journey from "the Bay," as Port Elizabeth, like San Francisco, is familiarly called [Annie Martin, *Home Life on an Ostrich Farm*, 1890].

(3) (Glenelg) Recent shells were collected on the shores of St. Vincent Gulf at 'the Bay' as Glenelg was mostly called then [*South Australiana*, September 1933].

(4) (Port Phillip Bay) In Melbourne ... a ship was ... just 'going down the Bay' to Queenscliff, Portarlington or Geelong [Graham McInnes, *The Road to Gundagai*, 1965].

**Bay City** *(1) Napier, New Zealand; (2) San Francisco, California, USA*. The nickname is commonly found for a town or city on a bay. Napier is on Hawke Bay, North Island, while San Francisco is on the bay of the same name. There are also US cities formally so named, as Bay City, Michigan, on Saginaw Bay. (The Bay City in Raymond Chandler's detective fiction, however, is generally held to be Oakland, California.)

(Napier) The 'bay city,' as locals know it, has smartened itself up in recent years [Nick Hanna, *Explore New Zealand*, 2d ed., 1999].

**Bayou State, the** *(1) Louisiana, USA; (2) Mississippi, USA*. Louisiana lies in the vast delta of the Mississippi River, where there are many bayous (marshy tributaries), as there are in the neighboring state of Mississippi.

**Bay State, the** *Massachusetts, USA*. The name refers both geographically to Massachusetts Bay, forming the state's eastern boundary, and historically to the Massachusetts Bay Colony founded here in 1630.

(1) He was from the Down-East country; a representative of the Bay State [Robert Montgomery Bird, *Nick of the Woods*, 1837].

(2) The War of 1812 between the United States and Great Britain was a disaster for the Bay State's mercantile economy [Thomas H. O'Connor, *Boston A to Z*, 2000].

**Bay Town** *Robin Hood's Bay, England.* A shortened name for the Yorkshire coastal resort and fishing port.

(1) In the 19th century 'Bay Town,' as it is also known, outranked Whitby as a fishing centre [*RD Britain's Coast*, p. 160].

(2) 'Bay Town' fishermen fish for crab, lobster and white fish on the long line [Christopher Somerville, *Coast: A Celebration of Britain's Coastal Heritage*, 2005].

**BC** *British Columbia, Canada.* A straightfoward initialism of the province's name.

Just over the horizon ... is the silhouette of Vancouver Island, just a BC ferry ride away [Dodd/Donald, p. 201].

**Beach City** *Fort Lauderdale, Florida, USA.* Fort Lauderdale is a residential and resort city on the Atlantic coast. Hence the nickname.

**Bean Town** or **Beantown** *Boston, Massachusetts, USA.* The original Boston beans were baked with molasses made from the rum and sugar imported from the West Indies. The distinctive food became popular as a Puritan dish, since the beans could be cooked for supper on Saturday night then kept simmering over a slow heat for breakfast on the Sunday, a day devoted to religious worship. Hence the name.

(1) He's what they call a functioning alcoholic, something of a character in Bean Town's shadier districts [Robert Ludlum, *The Bourne Ultimatum*, 1990].

(2) Never forget that Boston is also known as Beantown, offering a good strong dose of honest, plain fare as much as preppy refinement [Dodd/Donald, p. 109].

**Bear, the** *Russia.* The brown bear, a denizen of the Siberian forests, has long served as the fierce and fearsome emblem of **Russia** and the Soviet Union, despite the latter's aim to promote itself in the persona of the animal's gentler and friendlier relation, the *mishka* ("teddy bear"). (The actual Russian name of the bear is *medved'*, literally "honey eater," involving a similar sweetening.) The epithet is sometimes qualified as Brown Bear or Northern Bear (*cp.* **Northern Giant**).

(1) France turns from her abandoned friends afresh, And soothes the Bear that prowls for patriot flesh [Thomas Campbell, *Works*, 1831 (1901)].

(2) For ourselves, we believe that in arranging the terms of peace he [i.e. the French emperor] was as little inclined to clip the claws of the Northern Bear as his ally [*The Christian Examiner*, quoted in Wheeler, p. 261].

(3) English they be and Japanee that hang on the Brown Bear's flank [Rudyard Kipling, "The Rhyme of the Three Sealers," 1896].

(4) The left paw of the Bear bars Germany from the Black Sea [Winston S. Churchill, *Into Battle*, 1939].

(5) When he allowed himself to be flown back to Moscow ... he was consciously putting his head in the Bear's mouth [*The Observer*, January 15, 1967].

(6) In the south, oil-producing Iran and Iraq, isolated by United States' Middle East diplomacy, are quietly and slowly sliding further into the deadly embrace of the northern bear [Claudiu A. Secara, *The New Commonwealth*, 1998].

(7) Beware the Russian bear, [Polish trade unionist] Lech Walesa warns West [Headline, *The Times*, August 30, 2005].

**Bear Flag Republic, the** *California, USA.* A historic name for the state, still current in certain contexts. It relates to June 14, 1846, when settlers at Sonoma declared a republic independent from Mexico and raised a makeshift flag showing a grizzly facing a red star. The republic lasted only until July 9, when California was claimed for the United States and the bear flag was replaced by the US flag.

**Bearflanks** *Fairbanks, Alaska, USA.* A whimsical metathesis of the name, as if referring to a town fringed by the grizzly bears which are native to the state.

**Bear State, the** *Arkansas, USA.* The name is said to refer more to the gruffness or grumpiness of the state's rural residents, especially in the Ozarks, than to the bears that inhabited the region. (In its issue of December 23, 1944, *This Week Magazine* reported that only 30 grizzlies remained in Arkansas.)

Mr. [John R.] Bartlett, the author of a standard work on "Americanisms," says: "I once asked a Western man if Arkansas abounded in bears that it should be designated as The Bear State. 'Yes,' said he, 'it does; for I never knew a man from that State but he was a *bar*, and, in fact, the people are all barish to a degree'" [Wagner 1893, p. 31].

**Bear Town, the** *Congleton, England.* The Cheshire town was long a noted center of bear-baiting and on one occasion, when a bear died, the town clerk is said to have sold the parish Bible to buy a new bear. Hence the name.

**Beautiful Barmouth** *Barmouth, Wales.* An alliterative touristic name for the seaside resort on the lines of **Smiling Somerset**.

**Beautiful Bruges** *Bruges, Belgium.* The city promotes itself thus (French *Bruges la belle*,

Flemish *Brugge die scone*) for its many fine gothic and baroque buildings.

**Beaver State, the** *Oregon, USA.* The name associates Oregon's leading timber-producing industry with the tree-gnawing animal, whose resourcefulness and industriousness are qualities ascribed to the state's inhabitants. Beaver pelts have also played a part in Oregon's economy.

**Bedlam** *Bethlehem, West Bank.* An early form of the city's name found in medieval writings down to the 16th century, when it became familiar as the popular name of the Hospital of St. Mary of Bethlehem, London, England, founded as a priory in 1247 and later becoming a lunatic asylum (madhouse). Hence the use of the name as a modern word meaning "scene of noisy confusion." The asylum, later renamed Bethlehem Royal Hospital, was moved from its original site in Bishopsgate to Moorfields in 1676, to Lambeth in 1815, to Addington, Surrey, in 1930, and finally to Beckenham, Kent, where it is now known as Bethlem [*sic*] Royal Hospital.

> A cite of Dauith that is cleped Bedleem [Luke 2:4 in Wycliffe's Bible, 1382; King James Version, 1611: "the city of David, which is called Bethlehem"].

**Beds** *Bedfordshire, England.* A semiofficial abbreviation of the county name. *See also* Appendix 6, p. 325.

> House prices fell by 0.2 per cent in the South East last month. The counties of Beds and Bucks were the worst hit with 0.5 per cent falls [*The Times*, September 30, 2005].

**Bedsit Jungle, the** *Earls Court, London, England.* The district was formerly noted for its rented accommodation, especially "bedsits" (bedsitting rooms, or one-room apartments), located randomly as if in a "jungle."

> In recent years the area ... has been called 'Kangaroo Valley' ... and the 'Bedsit Jungle' [Weinreb/ Hibbert, p. 354].

**Bed-Stuy** *Bedford-Stuyvesant, New York City, USA.* A colloquial short name for the residential district of Brooklyn, the largest black neighborhood in New York City. An occasional elaboration is "Do-or-Die Bed-Stuy."

> (1) 'I've worked the Bronx, Bedford-Stuyvesant, and Harlem ... Bed-Stuy's the worst' [Tom Wolfe, *The Bonfire of the Vanities*, 1987].
> (2) Bed-Stuy is the nation's largest African-American community after Chicago's South Side [*The Rough Guide to New York City*, 2004].

**Beechy Bucks** *Buckinghamshire, England.* The county, short name **Bucks**, is so alliteratively nicknamed for its extensive wooded region known as Burnham Beeches. An alternate name is "Leafy Bucks." Despite quote (3) below,

the county's name does not derive from its beech trees but from an Anglo-Saxon called Bucc.

> (1) Our beloved and beechy Bucks [Benjamin Disraeli, *Home Letters*, 1830].
> (2) The houses of Metroland and beechy Bucks dot the landscape [John Betjeman, *An Oxford University Chest*, 1938].
> (3) It is the beech which is the peculiar glory of the chalk ... The very name Buckinghamshire proclaims this fact if the derivation from buccan (beech) is correct. "Leafy Bucks." it is indeed, and nowhere more gloriously so than at Burnham beeches [Laurence W. Meynell in Hadfield 1981, p. 448].

**Beef City** *(1) Kansas City, Missouri, USA; (2) Omaha, Nebraska, USA.* Both cities are noted for their beef production, and Omaha has one of the largest livestock markets in the world.

**Beef State, the** *(1) Nebraska, USA; (2) Texas, USA.* The two named states are noted for their beef production, while Texas leads the country in the raising of beef cattle.

**Beehive State, the** *Utah, USA.* The state flag depicts a beehive surrounded by a swarm of bees, symbolizing the industriousness of the Mormon inhabitants of Utah. Hence the name. The same symbol gave Utah's alternate name as the **Deseret State**.

**Beer Capital of the World, the** *Munich, Germany.* Several of the largest breweries in Germany are located in Munich and the city is famous for its annual international beer festival, the *Oktoberfest*. Hence its self-promoting sobriquet.

**Beer City** or **Town** *Milwaukee, Wisconsin, USA.* Milwaukee's beer-brewing industry once dominated the country. Hence the name, and hence also the slogan of the Jos. Schlitz Brewing Company, founded in Milwaukee in 1849: "the beer that made Milwaukee famous."

**Bel Eire** *Killiney, Ireland.* The Co. Dublin village is punningly so nicknamed (after Bel Air, Los Angeles, and *Eire*) for the rock stars who live there. (The quote below relates to Irish singer Sinead O'Connor.)

> She's off to a new seaside home at Killiney, nicknamed Bel Eire for its celebrity residents [*Sunday Times*, June 19, 2005].

**Belerium** *Land's End, England.* The tip of the Cornish peninsula was perhaps poetically so named after a mythical giant.

> Whom not th' extended Albion could contain,
> From old Belerium to the northern main
> [Alexander Pope, *Windsor Forest*, 1713].

**Belgia** *Belgium.* A literary name of the country, which began its history as the Roman province of Belgica.

> What counsel, lords? Edward from Belgia,

With hasty Germans and blunt Hollanders,
Hath pass'd in safety through the narrow seas
[William Shakespeare, *Henry VI, Part 3*, 1595].

**"Believe It or Not" Town, the** *Eureka Springs, Arkansas, USA.* The resort town, with its mineral springs, derives its nickname from its special features, such as the Basin Park Hotel, with "eight floors, every one the first," and the perfectly balanced Pivot Rock, whose height is 15 times its base.

**Bella Firenze, la** *Florence, Italy.* A regular laudatory name, "beautiful Florence," for the historic city and its many treasures. See also quote at **Superba.**

**Bella Italia, la** *Italy.* A regular epithet, "beautiful Italy," for one of Europe's loveliest lands. The name is both literal and metaphorical, in the latter sense describing a cultured and civilized country.

La Bella Italia was a site of loss, a great beauty scarred by the soldiers of foreign realms who had plundered and abandoned her [Esther Schor, reviews of Roderick Cavaliero, *Italia Romantica*, Jonah Siegel, *The Haunted Museum*, George Dekker, *The Fictions of Romantic Tourism*, *Times Literary Suppplement*, November 25, 2005].

**Belle France, la** *France.* A standard sobriquet on the same lines as **Bella Italia**, for a blessed and beautiful land.

(1) When talking to Frenchmen, he should always be soppy about La Belle France [Guy Egmont, *The Art of Egmontese*, 1951].
(2) His lifelong passion for La Belle France has lost none of its ardour [*Sunday Times*, August 1, 2004].

**Belle of the South Coast, the** *Brighton, England.* A former nickname of the popular Sussex resort, tying in with "Brighton Belle" (originally "Southern Belle") as the name of the Pullman train that ran between London and Brighton.

**Belle Province, la** *Quebec, Canada.* Canada's largest province is noted for its fine scenery, with a mix of mountains, hills, lakes, and forests. Hence the deserved French sobriquet.

**Bells, Smells, and Yells** *Malta.* A sailors' name for the Mediterranean island, with its many churches, channels, and children.

**Bel Paese, il** *Italy.* The name, Italian for "the beautiful country," is sometimes applied to Italy as a whole, although more precisely it relates to the northern part of the country. (Italian *paese*, like French *pays*, means both "countryside" and "nation.") The name was popularized by the title of Antonio Stoppani's book *Il bel paese* (1875), describing this part of Italy, and as *Bel Paese* it was later adopted for a make of creamy cheese originating from here. *Cp.* **Bella Italia.**

**Beltway, the** *Washington, DC, USA.* The nickname properly applies to the ringroad around Washington, but has been extended to the city itself, especially with reference to the perceived insularity of the US government.

(1) Spreading the government around a bit ought to reduce that self-feeding and self-regarding Beltway culture that Washington-phobes claim to dislike so much [*Time*, January 20, 1992].
(2) "Let me say to the money boys and the Beltway elite, who think that at long last they have pulled up the drawbridge and locked us out forever, you don't know this peasant army," he [i.e. presidential contender Pat Buchanan] said [*The Times*, October 26, 1999].

**Benares** *Varanasi, India.* The old name of the Indian city is still sometimes found as a corrupt form of the original.

**Benares of Bengal, the** *Nabadwip, India.* Like Varanasi, Nabadwip is a noted pilgrimage center, famous for its sanctity.

**Benidorm of Britain, the** *Newquay, England.* The Cornish seaside resort has a popular appeal on the lines of its larger Spanish equivalent.

**Berdoo** or **San Berdoo** *San Bernardino, California, USA.* A colloquial shortening of the city's formal name.

(1) We sauntered over to San Bernardino—"San Berdu," as the tramps call it [Harry Kemp, *Tramping on Life*, 1922].
(2) A flat-out high-speed burn through Baker and Barstow and Berdoo and then on the Hollywood Freeway straight into frantic oblivion [Hunter S. Thompson, *Fear and Loathing in Las Vegas*, 1971].

**Berg, the** *Drakensberg, South Africa.* A colloquial short name for the mountain range, especially that part of it in KwaZulu-Natal.

The total number of wagons that crossed the Berg during the Great Trek is estimated at more than one thousand [Julian Mockford, *Here Are South Africans*, 1944].

**Bergerac Country** see in Appendix 1, p. 269.

**Berks** *Berkshire, England.* The semiofficial abbreviated name of the English county (pronounced "Barks") gave the name of the US Pennsylvania county (pronounced "Burks"). *See also* Appendix 6, p. 325.

**Berloo** *see* **Balloo**

**Berm-on-Sea** *Bermondsey, London, England.* A Cockney nickname for the Thames-side district.

**Bermoothes, the** *Bermuda.* An early form of the name, reflecting the original Spanish pronunciation. (The islands take their name from the 16th-century Spanish explorer Juan Bermúdez.) The name became familiar from Shakespeare's use of it in the quote below.

Thou call'dst me up at midnight to fetch dew
From the still-vex'd Bermoothes [William
Shakespeare, *The Tempest*, 1611].

**Bermuda Triangle, the** *Mogadishu, Somalia.*
A nickname for the Somali capital seen as bandit country, based on the North Atlantic **Bermuda Triangle** (see in Appendix 1, p. 269), the
site of numerous reported disappearances of
planes and ships.

**Berzerkely** *Berkeley, California, USA.* A punning name deriving from the campus of the University of California at Berkeley, a center of student unrest and the "counterculture" movement
in the 1960s and early 1970s.

**Best Small Town in America, the** *Essex,
Connecticut, USA.* A promotional name for a
town with a population (including Essex village)
of around 6,000.

**Bethnal Green in the Sun** *Marbella, Spain.*
The popular Spanish resort lies not only in the
**Costa del Sol** but the **Costa del Crime** (see both
in Appendix 1, p. 269). Hence its British nick-
name, from the east London district of Bethnal
Green, notorious for its criminal elements.

**Between the Commons** *see* **Nappy Valley** in
Appendix 1, p. 269.

**Beulah** *Israel.* According to the Bible, this
was the symbolic name, meaning "married" (literally "possessed"), that was to be given to Israel
to denote its future prosperity. Instead of being
forsaken and desolate, Israel would be married and
its inhabitants would remove the existing reproach
of its widowhood. (In the verses quoted below,
Hephzibah, meaning "my delight in her," is a
name symbolizing Jerusalem's restored status.)

Thou shalt no more be termed Forsaken; neither
shall thy land any more be termed Desolate: but
thou shalt be called Hephzi-bah, and thy land
Beulah; for the Lord delighteth in thee, and thy
land shall be married. For as a young man marri-
eth a virgin, so shall thy sons marry thee: and as
the bridegroom rejoiceth over the bride, so shall
thy God rejoice over thee [Isaiah 62:4–5].

**Beyond the Black Stump** see in Appendix 1,
p. 269.

**BH** *Beverly Hills, California, USA.* A local
initialism of the Los Angeles suburb's name.

You will find the restaurants and the lifestyle in
BH to be much quieter than in West Hollywood
[*Fodor's Los Angeles 2006*].

**B'ham** *see* **So'ton**
**B'head** *see* **So'ton**
**Biarritz of the North, the** *North Berwick,
Scotland.* An aspirational name for the seaside
resort, comparing its beaches with those of the
famous French tourist center.

**Biarritz of Wales, the** *Aberystwyth, Wales.* An
image name for Wales's liveliest seaside resort,
designed to point up its touristic appeal rather
than its prestigious academic status as a university town. *See* **Aber**.

**Bible Belt** see in Appendix 1, p. 269.

**Big A, the** *(1) Albuquerque, New Mexico,
USA; (2) Amarillo, Texas, USA; (3) Atlanta,
Georgia, USA; (4) Australia; (5) New York City,
USA.* A name based on the initial of the given
city or country, emphasizing its size or importance. In the case of New York, the reference is
to the familiar sobriquet **Big Apple.**

**Big Apple, the** *New York City, USA.* The
name was apparently first promoted (but not invented) by turf reporter John J. Fitz Gerald,
whose following letter appeared in the *Morning
Telegraph* of December 1, 1926:

So many people have asked the writer about the
derivation of his phrase "the big apple" that he is
forced to make another explanation... A number
of years back, when racing a few horses at the Fair
Grounds with Jack Byer, he was watching a couple of stable hands cool out a pair of "hots" in a
circle outside the stable. A boy from an adjoining
barn called over, "Where are you shipping after
the meeting?" To this one of the lads replied,
"Why, we ain't no bull ring [i.e. third-rate] stable;
we's goin' to the big apple." The reply came back
bright and snappy: "Boy, I don't know why you're
goin' to that apple with those hides for. All you'll
get is the rind."

According to Gerald Cohen, quoting this letter in "The Origin of NYC's Nickname *The Big
Apple*" (*Names*, Vol. 41, No. 1, March 1993), the
phrase "big apple" is of black origin (the stable
lad's speech in the text suggests he is African
American) and evolved from an actual big red
delicious apple served as a dessert, and so regarded as special. In 1971, as part of a publicity
campaign for the city, the name was revived by
Charles Gillett, president of the New York Convention & Visitors Bureau (see quote for **Big
Stem** in Appendix 2, p. 307).

A rival account of the name links it to the jazz
club Smalls' Paradise, which opened on 7th Avenue in 1925, billing itself as "Harlem's House
of Mirth and Music." It is said that when jazz-
men met on the road in the 1930s, they called to
each other, "See you at the Big Apple," referring
to the decoration on the outside of Smalls'. But
this origin lacks attested support.

(1) As soon as we hit The Big Apple we'll ditch
the buggy, and when the New York cops find it
your insurance company will have to ... ship it
back to you [Milton Mezzrow and Bernard Wolfe,
*Really the Blues*, 1946].

(2) All of them are well aware of the negative as-

pects of life in New York. They are familiar with the pits in the Big Apple [*Women's Wear Daily*, March 23, 1973].

(3) In every way but formally the city went bankrupt [in the mid-1970s] ... Much of the country, always suspicious of New York's foreignness and arrogance, cheered as the Big Apple was shown to be full of worms [*Britannica*, vol. 24, p. 914].

(4) If you fancy a well-deserved evening on the town after a long day of meetings, our 11.35pm from JFK to Heathrow should allow you plenty of time to take a bite out of the Big Apple [American Airlines ad, *The Times*, November 7, 2005].

**Big Arch, the** *St. Louis, Missouri, USA.* The name refers to the striking stainless steel Gateway Arch in the city's Jefferson National Expansion Memorial, designed in 1965 to commemorate the historic role of St. Louis as **Gateway to the West.**

**Big B, the** *Baltimore, Maryland, USA.* An initial-based name on the lines of **Big A.**

**Big Bend** see in Appendix 1, p. 269.

**Big Bend State, the** *Tennessee, USA.* The name refers to the Tennessee River, which flows through the state and gave it its name, itself said to derive from an American Indian word meaning "river of the big bend."

**Big Brother** *Philadelphia, Pennsylvania, USA.* A name punning on the city's well-known sobriquet as the **City of Brotherly Love.**

**Big Burg, the** *New York City, USA.* A nickname for the city popular in the early 20th century.

**Big Butte, the** *Butte, Montana, USA.* An alliterative name for Montana's largest city.

**Big C, the** *Chicago, Illinois, USA.* An initial-based name on the lines of **Big A.**

**Big City, the** *(1) Berlin, Germany; (2) London, England.* A name that could be applied to any large or important city. London is also known as simply the **City.** The Berlin nickname is probably based on this, and was first used for the German capital by members of British Bomber Command in World War II.

(London) If you're going to London, there's another little book by Victor Hilton you may find both useful and amusing. This is the *Country Cousins Guide to London*— a gay and practical helping hand for innocents abroad in the Big City [Advertisement, *Holiday Haunts 1961: Area No. 4, West of England and South and Central Wales*].

**Big Country, the** *(1) Canada; (2) Wales.* Canada is the the second-largest country in the world (after Russia), so deserves its descriptive title. For Wales the name is a different matter. It is self-promotional, designed to denote the small country's many and varied attractions and growing modern economy. The name courts derision, as in quote (1) below. The title itself was popularized by that of the 1958 Western movie starring Gregory Peck.

(1) (Wales) It is not very clever to advertise yourself as "The Big Country," given that aficionados of big countries have Canada, Australia, Mongolia, the United States, China and, frankly, even Luxembourg to consider [*The Times*, June 17, 2004].

(2) (Canada) Oh, Canada! The best of the big country [Headline, *Sunday Times*, June 19, 2005].

**Big D, the** *(1) Dallas, Texas, USA; (2) Denver, Colorado, USA ; (3) Detroit, Michigan, USA; (4) Disneyland, California, USA.* Just four famous US places to which the initial-derived name has been given. *Cp.* **Big A.**

(1) (Dallas) You're from Big D,
My, oh yes, I mean Big D, little a, double l-a-s
And that spells Dallas, my darlin' darlin' Dallas,
Don't it give you pleasure to confess
That you're from Big D?
My, oh yes! [Frank Loesser, "Big D," *The Most Happy Fella*, 1956].

(2) (Disneyland) Anaheim, Orange County's tourist hub, which centers on the big D [*Fodor's Los Angeles 2006*].

**Big Ditch, the** *(1) Atlantic Ocean; (2) Erie Canal, New York, USA; (3) Manchester Ship Canal, England; (4) Pacific Ocean; (5) Panama Canal, Panama.* A colloquial name for any large or lengthy stretch of water, with mock-derisory "ditch" more obviously applicable to a canal than an ocean. A plane could "ditch" in the latter, however.

(1) (Panama Canal) What's the big deal about corruption? This is *Panama*, for God's sake. The whole country is a put-up job, sleazed into existence by Teddy Roosevelt so he'd have somewhere to put the Big Ditch [P.J. O'Rourke, *Holidays in Hell*, 1988].

(2) (Manchester Ship Canal) The Manchester Ship Canal is one of the Victorian era's greatest engineering feats. Built to bring deep-sea shipping right to the heart of the city, the 'big ditch' runs for 36 miles from the tidal river Mersey at Eastham to Salford in Manchester [Tourist brochure *Waterside England*, 2005].

**Big Drink, the** *(1) Atlantic Ocean; (2) Mississippi River, USA; (3) Pacific Ocean.* A colloquial name for an important waterway, similar to the **Big Ditch.** "The drink" is also a nickname for any river or sea.

(1) (Mississippi) There never would have been any Atlantic ocean if it hadn't been for the Mississippi, nor never will be after we've turned the waters of that big drink into the Mammoth Cave! [*Daily Picayune* (New Orleans), March 24, 1844].

(2) (Atlantic) I was coming across the Big Drink as fast as a Cunard could bring me [Mary Elizabeth Braddon, *Mount Royal*, 1882].

**Big E, the** *(1) Elizabeth, New Jersey, USA; (2) Erie, Pennsylvania, USA.* An initial-based name on the lines of **Big A**.

**Big Easy, the** *New Orleans, Louisiana, USA.* The name, referring to the city's perceived relaxed mode of living, is usually traced to James Conaway's 1970 crime novel so titled, set in New Orleans, or to the 1986 movie based on it. But the phrase almost certainly originated among jazz musicians, and the first great jazz legend Buddy Bolden played at a New Orleans dance hall called the Big Easy at the turn of the 20th century. The sobriquet was popularized by Betty Guillaud, a columnist for the *Times-Picayune*, who in the early 1970s wrote an article comparing the laid-back style of New Orleans with the pick-up pace of New York.

> (1) The town's unofficial motto is *Laissez les bons temps rouler* (let the good times roll) [and it is] nicknamed 'the Big Easy' for its laid-back vibe [*Lonely Planet USA*, 2004].
> (2) The city has sold a little of its soul ... but the Big Easy flavours of intrigue, romance and decadence are still palpable on the sultry air [Dodd/Donald, p. 164].
> (3) In a country inclined to puritanism, the Big Easy is the almost Mediterranean enclave where America came to eat and drink too much, to stay up late and behave badly [*The Times*, September 2, 2005].

**Big Ferry, the** *Atlantic Ocean.* A colloquial name for the ocean seen as providing a passage between Britain and the USA.

**Big Fog, the** *Pittsburgh, Pennsylvania, USA.* The nickname alludes to the fogs caused by the heavy pall of smoke that formerly hung over the city. *Cp.* **Big Smoke**.

**Biggest Little City in the World, the** *Reno, Nevada, USA.* The mock self-deprecatory name refers to the (big) city's fast mode of life, with its many nightspots and casinos.

> Reno repeatedly reminds you that it's 'The Biggest Little City in the World' ... and as hokey as that slogan will always be, there's something refreshing about it, too [*Lonely Planet USA*, 2004].

**Big Heart of England, the** *Birmingham, England.* A promotional name for the manufacturing and commercial city, formerly located in the county of Warwickshire, the **Heart of England**.

> Birmingham is fast gaining an international reputation as one of Britain's leading cultural, conference and exhibition centres, actively promoted as 'The Big Heart of England' [Robin Whiteman, *The Heart of England*, 1992].

**Big Hole, the** *Kimberley Mine, South Africa.* A semiofficial name for the former diamond mine, the richest in the world, closed in 1914.

> (1) The Prince made an unofficial visit to Kimber-

ley's 'big hole,' 1,700 feet deep [*Eastern Province Herald*, July 24, 1925].
> (2) Before leaving Kimberley I motored with Mr. Grimmer to a place rich in memories, the 'Big Hole' of the abandoned Kimberley Mine [Lawrence George Green, *Secret Africa*, 1936].
> (3) Day 4. Arrive Kimberley for a tour of the 'Big Hole' [Travel ad, *The Times Magazine*, August 20, 2005].

**Big Island, the** *Hawaii, Hawaii, USA.* A common local name for the largest island in the Hawaii group.

> The island of Hawaii is suitably dubbed the 'Big Island,' as it's larger than all the other Hawaiian islands combined [*Lonely Planet USA*, 2004].

**Big Lady, the** *New York City, USA.* A female personalization of the great city.

**Big M, the** *Memphis, Tennessee, USA.* A name on the lines of **Big A** and other initialisms.

**Big Moose, the** *Canada.* The nickname refers to the animal that is traditionally associated with Canada and that gave the name of the Saskatchewan city of Moose Jaw. *Cp.* **Big Country**.

> Canada is immense, second only to Russia for bulk. So how should a first-timer tackle the Big Moose in a two-week holiday? [*Sunday Times*, June 19, 2005].

**Big Muddy, the** *(1) Mississippi River, USA; (2) Missouri River, USA.* The two major rivers are notoriously sediment-laden, and the Mississippi becomes a brown flood as it flows toward the Gulf of Mexico. It is "big" as it is both lengthy and a mile or more wide in places. *Cp.* **Old Muddy**.

> (1) (Missouri) Our good friends out here, though they made light of their river by calling it the Big Muddy, nevertheless declared that it was the parent of the Mississippi [William Black, *Green Pastures and Piccadilly*, 1877].
> (2) (Mississippi) When it was daylight, here was the clear Ohio water inshore, sure enough, and outside was the old regular Muddy! [Mark Twain, *Huckleberry Finn*, 1884].

**Big Nipple, the** *Hollywood, Los Angeles, California, USA.* The nickname, a spin on **Big Apple**, stems from Italian filmmaker Bernardo Bertolucci, who used it, presumably inadvertently, during his acceptance speech at the Academy Awards ceremony for his epic movie *The Last Emperor* (1987). The sobriquet nicely encapsulates the particular genre of movie associated with Hollywood and other film studios, including Bertolucci's own explicit *Last Tango in Paris* (1972).

**Big O, the** *Omaha, Nebraska, USA.* An initial-based nickname similar to the **Big A**.

**Big Oak** *Oakland, California, USA.* A shortening of the city's name that also alludes to its size. "Big" is in any case a common adjective applied to an oak tree.

**Big Onion, the** *New York City, USA.* An allusion to a city that is both "pungent" and has "layers" of identity.

**Big Orange, the** *Los Angeles, California, USA.* A name based on New York's familiar **Big Apple**, referring to the orange groves for which Los Angeles is noted. It may also imply a city that is "juicier" and more exotic than the other.

**Big Peach, the** *Atlanta, Georgia, USA.* The name, punning on the **Big Apple**, refers to the peaches that are associated with Georgia (*see* **Peach State**) while also implying a city that is a "peach," or one of the best of its kind.

**Big Pond, the** *Atlantic Ocean.* A name that adds a descriptive to the ocean's common nickname of the **Pond**.

> [They] have hardly sustained their reputation on either side of the big pond [*Outing* (United States), June 1902].

**Big Port, the** *Portland, Oregon, USA.* A nickname that is both descriptive of the state's principal port and that puns on its name.

**Big Potato, the** *(1) Boise, Idaho, USA; (2) Moscow, Russia.* The state capital's nickname refers to the potatoes that are virtually synonymous with Idaho. *Cp.* **Famous Potatoes.** The Russian capital's sobriquet has a similar reference, but to potatoes as a constituent of vodka. Both names are a variation on the **Big Apple**.

**Big Pretzel, the** *Philadelphia, Pennsylvania, USA.* The first commercial pretzel bakery in the USA was set up in 1861 in Philadelphia, where the popular pretzel is usually eaten with a dash of yellow mustard or a daubing of melted butter.

> So famous are Philadelphia's pretzels that the city is nicknamed the 'Big Pretzel' [John Mariani, *The Dictionary of American Food and Drink*, 2d ed., 1994].

**Big PX, the** *United States.* As explained in the quote below, the nickname is of military origin.

> "You know what locals over here call the United States? ... The land of the big P.X. (The P.X. is the Post Exchange in military parlance, it is where military families shop for groceries on the reservation.)" [Steve Cochran, *Caught in the Gap*, <http://www.journalism.sfsu.edu/fluxForum/generationp1.html>, accessed September 29, 2004].

**Big Run, the** *Victoria River Downs, Australia.* A colloquial name for what at one time was the country's biggest cattle station, established in the Northern Territory in the 1880s. "Run" denotes a tract of pasture.

**Big Salty** *Salt Lake City, Utah, USA.* A fairly obvious nickname for the state capital, east of the Great Salt Lake.

**Big Sky Country, the** *Montana, USA.* The nickname refers to Montana's many open spaces, especially in the east of the state, where grazing cattle and sheep easily outnumber human inhabitants.

**Big Smear, the** *New York City, USA.* A not entirely complimentary name for the city, as if a "blot on the landscape" or at best an extended smudge or stain from the original **Melting Pot.**

**Big Smoke, the** *(1) London, England; (2) Melbourne, Australia; (3) Pittsburgh, Pennsylvania, USA; (4) Sydney, Australia.* A name referring to the smoke and fumes formerly emitted by industrial and domestic chimneys in the respective cities. A parallel name is that of **Auld Reekie.** *Cp.* **Smoke.**

> (1) (Sydney) The suburbs of Brisbane are full of such figures ... thumbing their way [south] up the Ipswich Road to that mecca of youth — Sydney and the Big Smoke [Dorothy Hewett, "The Strawberry Pickers," *Australians Have a Word for It*, 1964].
> (2) (Sydney) During the summer months, ... holiday-makers escape here [i.e. the south coast of New South Wales] from the "big smoke" up north [*The Rough Guide to Australia*, 2001].
> (3) (London) The other interesting news from Financial Accountancy is that Lisa Hawcroft has resigned and leaves us on 4th June to start a new life in the Big Smoke. She is moving to London to be with boyfriend Colin [*The Bews News* (Aberdeen University), Scotland], April 2004].

**Big South, the** *Atlanta, Georgia, USA.* The state capital symbolizes Georgia as the **Empire State of the South.**

**Big T, the** *(1) Tampa, Florida, USA; (2) Tucson, Arizona, USA.* An initial-based name similar to many others, as **Big A.**

**Big Town, the** *(1) Chicago, Illinois, USA; (2) New York City, USA.* A former name similar to **Big City** for these two major cities, among others. *Cp.* **Big Burg.**

**Big Twin, the** *Minneapolis, Minnesota, USA.* The name refers to St. Paul, with which Minneapolis was incorporated as the larger half of the "twin" in 1867. *Cp.* **Twin Cities.**

**Big V, the** *Las Vegas, Nevada, USA.* An initial-based name for the city, often known as simply **Vegas.**

**Big Water, the** *Atlantic Ocean.* A name on the lines of the **Big Ditch** or **Big Pond**, but lacking the mock denigration.

**Big Wind** or **Windy** *see* **Windy City**

**Bikini State, the** *Florida, USA.* The allusion

is to the perennial presence of bikini-clad women on the state's many beaches.

**Bilgewater** *Bridgwater, England*. A punning deprecatory alteration of the Somerset town's name, referring to pollution of the river here by effluvia from the local cellophane factory. Its closure was announced in 2005.

> The inhabitants seem undeterred by the acrid air or recent disclosures that Bilgewater has a lower average IQ than anywhere else in Somerset [Sam Jordison and Dan Kieran, eds., *The Idler Book of Crap Towns*, 2003].

**Biljam** *Belgium*. A World War I British soldiers' corruption of the country's name, suggesting "bilge."

**Billy Ricky** *Billericay, England*. A former personalization of the Essex town's name, as mainly current among vagrants.

**Bimshire** *Barbados, West Indies*. "Bim" is a colloquial term for a Bajan (Barbadian), with "shire" added to name their territory. The origin of the term is unclear. Igbo *bem*, "my home," has been proposed.

> Barbadoes is known to the initiated as Bimshire — a Barbadian as a Bim [W.A. Paton, *Down the Islands*, 1887].

**Binge-Drinking Capital of Britain, the** *Cardiff, Wales*. The Welsh capital earned this nifty nickname at the turn of the 21st century for its many pubs and bars, which are daily (or nightly) filled with dedicated drinkers. The city's carousers are said to spend more on drinking than in any comparable city in Britain.

> The title of Binge-drinking Capital of Britain is hotly contested, but Cardiff is named as the top spot more often than most [*The Times Magazine*, March 26, 2005].

**Birmingham of America, the** *Pittsburgh, Pennsylvania, USA*. A reference to Pittsburgh's fame as a steel-producing city, like that of its English counterpart.

> Pittsburgh is like Birmingham in England; at least its townspeople say so [Charles Dickens, *American Notes*, 1842].

**Birmingham of Belgium, the** *Liège, Belgium*. Liège is noted for its steel production, as is the English city.

**Birmingham of Russia, the** *Tula, Russia*. Tula has long been famed for its steel production, like that of the English city.

**Birthplace of American Liberty, the** *(1) Lexington, Massachusetts, USA; (2) Philadelphia, Pennsylvania, USA*. Both cities can lay claim to the title. Lexington was the scene of the opening engagement of the American Revolution, the battle of April 19, 1775, in which a force of minutemen resisted a British contingent marching to seize stores at Concord. The Declaration of Independence was signed in Philadelphia in 1776 and the Constitution of the United States adopted there on September 17, 1787.

**Birthplace of Aviation, the** *Dayton, Ohio, USA*. An alternate name for **Aviation City**.

**Birthplace of Cricket, the** *Hambledon, England*. The Hampshire village was long popularly so nicknamed, and although the rules of the English national sport were first formulated here by the Hambledon Club in the 18th century, the game itself is thought to date from some time before this. The name is thus a misnomer.

> An air of discreet Georgian prosperity pervades Hambledon, recalling the era when it was dubbed, erroneously, 'the birthplace of cricket' [*AA Book of British Villages*, 1980].

**Birthplace of Jazz, the** *New Orleans, Louisiana, USA*. The name is justified on the grounds that jazz bands first arose in New Orleans in the 1890s.

**Birthplace of the British Empire, the** *St. John's, Newfoundland, Canada*. The provincial capital, one of the oldest cities in North America, is so nicknamed as Britain's first overseas colony, founded in 1583.

**Birthplace of the Confederacy, the** *Abbeville, South Carolina, USA*. It was in Abbeville that a secessionist meeting was held on November 22, 1860, and here that Jefferson Davis, the Confederate president, held one of his last cabinet meetings, on May 2, 1865. Hence the city's alternate nickname as the "Cradle and Grave of the Confederacy."

**Birthplace of the Industrial Revolution, the** *West Midlands, England*. The term "industrial revolution" was first used by the French revolutionary Louis-Auguste Blanqui in 1837 to describe the transformation undergone by Britain over the previous half-century, from a predominantly rural society to a rapidly urbanizing country whose wealth came from commerce and manufacturing. One of the main agents in effecting the change was the use of coal as energy, as notably happened in the **Black Country** (see in Appendix 1, p. 269). If there is one city that can be pinpointed as the birthplace of the title, it is Birmingham, **Capital of the Midlands**.

> Welcome to the West Midlands — birthplace of the Industrial Revolution, the pneumatic tyre and state education [*The Times*, February 22, 2005].

**Birthplace of the Nation, the** *Northland, New Zealand*. An alternate name for the North Island region, also known as the **Cradle of New Zealand**, where the first Anglican mission was set up in 1841.

**Birthplace of the Nation's Wealth, the** *Camden, Australia*. It was in this suburb of Sydney, New South Wales, that in the early 19th century John and Elizabeth Macarthur carried out the sheep-breeding experiments that laid the foundation of Australia's wool industry. Hence the sobriquet.

**Biscuitopolis** *Reading, England*. A former humorous nickname for the Berkshire town, from the famous Huntley and Palmer biscuit (cookie) factory here. The jail alongside was known as the Biscuit Factory.

**Bitches' Heaven, the** *Boston, Massachusetts, USA*. A vagrants' nickname for the city, as described in the quote below. ("Bitch" was formerly a slang term for a prostitute. Hence the literal sense of "son of a bitch.")

> The city was once noted for the number of cheap prostitutes to be found there; and hobohemia, concluding that conditions must be ideal for the sisterhood, coined the phrase [Godfrey Irwin, *American Tramp and Underworld Slang*, 1931].

**Bitter Buxton** *Buxton, England*. The Derbyshire town, a former hot-water health resort, stands at a high altitude in the center of the Peak District and is noted for its cold climate. Hence the sobriquet.

> [The heated mineral baths] may well have been thought the only warm place in 'bitter Buxton' on a winter's day [Phil Drabble in Speaight, p. 189].

**Black Africa** see in Appendix 1, p. 269.

**Black Belt** see in Appendix 1, p. 269.

**Black City, the** *Angers, France*. The city derives its nickname from its important slate quarries, the largest in France.

**Black Country** see in Appendix 1, p. 269.

**Black Harlem** see in Appendix 1, p. 269.

**Black Hole, the** *Cheltenham, England*. The genteel Gloucestershire town was so dubbed for the many British army officers and civil servants who retired here from the late 19th century after service in India. The nickname alludes to the infamous Black Hole of Calcutta (1756).

**Black Indies, the** *Newcastle upon Tyne, England*. Both East Indies and West Indies were a source of great mercantile wealth. Hence the former nickname of the Tyneside city and port, whose coalmines provided comparable riches.

**Black North, the** *Northern Ireland*. A former nickname given by Catholics in the Republic of Ireland to the Protestant province.

**Blackpool of the South, the** *Margate, England*. The Kent seaside resort, long popular among Londoners, is noted for its "cheap and cheerful" attractions and entertainments, like those offered by Blackpool. Hence the nickname.

> (1) Margate is the Blackpool of the South [Theodora Benson and Betty Askwith, *Muddling Through, or Britain in a Nutshell*, 1936].
> (2) Pre-eminently a pleasure resort, the oldest and most famous in Kent, and one of the best known in England; it is sometimes called the Blackpool of the South [Hadfield 1981, p. 177].

**Black Republic, the** *Haiti, West Indies*. The name refers to the dark-skinned inhabitants of the country, which first became a republic in 1804 following a slave revolt. *See also* **First Black Republic**.

**Black Town, the** *(1) Agde, France; (2) Chinnai (Madras), India*. The French town is so named for the dark color of its houses, most of which are built from basalt. The Indian city was so nicknamed for its dark-skinned Indian inhabitants, living in the oldest part of the town, as distinct from the white English residents in the southern suburbs.

> (1) (Chinnai) The Black Town is inhabited by *Gentows, Mahometans*, and *Indian Christians* [Alexander Hamilton, *A New Account of the East Indies*, 1727].
> (2) (Chinnai) Hartley hastened from the Black Town, more satisfied than before that some deceit was about to be practised towards Menie Gray [Sir Walter Scott, *The Surgeon's Daughter*, 1827].

**Black Wantage** *Wantage, England*. The Oxfordshire town was formerly so nicknamed from its severe depression in the 19th century, having narrowly failed to benefit from the Industrial Revolution. The situation was redeemed by Robert Loyd-Lindsay, Baron Wantage (1832–1901), who revived the ironworks and linked the town with the railroad.

**Blackwater State, the** *Nebraska, USA*. The state is sometimes so nicknamed for the murky waters of its rivers and streams, resulting from the rich, dark soil over which they flow.

**Bleeding Kansas** *Kansas, USA*. A nickname referring to the warring proslavery and antislavery factions in Kansas in the second half of the 1850s. One of the bloodiest incidents was the Pottawatomie Massacre of 1856, in which five men from a proslavery settlement on Pottawatomie Creek were murdered by an antislavery party.

**Blenheim** *Blindheim, Germany*. The English form of the village's name became familiar from the battle of 1704 in which the English and Dutch under the Duke of Marlborough defeated the Franco-Bavarian forces under Marshal Tallard. The name is preserved in that of Blenheim Palace, Woodstock, Oxfordshire, given to the duke in gratitude for his victory, and the home of subsequent dukes. The Blenheim Orange apple came from its grounds.

**Blighty** *England.* An enduring (and endearing) nickname for England that first gained popularity from its use among British soldiers fighting in France in World War I. The word is an Anglo-Indian corruption of Hindi *bilāyatī,* "foreign," "European," which itself originated in the Indian army in the late 19th century. The name is found as the subject of popular songs of World War I vintage, one of the best-known being Fred Godfrey, A.J. Mills, and Bennett Scott's "Take Me Back to Dear Old Blighty" (1916).

(1) As far as ageing romantics are concerned Dover is the only way to return to good old Blighty [*The Times,* August 17, 1999].

(2) I saw the green, brown and yellow patchwork of Blighty down below and allowed myself to feel the beginnings of relief [*The Times Magazine,* July 10, 2004].

(3) Cyprus, so the brochures say, is just like Old Blighty. Everyone speaks English, they drive on the left and the legal system is based on ours [*The Times,* February 25, 2005].

**Blizzard State, the** *(1) South Dakota, USA; (2) Texas, USA.* Both states experience blizzards, although those in Texas only rarely bring snow.

**Block** see in Appendix 1, p. 269.

**Bloem** *Bloemfontein, South Africa.* A regular short name for the Free State provincial capital.

**Bloody Breathitt** *Breathitt County, Kentucky, USA.* The nickname alludes to the feuds between family clans that occurred in the county.

**Bloody Halfway** *Wadi Halfa, Sudan.* A cynical pun devised by British forces in North Africa in the 1880s, when the town, on the Nile midway between Alexandria, Egypt, and Khartoum, Sudan, was the headquarters of the Anglo-Egyptian army as it prepared to reclaim Sudanese territory from the Mahdi.

The War Office had already consulted [English tourist agent] John Cook about navigation on the Nile and his firm tendered to transport the entire expedition from Alexandria to Wadi Halfa, aptly known to the troops as 'Bloody Halfway' [Piers Brendon, *Thomas Cook: 150 Years of Popular Tourism,* 1991].

**Bloody Orkney** *Orkney Islands, Scotland.* The adjective in this nickname is not meant literally, but simply by way of disparagement. The islands lack some of the facilities and sophistication available on the mainland.

This bloody town's a bloody cuss —
No bloody trains, no bloody bus,
And no one cares for bloody us —
In bloody Orkney [Hamish Blair, "In Bloody Orkney," 1952].

**Blue Banana** see in Appendix 1, p. 269.

**Blue City** or **Town, the** *Jodhpur, India.* The city is so named for its many blue-painted houses. The reason for the choice of this particular shade is uncertain. It may be because blue is the color of the Brahmin caste, or because it repels insects, or because it is cooling. A combination of factors may be at work.

(1) Drive to the 'blue city'of Jodhpur [Travel ad, *The Times Magazine,* November 27, 2004].

(2) Full day excursion to Jodhpur, including ... a walking tour through the "blue town" [Travel brochure issued with *Sunday Times,* November 27, 2005].

**Blue Continent, the** *Antarctica.* The name describes the blue color of the ice on the continent's many frozen lakes when they are free of snow. *Cp.* **White Continent.**

**Blue Danube, the** *Danube River, Europe.* Europe's second-longest river, rising in southern Germany and flowing east then south through the capitals of Austria (Vienna), Slovakia (Bratislava), Hungary (Budapest), and Serbia (Belgrade) to enter the Black Sea in Romania, derives its nickname from Johann Strauss the Younger's famous waltz, titled in German *An der schönen, blauen Donau* ("On the beautiful blue Danube") (1866), a phrase from a poem by Karl Isidor Beck first published in his *Gesammelte Gedichte* ("Collected Poems") (1844). The waters of the Danube can appear blue when reflecting a sky of that color, as indeed can those of any river. The name appears in the Bulgarian national anthem, as in quote (1) below, written in 1885 by Tsvetan Radoslavov, a 22-year-old student on his way to fight in the Serbo-Bulgarian War.

(1) Gorda Stara planina,
Do ney Dunava siney
(Proud are the Balkans,
Below them the Blue Danube).

(2) Vienna was famous for illusions. Even the Blue Danube, which is not blue, is also not really in Vienna at all, but diverted to a channel beyond to let the great city grow [Malcolm Bradbury, ed., *The Atlas of Literature,* 1996].

**Bluegrass State, the** *Kentucky, USA.* The central region of Kentucky is noted for its abundance of bluegrass (*Poa pratensis*), used to provide rich pasture for horses and thus make the state a center of racehorse breeding.

(1) He fathered two sons, Todd and Charles Jr., both born in Kentucky, where their mother had gone in order that they could claim to be natives of the bluegrass state [Truman Capote, *The Grass Harp,* 1951].

(2) The limestone-rich pastures with green grasses that bloom blue buds in spring (earning Kentucky the moniker 'Bluegrass State') showed

early pioneers the state's horse-breeding potential [*Lonely Planet USA*, 2004].

**Blue Hen State, the** *Delaware, USA.* The name arose from the sobriquet "Blue Hen's Chickens" applied to soldiers from Delaware during the Revolutionary War, as a blue hen is said to breed the best fighting cocks. The original nickname was simply "the Blue Hen," as described in the quotes below.

(1) In the revolutionary war ... Captain Caldwell [of Delaware] had a company called by the rest "Caldwell's game cocks," and the regiment after a time in Carolina was nicknamed from this, "the blue hen's chickens" and "the blue chickens" ... But after they had been distinguished in the south the name of the *Blue Hen* was applied to the state [*Niles' National Register*, May 9, 1840].

(2) This sobriquet is said to have had its origin in a certain Captain Caldwell's fondness for the amusement of cock-fighting. Caldwell was for a time an officer of the First Delaware Regiment in the war of the Revolution, and was greatly distinguished for his daring and undaunted spirit. He was exceedingly popular in the regiment, and its high state of discipline was generally conceded to be due to his exertions; so that when officers were sent on recruiting service to enlist new men ... it was a saying, that they had gone home for more of Caldwell's game-cocks; but, as Caldwell insisted that no cock could be truly game unless the mother was a blue hen, the expression "Blue Hen's chickens" was substituted for "game-cocks" [*Delaware State Journal*, July 1860, quoted in Wheeler, pp. 49–50].

**Blue Law State, the** *Connecticut, USA.* The name relates to the severe laws, printed on blue paper, that were imposed in the 17th century on the citizens of some New England colonies by Puritans based at New Haven, Connecticut. The 45 blue laws listed by Samuel A. Peters in his *General History of Connecticut* (1781) include the following: "The judges shall determine controversies without a jury"; "Married persons must live together or be imprisoned"; "A wife shall be good evidence against her husband."

**Blue Water Paradise** see in Appendix 1, p. 269.

**Bluff City** *(1) Hannibal, Missouri, USA; (2) Memphis, Tennessee, USA.* The nickname of both cities relates to their location on bluffs overlooking the Mississippi.

**B'mouth** *see* **So'ton**

**Boardwalk, the** *Atlantic City, New Jersey, USA.* Atlantic City is nicknamed for its famous 6-mile-long boardwalk, lined with hotels, shops, casinos, and amusements. The first boardwalk was built in 1870, the present one in 1896.

**Bob, the** *Bob Marshall Wilderness Complex, Montana, USA.* A friendly personalization of the name of the vast complex in the northwest of the state.

Trails generally start steep, reaching the wilderness boundary after about 7 miles. It takes another 10 miles or so to really get into the heart of the Bob [*Lonely Planet USA*, 2004].

**Bocheland** *Germany.* A former derogatory nickname for the land of the Boches, as French soldiers called the Germans, especially in World War I. The name itself is said to derive from *Alboche*, a French argot alteration of *Allemand*, "German."

**BoCoCa** see in Appendix 1, p. 269.

**Bogland** *Ireland.* A former supposedly humorous name for the country, and especially its rural regions, where there are large areas of peat bog.

Go, Conqu'rors of your Male and Female Foes;
Men without Hearts, and Women without Hose.
Each bring his Love a *Bogland* Captive home;
Such proper Pages will long Trains become [John Dryden, Prologue to *The Prophetess*, 1690].

**Bogue** see in Appendix 1, p. 269.

**Bollywood** *Mumbai (Bombay), India.* Bombay has long been the center of the Indian motion picture industry, and the name accordingly substitutes the first letter of the city's name for the initial of "Hollywood."

It is possible to be ushered into the presence of a Bollywood star. Not Mollywood, note — while the city is now officially Mumbai, even the locals still call it Bombay [Dodd/Donald, p. 295].

**Bolong** or **Boolong** *Boulogne, France.* A former facetious representation of a popular pronunciation of the French seaport's name. The lines from the music-hall song in quote (2) below relate to the Bois de Boulogne, the famous Paris park, itself named for another Boulogne, now a suburb of the French capital.

(1) "Oho!" the Captain said, "I see!
And is she then so very strong?"
"She'd take your honour's scruff," said he
"And pitch you over to Bolong!" [W.S. Gilbert, "Babette's Love," *The "Bab" Ballads*, 1869].
(2) As I walk along the Bois Boolong
With an independent air,
You can hear the girls declare,
"He must be a Millionaire!" [Fred Gilbert, "The Man that Broke the Bank at Monte Carlo," 1892].

**Bolthole, the** *Channel Islands, UK.* The islands are noted for their low income tax, and so serve as a place of refuge for high taxpayers.

**Bomb Alley** see in Appendix 1, p. 269.

**Bombay** *Mumbai, India.* The corrupted name of the Indian city, which officially adopted its Marathi name in 1995, is still widely current, both locally and internationally as noted in the quote for **Bollywood**. The altered form does not affect such culinary terms as Bombay duck (a fish) and Bombay mix.

(1) The name Bombay is rapidly disappearing. Mumbai is used by all Indian newspapers and is officially recognised by Delhi [*The Times*, August 31, 1996].

(2) [In writing Indian placenames] continue to use Bombay rather than Mumbai, Madras rather than Chennai, Calcutta rather than Kolkata, and Delhi rather than New Delhi [*The Times Style and Usage Guide*, 2003].

(3) Surely we should start writing Mumbai and Myanmar? [*The Times* chief revise editor Richard] Nixon's answer is that *Times* readers are more likely to be familiar with Bombay and Burma [*The Times*, August 19, 2005].

**Bombingham** *Birmingham, Alabama, USA.* A wryly punning nickname applied to the city during the 1960s race riots.

Violence was turning her hometown into "Bombingham" as Alabama's governor George Wallace fought a federal court order to integrate the city's schools [*Sunday Times*, November 21, 2004, quoting from Antonia Felix, *Condi: The Condoleezza Rice Story*, 2002].

**Bom-Bom Bay** *Mumbai (Bombay), India.* A nickname popularized by Harry Carroll's song "Down in Bom-Bom Bay" (1923). The city is not actually on a bay.

**Bo-Mo** *Bournemouth, England.* A casual abbreviation of the south-coast resort's name, mainly used by its younger residents.

**Bonanza State, the** *(1) Montana, USA; (2) Nevada, USA.* The great mineral wealth of Montana was first exploited in the 1860s, when gold prospectors arrived following the discovery of rich placer deposits. Hard-rock mining began in the late 1880s, when vast deposits of copper were found at Butte, the **Richest Hill on Earth**. Gold and copper have also been extensively mined in Nevada, where the original "bonanza" was the rich deposit of silver discovered in the Comstock Lode in 1859 (*cp.* **Silver State**).

**Bongo Bongo Land** *Africa.* A racially offensive nickname for the continent, based on a popular association with bongo drums.

[British politician Alan Clark] delighted in outrageous behaviour ... The French were "bum boys," the African continent "bongo bongo land" [Anthony Blond, *Jew Made in England*, 2004].

**Bonkersville** *Camberwell, London, England.* A nickname referring to the perceived eccentricity of some of the district's inhabitants.

Christened Bonkersville by the comedienne Jenny Eclair, a resident for ten years, Camberwell is crazy in parts but much calmer away from the Green [*The Times*, September 12, 2003].

**Bonnie Strathyre** *Strathyre, Scotland.* The village in central Scotland, in the valley of the same name, derives its sobriquet from a popular song. The epithet properly applies to the valley, as mentioned in quote (2) below, in which "circumstances" has the literal sense "surroundings."

(1) A most attractive village, ... "Bonnie Strathyre" is inclined to get even bonnier with the years [*Holiday Haunts 1962: Scotland*].

(2) The valley of Strathyre is the subject of the well-known song 'Bonnie Strathyre'; the village of that name is not, save for a few good old 18th-cent. Scottish-style stone cottages, 'bonnie' in itself, but its circumstances undoubtedly are ... It is bonnily set among hills [Macnie/McLaren, p. 242].

**Bonny Dundee** *Dundee, Scotland.* The nickname is sometimes applied to the city, although it is more usually associated with John Graham of Claverhouse, 1st Viscount Dundee (*c.*1649–1689), victor of the battle of Killicrankie, on July 17, 1689, in which he defeated the rebeling Scots at the price of his own life. "Bonny" (in Graham's case usually "Bonnie") is a general Scots term of approval.

(1) Dundee, a pleasant, large, populous city, and well deserves the title of Bonny Dundee, so often given it in discourse, as well as in song (bonny, in Scots, signifying beautiful) [Daniel Defoe, *A Tour thro' the Whole Island of Great Britain*, 1724–6].

(2) Come fill up my cup, come fill up my cann,
Come saddle my horses, and call up my man;

Come open your gates, and let me gae free,
I daurna [i.e. dare not] stay langer in bonny Dundee [Sir Walter Scott, *Rob Roy*, 1818].

**Book Town of Norway, the** *Fjærland, Norway.* In 1996 the popular resort at the head of the fjord of the same name decided to broaden its touristic appeal by styling itself "The Book Town of Norway" (*Den Norske Bokbyen*). Several secondhand bookhops soon opened and an annual book fair was instituted.

**Boomers' State, the** *Oklahoma, USA.* The name alludes to the "boomers," the bands of white settlers who sought work and property on land held by the American Indians in the late 19th century.

**Boomingest Boom on the Continent, the** *Dakar, Senegal.* The name refers to the Senegalese capital's rapid economic and cultural growth in the years immediately after World War II.

Dakar has been fittingly called "the boomingest boom on the continent." It is a real city, in the European manner [John Gunther, *Inside Africa*, 1955].

**Bop** *Bophuthatswana, South Africa.* A short form of the name of the former black "homeland," reintegrated with South Africa in 1994. Its national airline, radio service, and television service were respectively known as Bop-Air, Bop-Radio, and Bop-TV.

> Most of Bop's unrest of recent years has stemmed from attempts to incorporate further segments of territory into its jigsaw borders [*Sunday Star*, March 11, 1990].

**Border Counties** see in Appendix 1, p. 269.

**Border Country** see in Appendix 1, p. 269.

**Border Eagle State, the** *Mississippi, USA.* The name refers to the eagle on the state's coat of arms.

**Border State, the** *Maine, USA.* Maine lies in extreme southeast New England, where it borders Canada. It was not one of the Border States (Delaware, Maryland, Virginia, Kentucky, and Missouri), which as "Slave States" bordered the "Free States" before the Civil War.

**Border Town** *(1) El Paso, Texas, USA; (2) Rye, New York, USA.* El Paso is a port of entry in far western Texas on the Rio Grande opposite Ciudad Juárez, Mexico. Rye is so named because it was settled (in 1660) on the border of present Connecticut and New York, and for some years vacillated between the two states.

**Boring Brussels** *Brussels, Belgium.* Belgium is popularly regarded as a dull and dismal country by its European neighbors, and especially France, so its capital city is regarded as encapsulating this negative attribute.

> "Boring Brussels" is the bolthole of choice for French tax exiles [*Sunday Times*, September 25, 2005].

**Boro** *Middlesbrough, England.* The abbreviated form of the town's name derives from the nickname of its football club, founded in 1876.

> Last summer I visited Middlesbrough for a few days on business. I checked in at the hotel ... and was politely and helpfully informed by the young lady at the desk that it wasn't a good idea to go out in the centre of 'Boro after dark [Sam Jordison and Dan Kieran, eds., *The Idler Book of Crap Towns II*, 2004].

**Borough, the** *Southwark, London, England.* The district came to be known as a borough (in the sense "suburb") as it lay to the south of the City of London across the Thames. It is now a London borough in the regular sense of the term. The historic name is preserved in Southwark's Borough High Street and famous Borough Market, and usually appears on London maps. It is also current without "the."

> (1) A dreadful fire broke out yesterday morning in the High-Street in the Borough [*Annual Register*, 1797].
>
> (2) In the Middle Ages Southwark became a flourishing borough (in common parlance it is still 'the Borough') [F.R. Banks, *The New Penguin Guide to London*, 1988].

> (3) If you like literature, you'll love Borough [*Time Out London Guide*, 5th ed., 1997].

**Borscht Belt** see in Appendix 1, p. 269.

**Bosnywash** see in Appendix 1, p. 269.

**Bosphorus** *Bosporus, Turkey.* This popular spelling of the name of the strait connecting the Sea of Marmara with the Black Sea is generally regarded as incorrect. It appears to have been influenced by Greek *-phoros*, "bearing," as if related to the name's traditional derivation from Greek *bous*, "ox," and *poros*, "passage," "ford." In Greek mythology, the Cimmerian Bosporus, the modern Kerch Strait, connecting the Sea of Azov with the Black Sea, was swum by Io after she had been changed into a heifer by Zeus.

**Bourbon Capital of the World, the** *Bardstown, Kentucky, USA.* The city is noted for its distilleries. Hence the nickname.

**Bourne** *see* **City of Pines**

**Bournemouth of the Riviera, the** *St.-Raphaël, France.* A 19th-century nickname for the French resort, comparing it to the much larger English seaside town, traditionally regarded as serene and sedate.

> Perhaps the label is still to some extent appropriate ... for not only does St-Raphaël boast an Anglican church which functions during the tourist season but there is a a golf course at Valescure close by dating back to pre-1914 — a product ... of British enterprise. Even today there is something rather sedate about much of St-Raphaël [Young, p. 425].

**Bowie State, the** *Arkansas, USA.* The nickname alludes to the fact that in the early days of the state's existence, many of its inhabitants carried a bowie knife.

**Boystown** or **Boyz Town** *West Hollywood, Los Angeles, California, USA.* The residential suburb is nicknamed for its sizeable gay and lesbian population. The name was presumably suggested by that of Boys Town, Nebraska (*see* **City of Little Men**).

> Beauty reigns supreme in "Boyz Town" [*Lonely Planet USA*, 2004].

**Bradders** *Bradford, England.* A colloquial name for the Yorkshire city with the so-called "Oxford -er," as for **Honkers.**

> Traditionally viewed as a poor relation by residents of Leeds, 'Bradders' has finally managed to beat its pretentious neighbours at something [Sam Jordison and Dan Kieran, eds., *The Idler Book of Crap Towns II*, 2004].

**Brasilia of the North** *see* **New Brasilia**

**Brass, the** *Butte, Montana, USA.* The nickname refers to the copper mine for which the city is famous. *Cp.* **Richest Hill on Earth.**

**Brave New World, the** *United States.* The

well-known phrase, spoken by Miranda in Shakespeare's play *The Tempest*, as in quote (1) below, is said to refer to the newly discovered America, as explained in quote (2). Jamestown, Virginia, was founded in 1607 as the first permanent English settlement in America. The phrase was adopted by Aldous Huxley as the title of his satirical novel of 1932. *See also* **New World**.

> (1) O, wonder!
> How many goodly creatures are there here!
> How beauteous mankind is! O brave new world,
> That has such people in't! [William Shakespeare, *The Tempest*, 1611].
> (2) The "brave new world" in Shakespeare's *The Tempest* (1611) refers to the first British settlement in the New World, Jamestown, Virginia, and Miranda's words reflect the Renaissance sense of wonder [Malcolm Bradbury, ed., *The Atlas of Literature*, 1996].

**Brave Toun, the** *Aberdeen, Scotland.* The nickname alludes to the city's stalwart role in the many battles in which it was involved down to the 1745 rebellion.

**Bread and Butter State, the** *Minnesota, USA.* The nickname alludes to the state's formerly prominent flour and dairy industry. The sobriquet originated in 1901 at the time of the Pan-American Exposition in Buffalo, New York, where wheat and dairy products from Minnesota were displayed. *Cp.* **Wheat State.**

**Bread and Cheese County, the** *Durham, England.* The county was formerly so nicknamed by vagrants, from the free basic food doled out there.

**Breadbasket of Romania, the** *Walachia, Romania.* The title describes the historic region as a rich agricultural area.

**Breadbasket of Serbia, the** *Voyvodina, Serbia.* The fertile plains of the province justify its nickname.

**Breadbasket of the Nation, the** *Kansas, USA.* The state's many farms and ranches rank it first for wheat production in the USA and also first for sorghum grains. Hence its alternate nickname as the **Wheat State.**

**Breadbasket of the Philippines, the** *Central Luzon, Philippines.* The region is noted for its rice growing. Hence the nickname.

**Breakneckshire** *Breconshire, Wales.* The dated nickname puns on the alternate form of the county's name as **Brecknockshire**, and alludes to its mountainous terrain.

> Brecknockshire is a meer inland county, as Radnor is; the English jestingly ... call it Breakneckshire [Daniel Defoe, *A Tour thro' the Whole Island of Great Britain*, 1724–6].

**Brecknockshire** *Breconshire, Wales.* The now dated or archaic form of the county's name derives from Welsh *Brycheiniog*, meaning "territory of Brychan," after a 5th-century prince. The county town of Brecon is still sometimes referred as Brecknock, and the name is preserved in that of Brecknock Museum.

**Bree** *Brewarrina, Australia.* A short colloquial local name for the small New South Wales town.

**Brick City** *Newark, New Jersey, USA.* The city is so nicknamed because many of its buildings have brick façades.

**Brid** *Bridlington, England.* A colloquial shortening of the name of the popular Yorkshire seaside resort.

> (1) A surprise even to me, who must have been to Brid 50 times as a child [*The Times*, May 21, 2004].
> (2) Bridlington (Brid in the vernacular) bursts into life with its traditional seaside attractions [*The Times*, November 4, 2005].

**Bride of the Sea, the** *Venice, Italy.* The name relates to the annual Ascension Day ceremony marking the traditional role of Venice as a major sea power. During this ceremony, known as the "Marriage of the Adriatic," the doge symbolically dropped a consecrated ring into the Adriatic from his official barge, pronouncing the Latin words cited in the quote below. The ceremony was instituted to commemorate the victory over the Holy Roman emperor Frederick I (Barbarossa) at Legnano in 1176 and and the subsequent Peace of Venice (1177) by which Frederick acknowledged Alexander III as the true pope.

> [The doge said] *"Desponsamus te, mare, in signum veri perpetuique dominii"* (Italian *Ti sposiamo, o mare nostro, in signo di vero a perpetuo domino*), "We wed thee, O sea, in sign of a true and perpetual dominion."

**Bridge between the Oceans, the** *Panama City, Panama.* The promotional name sees the city as linking the Atlantic and Pacific via the Panama Canal.

**Brigadoon** *Scotland.* The name denoting an idealized Scotland comes from the 1947 Lerner and Loewe musical so titled, about a quaint village that comes to life for only one day every century. The name itself suggests a Scottish placename Brig o' Doon, "bridge of the Doon (River)."

**Brighton of Russia, the** *Yalta, Ukraine.* Any comparison with England's Brighton implies a flourishing seaside resort. Yalta lies on the Black Sea.

> Yalta is called the Brighton of Russia. It is not that [John Foster Fraser, *Round the World on a Wheel*, 1899].

**Brighton of Scotland, the** *St Andrews, Scot-*

*land*. The historic town is better known by many for its university and prestigious golf course than as a seaside resort, although its West Sands make it Scotland's prime beach town.

**Brighton of the North, the** *(1) Morecambe, England; (2) Nairn, Scotland*. The name is adopted for any northern British resort regarded as comparable with its southern equivalent. The Lancashire seaside resort has long shared the popularity of Brighton, as to a lesser extent has the Scottish town on the Moray Firth, an inlet of the North Sea.

> (1) (Nairn) The 'Brighton of the North' owed much of its success to Dr John Grigor, who recommended its invigorating air and sunny climate to his patients [John Julius Norwich, ed., *Treasures of Britain*, 2002].
> (2) (Morecambe) The Midland Hotel ... is the centrepiece of [a] bold campaign to turn the resort into the "Brighton of the North" [*The Times*, August 23, 2005].

**Brighton of Wales, the** *Aberystwyth, Wales*. The popular seaside resort is also known more exotically as the **Biarritz of Wales**.

**Bris** or **Brissie** *Brisbane, Australia*. A colloquial shortening of the Queensland capital city's name.

**Bristol of America, the** *Boston, Massachusetts, USA*. The Massachusetts city has been compared with many others around the world. The identity with England's Bristol is as a major seaport.

> Boston is the Bristol, New York, the Liverpool, and Philadelphia, the London of America [Henry Wallsey, *An Excursion to the United States of North America in 1794*, 1796].

**BrisVegas** *Brisbane, Australia*. A blend of the Queensland capital's name and that of America's Las Vegas, denoting a city with much to offer its many visitors.

**Britain's Coolest City** *Bournemouth, England*. The south coast resort shook off its staid image with this accolade from *Harpers & Queen*.

> The one time sleepy town with a reputation as a genteel place to retire next to the sea is now one of Britain's most vibrant cosmopolitan coastal spots and has been billed as "Britain's coolest city" by Harpers & Queen [Travel writer Judith Chalmers in *Bournemouth: Holidays and Short Breaks Guide 2006*].

**Britain's Largest Village** *Totton, England*. The Hampshire town (former village) is a near neighbor of Southampton, across the Test River.

> Totton was once proud to be 'Britain's largest village' until this accolade was stolen from it by unwelcome inside forces [Sam Jordison and Dan Kieran, eds., *The Idler Book of Crap Towns II*, 2004].

**Britain's 100% Spa** *Harrogate, England*. A rather unusual promotional name for the Yorkshire town, a former leading health resort. The sobriquet appears in a Great Northern Railway poster of *c*. 1921.

**Britannia** *England or Britain*. The Roman name of Britain was adopted for literary use and personalized in the form of a seated female figure holding a spear and a shield, long familiar on coins. (In the 19th century her persona was in a sense popularly identified with that of Queen Victoria, whose royal title was *Britanniae Regina, Fidei Defensor*, "Queen of Britain, Defender of the Faith.")

> (1) When Britain first, at heaven's command,
> Arose from out the azure main,
> This was the charter of the land,
> And guardian angels sung this strain:
> "Rule, Britannia, rule the waves;
> Britons never will be slaves" [James Thomson, *Alfred: A Masque*, 1740].
> (2) Nelson was once Britannia's god of war, And still should be so, but the tide is turn'd [Lord Byron, *Don Juan*, 1819].
> (3) England is also a supernatural person, Britannia, a kind of sea goddess, from our long addiction to the sea and our island status [Maureen Duffy, *England*, 2001].
> (4) Let Britannia have her identity, let Britain be herself, proud and confident, "mother of the free" [Letter to the Editor, *The Times*, August 6, 2005].

**British Lion, the** *England or Britain*. The sobriquet refers to the beast that is the country's national emblem and that appears in the royal coat of arms. The symbol first appears in the writings of Dryden, as in quote (1) below.

> (1) Such pity now the pious Pastor shows, Such mercy from the *British* Lyon flows, That both provide protection for their foes [John Dryden, *The Hind and the Panther*, 1687].
> (2) She [i.e. Chicago] is young, and may be forgiven her conceit when our elder, the British lion, has not yet outgrown it [Rudyard Kipling, *American Notes*, "Kipling Brought to Book," 1899].

**Britsville** *(1) England or Britain; (2) London, England*. A mainly Australian nickname for the country and city populated by "Brits."

**Brizzie** *(1) Brisbane, Australia; (2) Bristol, England*. The Australian city is also known even more briefly as **Bris**.

> (Bristol) Bristol — or Brizzie — as the locals call it [Sam Jordison and Dan Kieran, eds., *The Idler Book of Crap Towns II*, 2004].

**Broad Acres** *see* **Land of the Broad Acres**

**Broadland** see in Appendix 1, p. 269.

**Broads** see in Appendix 1, p. 269.

**Brocéliande** *Forest of Paimpont, France*. The former French name of the Brittany forest has been preserved in medieval legend and modern poetry, as the legendary country of King Arthur and Merlin.

(1) The deep forest-glades of Broce-liande,
Through whose green boughs the golden sun-shine creeps,
Where Merlin by the enchanted thorn-tree sleeps [Matthew Arnold, *Tristram and Iseult*, 1852].
(2) It is on the well-marked footpaths leading into the forest depths that the solitude and unique atmosphere of the Brocéliande can be best enjoyed [Young, p. 175].

**Broch, the** *(1) Burghead, Scotland; (2) Fraserburgh, Scotland.* In each case the short name represents a Scots form of the "burg(h)" element, related to English "borough." Burghead and Fraserburgh are fishing ports some 55 miles (88 km) apart on the same north-facing coast. *Cp.* **Boro, Burgy.**

**Brollywood** *Vancouver, British Columbia, Canada.* The city is famed for its thriving film industry. Hence the nickname, combining "Hollywood" with "brolly" (umbrella), alluding to the heavy local rainfall. *Cp.* **Bollywood.**

**Brontë Country** see in Appendix 1, p. 269.

**Brosie Forfar** *Forfar, Scotland* The first word of the town's nickname derives from "brose," a Scots dish made of oatmeal mixed with boiling water or milk. (It differs from porridge in that the oatmeal is not cooked.)

**Brothel of Europe, the** *Venice, Italy.* The pejorative tag refers to the profusion of prostitutes found in the city in former times. The sobriquet is in marked contrast to the many honorifics bestowed on Venice, such as **Bride of the Sea** and **Queen of the Adriatic.**

**Brothels** *Brussels, Belgium.* A punning British military name for the Belgian capital dating from World War II.

**Brow, the** *Hillbrow, Johannesburg, South Africa.* A short name for the tough, densely-populated suburb of the country's largest city.
'I hailed the first cab I saw and asked him to head for the "Brow" (Hillbrow),' he said [*Sunday Times* (Johannesburg), June 15, 1975].

**Brown Bear** *see* **Bear**

**Brown Bottle City** *Milwaukee, USA.* The nickname alludes to the city's noted beer-brewing industry. *Cp.* **Beer City**

**Brownstone State, the** *Connecticut, USA.* The name refers to the state's sandstone and feldspar quarries, especially around Portland.

**BR Town** *Baton Rouge, Louisiana, USA.* A simple initialism of the city's full name.

**Bru-Bru Land** *Brussels, Belgium.* A journalistic nickname for the Belgian capital based on its role as host of the European Union and thus as a stage of political play. The name obviously puns on that of **La-La Land.**

There is one big difference between Los Angeles and Brussels. In Hollywood the dream-makers only *think* they run the continent; in Bru-Bru land, if we're not careful, they really will [*The Times*, December 9, 2005].

**Bruce, the** *Bruce Peninsula, Ontario, Canada.* A familiar name for the peninsula extending between Lake Huron and Georgian Bay.

**Brum** or **Brummagem** *Birmingham, England.* The name of the industrial city was at one time popularly pronounced as "Brummagem," possibly by association with the names of nearby Castle Bromwich and West Bromwich. This was then shortened to "Brum." The longer form is now rarely used as a nickname, but came to acquire a generic sense to refer to a cheap or showy manufactured article, especially an imitation one. Inhabitants of Birmingham are colloquially called "Brummies."

(1) Poor babby cried ... till we got to Brummagem for the night [Elizabeth Gaskell, *Mary Barton*, 1848].
(2) Becoming dissatisfied with his native soil he passed over to England, and settling for some time at "Brummagem," took lessons from certain cunning smiths in the art of making *fashiono vangusties* [i.e. false rings, supposedly made of gold but actually of brass or copper] [George Borrow, *Romano Lavo-Lil*, 1874].
(3) Sutton for mutton,
Tamworth for beeves,
Walsall for knockknees,
And Brummagem for thieves [Old rhyme, quoted in Walter Showell, *Dictionary of Birmingham*, 1885].
(4) Whereas many northern and Midland cities grew on a handful of staple industries, "Brum" turned its hand to every kind of manufacturing [*The Rough Guide to England*, 1998].
(5) There are countless reasons why Brum is the only English city other than London where I could bear to live [Jonathan Meades, "Motor City, UK," *The Times*, March 5, 2005].
(6) England's second-largest city — known colloquially as Brum, the inhabitants as Brummies and the dialect as Brummie — has long held a reputation as an industrial wasteland [*Lonely Planet Great Britain*, 2005].

**Brummagem** *Bergen, Norway.* A British soldiers' World War II corruption of the Norwegian name, adopted from the former colloquial name of Birmingham (*see* **Brum**).

**Brunswick** *Braunschweig, Germany.* An English form of the city's name that is linguistically closer to the original (meaning "Bruno's settlement").
Hamelin Town's in Brunswick [Robert Browning, "The Pied Piper of Hamelin," 1842].

**Brutal Bootle** *Bootle, England.* A derisory name for the Merseyside seaport town, current among residents of neighboring Liverpool. An extended form of the name is "Brutal Bootle where the bugs wear clogs."

**Brute's City** *London, England.* A literary name for the British capital, derived from the legendary Trojan hero Brutus, supposedly the first king of Britain and founder of London under the name of **Troynovant**. His own name is popularly related to that of Britain itself.

> The goodly Thames near which Brute's city stands [Michael Drayton, *Poly-Olbion*, 1612].

**Bs. As.** *Buenos Aires, Argentina.* A Spanish abbreviation of the Argentine capital's name, as in the street magazine title *Hecho en Bs.As.* ("Made in Buenos Aires").

**BSB** *Bandar Seri Begawan, Brunei.* An initial-derived short form of the capital city's name.

> Bandar Seri Begawan (usually called BSB or Bandar for short) [*Lonely Planet Malaysia, Singapore & Brunei*, 1999].

**Bu, the** *Malibu, California, USA.* A local truncation of the coastal community's name. *Cp.* **Maliboo-boo.**

> British and Irish stars are setting the pace for summer leases along the 27 miles of palm-fringed sands known to locals as "the Bu" [*Sunday Times*, July 3, 2005].

**Buckeye State, the** *Ohio, USA.* The nickname refers to the former proliferation of the buckeye tree (*Aesculus glabra*) in the state. The tree itself is so called because its dark-brown chestnut resembles a buck's eye on first cracking open in its shell. The name is also associated with William Henry Harrison (1773–1841), 9th president of the United States, a Virginia-born Ohioan, who in his 1840 presidential campaign was portrayed as the occupant of a log cabin, with his campaign emblem a log cabin made of buckeye timbers.

> (1) The very author of the tariff plank in the Chicago platform was last fall buried beneath more than 80,000 votes in that grand old "Buckeye" State [*The Congressional Record*, January 1894].
> (2) Republicans and Democrats agree on this: the "Buckeye" state is the most closely contested [*Financial Times*, October 4, 2004].

**Bucks** *Buckinghamshire, England.* A semi-official abbreviation of the county's name. *See also* Appendix 6, p. 325.

> The high plateau on the other side of the [railroad] line towards Newlands Park is no less beautiful. Here the beech woods of Bucks begin [*Metro-land*, 1932].

**Buffer, the** *Buffalo, New York, USA.* A colloquial form of the city's name.

**Bug-Eating State, the** *Nebraska, USA.* The state is said to derive its nickname from its inhabitants' endeavor to utilize its abundance of hoppers as food, as in North Africa and Arabia (and by some American Indians).

**Bulgaria** *Thessaloníki, Greece.* The name of neighboring Bulgaria is used both within and beyond Greece as a term of abuse (it gave English "bugger"). Football clubs from Greece's two largest cities, Athens and Thessaloníki (Salonica), first met in contest in 1928.

> Athenians, especially the capital's football fans, disparagingly dub Thessaloniki "Bulgaria" [Dodd/Donald, p. 381].

**Bullion State, the** *Missouri, USA.* The nickname originated in the 19th century with Senator Thomas Hart Benton, known as "Old Bullion" for his advocation of gold and silver instead of paper currency. His sobriquet then passed to that of the state.

**Bulwark of the Indies, the** *Havana, Cuba.* The Cuban capital came to be so nicknamed in the 18th century, when it was the most heavily fortified city in the New World. The "Indies" are the West Indies.

**Bulwark of the North, the** *Stirling, Scotland.* The fortified town, associated with two great Scottish battles (Stirling Bridge in 1297 and Bannockburn in 1314), is said to have been so nicknamed by Scott, as in the quote below.

> And soon the bulwark of the North,
>   Grey Stirling, with her towers and town,
> Upon their fleet career look'd down [Sir Walter Scott, *The Lady of the Lake*, 1810].

**Bundie** *Bundaberg, Australia.* A colloquial shortening of the Queensland seaport town's name.

> "Bundie" is synonymous with dark rum throughout Australia [*The Rough Guide to Australia*, 2001].

**Burberry** *Burbure, France.* A British soldiers' corruption of the French placename during World War I, presumably from the Burberry clothing (especially raincoats) that first became widely known at that time. Burbure is a village just outside Béthune in extreme northern France.

**Burghs, the** *Pittsburgh, Pennsylvania, USA.* A colloquial shortening of the city's name. *Cp.* English **Boro** and Scottish **Broch**.

**Burgy** *Williamsburg, Virginia, USA.* A colloquial abbreviation of the city's name. *Cp.* English **Boro** and Scottish **Broch**.

**Burma** *Myanmar.* Although the Asian country's official English name was changed from the Union of Burma to the Union of Myanmar in

1989, the familiar name is still found in many media reports.

> (1) In 1988 [*sic*], Burma went and changed its name to the "Union of Myanmar," thinking they could fool us. I say let's give them a Burma Shave [Michael Moore, *Downsize This!*, 1996].
> (2) Continue to call the country Burma [*The Times Style and Usage Guide*, 2003].

**Burning River City, the** *Cleveland, Ohio, USA*. The name relates to an incident in 1969, when an oilslick on the Cuyahoga River, which flows through the city, was inadvertently set on fire. The blaze was soon extinguished, but the image of the "burning river" persisted long after. (The event was even commemorated in Randy Newman's song "Burn On Big River" in his 1972 album *Sail Away*.) Cleveland later flaunted the potentially damaging nickname as a proud slogan. *Cp.* **Mistake on the Lake.**

**Burns Country** see in Appendix 1, p. 269.

**Burp** *Belchertown, Massachusetts, USA*. An obvious punning variant on the town's name.

**Bury** *Bury St Edmunds, England*. A common short name, especially in local use, for the Suffolk town, causing potential confusion with the much larger town of Bury near Manchester. *Cp.* **St. Edmundsbury,**

> (1) Away toward Bury; to the Dauphin there! [William Shakespeare, *King John*, c. 1596].
> (2) St. Edmund's Bury, or Bury St. Edmund's, or simply Bury, as it is termed by some [William Pulleyn, *The Etymological Compendium*, 3d ed., revised and improved by Merton A. Thoms, 1853].
> (3) 'Bury' to the locals, it's long been the pride of Suffolk [Charlie Godfrey-Faussett, *Footprint England*, 2004].

**Bush, the** *Shepherd's Bush, London, England*. A colloquial short form of the district's name.

> TV cook Nigella Lawson made waves by describing the Bush, her home for some years, as 'not especially nice' [Carrie Segrave, *The New London Property Guide*, 2003].

**Bush Capital, the** *Canberra, Australia*. An early derisory nickname for the capital city.

> It is all very well to laugh at the 'Bush Capital'; but Washington was laughed at in just the same way before it grew to be the fine city it is [Archibald Marshall, *Sunny Australia*, 1911].

**Bushistan** *United States*. An Asian-style sobriquet for the USA under the presidency of George W. Bush (elected 2001, re-elected 2004), whose foreign policy caused controversy following the US-led invasion of Iraq in 2003.

> The Indian-born novelist Abha Dawesar ... urges American writers not to "flee Bush-i-stan" [*Times Literary Supplement*, December 3, 2004].

**Butternut State, the** *Missouri, USA*. A nickname from the butternut tree (*Juglans cinerea*) which grows in the state. The brownish-gray color of the nut became associated with the color of Southern uniforms during the Civil War.

**Buzzard State, the** *Georgia, USA*. The state came to be known by this name when the buzzard became a protected bird there.

**BVIs, the** *British Virgin Islands, West Indies*. A colloquial initialism for the Caribbean island group, a British dependent territory.

> The BVIs are yachting's nursery slopes [*Sunday Times*, November 27, 2005].

**Bytown** *Ottawa, Ontario, Canada*. Bytown was the original name of the Canadian capital, from the English army officer John By. The former logging town took its present name in 1855, but the earlier name remains as a nickname, as chiefly applied by cities who reckoned *they* had a worthier claim as capital, and that Ottawa is really a bureaucratically boosted small town or "backwoods 'burb."

**Byzantium** *Istanbul, Turkey*. The ancient name of the former Turkish capital is familiar in historical references. The city was renamed **Constantinople** in the 4th century AD and took its present name only in 1930.

**Cabbage Garden** or **Patch, the** *Victoria, Australia*. The name is said to refer to the mallee, a small type of eucalyptus tree, which grows widely in Victoria, although there could equally be a more general reference to the crops grown in the state (*see* **Garden State**) or even to its smallish size by comparison with other states.

> There is a town in the "Cabbage Garden," where, after a lot of exertion, two or three were gathered together to petition for rain [*The Bulletin* (Sydney), April 8, 1882].

**Cactus City** *Amarillo, Texas, USA*. The name refers to the profusion of cacti around the city.

**Cactus Patch, the** *Phoenix, Arizona, USA*. The cactus is widely found in the vicinity of the city. Hence the name.

**Cactus State, the** *New Mexico, USA*. The cactus is widely found in the state, especially near the border with Mexico, where the plant grows in great numbers and varieties.

**Cadfael Country** see in Appendix 1, p. 269.

**Cadiz the Joyous** *Cádiz, Spain*. The seaport city has been known by its hedonistic sobriquet since Roman times, as described in the quote below.

> It was more renowned for gaiety and luxury than for learning. Juvenal and Martial write of Jocosae Gades, Cadiz the Joyous, as naturally as the modern Andalusian speaks of Cadiz la Joyosa; and throughout the Roman world its cookery and its dancing-girls were famous [*Encyclopædia Britannica*, 1911].

**Caesarea** *Jersey, Channel Islands, UK.* The island is sometimes referred to by this Roman name, which is said to derive from its present name, itself of Scandinavian origin and meaning "Geirr's island." It has recently been shown, however, that Caesarea was really the Roman name of the smaller island of Sark.

**Cajun Country** see in Appendix 1, p. 269.

**Cajun Music Capital, the** *Mamou, Louisiana, USA.* A self-promotional name for the town as a center of the lively syncopated music known as Cajun music. *See* **Cajun Country** in Appendix 1, p. 269.

**Cal** *(1) California, USA; (2) Kolkata (Calcutta), India.* A simple shortened form of the names of both state and city, in the former case equating to the standard abbreviation. *Cp.* **Cali.**

**Caledonia** or **Caledon** *Scotland.* The Roman name of Scotland has been preserved in that of the Caledonian Canal which extends diagonally across northern Scotland, as well as in various commercial names, such as the former Caledonian Airways and present Caledonian MacBrayne ("CalMac") ferry company. It is also found in poetry, especially of Scottish origin. Although now applied to the whole of Scotland, the name is more narrowly applied, as in quote (1) below, to the region lying to the north of the Firth of Forth.

(1) I am now to enter the true and real Caledonia, for the country on the north of the firth [of Forth] is alone called by that name, and was anciently known by no other [Daniel Defoe, *A Tour thro' the Whole Island of Great Britain,* 1724–6].
(2) Mourn, hapless Caledonia, mourn
Thy banished peace, thy laurels torn [Tobias Smollett, "The Tears of Scotland," 1746].
(3) There was once a day, but old Time then was young,
That brave Caledonia, the chief of her line,
From some of your northern deities sprung:
(Who knows not that brave Caledonia's divine?)
[Robert Burns, "Caledonia," 1791].
(4) O Caledonia! stern and wild,
Meet nurse for a poetic child! [Sir Walter Scott, *The Lay of the Last Minstrel,* 1805].
(5) Not thus, in ancient days of Caledon,
Was thy voice mute amid the festal crowd [Sir Walter Scott, *The Lady of the Lake,* 1810].

**Cales** *Cádiz, Spain.* An old English form of the seaport city's name, as in the rhyme quoted below.

A knight of Cales, a gentleman of Wales,
And a laird of the north countree;
A yeoman of Kent, with his yearly rent,
Will buy them out all three [Rhyme quoted in Thomas Fuller, *The History of the Worthies of England,* 1662].

**Cali** or **Cally** *California, USA.* Two of the many short forms of the state's name. *Cp.* **Cal.**

**Calicut** *Kozhikode, India.* The traditional form of the city's name is still in use alongside its indigenous form. It should not be confused with Calcutta (now officially Kolkata).

**California of Wales** see in Appendix 1, p. 269.

**California's Galápagos** *Channel Islands, California, USA.* The islands off the south coast of California are so nicknamed for their unique flora and fauna, like those of the Galápagos.

**Californ-i-ay** *California, USA.* A playful form of the state name, popularized by Jerome Kern and E.Y. Harburg's song so titled in the musical *Can't Help Singing* (1944).

**Cally** *see* **Cali**

**Calpe** *(Rock of) Gibraltar.* The original Greek name has remained in latinized form for poetic use. Together with **Abyla** it formed the **Pillars of Hercules.**

(1) Heaves up huge Abyla on Afric's sand,
Crowns with high Calpë Europe's salient strand
[Erasmus Darwin, *The Economy of Vegetation,* 1792].
(2) Through Calpe's straits survey the steepy shore;
Europe and Afric on each other gaze! [Lord Byron, *Childe Harold's Pilgrimage,* 1812].

**Calvinist Rome, the** *Debrecen, Hungary.* The city gained its sobriquet as the country's Protestant capital under the Austrian Habsburg rulers. It finally broke free from Austria in 1849.

**Cambria** *Wales.* The literary name is preserved not only in poetry but also in the Cambrian Mountains, running from north to south through Wales, the **Cambrian Coast** (see in Appendix 1, p. 269), and the geological Cambrian period. According to legend, Cambria was named for Camber, one of the sons of Brutus (*see* **Brute's City**), king of Britain, but it is really a latinized form of Welsh *Cymry,* "Welshmen." *See also* **Cymru.**

(1) *Locrine* was left the soueraine Lord of all;
But *Albanact* had all the Northrene part,
Which of himself *Albania* he did call;
And *Camber* did possesse the Westerne quart,
Which *Seuerne* now from *Logris* doth depart
[Edmund Spenser, *The Faerie Queene,* 1590].
(2) Take notice that I am in Cambria, at Milford-Haven [William Shakespeare, *Cymbeline,* c. 1609].
(3) Nor e'en thy virtues, Tyrant, shall avail
To save thy secret soul from nightly fears,
From Cambria's curse, from Cambria's tears
[Thomas Gray, *The Bard,* 1757].
(4) And Cambria, but of late subdued,
Sent forth her mountain multitude [Sir Walter Scott, *The Lord of the Isles,* 1815].

**Cambrian Coast** see in Appendix 1, p. 269.

**Cambridge of the North** *see* **Oxford of the North**

**Cambs** *Cambridgeshire, England.* A semi-official abbreviation of the county's name. *Cp.* **Cantab.** *See also* Appendix 6, p. 325.

**Camcreek** *Cambridge, England.* A rarish university students' form of the city's name, the "creek" being the Cam River.

**Camellia State, the** *Alabama, USA.* The state takes its nickname from the flowering shrub for which, among others, it is noted. The name was perhaps chosen to rival neighboring Mississippi as the **Magnolia State.**

**Camelot** *(1) Cadbury Castle, England; (2) Caerleon, Wales; (3) Camelford, England; (4) Colchester, England; (5) Winchester, England.* The name of the legendary court of King Arthur has been applied to the various English locations where the original is said to have been situated, mainly because of the traditional setting of the stories and, in the case of the first three, the similarity between the two names. The case for Colchester is based partly on the similarity between that city's Roman name *Camulodunum* and the Arthurian location, and partly because Geoffrey of Monmouth's description of the Camelot countryside in *Historia Regum Britanniae* (*c.*1136) fits the northern part of Essex better than any of the West-Country sites. Shakespeare, in quote (1) below, appears to have sited Arthur's court at Cadbury Castle, Somerset, and this site is popularly regarded as the true contender.

(1) (Cadbury Castle) Goose, if I had you upon Sarum plain,
I'd drive ye cackling home to Camelot [William Shakespeare, *King Lear, c.* 1604].
(2) (Cadbury Castle) Cadbury Castle, an Iron Age hill fort beside the village of South Cadbury in Somerset, has three features of Arthurian interest: first, its longstanding designation by the name *Camelot*; second, a miscellany of local folklore relating to this; and third, its proved reoccupation and refortification during the period within which Arthur supposedly lived [Norris J. Lacy, ed., *The New Arthurian Encyclopedia*, 1991].
(3) (Cadbury Castle) This is a mighty day to take on the elements here at the legendary Camelot — the wind nearly blew me off the highest bank [Julian Cope, *The Modern Antiquarian*, 1998].
(4) (Cadbury Castle) Those seeking a taste of Camelot today should consider a visit to Cadbury Castle in Somerset [Charlie Godfrey-Faussett, *Footprint England*, 2004].

**Camp, the** *(1) Hobart, Australia; (2) Sydney, Australia.* The historic nickname relates to the temporary settlements from which a number of Australian cities grew, including the two men-tioned, now respectively the capitals of Tasmania and New South Wales.

(1) (Sydney) I walked by myself to the Brick fields, about a mile from the Camp, for so Sydney is call'd, from its having been on the Spot they pitch'd their tents on the first landing [R. Atkins, *Journal*, April 4, 1792].
(2) (Hobart) A bark hut, under a great gum tree, in the very middle of *Camp* as they then called the charming port of Hobart Town [*South Briton* (Hobart), May 1843].

**Campo** see in Appendix 1, p. 269.

**Camptown** *Kemp Town, Brighton, England.* The nickname of the eastern district of Brighton puns on its prominent gay community.

(1) Brighton is Britain's gay capital, focused around Kemptown — affectionately branded Camptown [Dodd/Donald, p. 10].
(2) Kemptown (aka Camptown) ... is where it's all at [*Lonely Planet Great Britain*, 2005].

**Canada's Pride** *Banff, Alberta, Canada.* The famous tourist center and winter resort boasts wide-ranging facilities and amenities. Hence the self-promotional name.

Day 6. Free to explore Banff—"Canada's Pride" [Travel brochure issued with *The Times*, August 20, 2005].

**Canady** *Canada.* A dialect or local colloquial form of the country's name.

'Can't tell me I don't know my way around here. Been walkin this country for years. I'm headed for Canady.' 'But this ain't the road to Canada, this is the road to Pittsburgh and Chicago' [Jack Kerouac, *On the Road*, 1957].

**Canal County, the** *Staffordshire, England.* The county is famous for its canals, such as the early Staffordshire and Worcestershire Canal and the famous Shropshire Union Canal (*see* **Shroppie**), formerly used to carry china from the **Potteries** and beer from Burton upon Trent but now exploited for pleasure purposes.

Get on your bike and cycle the towpaths, perhaps through the 'canal county' of Staffordshire [Tourist brochure *Waterside England*, 2005].

**Candia** or **Candy** *(1) Crete, Greece; (2) Heracleum (Iráklion), Crete, Greece.* The Latin name of both the island and its seaport capital was long in literary use and is preserved in the name of the candytuft plant.

(1) (Heracleum) Orsino, this is that Antonio
That took the Phœnix and her fraught [i.e. freight] from Candy [William Shakespeare, *Twelfth Night*, 1601].
(2) (Heracleum) Witness Troy's rival, Candia!
Vouch it, ye
Immortal waves that saw Lepanto's fight! [Lord Byron, *Childe Harold's Pilgrimage*, 1812].

**Candy** *see* **Candia**

**Canny Newcastle** *Newcastle upon Tyne, En-*

*gland.* The northern city is regarded as generally agreeable or "nice." Hence the epithet, in origin the Scottish word meaning "knowing," "cautious."

> "Where d'ye come from?" "Canny-newcassel," replied Pigg [R.S. Surtees, *Handley Cross*, 1843].

**Cantab** *Cambridge, England.* The name, used in academic contexts with regard to Cambridge university, as "BA, Cantab," is an abbreviation of Latin *Cantabrigiensis,* "of Cambridge." The name is not used for Cambridgeshire in the way that **Oxon** is used for Oxfordshire, nor is it found as an episcopal signature, as there is no bishop of Cambridge. *Cp.* **Cambs.**

**Canton** *Guangzhou, China.* The traditional European name of the seaport city is a corruption not of its Chinese name but of that of Kwangtung, the province of which it is the capital. The form of the name may have been influenced by French (also English) *canton,* as a geographical administrative region. The Chinese name of the city has only recently begun to prevail over the popular form.

> The chief towns [in China] are Pekin, Nanking, Shanghai, Hankow, Canton and Chungking [Johnson, p. 72].

**Cape, the** *(1) Cape of Good Hope, South Africa; (2) Cape Peninsula, South Africa; (3) Cape Province; South Africa; (4) Cape Town, South Africa.* The name is used not only for the Cape of Good Hope and the Cape Peninsula but also for the former Cape Province and its capital city of Cape Town. (In 1994 the province was divided into Eastern Cape, Northern Cape, and Western Cape.) When "Cape" precedes a generic word, as Cape gooseberry, the reference is almost always to the Cape of Good Hope.

> (1) They on the trading flood,
>   Through the wide Ethiopian to the Cape,
>   Fly stemming nightly toward the pole [John Milton, *Paradise Lost*, 1667].
> (2) There are thousands of capes in the World, but, when people speak of *The* Cape, they always mean the Cape of Good Hope [Johnson, p. 63].
> (3) Before Union [in 1910], 'the Cape' popularly stood for the Cape Colony, the political entity which ... became the Cape Province. The same appellation therefore stood and still stands for the Cape of Good Hope... Furthermore, the 'Cape' may mean the Cape Peninsula, or even, in popular parlance, Cape Town [*Standard Encyclopaedia of Southern Africa*, 1971].

**Cape Stiff** *Cape Horn, Chile.* The cape at the southern extremity of South America was formerly so nicknamed by crews of sailing ships, for whom it was stiff work to beat round it.

**Cape Trib** *Cape Tribulation, Australia.* A colloquial abbreviated name for the Queensland cape and surrounding area, originally so named when Captain Cook's vessel hit a reef offshore here in 1770.

**Capital City, the** *(1) Columbus, Ohio, USA; (2) Washington, DC, USA.* The name could obviously apply to the capital of any state or country, but in the USA usually means the national capital or that of the state in question.

**Capital J** *Jackson, Mississippi, USA.* A punning name, referring to Jackson as the state capital of Mississippi and as spelled with a capital letter.

**Capital of All Music, the** *New York City, USA.* New York was so named by E.L. Doctorow in his novel *City of God* (2000).

**Capital of Capital, the** *New York City, USA.* The name was applied to the city for its dominant position in the world of global finance by Thomas Bender in *The Unfinished City* (2002). *Cp.* **Economic Capital of the World.**

**Capital of Civilization, the** *Paris, France.* A 19th-century sobriquet for the French capital which retains much of its validity today. The theme of the international Exposition of 1900 held in Paris was "Paris, Capital of the Civilized World."

> An 1846 tourist guidebook caught the tone by describing Paris as 'the heart of Europe, the capital of civilisation' [Colin Jones, *Paris*, 2004].

**Capital of Exhausted Trees, the** *New York City, USA.* New York was so named by E.L. Doctorow in his novel *City of God* (2000).

**Capital of Fife, the** *Glenrothes, Scotland.* The New Town, designated in 1948, made this claim for itself when flourishing as **Silicon Glen,** although the historic capital of the county and ancient kingdom has long been Cupar.

> A sign ... boldly announced, "Welcome to Glenrothes, the Capital of Fife." So outraged at this audacity were the residents of Cupar ... that the sign had to be removed [*The Rough Guide to Scotland*, 1998].

**Capital of Money, the** *London, England.* The British capital was so portrayed in Tobias Hill's novel *The Cryptographer* (2003), set in the near future, when a new type of currency has replaced existing world's currencies.

**Capital of Pleasure, the** *Paris, France.* The sobriquet denotes the hedonism for which the capital is famed. *Cp.* **Gay Paree.**

> Where between granite terraces
>   The blue Seine rolls her wave,
>   The Capital of Pleasure sees
>   Thy hardly-heard-of grave [Matthew Arnold, "Obermann," 1852].

**Capital of Pop, the** *Liverpool, England.* A

sobriquet for the seaport city dating from the 1960s, the heady heyday of the Beatles.

> Take a ferry across the Mersey to Liverpool, the official 'Capital of Pop' [Tourist brochure *Chester and Cheshire*, 2006].

**Capital of Prehistory, the** *Les Eyzies, France.* The village owes its nickname to the major archaeological discoveries in its many caves, notably type specimens of Cro-Magnon man in the cave so named in 1868, and paleolithic paintings and carvings in the caves Les Combarelles and Font-de-Gaume in 1901.

**Capital of Progress, the** *Paris, France.* The nickname relates to the sweeping improvements in the layout of the French capital made by Baron Haussmann in the second half of the 19th century, notably by widening streets, laying out boulevards and parks, and building bridges. His visionary work was the model for town planning in a number of other cities, such as Cairo and Buenos Aires.

**Capital of Romance, the** *Paris, France.* The French capital has long been a favorite venue for lovers and honeymooners, and many couples visit it on Valentine's Day. (*Cp.* **City of Love.**) The Golden Arrow express train that formerly ran from London, England, to Paris (where it was known as *La Flèche d'Or*) was so named from the tale in which a pair of lovers seek a golden arrow in the land of their dreams.

> I knew I would be conspicuous as a single woman in the capital of romance: more than 100,000 people had come to the city for a romantic break on Eurostar alone [*The Times*, March 26, 2005].

**Capital of Salt, the** *Zigong, China.* The city has been known for its salt extraction since ancient times. Hence the nickname.

**Capital of Smoke, the** *Osaka, Japan.* The sobriquet was at first adopted proudly by local residents, who regarded the city's smoky atmosphere as a sign of industrial progress. By the 1970s, however, they realized that the smog and pollution was actually harmful, and measures were introduced to improve the air quality. The English name translates Japanese *kemuri no miyako*, from *kemuri*, "smoke," *no*, "of," and *miyako*, "capital."

**Capital of Steel, the** *Anshan, China.* The city owes its nickname to its predominant production of iron and steel products.

**Capital of the Black Country, the** *Dudley, England.* Dudley is not the biggest city in the **Black Country** (see in Appendix 1, p. 269), which is Birmingham. But it can claim the given title as it was here in the 17th century that coal was first used for smelting iron, and its major

iron, coal, and limestone industries subsequently brought it fame. The industries have been in gradual decline, however, since the last quarter of the 19th century.

**Capital of the Cornish Riviera, the** *Penzance, England.* The resort and port lies on Mounts Bay in the center of the **Cornish Riviera** (see in Appendix 1, p. 269).

> [Penzance] is called the capital of the "Cornish Riviera," which will strike the tourist as an unfortunate label [Ruth McKenney and Richard Bransten, *Here's England*, 1955].

**Capital of the Cotswolds, the** *Cirencester, England.* The Gloucestershire town arose on the site of the important Roman settlement of **Corinium** and has been a flourishing trading center from medieval times. Five of the nine roads that radiate from the town in the Cotswold Hills are Roman.

> (1) Cirencester ... well deserves its title of "The Capital of the Cotswolds" [*Holiday Haunts 1961: Area No. 4, West of England and South and Central Wales*].
> (2) The self-styled "capital of the Cotswolds" sits at the intersection of three ancient thoroughfares [*The Times*, August 6, 2004].

**Capital of the Devonshire Highlands, the** *Okehampton, England.* The Devon town lies below the northern edge of Dartmoor, and the latter's upland area would be the "highlands" of the nickname.

> Okehampton, which claims to be the "Capital of the Devonshire Highlands," is ... situated ... on the north-western fringe of Dartmoor [*Holiday Haunts 1961: Area No. 4, West of England and South and Central Wales*].

**Capital of the Highlands, the** *(1) Inverness, Scotland; (2) Oban, Scotland.* Each of the two Scottish towns claims the title, with Inverness, the larger town, a seaport on the northwest coast and Oban a port and resort on the west coast. *See* **Highlands** in Appendix 1, p. 269.

> (1) (Inverness) Inverness, the Capital of the Highlands, is a pleasant town [*Holiday Haunts 1962: Scotland*].
> (2) (Inverness) Inverness is rapidly reinforcing its claim to be one of Europe's fastest growing cities. It was already the undisputed capital of the Highlands and the impression of its stature grows as you approach [*The Times* (Scotland Supplement), September 10, 2005].

**Capital of the Landsker Borderlands, the** *Narberth, Wales.* The Pembrokeshire town lies on the border that formerly divided the Welsh-speaking region to the north from **Little England Beyond Wales** to the south. ("Landsker," literally "land division," itself means "boundary," so the title is essentially a tautology.)

**Capital of the Mendips, the** *Wells, England.* The small Somerset city derives its nickname from its site below the southern slopes of the Mendip Hills.

> Wells, as the acknowledged "Capital of the Mendips," is ideally situated for the exploration of the whole range [*Holiday Haunts 1961: Area No. 4, West of England and South and Central Wales*].

**Capital of the Midlands, the** *(1) Athlone, Ireland; (2) Birmingham, England.* The Co. Westmeath town, on a crossing of the Shannon River, has long served as a key link between eastern and western Ireland. Hence the name, referring to its status in the Irish Midlands. Britain's second city has a like claim in England. *Cp.* **Midland Metropolis.**

> (Birmingham) The restaurants ... have finally allowed the capital of the Midlands to take its "long overdue ... place on the culinary map" [*The Times*, January 21, 2005]

**Capital of the Mind, the** *Edinburgh, Scotland.* The sobriquet describes the Scottish capital in the 18th century, according to James Buchan's 2003 novel of this title. Many noted writers and thinkers then lived in Edinburgh, such as the philosopher David Hume.

**Capital of the Miracle, the** *Milan, Italy.* The nickname refers to the economic miracle experienced in Milan during Italy's boom period following World War II.

**Capital of the New Forest, the** *Lyndhurst, England.* The Hampshire town lies in the middle of the New Forest. Its Old English name means "wooded hill with lime trees," although the lime is not the most common tree in the forest. *Cp.* **Gateway to the New Forest.**

> As befits the "capital" of the New Forest, Lyndhurst lies in the heart of this wild and lovely country [*Holiday Guide 1952: Area No. 5, South & South East England*].

**Capital of the Nineteenth Century, the** *Paris, France.* The French capital was so described by the 20th-century cultural critic Walter Benjamin. *Cp.* **Queen City of the World.**

**Capital of the North, the** *(1) Mzuzu, Malawi; (2) York, England.* A promotional name for the African town, in the north of the country. As such it balances Lilongwe, the political capital, in the center, and Blantyre, the commercial capital, in the south. Historically, the English city is in many ways the northern equivalent of London, and the Romans made Eboracum, as they called it, their military headquarters in northern Britain.

> (York) Known for centuries as the capital of the North, York ... was somehow overlooked by the Industrial Revolution [Charlie Godfrey-Faussett, *Footprint England*, 2004].

**Capital of the Resistance, the** *Milan, Italy.* The nickname relates to World War II, when the Germans occupied Milan and partisans led sabotage campaigns in the city.

**Capital of the Twentieth Century, the** *Detroit, Michigan, USA.* The city was so adjudged by Jerry Herron, as in the quote below.

> Nowhere else has American modernity so completely had its way with people and place alike. Reputedly "historic" towns, like Philadelphia, New Orleans and San Francisco, merely seem *old* by comparison. Others, such as New York, Los Angeles and Miami, are not American at all... This makes Detroit the revealed "Capital of the Twentieth Century," ... because this is the place, more than any other, where the native history of modernity has been written [Jerry Herron, "Three meditations on the ruins of Detroit," in G. Dalaskalis, C. Waldheim, and J. Young (eds.), *Stalking Detroit*, 2001].

**Capital of the Vale, the** *Cowbridge, Wales.* The small but prosperous town was so nicknamed for its location in the Vale of Glamorgan. (The reference to Cranford in the quote below is to the fictional village that is the setting of Elizabeth Gaskell's 1853 novel titled with its name. It is based on Knutsford, Cheshire, and features as a genteel community of ladies.)

> It has been christened the Capital of the Vale, and even the Cranford of Glamorgan [Vaughan-Thomas/Llewellyn, p. 153].

**Capital of the Vanished World, the** *Rome, Italy.* The name evokes the former greatness of the Roman empire. A similar sentiment was expressed by Edgar Allan Poe in his lines on "the glory that was Greece / And the grandeur that was Rome" ("To Helen," 1831).

> Behold me in the capital of the vanished world! [P.B. Shelley, letter to Thomas Love Peacock, November 20, 1818].

**Capital of the Weald, the** *Cranbrook, England.* The former cloth-weaving town is so nicknamed for its location in the Weald, a region of southeastern England known in this county as the Weald of Kent. ("Weald" properly denotes a wooded district, although the definition here is no longer valid.) *Cp.* **Jewel of the Weald.**

> Known as 'The Capital of the Weald,' it was once the centre of the region's medieval cloth industry [Heart of Kent Holiday Guide, 2005].

**Capital of the World, the** *(1) London, England; (2) New York City, USA; (3) Varanasi, India.* Each of the two great Western cities can with some justification claim the title on grounds of size and importance. New York gained its nickname in 1939 when the World's Fair was held there, and it became popular again when the United Nations made the city its home after

World War II. London has been unofficially so known over more or less the same period, having earlier been patriotically promoted as the capital of the British Empire. Varanasi, one of India's most ancient cities, is the **Holy City** of the Hindus and so a world religious capital.

> (1) (Varanasi) You hear the same mournful wail by the rotted walls of Cádiz, Spain, that you hear 12,000 miles around in the depths of Benares the Capital of the World [Jack Kerouac, *On the Road*, 1957].
>
> (2) (London) "There was no need to advertise this type of product," says Rapp gnomically. "London is the capital of the world. And people who can afford this type of apartment want to be here" [*Sunday Times*, August 8, 2004].
>
> (3) (New York) Today the city will mark the exact centenary of the first nine-mile ride on the 722-mile underground railway that enabled it to grow into the "capital of the world" [*The Times*, October 27, 2004].
>
> (4) (New York) The pope [i.e. John Paul II] even came to town [in 1979] and called New York "the capital of the world" [*The Rough Guide to New York City*, 2004].

**Captain Cook Country** see in Appendix 1, p. 269.

**Carcassonne of Poland, the** *Paczków, Poland.* The town of southern Poland, near the Czech border, is so nicknamed for its medieval fortifications, which to some extent suggest those of the town in southern France.

**Carcassonne of Wales, the** *Conwy, Wales.* The town and port in northwest Wales owes its nickname to its medieval turreted castle, which bears some resemblance to that of the town in southern France.

**Caribbees, the** or **Caribbee** or **Cariboo** *West Indies.* A popular poetic name for the Caribbean islands or the sea in which they lie, especially in the context of adventure on the "high seas."

> (1) 'Say, come ye from the shore of the holy Salvador,
> Or the gulf of the rich Caribbees?' [Lord Macaulay, "The Last Buccaneer," 1839].
>
> (2) The story of Frederick Gowler,
> A mariner of the sea,
> Who quitted his ship, the *Howler*,
> A-sailing in Caribbee [W.S. Gilbert, "The King of Canoodle-Dum," *The "Bab" Ballads*, 1869].
>
> (3) The *Ballyshannon* foundered off the coast of Cariboo,
> And down in fathoms many went the captain and the crew [W.S. Gilbert, "Etiquette," *The "Bab" Ballads*, 1869].

**Carib Sea, the** *Caribbean Sea.* The poetic form of the sea's name is found in the opening line of the national anthem of Belize, as in quote (3) for **Land of the Free**.

**Carlsbad of Mexico, the** *Tehuacán, Mexico.*

The city earned its nickname through its famed mineral springs, like those of Carlsbad (modern Karlovy Vary, Czech Republic).

**Carnarvon** *Caernarfon, Wales.* The older spelling of the town's name, and that of its county, Carnarvonshire, is preserved in the title of the earls of Carnarvon, beginning with Henry Herbert, created earl of the town and county of Carnarvon in 1793.

> In faith, for little England
> You'd venture an emballing: I myself
> Would for Carnarvonshire [William Shakespeare, *Henry VIII*, 1623].

**Carnival Island** *Isle of Wight, England.* The promotional nickname aims to draw visitors to the island county's varied entertainment.

> Throughout the year the Island is alive with carnival celebrations, confirming its reputation as England's own 'Carnival Island' [Isle of Wight travel brochure, 2005].

**Carport** see in Appendix 1, p. 269.

**Carrousel Capital of the World, the** *Binghamton, New York, USA.* The city styles itself thus for the many merry-go-rounds in its parks.

**Carthage of the North, the** *Lübeck, Germany.* Lübeck, a city and seaport on two rivers near the Baltic Sea, was head of the Hanseatic League, the defensive commercial confederacy of Europe founded in the 13th century. It was thus akin to Carthage, the ancient fortified city of North Africa that came to dominate the western Mediterranean.

**Casa** *Casablanca, Morocco.* A colloquial abbreviation of the seaport city's name

> Casablanca (Dar el-Baïda in Arabic and popularly known as Casa) [*Lonely Planet Morocco*, 2001].

**Casey** *Kansas City, Missouri, USA.* A personalized form of the city's initialism, **KC**.

**Catfish Capital of the World, the** *Belzoni, Mississippi, USA.* The town is surrounded by ponds of farm-raised catfish. Hence its self-promotional name.

**Cathay** *China.* An early name for China preserved in poetry. It was popularized by Marco Polo in the 13th century and derives from the Khitan (or Khitai), a Manchurian people who conquered northern China and founded the Liao dynasty in 937. It is directly related to *Kitay* as the modern Russian name of China and is preserved in the name of the Hong Kong airline Cathay Pacific.

> (1) *A Discovrse of a Discouerie for a New Passage to Cataia.* Written by Sir Hvmfrey Gilbert [Book title, 1576].
>
> (2) The lands on either side are his; the ship
> From Ceylon, Inde, or far Cathay, unloads
> For him the fragrant produce of each trip [Lord Byron, *Don Juan*, 1823].

(3) Better fifty years of Europe than a cycle of Cathay [Alfred, Lord Tennyson, "Locksley Hall," 1842].

(4) They rested there, escaped awhile
From cares that wear the life away,
To eat the lotus of the Nile,
And drink the poppies of Cathay [John Greenleaf Whittier, *The Tent on the Beach*, 1867].

**Catherine Cookson Country** see in Appendix 1, p. 269.

**Causeway Coast** see in Appendix 1, p. 269.

**Cavalier State, the** *Virginia, USA.* The nickname refers historically to the English "cavaliers" or royalists in Virginia who supported Charles I against Parliament in the civil wars of the mid–17th century.

**Cawnpore** *Kanpur, India.* An anglicized form of the city's Hindi name that was still current in the 20th century.

**CDM** *Corona del Mar, California, USA.* A local initialism for the name of the section of Newport Beach city, on the Pacific coast.

Corona del Mar (known by locals as "CDM") [*Fodor's Los Angeles 2006*].

**Celebes** *Sulawesi, Indonesia.* The europeanized form of the island's name is still sometimes found and is regular for the Celebes Sea, to the north of the island, as part of the western Pacific Ocean.

**Celestial City, the** *Beijing, China.* The name is sometimes found for the city that is the capital of the **Celestial Empire**. More commonly, however, the Celestial City is thought of as a name for heaven, and is so applied in John Bunyan's *The Pilgrim's Progress* (1678, 1684).

**Celestial Empire, the** *China.* The name translates Chinese *tiān cháo,* "heavenly dynasty," meaning a kingdom ruled over by a dynasty appointed by heaven.

He possessed the most delightful *chinoiseries*— trophies of his sojourn in the Celestial Empire [Henry James, *The Europeans*, 1878].

**Celtic Fringe** see in Appendix 1, p. 269.

**Celtic Tiger, the** *Ireland.* The country was so nicknamed for its rapid economic development from the mid–1990s. The name itself is based on the so-called "tiger" economies of Southeast Asia.

(1) At the risk of a horrible mixed metaphor, we can say that the Celtic Tiger needs a human face and a human heart [Cardinal Cahal Daly, quoted in *Irish Times*, January 10, 1998].

(2) Transformed from the 'sick economy' of Western Europe into a 'model economy,' Ireland emerged as the Celtic Tiger [Brigid Laffan in *The Hutchinson Encyclopedia of Ireland*, 2000].

(3) Dark underbelly of the Celtic Tiger. Among the frothy romcoms of prosperous Ireland one

gritty film stands out [Heading, review of Irish romantic comedy *Adam & Paul*, *The Times*, May 26, 2005].

(4) Today's Dublin is enjoying the "Celtic Tiger" economic boom [*The Times*, December 10, 2005].

**Centennial State, the** *Colorado, USA.* The state was admitted into the Union in 1876, a hundred years after the signing of the Declaration of Independence. Hence its nickname.

But for the protrusion of this [mountainous] wedge the 'Centennial State' would have been a quiet pastoral or agricultural territory [Archibald Geikie in *Macmillan's Magazine*, 1881].

**Center of Black Culture, the** *Esmeraldas, Ecuador.* The major seaport, in northwestern Ecuador, has a sizable black population, many of whom attend the city's technical university, founded in 1970.

**Centralia** see in Appendix 1, p. 269.

**Central State, the** *Kansas, USA.* Kansas lies almost in the geographical center of the United States.

**Centre** see in Appendix 1, p. 269.

**Ceylon** *Sri Lanka.* The former British crown colony was officially renamed as now on gaining its independence in 1972. The traditional name, representing the Sanskrit word for "lion," has been preserved in literary contexts and is still sometimes used by travel companies and the older generation.

(1) What though the spicy breezes
Blow soft o'er Ceylon's isle [Bishop Reginald Heber, hymn, 1821; he later altered "Ceylon's" to "Java's"]

(2) Every slip is seized on by the gossip columns as proof of the 65-year-old's decrepitude — last Sunday it was for calling Sri Lanka "Ceylon" [*Sunday Times*, January 16, 2005].

(3) Sri Lanka, the island of Ceylon, is a very special place [Travel ad, *The Times Magazine*, September 17, 2005].

**Chain, the** *Aleutian Islands, Alaska, USA.* The Aleutians are a chain of volcanic islands extending west from the Alaskan Peninsula.

**Chair City** *Grand Rapids, Michigan, USA.* The city is a noted manufacturer of furniture, and especially office furniture. Hence the nickname.

**Chamonix of Wales, the** *Llanberis, Wales.* The location of the Welsh town at the base of Snowdon invites comparison with that of the French Alpine town at the foot of Mont Blanc.

**Channel, the** *English Channel.* On the British side, the shortened name is generally taken to mean the English Channel, especially in such phrases as "Channel crossing," "Channel ferry." On the French side, the Channel is known as *la Manche* (*see* **Manche**).

(1) I go of message from the queen of France;
I charge thee, waft me safely cross the Channel
[William Shakespeare, *Henry VI, Part 2*, 1594].
    (2) Dirty British coaster with a salt-caked smoke
stack,
Butting through the Channel in the mad March
days [John Masefield, "Cargoes," 1903].
    (3) Friendly pub staff give customers a warmer
welcome than "surly" waiters across the Channel
[*The Times*, November 21, 2005].

**Channel City** *Santa Barbara, California,
USA.* The city lies on the Santa Barbara Channel, the strait between the California mainland
and the Santa Barbara Islands. Hence the nickname.

**Channel Country** see in Appendix 1, p. 269.

**Chapel, the** *Whitechapel, London, England.* A
Cockney shortening of the name of the district,
where there once was a "white chapel."

**Chapelouze, la** *La Chapelle, Paris, France.* A
colloquial name for the district, centering on the
church of St.-Denis de la Chapelle.

**Charing Cross of the Highlands, the** *Oban,
Scotland.* The name compares the Scottish port
and resort with the busy London district, the location of Charing Cross station, the mainline
station nearest to central London. *See* **Highlands**
in Appendix 1, p. 269.

Oban is the starting-point for so many excursions
and the centre of so much traffic by train and
steamer that it has been called the 'Charing Cross
of the Highlands' [Karl Baedeker, *Handbook to
Great Britain*, 1890].

**Charleston of Nicaragua, the** *Granada,
Nicaragua.* The comparison is with Charleston,
South Carolina, a city of old colonial homes and
picturesque streets, popular as a tourist resort.

Charming, characterful, timeless ... Granada has
often been dubbed "the Charleston of Nicaragua"
[Dodd/Donald, p. 158].

**Charlie** *Charleston, South Carolina, USA.* A
pet personalization of the city's name.

**Charter Oak City, the** *Hartford, Connecticut,
USA.* The nickname alludes to the oak tree in
which Captain Joseph Wadsworth supposedly
hid the colony's royal charter when Governor Sir
Edward Andros attempted to seize it in 1687.

**Château Country** see in Appendix 1, p. 269.

**Chats** *Chatham, England.* A naval shortening of the name of the Kent town, a historic port
and Royal Marine base.

**Chelsea-on-Sea** *Polzeath, England.* The Cornish resort on the **Costa del Sloane** (see in Appendix 1, p. 269) is one of the best surfing sites
in the county, frequented both by regular vacationers and the young well-to-do. The latter
gave its nickname, for the wealthy and fashionable London district.

Polzeath is Chelsea-on-sea and when there is a
"zoo" (crowded surf), it's either "O Hello!" or
"Oi!" if you collide with someone, reflecting the
social polarities of the area [Hugo Williams in
*Times Literary Supplement*, September 15, 2005].

**Chemical Capital of the World, the** *Wilm-
ington, Delaware, USA.* The city is a major
chemical center, with many manufacturing
plants. The headquarters of the vast Du Pont
Corporation are also here, together with their
experimental laboratories.

**Cher, the** *Cherwell River, England.* An abbreviation used mainly by Oxford university students. The Cherwell flows into the Thames at
Oxford.

**Cherry Capital of the World, the** *Traverse
City, Michigan, USA.* The city derives its nickname from its location in a noted cherry-
growing region.

Michigan's Cherry Capital is the largest city in
the northern half of the Lower Peninsula [*Lonely
Planet USA*, 2004].

**Cherry Ripe** *Centuripe, Italy.* A British soldiers' World War I perversion of the Italian placename. Centuripe is a small town in Sicily.
"Cherry Ripe" was a well-known 19th-century
song title adopted by Millais for a popular child
portrait of 1879.

**Chi** (1) *Chicago, Illinois, USA; (2) Chichester,
England.* The abbreviated name of the English
city is pronounced as in "chime," but that of the
US city as "shy." Chicago is also known as **Chi
Town.**

(1) (Chicago) Throughout the Under World, Chicago is known by its nickname, "Chi"... Other
cities have similar nick-names. New York is called
"York"; Philadelphia, "Phillie"; Cincinnati, "Cin-
cie"; Boston, "Bean-Town"; Detroit, "Slow-
Town"; Baltimore, "Balt," and Kansas City,
"Kay See" [Josiah Flint, *The World of Graft*,
1901].
    (2) (Chicago) 'Oh, and are we going to cut
around old Chi with this thing! Think of it, Sal,
I've never been to Chicago in all my life, never
stopped' [Jack Kerouac, *On the Road*, 1957].

**Chiantishire** *Tuscany, Italy.* The region of
western Italy became popular with middle-class
English vacationers and vacation-home buyers
from the 1970s, Chianti being the local wine,
from the Chianti Hills. The name was popularized by the English writer John Mortimer. *Cp.*
**Paradise of Exiles.**

(1) The British are coming, flooding into Pisa airport, known as Pizza to the BA hostesses. They're
invading Tuscany, part of Italy which has become
part of England, so that it's known as Chiantishire
to the natives [John Mortimer, *Mortimer in Tuscany*, TV program, May 17, 1988].
    (2) We chose to head north, away from Chi-

antishire, to the Garfagnana region, northwest of Lucca [*The Sunday Times*, September 11, 2005].

**Chicagoland** *Chicago, Illinois, USA.* A form of the city's name that is popular with the local media.

**Chicago of New Zealand, the** *North Palmerston, New Zealand.* An early nickname for the North Island city, settled in 1870, referring to its rapid growth.

> If not quite warranting [the] title given it in the 1890s of 'the Chicago of New Zealand,' [the] seventh city in New Zealand does continue to exceed national growth by a good margin [Shadbolt, p. 158].

**Chicago of South America, the** *São Paolo, Brazil.* The name refers to each city as a leader of commerce and industry, although such a role is more obviously played by the Brazilian city in South America than the American in the USA.

**Chicago of the Caspian, the** *Baku, Azerbaijan.* The city and seaport is said to derive its name from a word meaning "windward," referring to its location on the western shore of the Caspian Sea. The association with wind thus suggests a comparison with Chicago, the **Windy City.**

> A more popular etymology [of the name] is the Azeri *Bad Kube*, meaning "blustering wind," on account of the wind that gives Baku its nickname, "the Chicago of the Caspian" [Dodd/Donald, p. 313].

**Chicago of the East, the** *Harbin, China.* The nickname compares the city's rapid growth in the early 20th century with that of Chicago half a century earlier.

> Harbin is now called the Chicago of the East. This is not a compliment to Chicago [Maurice Baring, *What I Saw in Russia*, 1913].

**Chicago of the North, the** *Anchorage, Alaska, USA.* The name equates the city's rapid growth in the mid–20th century with that of Chicago a century earlier.

**Chicago of the South, the** *Houston, Texas, USA.* The sobriquet compares the rapid growth of Houston in the mid–20th century with that of Chicago a hundred years earlier.

**Chicago on the Main** *see* **Mainhattan**

**Chichi** *Chichicastenango, Guatemala.* A local short form of the town's name.

> *Chichi*, as it is known, has an atmosphere all of its own [Natascha Norton and Mark Whatmore, *Cadogan Guides: Central America*, 1993].

**Child of the Mississippi River, the** *Louisiana, USA.* Louisiana arose on alluvial lands in the Mississippi basin, as if "born" from that great river. Hence the nickname.

**Children's Paradise, the** *(1) Littlehampton,* *England; (2) Rhyl, Wales.* The sandy beaches of both resorts, one on England's south coast, the other on the north coast of Wales, were promoted in the early 20th century as happy places for young children, with entertainment for all the family.

**Chili Switch** *San Antonio, Texas, USA.* A pun on the hot chili pepper, as a typical ingredient of Mexican food, in a city that has a huge Mexican quarter. San Antonio was formerly noted for its "chili queens," young ladies who set up stalls in the Market Square to sell plates of chili con carne.

> Sure wish we had a Fry's here in Chili Switch... Seems to me the San Antonio market would be big [Message, Jay Emrie to Charles Scaglione, *FidoNet EchomailArchive*, September 18, 2004].

**Chimney of the World, the** *Manchester, England.* A name for the city's smoke-belching factory chimneys of the late 1830s, as given by British army officer Sir Charles James Napier (who also dubbed Manchester "the entrance to hell").

**Chimneyville** *Jackson, Mississippi, USA.* The city acquired the nickname when it was virtually destroyed by fire during the Civil War leaving only its chimneys standing.

**China Clay Country** see in Appendix 1, p. 269.

**China's Mouth** *Jiayuguan, China.* The city in Gansu province arose as a fortified town at the western limit of the Great Wall of China on the Silk Road, the main route linking China to the Mediterranean. It was thus a major key point of entry to China. Hence its name.

> Into any region beyond the Great Wall, disgraced Chinese were banished in despair. Jiayuguan was "China's Mouth." Those beyond it were "outside the mouth," and its western gate ... used to be covered with farewell inscriptions [Colin Thubron, "The end of the world," *Sunday Times*, December 11, 2005].

**China's Sorrow** *Huang Ho, China.* The Huang Ho (known in English as the Yellow River) often overflows its banks in its lower reaches, sending ruinous floodwaters across the North China Plain. Hence its sobriquet.

> (1) So named [in the 19th century] by the Emperor Tao Kuang because of the devastation caused by its oft-recurring floods [Giles, p. 47].
> (2) It is called "China's Sorrow," as it often alters its course without warning and then drowns all the people in its new path [Johnson, p. 125].

**Chinatown** see in Appendix 1, p. 269.

**Chinook State, the** *Washington, USA.* The state takes its name from the Chinook, the American Indian people originally inhabiting the region around the mouth of the Columbia River, which flows through the state.

**Chippitts** see in Appendix 1, p. 269.

**Chippy** *Chipping Campden, England.* A colloquial local name for the Gloucestershire market town.

> Londoners flock to [buy houses in] "Chippy" (Chipping Campden) [*Sunday Times*, November 13, 2005].

**Chi Town** *Chicago, Illinois, USA.* An abbreviated name for the city, pronounced "shy town." A shorter form is simply **Chi.**

**Chizzie** *Chizumulu Island, Malawi.* A colloquial name for the island in Lake Malawi.

**Chocolate City** *(1) Hershey, Pennsylvania, USA; (2) Perugia, Italy; (3) Washington, DC, USA.* Hershey was founded in 1903 by Milton Snavely Hershey as the site for his chocolate factory, the germ of the Hershey Chocolate Corporation. Hence the nickname. The Italian city is equally noted for its chocolate manufacture and hosts an annual chocolate festival. The ethnic composition of Washington's population is around three-fifths African-American and less than one-third white, with the remaining tenth a mixture of Asians, Africans, Latin Americans, and other ethnic minorities. The nickname thus has a different sense here.

> (Perugia) Perugia (the self-styled Citta del Cioccolato) [*Sunday Times*, July 31, 2005].

**Choo Choo Town** *Chattanooga, Tennessee, USA.* The noted railroad center took its nickname from Mack Gordon's 1941 song "Chattanooga Choo-choo" (opening line: "Pardon me boy is that the Chattanooga Choo-choo").

**Chopburg** *Hamburg, Germany.* A punning name for the city used by British Royal Air Force flyers in World War II. (Some of them may also have feared "getting the chop," or being shot down over Hamburg.)

**Chopper City** *New Orleans, Louisiana, USA.* A nickname referring to the city's repute for gangsterism, a "chopper" being a gangster with a submachine gun (which "chops" its victims). *Cp.* **Click-Click.**

**Chops of the Channel** see in Appendix 1, p. 269.

**Chowland** *Queensland, Australia.* The state was so nicknamed for its many Chinese ("Chow") immigrants, themselves so dubbed from the "chow" (mixed food) that they ate.

**Christiania** *Oslo, Norway.* The former name of the Norwegian capital (from 1625 to 1924), also spelled Kristiania, is still found in certain contexts. It should not be confused with the modern hippie "free city" (commune) of Kristia-

nia in the center of Copenhagen, the Danish capital.

**Christmas Island** *Kiritimati, Kiribati.* The alternate name of the island should not be confused with that of Christmas Island, an Australian territory in the Indian Ocean. The name Kiritimati represents a local pronunciation of "Christmas," just as Kiribati represents the "Gilbert" of the Gilbert Islands.

**Ch'town** *Charlottetown, Prince Edward Island, Canada.* A colloquial short form of the provincial capital's name.

**Cicester** *Cirencester, England.* The old spelling of the Gloucestershire town's name was long represented by the supposedly "correct" pronunciation of the name as "Sissiter," a form now rarely heard. *See also* **Ciren.**

> (1) Kind uncle York, the latest news we hear
> Is that the rebels have consum'd with fire
> Our town of Cicester in Gloucestershire [William Shakespeare, *Richard II*, 1597].
> (2) In the year 1924 a controversy raged in the *Sunday Times* as to the pronunciation of *Cirencester*. One critic told us that 'the correct pronunciation of *Cirencester* should be in full. It is the locals who abbreviate, sometimes beyond recognition.' This authoritative gentleman ain't arguing, he's a-telling you [Ernest Weekley, *Adjectives—And Other Words*, 1930].
> (3) The name of 'Cirencester' has always attracted attention, and occasional flutters of letters to *The Times* about its proper pronunciation. Some of its natives pronounce it 'sissiter,' others pronounce it 'syren-sester,' and most strangers find some variant between the two [C. Stella Davies and John Levitt, *What's in a Name?*, 1970].
> (4) Cirencester ... 'Sister' to the sophisticated and 'Siren' to the locals [Hogg, p. 208].

**Cidade de Deus** *see* **City of God**

**Cider Country, the** *(1) Herefordshire, England; (2) Worcestershire, England.* Both counties, which merged to form the united county of Hereford and Worcester from 1971 to 1998, are famous for their many apple orchards. Hence the name. (Administratively, Herefordshire became a unitary authority in 1998 and did not revert to county status.) Just to the south is the **Cider County** of Somerset.

> (Worcestershire) The lucrative see of Worcester was vacant; and some powerful Whigs of the cider country wished to obtain it for John Hall [Thomas Babington Macaulay, *The History of England*, 1849].

**Cider County, the** *Somerset, England.* The county has long been noted for its production of cider, especially the strong "rough" variety known as "scrumpy." *Cp.* **Cider Country.**

> Somerset is the cider county, although few of its

traditional orchards remain [Charlie Godfrey-Faussett, *Footprint England*, 2004].

**Cigar City** *Ybor City, Tampa, Florida, USA.* At one time the historic area of Tampa had the world's largest cigar factory. Hence the nickname, sometimes extended to Tampa itself.

**Cinci** or **Cincy** *Cincinnati, Ohio, USA.* A colloquial shortening of the city's name.

**Cinderella City** *Disneyland, Anaheim, California, USA.* An appropriate nickname for an amusement park where the workaday visitor is transported to a glittering fantasy world, as Cinderella was when she went to the ball. The name is all the more apt from its association with the Disney animation romance *Cinderella* (1950).

**Cinque Ports** see in Appendix 1, p. 269.

**Cipango** *Japan.* The name emerged in medieval legend as that of an island or islands to the east of Asia. It was described by the 13th-century Venetian traveler Marco Polo and was later sought by Christopher Columbus and other navigators. Its name alone suggests an identity as Japan and this is generally confirmed by the early accounts.

**Circle City** *(1) Corona, California, USA; (2) Indianapolis, Indiana, USA.* Corona, a suburb of Riverside, derives its nickname (and its actual name, Latin for "crown," "circle") from the circular boulevard around the city center, at one time used for car racing. Indianapolis, still famed for auto racing, was founded in 1821 as a planned radial city. Hence the respective names.

**Ciren** *Cirencester, England.* A local nickname for the Gloucestershire town, pronounced as "siren." An alternate spelling (and pronunciation) with initial "z" also exists, as in quote (2) below. *See also* **Cicester**.

(1) Ciren, as the locals calls it (*not* 'Cisiter'), was the Roman town of Corinium [John Moore in Speaight, p. 154].

(2) 'Ziren,' as it is sometimes known locally [John Julius Norwich, ed., *Treasures of Britain*, 2002].

**Cisco** *San Francisco, California, USA.* A rarish shortening of the city's name, familiar from the Cisco Kid, a romantic Latin cowboy who first appeared as a Mexican bandit in O. Henry's story "The Caballero's Way" in *Heart of the West* (1907) and who subsequently became a hero of Hollywood movies.

In Cisco's Dewdrop Dining Rooms
They tell the tale anew [Rudyard Kipling, "The Rhyme of the Three Sealers," 1893].

**Cities of the Plain, the** *Sodom and Gomorrah, Palestine.* A unified name for the two biblical cities in the region of the valley of the Jordan River and the Dead Sea. As described in Genesis 19:24–29, the cities were destroyed by God because of their corruption.

**City, the** *(1) London, England; (2) New York City, USA; (3) St. Louis, Missouri, USA.* The name could obviously apply at a local level to any city, but it is particularly associated with the three mentioned. For London, it applies to the capital's historic center, the City of London, as the business quarter or financial center otherwise known as the **Square Mile**. For New York, it implies New York City, or more precisely Manhattan, as distinct from New York State, and for St. Louis, similarly, it denotes the city as opposed to the **County**.

(1) (London) In every weather, every day,
  Dry, muddy, wet, or gritty,
  He took to dancing all the way
  From Brompton to the City [W.S. Gilbert, "A Discontented Sugar Broker," *The "Bab" Ballads*, 1869].

(2) (New York) That wonderful town known among vagrants as the "City" and also as "York" [Josiah Flynt, *Tramping with Tramps*, 1899].

(3) (St. Louis) Heading toward the year 2000, what happened to "the City" was happening to "the County" [Cohen, p. 2697].

(4) (New York) Teachers who venture into The City, Manhattan, tell me they see Malachy in plays [Frank McCourt, '*Tis*, 1999].

(5) (New York) Manhattan is the original New York... Even to residents of the other boroughs, Manhattan is "the city," the administrative, business, and financial centre of the metropolis [*Britannica*, vol. 24, p. 904].

(6) (London) The city of London is not to be confused with the City of London... "The City" is the financial heart of the capital, a small geographical area with defined boundaries [*The Times*, November 17, 2005].

**City at the End of the World, the** *Ushuaia, Argentina.* Ushuaia, in southern Tierra del Fiego, is the southernmost city in the world. Hence the name.

In a bid to appeal to explorers ... Ushuaia calls itself "the city at the end of the world" [Dodd/Donald, p. 104].

**City between the Bridges, the** *Stockholm, Sweden.* The nickname is that of the historical heart of the Swedish capital, now known as Gamla Stan ("old town"), located on the islands of Stadsholmen, Helgeandes-holmen, and Riddarholmen. The bridges connect these islands to districts north and south of the city's original nucleus.

**City Built on Bones, the** *St. Petersburg, Russia.* Construction of the former Russian capital is believed to have cost the lives of thousands, notably Swedish prisoners of war, conscripts, and criminals. Hence the grisly nickname.

**City Built on Water, the** *Matsue, Japan.* The city owes its nickname to its location on Lake Shinji and the Tenjin River, near the Sea of Japan.

**City by the Sea, the** *(1) Brighton, England; (2) Long Beach, New York, USA.* The Sussex resort so styled itself on gaining city status in 2000. *Cp.* **London-by-the-Sea.** Long Beach, a residential city and seaside resort on Long Island, featured under this name in the 2001 movie *City by the Sea* directed by Michael Caton-Jones.

**City Different, the** *Santa Fe, New Mexico, USA.* The state capital is said to be so named because it was founded by the Spanish, not the British or the French, because it is the oldest state capital in the USA, and because there are more Native Americans living on ancestral lands in New Mexico than in the whole of the USA east of the Mississippi. The reference could also be to the city's "unique" inhabitants.

> (1) Santa Fe is known as the City Different. But not just because of its beautiful scenery, its rich traditions or historical heritage. I think it's the people — those wonderful individuals whose proclivities have labeled them a little the other side of center [Berry Bauer, *My City Different*, 2004].
> (2) The soothing and addictive effect of the self-styled "City Different" [Dodd/Donald, p. 186].

**City in an Orchard, a** *Norwich, England.* The historic Norfolk city is noted for its picturesque setting in a broad bend of the Wensum River, with many parks and gardens.

> (1) Norwich is (as you please) either a city in an orchard or an orchard in a city, so equally are houses and trees blended in it [Thomas Fuller, *The History of the Worthies of England*, 1662].
> (2) Its environs are charming, and preserve to it the old description of "a city in an orchard" or "a city of gardens" [J.H.F. Brabner, ed., *A Comprehensive Gazetteer of England and Wales*, c. 1893].

**City in the Country, a** *(1) Hanover, Germany; (2) Paris, France.* The extensive parks of the German city justify its claim to the nickname, while the French capital is ringed with great forests soon reached from the city center. *Cp.* **City in the Sea.**

> (Paris) It's a splendid city — a city in the country, as Venice is a city in the sea [Elizabeth Barrett Browning, letter, 1851].

**City in the Country near the Sea, the** *Exeter, England.* The Devon county capital so designated itself in the early years of the 21st century, hoping to attract visitors or businesses to one or other (or both) of these attributes. The city lies on the Exe River, which flows south via a broad estuary into the English Channel.

**City in the Sea, the** *Venice, Italy.* Venice is a "water city" and seaport situated on over 100 islands in the Lagoon of Venice. *Cp.* **City in the Country.**

**City Linking Nine Provinces, the** *Wuhan, China.* The city has long borne its name for its role as a major transportation center in the heart of China.

**City of a Hundred Bell Towers, the** *Valencia, Spain.* Of the city's many bell towers, the most outstanding are the Miguelete Tower, adjoining the cathedral, and the Tower of Santa Catalina.

**City of a Hundred** or a **Thousand Spires, the** *Prague, Czech Republic.* The Czech capital is so nicknamed for its many church steeples, especially as viewed from the surrounding hills.

> Prague is described in many ways — 'City of a Hundred Spires,' 'Paris of the East' or 'The Golden City' [Travel brochure issued with *The Times*, July 9, 2005].

**City of a Hundred Temples, the** *T'ainan, Taiwan.* The sobriquet is overmodest, as the city actually has over 200 temples.

**City of a Hundred Thousand Novels** *see* **City of a Thousand Novels**

**City of a Hundred Towers, the** *(1) Pavia, Italy; (2) Prague, Czech Republic.* The Italian city was so nicknamed for its many churches and other prominent buildings. The Czech capital is more commonly known as the **City of a Hundred Spires.**

> (Prague) Jan Kaplan has compiled ... this ... anthology in which a diverse range of writers takes us on an anecdotal tour of the "city of a hundred towers" [Adam Preston, review of Jan Kaplan, *A Traveller's Companion to Prague*, Times Literary Supplement, July 15, 2005].

**City of a Hundred Villages, the** *Paris, France.* The sobriquet, in the original French and neater form, *La Ville de cent villages*, sees Paris as a composite of many distinctive quarters, each with its own character. *Cp.* **City of Villages.**

> Keep a joie-ful spring in your step with the help of our guide to a short stay in the "city of 100 villages" [*The Times*, January 13, 2005].

**City of Ambition, the** *New York City, USA.* The city was so titled in a famous photograph of New York taken by Alfred Stieglitz in 1910.

**City of a Million Dustbins, the** *London, England.* George Orwell so referred to the British capital as in the quote below.

> He seemed to see a vision of London, vast and ruinous, city of a million dustbins [George Orwell, *Nineteen Eighty-Four*, 1949].

**City of (the) Angels, the** *(1) Bangkok, Thailand; (2) Los Angeles, California, USA.* For the capital of Thailand, the name is a traditional translation of its abbreviated name, *Krung Thep*, which more precisely means "city of gods." (It represents the opening words of the city's lengthy official name, which according to one authority translates from the Thai as "the city of gods, the great city, the residence of the Emerald Buddha, the impregnable city of the god Indra, the grand capital of the world endowed with nine precious gems, the happy city abounding in enormous royal palaces which resemble the heavenly abode wherein dwell the reincarnated gods, a city given by Indra and built by Vishnukarm.") For Los Angeles, the nickname obviously derives from the city's Spanish name, which in full translates as "the city of Our Lady of the angels," a title of the Virgin Mary. It was adopted for the 1998 movie *City of Angels*, in which an angel watching over Los Angeles becomes human.

(1) (Los Angeles) Smog was something that God ... had visited only on the vast, blowsy city two hundred and forty miles to the south [of San Francisco] — the city of the angels (a misnomer if ever there was one): Los Angeles [Alistair Cooke, *Letter from America*, "John McLaren's Folly," June 26, 1966 (2004)].

(2) (Los Angeles) The highroad between Los Angeles, City of the Angels, and Las Vegas, City Without Clocks, cuts through the mountains and across the desert for a distance of three hundred miles [Harry Mark Petrakis, *Nick the Greek*, 1979].

**City of Art, the** *Kwangju, South Korea*. The city gained its name as home of the Kwangju Biennale, an international art exhibition.

**City of a Thousand and One Trades** *see* **City of a Thousand Trades**

**City of a Thousand Columns, the** *Palmyra, Syria*. The ancient oasis city, also known as Tadmur, is so nicknamed for its columned remains, especially the Great Colonnade, with its buildings and monuments, and the Temple of Bel.

**City of a Thousand Fountains, the** *Aix-en-Provence, France*. The city is noted not only for its thermal waters but for its many fountains, such as the Fontaine de la Rotonde in the Place de la Libération and, on the Cours Mirabeau, the Fontaine d'Eau Chaude and Fontaine du Roi René.

Aix en Provence is a stunningly beautiful place. Originally a spa town founded by the Romans, today it is ... known as the 'City of a Thousand Fountains' [Travel brochure issued with *The Times*, July 9, 2005].

**City of a Thousand** or **a Thousand and One Trades, the** *Birmingham, England*. The city was so dubbed for its great range of manufactured articles.

(1) Whereas many northern and Midland cities grew on a handful of staple industries, "Brum" turned its hand to every kind of manufacturing, gaining the epithet "the city of 1001 trades" [*The Rough Guide to England*, 1998].

(2) Birmingham, the "city of a thousand trades," has famous forefathers to match any of your Michelangelos [*The Times*, February 4, 2005].

**City of a Thousand** or **a Hundred Thousand Novels, the** *Paris, France*. The French capital was so named by Balzac in his novel *Ferragus* (1834), referring to the many novels published both in Paris and about Paris, the latter including such 19th-century classics as Victor Hugo's *Notre-Dame de Paris* (1831) and Eugène Sue's *Les Mystères de Paris* (1843). *Cp.* **World Capital of Literature.**

The imagination of Pissarro and Degas, Hugo and Baudelaire, is written into the very stone of Paris... It is infinitely suggestive, a 'city of a hundred thousand novels,' as Balzac said [Michael Peppiatt in Young, p. 68].

**City of a Thousand Spires** *see* **City of a Hundred Spires**

**City of a Thousand Temples, the** *(1) Kathmandu, Nepal; (2) Pagan, Myanmar*. Both cities are famed for their many temples. Pagan is now ruined, but in medieval times was home to thousands of Buddhist shrines and temples, several of which still survive.

(Kathmandu) In the modern parts of the "city of a thousand temples" the cleansing mist is replaced by smelly gases from car and moped exhausts [Leier, p. 163].

**City of Bad Men, the** *Carson City, Nevada, USA*. The state capital was at one time associated with lawlessness, as in the 1953 movie so titled, in which outlaws plan to steal the receipts from the notorious 1897 Carson City boxing match between Jim Corbett and Bob Fitzsimmons.

**City of Beauty, the** *Bath, England*. The former Somerset town is noted for its elegant streets and buildings and for its picturesque setting, as described in the quote below. Hence the sobriquet, which may owe something to the musical play *Beauty of Bath* (1906) and the variety of apple so named.

Bath is a city of incomparable beauty, where the elegance and grandeur of the 18th-century architecture is set against a perfect background of green hills and open countryside [*Holiday Haunts 1961: Area No. 4, West of England and South and Central Wales*].

**City of Bells, the** *Strasbourg, France*. The name alludes to the city's many church bells and chiming clocks.

**City of Benjamin Franklin, the** *Philadelphia, Pennsylvania, USA*. Born in Boston, Massachusetts, Benjamin Franklin migrated to Philadelphia at the age of 17 and there became a leader in scientific and intellectual affairs, founding the nation's first free library, its first hospital, and its first learned society, the American Philosophical Society.

**City of Big Shoulders, the** *Chicago, Illinois, USA.* The name, popularized by Carl Sandburg (*see* **Hog Butcher for the World**), refers to the sturdy physique of the immigrant European laborers from whom many of the city's present-day inhabitants are descended.

> The City of Big Shoulders has always thought big [*Lonely Planet USA*, 2004].

**City of Bon Accord, the** *Aberdeen, Scotland.* Following the support of Aberdeen citizens for Robert the Bruce in the War of Independence at the beginning of the 14th century, they were rewarded with hunting land and a coat of arms with the motto "Bon Accord," a Scottish term from the French meaning "good will." A fast train running between Glasgow and Aberdeen was formerly named the "Bon Accord."

**City of Bridges, the** *Matanzas, Cuba.* The city is so nicknamed for the six bridges across the San Juan and Yumurí rivers here.

**City of Brotherly Love, the** *Philadelphia, Pennsylvania, USA.* When the English Quaker William Penn founded Philadelphia in 1682, he gave it the name of the ancient city in what is now western Turkey, the seat of one of the "Seven Churches" mentioned in the Bible (Revelation 1:11), apparently interpreting this as "brotherly love," from Greek *philo-* "loving," and *adelphos*, "brother." However, the biblical city was actually named for its founder, Attalus II Philadelphus, 2d-century BC king of Pergamum, whose title or byname meant "loving the brethren," which is not quite the same. Even so the city's nickname is traditionally interpreted the way Penn intended.

> (1) The city of Brotherly Love, or, according to the disparaging assertion of New Yorkers, the city of "brotherly love and riots" [Charles Mackay, *Life and Liberty in America, 1857–8*, 1859].
> (2) Philadelphia, a metropolis sometimes known as the City of Brotherly Love, but more accurately as the City of Bleak November Afternoons [S.J. Perelman, *Westward Ha!*, 1948].
> (3) Philadelphia may be the city of brotherly love, but that affection is lavished only on those willing to root for the local teams [*Financial Times*, September 28, 2004].

**City of Caves, the** *Nottingham, England.* The name refers to the caves that lie beneath the rock on which the city's medieval castle formerly stood. It is said to render a Celtic name *Tigguo*

*Cobauc* meaning "house of caves," from words related to modern Welsh *tŷ*, "house," and an adjectival form of *ogof*, "cave."

**City of Ceramics, the** *Talavera de la Reina, Spain.* The town was formerly noted for its manufacture of pottery and tiles. Its ceramic industry declined in the 18th century but revived to some extent in the 20th, justifying the sobriquet.

**City of Champions, the** *Edmonton, Alberta, Canada.* The provincial capital adopted its title in the 1980s, referring to the successes of its professional hockey team, the Edmonton Oilers, who won five championships in that decade.

**City of Churches, the** *(1) Adelaide, Australia; (2) Brooklyn, New York City, USA; (3) Norwich, England.* The South Australia capital, the New York borough, and the Norfolk city are noted for their many churches, in the first two cases the result of colonial expansion. (Norwich has over 30 parish churches clustered around its medieval cathedral, and in the 16th century there were many more.) Adelaide is also known as the **Holy City** and Brooklyn as the **City of Homes**.

> (1) (Adelaide) Supposed to be the "City of Churches," but actually a city as sinful as they come [John Hepworth, *Great Australian Cities: Adelaide*, 1983].
> (2) (Brooklyn) The immigrant growth led to a proliferation of churches and ethnic social service organizations, and Brooklyn became known as both the "city of homes" and the "city of churches" [Jackson, p. 151]
> (3) (Norwich) Norwich, City of Churches, has great musems and a castle too [*Enjoy England Holiday Planner 2005*].

**City of Clones, the** *Atlanta, Georgia, USA.* The state capital was so dubbed by Dutch architect Rem Koolhaas in his 1995 book *S, M, L, XL* (initials of "Small, Medium, Large, Extra Large"), referring to the city's sprawl of suburbs, each virtually indistinguishable from the next.

**City of Conferences, the** *Cardiff, Wales.* A promotional name appearing in a railroad bill of 1932, showing an aerial view of the future Welsh capital's center reprinted from the *Western Mail & South Wales News*. Concerts and conferences are now held in the city's International Arena.

**City of Conversation, the** *Washington, DC, USA.* The national capital earned its sobriquet more from its self-admiration in its earlier days than from its role as a focus of conversation by others.

> Washington talks about herself and about almost nothing else... It is about herself *as* the City of Conversation precisely that she incessantly converses [Henry James, *The American Scene*, 1907].

**City of David, the** *(1) Bethlehem, West Bank; (2) Jerusalem, Israel.* Most biblical references to the "city of David" are to Jerusalem, as in quote (1) below. But some are to Bethlehem, David's hometown, as in quote (2). This happened because Ruth came to Bethlehem with her mother Naomi, married Boaz, and became the ancestor of David through Obed, his grandfather, and Jesse, his father. It is Bethlehem that is named in the opening line of Mrs. Alexander's well-known Christmas hymn "Once in royal David's city." *See also* **Zion.**

> (1) Nevertheless David took the strong hold of Zion: the same is the city of David [2 Samuel 5:7].
> (2) And Joseph also went up from Galilee, out of the city of Nazareth, into Judæa, unto the city of David, which is called Bethlehem [Luke 2:4].

**City of Destiny, the** *Tacoma, Washington, USA.* The seaport city is so nicknamed because it arose around the terminus of the Northern Pacific Railway, built on Puget Sound in 1873.

> Its nickname, 'City of Destiny,' ... once seemed like a grim joke. But these days destiny is coming through for Tacoma [*Lonely Planet USA*, 2004].

**City of Discovery, the** *Dundee, Scotland.* A former self-promotional name for the city.

> 'City of Discovery' is an ingenious promotional slogan, but is meaningless unless it is accompanied by self-discovery and self-awareness on the part of all Dundee's citizens [David Dorward, *Dundee*, 1998].

**City of Djinns** *Delhi, India.* The city was so dubbed by British travel writer William Dalrymple in his 1993 book of this title, where he describes Delhi as "a city disjointed in time, a city whose different ages lay suspended side by side in aspic, a city of djinns." A djinn is a genie, or invisible spirit.

**City of Dreadful Height, the** *New York City, USA.* A nickname punning on the **City of Dreadful Night** in its original, literary sense. It was the title of a 1927 essay by US architect Thomas Hastings warning against the increasing density of development in Manhattan.

**City of Dreadful Joy, the** *Los Angeles, California, USA.* The city was so described by Aldous Huxley as in the quote below.

> Thought is barred in this city of Dreadful Joy, and conversation is unknown [Aldous Huxley, *Jesting Pilate*, 1926].

**City of Dreadful Knights, the** *(1) Birmingham, England; (2) Cardiff, Wales; (3) Dublin, Ireland; (4) Glasgow, Scotland.* The ironic name, punning on the title of James Thomson's poem (*see* **City of Dreadful Night**), refers to certain wealthy businessmen in the named cities who,

under Lloyd George's coalition government after World War I, were permitted to purchase their knighthood honors. The scandalous situation was rectified by a Royal Commission set up in 1923.

> (1) (Dublin) The survivor of Protestant ascendancy ... was a quiet and industrious fellow. It was not by such as he that Dublin won its title, the City of Dreadful Knights [Terence de Vere White, in Francis Mac Manus, ed., *The Years of the Great Test 1926–39*, 1967].
> (2) (Birmingham) The man who after the First World War called Birmingham the City of Dreadful Knights ... deserved the accolade far more than those who actually got it [Godfrey Smith, *The English Companion*, 1996].

**City of Dreadful Night, the** *Kolkata (Calcutta), India.* The name was used by Rudyard Kipling writing about Calcutta for a newspaper in Lahore. He adopted the title of James Thomson's pessimistic poem about London published in 1874 and included in his volume of verse *The City of Dreadful Night and other Poems* (1880).

> Kipling called Calcutta "the city of dreadful night" and wrote a verse: "Chance-directed, chance-erected, laid and built / On the silt —/ Palace, byre, hovel — poverty and pride —/ Side by side." That's still a pretty apt description [A.A. Gill in *Sunday Times Magazine*, January 23, 2005].

**City of Dreaming Spires, the** *Oxford, England.* The name, from the poetic line in quote (1) below, refers to the spires of the city's churches and college chapels. *Cp.* **City of Perspiring Dreams.**

> (1) And that sweet City with her dreaming spires [Matthew Arnold, *Thyrsis*, 1866].
> (2) Oxford without its dreaming spires is unthinkable [Dodd/Donald, p. 18].
> (3) *The Rumpus*, a shortlived [Oxford student] newspaper that caused a stir amid the dreaming spires [*The Times*, December 10, 2005].

**City of Dreamless Spires, the** *New York City, USA.* The sobriquet puns on that of Oxford as the **City of Dreaming Spires.** But whereas Oxford's spires are of churches and chapels, those of New York are of mostly secular buildings. The sobriquet was apparently created by British author Baron Kinross, as in the quote below.

> The classic view of the New York skyline ... is from the Brooklyn waterfront. Here, on my third evening in New York, I look across the river ... to see range upon range of towers ... I was reminded of the serried church-towers of San Gimignano... But these were not church-towers. They were towers filled with men. And to what purpose? Was New York, perhaps, the City of Dreamless Spires? [Lord Kinross, *The Innocents at Home*, 1959].

**City of Dreams, the** *(1) Los Angeles, California, USA; (2) Vienna, Austria.* The sobriquet subtly presents a city as a waking equivalent (but not necessarily realization) of one's dreams. Vienna was so known in the years before World War I.

(1) (Vienna) "Vienna, City of My Dreams" [Rudolph Sieczynski, Edward Lockton, song title, 1931, sung by Richard Tauber in movie *Heart's Desire*, 1935].

(2) (Los Angeles) Los Angeles may have bagged the epithet "City of Dreams" but that's okay, because Miami would probably prefer to be known as the "City of Dreams Come True" [*Sunday Times*, January 30, 2005].

**City of 18 Mountains, the** *Man, Côte d'Ivoire.* The town derives its nickname (French *Cité des 18 montagnes*) from its setting at the foot of the Toura mountains.

**City of Elms, the** *New Haven, Connecticut, USA.* The city gained its nickname from the tall elms that shaded many of its streets.

When happier days shall return, and the South ... shall remember who it was that sowed her sunny fields with the seeds of those golden crops with which she thinks to rule the world, she ... will rear a monument of her gratitude in the beautiful City of Elms, over the ashes of her greatest benefactor,—Eli Whitney [Edward Everett, 1861, quoted in Wheeler, p. 76].

**City of Entertainment, the** *Birmingham, England.* A touristic title designed to attract visitors and vacationers to England's **Second City**.

Birmingham has reinvented itself as the City of Entertainment [*Enjoy England Holiday Planner 2005*].

**City of Eternal Spring, the** *(1) Cuernavaca, Mexico; (2) Kunming, China.* Both the popular Mexican resort and the city of southwestern China are noted for their pleasant climate. Hence their respective nicknames. *Cp.* **City of Everlasting Spring**.

Fly to Kunming, the 'eternal city of spring' [*sic*] [Travel brochure issued with *Sunday Times*, August 14, 2005].

**City of Everlasting Spring, the** *Arica, Chile.* The seaport and popular resort, Chile's northernmost city, is noted for its mild climate. Hence its name, translating the Spanish original: *la ciudad de la eterna primavera*.

**City of Fear, the** *Oujda, Morocco.* Fought over successively by Berbers, Arabs, and Turks, the city was destroyed and rebuilt so many times that it gained this (originally Arabic) nickname.

**City of Festivals and Temples, the** *Madurai, India.* The second-largest city in Tamil Nadu state is famous for its temples, especially the Meenakshi temple with 1,000 carved pillars, and its many festivals. Hence its nickname.

**City of Firsts, the** *(1) Kokomo, Indiana, USA; (2) Philadelphia, Pennsylvania, USA.* Kokomo gained its nickname for its industrial innovations, including the first commercially built automobile (invented and tested in 1894 by Elwood Haynes), first mechanical cornpicker, first push-button car radio, and first canned tomato juice. Philadelphia was the nation's first capital and the first town in the New World to have a planned layout. The first medical school, art school, university, and library in the United States were founded here, and the first US locomotive, piano, cotton mill, and steam automobile were built here.

(Philadelphia) Philadelphians take a weary pleasure in the fame of their "city of firsts"—first in the idealism of the Founding Fathers, first in the political corruption that followed [Peter Stothard in *Times Literary Supplement*, July 1, 2005].

**City of Five Flags, the** *Mobile, Alabama, USA.* The city is so nicknamed because it was in territory under the successive sovereignty of France, Britain, Spain, the Confederacy, and finally the United States.

**City of Flowers, the** *(1) Angers, France; (2) Da Lat, Vietnam; (3) Guangzhou, China; (4) Pietermaritzburg, South Africa.* All of the named cities are noted for their parks and gardens.

(1) (Angers) The city is rich in gardens and is surrounded by nurseries, so that it has been called 'the city of flowers' [*AA Road Book of France*, 1972].

(2) (Guangzhou) Apart from the Orchid Gardens (Guangzhou is known as the City of Flowers) and the temples — there is little peace or gentility to be had [Dodd/Donald, p. 247].

**City of Fountains, the** *Kansas City, Missouri, USA.* Kansas City is famous for its fountains and claims to have more than any city except Rome.

**City of Gardens, the** *Norwich, England.* An alternate name for Norwich as a **City in an Orchard**.

**City of Ghosts, the** *(1) Fengdu, China; (2) Thessaloníki, Greece.* The Chinese town is so nicknamed for its deserted population. The Greek city (*see* **Salonica**) has a sobriquet made familiar by Mark Mazower's book *Salonica, City of Ghosts* (2004). The "ghosts" are the Christians, Muslims, and Jews who lived there, more or less in harmony, from 1430 to the turn of the 20th century.

(Fengdu) Visit the 'city of ghosts,' Fengdu, and see its 700 hilltop temples [Travel ad, *Sunday Times Magazine*, January 23, 2005].

**City of Glass, the** *(1) La Coruña, Spain; (2) Shahe, China.* The Spanish city is noted for the glassed-in window balconies of its multistory houses, thus equipped for protection against the wind. The Chinese city is a famous glass-manufacturing center. Hence the respective nicknames.

**City of God, the** *Rio de Janeiro, Brazil.* The city's sobriquet, properly that of the Christian church, was promoted by the 2002 film so titled, based on a novel by Paulo Lins, about a poor boy in the slum area of Rio de Janeiro known as Cidade de Deus who wants to better himself but who sees his friends turn to a life of crime. Mainly because of the movie, the name became associated with Rio itself.

> [The film] tells the story of Rio de Janeiro's crime-ridden housing projects ... and in particular the eponymous Cidade de Deus ... Leandro Firmino, who played gangster Li'l Ze, still lives in Cidade de Deus [*Four*, 2004].

**City of Gods, the** *Angkor, Cambodia.* The name of the ruined ancient city refers to the Hindu gods worshiped in its many temples.

**City of Gold, the** *(1) Dawson (City), Yukon Territory, Canada; (2) Dubai, United Arab Emirates; (3) Johannesburg, South Africa; (4) London, England.* Dawson sprang to fame in 1896 as a result of the Klondike gold rush. Dubai became wealthy through "black gold," or oil. Johannesburg, also known as **Egoli** and the **Golden City**, was founded in 1886 as a mining settlement when gold was found on the Witwatersrand. The 1957 movie *City of Gold* told the story of Dawson. London was once so known for its wealth, and it was popularly believed that any poor person who went there would soon be rich.

> (1) (London) Oh, London is a fine town,
> A very famous city,
> Where all the streets are paved with gold,
> And all the maidens pretty [George Colman, the Younger, *The Heir at Law*, 1808].
> (2) (Johannesburg) The City of Gold — more or less — does not pride itself on his matured glories [Louis Cohen, *Reminiscences of Johannesburg and London*, 1924].
> (3) (Johannesburg) "Just now" (as Jo'burgers would say) ... the "City of Gold" is moving on [Dodd/Donald, p. 366].

**City of Grain** *see* **City of Rams**

**City of Heroes, the** *Leipzig, Germany.* The city gained this name (German, *Stadt der Helden*) for its role in the 1989 democratic revolution, when huge but peaceful demonstrations by its citizens played a significant part in ending the Communist regime in East Germany.

**City of Homes, the** *(1) Brooklyn, New York City, USA; (2) Philadelphia, Pennsylvania, USA.* The immigrant growth of Brooklyn in the mid–19th century led to a proliferation of new houses. Philadelphia, on the other hand, earned

its nickname because the orientation of its inhabitants was to their homes rather than to their street, as in many other cities.

**City of Intelligence, the** *Berlin, Germany.* A former nickname for the German capital as a center of academic achievement. *Cp.* **Athens on the Spree.**

**City of Isms, the** *Syracuse, New York, USA.* The city earned its nickname in the early days as a center of abolitionists and reformers.

**City of Joy, the** *Kolkata (Calcutta), India.* The somewhat cloying title was that of a 1992 movie telling how an American doctor strives to help Calcutta's poor against their exploitation by gangsters.

> It may be the "City of Joy," but Mother Theresa's mission for the destitute and the dying only highlighted the city's overcrowding and areas of poverty [Dodd/Donald, p. 272].

**City of Kind Hearts, the** *Boston, Massachusetts, USA.* The name was bestowed on Boston by the blind reformer Helen Keller, because her teacher, Anne Mansfield Sullivan, and many of those who helped and inspired her, came from there.

**City of Kings, the** *(1) Blois, France; (2) Bulawayo, Zimbabwe.* The French city on the banks of the Loire River was so nicknamed by the 16th-century poet Pierre de Ronsard for the French kings who lived here. When Charles, duc d'Orléans, returned from England in 1440 he took up residence here and his son, later Louis XII, was born here. Various kings spent time here after him. Zimbabwe's second-largest city is nicknamed both specifically for Lobengula, king of the Ndebele, who fought a major battle against his rivals here in 1893, and for its general prosperity.

**City of Legions, the** *Caerleon, Wales.* The name is an effective translation of the town's name, a combination of Welsh and Latin meaning "fort of the legion," referring to the Roman Second Legion stationed here.

**City of Light, the** *(1) Lyon, France; (2) Paris, France.* The French capital was a "City of Light" (French *Ville-Lumière*) as a center of learning and culture during the Enlightenment of the 18th century. The epithet is said to date from 1470, when the *Recueil des lettres de Gasparin de Bergame* ("Collection of Letters of Gasparinus Barzizius") was the first book to be printed and published in France. The work was dedicated to Paris: "*De même que le soleil répand partout la lumière, ainsi toi, ville de Paris, capitale du royaume, nourricière des Muses, tu verses la science sur le monde*" ("Just as the sun casteth light everywhere, so dost thou, city of Paris, capital of the kingdom, nurturer of the Muses, pour knowledge on the world"). The name could also be applied literally both to the "lightening" of the city in the 19th century by the boulevards that Baron Haussmann drove through its slum areas (*see* **Capital of Progress**) and to its illuminations. (The international Expositions of 1889 and 1890, held in Paris, highlighted the capital as "the City of Light" and were both illuminated by electric lighting.) The latter sense applies to Lyon, which introduced a program of illuminating buildings in the city center to promote the lighting-design industry. The title for Paris is still valid in the original sense, as the city remains a major educational and intellectual center in its role as the **Capital of Civilization**.

(1) (Paris) S'il est vrai que la France a souvent joué à l'égard de l'Europe un rôle de "plaque tournante," elle le doit surtout à Paris, qui s'enrichit depuis des siècles de l'apport des autres cultures: dialogue sans fin, échange réciproque qui, au cours des âges, a fait de la "Ville-Lumière" un monde en réduction. (While it is true that France has often served as the "hub" of Europe, it owes this role above all to Paris, which for centuries has been enriched by other cultures. Continuing dialogue and mutual exchange down the ages have made the "City of Light" a world in miniature.) [Guy Michaud et Georges Torrès, *Le Nouveau Guide France*, 1983].

(2) (Paris) Wearing haute couture to the office and sipping fine wine in side-street bistros ... follow our guide to relocating in the City of Light [*The Times*, April 14, 2005].

**City of Lights, the** *Tamworth, Australia*. A self-promotional name for the New South Wales city, as the first town in Australia to be fitted with electric street lighting, in 1888.

**City of Lilies, the** *(1) Florence, Italy; (2) Paris, France*. Both cities are named for the lilies on their respective coats of arms. In the case of Paris, there is also a pun between French *lys*, "lily" (as in *fleur de lys*, "flower of lily"), and the name of the many French kings *Louis*. *Cp.* **Empire of Lilies**.

**City of Little Men, the** *Boys Town, Nebraska, USA*. A sentimental sobriquet for the town founded in 1917 as a community of homeless or abandoned boys.

**City of Living Crafts, the** *Hereford, England*. A self-promotional name for the city, referring to the growing reputation of its technical college.

**City of Love, the** *Paris, France*. The city is traditionally regarded as a favorite resort of lovers and honeymooners, both for its own seductive attractions and for the romantic reputation of

the French, whose capital it is. The equation has been popularized on stage and screen. The words "Paris is for lovers" are heard in Billy Wilder's 1954 movie *Sabrina*, while Cole Porter's lyric "Paris Loves Lovers" features in the 1955 musical *Silk Stockings*. *Cp.* **Capital of Romance**.

(1) Staying with her uncle ... while her mother tests ... the clichés about Paris as the city of love, Zazie [in the 1960 movie *Zazie dans le Métro*] has her heart set on visiting the Métro [Colin Jones, *Paris*, 2004].

(2) The winner of the Pink Lady(™) apples love poem of the year competition will be treated to a weekend in Paris, "city of love" [*Times Literary Supplement*, March 11, 2005].

(3) Somebody needs to remind our young folk that Paris, not London, is the City of Love [*The Times*, August 15, 2005].

**City of Magnificent Distances, the** *Washington, DC, USA*. The impressive nickname refers to Washington's wide avenues and fine vistas, especially as envisioned by the city's original planner, the French army engineer Pierre-Charles L'Enfant. The original effect has now to some extent been lost by the addition of trees along most major avenues and streets. The sobriquet was first applied to the young city in 1816 by the Portuguese minister to the United States, José Correa da Serra. Charles Dickens described Washington as "The City of Magnificent Intentions" in his *American Notes* (1842).

What was conceived as a "city of magnificent distances" or, in Washington's words, "the Emporium of the West," was referred to by various statesmen and congressmen as "wilderness city," "Capital of Miserable Huts," "A Mud-Hole Equal to the Great Serbonian Bog," and similar epithets [*Britannica*, vol. 29, p. 716].

**City of Masts, the** *London, England*. A former nickname of the capital city for the profusion of ships' masts in the days when it was a major port.

**City of Monuments** *see* **Monument City**

**City of Millionaires, the** *Ipoh, Malaysia*. The city made a fortune from its rich tin mines. Hence its nickname.

**City of Mosaics, the** *Madaba, Jordan*. The ancient city derives its nickname from the 6th-century mosaic map of the Holy Land that formed the floor of one of its many ruined churches. It was discovered only in 1884 and after suffering damage over the next few years was restored by German archaeologists in 1966.

**City of Mosques, the** *Fallujah, Iraq*. The city numbers over 200 mosques. Hence its nickname.

Thirteen months ago the Sunni minority's city of mosques was aflame after a ground and air assault by 15,000 American troops [*The Times*, December 16, 2005].

**City of Music, the** *Leipzig, Germany.* The city has a long tradition of sacred and secular music and was the home of famous composers such as Bach, Mendelssohn, and Schumann, while Mozart gave a concert of his works there in 1789 and Brahms conducted all of his symphonies there.

> A morning sightseeing tour [in Leipzig] is followed by free time in this city of music [Travel ad, *Sunday Times Magazine*, January 25, 2005].

**City of Nations, the** *London, England.* The British capital has been so called for its cosmopolitan character. *Cp.* **Diaspora City.**

**City of Notions, the** *Boston, Massachusetts, USA.* The name refers to the "Yankee notions," or inventive wares and manufactured articles, for which Boston became famous.

**City of Oaks, the** *Raleigh, North Carolina, USA.* The city became noted for its many oak trees. Hence the name.

**City of Palaces, the** *(1) Edinburgh, Scotland; (2) Genoa, Italy; (3) Kolkata (Calcutta), India; (4) Mexico City, Mexico; (5) Paris, France; (6) Rome, Italy; (7) St. Petersburg, Russia.* All of the named cities are noted for their palaces, from the early marble palaces of Rome to the Winter Palace at St. Petersburg and the palatial residences in the British part of Calcutta in the days when it was the capital of British India. The epithet is no longer entirely apt for Mexico City, despite some notable buildings of colonial and modern architecture, but Paris has or had many famous buildings named "palace" (*palais*), as the Palais-Bourbon, Palais de Justice, and Palais-Royal, while Edinburgh is famed for the Palace of Holyroodhouse.

> (1) (Kolkata) The City of Palaces really deserves that appellation. Nothing can be more imposing than the splendid houses of Chowringhee, viewed from the Course, which is a broad carriage-road on the esplanade of Fort William, adjoining the race-course, from which, I presume, it derives its name [*Blackwood's Magazine*, quoted in Wheeler, p. 76].
> (2) (Kolkata) [English tourist agent Thomas] Cook was glad to return to the ship. Four days later it sailed up the Hooghly to Calcutta, then the capital of India and the City of Palaces [Piers Brendon, *Thomas Cook: 150 Years of Popular Tourism*, 1991].

**City of Palms, the** *McAllen, Texas, USA.* The city derives its nickname from the 40 varieties of palm growing here.

**City of Palm Trees, the** *Jericho, West Bank.* The byname of the biblical city refers to the palms for which it was noted.

> (1) The plain of the valley of Jericho, the city of palm trees [Deuteronomy 34:3].
> (2) And took the captives ... and brought them to Jericho, the city of palm trees [2 Chronicles 28:15].

**City of Parks, the** *(1) Holguín, Cuba; (2) Malmö, Sweden.* Both cities are nicknamed for their many parks. Holguín has six in the city center alone.

> (Malmö) Malmö, "City of Parks," boasts a sandy beach known as the Scandinavian Copacabana [*The Times*, August 11, 2004].

**City of Paved Streets, the** *Winnemucca, Nevada, USA.* A self-descriptive, self-promotional name for the town.

**City of Peace, the** *(1) Baghdad, Iraq; (2) Jerusalem, Israel; (3) Sharm el Sheikh, Egypt.* The name of Baghdad means "city of God," but that of Jerusalem is generally understood as "city of peace," from a word related to the Jewish salutation "shalom." The Red Sea resort of Sharm el Sheikh received its sobriquet following the conference of 1996 in which 27 nations, including 14 Arab states, met to discuss and promote Middle Eastern peace. The name seemed ironic in the wake of an attack by bombers in 2005 in which 88 people were killed.

> (1) (Baghdad) Baghdad painfully prepared itself ... to welcome visitors once more to "the City of Peace" [Dodd/Donald, p. 317].
> (2) (Jerusalem) The meaning of the city's name — Ursalim, "city of peace" — seems poignantly inappropriate [Dodd/Donald, p. 341].

**City of Perspiring Dreams, the** *Cambridge, England.* A punning inverted alteration of Oxford's poetic sobriquet, **City of Dreaming Spires.**

> He glanced with disdain at the big centre table where the famous faces of the Cambridge theatre were eating a loud meal. 'So this is the city of dreaming spires,' Sheila said. 'Theoretically speaking that's Oxford,' Adam said. 'This is the city of perspiring dreams' [Frederic Raphael, *The Glittering Prizes*, 1976].

**City of Pines, the** *Bournemouth, England.* The south-coast resort is noted for its pine-clad "chines" or valleys, and an express train running between Manchester and Bournemouth was known as the "Pines Express."

> (1) The country folk who live in the background of this oft-styled "City of Pines" still call it merely "Bourne" [Charles G. Harper, *The Hardy Country*, 1904].
> (2) One of the most attractive features of the "Resort among the Pines" is the series of leafy clefts or chines that sweep down to the shore [*Holiday Guide 1952: Area No. 5, South & South East England*].

**City of Posters, the** *Kolkata (Calcutta), India.* The nickname refers to the popular custom of using the walls of the city as a medium for the dissemination and exchange of political viewpoints.

**City of Punishment, the** *Los Angeles, California, USA.* As indicated in the quote below, the nickname arose among the city's British residents.

> What really killed [heiress] Sita [White] was Los Angeles, what we young expats used to call the City of Punishment. Living in LA ... can be addictive and dangerous [*Sunday Times*, May 23, 2004].

**City of Rams, the** *Guangzhou (Canton), China.* The city derived its nickname from the legend outlined in the quote below.

> Five Immortals are said to have entered this city during the Chou dynasty, riding on five rams, and each holding an ear of grain. When they dismounted, the rams were changed into stone, and may be seen to this day on an altar in the Five Genii shrine. Hence Canton is sometimes called the City of the Genii, and also the City of Grain [Giles, p. 235].

**City of Refuge, the** *Medina, Saudi Arabia.* Medina was so named by Muslims as the city to which the prophet Muhammad fled after being driven from Mecca by conspirators. There are also various "cities of refuge" mentioned in the Bible, as places of asylum for anyone who killed a person unintentionally. (Numbers 35:6 has God commanding Moses: "And among the cities which ye shall give unto the Levites there shall be six cities for refuge, which ye shall appoint for the manslayer, that he may flee thither." Three of these were east of the Jordan River and three west of it.)

**City of Roses, the** *Orléans, France.* The city is a noted horticultural center and its roses are famous. Hence the nickname.

> Orléans, once capital of the Orléanais, city of roses and vinegar, is a busy, commercial town [Young, p. 205].

**City of Sails, the** *Auckland, New Zealand.* Set around two harbors on the west coast of North Island, Auckland is the country's largest seaport, and reportedly has more boats per person than any other city in the world. Every weekend, a whole flotilla of yachts, dinghies, and other craft sets sail from the marinas.

> (1) Auckland's known as the 'City of Sails'—so the ideal way to appreciate it was an organised tour that took in a sail round the harbour on a fifty foot yacht [Travel ad, *Sunday Times Magazine*, June 5, 2005].
>
> (2) Stroll the newly developed pier-side area and admire the many yachts moored in the lively harbour of this, the 'City of Sails' [Travel brochure issued with *The Times*, August 20, 2005].

**City of St. Francis, the** *San Francisco, California, USA.* An English rendering of the city's Spanish name.

> Again tonight the moon advances,
> A casual crescent, fine and high,
> A sort of innocent passerby
> Across the city of Saint Francis [Vikram Seth, *The Golden Gate*, 1986].

**City of St. Michael, the** *Dumfries, Scotland.* The city is so named for its patron saint, to whom its parish church is dedicated.

**City of Saints, the** *(1) Grahamstown, South Africa; (2) Montreal, Quebec, Canada.* Grahamstown is generally so known for its many places of worship, although the name is sometimes given a more colorful explanation, as in quote (1) below. Montreal, in the French Catholic province of Quebec, is so called because many of its streets are named after saints.

> (1) (Grahamstown) The most popular version of how Grahamstown earned this nickname has it that, during the early Frontier days, an outlying fort sent to town to fetch a vice [i.e. a vise]. After calling at the various trading stores, the trooper returned to his outpost and reported, "There is no vice in Grahamstown" [Grahamstown Publicity Association, *Grahamstown, Cape Province*, c.1970].
>
> (2) (Grahamstown) The city of Grahamstown has been given many picturesque names: the 'City of Saints' because there are more than 40 places of worship here [*Reader's Digest Illustrated Guide to Southern Africa*, 1978].

**City of Screaming Tyres, the** *Oxford, England.* A pun on the university city's better-known sobriquet **City of Dreaming Spires**. It first arose in the 1980s to refer to the squealing wheels of young joyriders on night-time roads but later came to refer more generally to the city's clogging traffic and pernicious parking problems.

> Oxford is proud of its reputation as the city of screaming tyres. Cars are ferociously ticketed, clamped and impounded by legions of fanatical traffic wardens. I guess they just want to make sure you can see the architecture properly [*The Independent*, January 11, 2004].

**City of Ships, the** *New York City, USA.* New York is one of the greatest seaports in the world, and Brooklyn Navy Yard, on the East River, is a main base and shipbuilding center of the US Navy. Hence the name.

> City of Ships!
> (O the black ships! O the fierce ships!
> O the beautiful sharp-bow'd steam-ships and sail-ships!) [Walt Whitman, "City of Ships," *Drum-Taps*, 1865].

**City of Snow and Sea, the** *Kemi, Finland.* A touristic nickname for the northern seaport town on the Gulf of Bothnia, describing its twin attractions.

> Known as the "City of Snow and Sea," Kemi offers the chance to ... take a Lapland/Arctic Circle tour [Travel ad, *The Times*, October 22, 2005].

**City of Souls, the** *Colma, California, USA.* The city is so nicknamed for its many cemeteries.

**City of Spindles, the** *Lowell, Massachusetts, USA.* The city's former nickname alludes to the spindles used for spinning cotton in its mills.

**City of Springs, the** *Jinan, China.* The city is rich in springwater and has many lakes. Hence its nickname.

**City of Strife, the** *Milan, Italy.* The city is sometimes so named for the many battles fought in the surrounding plain.

**City of the Angels** *see* **City of Angels**

**City of the Beautiful Towers, the** *San Gimignano, Italy.* The town is so known for its medieval towers, 14 of which remain out of the original 72.

**City of the Blind, the** *Kadıköy (Chalcedon), Turkey.* The ancient city, now a suburb of Istanbul, was so nicknamed because the Greeks who founded it in 685 BC chose this site rather than the more suitable one across the Bosporus.

> Chalkedon was called the city of the blind, because its founders passed by the then unoccupied site of Byzantium [E.A. Freeman, *Historical Essays*, 1871].

**City of the Blue Mountains** see in Appendix 1, p. 269.

**City of the Century, the** *Chicago, Illinois, USA.* Chicago was so called by Donald L.Miller in his book *City of the Century: The Epic of Chicago and the Making of America* (1996). He meant the 19th century, when the city arose.

**City of the Cockerel, the** *Morón, Cuba.* The town is so named for a local legend about a cock that kept on crowing when defeathered.

**City of the Czars, the** *Veliko Tŭrnovo, Romania.* The second Bulgarian kingdom came into existence in the majestic old town in 1186 when Ivan Asen I was proclaimed czar here. It remained the imperial capital until 1393, when it was sacked and burned by the Turks. Hence the royal sobriquet.

> Day 9 ... Drive to the Balkan Mountains and wonderfully picturesque Veliko Turnovo, the 'City of the Tsars' [Travel ad, *The Times*, November 19, 2005].

**City of the Future, the** *Brasília, Brazil.* The Brazilian capital, inaugurated in 1960, came to be so known for its radical design.

**City of the Genii** *see* **City of Rams**

**City of the Golden Gate, the** *San Francisco, California, USA.* San Francisco lies on the southern shore of the Golden Gate, the strait leading from the Pacific into San Francisco Bay. Hence its descriptive sobriquet. *Cp.* **Golden Gate City.**

**City of the Golden Stool, the** *Kumasi, Ghana.* The city was founded in the 1670s as the capital of the Ashanti people. Hence its sobriquet, referring to the golden stool on which all Ashanti kings have subsequently been enthroned.

**City of the Great King, the** *Jerusalem, Israel.* The biblical byname refers to King David. *See* **City of David.**

> (1) Beautiful for situation, the joy of the whole earth, is mount Zion, on the sides of the north, the city of the great King [Psalm 48:2].
> (2) But I say unto you, Swear not at all; neither by heaven; for it is God's throne: nor by the earth; for it is his footstool: neither by Jerusalem; for it is the city of the great King [Matthew 5:34–35].

**City of the Horse, the** *Pompadour, France.* The town is a noted horse-breeding center with a famous racecourse. Hence its nickname.

> In a bowl below the walls of the château is the well-known racecourse, scene of colour and excitement during the meetings held throughout the summer. No wonder that today Pompadour ... is known as 'the city of the horse' [Young, p. 301].

**City of the Knights, the** *Rhodes, Greece.* The major city, on the island of the same name, is so named for the Knights of St. John of Jerusalem (Knights Hospitalers), who in the 14th century built the walls of the old city of Rhodes as part of their conversion of the entire island into a virtually impregnable fortress.

**City of the Midnight Sun, the** *London, England.* A former nickname for the British capital, referring not to its proximity to the Arctic Circle but to its reputation as a place of nocturnal pleasure.

**City of the Prophet, the** *Medina, Saudi Arabia.* A familiar name for the city to which Muhammad fled after he and his followers were driven out of Mecca by conspirators and in which he died and is buried. *Cp.* **City of Refuge.** The flight, known as the Hegira, took place in AD 622 and marked the start of the Muslim era.

> [Medina] is called the city of the prophet, on account of Mahomet's being received and protected by the inhabitants on his flight hither from Mecca [*Encyclopædia Britannica*, 1771].

**City of the Sacred Serpent, the** *Trivandrum, India.* The nickname is in effect a translation of the city's Hindi name, which literally means "town sacred to Ananta," a name of the god Vishnu and of the thousand-headed serpent Sheshnag who symbolizes eternity.

Built over seven hills, the "City of the Sacred Serpent" retains some of old Kerala's ambience [Travel ad, *The Times*, July 17, 2004].

**City of the Saints, the** *Salt Lake City, Utah, USA.* Salt Lake City is the home of the Church of Jesus Christ of Latter-Day Saints (Mormons). Hence the sobriquet.

**City of the Sea, the** *Venice, Italy.* A variant name for the **City in the Sea**.

Near the celebrated Lido where the breeze is fresh and free
  Stands the ancient port of Venice called the City of the Sea [John Betjeman, "Longfellow's Visit to Venice," *Collected Poems*, 1958].

**City of the Seven Hills** *see* **Seven-Hilled City**

**City of the Seven Lakes, the** *San Pablo, Philippines.* The city, in southern Luzon, is so nicknamed for the seven small crater lakes here.

**City of the Spire, the** *Salisbury, England.* The Wiltshire city is so nicknamed for its cathedral spire, the loftiest in England.

After I had looked from the Roman rampart [of Old Sarum] for a long time, I hurried away, and, retracing my steps along the causeway, regained the road, and, passing over the brow of the hill, descended to the city of the spire [George Borrow, *Lavengro*, 1851].

**City of the Stare, the** *Glasgow, Scotland.* The sobriquet alludes to the traditional wariness of the Scots, as they size up a stranger. (*Cp.* **Furry Boots City.**) It was applied to Glasgow by the suspense novelist William McIlvanney, as in quote (1) below, and was taken up by columnists and other writers.

(1) It was Glasgow on a Friday night, the city of the stare [William McIlvanney, *The Papers of Tony Veitch*, 1983].
  (2) The Queen was deliriously welcomed back to Glasgow yesterday, her first visit in three years to the "city of the stare," which softened the look in its eye just for her and Prince Philip [*The Scotsman*, May 24, 2002].

**City of the Stars, the** *Beverly Hills, Los Angeles, California, USA.* The name refers to the many movie stars who made the city their home.

**City of the Straits, the** *Detroit, Michigan, USA.* The name refers to the city's geographical location on the strait connecting Lake St. Clair with Lake Erie. (The city's French name actually means "strait," and English *strait* and French *détroit* are related words.)

**City of the Sun, the** *(1) Baalbek, Lebanon; (2) Cuzco, Peru; (3) Heliopolis, Egypt; (4) Rhodes, Greece.* The name in each case related to sun worship. Baalbek is identified with the worship of Baal as a Semitic sun god and its Greek name was Heliopolis ("city of the sun"). As such it should not be confused with the Egyptian He-liopolis which is the biblical On, where there was a Temple of the Sun. Rhodes had Apollo, Greek god of the sun, as its tutelary deity, while Cuzco also had a Temple of the Sun as an Inca center of sun worship.

**City of the Three Cultures, the** *Toledo, Spain.* The city earned its nickname (Spanish *la ciudad de las tres culturas*) as the historic capital of Jewish, Muslim, and Christian rulers. *See also* **Imperial City**.

**City of the Three Kings, the** *Cologne, Germany.* Cologne claims to be the burial place of the biblical Magi, the three kings or "wise men" Gaspar, Melchior, and Balthazar who brought gifts from the East to the infant Jesus. The city's coat of arms bears three crowns to represent this association and the cathedral houses a gold shrine containing what are said to be the relics of the Magi, sent from Milan in 1164.

**City of the Three Rivers, the** *Passau, Germany.* The Bavarian city lies on the Austrian frontier at the confluence of the Danube, Inn, and Ilz rivers. Hence its nickname.

**City of the Tribes, the** *Galway, Ireland.* The town's nickname alludes to the so-called "tribes of Galway," the 14 Irish families whose Anglo-Norman ancestors settled here in the 13th century: Athy, Blake, Bodkin, Browne, Darcy, Deane, Font, French, Joyce, Kirwan, Lynch, Martin, Morris, and Skerret.

A day at least must be given to Galway — the "City of the Tribes" [*Westminster Gazette*, October 10, 1898].

**City of the Violated Treaty, the** *Limerick, Ireland.* The name refers to the Treaty of Limerick signed by Jacobites (supporters of the Catholic king James II) and Williamites (supporters of the Protestant king William III) in 1691. It concluded the siege of Limerick and ended the war but was often dishonored subsequently.

Many of the quaint old sayings about Irish places seem to be dying out. We have even forgotten the meaning of many of them. Some, like "The City of the Tribes," "The City of the Violated Treaty," "The County of Short Grass" and "Tyrone of the Bushes" explain themselves [*Irish Times*, August 22, 1930].

**City of the Violet Crown, the** *Athens, Greece.* The sobriquet translates Greek *iostephanos*, "violet-crowned," an epithet applied by Aristophanes to Athens that may have referred to the purple-headed mountains surrounding the city. There is also a pun on the name of Ion, the legendary king of Athens, giving an alternate interpretation "Ion-crowned," i.e. "city of Ion."

Round the hills whose heights the first-born olive blossom brightened,

Round the city brow-bound once with violets like a bride [A.C. Swinburne, "Athens," *Erechtheus*, 1876].

**City of the West, the** *Glasgow, Scotland.* The name alludes to the location of Glasgow in west central Scotland. The city is on the Clyde, which flows northwest into the Firth of Clyde.

**City of the World, the** *New York City, USA.* The name describes New York as a city of many nationalities. *Cp.* **Melting Pot.**

City of the world! (for all races are here,
  All the lands of the earth make contributions here) [Walt Whitman, "City of Ships," *Drum-Taps*, 1865].

**City of Trees, the** *Milton Keynes, England.* The Buckinghamshire New Town, designated in 1967, was so named by its development corporation in 1971. Open spaces with lawns and trees were an integral part of the city's original plan, especially in residential areas.

**City of Victory, the** *Cairo, Egypt.* The sobriquet refers to the city's name, which in the Arabic original meant "the victorious," referring to its foundation by the Fatimid dynasty in AD 969. The name was given when it became their capital in 973.

**City of Villages, the** *(1) London, England; (2) San Diego, California, USA.* The British capital was so designated by the Greater London Authority in 2002, seeing the city as a composite of many distinctive neighborhoods. The concept was not new, and in 1956 English writer and critic V.S. Pritchett described London as "an agglomeration of villages which have been gummed together in the course of centuries." California's second-largest city was similarly envisaged at the time of its rapid growth in the 1980s. *Cp.* **City of a Hundred Villages.**

(London) London is a city of villages. Chicago is a city of neighbourhoods [*The Times*, May 20, 2005].

**City of Waters, the** *Amman, Jordan.* The Jordanian capital is so named in the Bible (when it was known as Rabbah Ammon) for its location at the headwaters of the Jabbok near the Jordan River.

And Joab sent messengers to David, and said, I have fought against Rabbah, and have taken the city of waters [2 Samuel 12:27].

**City of Witches, the** *Salem, Massachusetts, USA.* The name refers to the notorious execution of 20 persons for witchcraft here in 1692.

**City on Fourteen Hills, the** *San Francisco, California, USA.* The most prominent of the city's many hills are Twin Peaks, Mount Davidson, and Mount Sutro, while the best known are Nob Hill and Telegraph Hill. The name in-

evitably invites comparison with ancient Rome, the **Seven-Hilled City.**

The greatness of Rome is somehow associated ... with the fact that it was built on seven hills. How much greater, then, should San Francisco be, standing on fourteen hills? ... The answer, so it seemed to me, surely must be 'Twice' [A.G. Macdonell, commenting on US railroad guide, *A Visit to America*, 1935].

**City on Seven Hills, the** *(1) Birmingham, England; (2) Sheffield, England.* Both industrial cities have been so nicknamed from a favorable kinship with ancient Rome, the **Seven-Hilled City**, Birmingham as described in the quote below, Sheffield for its location at the foot of the Pennine highlands in an amphitheater of seven hills.

(Birmingham) Like unto Rome this town may be said to be built on seven hills, for are there not Camp Hill and Constitution Hill, Summer Hill and Snow Hill, Ludgate Hill, Hockley Hill, and Holloway Hill [Walter Showell, *Dictionary of Birmingham*, 1875].

**City on the Lake, the** *Chicago, Illinois, USA.* A straightforward descriptive name referring to Chicago's location on Lake Michigan.

**City that Care Forgot, the** *New Orleans, Louisiana, USA.* New Orleans is famous for its facilities for recreation and relaxation, and anyone looking for a good time is sure to find satisfaction here. Hence the nickname, which took a bitter turn following the devastating floods of 2005. *Cp.* **Mardi Gras City.**

The "city that care forgot" will never be as carefree again; the Big Easy has never faced a harder moment [*The Times*, September 2, 2005].

**City that Has Everything, the** *New York City, USA.* A sobriquet for the **Maximum City** that implies the presence of all that one could need or desire.

New York, the city that has everything, does not have a Topshop [*The Times Magazine*, September 10, 2005].

**City that Hitler Built on His Way Home, the** *Sheffield, England.* The industrial city suffered severely from German bombing in World War II and was hastily and tastelessly reconstructed after the war. Hence its former wry nickname.

**City that Knows How, the** *San Francisco, California, USA.* A label designating a city that has gotten its act together, that is "streetwise and savvy."

Vibrant, beautiful and hedonistic, the 'City that Knows How' is worth [a visit of] three to four days [*Lonely Planet USA*, 2004].

**City that Never Sleeps, the** *New York City, USA.* The name denotes a city where people are awake and active at any time of the day or night. (The 1953 movie of this title was about Chicago, not New York.)

(1) A place for 40 winks in the city that never sleeps [Headline, *The Times*, July 16, 2004].

(2) What does the City That Never Sleeps have to offer the Man Who Rarely Wakes? [*The Times*, March 9, 2005].

(3) There's nowhere quite like New York, the city that never sleeps [Travel ad, *The Times*, October 15, 2005].

**City that Perfumed the World, the** *Papantla de Olarte, Mexico.* The city's self-promotional name refers to its vanilla production, the largest in the country.

Tim Ecott's book ... takes him from Papantla in Mexico — "the city that perfumed the world" — to the "Bourbon" Island of the Indian Ocean [Piers Moore Ede, review of Tim Ecott, *Vanilla*, *Times Literary Supplement*, September 30, 2005].

**City that Reads, the** *Baltimore, Maryland, USA.* Mayor Kurt L. Schmolke created this slogan for Baltimore when running for office in 1987, tying it in with his promotion of a major literacy campaign. Cynics claimed a more realistic slogan would have been "The City that Breeds."

**City that Works, the** *Chicago, Illinois, USA.* A city that works is one that is successful, as well as one whose inhabitants are hard workers. The name was said to be "recently traditional" when quoted in the *The Economist* of March 3–9, 1979.

The City That Works went to work on itself, and ... cleaned up its image [*Lonely Planet USA*, 2004].

**City Too Busy to Hate, the** *Atlanta, Georgia, USA.* The epithet reflects Atlanta's determination to rise above racism by concentrating on the job in hand. The city was the birthplace of Martin Luther King and one of its first black millionaires was Alonzo F. Herndon, founder of Atlanta Life Insurance.

During the early 1960s Atlanta made a conscious decision to desegregate at a time other cities ... were doing their damnedest to obstruct even a hint of civil rights. It became known as "the city too busy to hate" [Dodd/Donald, p. 157].

**City Where Everything Is Produced, the** *St.-Étienne, France.* The city earned its nickname as a result of its broad diversification of industry from the second half of the 19th century.

**City Without Clocks, the** *Las Vegas, Nevada, USA.* The city is so nicknamed as there are no clocks in its casinos, so that gamblers are unaware of the passage of time. The name was popularized by the title of Ed Reid's novel *Las Vegas: City Without Clocks* (1961).

The highroad between Los Angeles, City of the Angels, and Las Vegas, City Without Clocks, cuts through the mountains and across the desert for a distance of three hundred miles [Harry Mark Petrakis, *Nick the Greek*, 1979].

**Clam State, the** *New Jersey, USA.* The state, bordering the Alantic on the east and south, is so nicknamed for its seafood products.

**Cleanest City in the World, the** *Broek, Netherlands.* The Dutch city was renowned for its neatness and tidiness. Hence the nickname.

**Cleckheckmondsedge** see in Appendix 1, p. 269.

**Cleveland Matterhorn, the** *Roseberry Topping, England.* The small but prominent summit in the Cleveland Hills is so nicknamed for its rocky profile, the result of mining and quarrying, which evokes that of the Matterhorn in the Pennine Alps.

**Cleveland of Latin America, the** *Montevideo, Uruguay.* The nickname compares the Uruguayan capital unfavorably but unjustly with the US city. *Cp.* **BA without the LA.**

Montevideo has had to be judged in comparison to the Argentinian capital... Those comparisons have frequently been derogatory: "the Newark of Buenos Aires" or the "Cleveland of Latin America." More fool those who coined such analogies [Dodd/Donald, p. 92].

**Click-Click** *New Orleans, Louisiana, USA.* The nickname imitates the cocking (or firing) of a submachine gun, referring to the high murder rate in the **Crime Capital of the South.** *Cp.* **Chopper City.**

**Clinton's Ditch** *Erie Canal, New York, USA.* A derisory nickname for the canal, referring to the unrelenting vigor with which De Witt Clinton, when governor of New York, promoted its construction, despite keen opposition. It opened in 1825. *Cp.* **Big Ditch.**

**Cloggy** *Clogwyn Du'r Arddu, Wales.* A pet name for the Snowdon mountain, popular among tyro climbers.

**Cloth-Making Capital of the World, the** *Lawrence, Massachusetts, USA.* A former nickname for the city as one of the world's greatest centers for woolen textiles.

**Cloud City** *Leadville, Colorado, USA.* The town lies in the Rocky Mountains at an altitude of *c.*10,152 ft (3,094 m), and claims to be the highest incorporated city in the USA. Hence the nickname.

**Clubland** see in Appendix 1, p. 269.

**Cluster of Suburbs in Search of a City, a** *Canberra, Australia.* The capital city was so tagged for its inexorable sprawl in the latter half of the 20th century. The suburb of Woden, south of the city center, arose in the mid–1960s, then Belconnen to the northwest in the early 1970s, then Tuggeranong, again to the south, in the mid–1970s. *Cp.* **Nineteen Suburbs in Search of a Metropolis; Seventy-Two Suburbs in Search of a City.**

**Clydeforth** see in Appendix 1, p. 269.

**Coalopolis** *Newcastle, Australia.* The nickname is appropriate for the city as one of the largest coal-mining areas in the country. It was founded in 1804 as a penal settlement named for Newcastle upon Tyne in England, a city famous for its coal-shipping industry.

> (1) The honest miners of Coalopolis [*Truth* (Sydney), February 8, 1891].
>
> (2) Newcastle, the coalopolis and second city of New South Wales [George Mackaness, *The Art of Book-Collecting in Australia*, 1956].

**Coal State, the** *Pennsylvania, USA.* The state is nicknamed for its seemingly inexhaustible supplies of coal.

**Coast** see in Appendix 1, p. 269.

**Coast of Dreams, the** *California, USA.* A sobriquet for the coastal state that reflects the aims and ambitions of its multiracial, multicultural community ever since gold was discovered in the mid–19th century. Some of the dreams were realized in Hollywood. Others came to nothing, or remain unfulfilled, although a tone of hope and optimism is generally regarded as prevailing.

> [Kevin Starr] considers whether California is now "one vast failed experiment," or whether it remains true to its mythic status as a coast of dreams [Review of Kevin Starr, *Coast of Dreams: California on the Edge, 1990–2003, Sunday Times*, June 19, 2005].

**Cocaine Country** see in Appendix 1, p. 269.

**Cockade City** *Petersburg, Virginia, USA.* The city derives its nickname from the cockade worn by soldiers recruited there during the War of 1812.

**Cockade State, the** *Maryland, USA.* The state gained its nickname from the cockades worn by soldiers of the Old Line during the War of Independence.

**Cockaigne** or **Cockayne** *London, England.* The name originally denoted an imaginary land of luxury and idleness. By association with *Cockney* (*see* **Cockneyshire**) it then came to be punningly applied to London, as if such a land. Hence, for example, the title of Edward Elgar's concert overture *Cockaigne* (*In London Town*) (1901). The name is of uncertain origin, but has been popularly derived from Latin *coquere,* "to cook," since it was fancied that the houses in Cockaigne were covered in cakes.

> The writer is evidently a Cockney, accustomed to

the ways and feeling of Cockaigne [*Athenæum*, July 30, 1881].

**Cockney's Back Yard, the** *Surrey, England.* The county west of London is so nicknamed for its proximity to the home of the Cockney (*see* **Cockneyshire**).

> The 'Cockney's back yard,' Surrey has been called; but it is really a neat green back garden [John Montgomery in Speaight, p. 103].

**Cockneyshire** or **Cockneyland** *London, England.* A former nickname for the British capital, seen as the home of the Cockney, or native Londoner. (The name itself comes from Middle English *cokeney,* "cock's egg," a colloquial term for a small or misshapen egg, as distinct from a proper hen's egg, and thus a derogatory epithet for a puny townsman, as distinct from a robust countryman.) *Cp.* **Cockaigne.**

**Cockpit of Christendom, the** *Netherlands.* The Netherlands was the scene of many theological disputes at the time of the Reformation.

> For the *Netherlands* have been for many yeares ... the very Cockpit of Christendom, the Schoole of Armes, and Rendezvous of all adventurous Spirits [James Howell, *Instructions for Forreine Travell*, 1642].

**Cockpit of Europe, the** *Belgium.* The small country of Belgium has been the arena of many European battles and forays, including Ramillies (1706), Waterloo (1815), Mons and Ypres in World War I, and the "Battle of the Bulge" in World War II. The concept of Belgium as a cockpit (properly an enclosure where cockfights are held) began with James Howell's **Cockpit of Christendom.**

> The part of Belgium through which our route lies, has been called the "Cock-pit" of Europe [*Murray's Hand-Book for Travellers in Northern Germany*, 1858].

**Cockpit of India, the** *Rajasthan, India.* The state, formerly familiar as Rajputana, has been an arena of bloody battles fought between rival royal houses. Hence the epithet, given by Rudyard Kipling, as noted in the quote below.

> Rudyard Kipling described this vast desert region as "the cockpit of India." The 36 royal houses of Rajputs that presided here ... fought as royal houses know best — brother against brother, son against father [*Sunday Times*, January 30, 2005].

**Cocktail Isles** see in Appendix 1, p. 269.

**Cod Preserves, the** *Atlantic Ocean.* An old nautical nickname for the ocean, punning on the sailors' prayer "God preserve us."

**Coffs** *Coffs Harbour, Australia.* A colloquial short name for the coastal city in New South Wales.

**Coketown** *(1) Hanley, England; (2) Manchester, England; (3) Preston, England.* All three towns gained their nickname from their 19th-century coke furnaces, Preston being so disguised in Charles Dickens's *Hard Times* (1854), where it is described as "a town of machinery and tall chimneys out of which interminable serpents of smoke trailed themselves for ever and ever."

**Cold Country, the** *England or Britain.* A former Australian nickname for the land that colonized the island continent, with an implied punning reference to the original **Old Country**.

> He could tell on sight whether any man he met came from Queensland, N.S. Wales, Victoria, Tasmania, or the Cold Country. [*The Bulletin* (Sydney), May 24, 1906].

**Cold Shoulder of Scotland, the** *Buchan, Scotland.* The region of northeastern Scotland is so nicknamed as it juts out into the North Sea.

**Coleville** *see* **Albertopolis** in Appendix 1, p. 269.

**Colonies** see in Appendix 1, p. 269.

**Colorado of the East, the** *West Virginia, USA.* Like Colorado, especially in its western half, West Virginia is a mountainous state. Hence its nickname. (The quote below describes the Monongahela National Forest, which contains Spruce Knob, the state's highest peak.) *See also* **Mountain State; Top of the World**.

> This vast expanse of rugged terrain in the Allegheny Mountains is the kind that earned West Virginia the nickname the 'Colorado of the East' [*Lonely Planet USA*, 2004].

**Colorful Colorado** *Colorado, USA.* A promotional alliterative nickname that is perhaps more subtle than it seems, as the actual name of Colorado is Spanish for "colored."

**Columbia** *United States.* The name, from that of the explorer Christopher Columbus, has been poetically applied to the New World, and in particular to the United States, for which it was at one time officially proposed. It dates from the Revolutionary period and is found in Philip Freneau's patriotic poem "American Liberty" (1775). Although not adopted for the nation, the name is widely found throughout the USA, not least for the District of Columbia, formed in 1791. It was also that of the female figure who came to personify the nation, as popularly portrayed in the trademark for the movie company Columbia Pictures, a draped maiden in a Statue of Liberty pose. The equation of Columbia with Liberty is well established, as exemplified in quote (2) below, although the Statue of Liberty figure herself does not explicitly represent Columbia.

It has been pointed out that a country may be personified either by a woman, as here, and also as **Britannia**, **Germania**, and **Marianne**, or by a man, as **John Bull** and **Uncle Sam** (and even the Russian **Bear**), but the more precise identity of the male figure is with a national government, involving politics, diplomacy, and war. From a feminist viewpoint, this means that the female figure is to be fought for, while the male does the actual fighting. Etymologically, too, the name Columbia (also Columbus) derives from Latin *columba*, "dove," a bird representing the traditional female attributes of peace, love, purity, and hope.

> (1) Hail, Columbia! happy land!
> Hail, ye heroes! heaven-born band! [Joseph Hopkinson, "Hail, Columbia!," 1798].
> (2) Can tyrants but by tyrants conquer'd be,
> And Freedom find no champion and no child
> Such as Columbia saw arise when she
> Sprung forth a Pallas, arm'd and undefiled?
> [Lord Byron, *Childe Harold's Pilgrimage*, 1812].

**Combat Zone** see in Appendix 1, p. 269.

**Comeback City, the** *Cleveland, Ohio, USA.* The city and port was so designated by its promoters in the 1990s with reference to its attempts to limit its outward sprawl and revert to a contained and coherent urban community.

**Conch Republic, the** *Florida Keys, Florida, USA.* The island chain, noted for its coral formations and resort developments, informally declared its independence from the USA in 1982. Hence the nickname.

> With your stash of shells, there's only one other place in Florida to go: the "Conch Republic," where natives name themselves after their indigenous spiral-shelled marine gastropod molluscs [*Sunday Times*, January 30, 2005].

**Constable Country** see in Appendix 1, p. 269.

**Constant** *Istanbul, Turkey.* A former nickname for the Turkish city in the days when it was **Constantinople**, as current among Britons living or working in the Middle East.

**Constantinople** *Istanbul, Turkey.* A name still associated with the former capital of the Turkish Empire, although officially superseded in 1930, following the removal of the new Turkish Republic capital to Ankara in 1923. As Jimmy Kennedy and Nat Simon's 1953 hit reminds us, "Istanbul, not Constantinople now." *See also* **Byzantium**.

> [Constantinople is] the name of a very old and famous town in Turkey — but it will not be found mentioned on up-to-date maps, because the people of Turkey have renamed it. It has been changed to Istanbul [Johnson, p. 77].

**Constitution State, the** *Connecticut, USA.* The state is so nicknamed because the Fundamental Orders of Connecticut drawn up here in 1638 are believed to be the first formal constitution written on American soil. The Constitution of the United States is said to be closer to this constitution than to that of any of the other states. The nickname (which bears a coincidental similarity to the actual state name) was officially adopted in 1959.

**Continent, the** *Europe.* A name common in insular Britain for mainland Europe, in itself suggesting a certain "foreignness," with an implied fashionable discernment and even exoticism. *Cp.* **Continong.**

(1) *Memorials of a Tour on the Continent, 1820* [William Wordsworth, title, 1822].

(2) She was going back to the Continent with her husband [Mrs. Alexander, *The Wooing O't*, 1873].

(3) Another excellent way of making contacts is, of course, 'swanning' on the Continent [Guy Egmont, *The Art of Egmontese*, 1961].

(4) The inhabitants [of Britain] look out to the sea all around them from the fastness of their 'tight little island.' Nobody would ever question the aptness of the newspaper report: 'Fog in the Channel — Continent cut off' [Anthony Miall, *The Xenophobe's Guide to the English*, 1993].

**Continent in Miniature, a** *Gran Canaria, Canary Islands.* The island, one of the largest in the group, is so titled as a lure to tourists who might otherwise think there was little but sea, sun, and sand and overlook the presence of the seaport city of Las Palmas, capital of the Spanish province of the same name.

Guests looking for an unusual destination that offers both beaches and mountains, as well as cultural and urban attractions, need look no further than Gran Canaria. Known as a 'continent in miniature,' it offers ... the most dynamic capital city in the Canaries [Holiday brochure, 2005].

**Continong, the** *Europe.* A humorous "low" English rendering of the French pronunciation of *continent*, meaning the **Continent**, otherwise Europe, and especially implying France.

(1) "On the Continong" [G.W. Hunt, song title, *c.*1870].

(2) *Mr Punch on the Continong* [Humorous book series, *c.*1900].

**CONUS** *United States.* A not very common acronym for the *con*tinental *U*nited *S*tates.

**Cook Country** *see* **Captain Cook Country** in Appendix 1, p. 269.

**Cool** *Coolgardie, Australia.* A local shortened name for the former gold-mining town in Western Australia.

**Cool Britannia** *Britain.* The name, associated with a new, revitalized Britain under the premiership of Tony Blair, is punningly based on the familiar phrase "Rule, Britannia," from James Thomson's patriotic poem *Alfred* (*see* **Britannia**). The pun was apparently first perpetrated as in quote (1) below. The tag then lay dormant for 30 years until the late 1990s, when it appeared on a *Newsweek* cover and became widely known. *Cp.* **Swinging London.**

(1) Cool Britannia
  Britannia take a trip
  Britons ever ever ever will be hip [Vivian Stanshall, "Cool Britannia," song on Bonzo Dog Doo-Dah Band album *Gorilla*, 1967].

(2) The silly slogan for selling this new country [under a Labour government] was 'Cool Britannia' ... The 'Britain' element was significant, though: no one talked of a Cool England [Jeremy Paxman, *The English*, 1998].

(3) After eight years of Tony Blair and several clumsy wars, how does "Cool Britannia" fare now? [*The Times*, June 11, 2005].

**Copper City, the** *Rome, New York, USA.* The name arose from the city's reputation as a center of copper and brass manufacturing.

**Copperopolis** *(1) Anaconda, Montana, USA; (2) Swansea, Wales.* The original name for Anaconda, for its famous copper smelter, remained a nickname following the city's adoption of its present name in 1888, when it was renamed to avoid confusion with Copperopolis in Meagher County. The copper smelter was closed in 1980. The town and port of Swansea became a major copper-smelting center in the 18th century.

(Swansea) During the Industrial Revolution, Swansea expanded dramatically to become 'Copperopolis,' the epicentre of the global copper-smelting trade [*Lonely Planet Great Britain*, 2005].

**Copper State, the** *Arizona, USA.* Arizona abounds in minerals, including copper. Hence its nickname.

**Corea** *Korea.* A once common spelling of the country's name that is still occasionally found, and that perhaps originated from French *Corée.* Yet as can be seen from quote (1) below, it has long been regarded by careful writers as erroneous.

(1) It is inexcusable ... to reproduce the obsolete and indefensible spelling, "Corea." All modern geographers and travellers adopt the official spelling originally promulgated by the Royal Geographical Society, acording to which the hard sound in question is always represented by "K" [C.E. Clark, *The Mistakes We Make*, 1898].

(2) Korea. Sometimes spelt Corea [Johnson, p. 143].

**Corinium** *Cirencester, England.* The Roman name of the Gloucestershire town remains active for its Corinium Business Park and Corinium Museum, as well as a street named Corinium Gate.

**Corkassonne** *Carcassonne, France.* The name of the Irish city of Cork was punningly adopted when the Irish airline Ryanair introduced a direct flight from England to the French city.

> You can now fly every day from Stansted to Carcassonne (dubbed Cork-assonne by grateful passengers of the Irish-owned budget airline) [*Sunday Times*, July 10, 2005].

**Corn Belt** see in Appendix 1, p. 269.

**Corncracker State, the** *Kentucky, USA.* The nickname "Corncrackers" came to be given to the "poor whites" of the Southern states, supposedly because they subsisted on corn or because they earned a living cracking corn to make cornmeal.

**Corner Country** see in Appendix 1, p. 269.

**Cornhusker State, the** *Nebraska, USA.* The state derives its nickname from that of the University of Nebraska football team in the 1920s, a cornhusker being literally a person who strips the husk from corn. The term came to be associated with so-called "husking bees," when neighbors would gather at a farmer's house to assist him in husking the corn, after which there would be feasting and dancing.

**Cornish Alps** *see* **China Clay Country** in Appendix 1, p. 269.

**Cornish Riviera** see in Appendix 1, p. 269.

**Corn State, the** *Iowa, USA.* The nickname refers to Iowa as one of the country's leading corn producers.

**Cornubia** *Cornwall, England.* The latinized form of the county's name is mostly found in poetic adjectival form, as in quotes (1) and (2) below, where the subject is Cornwall's tin mines.

> (1) From the bleak Cornubian shore
> Dispense the mineral treasure, which of old
> Sidonian pilots sought [Mark Akenside, "Hymn to the Naiads," 1746].
> (2) 'Tis heard where England's eastern glory shines,
> And in the gulphs of her Cornubian mines [William Cowper, "Hope," 1782].
> (3) Cornwall is also known as the Land of the Saints or Cornubia [*The Times* (Travel West Supplement), September 24, 2005].

**Corpus** *Corpus Christi, Texas, USA.* A conventional and convenient abbreviation of the port city's name.

> Corpus is a pleasant enough port town, but you wouldn't book your honeymoon here [*Lonely Planet USA*, 2004].

**Corunna** *La Coruña, Spain.* A common English form of the city's name, familiar from Charles Wolfe's well-known poem "The Burial of Sir John Moore at Corunna" (1817) and other works.

**Costa** For any name beginning thus, see in Appendix 1, p. 269.

**Costas** see in Appendix 1, p. 269.

**Côte d'Azur** see in Appendix 1, p. 269 (where this entry lists other *Côte* names)

**Cotton Belt** see in Appendix 1, p. 269.

**Cottonopolis** *Manchester, England.* The sobriquet, meaning "cotton city," was in common use for Manchester in its 19th-century heyday as Britain's leading cotton manufacturer. (An old tag ran: "The nation's bread hangs on Lancashire's thread.")

> (1) Cottonopolis, Manchester. A term much in use among the reporters of the sporting press engaged in that locality [*The Slang Dictionary*, 1894].
> (2) The spectacular rise of Cottonopolis, as it became known, came from the production of competitively priced imitations of expensive Indian calicoes, using machines evolved from Arkwright's first steam-powered cotton mill [*The Rough Guide to England*, 1998].
> (3) The drear rain ... came into its own, as it provided the perfect climate for spinning cotton. "Cottonopolis" was all-conquering [Dodd/Donald, p. 27].

**Cotton** or **Cotton Plantation State, the** *Alabama, USA.* Cotton production was long important in Alabama's **Black Belt** (see in Appendix 1, p. 269) until 1915, when the industry was affected by boll weevil blight and began to decline. It retains local importance, however.

> Alabama is known as the "Cotton State," it having some of the best cotton-growing soil in the world [Johnson, p. 16].

**Cotzbus** *Cottbus, Germany.* The respectable city's derisory nickname, favored by local students and graffiti artists, puns on German *kotzen*, "to puke."

**Country** see in Appendix 1, p. 269.

**Country Music Capital of the World, the** *Nashville, Tennessee, USA.* The name relates to 1925, when regular radio broadcasts of a country music program later known as the Grand Ole Opry began. Nashville is now the recording center of country music.

> Yee haw! The country music capital of the world, Nashville ... offers a musical experience that'll get anyone tapping toes [*Lonely Planet USA*, 2004].

**County, the** *St. Louis County, Missouri, USA.* The name is used to distinguish the county from St. Louis, the **City.**

**County Bondi** *Bondi, Sydney, Australia.* The residential area, famous for Bondi Beach, came to be so known for the young Irish people living there on temporary visas in the late 20th and early 21st century. The name copies Irish county names such as Co. Clare.

**County of Squires and Spires, the** *Northamptonshire, England.* The Midlands county has been so nicknamed for the many ancestral homes of "landed gentry" (squires) found here and for its numerous churches (spires). The title is prone to permutation, as in the quotes below.

(1) [Stanwick and Higham Ferrers are] lovely towns, famous in this countryside of "Springs, Spires, and Squires" [Ruth McKenney and Richard Bransten, *Here's England*, 1955].

(2) Northamptonshire, that 'county of squires,' is still great hunting country [Laurence W. Meynell in Hadfield 1981, p. 450].

(3) The county of 'squires, spires and mires' attracts fewer visitors than it deserves [Charlie Godfrey-Faussett, *Footprint England*, 2004].

**County Palatine, the** *(1) Cheshire, England; (2) Lancashire, England*. The historic label was used in medieval times for an English county whose earl or lord held certain royal privileges, such as pardoning treason. There were formerly more counties so designated than the two mentioned. "Palatine" means literally "pertaining to a palace."

**Cowboy Capital of the World, the** *Bandera, Texas, USA*. The town is in a famous ranching area, as more precisely defined by the quote below.

The little town is the self-proclaimed 'Cowboy Capital of the World,' and wanna-be cowpokes can saddle up at one of the many dude ranches dotting the surrounding hills [*Lonely Planet USA*, 2004].

**Cowboy City** *Cheyenne, Wyoming, USA*. The state capital has long been famous for its cattle and its rodeos. *See* **Rodeo Town**.

**Cowboy State** *Wyoming, USA*. The state has long been noted for its ranching. Hence the sobriquet.

The Wild West image in the 'Cowboy State' can be a lot of fun [*Lonely Planet USA*, 2004].

**Cow Country** see in Appendix 1, p. 269.

**Cow Town** *(1) Calgary, Alberta, Canada; (2) Fort Worth, Texas, USA*. Calgary gained fame for its cattle production and its Calgary Stampede is still held as an annual rodeo and agricultural fair. Fort Worth became a cow town after the Civil War, and its first railroad helped establish it as a meat-packing and cattle-shipping center.

(1) (Fort Worth) This city is proud of its nickname, 'Cowtown,' but the livestock industry is just a small part of what's happening here [*Lonely Planet USA*, 2004].

(2) (Calgary) When [snackbar chain founder] Faith MacArthur was a child, she'd pluck chickens and pick potatoes during the harvest. She lived in "Cow Town"—Calgary, Alberta—in the Prairies [*The Times Magazine*, June 5, 2004].

**Coyote State, the** *South Dakota, USA*. The official nickname refers to the coyote (prairie wolf) that frequents the state's prairies.

**Crabtown** *Annapolis, Maryland, USA*. The nickname refers to the crab fishing and seafood packaging carried on in the seaport city.

**Cracker State, the** *Georgia, USA*. There are three main contenders for the origin of the nickname: (1) It alludes to the whips that early settlers cracked over their mules; (2) It refers to the corn that the poorer settlers cracked and ate (*cp.* **Corncracker State**); (3) It describes the harsh, "cracked" speech of these settlers in their Georgian dialect.

Through November the "Cracker State" has occupied the center of motordom's stage [*Washington Herald*, November 27, 1910].

**Cradle of Aviation, the** *Hammondsport, New York, USA*. The village earned its nickname as the birthplace of the aeronautical pioneer Glenn Hammond Curtiss (1878–1930).

**Cradle of Civilization, the** *(1) Çatal Höyük, Turkey; (2) Fertile Crescent, Africa; (3) Greece; (4) Jericho, West Bank; (5) Kenya; (6) Tassili-n-Ajjer, Algeria*. The epithet has been applied to any place that is historically regarded as a point of origin of human culture, such as the Middle East. Of these six candidates for the title, Çatal Höyük ("Fork Mound"), near Konya, is the most famous neolithic site of western Asia, dating from around 7000 BC. Greece obviously qualifies for the tag, as does Kenya, for the reasons mentioned in quote (3) below. Jericho, despite quote (2), dates from around 9000 BC and so can claim to be the oldest city in the world. Tassili is a rugged massif, noted for its rock art. Some of the above archaeological sites are alternately known as the "Cradle of Humanity." For the **Fertile Crescent**, see Appendix 1, p. 269.

(1) (Tassili) This remote desert region can rightly claim the overworked title "cradle of civilisation" for what it teaches us of our prehistory [*The Times*, December 4, 2004].

(2) (Çatal Höyük) As far as anyone knows, the fertile plain around Konya is the real cradle of civilisation—beneath one vast mound, archeologists found Catalhoyuk, the world's oldest city [*Sunday Times*, February 6, 2005].

(3) (Kenya) Known as "the cradle of civilisation" because the earliest evidence of Man was discovered there, Kenya has remained remarkably stable since independence from Britain in 1963 [*The Times*, July 26, 2005].

**Cradle of Confederation, the** *Prince Edward Island, Canada*. The province gained its sobriquet because the Charlottetown Conference, held there in 1864, prepared the way for the confederation of all Canadian provinces. Prince Edward Island itself did not finally join the union until 1873.

**Cradle of English Christianity, the** *Glaston-*

*bury, England.* The Somerset town is associated with Joseph of Arimathea, who is said to have buried the Holy Grail here and to have made the first conversions to Christianity here. There is also a legend that Jesus was here as a young man. *See also* **Avalon.**

**Cradle of Finnish Culture, the** *Turku, Finland.* The former capital of Finland (to 1812) is one of the country's oldest cities, and the site of the national university from 1640 to 1827. Hence the sobriquet.

**Cradle of Humanity** *see* **Cradle of Civilization**

**Cradle of Islam, the** *Hejaz, Saudi Arabia.* The region of western Saudi Arabia is so nicknamed as the seat of Mecca and Medina (*see* **Holy City**), the original centers of Islam.

**Cradle of Liberty, the** *Boston, Massachusetts, USA.* Boston was the center of opposition to the British both before and during the War of Independence. The name is chiefly associated with Faneuil Hall, the meeting place of the rebels at this time.

**Cradle of Mankind, the** *Olduvai Gorge, Tanzania.* The northern locality contains a series of sites in sediments from which the longest cultural sequence in the world has been recorded. Hence the nickname. *Cp.* **Cradle of Civilization.**

> This morning head for Lake Manyara National Park. En route stop at Olduvai Gorge, 'the cradle of mankind' [Travel ad, *The Times Magazine*, February 12, 2005].

**Cradle of New Zealand, the** *Northland, New Zealand.* The North Island region justifies its sobriquet from its site of Waitangi, where a treaty between Maori chiefs and Great Britain was signed in 1840, and from its many early mission stations. *Cp.* **Birthplace of the Nation.**

**Cradle of Scottish Christianity, the** *Whithorn, Scotland.* One of the oldest Christian centers in Britain, Whithorn claims its title on the grounds that the 5th-century British missionary St. Ninian founded a church here and is buried here.

**Cradle of the Bantu, the** *Central African Republic.* The Bantu are said to have originated in central Africa. The name occurs in the opening line of the country's national anthem, as quoted below. It was written by Barthélémy Boganda (1910–1959), first president of the republic, and adopted in 1960.

> Ô Centrafrique, ô berceau des Bantous!
> (O Central Africa, cradle of the Bantou.)

**Cradle of the Confederacy, the** *Montgomery, Alabama, USA.* The state capital derives its nick-

name as the city where the seceded Southern states met in 1861 to form the Confederate States of America. For a few months that year Montgomery was the first capital of the Confederacy, until this status was granted to Richmond, Virginia.

**Cradle of the Law, the** *Bury St Edmunds, England.* The Suffolk town is so nicknamed as it was here in 1215 that the local barons vowed to obtain from King John the ratification of the Magna Carta, the basis of English personal and political liberty. The phrase forms part of the town's motto, "Shrine of a King, Cradle of the Law," the king being Edmund, for whom the town is named.

**Cradle of the Nation, the** *(1) Guimarães, Portugal; (2) Lower Austria, Austria.* The Portuguese city is so nicknamed as the birthplace in *c.*1109 of Afonso I, first king of Portugal. Austria's largest state, known in German as Niederösterreich, is so called as the historical heartland of the country as a whole.

**Cradle of the US Textile Industry, the** *Pawtucket, Rhode Island, USA.* Located on the Blackstone River at Pawtucket Falls, Pawtucket has been a textile center since Samuel Slater built the nation's first successful water-powered cotton mill here in 1793. Hence the sobriquet.

**Crawfish Town, the** *New Orleans, Louisiana, USA.* The city is noted for its seafood products, served in many of its famous restaurants.

**Crazy City, the** *Barranquilla, Colombia.* The city and port justifies its name (Spanish *la ciudad loca*) once a year when in the week before Lent it holds a wild carnival.

**Cream City, the** *Milwaukee, Wisconsin, USA.* The city is so nicknamed from the cream color of the bricks manufactured here.

**Cream of Antarctica, the** *South Georgia, South Atlantic.* A touristic name for the island, whose beaches are backed by glaciers and snow-clad mountains. The name is a variant of the popular "pearl" tag (which would have been equally appropriate, considering the colors involved).

> South Georgia is generally agreed by all visitors to represent the 'Cream of Antarctica' [Travel ad, *The Times Magazine*, June 4, 2005].

**Creative County, the** *Staffordshire, England.* The promotional name refers primarily to the county's manufacturing enterprise, notably that of china and earthenware in the **Potteries**, with which famous names such as Wedgwood and Spode are associated. The title can also be interpreted generally in terms of modern crafts.

> (1) The energy of our home-grown talent has

fashioned a unique experience from art, design, skill and engineering into the best short break you'll ever have. Welcome to Staffordshire ... The Creative County [Staffordshire travel brochure, 2005].

(2) Known as the Creative County, you'll find handicrafts, fine china, crystal glass and distinctive ales made here [*Enjoy England Holiday Planner 2005*].

**Creative Town, the** *Huddersfield, England.* The industrial Yorkshire town was so dubbed in the late 20th century following a European Union project to encourage creativity in both individual residents and the town as a whole.

**Creek, the** *Strait of Messina, Italy.* The nickname for the strait between southern Italy and Sicily was current among British naval personnel in World War II. The name was also expanded as "Crazyman's Creek."

**Creole State, the** *Louisiana, USA.* The state derives its nickname from the many Creoles of French and Spanish descent among its population.

**Crescent City** *New Orleans, Louisiana, USA.* The nickname refers to the city's location on the east bank of a great bend in the Mississippi. *Cp.* **Silver Smile.**

(1) The mint julep, that in the Crescent City you may enjoy for ten cents, costs you twelve and a half in the Empire city [William Chandless, *A Visit to Salt Lake*, 1857].

(2) New Orleans is ... a comfortable metropolis which has a certain apathy and stagnation which I find inoffensive. At least its climate is mild; too, it is here in the Crescent City that I am assured of having a roof over my head [John Kennedy Toole, *A Confederacy of Dunces*, 1980].

(3) Around the headland that is called Algiers the Mississippi describes the majestic curve that gave to New Orleans its ekename of The Crescent City [John Brunner, *The Great Steamboat Race*, 1983].

**Cricklewitch** *Cricklewood, London, England.* A punning alteration of the district's name, referring to its Jewish population. The "-witch" represents the "-vich" typically found in Jewish names, as Abramovich (*cp.* **Abrahampstead**).

**Cricklewood** *Crich el Oued, Tunisia.* A British soldiers' punning corruption of the Arabic name during the North Africa campaign of World War II, referring to Qarish al-Wadi (as it is now usually spelled) in Tunisia.

**Crimean Riviera** see in Appendix 1, p. 269.

**Crime Capital of the South, the** *New Orleans, Louisiana, USA.* The nickname gained validity in the early 21st century, when murder rates were falling in many parts of the USA but rising in New Orleans. In 2002 there were 53.1 murders per 100,000 inhabitants in the city as against 7.3 in New York and 17.1 in California, while robberies and motor vehicle thefts were almost four times the national average. *See also* **Chopper City; Click-Click.**

[Singer Ray Davies] could count himself lucky not to be killed in what is, or was, the crime capital of the South [*Sunday Times*, September 4, 2005].

**Croakumshire** *Northumberland, England.* As indicated in the quote below, the county is or was nicknamed from the distinctive "croak" or speech peculiarity of its inhabitants.

CROAKUMSHIRE. Northumberland, from the particular croaking in the pronunciation of the people of that county, especially about Newcastle and Morpeth, where they are said to be born with a burr in their throats, which prevents their pronouncing the letter *r* [Grose].

**Cronian Sea, the** *Arctic Ocean.* A somewhat lofty poetic name, denoting a sea belonging to Cronus (Kronos), the Titan god of Greek mythology, equated with the Roman Saturn, who in later literature is said to have been lord of the Islands of the Blessed in the Western Ocean.

As when two Polar Winds, blowing adverse
  Upon the Cronian Sea, together drive
  Mountains of Ice [John Milton, *Paradise Lost*, 1667].

**Crookland** *Brooklyn, New York City, USA.* A nickname referring to Brooklyn's criminal reputation in the 1920s, when it was the most populous borough in New York City. A punning alternate form of the name is Crooklyn.

**Crooklyn** *see* **Crookland**

**Cross, the** *(1) Draperstown, Northern Ireland; (2) Kings Cross, Sydney, Australia.* The Co. Londonderry village is locally so known as an abbreviated translation of its Irish name, *Baile na Croise,* "town of the cross." The colloquial name of the cosmopolitan city district is a similar shortening.

(1) (Kings Cross) Just where is King's Cross? — or as it is referred to affectionately by those who live there — The Cross [H.C. Brewster, *King's Cross Calling*, 1945].

(2) (Kings Cross) He took me up to the Cross, the city's playground [Max Williams, *Dingo! My Life on the Run*, 1980].

(3) (Kings Cross) The two sides of "the Cross" (as locals call it) coexist with little trouble [*The Rough Guide to Australia*, 2001].

**Crosser** *Crosshaven, Ireland.* A short name for the Co. Cork resort.

**Crossroads of America, the** *Indiana, USA.* The nickname, officially adopted in 1937, refers to the state's location between Michigan, Kentucky, Ohio, and Illinois, as an integral region of the Midwest.

**Crossroads of Europe, the** *Belgium*. The country, bounded by the North Sea, France, the Netherlands, Germany, and Luxembourg, lies on one of the main road and rail routes into and out of continental Europe. Hence the nickname.

**Crossroads of the Pacific, the** *Honolulu, Hawaii, USA*. The state capital is so nicknamed for its location on major shipping and air routes.

**Crump Dump, the** *Ruhr, Germany*. The nickname was used by British Royal Air Force pilots when on bombing raids over this industrial region in World War II, "crump" denoting the sound of an exploding bomb.

> In action, one may bomb the *Crump Dump* or Ruhr, in which our airmen have made so many 'crump holes' or bomb-craters [Eric Partridge, *A Dictionary of RAF Slang*, 1945].

**Crustonbury** *Glastonbury, England*. A punning name referring to the cloying, clinging mud of the open fields at the site of the annual rock festival near the Somerset town of Glastonbury. *Cp.* **Glasto**.

> These days the thought of Glastonbury just exhausts me. All that mud? I just cannot be bothered ... Are you post–Crustonbury too? [*Sunday Times*, April 25, 2004].

**Crystal Coast** see in Appendix 1, p. 269.

**Crystal Hills, the** *White Mountains, New Hampshire, USA*. The name has been applied poetically to the mountains, as in the quote below.

> We had passed
> The high source of the Saco; and, bewildered
> In the dwarf spruce-belts of the Crystal Hills,
> Had heard above us, like a voice in the cloud,
> The horn of Fabyan sounding [John Greenleaf Whittier, "The Bridal of Pennacook," 1848].

**Cuba of America, the** *Miami Beach, Florida, USA*. The nickname arose in the 1950s, partly for the gamblers and gangsters attracted by the city's gaming, and partly because of its proximity to sunny, swinging Cuba. *Cp.* **Little Cuba**.

**Cubist Town, the** *Olhão, Portugal*. The nickname refers to the town's white, cube-shaped, flat-roofed houses.

**Cubitopolis** see in Appendix 1, p. 269.

**Cuchulainn Country** see in Appendix 1, p. 269.

**Cumberland** *Cumbria, England*. The name of the former northwestern county is sometimes erroneously used for that of the present county, itself a revival of the name of the ancient Celtic kingdom. *Cp.* **Northumbria**.

**Cupid Capital of Nebraska, the** *Valentine, Nebraska, USA*. The nickname playfully puns on the city's real name, in fact that of a Union army officer.

**Curry, the** *Cloncurry, Australia*. The colloquial short name of the Queensland town is associated with its fame as a former copper producer. For the characteristic prefixed "the" see quote (3) for **Alice**.

> (1) Cloncurry, generally called "The Curry," is the western Queensland base of the incomparable Flying Doctor Service [Jock Marshall and Russell Drysdale, *Journey among Men*, 1962].
> (2) The Curry was the largest copper producer in the British Empire in 1916 [*Lonely Planet Australia*, 2004].

**Cushy** *La Cauchie, France*. A British soldiers' World War I version of the name of the village near Arras.

**Cutlery Capital of France, the** *Thiers, France*. The town has been known for its cutlery since medieval times, and in the late 20th century was producing over half of the knives made in France. Hence the name.

**Cyclone State, the** *Kansas, USA*. The state is notorious for its cyclones, as graphically described in L. Frank Baum's children's novel *The Wonderful Wizard of Oz* (1900), and as depicted in the 1939 movie based on it. It is said that whenever the movie is shown on TV, there are calls to the local weather center asking if a cyclone is expected (Findley Rowe, "Kansas City, Heartland U.S.A," *National Geographic Magazine*, July 1976).

**Cymru** *Wales*. The Welsh name of Wales is familiar to those entering the country by road from England, who will pass a sign in Welsh and English saying "Croeso i Gymru / Welcome to Wales," the Welsh name being in its mutated form (after the preposition *i*). *See also* **Cambria**.

**Czecho** *Czech Republic*. An abbreviated form of the name of the former Czechoslovakia, used mainly among Central European specialists.

**Daggarramereens, the** *Diego Ramírez, Chile*. A former sailors' corruption of the name of the island group, the southernmost of the Tierra del Fuego Archipelago, east of the potentially hazardous Cape Horn.

**Dago** *San Diego, California, USA*. An abbreviated form of the city's name that seems to suggest "dago" as a nickname for a foreigner, especially a Spaniard or Italian. San Diego was settled by the Spanish.

> I think there were five of us, all of us boots just out of Dago [William Styron, *The Long March*, 1952].

**Daintry** *Daventry, England*. The name of the Northamptonshire town was long spelled (and pronounced) thus.

> (1) Where is the post that came from Montague?

By this at Daintry, with a puissant troop
[William Shakespeare, *Henry VI,Part 3*, 1595].

(2) 'Education' and the railway are responsible
for the replacement of the old local forms by pro-
nunciations based on a traditional spelling. Daintry is giving way to *Daventry*, and Sapsworth has
quite yielded to *Sawbridgeworth* [Ernest Weekley,
*Adjectives — And Other Words*, 1930].

(3) Fifty years ago, many places preserved distinctive local fashions ... Daventry was pronounced 'Daintry,' Sawbridgworth [*sic*] in Hertfordshire is said to have been 'Sapsed' [*sic*] [C.
Stella Davies and John Levitt, *What's in a Name?*,
1970].

**Dales** see in Appendix 1, p. 269.

**Dallas of South England, the** *Basingstoke,
England*. A journalistic nickname for the Hampshire town alluding to its ultramodern architecture.

[The Churchill Plaza is] an unnecessarily huge
glass-fronted building which, along with a series
of smaller but no less glazed buildings, earned
Basingstoke the title of 'The Dallas of South England' in the *Independent* [Sam Jordison and Dan
Kieran, eds., *The Idler Book of Crap Towns*, 2003].

**'Dam, the** *Amsterdam, Netherlands*. A colloquial short form of the Dutch capital city's
name.

Many of us [have been led] to sideline the 'Dam
as a venue for ritual rites of passage and seedy
sales conferences [*Sunday Times*, December 4,
2005].

**Damascus of the North, the** *Sarajevo,
Bosnia-Hercegovina*. The country's capital earned
its sobriquet for its trees and gardens, like those
at Damascus.

**Dandies, the** *Dandenong Ranges, Australia*.
A friendly nickname for the national park east of
Melbourne, Victoria, a favorite location for
bushwalking.

**Danum** *Doncaster, England*. The Roman
name of the South Yorkshire town (from the
Don River on which it lies) remains in active
service for Danum Grammar School and
Danum Street.

**Danzig** *Gdańsk, Poland*. Long familiar under
this German form of its name, the city was incorporated in Germany in 1939. (Germany's de-
mands for its secession from Poland were an issue
of conflict between the two countries and precipitated World War II.) It passed to Poland in
1945.

**Dar** *Dar es Salaam, Tanzania*. A handy short
name for the Tanzanian capital.

Dar's history as a city ... is relatively recent
[Dodd/Donald, p. 324].

**Dards, the** *Dardanelles, Turkey*. A British soldiers' World War I nickname for the strait between Europe and Asia, the scene of severe fighting during the Gallipoli campaign.

**Dark and Bloody Ground, the** *Kentucky,
USA*. The nickname is sometimes said to be a
translation of the state's Native American name.
It refers to the battles fought here between the
Indian tribes of the North and South, and was
popularized by Theodore O'Hara in the line
"Sons of the dark and bloody ground" in his
poem "The Bivouac of the Dead" (1847).

That beautiful region which was soon to verify its
Indian appellation of the dark and bloody ground
[C.J. Latrobe, *The Rambler in North America*,
1835].

**Dark City, the** *Alexandra, South Africa*. The
township near Johannesburg had a predominantly black (dark-skinned) population. Hence
the former nickname. *Cp.* **Kofifi**.

(1) A velvet pall ... hung over Alexandra Township... In this evening frock, the "Dark City," as it
is called, could compete for loveliness with any
other town [W.M. Manqupu in *Drum*, 1955].

(2) Former famous black residential areas like
Sophiatown, Western Native Township and
Alexandra went under quaint names like "Kofifi,"
"Casbah" and "Dark City" [*Rand Daily Mail*, Oc-
tober 14, 1982].

**Dark Continent, the** *Africa*. The name became familiar from H.M. Stanley's two books
describing his explorations and experiences in
Africa, *Through the Dark Continent* (1878) and
*In Darkest Africa* (1890). The adjective "dark"
refers metaphorically to a continent that was
then unknown and mysterious, and literally to
its dark-skinned inhabitants. It is possible that
Stanley invented the epithet.

The first thing you notice is the light. Light
everywhere. Brightness, everywhere. Not the
"Dark Continent" as so often described by writers
from the gloomy northern skies of Europe. Not
the Dark Continent at all. This is the luminous
continent; drenched in sun; pounded by heat;
and shimmering in its blinding glare [Bob Geldof, *Geldof in Africa*, BBC One TV program,
June 20, 2005].

**Dark Town** *Harlem, New York City, USA*. A
name alluding to the neighborhood's predominantly black population.

**Darling-it-hurts** *Darlinghurst, Sydney, Australia*. A punning alteration of the city district's
name.

**Darlo** *(1) Darlinghurst, Sydney, Australia; (2)
Darlington, England*. Identical abbreviated
names for the Australian city district and English town, the former having the characteristic
Australian -o as in **Kenso**. The English name is
chiefly used by army troops stationed at nearby
Barnard Castle, Co. Durham.

(Darlinghurst) Oxford Street in Darlinghurst (nicknamed Darlo) is the "pink strip" of this Queen of gay cities [Dodd/Donald, p. 213].

**Daughter of the Baltic, the** *Helsinki, Finland.* A semiofficial title of the Finnish capital used in the local media. Helsinki is on the Gulf of Finland, an arm of the Baltic Sea.

**David's City** *see* **City of David**

**Davos of Styria, the** *Aflenz Kurort, Austria.* The resort village is so nicknamed as a local equivalent to the famous Swiss health resort.

**Dawdoink, the** *Dordogne, France.* The name represents a mangling of the name of the French region, popular among British vacationers and vacation-home owners. The spelling has the illiterate "-ink" ending heard among some speakers in words ending in "-ing," as "nothink" for "nothing." ("Lottungerron" in the quote below is Lot-et-Garonne, the department south of Dordogne. The sentence as a whole illustrates the typical British reluctance to pronounce French placenames correctly.)

> I am francophilephobic—but, then, so too are the 50 million Brits who live in the Dawdoink and Lottungerron [Jonathan Meades in *The Times*, January 15, 2005].

**DC** *(1) District of Columbia, USA; (2) Washington, DC, USA.* An initialism used equally for the federal district and the city with which it is coextensive.

> (1) (Washington) Then it was time to go to DC. *Our nation's capital* [Rick Moody in *Mortification*, 2003].
>
> (2) (District of Columbia) As a federal protectorate, DC has a political life that resembles that of a colony more closely than a state [*Lonely Planet USA*, 2004].
>
> (3) (Washington) DC is a business town, so hotel rates can drop as much as 50% on weekends and in summer [*Lonely Planet USA*, 2004].

**Dead Heart** *see* in Appendix 1, p. 269.

**Dead Heart of France, the** *Massif Central, France.* The vast upland region lies geographically in the heart of France but seems alien to many urban French, who have thus nicknamed it accordingly.

**Dead Man's Island** *North Coronado, Mexico.* The northern island of Los Coronados, a small group of islands in the Pacific Ocean off Tijuana, northwestern Mexico, was so nicknamed from its fancied resemblance to a corpse floating in the sea. It was used by smugglers as a transfer point, and in turn gave the nickname of Dead Man's Canyon, a canyon leading from Tijuana into southern California, used by drug smugglers and illegal immigrants.

**Dead Moans** *Des Moines, Iowa, USA.* A local punning nickname for the state capital, regarded by some as dull and lifeless.

**Dear Green Place, the** *Glasgow, Scotland.* The epithet, translating the city's Gaelic name (more precisely "green hollow"), is attributed to St. Kentigern, who founded a monastery by the Clyde River here in the 6th century.

> With its grey and claustrophobic climate, one wonders how Glasgow got its Celtic name, Glas-cu, meaning "dear green place" [Dodd/Donald, p. 44].

**Debatable Land** see in Appendix 1, p. 269.

**Debtors' Retreat, the** *Wallasey, England.* A derisory nickname for the Merseyside resort by residents of nearby Liverpool, as a town to which debtors supposedly retire in order to escape their creditors.

**Deep North, the** *Queensland, Australia.* The nickname is based on the US **Deep South** (see in Appendix 1, p. 269), partly as a geographical analogy, as the state of Queensland occupies northeastern Australia, just as the Deep South is located in the southeastern United States, but partly also because of a supposed identical conservatism.

> (1) Perhaps the author thinks that with our "Deep North" of Queensland, there is little hope for a crocodilian future [*The Bulletin* (Sydney), August 26, 1972].
>
> (2) In the Deep North it is well-known that a bloodthirsty socialist and, more than likely, a communist tries to hide behind every peanut and pumpkin scone [*The Bulletin* (Sydney), July 30, 1985].

**Deep South** see in Appendix 1, p. 269.

**Delightsome State, the** *Maryland, USA.* The name comes from a description of the region in the logbook of Captain John Smith in 1608, an era when the adjective was regularly used in the sense of today's "delightful."

**Delta City** *Venice, Italy.* Venice lies on the northwestern shore of the Gulf of Venice, an arm of the Adriatic, between Istria and the Po river delta. Hence the descriptive name.

> Delta City downpours [Heading to article on Venice floods, *The Times*, November 8, 2004].

**Demon's Land** *Tasmania, Australia.* A corruption of the former name of the island state, Van Diemen's Land, given by Abel Tasman, its discoverer in 1642, in honor of Anthony Van Diemen, governor of the Dutch East Indies (or according to some, that of his daughter Maria). The name was later associated with the island as a penal colony, as which it was also nicknamed **Vandemonia**.

> In consequence of an ignorant prejudice, which was supposed to deter intending colonists, the name of Van Diemen's Land, or Demon's Land, as

it was called, has after the lapse of two centuries been changed to TASMANIA, in honour of the sailor who preferred the name of his mistress to his own [Isaac Taylor, *Words and Places*, edited with corrections and additions by A. Smythe Palmer, *c.*1908].

**Den, the** *New Cross, London, England.* The name refers to the district's low-lying location amid hills south of the Thames. The name gave that of The Den, the old ground of Millwall football club here. (In 1993 it was sold to a housing company and a new stadium was built at a nearby site now known as the New Den.)

**Den Bosch** *'s Hertogenbosch, Netherlands.* A local short form of the city's awkward name, itself originally *des Hertogen Bosch*, "The duke's forest." (The shortened name gave that of the medieval painter Hieronymus Bosch.)

[The city is] known to locals and visitors as Den Bosch (pronounced Den Boss) [Netherlands Board of Tourism & Conventions tourist brochure, 2005].

**Denmark of Latin America, the** *Uruguay.* The nickname, of anonymous origin, is quoted in John Gunther, *Inside South America* (1961), and compares Uruguay, the smallest of the South American states, with Denmark, the smallest of the Scandinavian countries. Like Denmark, too, Uruguay is a generally flat country, without the mountains found elsewhere in South America and Scandinavia.

**Denver of the Gold** *Denver, Colorado, USA.* The state capital was so nicknamed following the gold rush of 1859. The name partly reflects the city's history. It arose in 1860 when a settlement called Auraria (Latin for "goldmine"), set up in 1858 by by gold prospectors and miners, united with two other villages.

What we had wanted was that Denver of the Gold should provide for us Fifth Avenue by day and by night the Great White Way [Ford Madox Ford, "Denver," 1937, in Sara Haslam, ed., *Ford Madox Ford and the City*, 2005].

**Derby Town** or **Derbyville** *Louisville, Kentucky, USA.* Louisville is the home of the Kentucky Derby, the classic horse race established in 1875.

**Derry** *see* **Stroke City**

**Des** or **Dez Minnies** *Des Moines, Iowa, USA.* An abbreviated or playfully corrupted form of the city's name.

**Deseret State, the** *Utah, USA.* Deseret was the name of the provisional state organized in 1849 by a convention of Mormons, who had settled at Salt Lake City two years earlier. The word comes from the Book of Mormon and means "honeybee," as a symbol of hard work and co-

operation. In 1850 Utah Territory was created in its stead. *See also* **Mormon State**.

**Detroit of Britain, the** *Coventry, England.* The Warwickshire city was so formerly nicknamed for its manufacture of motor vehicles, as is Detroit (*see* **Motor City**).

**Detroit of India, the** *Chennai (Madras), India.* As intimated in the quote below, Chennai is noted for its vehicle works, like those of Detroit.

The modern city has brought ... the heavy industry of the Ford car plant that has had Chennai dubbed the Detroit of India [Dodd/Donald, p. 279].

**Deva** *(1) Chester, England; (2) Dee River, Wales/England.* A poetic adoption of the Roman name for the Cheshire city and the river on which it lies. The name is also in use for the heritage museum known as the Deva Roman Experience, as well as for the nearby Deva Business Park and Deva Industrial Park. In connection with the quote below, *see* **Wizard Stream**.

(Dee) Nor on the shaggy top of Mona high,
Nor yet where Deva spreads her wisard stream [John Milton, *Lycidas*, 1638].

**Devil's Drawing Room, the** *London, England.* An 18th-century sobriquet for the British capital, referring to the deceit and deviousness of much of its society, especially as portrayed in the theater.

(1) [I] made him repeat with great energy an observation which was often in his mouth, viz. "London is the devil's drawing room" [Tobias Smollett, *Roderick Random*, 1748].
(2) *Jenny:* So, Mr. Jonathan, I hear you were at the play last night.
*Jonathan:* At the play! why, did you think I went to the devil's drawing room?
*Jenny:* The devil's drawing room!
*Jonathan:* Yes, why an't cards and dice the devil's device, and the play-house the shop where the devil hangs out the vanities of the world upon the tenter-hooks of temptation? [Royall Tyler, *The Contrast*, 1787].
(3) The sun went down, the smoke rose up, as from
A half-unquench'd volcano, o'er a space
Which well beseem'd the "Devil's drawing-room,"
As some have qualified that wondrous place [Lord Byron, *Don Juan*, 1823].
(4) How few years is it since [Scottish judge] Henry Cockburn, hating London, and coming but rarely to what he called the "devil's drawing-room," stood near him? [Grace and Philip Wharton, *The Wits and Beaux of Society*, 1860].

**Devil's Triangle** *see* **Bermuda Triangle** in Appendix 1, p. 269.

**Devil's Wood** *Bois de Delville, France.* The name of the wood in northern France was rendered thus by British soldiers in World War I during (and after) the battle of the Somme (1916).

**Dez Minnies** *see* **Des**

**Diamond City** *(1) Amsterdam, Netherlands; (2) Kimberley, South Africa.* The Dutch capital is so nicknamed for its repute as a diamond-cutting center, while Kimberley, in Northern Cape province, is the headquarters of the world's diamond industry. (The city was founded in 1871 following the discovery of diamonds locally.) Kimberley has also been called Diamondia and Diamondopolis, as well as simply Diamond Town. *See also* **Big Hole**.

(1) (Kimberley) A good tale is told of Couper during the time he kept a boxing school in Diamondopolis [Louis Cohen, *Reminiscences of Johannesburg and London*, 1924].
(2) (Kimberley) In order to bring that affair to a successful conclusion the Major had been obliged to move to the Diamond Town [L. Patrick Greene, *The L. Patrick Greene Adventure Omnibus*, 1928].
(3) (Kimberley) J.B. Robinson Diamond Merchant, of Diamondia, Begs to announce to the Diggers that he has removed to the New Rush, De Beers, where he will continue to buy Diamonds at the highest market prices [George Beet, *Grand Old Days of the Diamond Fields*, 1931].
(4) (Kimberley) Then came the South African War and the siege of Kimberley, with the Boers at the gates of Diamond City [*Personality*, March 13, 1989].

**Diamond Coast** see in Appendix 1, p. 269.

**Diamondia** *see* **Diamond City**

**Diamondopolis** *see* **Diamond City**

**Diamond State, the** *Delaware, USA.* The nickname is not literal but metaphorical, denoting the state's small size but great value, the latter with reference to its economic role. *Cp.* **Small Wonder**.

Delaware gets the nickname, the Diamond State, from the fact that it is small in size but great in importance [G.E. Shankle, *State Names*, 1934].

**Diamond Town** *see* **Diamond City**

**Diaspora City** *London, England.* A nickname for the British capital that refers to its cultural diversity. *Cp.* **City of Nations**.

**Dice City** *Las Vegas, Nevada, USA.* The nickname refers to the city as a center of gaming, in which a roll of the dice can make or break a player.

**Dickensland** see in Appendix 1, p. 269.

**Diggerland** *New Zealand.* The nickname derives from "digger" as a friendly form of address among Australians and New Zealanders, and especially among soldiers in World War I (and later in World War II), in turn from the miners ("diggers") in the Australian gold fields in the 19th century.

**Dilli** *New Delhi, India.* A local form of the Indian capital's name, said to represent the original Hindi.

(1) *Dilli* is, according to Cunningham, the old Hindu form of the name; *Dihli* is that used by Mahommedans [Henry Yule and A.C. Burnell, *Hobson-Jobson: The Anglo-Indian Dictionary*, 1886].
(2) New Delhi keeps its name, although locals call it Dilli [*The Times*, December 24, 2000].

**Dimple of the Universe, the** *Nashville, Tennessee, USA.* The name, quoted in John Gunther, *Inside the U.S.A.* (1947), refers not to the city's location in a hollow but to its attraction, like a dimple on a human face. Nashville has been admired for its rolling hills, its pleasant seasons, and its farms surrounded by long white picket fences.

She stood up ... and extended her hand to me. "Welcome to the dimple of the universe, Baby Girl" [Phoebe Kate Foster, "The Head of the Clan: A Southern Homecoming," *Mid-South Review*, Fall 2003].

**Dinosaur Coast** see in Appendix 1, p. 269.

**Dinosaurland** see in Appendix 1, p. 269.

**Dirty Old Town, the** *Salford, England.* The former cotton-spinning and coal-mining city across the river from Manchester owes its insalubrious tag to Scottish folksinger Ewan MacColl's song of this name (1946). Understandably, the local council is keen to shake off the grimy image.

"We are not trying to divorce ouselves from our industrial past, far from it," says a spokesperson. "The council simply wants to change some of the preconceptions about Salford as the 'Dirty Old Town'" [*The Times*, November 7, 2005].

**Dish, the** *Mogadishu, Somalia.* A colloquial anglicized abbreviation of the Somali capital's name.

**Dismal Swamp** see in Appendix 1, p. 269.

**Disputed Lands** see in Appendix 1, p. 269.

**District, the** *(1) Storyville, New Orleans, Louisiana, USA; (2) Washington, DC, USA.* The nickname was applied to Storyville as the red-light district of New Orleans, where jazz had its beginnings among blacks in the early 20th century. For Washington, the name is used as an alternate designation by the city's residents. *Cp.* **DC**.

**Disunited Kingdom, the** *United Kingdom.* An ironic name for the United Kingdom of Great Britain and Northern Ireland, historically that of England, Scotland, Wales, and Ireland, as a country in which, since the 1707 Act of Union, there has been a continuous evolution of territorial politics and a trend towards national or regional devolution. The latter resulted in an independent Scottish parliament and Welsh assembly in 1999, but with authority only over domestic issues. The name has been adopted for various studies, books, and TV and radio programs on the subject.

It is five years ago this week that New Labour came to power ... heralding a new dawn for the Disunited Kingdom [*Scots Independent Newspaper Online*, May 3, 2002].

**Ditch, the** *(1) Atlantic Ocean; (2) English Channel; (3) Kolkata (Calcutta), India; (4) North Sea; (5) Suez Canal, Egypt.* A mock-belittling term for any stretch of water, from an ocean to a canal. The English Channel and North Sea were usually so dubbed by members of the British Royal Air Force, while the Suez Canal received the label from the time it was built in the 1860s by the French engineer Ferdinand de Lesseps. The sobriquet is more subtle for the Indian city, where it refers to the Mahratta Ditch, built by the East India Company in 1742 to protect Calcutta from the Mahratta tribesmen, but never completed. *See also* **Big Ditch.**

(1) (Kolkata) MAHRATTA DITCH, n.p. An excavation made in 1742 ... on the landward side of Calcutta, to protect the settlement from the Mahratta bands. Hence the term, or for shortness 'The *Ditch*' simply, as a disparaging name for Calcutta [Henry Yule and A.C. Burnell, *Hobson-Jobson: The Anglo-Indian Dictionary*, 1886].
(2) (Suez Canal) As I was spittin' into the Ditch aboard o' the *Crocodile,*
I seed a man on a man-o'-war got up in the Reg'lars' style [Rudyard Kipling, "Soldier an' Sailor Too," *The Seven Seas*, 1896].
(3) (Suez Canal) The French mind set the Egyptian muscle in motion and produced a dismal but profitable ditch [Joseph Conrad, *An Outcast of the Islands*, 1896].
(4) (English Channel) We had a beautiful journey across the ditch [Letter from repatriated wounded English soldier, April 1916, quoted in Olive Dent, *A V.A.D. in France*, 1917].
(5) (Suez Canal) 'Stagnant ditch' is a cynical phrase that ... Ferdinand de Lesseps was greeted with time and again when he appealed to England for financial backing [Donough O'Brien, *Fame by Chance*, 2003].

**Divorce Capital of the World, the** *Reno, Nevada, USA.* The former nickname alludes to the city's liberal divorce laws in an era before other states liberalized their laws.

**Dixie** see in Appendix 1, p. 269.

**Dixie Town** *New Orleans, Louisiana, USA.* New Orleans is in **Dixie** (see in Appendix 1, p. 269). Hence the nickname.

**Docklands** see in Appendix 1, p. 269.

**Doctor Brighton** *Brighton, England.* The sobriquet is said to have been applied to the Sussex seaside resort for its salubriousness by the Prince Regent (the future George IV), who paid visits here from 1782. To modern ears the name may suggest "Dr. Bright 'Un."

(1) Kind, cheerful, merry Dr. Brighton [W.M. Thackeray, *The Newcomes*, 1854].
(2) It is perhaps natural that Thackeray should comment that countless Londoners had George IV to thank for inventing 'the kind, merry and cheerful Dr Brighton' [Robinson/Millward, p. 306].

**Doctor Town, the** *Rochester, Minnesota, USA.* The city derives its nickname from the famed Mayo Clinic, founded in 1889.

**Dodge** *Dodge City, Kansas, USA.* A short name for the city that was laid out in 1872 and named for Richard I. Dodge. This form of the name became familiar from the phrase "to get the hell out of Dodge," as badmen in Dodge City were ordered to do in cowboy movies and the 1950s TV western *Gunsmoke.*

Modern Dodge ... revels in its infamous Wild West past [*Lonely Planet USA*, 2004].

**Dodger Town** *Los Angeles, California, USA.* A nickname from the baseball team that originated as the Brooklyn Dodgers, formed in Brooklyn, New York, in 1883 and said to be so named for the skill of Brooklyn residents at evading ("dodging") the streetcars. The team came to Los Angeles in 1927.

**Doin' It** *Doingt, France.* A British soldiers' World War I corruption of the name of the village near Péronne.

**Dolphin Capital of Australia, the** *Nelson Bay, Australia.* Dolphins can be seen year-round at many places on the east coast of Australia, but especially at this small town on the bay of the same name in New South Wales.

**Dome City** *Houston, Texas, USA.* A nickname referring to Houston's famous Astrodome, opened as a sports stadium in 1965. *Cp.* **Astrodome City.**

**Dominion, the** *(1) Canada; (2) New Zealand.* In 1867 Canada became the first Dominion within the British Empire. It retained this status (implying self-government and equality with Britain) until 1982, when it became fully responsible for its own constitution. New Zealand became a Dominion in 1907, but likewise became legally independent in 1947. Australia, the Irish Free State (*see* **Eire**), South Africa, and Newfoundland were also Dominions, but the title became particularly associated with the two countries mentioned. After 1947, the use of the term was abandoned, as it was felt to imply a form of subordination, and all "Dominions" were "members of the Commonwealth."

(1) (New Zealand) The Dominion consists of two large islands ... and several smaller islands [Johnson, p. 181].

(2) (Canada) The words "British Dominions beyond the Seas" had disappeared from the Proclamations in the United Kingdom, Australia, and New Zealand ... At the same time Canada had substituted "Canada" for "Dominion of Canada" [*The Times*, February 21, 1952].

(3) (New Zealand) The country's firm legislative link with England was struck off in 1947, thus ending the transient period when New Zealand saw itself as 'the Dominion,' an expression which still fitfully survives [Shadbolt, p. 33].

**Dom Rep, the** *Dominican Republic, West Indies.* A neat abbreviation of the country's formal name. *Cp.* **DR.**

(1) On a recent visit to the Dom Rep our rep told us to ... ask a member of hotel staff to remove any unattended towels [*The Times*, May 15, 2004].

(2) The "Dom Rep" has one of the largest concentrations of all-inclusive beach hotels on earth [*Sunday Times*, September 18, 2005].

**Donbass** *Donets Basin, Ukraine.* The short name of the coal-producing region was adopted into English and other languages from the original Russian abbreviation of *Donetsky basseyn*, "Donets basin," after the river.

**Donny** *Doncaster, England.* A colloquial local name for the South Yorkshire town.

**Doorway to Britain, the** *Dover, England.* The Kent town is the main port of arrival and departure in England for passengers from or to France and other countries of continental Europe. The entry point has long been guarded by Dover Castle, dubbed "the key to England." ("Doorway" rather than "gateway" may have been partly prompted the name of the town and that of the Dour River on which it lies.)

Dover is the doorway, inward and outward, to Britain and the rest of the world ... Its castle claims that office [Richard Church in Hadfield 1981, p. 133].

**Doorway to Mecca, the** *Banda Aceh, Indonesia.* The city, in northwestern Sumatra, derives its nickname from its traditional role as a stopping place for Muslim pilgrims journeying to Mecca.

**Dormitory of Liverpool, the** *Wirral, England.* The Wirral peninsula, between the estuaries of the Dee and the Mersey, is a favored region of residence, especially on its western side, for commuters to Liverpool. Hence the name.

**Dormitory of New York, the** *Brooklyn, New York City, USA.* Brooklyn is sometimes so nicknamed as many of its residents work in Manhattan. *See also* **Nation's First Commuter Suburb.**

**Dorset Lakeland, the** *Poole, England.* The Dorset port and resort derives its nickname from the waterways that flow into its capacious harbor, which itself gave the town's regular name ("pool").

"The Dorset Lakeland" is no far-fetched nickname for the large land-locked Harbour of Poole [*Holiday Guide 1952: Area No. 5, South & South East England*].

**Douay** *Douai, France.* The variant spelling of the town's name is found for the Douay Bible, the English translation of the Bible completed at Douai in the 17th century and formerly used by Roman Catholics.

**Double Pay** *Double Bay, Sydney, Australia.* A punning nickname for the city suburb, with its swanky sidewalk cafés and stylish shops.

**Down Along** see in Appendix 1, p. 269.

**Down East** see in Appendix 1, p. 269.

**Down East State, the** *Maine, USA.* The state is so nicknamed for its location in the eastern coastal region of New England, known as **Down East** (see in Appendix 1, p. 269).

**Down South** see in Appendix 1, p. 269.

**Downtown** see in Appendix 1, p. 269.

**Down Under** *Australia and New Zealand.* The name refers to the **Antipodes**, which are "down under" the feet of a person in Europe. The term is rarely used by Australians themselves, although the Australian band Men at Work scored a hit with their popular 1983 song "Down Under" during Australia's successful challenge for the America's Cup, as described in quote (2) below.

(1) The second concert in Auckland brought to an end John's first visit Down Under [L.A.G. Strong, *John McCormack*, 1941].

(2) Men from Down Under are conquering America, and the latest to infiltrate the airwaves walked off with a major Grammy award at the 25th annual homage the record industry pays to itself. The Australian New Wave band "Men at Work" ... won the best prize for their debut album [*Newsweek*, March 7, 1983].

(3) When it's winter or summer in the northern hemisphere, the opposite season prevails Down Under [*The Rough Guide to Australia*, 2001].

**Down Where the South Begins** *Virginia, USA.* Virginia is the southernmost of the Middle Atlantic states. Hence its sobriquet, usually found in spoken form, as by radio commentators.

**DR, the** *Dominican Republic, West Indies.* A mainly local abbreviation for the island republic. *Cp.* **Dom Rep.**

The DR, as Dominicans commonly call their homeland [*Lonely Planet Dominican Republic & Haiti*, 2002].

**Drier Side of Britain, the** *Lincolnshire, England.* The eastern county promotes itself thus, comparing its generally drier climate with the notorious wet weather of North Wales and Merseyside, on the west side of the country.

(1) Lincolnshire ... advertises itself as the 'drier side of Britain.' There's some truth in that strapline, as regards both the prevailing weather and sense of humour [Charlie Godfrey-Faussett, *Footprint England*, 2004].

(2) Lincolnshire receives only half the national average of rainfall, a fact that earned it the slogan 'the drier side of Britain' [*Lonely Planet Great Britain*, 2005].

**Driff** *Driffield, England.* A colloquial truncation of the name of the Yorkshire town (earlier known as Great Driffield).

**Drisheen City** *Cork, Ireland.* The name, from Irish *drisín*, "intestine," is that of a popular local dish, a kind of blood pudding made of sheep and beef blood, which became associated with Cork from the city's former role as a major exporter of salted beef. The blood byproduct of the slaughterhouses was used to make the pudding.

**Drukken Dunblane** *Dunblane, Scotland.* The first word of the uncomplimentary nickname is a Scots form of "drunken," referring to the alleged alcoholic indulgence of the townsfolk.

**Drumlin Belt** see in Appendix 1, p. 269.

**D-Town** *Dallas, Texas, USA.* A colloquial initialism of the city's name.

**Dublin of the East, the** *Prague, Czech Republic.* The nickname compares the Czech capital with the Irish one, to which at one time it bore an artistic and academic similarity, as a city of learning and legend.

Prague ... was the "city of a thousand golden spires," the "Dublin of the East" [Malcolm Bradbury, ed., *The Atlas of Literature*, 1996].

**Duchy, the** *Cornwall, England.* The name refers to the county of Cornwall as the estate of the Duke of Cornwall, the title of the heir to the British throne. The title dates from 1337, when Edward III created his eldest son, Edward the Black Prince, Duke of Cornwall. He also laid down the principle that the Duke of Cornwall must succeed to the throne and that only the eldest son of the monarch can be Duke of Cornwall. Charles, Prince of Wales, became Duke of Cornwall in 1952 on the succession of his mother as Queen Elizabeth II. *Cp.* **Principality.**

**Dukeries** see in Appendix 1, p. 269.

**Dumbo** see in Appendix 1, p. 269.

**Dunedin** *Edinburgh, Scotland.* The poetic name of the Scottish capital represents an anglicized form of the city's Gaelic name *Dùn Eideann*, which may mean "fort on a slope," referring to the site of the present Edinburgh Castle. (The -burgh of the present name represents an English equivalent of Gaelic *dùn*, "fort.") The English form was adopted for the name of Dunedin, New Zealand, a city founded by Scottish Presbyterians in 1848. *See also* **Edin; Edinburgh of the South.**

(1) When the streets of high Dunedin
Saw lances gleam and falchions redden [Sir Walter Scott, *The Lay of the Last Minstrel*, 1805].
(2) Stern then, and steel-girt was thy brow,
Dun-Edin! [Sir Walter Scott, *Marmion*, 1808].
(3) No! not yet, thou high Dunedin!
Shalt thou totter to thy fall;
Though thy bravest and thy strongest
Are not there to man the wall [W.E. Aytoun, *Lays of the Scottish Cavaliers*, "Edinburgh after Flodden," 1849].

**Dunelm** *Durham, England.* An abbreviation of Latin *Dunelmensis*, "of Durham," found in academic titles relating to Durham University, as "BA, Dunelm," and as the official signature of the bishop of Durham.

**Dunkirk** *Dunkerque, France.* A regular anglicized form of the name of the French seaport city, itself of Middle Dutch origin and meaning "church on the dune." The English form became familiar from the role played by the city in World War II, as the scene of the evacuation of thousands of Allied troops after the fall of France in 1940. The name was known in Britain long before this, however, and there are places in England that have adopted it, such as the village of Dunkirk near Canterbury in Kent, first recorded in 1790.

**Durbs** or **Durbs-by-the-sea** *Durban, South Africa.* A familiar abbreviated form of the seaport city's name.

(1) 'What's it *like* up there?' I ask again. 'Like Durbs at Christmas time but without the sea,' someone answers [*Darling*, February 7, 1979].
(2) These holidays, head for Durbs-by-the-sea. You could catch far more than a tan [*Sunday Times* (Johannesburg), December 2, 1990].

**Dust Bowl** see in Appendix 1, p. 269.

**Dust Bowl State, the** *Kansas, USA.* The name refers to the location of the southwestern part of the state in the **Dust Bowl** (see in Appendix 1, p. 269).

**Dutch Paradise, the** *Gelderland, Netherlands.* The name was formerly given to the Dutch province for its fertility, especially in the marshy area between the Rhine and the Waal, with its cherry and apple orchards. (*See* **Batavia** in connection with this region.)

**Dykehart** or **Dyke Hart** *Leichhardt, Sydney,*

*Australia*. A pun on the name of the city district, as a popular place of resort for gays and lesbians.

> (1) Leichhardt (known affectionately as "Dykehart") [*The Rough Guide to Australia*, 2001].
>
> (2) The art deco Little Italy of Leichhardt (or Dyke Hart) is navel of the lesbian scene [Dodd/Donald, p. 213].

**E1** *Whitechapel, London, England*. The postal district designation (east 1) essentially represents London's **East End** (see in Appendix 1, p. 269), formerly in sharp social contrast to fashionable **W1**.

> Stepney, Whitechapel and Wapping, an area defined quite precisely by the E1 postal district, ... is the heart of the old East End [Carrie Segrave, *The New London Property Guide*, 2003].

**E17** *Walthamstow, London, England*. The postal district designation (east 17) serves as a synonym for the former densely populated district, now increasingly fashionable. (See the quote at **Jewel in the East**.)

**Eagle State** *see* **Border Eagle State**

**Earthly Paradise, an** *(1) Damascus, Syria; (2) Hangzhou, China; (3) St. Petersburg, Russia; (4) Sana, Yemen; (5) Suzhou, China*. Various cities in the world have been built or preserved as a "earthly paradise," as distinct from the paradise that is in heaven. The Syrian capital was so termed in A.W. Kinglake's novel *Eothen* as in quote (1) below, while *The Earthly Paradise* was the title of two volumes of poetry by William Morris published in 1868. The two Chinese cities of Hangzhou and Suzhou, some 80 miles apart, have been called "paradise on earth" since ancient times, while Russian czar Peter the Great declared that his city of St. Petersburg, founded in 1703, would be an "earthly paradise." Sana, Yemen's largest city, has also long been so known.

> (1) (Damascus) This "Holy" Damascus, this "earthly paradise" of the Prophet ... she is a city of hidden palaces, of copses, and gardens, and fountains, and bubbling streams [A.W. Kinglake, *Eothen*, 1844].
>
> (2) (Hangzhou) Above, there is the Hall of God; below there is Soochow and Hangchow [Chinese saying, quoted in Giles, p. 117].
>
> (3) (St. Petersburg) It is now about two hundred years since Peter laid the foundation of his "Earthly Paradise" [W. Barnes Steveni, *Things Seen in Russia*, 1914].
>
> (4) (Sana) "There are three earthly paradises," said the Prophet. "Merv of Khurasan, Damascus of Syria, and San'a of Yemen. And San'a is the paradise of paradises" [Tim Mackintosh-Smith, *Yemen: The Unknown Arabia*, 2000].

**East** see in Appendix 1, p. 269.

**East Coast** see in Appendix 1, p. 269.

**East Country** see in Appendix 1, p. 269.

**East End** see in Appendix 1, p. 269.

**Eastern States** see in Appendix 1, p. 269.

**East Side** see in Appendix 1, p. 269.

**Eat-Apples** *Étaples, France*. A British soldiers' version of the French town's name in World War I. Étaples, near Boulogne, was an important British base at that time.

**Eblana** *Dublin, Ireland*. The ancient form of the Irish capital's name, first recorded by the geographer Ptolemy in the 2d century AD, has been adopted in modern times as an academic imprint for Dublin.

> Dublin the beautie and eie of Ireland, hath been named by Ptolome, in ancient time, Eblana [Richard Stanhurst, *De Rebus in Hibernis Gestis*, in Raphael Holinshed, *Chronicles*, 1577].

**E-Boat Alley** see in Appendix 1, p. 269.

**Ebor** *York, England*. The name is an abbreviation of either *Eboracum*, the Roman name of York, or of Latin *Eboracensis*, "of York." It occurs in various contexts, but notably for the Ebor Handicap (now the totesport Ebor), a horse race run annually at York, and as the official signature of the archbishop of York. The quote below assumes a knowledge of these two applications.

> Little excitement has arisen over who will be the next Archbishop of York. Two years ago there was much speculation on the Canterbury Stakes — and it looked for a period as if Dr Michael Nazir-Ali was a likely winner. But ... since then his star has faded and I would not put money on his ability to capture the Ebor Handicap [Anthony Howard in *The Times*, December 14, 2004].

**EC2** *(City of) London, England*. A fairly frequent substitution of the postal district designation (east central 2) for the formal title of the **City**.

**Economic Capital of the World, the** *New York City, USA*. The name encapsulates the city's longstanding financial supremacy. *Cp.* **Capital of Capital**.

> New York marketed its monetary expertise to the globe ... and in the process the city became the "economic capital of the world" [*Britannica*, vol. 24, p. 910].

**Écosse** *Scotland*. The French name of Scotland is sometimes found as a nameplate on automobiles of Scottish tourists and in the names of some Scottish commercial organizations, such as the travel firm Ecosse Unique. It preserves the memory of the "Auld Alliance," the medieval alliance of France and Scotland to prevent England from conquering either of those two countries.

**Eden of Germany, the** *Baden, Germany*. The name was applied to the former German state (now part of Baden-Württemberg) on account of its fine scenery.

**Edge of the World** see in Appendix 1, p. 269.

**Edin** or **Edina** *Edinburgh, Scotland.* A poetic name for Edinburgh as a shortened form of the city's ancient name **Dunedin**. The name is said to have been introduced by the 16th-century Scottish writer George Buchanan.

> Edina! *Scotia's* darling seat!
> All hail thy palaces and tow'rs [Robert Burns, "Address to Edinburgh," 1786].

**Edinbro** *Edinburgh, Scotland.* A local form of the city's name, typically found in verse, as quoted below. *Cp.* **Embro**.

> When we cam' in by Edinbro' town
> My mother and father they met me ["Jamie Douglas," *The Oxford Book of Ballads,* 1910].

**Edinburgh of America, the** *Albany, New York, USA.* The state capital's nickname is said to refer to its fine buildings, like those of the Scottish capital. (It so happens that Albany is named for the Duke of Albany, the Scottish title of the Duke of York, itself from Albany as an old name of Scotland. *See* **Albion**.)

**Edinburgh of the South, the** *Dunedin, New Zealand.* The South Island city was founded in 1848 by Scottish Presbyterians and named with the historic name of Edinburgh. (*See* **Dunedin**.) The nickname thus preserves the historic link, despite the absence of any physical or even geographical resemblance to the Scottish capital.

> That saddening phrase 'Edinburgh of the South,' the silliest description any city contrived about itself (silly because it emphasises imitation, invites foolish comparison, and denies Dunedin's truly indigenous and original quality) [Shadbolt, p. 297].

**Edmonchuk** *Edmonton, Alberta, Canada.* The provincial capital is sometimes known by this humorous nickname, for the Ukrainians who have influenced the city's development. Many Ukrainian family names end in *-chuk*.

**Egee Pete** *Egypt.* A mostly pre–World War I perversion of the country's name in the talk of British soldiers.

**Egg Wiped** *Egypt.* A whimsical alteration of the country's name among British soldiers during World War I.

**Egoli** *Johannesburg, South Africa.* A Zulu name for the **City of Gold**, with an identical meaning (adopted from English "gold").

> (1) In Britain, with forty times the population of the Reef, there is only one murder every three days. Egoli has a worse record than anywhere else in the civilised world [*Drum*, October 6, 1951].
> (2) The Bantu usually refers to Johannesburg as 'Goli' ('Goldie'). The Whites sometimes refer to Johannesburg as the 'City of Gold' [H.H.W. De Villiers, *Rivonia*, 1964].

**Egypt** *Illinois, USA.* The nickname came about because the Illinois city of Cairo (pronounced "Kayro") was named after the Egyptian capital. The story also goes that as the northern part of the state was settled after the southern, settlers would say "we must go down into Egypt to buy corn," alluding to the biblical story of Joseph and his brethren (Genesis 42).

**Egypt of the North, the** *Rousay, Scotland.* The Orkney island is noted for its rich archaeological sites. Hence its ambitious sobriquet.

> This wild and windswept hilly island ... is known (more by tourist brochures than locals admittedly) as 'the Egypt of the North' [*Lonely Planet Great Britain*, 2005].

**Eiderdown** *Ouderdon, Belgium.* A British soldiers' World War I version of the name of the village near Ypres.

**Eighth Wonder of the Natural World, the** *Ngorongoro Crater, Tanzania.* The extinct volcano crater is noted for its great size and its vast array of African wildlife. Hence its nickname.

> Our very special journey takes you ... to the stunning Ngorongoro crater, known as the eighth wonder of the natural world [Travel ad, *The Times Magazine*, February 12, 2005].

**Eighth Wonder of the World, the** *Erie Canal, New York, USA.* The promotional tag accompanied the grand opening of the canal in 1825.

**Eine** *London, England.* A late 19th-century parlyaree (showmen's slang) name for the British capital, in origin apparently a corruption of its Italian name of *Londra*.

**Eire** *Ireland.* A name still sometimes found for Ireland, as in postal addresses, but officially used only from 1937, when it replaced the title of Irish Free State, to 1949, when the Republic of Ireland was created. It supposedly derives from Eriu, one of the three sister goddesses (the others were **Banba** and **Fódla**) whose names competed to be chosen for the country. *See also* **Erin**.

> (1) Eire (which is the Irish word for Ireland) should be used only in headlines [*The Times Guide to English Style and Usage*, 1992].
> (2) (Avoid Eire except in direct quotes or historical context.) [*The Times Style and Usage Guide*, 2003].
> (3) Irish people are not pleased to hear their country referred to as *Éire*, preferring 'Ireland,' 'the Irish Republic,' or more briefly 'the Republic' (Northern Ireland politicians frequently refer to the south as *Éire*, conscious of its offensive potential) [Brian Lalor, *Blue Guide Ireland*, 2004].

**EL** *East London, South Africa.* The abbreviation of the port city's name is frequently found in newspaper headlines.

EL man wins six jackpots [Headline, *Eastern Province Herald*, June 1, 1979].

**El Dorado State, the** *California, USA.* The name is apt when it is recalled that *El Dorado* literally means "the gilded one." *Cp.* **Golden State.**

**Electric City, the** *Great Falls, Montana, USA.* The city, at the confluence of the Missouri and Sun rivers, near the falls that gave it its name, is the center of extensive hydroelectric power development. Hence the sobriquet.

**Elektropolis** *Berlin, Germany.* The nickname was current for the German capital between 1880 and 1913, when it was the center of the world's electrical industry. The noted German electrical manufacturer Siemens was founded in Berlin in 1847.

**Elie** see in Appendix 1, 269.

**Ellay** *Los Angeles, California, USA.* An alternate spelling of the familiar initialism **LA.**

**Elm City** *see* **City of Elms**

**El Paso** *Dundalk, Ireland.* The Co. Louth town stands on the main Dublin to Belfast road near the border with Northern Ireland, just as El Paso stands on the border between the United States and Mexico.

> Residents saw the visit [of President Clinton] as a formal end to the bad old days during which ... the town was known as "El Paso," especially in the North. There was a geographical contradiction in this because the Republic as a whole used to be referred to in the North as "Mexico," partly on account of it being south of the border, and partly because of its poverty in the eyes of the *gringos* who lived north of the Forkhill customs post [*Irish Times*, December 16, 2000].

**Elsinore** *Helsingør, Denmark.* The name of the seaport became familiar in this form thanks to Shakespeare's use of it.

> (1) But what is your affair in Elsinore? [William Shakespeare, *Hamlet*, 1603].
> (2) Just two railway stops to the south of Elsinore in northern Denmark, where Hamlet fretted and fumed his vengeful life, is the Louisiana Museum [*The Times*, February 1, 2005].

**Embro** or **Embra** *Edinburgh, Scotland.* A phonetic representation of a local pronunciation of the Scottish capital's name.

> Hech, sirs, but ye've gotten a nasty, cauld, wet day for coming into Auld Reekie, as you kintra [i.e. country] folks ca' Embro [M. Lindsay, quoted in Wheeler, p. 29].

**Emerald City, the** *Seattle, Washington, USA.* The city and port is nicknamed for its lushness and greenness, the result of mild winters and cool summers.

> One of the fastest-growing metropolitan areas in the USA, the 'Emerald City' has become an exporter of trends [*Lonely Planet USA*, 2004].

**Emerald Isle, the** *(1) Ireland; (2) Ischia, Italy; (3) Montserrat, West Indies.* The familiar poetic name of Ireland refers to the rich verdure of its countryside, as any film or photo will confirm. The epithet is said to have been created by the Irish patriot William Drennan, as in quote (1) below. *Cp.* **Green Isle.** The island of Ischia is nicknamed similarly. Montserrat is not only an island with an Irish history (it was first settled in 1632 by Irish Catholics from St. Kitts) but was once also a lush green, although the southern part was laid waste by the 1995 eruption of the supposedly dormant Soufrière Hills volcano and a further eruption in 1997, which wiped out the capital, Plymouth (*see* **Pompeii of the Caribbean**).

> (1) (Ireland) Arm of Erin, prove strong; but be gentle as brave,
>   And, uplifted to strike, still be ready to save;
>   Nor one feeling of vengeance presume to defile
>   The cause, or the men, of the Emerald Isle [William Drennan, "Erin," 1795].
> (2) (Ireland) The Emerald Isle, where honest Paddy dwells,
>   The cousin of John Bull, as story tells [Sir Walter Scott, *The Search after Happiness*, 1817].

**Emerald of the Desert, the** *Bam, Iran.* The town derives its nickname from its favorable location on a small river in an otherwise barren landscape, as described in the quote below.

> Bam, celebrated as Iran's "emerald of the desert" for its improbable fertility in the arid Dasht-e Lut desert from which it rose [*Sunday Times*, December 28, 2003].

**Emmerdale Country** see in Appendix 1, p. 269.

**Emperor's Cradle, the** *Ajaccio, France.* The traditional capital of Corsica is so nicknamed (French, *le Berceau de l'Empéreur*) for the French emperor Napoleon, who was born here in 1769.

**Empire City** *(1) New York City, USA; (2) Wellington, New Zealand.* New York takes its name from the **Empire State** in which it lies. Wellington, founded in 1840, was so nicknamed because it was popularly seen as the colonial capital of the British Empire, as well as the national capital of New Zealand.

> (1) (New York) Broadway Swell, a New York term for a great dandy, Broadway being the principal promenade in the "Empire City" [*The Slang Dictionary*, 1894].
> (2) (Wellington) Back again in what the New Zealanders proudly call the Empire City, oblivious entirely of the misnomer [F.T. Bullen, *Advance Australasia*, 1907].

**Empire of Lilies, the** *France.* The name puns between French *l'empire des lys*, "empire of the lilies," and *l'empire des Louis*, "empire of the

Louis," in the same way that Paris has been nick-named **City of Lilies**.

**Empire State, the** *(1) Delaware, USA; (2) Illinois, USA; (3) New York, USA.* The well-known nickname is usually associated with New York, not only generally from its earlier preem-inence in population, wealth, and industry, but more specifically from the words of George Washington, who in reply to an address by the common council of New York City on Decem-ber 2, 1784, called New York "the seat of Em-pire." The title has been claimed by other states, as indicated by quotes (2) and (3) below.

(1) (New York) We are told, sir, of ... the empire State of New York [*Register of Debates in Congress,* 1834].

(2) (Delaware) If there is an "Empire State" in this Union, it is Delaware ... [but] if my forty friends from New York choose to call it the Em-pire State, I will not quarrel with them [John Quincy Adams in *The Congressional Globe,* Sep-tember 1841].

(3) (Illinois) Illinois, the "Empire State" of the mighty West [*The Leisure Hour,* November 29, 1860].

(4) (New York) It rained in New York State, the Empire State, rained cold and pitiless [John Steinbeck, *Travels with Charley in Search of Amer-ica,* 1962].

**Empire State of the South, the** *Georgia, USA.* The state was so nicknamed in 1872 for its leading role in the industrial growth of the South. It is also the largest of the US states east of the Mississippi, while its capital, Atlanta, has long been the economic and cultural center of the Southeast. The comparison is with New York as the **Empire State**.

**Emporium of South Wales, the** *Carmar-then, Wales.* The nickname alludes to the wide variety of goods sold in the town's shops and markets.

Carmarthen (the 'Emporium of South Wales') [Ruth Thomas, *South Wales,* 1977].

**Empress of All Cities, the** *London, England.* A royal personification of the British capital.

The British capital has been called ... the empress of all cities [*Blackwood's Magazine,* February 1832].

**Empress of the Ancient World, the** *Rome, Italy.* A poetic personification of the city that was the capital of the Roman empire. (A pictorial representation exists as Mel Ramos's 1963 paint-ing *Roma — Empress of the Ancient World.*)

**Empress of the North, the** *Edinburgh, Scot-land.* A royal personification of the Scottish cap-ital, introduced by Scott as in the quote below.

"Nor less," he said, — "when looking forth,
I view yon Empress of the North

Sit on her hilly throne" [Sir Walter Scott, *Marmion,* 1808].

**Empress of Watering Places** *see* **Queen of Watering Places**

**Empty North** see in Appendix 1, p. 269.

**Empty Quarter, the** *(1) El Djouf, Maurita-nia; (2) Rub' al Khali, Saudi Arabia.* Both desert regions are known by this English name, which translates the Arabic name of the Saudi Arabia expanse (literally "quarter of the desert"). "Quar-ter" denotes the crescent shape of the desert, like that of the moon in its first quarter. It is "empty" because it is deserted (uninhabited). The Rub' al Khali is also known in English as the Great Sandy Desert.

**Encantadas, Las** *Galápagos Islands, Ecuador.* A touristic name for the Pacific islands, obtained by resurrecting their original Spanish name *Las Encantadas,* "the enchanted ones," given them for their spectacular rugged landscape by their discoverer in 1605, Tomás de Berlanga, bishop of Panama.

This tour cleverly unites the two greatest attrac-tions of South America — 'Las Encantadas' or En-chanted Islands of Galapagos, and the 'lost' Inca city of Machu Picchu [Travel ad, *Sunday Times Magazine,* January 23, 2005].

**Energy Capital of the United States, the** *Gillette, Wyoming, USA.* The city is noted for its coal and oil production. Hence the nick-name.

**Engineering Burgh, the** *Johnstone, Scotland.* The town near Paisley was founded in 1781 and grew quickly as a product of the industrial rev-olution, with engineering as its staple industry. Hence the nickname.

**England, Home and Beauty** *England.* The old patriotic sobriquet for England derives from the lines cited in quote (1) below.

(1) In honor's call I fall at last.

For England home and beauty,

For England, home and beauty [John Braham, song, "Death of Nelson," *The Americans,* 1811].

(2) Let it be ... said of me, as of a gallant and eminent naval Hero, ... that what I have done, I did ... "For England, home, and Beauty" [Charles Dickens, *David Copperfield,* 1850].

(3) "England, home, and beauty!" said Vetch, with a mock-heroic air [Marcus Clarke, *His Nat-ural Life,* 1875].

(4) The youthful governess [in Henry James's short story "The Turn of the Screw" (1898)] sees Bly as a symbol of a beloved aristocratic country house culture — a vision, extreme and narrow, of England, Home and Beauty [Barbara Everett, "The last turn," *Times Literary Supplement,* De-cember 23 & 30, 2005].

**England-land** *England.* The colloquial term represents England promoted as a land of touristic treasure and historical "heritage," encapsulating everything that is (or is felt to be) quintessentially "English."

> This ordinary little place [i.e. Stratford-upon-Avon, Shakespeare's birthtown] is nowadays all but smothered by packet-tourist hype and tea-shoppe quaintness, representing the worst of "England-land" heritage marketing [*The Rough Guide to England*, 1998].

**England of South America, the** *Chile*. The country was so nicknamed in the 19th century for the constitutional model of its government and its healthy respect for law, as at the time in England.

**England's** or **Britain's Finest Tudor Town** *Shrewsbury, England*. The Shropshire town is one of the best-preserved medieval towns in the country, boasting many 16th-century Tudor buildings, as described in the quotes below.

> (1) The higgledy-piggledy charms of its [i.e. Shrewsbury's] ancient half-timbered buildings make it Britain's finest Tudor town. Buckled black-and-white houses line the passageways and lanes [*Lonely Planet Great Britain*, 2005].
>
> (2) It's been called England's finest Tudor town, and with good reason. Black and white magpie buildings are everywhere, as are the "shuts" or ancient passageways which connect them [Tourist brochure, *Shrewsbury*, 2005].

**England's Garden Isle** *Isle of Wight, England*. The island off the south coast of mainland Britain is sometimes so known, and is promoted as such on a railway poster of 1914. *Cp.* **Garden of England**.

**England's Island of Flowers** *Tresco, England*. The second largest of the Isles of Scilly, off the southwest coast of England, is noted for its subtropical gardens. Hence the nickname.

> Tresco ... is utterly unspoilt, basks in a balmy climate and is renowned as 'England's Island of Flowers' [Travel ad, *The Times*, November 3, 2005].

**England's Nazareth** *Walsingham, England*. The Norfolk village (properly Little Walsingham) is so nicknamed not just because it is a place of Christian pilgrimage, like the Israeli city, the boyhood home of Jesus, but because this came about when in the 11th century a local widow was inspired by a vision to build a replica of the house in Nazareth in which the angel Gabriel appeared to the Virgin Mary.

> Even the sky at night provided sign-posts to the shrine — the Milky Way was renamed the Walsingham Way as it was said to point pilgrims in the right direction for what became known as England's Nazareth [Quentin Cooper and Paul Sullivan, *Maypoles, Martyrs and Mayhem*, 1994].

**England's Prettiest Village** *Castle Combe, England*. The Wiltshire village, set beside a trout stream in a deep valley with a market cross and old stone cottages, is famous for its "chocolate box" charm.

> (1) Chosen in 1962 as the prettiest village in England, Castle Combe survived a Hollywood invasion four years later [when the movie *Doctor Doolittle* was filmed here] [*AA Book of British Villages*, 1980].
>
> (2) Castle Combe ... has been voted England's prettiest village (it is pretty, but not that pretty, by any means) [Geoffrey Grigson in Speaight, p. 73].
>
> (3) Castle Combe claims to be the prettiest village in England and, frankly, this is hard to dispute [*Lonely Planet Great Britain*, 2005].

**England's Umbrella** *Ireland*. The reference is to Ireland's heavy rainfall. Most rain in England arrives from the southwest, so falls first on Ireland before reaching the larger country. *Cp.* **Urinal of the Planets**.

**English Alps, the** *Malvern Hills, England*. An old nickname for the hills in western England, southwest of Worcester. They are a modest equivalent of the Alps, and their highest point rises to only 1,394 ft (425 m).

> Mauborn hills or as some term them the English Alps [Celia Fiennes, *Journeys, c.* 1685–96].

**English Jerusalem, the** *Torrington, England*. The Devon hilltop town, also known as Great Torrington, has been so nicknamed not for its religious associations but for its geographical situation, as indicated in the quote below.

> Sometimes known as the 'English Jerusalem' — because of its position on a high escarpment, clustering around the castle and protected by a horseshoe bend in the River Torridge — the town is visited principally by those interested in its large glassworks [John Julius Norwich, ed., *Treasures of Britain*, 2002].

**English Lakes** see in Appendix 1, p. 269.

**English Lucerne, the** *Ullswater, England*. The second-largest lake in the Lake District is so advertised in a Great Northern Railway poster of 1901, comparing its scenic mountain setting with that of the Swiss lake.

**English Mentone, the** *Parkstone, England*. The resort and residential district of Poole, Dorset, received its nickname by virtue of its sheltered situation, suggesting that of the famous French resort of Menton (Italian Mentone), on the Mediterranean coast below a rocky amphitheater.

> It lies almost hidden among its pine trees, and, being so well screened from cold winds, it has been called the "English Mentone" [*Holiday Guide 1952: Area No. 5, South & South East England*].

**English Naples, the** *Bournemouth, England*. A grandiose name for the popular resort, which lies on the south coast of England, as Naples lies on the south coast of Italy.

**English Riviera** see in Appendix 1, p. 269.

**English Town, the** *Pau, France.* The town in southwestern France was a favorite resort with English aristocrats in the 19th century, and some of the English institutions, such as a hunt and a golf club, remain today.

> For 100 years, the place was was barely out of the society pages in Britain and, later, the United States. They called it "Pau, *ville anglaise*" [*Sunday Times*, January 2, 2005].

**Entertainment Capital of the World, the** *Las Vegas, Nevada, USA.* A self-promotional name for the city, implying that it has more to offer the visitor than its famous casinos, which gave it the narrower epithet **Gambling Capital of the World.** *Cp.* **America's Playground.**

**Environment City** *Leicester, England.* A self-promotional title for the city, referring to the various environmental initiatives planned by the city council.

**Enzed** *New Zealand.* A phonetic spelling of the more usual abbreviation **NZ.**

> (1) We christened the Adjutant "Kiwi"—the symbol of En-Zed [*Chronicles of the New Zealand Expeditionary Force*, June 21, 1918].
> (2) 'I swear that mare has the hardest mouth in En Zed' [Colleen McCullough, *The Thorn Birds*, 1977].

**EP** *Eastern Province, South Africa.* The province's abbreviated name is frequently found in sports reports.

> A former EP rugby player had been at the forefront of it all [*Daily Dispatch*, June 5, 1984].

**Epitome of the Universe, the** *Paris, France.* The French capital was so microcosmically described by the historian and political writer Charles de Peyssonel in his book *Les Numéros* (1782).

> Paris was, Charles de Peyssonel agreed in 1782, 'the Epitome of the Universe, a vast and shapeless city, full of marvels, virtues, vices and follies' [Colin Jones, *Paris*, 2004].

**Equality State, the** *Wyoming, USA.* The Territory of Wyoming granted women the right to vote in all elections in 1869, when the National Woman Suffrage Association was formed. Later, the state's constitution, approved in 1889, was the first in the world to grant full voting rights to women, while in 1924 Wyoming was the first state to elect a woman governor. Hence the nickname.

> Wyoming is called The Equality State because, according to Mr. [Moses F.] Sweetser, the author of a most comprehensive "Handbook of the United States," ... "ever since its organisation men and women have been accorded equal rights to

vote, and the people have ratified the same principle in the State Constitution. This was the first community in the world to inaugurate woman suffrage, and twenty years of trial have shown that the best class of women vote, without detriment to themselves, and with increasing detriment to the States. They give their ballots to the best and truest men, and for this reason both parties are compelled to nominate worthy candidates" [Wagner 1893, p. 35].

**Eridan** *Po River, Italy.* The river's poetic name derives from the Eridanus of classical mythology, which was dubiously identified with it.

> So down the silver streams of Eridan,
>   On either side bankt with a lily wall
>   Whiter than both, rides the triumphant swan
> [Giles Fletcher, *Christs Victorie, and Triumph in Heaven, and Earth, Over, and After Death*, 1610].

**Erin** *Ireland.* The poetic name of Ireland is an anglicized form of its Irish name of *Éirinn*, grammatically the dative form of *Éire* (*see* **Eire**). It occurs frequently in the works of 19th-century romantic poets, and notably in the *Irish Melodies* of Thomas Moore, as in quote (3) below.

> (1) Dear Erin, gow sweetly thy green bosom rises!
>   An emerald set in the ring of the sea [John Philpot Curran, "Cushla ma-Cree," late 18th century].
> (2) The natives call this island Erin; from which the names Ierna, Juverna, Iouernia, Overnia, and Hibernia are plainly derived [Thomas Comerford, *The History of Ireland*, 1807].
> (3) Erin, O Erin! thus bright through the tears
>   Of a long night of bondage thy spirit appears
> [Thomas Moore, "Erin, O Erin!," *Irish Melodies*, 1821].
> (4) "God save Ireland!" said the heroes;
>   "God save Ireland," say they all:
>   Whether on the scaffold high
>   Or the battlefield we die,
>   Oh, what matter when for Erin dear we fall
> [Timothy Daniel Sullivan, "God Save Ireland," 1867].

**Erythraean Sea** or **Main, the** *Indian Ocean.* A classical name for the Arabian Sea, Red Sea, and Persian Gulf, or more generally for the Indian Ocean. It is based on Greek *erythros*, "red," referring to the Red Sea.

> Wandering in those deserts of Africa that border the Erythræan Sea, I came to the river Nile [Benjamin Disraeli, *Contarini Fleming*, 1832].

**Eskimo Pie Land** *Alaska, USA.* A humorous nickname for the state, with its proportion of Inuit (Eskimo) inhabitants. The pun is on the name of the chocolate-coated ice cream.

**Etchil** *Etchilhampton, England.* A short colloquial name for the Wiltshire village.

**Eternal City, the** *Rome, Italy.* The sobriquet arose in the writings of classical authors, who called Rome *urbs aeterna*, as a city supposedly built by the gods. As the gods were immortal, so the city would be eternal.

(1) When, at last, you come to the Eternal City, the first impression is, I think, a feeling of disappointment [Henry Matthews, *The Diary of an Invalid*, 1820].

(2) Twice had the eternal city bowed her low
In sullen homage to the invader's might
[Matthew Arnold, "Alaric at Rome," 1840].

(3) Michael Angelo ... designed the Eternal City [Mark Twain, *The Innocents Abroad*, 1869].

(4) "What happened to your nose," he asked. "A drunk hit me outside the hotel," Jack said feeling embarrassed. "It didn't take you long to enter into the thrilling life of the Eternal City, did it? I've been here five months and I haven't been hit yet" [Irwin Shaw, *Two Weeks in Another Town*, 1960].

(5) Rome may be the Eternal City, but Tuscany is the eternal countryside [*Sunday Times*, January 9, 2005].

**Eternal City of the West, the** *Chicago, Illinois, USA.* A name equating the great city with the **Eternal City** that was Rome.

Where was the architecture of the great city — the "Eternal City of the West"? Where was it? ... Chicago! Immense gridiron of dirty, noisy streets [Frank Lloyd Wright, *An Autobiography*, 1932 (written *c.*1887)].

**Etruria** *Tuscany, Italy.* The ancient country so named is generally equated with the modern region. The names are related, as Tuscany takes its name from the Etruscans who inhabited Etruria.

**Eureka State, the** *California, USA.* The name is that of the state's motto, "Eureka," a Greek word meaning "I have found it!," denoting the discovery of gold in 1848.

**Europe's Food Town** *Grimsby, England.* The North Lincolnshire city was long famous as one of the world's great fishing ports, and is now a major center of frozen-food production. Hence the nickname.

**Euxine Sea, the** *Black Sea.* The poetic name has a devious origin. The Old Persian word for the sea was *akhshaena*, meaning "dark," referring to its frequent storms. This was adopted untranslated by the Greeks, who called it *Pontos Axeinos, pontos* meaning "sea." But *Axeinos* came to be interpreted as *Axenos*, "inhospitable" (from *a-*, "not," and *xenos*, "friend") so that it was the "inhospitable sea." Later, the Greeks altered this unfavorable name to the favorable *Pontos Euxenos*, "hospitable sea," and English adopted this, also untranslated, in the present form.

(1) There's not a sea the passenger e'er pukes in,
Turns up more dangerous breakers than the Euxine [Lord Byron, *Don Juan*, 1823].

(2) Flooded plains

Through which the groaning Danube strains
To the drear Euxine [Matthew Arnold, "Resignation," 1849].

**Everglades State, the** *Florida, USA.* The name comes from the Everglades, the great tract of marshland in the south of the state.

**Evergreen State, the** *Washington, USA.* The name alludes to Washington's many evergreen forests and to its green grass, which does not fade even in winter thanks to the mild, moist climate. The state flag is also green.

**Ever-Loyal City, the** *Oxford, England.* The city was given this name for its steadfast loyalty to Charles I during the Civil War.

**Evil Empire, the** *Soviet Union.* A highly charged nickname for **Russia** in its incarnation as the Soviet Union. The name was generally prevalent in the West, and especially in the USA, during the Cold War between the superpowers. *Cp.* **Red Empire**.

(1) I urge you to beware the temptation of pride — the temptation of blithely declaring yourselves above it all and label both sides equally at fault, to ignore the facts of history and the aggressive impulses of an evil empire [Ronald Reagan, speech at Annual Convention of the National Association of Evangelicals, Orlando, Florida, March 8, 1983].

(2) From 1946 to 1988, our American leaders pounded into us that the Soviet Union was the Evil Empire, a huge Red Menace that would brainwash our youth and that ... had the capacity to blow us to smithereens [Michael Moore, *Downsize This!*, 1996].

**Excelsior State, the** *New York, USA.* The state takes its nickname from its motto ("Excelsior"), adopted on March 16, 1778, and appearing on the state seal, where it is accompanied by the device of a rising sun. The word itself, as in the well-known quote below, is traditionally explained to mean "Ever Upward," but grammatically it is a Latin adjective ("higher"), not an adverb.

The shades of night were falling fast,
As through an Alpine village passed
A youth, who bore, 'mid snow and ice,
A banner with a strange device,
Excelsior! [H.W. Longfellow, "Excelsior," 1841].

**Exon** *Exeter, England.* An abbreviation of Latin *Exoniensis*, "of Exeter," used in the official signature of the bishop of Exeter and also in the title of the Exon Domesday, an abstract of the Domesday Book covering Cornwall, Devon, Dorset, Somerset, and Wiltshire and kept at Exeter Cathedral.

**External City, the** *Rome, Italy.* The sobriquet, punning on the famous **Eternal City**, takes the Italian capital as a city whose nature and spirit are not hidden or allusive but everywhere ready to be experienced. Rome has many museums and galleries, but the city is really its own museum and its own gallery.

**Extra** *see* **Kirton**

**Eye of Greece, the** *(1) Athens, Greece; (2) Corinth, Greece; (3) Sparta, Greece.* The name was given in classical times to either of the famous cities Athens and Sparta, or to both together, as "the Two Eyes of Greece," seeing them as a source of light or intelligence. Corinth has also been so called.

(Athens) Behold
Where on th' Ægean shore a city stands,
Built nobly, pure the air and light the soil —
Athens, the eye of Greece, mother of arts
And eloquence [John Milton, *Paradise Regained*, 1671].

**Eye of the Baltic, the** *Gotland, Sweden.* The name has been applied to the island as a Swedish "lookout" in the Baltic Sea.

**Fair City, the** *(1) Dublin, Ireland; (2) Perth, Scotland.* Both the Irish city and the Scottish town are so nicknamed for their picturesque riverside setting, beautiful buildings, and elegant layout. (Dublin's impressive architectural heritage has made it one of Europe's finest cities.) The former Scottish capital is additionally associated with the Fair Maid of Perth, the beautiful young heroine of Sir Walter Scott's novel so titled (1828), as if the town had adopted her female persona. (The Fair Maid's House in Perth is the town's best-known attraction.)

(1) (Dublin) In Dublin's fair city,
Where girls are so pretty [James Yorkston, "Cockles and Mussels," 1884].
(2) (Perth) It is a pleasant town, in splendid surroundings and is nicknamed "The Fair City" [Johnson, p. 198].
(3) (Dublin) The Fair City today is a monument to past periods of prosperity and civil strife [Simon Heffer, review of Christine Casey, ed., *The Buildings of Ireland: Dublin, Times Literary Supplement*, December 2, 2005].

**Fairest Cape, the** *Cape of Good Hope, South Africa.* The sobriquet has been attributed to Sir Francis Drake, but probably originated with a crew member accompanying him on his voyage around the world (1577–80). By extension the name can also apply to Cape Town and the surrounding area.

Please don't leave your empty, broken bottles on beaches — or anywhere else in scenic and picnic spots in our Fairest Cape [*Cape Times*, December 28, 1987].

**Fairest Jewel in the Imperial Crown, the** *India.* In Victorian times, India was traditionally regarded, partly for exotic reasons, as the most valuable possession of the British Empire, the "imperial crown" being that of the monarch. *Cp.* **Jewel in the Crown.**

**Faithful City, the** *Worcester, England.* The sobriquet refers to the city's royalist allegiance in the civil wars of 1642–51, and the city motto is still "Faithful in war and peace."

The Faithful City saw the King's downfall [in 1651] and the triumph of the hated Roundheads [Harry Soan and John Moore in Speaight, p. 162].

**Faithful County, the** *Offaly, Ireland.* The nickname has a sporting reference, from the successes of the county's Gaelic Athletic Association teams. The name itself is said to have been given in the mid–1930s by Association President Bob O'Keeffe.

**Faithfu' Toun, the** *Linlithgow, Scotland.* The town was so nicknamed by the Stuarts for its loyalty to James VI of Scotland (James I of England), offering refuge to the royal court, privy council, and court of session in 1596 when there was disorder in the capital, Edinburgh.

**Falls City** *Louisville, Kentucky, USA.* The city is so nicknamed for its location opposite the Falls of the Ohio River. Falls elsewhere have given a regular name, as Falls City, Nebraska, near the falls of the Big Nemaha River.

**Fame Town** *Canton, Ohio, USA.* The city is so known for the Professional Football Hall of Fame located here.

**Famous Foodie Capital, the** *Ludlow, England.* The Shropshire town holds an annual food festival and boasts three highly-rated restaurants. *Cp.* **Gourmetville.**

A small Shropshire village near the "famous foodie capital" of Ludlow [*The Times Magazine*, 17 January 2004].

**Famous Potatoes** *Idaho, USA.* The state is noted nationwide for its potatoes.

**Fanning Island** *Tabuaeran, Kiribati.* The island was discovered in 1798 by the American navigator Captain Edward Fanning and is still sometimes known by its former name.

**Far East** see in Appendix 1, p. 269.

**Farinaceous City, the** *Adelaide, Australia.* The former nickname of the South Australia capital refers to the wheat that was the state's chief export.

[Adelaide] has also been nicknamed the Farinaceous City ... The colony ... is regarded as one devoted in a special manner to the production of flour [Anthony Trollope, *Australia and New Zealand*, 1873].

**Farm Belt** see in Appendix 1, p. 269.
**Far West** see in Appendix 1, p. 269.
**Fashionable Frinton** *Frinton-on-Sea, En-*

*gland.* The genteel Essex resort acquired its epithet following visits here in the 1920s by film stars and royalty.

**Fashion Capital of Europe, the** *London, England.* A self-promotional name for the British capital from the last quarter of the 20th century.

> "Fashion capital" is another phrase often used to describe England's bustling metropolis [Travel brochure issued with *The Times*, May 21, 2005].

**Fat City, the** *Bologna, Italy.* The city is famous for its food and especially its pasta, of which spaghetti Bolognese is a well-known variety. Hence its nickname (Italian *la grassa*).

> (1) Bologna — the nation's gastronomic capital, known to Italians as La Grassa ("the fat") [*Sunday Times*, June 12, 2005].
>
> (2) It's La Grassa, the Fat One, the oh-my-god-I-can't-eat-another-thing-but-go-on-pass-me-that-prosciutto one, where you can eat like a medieval duke at medieval prices [*Sunday Times*, November 27, 2005].

**FAT DAD** *see* **FAT LAD**

**Father Knickerbocker** *New York City, USA.* The nickname ultimately derives from Washington Irving's *A History of New York, by Diedrich Knickerbocker* (1809), with George Cruikshank's illustrations of Dutchmen wearing knee breeches ("knickerbockers").

**Fatherland, the** *Germany.* The name translates German *der Vaterland* as a patriotic name for Germany. The title occurs in the opening lines of the national anthem, as in quote (1) below, adopted by West Germany in 1952 and reaffirmed by the united Federal Republic in 1991. (The words are now limited to the third verse of the original, which began "Deutschland, Deutschland über alles," and was the national anthem from 1922 to 1945.) The German word is itself sometimes used in an English context, as in quote (2). *Cp.* **Motherland.**

> (1) Einigkeit und Recht und Freiheit
> Für das deutsche Vaterland!
> (Unity and Right and Freedom
> For the German Fatherland!) [August Heinrich Hoffmann von Fallersleben, "Deutschland, Deutschland über alles," 1841].
>
> (2) A stone slab had carved upon it the ... names of the village boys dead for the Vaterland in '14–'18 [Nicolas Freeling, *Gadget*, 1977].
>
> (3) "Patriotism begins with honesty," Ijoma Mangold, a young novelist, said. "When [Chancellor] Schröder put his own grip on power at risk for the sake of the Fatherland, that was true patriotism" [*The Times*, January 3, 2005].
>
> (4) Germany's *Deutschland über Alles* is unthinkable without [mention of] the fatherland [*The Times*, September 27, 2005].

**Father Nile** *Nile River, Egypt.* The word "Father" is traditionally prefixed to the name of an important river. The Nile is the longest river in the world and flows through three African countries.

**Father of Rivers, the** *(1) Apidanus, Greece; (2) Lydias, Greece.* Two classical names for the Greek rivers. The Apidanus, in Thessaly, and the Lydias, in Macedonia, are both so termed by Euripides, the former in *Hecuba*, the later in *Bacchae.*

**Father of Waters, the** *(1) Irrawaddy River, Myanmar; (2) Mississippi River, USA; (3) Nile River, Egypt.* The three major rivers are equally so nicknamed. The many tributaries of the Mississippi, especially the Missouri, are regarded as its "offspring." The name of the Irrawaddy means literally "risen from the waters," a near equivalent, while the Nile is also **Father Nile.** The Mississippi equally has a like name, the Native American original meaning "great waters."

> (1) (Nile) The mighty emperour, in whose dominions the Father of Waters begins his course [Samuel Johnson, *Rasselas*, 1759].
>
> (2) (Mississippi) Not too far along I found a pleasant resting place where I could sit and munch and contemplate and stare out over the stately, brown, slow-moving Father of Waters as my spirit required [John Steinbeck, *Travels with Charley in Search of America*, 1962].
>
> (3) (Mississippi) Along the trade route that linked the towns of the Chickasaw nation with the river called Father of Waters there lay a wild and dark swamp that was sacred to the Chickasaw people [Thomas McNamee, *A Story of Deep Delight*, 1990].

**Father Thames** *Thames River, England.* A personification of the English river in the same vein as **Father Nile** and **Father Tiber,** among others. *Cp.* **Old Father Thames.**

> (1) In vain on Father Thames she calls for aid [Alexander Pope, "Windsor Forest," 1704].
>
> (2) Say, Father Thames, for thou hast seen
> Full many a sprightly race
> Disporting on thy margent green
> The paths of pleasure trace [Thomas Gray, "Ode on a Distant Prospect of Eton College," 1747].

**Father Tiber** *Tiber River, Italy.* A personification of the Italian river, which flows through Rome, on the lines of **Father Nile.**

> 'Oh, Tiber! father Tiber!
> To whom the Romans pray,
> A Roman's life, a Roman's arms,
> Take thou in charge this day!' [Lord Macaulay, "Horatius," *Lays of Ancient Rome*, 1842].

**FAT LAD** *Northern Ireland.* The nickname is an acronym of the initials of the **Six Counties.** Nationalists prefer FAT DAD, substituting Derry (*see* **Stroke City**) for Londonderry.

**Fattening-Up State, the** *Pennsylvania, USA.* A former vagrants' nickname for the state, referring to its rich pickings.

**Faulkner Country** see in Appendix 1, p. 269.

**Feather Capital of the World** *see* **Ostrich-Feather Capital of the World**

**Federal City, the** *Washington, DC, USA.* Washington is coextensive with the federal district of Columbia. Hence the nickname.

**Fens** see in Appendix 1, p. 269.

**Fernando Po** *Bioko, Equatorial Guinea.* The island is still sometimes popularly known by its original name, that of the Portuguese explorer (Fernão do Po) who discovered it.

**Ferry, the** *Broughty Ferry, Scotland.* A local short form of the name of the suburb of Dundee, where a ferry formerly crossed the Tay River.

**Fertile Crescent** see in Appendix 1, p. 269.

**Festival State, the** *South Australia, Australia.* The nickname reflects the importance of the Adelaide Festival of Arts, held in the state capital in even-numbered years.

**Festival Town of England, the** *Cheltenham, England.* The Gloucestershire spa town claims to host some type of arts, cultural, or sporting festival at least one day in every five. Hence its self-promotional title.

**Fifth Quarter of the Globe, the** *Romney Marsh, England.* The area of marshland in Kent earned its nickname through its distinctiveness, as a "world of its own."

(1) The World, according to the best geographers, is divided into Europe, Asia, Africa, America, and Romney Marsh. In this last-named, and fifth, quarter of the globe, a Witch may still be occasionally discovered [Richard Barham, *The Ingoldsby Legends*, "Mrs. Botherby's Story," 1840].

(2) In the Middle Ages they used to say: "These be the four quarters of the world: Europe, Asia, Africa, and the Romney Marsh." But that was before Columbus committed his indiscretion [Ford Madox Ford, *Return to Yesterday*, 1932].

**51st State, the** *(1) England or Britain; (2) Liverpool, England; (3) Puerto Rico, West Indies.* Puerto Rico is so nicknamed as its citizens have US citizenship. It is thus an "extra" state to the existing 50 states of the USA, and has been close to gaining official status as such. Liverpool was long Britain's main transatlantic port and regularly traded with America, while hundreds of emigrants to the USA set sail from here between 1830 and 1930. England is sometimes referred to as the 51st state when regarded as following the trends of the USA.

(England) If the fads of the young follow their usual practice and pass over into the settled habits of middle age, ... then in another quarter-century England indeed will be the fifty-first state [Alistair Cooke, "New Ways in English Life," *Manchester Guardian*, July 16, 1959].

**55 Degrees North** *Newcastle upon Tyne, England.* The nickname of the city, based on its geographical coordinates, became familiar as the title of a TV cop drama in 2004.

Why is the series called *55 Degrees North*? No clues are given. Is that supposed to be Newcastle's grid reference? [*The Times*, July 7, 2004].

**Fifty-Three** see in Appendix 1, p. 269.

**Filmdom** *Hollywood, Los Angeles, California, USA.* A fairly obvious nickname for the major movie center. *Cp.* **Moviedom.**

**Finger Lickin' Country** *Kentucky, USA.* The nickname is extracted from the commercial slogan "finger lickin' good" for Kentucky Fried Chicken (KFC), which had its beginnings in North Corbin, Kentucky, in the 1930s.

**First Black Republic, the** *Haiti, West Indies.* The republic of Haiti dates from 1804, when black slaves and freed mulattoes rebelled against French rule and declared their country's independence. Hence the unique title.

**First Capital, the** *Moscow, Russia.* The sobriquet translates the city's Russian title *Pervoprestolnaya* (from *pervo-*, "first," and *prestol,* "throne"), denoting that Moscow was Russia's first capital (from 1547 to 1712), before St. Petersburg (from 1712 to 1917), the throne being that of the czar. In 1918, after the Russian Revolution, the capital of Soviet Russia reverted to Moscow, where it remains today.

**First State, the** *Delaware, USA.* Delaware earned its title as the first state to ratify the US Constitution, on December 7, 1787.

**Fish-Hooks** *Ficheux, France.* A British soldiers' World War I version of the name of the village south of Arras.

**Fitzrovia** see in Appendix 1, p. 269.

**Fiume** *Rijeka, Croatia.* The ancient city and seaport is still alternately known by its Italian name, especially in Italy. Both names mean simply "river."

**Five Counties** see in Appendix 1, p. 269.

**Five Towns, the** *Stoke-on-Trent, England.* The five towns that came to make up the Staffordshire city are Tunstall, Burslem, Hanley, Longton, and Stoke itself, the first four of these now being districts. In the novels of Arnold Bennett, notably *Anna of the Five Towns* (1902), the five are disguised respectively as Turnhill, Bursley, Hanbridge, Longshaw, and Knype. *Cp.* **Potteries.**

It is doubtful whether the people of Southern England have even yet realized how much introspection there is going on all the time in the Five Towns [Max Beerbohm, *A Christmas Garland*, 1912].

**Flag Town** *Flagstaff, Arizona, USA.* A nickname based on the city's real name.

**Flatlands** see in Appendix 1, p. 269.

**Flemo** *Flemington, Melbourne, Australia*. A shortening of the city district name, with the typical Australian -o, as for **Darlo**.

**Fleuron of the Americas, the** *Brazil*. The name denotes a symbolic "flower" in the literal and metaphorical sense. (A fleuron is properly a flower-shaped ornament.) The phrase occurs in the words of the country's national anthem, by Joaquim Osório Duque Estrada (1870–1927), as in the lines quoted below.

> Fulguras, ó Brasil, florão da América,
> Illuminado ao sol do novo mundo!
> (You gleam, O Brazil, fleuron of the Americas,
> Illuminated by the sun of the New World.)

**Flickertail State, the** *North Dakota, USA*. The flickertail is another name for Richardson's ground squirrel, a rodent found in North Dakota and also in neighboring parts of Canada. Hence the nickname.

**Floating Garden of the Atlantic, the** *Madeira, Atlantic Ocean*. The Portuguese island is a year-round resort famed for its gardens and clement weather. Hence the sobriquet. *Cp*. **Island of Eternal Spring**.

> (1) Blessed by a climate that is almost perfect all year round, this subtropical island is known as the "Floating Garden of the Atlantic" [Travel brochure issued with *The Times*, August 20, 2005].
> (2) You'll also have a full day in Madeira, known as the "Floating Garden of the Atlantic" because of its abundant flora and stunning scenery [Cruise brochure, 2005].

**Floral Folkestone** *Folkestone, England*. The Kent resort is so nicknamed for the colorful flowerbeds which run along its seafront.

**Florence of Apulia, the** *Lecce, Italy*. The name compares the town's cultural heritage and noted architecture with those of the world-famous city.

> Known as the "Florence of Apulia" its sights include a very impressive Roman amphitheatre [Travel ad, *The Times*, August 14, 2004].

**Florence of Suffolk, the** *Ipswich, England*. A rather grand comparison between the Suffolk town and the famous Italian cultural center.

**Florence of the North, the** *Dresden, Germany*. The 18th-century sobriquet compared the city, famed for its art galleries and museums, with the great Italian cultural and artistic center.

**Florence of the West, the** *Chicago, Illinois, USA*. The city was so nicknamed by Theodore Dreiser as in the quote below.

> To whom may the laurels as laureate of this Florence of the West yet fall? This singing flame of a city, this all America, this poet in chaps and buckskin, this rude, raw Titan, this Burns of a city! [Theodore Dreiser, *The Titan*, 1914].

**Florence on the Elbe** *Dresden, Germany*. An alternate name for the **Florence of the North**, bestowed on the city on the Elbe River by the 18th-century German poet Johann Gottfried Herder. The name (German *Elbflorenz*) refers to the splendor of Dresden's baroque buildings, reflecting its rich cultural heritage.

> [The Allies] poured ... a firestorm of incendiary bombs onto "the Florence on the Elbe," the pride of Saxony [Dodd/Donald, p. 418].

**Florida's Crown** see in Appendix 1, p. 269.

**Flour City** *(1) Minneapolis, Minnesota, USA; (2) Rochester, New York, USA*. Both cities are noted for their flour milling, in the case of Rochester thanks to the Erie Canal.

**Flower City, the** *Springfield, Illinois, USA*. The state capital earned its sobriquet for its attractive setting on the Sangamon River.

**Flower of Scotland, the** *Aberdeen, Scotland*. The city takes its nickname from its attractive architecture and its agreeable seaside setting. "Flower of Scotland" is also the title of a popular song of the 1960s by the Corrie Folk Trio, a Scottish folk act, subsequently adopted as the unofficial Scottish national anthem.

> Aberdeen, "The Flower of Scotland," lies in a picturesque spot on the North Sea coast [*Baedeker's Scotland*, 3d ed., 1999].

**Flower of the East** or **Levant** or **Orient, the** *Zakynthos (Zante), Greece*. The beautiful Greek island, the third-largest of the Ionian group, was so named by the Venetians, who held it from c.1485 to 1797.

> (1) The Venetians, who ruled Zakynthos for more than 300 years, described it as "the flower of the east" [*The Times*, July 4, 2005].
> (2) The Venetians christened Zante 'the flower of the Orient,' and its [*sic*] easy to see why as this typically Greek island is one of outstanding beauty [Holiday brochure, 2005].

**Flower of the Indies, the** *Maldives*. The republic lies on a number of coral islands (atolls) in the Indian Ocean. The poetic nickname is said to have been bestowed by Marco Polo.

**Flower of the Levant** *see* **Flower of the East**

**Flower of the Orient** *see* **Flower of the East**

**Flower of the West Indies, the** *Jamaica, West Indies*. The nickname pays tribute to the island's natural attractions as well as its colorful African heritage.

**Flower State** *see* **Land of Flowers**

**Flowery Kingdom** or **Land, the** *China*. The epithet is a metaphorical description of a polished and civilized nation. It translates Chinese *huáguó*, from *huá*, "brilliant," "flourishing," and *guó*, "country," "nation." *Cp*. **Middle Kingdom**.

> (1) Two of the big Chinese companies have had

men at work ... exhuming the bodies of their dead countrymen for shipment home to China where all loyal citizens of the Flowery Kingdom wish to have their last resting place [*Daily Colonist* (Victoria, British Columbia), October 30, 1901].

(2) FLOWERY LAND, THE: A common Chinese name for China, similar to *la belle France*, and not necessarily implying the presence of flowers [Giles, p. 96].

**Flowery Land** *see* (1) **Flowery Kingdom**; (2) **Land of Flowers**

**Flowery Town, the** *Maubeuge, France.* The industrial town near the Belgian border was awarded its title (French, *La Ville Fleurie*) for its attractive gardens.

**Flu Capital of Scotland, the** *Kirriemuir, Scotland.* A rather unfair epithet for a town whose recent flu epidemics can hardly be attributed to its hilly setting.

[Scottish author Don] Paterson ... is quoted as calling Kirriemuir, his domicile in north-east Scotland, the country's "self-styled Flu Capital" [*Times Literary Supplement*, November 26, 2004].

**Flushing** *Vlissingen, Netherlands.* The English form of the Dutch seaport's name is still regularly in use. It rightly suggests "flush," relating to the current or stream of the West Scheldt estuary on which it lies.

**Fly Speck** or **Fly-Speck Isle, the** *Tasmania, Australia.* An old humorously belittling nickname for the island, which is tiny in comparison to the Australian mainland. It is not just a "speck" (*see* **Speck**) but a "fly speck," like the small stain made by an insect's excrement.

Tasmania has lost its oldest inhabitant. ... He had inhabited the Flyspeck Isle since 1828 [*The Gadfly* (Adelaide), April 25, 1906].

**Fódla** or **Fótla** *Ireland.* The old poetic name for Ireland derives from one of the three sister goddesses whose names vied to be chosen for the country. The other two were **Banba** and Eriu, the latter being the winner (*see* **Eire**). The name of the mountain area of Atholl in Scotland derives from Fódla's name and means "new Ireland."

**Foggieloan** *Aberchirder, Scotland.* The village northwest of Aberdeen is known by this informal Scots name, meaning "mossy bank," referring to its location. It was founded in 1764 in the form of three long parallel streets that slope gradually down from a hilltop.

Aberchirder has a nickname, Foggieloan, meaning 'mossy field,' an apt description of its site [Macnie/McLaren, p. 308].

**Fogland** *England or Britain.* The not entirely accurate blanket nickname for Britain originated in Australia. *Cp.* **Fogtown**.

An English chap and fast shearer ... used to go 'home' to Fogland every year [*The Bulletin* (Sydney), February 7, 1907].

**Fogtown** *London, England.* The Australian nickname for the British capital was formerly applied with some justification.

Writes my Fogtown correspondent:—'...all the South Australians ... who happened to be wandering loose about London just then gathered themselves into a bunch' [*The Gadfly* (Adelaide), June 20, 1906].

**Folkloric Capital of Bolivia, the** *Oruro, Bolivia.* The city is known as much for its silver (now tin) mines as for its self-promoted folkore.

**Folk Music Capital of the World, the** *Mountain View, Arkansas, USA.* The town is promoted under this name by its chamber of commerce for the various festivals organized by the Ozark Folk Center here.

**Food Capital of the World, the** *Iowa, USA.* The state leads the nation in hog, corn, and soybean production. Hence the nickname.

**Fool's Paradise, the** *London, England.* A former nickname for the British capital, referring to its false promise of riches and success.

[The Dammee Captain] makes *London* (by a new denomination called *Fool's Paradise*) his tenement, from which he receives good round summes of money for rent [Anon., *The Catterpillers of this Nation Anatomized*, 1659].

**Forbidden City, the** *(1) Beijing, China; (2) Lhasa, Tibet.* The familiar name of the Chinese capital properly applies to the imperial palace at its center, built in the early 15th century and the largest of its kind in the world. Entry was forbidden to all except members of the imperial family and their servants. The name translates Chinese *jìn chéng*, from *jìn*, "to forbid," and *chéng*, "city." For the Tibetan capital, Lhasa, the term is more generally applicable, referring both to the city's difficulty of access and to the potential hostility of its religious leaders to outside visitors.

(Beijing) While the Chinese speak of the Crimson City, in western countries the name Forbidden City has become common usage [Leier, p. 180].

**Forbidden Island, the** *Niihau, Hawaii, USA.* The smallest of the inhabited Hawaiian islands has long been closed to outsiders. Hence its nickname.

**Forbidden Land, the** *(1) Korea; (2) Tibet.* Both countries long closed their frontiers to foreigners. Korea's isolation caused it to be known as the **Hermit Kingdom**, while the Tibetan capital, Lhasa, was the **Forbidden City**.

**Foreigner State, the** *New Jersey, USA.* The nickname alludes to Joseph Bonaparte, king of

Spain, who fled to Bordentown, New Jersey, after the defeat of his brother, Napoleon I, at the Battle of Waterloo (1815). He bought himself an estate of around 1,500 acres on the outskirts of the city and developed a "little kingdom" from 1816 to 1839. For the same reason New Jersey was also dubbed "New Spain State" and even "State of Spain."

**Forest City** *(1) Cleveland, Ohio, USA; (2) Portland, Maine, USA; (3) Savannah, Georgia, USA.* All three cities are so nicknamed for their prominent trees. Cleveland became noted for the ornamental trees that bordered its streets, Portland for its elms and other shade trees, and Savannah for the pride of India trees (*Melia azederach*) that shaded its streets.

**Forge of Germany, the** *Ruhr, Germany.* The Ruhr was long a major mining area and key manufacturing center. Hence the sobriquet, now less valid than formerly since the decline of the coal and steel industries in the 1980s.

**Forgotten City, the** *Ouadane, Mauritania.* The oasis village was formerly a settlement of some size. Hence the name, which could equally apply to any place that once had a large and flourishing population.

> The seasonal Harmattan wind blows sand and dust south from the Sahara through the "forgotten city" of Ouadane in Mauritania [Photo caption, *The Times*, August 19, 2005].

**Forgotten Eden, the** *Praslin, Seychelles.* A promotional name that could apply to any remote or exotic "paradise." It is "forgotten," but invites the visitor or vacationer to "rediscover" it.

> The "Forgotten Eden," the second largest island of the Seychelles is a wonderful place [Travel ad, *Sunday Times Magazine*, October 31, 2004].

**Formosa** *Taiwan.* The name was long familiar for the island republic off southeastern China, and is still sometimes found as an alternate. It arose among the Portuguese, who visited the island in 1590 and named it *Ilha Formosa*, "beautiful island." Its Chinese name means "terrace bay."

> Tai-Wan is the name given to the island which was formerly called Formosa. The Japanese took it from China in 1894–5 ... Soon after, they changed the name from Formosa to Tai-wan. Now that the Japanese have been conquered, China will probably regain Tai-wan and rename it Formosa [Johnson, p. 237].

**Forster Country** see in Appendix 1, p. 269.

**Fort Bill** *Fort William, Scotland.* A friendly nickname for the town and tourist resort on Loch Linnhe in western Scotland.

> Fort William, known by the many walkers and climbers that come here as "Fort Bill," should be a gem [*The Rough Guide to Scotland*, 1998].

**Fort Liquordale** *Fort Lauderdale, Florida, USA.* A none too subtle punning alteration of the city's name, referring to one method of relaxation and recreation enjoyed by the visitors and vacationers who flock to the popular resort.

**Fortunate Isles** or **Islands, the** *(1) Canary Islands, Spain; (2) Madeira, Portugal.* In classical mythology, the Fortunate Isles, also known as the Islands of the Blessed (or Blest), were so called as the abode of the happy or blessed dead in the Western Ocean. They were later traditionally identified with the Canaries and Madeira, which appropriately lie to the west of the African continent. (The Islands of the Blessed is the older name, and originated among the Greeks. The Fortunate Isles is a Roman name, and came later.) *Cp.* **Hesperides**. In quote (2) below, the name is reflected (perhaps intentionally) in that of the cruise ship, where it is Spanish for "Fortune Coast." (The suggestion of "costs a fortune" is, quite literally, unfortunate.) *See also* **Islands of the Blessed**.

> (1) (Canaries) Contents, The fortunate Ilandes, otherwyse called the Ilandes of Canaria [Richard Eden, *A Treatyse of the New India*, 1553].
> (2) An unforgettable cruise of Morocco, the Canaries and Madeira aboard the new and spectacular *Costa Fortuna* [Travel ad, *The Times*, August 7, 2004].

**Fostershire** *Worcestershire, England.* An early 20th-century nickname for the English county, famous for its cricket team, which included the seven Foster brothers, sons of the Revd. Henry Foster of Malvern.

**Fótla** *see* **Fódla**

**Four Green Fields, the** *Ireland.* The sobriquet refers to Ireland as a united country, the "fields" being the four provinces Ulster, Munster, Leinster, and Connacht, which together make up the **Thirty-Two Counties**. The name became familiar as the title of a song by the Northern Ireland folk musician Tommy Makem. For the personification in the quote below, *see* **Kathleen Ní Houlihan**.

> "God Save Ireland" was the slogan of the middle class nationalist who dreamed of restoring to Kathleen Ni Houlihan her four green fields [James Plunkett in J.W. Boyle, ed., *Leaders and Workers*, 1966].

**Four Seas** see in Appendix 1, p. 269.

**Fourth Weimar Republic, the** *Los Angeles, California, USA.* The city came to be so nicknamed during World War II, when a number of talented German and Austrian refugees settled there, among them novelists such as the brothers Heinrich and Thomas Mann, playwrights and poets such as Bertolt Brecht, Lion Feuchtwanger, and Franz Werfel, and composers and conductors such as Arnold Schoenberg and Bruno Walter. It was so dubbed after the Weimar Republic, the nickname of Germany's republican regime from 1919, when it was established at Weimar, until the start of the Third Reich in 1933.

**Fourth World** *see* **Third World** in Appendix 1, p. 269.

**France Profonde, la** *France*. The byname, literally meaning "deep France," denotes the broad mass of French people, especially those living in rural areas, away from changing urban trends and influences.

(1) From Paris to La France Profonde, the country is profoundly anxious [*The Times*, September 1, 2005].

(2) [Limoges is] the largest city in the Limousin region. Generations have fled this very rural area of *la France profonde* for the cities [*Sunday Times*, November 20, 2005].

**Franchecaille, la** *France*. A corruption of the country's name as used by argot speakers. It is said to represent French *la France qui se caille*, "France that turns cold," referring to the changeable weather.

**Freaktown** *Gibsonton, Florida, USA*. As described in the quote below, the town is an annual venue for sideshow artists.

Burkhardt lived with his wife ... on the outskirts of Gibsonton, Florida — "Freaktown USA'"–where 7,000 [freak] sideshow performers adjourn for the winter [*The Times*, January 17, 2004].

**Free-O or Freo** *Fremantle, Australia*. A short colloquial name for the Western Australia seaport city, part of the Perth metropolitan area, with the typical Australian -o suffix as in **Darlo**.

(1) The "West End," as the old shipping office and freight district of Freo is known [*The Rough Guide to Australia*, 2001].

(2) Two stops before Freo is Cottesloe, Perth's premier beach [*Sunday Times*, November 20, 2005].

**Free State, the** *(1) Maryland, USA; (2) Orange Free State, South Africa*. Maryland was so nicknamed (originally as Maryland Free State) in 1923 by Hamilton Owens, editor of the *Baltimore Evening Sun*, by way of promoting the state's claim to be a place of refuge from the harsh legislation enforced elsewhere in the USA. The Orange Free State was so colloquially nicknamed before 1995, when it adopted the name formally. (The name was also in earlier official use for the Boer republic that existed from 1854 to 1901.)

(Orange Free State) Zondi was going it like a Free State farmer on his way to a Rugby international [James McClure, *The Steam Pig*, 1970].

**Freestone State, the** *Connecticut, USA*. The state is so nicknamed for its freestone quarries.

**French Riviera** *see* **Côte d'Azur** in Appendix 1, p. 269.

**Freo** *see* **Free-O**

**Friendliest Ghost Town in Alaska, the** *Hyder, Alaska, USA*. A touristic promotion for the mining village. The original town was destroyed by fire in 1948. There are still gold and copper mines, but a major copper mine closed in 1984. The name puns on that of Casper, the Friendly Ghost (*see* **Ghost Town**).

**Friendly City, the** *Port Elizabeth, South Africa*. A self-promotional name for the seaport city, which regards itself as welcoming for visitors.

(1) Can one really still call PE the Friendly City? I disagree. Call it Windy City by all means, but PE has lost its claim to be the Friendly City [*Weekend Post*, November 17, 1990].

(2) Port Elizabeth, the Friendly City, also cloudy tomorrow, I'm afraid [Weather forecast on Radio Algoa, October 25, 1994].

**Friendly Islands, the** *Tonga, Pacific Ocean*. The island kingdom's original name alludes to the welcome accorded Captain Cook when he landed here in 1773. It was officially replaced by the indigenous name in 1970, when the former British protectorate achieve independence, but is still occasionally used and found as an alternate name on many modern maps, e.g. in *Philip's Great World Atlas* (2001).

**Frisco** or **'Frisco** *San Francisco, California, USA*. A familiar abbreviation of the city's name, but one eschewed locally. In September 1966, two escapees from a Utah jail, Anthony Scott and Eric Neil Fischbeck, said they were from "Frisco" when questioned by University of California officers who found them sleeping on campus. The response triggered an alarm. "No one from here ever says that," said campus police sergeant David Eubanks (Dickson, p. 165).

(1) As for Frisco itself, it looked hopeless. Hundreds of tons of the wreckage had been cleared away, but hundreds of tons still remained [Martin Johnson, *Through the South Seas with Jack London*, 1913].

(2) Dance then wild guests of 'Frisco,
Yellow, bronze, white and red!
Dance by the golden gateway–
Dance tho' he smite you dead! [Vachel Lindsay, "The City that will not Repent," *Collected Poems*, 1923].

(3) "I been down and out myself. In Frisco. Nobody picked me up in no taxi either. There's one stony-hearted town." "San Francisco," I said mechanically. "I call it Frisco," he said. "The hell with them minority groups"[Raymond Chandler, *The Long Goodbye*, 1953].

(4) The bus trip from Denver to Frisco was uneventful except that my whole soul leaped to it the nearer we got to Frisco [Jack Kerouac, *On the Road*, 1957].

(5) 'Frisco is a vulgarism. It is San Francisco [Guy Egmont, *The Art of Egmontese*, 1961].

(6) Sophisticated, photogenic, foggy and fabulous, Frisco is the class act of California [*Sunday Times*, February 13, 2005].

**Frog Capital of the World, the** *Rayne, Louisiana, USA.* The town is so nicknamed for its edible frog industry. (By a strange coincidence, in this French-speaking region, the town's own name suggests an origin in Old French *raine*, "frog," although it actually derives from a 19th-century railroad employee, B.W.L. Rayne.)

The Rice Belt sports 19th-century railroad towns like Rayne, 'Frog Capital of the World,' and Crowley, the 'Rice Capital of Louisiana' [*Lonely Planet USA*, 2004].

**Frogland** *France.* The derogatory nickname derives from "Frog" as a colloquial term for a Frenchman, supposedly because the French enjoy frog's legs as a table delicacy. The name was earlier used for a low-lying district where frogs abound, as the Netherlands or the Fens in England (*see* **Fens** in Appendix 1, p. 269).

**Frogolia** *France.* A more original equivalent of **Frogland**, perhaps based on a name such as "Mongolia."

**Frostbelt** *see* **Snowbelt** in Appendix 1, p. 269.

**Frostbite Falls** *International Falls, Minnesota, USA.* The town frequently records the coldest daily temperature readings in the USA. Hence the name. *Cp.* **Icebox of the Nation.**

**Frozen Continent, the** *Antarctica.* Most of Antarctica consists of a thick ice sheet, while temperatures for the warmest month rarely rise above freezing point. *Cp.* **White Continent.**

The subject this year is Antarctica ... Footage filmed on the frozen continent shows [Professor Lloyd] Peck finding out how long he can last in the waters beneath the ice [*Four*, 2004].

**Frozen North** see in Appendix 1, p. 269.

**Frozen Wilderness, the** *Alaska, USA.* One third of Alaska lies within the Arctic Circle and has perennially frozen ground and treeless tundra. This in itself largely justifies the nickname of a state whose population is smaller than all other states except Vermont and Wyoming.

**Frying Pan of Andalusia, the** *Ecija, Spain.* The city, in southwestern Spain, is noted for its hot summers.

Since time immemorial Ecija, deep in southern Spain, has had a blazing sun in its coat of arms. Spaniards call it the "frying pan of Andalusia" [*Sunday Times*, July 25, 2004].

**F-Town** *Friedrichshain, Berlin, Germany.* A colloquial local abbreviation of the name of the capital's eastern district.

Friedrichshain (sometimes called 'F-Town' by the hipper-than-thou) [*Lonely Planet Germany*, 2004].

**Fu** or **Futa** *Futaleufú, Chile.* A shortened name of the village, used chiefly by those who visit it for sports such as rafting, kayaking, fishing, and hiking.

**Fuji of the West, the** *Mt. St. Helens, Washington, USA.* The volcanic peak, notorious for its violent eruption in 1980, was so nicknamed for its resemblance to Japan's famous sacred mountain.

If you want to know what the area around Mount St. Helens used to look like, look at Japan's Mount Fuji. Mount St. Helens was known as 'The Fuji of the west' [Donough O'Brien, *Fame by Chance*, 2003].

**Fulham-on-Sea** *Rock, England.* The Cornish seaside resort, also nicknamed **Kensington-on-Sea**, is sometimes so known for its popularity among vacationers from London (not necessarily from genteel Fulham itself).

The village of Rock has become known as 'Fulham-on-Sea' thanks to the influx of second-homers from London [Charlie Godfrey-Faussett, *Footprint England*, 2004].

**Fuming Freddie** *Fiumefreddo, Italy.* A British soldiers' World War II corruption of the name of one or other of two villages in southern Italy, now respectively distinguished as Fiumefreddo Bruzio (in Calabria) and Fiumefreddo di Sicilia (in Sicily). The name itself actually means "cold river."

**Fun City** *(1) Bletchley, England; (2) New Orleans, Louisiana, USA; (3) New York City, USA.* New Orleans and New York City can justifiably lay claim to the name, as vibrant cities noted as much for their business and commerce as their entertainment and extravagance. In the case of New York, the name is said to have originated with mayor John V. Lindsay, who during a severe transit strike in 1966 is said to have commented, "I still think it's a fun city." Newspaper writer Dick Schaap later capitalized the name in his *New York Herald Tribune* column, "What's New in Fun City." *Cp.* **Big Apple.** For Bletchley, Buckinghamshire, the name arose ironically among railroad workers for a town that grew up around a railway shed.

(1) (New York) Shortly after 10 p.m., in what tourists call the Big Apple and Fun City, Monty was in bed watching a western on black and white TV [*Maclean's*, March 1974].

(2) (New York) Whether the crowds who come to New York expect Fun City, the Big Apple, or Gotham, the city can fulfill every expectation of an admiring public [*Britannica*, vol. 24, p. 912].

**Funky Villas** *Foncquevillers, France.* A British soldiers' World War I rendering of the name of the village near Arras. At that time "funky" would have meant "nervous," "timid," as the present meaning ("trendy") dates from jazz jargon of the 1950s. (The American sense "bad-smelling" would not have applied.)

**Furry Boots City** *Aberdeen, Scotland.* A humorous nickname for the city and port, devised by a Scottish newspaper columnist in the 1980s from the local dialect question, "Fur aboots are ye from?" ("Whereabouts are you from?"), put cautiously to an unfamiliar visitor.

**Futa** *see* **Fu**

**Gabs** *Gaborone, Botswana.* An affectionate short form of the capital city's name.

**Gai Paris** *see* **Gay Paree**

**Galilee, Sea of** *Lake Tiberias, Israel.* The name is a biblical one for the freshwater lake. It occurs only in the Gospels (for example in Mark 1:16) and derives from the ancient region of northern Palestine known as Galilee.

**Gallia** *France.* The Roman name of **Gaul** was adopted as a poetic name for France.

> (1) I mean, my lords, those powers that the queen
>   Hath rais'd in Gallia, have arriv'd our coast
> [William Shakespeare, *Henry VI, Part 3*, 1595].
> (2) For gold let Gallia's legions fight,
>   Or plunder's bloody gain [Sir Walter Scott, *Minstrelsy of the Scottish Border*, 1802].

**Gallipoli** *Gelibolu, Turkey.* The English name of the Turkish seaport is still current as that of the peninsula on which it lies. The peninsula itself was the scene of heavy fighting in World War I and its name remains familiar in this historical context. (The Turkish name evolved from the Greek, meaning "beautiful city.")

**Gambling Capital of the Far East, the** *Macao, China.* The former Portuguese overseas territory is noted for its gambling casinos. Hence the name.

**Gambling Capital of the Far West** or **the World, the** *Las Vegas, Nevada, USA.* An unsurprising nickname for the leading center of gambling in the USA.

**Gamecock State, the** *South Carolina, USA.* The state gained the nickname for the supposed belligerence of its inhabitants, like that of a gamecock bred for cockfighting, and also for its opposition to the abolition of slavery.

**Gangland** *Chicago, Illinois, USA.* The city was notorious for its underground violence during and after the Prohibition era of the 1920s and 1930s. Hence the obvious nickname. *Cp.* **Sin City.**

**Gap, the** *Cumberland Gap, Tennessee, USA.* A short name for the pass through the Cumberland Plateau, famous from its use by Daniel Boone in his pioneer trips into Kentucky in the late 1760s.

> Daniel Boone told stories by Pennsylvania lamps and promised to find the Gap [Jack Kerouac, *On the Road*, 1957].

**Gaperies, the** *Paris, France.* The former nickname for the French capital, current at the turn of the 20th century, represents an elided form of **Gay Paree**, with a hint at the "gaping" English visitor.

**Garden City, the** *(1) Chicago, Illinois, USA; (2) Launceston, Australia; (3) Letchworth, England; (4) Port Harcourt, Nigeria; (5) Singapore; (6) Tsumeb, Namibia.* Chicago gained its nickname for its many private gardens. Launceston, Tasmania's second-largest city, is so called for its many public squares, parks, and reserves. The Hertfordshire town of Letchworth was the first planned "garden city" in England, founded in 1903. The concept, outlined in Ebenezer Howard's *Garden Cities of Tomorrow* (1898), was soon copied elsewhere. Port Harcourt, founded by the British in 1912, was so nicknamed for its beauty, Singapore is noted for its parks and tree-lined streets, and Tsumeb, amid desert landscapes, has contrastingly lush vegetation.

> (1) (Singapore) Singapore has been dubbed the 'Garden City' and with good reason; it's green and lush, with parks and gardens scattered everywhere [*Lonely Planet Malaysia, Singapore & Brunei*, 1999].
> (2) (Tsumeb) Streets lined with jacaranda and bougainvillea have led to it being known locally as the 'garden city' [Travel ad, *The Times Magazine*, September 3, 2005].

**Garden City by the Sea, the** *Peacehaven, England.* Peacehaven arose in World War I as a planned "plotland" on a coastal site in East Sussex. It was hardly a "garden city" in the conventional sense of the term.

> Every London tram ticket had on its obverse an advertisement for Peacehaven as "The Garden City by the Sea" [Dennis Hardy and Colin Ward, *Arcadia for All*, 1984].

**Garden City of India, the** *Bangalore, India.* The city's springlike weather, beautiful parks, dazzling flower displays, and lush vegetation all combine to give its well-deserved nickname.

> As India's garden city, Bangalore has a temperate climate that has been luring the British since the early days of the Raj [*Sunday Times*, October 30, 2005].

**Garden City of New Zealand, the** *Christchurch, New Zealand.* The city earned its nickname for its many public gardens and parks.

**Garden City of the East, the** *Yangon (Rangoon), Myanmar.* The nickname alludes to the capital city's extensive network of parks and gardens.

> A mass of shady groves, lush foliage and teak trees ... gave rise to its nickname, "the Garden City of the East" [Dodd/Donald, p. 268].

**Garden City of the Gulf, the** *Abu Dhabi, United Arab Emirates.* The capital of Abu Dhabi emirate and of the federation overall, on the southern shore of the Persian Gulf, is promoted by this name, describing its tree-lined thruways and parks, such as those laid out along the coast beside Corniche Road in the city center.

> Abu Dhabi is billed as the "garden city of the Gulf" and the InterContinental Hotel, set in parkland beside a long private beach, is the place to stay [*The Times*, March 3, 2005].

**Garden Colony** *see* **Garden Province**

**Garden County of England, the** *Cheshire, England.* A promotional name for a county that boasts many fine gardens, such as the Temple Gardens at Cholmondeley Castle, Dutch Garden at Lyme Park, and Japanese Gardens at Tatton Park. *Cp.* **Garden of England**.

> Walking in England's Garden County is a stroll in Lyme Park, or a wander through woodlands at Delamere Forest [Tourist brochure *Chester and Cheshire*, 2006].

**Garden Isle, The** *(1) England; (2) Kauai, Hawaii, USA.* England is poetically seen as a land of scenic beauty and natural bounty. *Cp.* **Garden of the World**. Kauai is the most verdant island in Hawaii. Hence its promotional name.

> (1) (England) He lived in "lotos land"— the Garden Isle of England [*Longman's Magazine*, January 1902].
>
> (2) (England) Our England is a garden that is full of stately views,
>
> Of borders, beds and shrubberies and lawns and avenues [Rudyard Kipling, "The Glory of the Garden," 1911].
>
> (3) (Kauai) Head into the valleys of Kauai, the 'Garden Isle' [Travel ad, *The Times*, January 15, 2005].

**Garden of Asia, the** *Kashgaria, China.* The region of Kashgaria, centering on the oasis city of Kashgar, is remarkable for its fertility, and this gives its nickname. *Cp.* **Land of Fruit and Melons**.

**Garden of China, the** *Kiangsi, China.* The province deserves its nickname as one of the richest agricultural regions in China.

**Garden of Cymodoce, the** *Sark, Channel Islands, UK.* The island is so called by A.C. Swinburne in a poem of this title in *Songs of the Springtides* (1880). In Greek mythology, Cymodoce ("wave-receiving") is one of the sea nymphs known as the Nereids. She is mentioned in Edmund Spenser's *The Faerie Queene* (1596).

**Garden of Ecuador, the** *Ambato, Ecuador.* The city is so named for the variety of fruit growing in its outskirts.

**Garden of Eden, the** *(1) Costa Rica; (2) Jamaica.* The name could obviously describe any paradisical place. It has been touristically applied to the Central American republic for its tropical-forest parks and nature reserves and to the **Flower of the West Indies** for its richly varied crops, mountain scenery, and fine beaches, as well as for the specific prelapsarian state enjoyed at the resort described in quote (2) below.

> (1) (Costa Rica) A kaleidoscope of vivid natural colour, Costa Rica corresponds more closely to what we imagine the Garden of Eden might have been like than any other country in the Americas [Travel ad, *The Times Magazine*, September 3, 2005].
>
> (2) (Jamaica) Hedonism II resort in Jamaica, which describes itself as a "real life garden of Eden" and which caters for many nudist holiday-makers [*The Times*, October 15, 2005].

**Garden of England, the** *(1) Herefordshire, England; (2) Isle of Wight, England; (3) Kent, England; (4) Surrey, England; (5) Worcestershire, England.* Of the five counties mentioned, the nickname is chiefly associated with Kent, in the fertile southeast of the country. Herefordshire and neighboring Worcestershire are famed for their orchards (*see* **Cider Country**), while the Isle of Wight, with its mild climate, is noted for its fruit and vegetables as well as its scenery. Surrey is so named by Jane Austen as in quote (1) below, but the epithet is not common for the county. *See also* **Garden County of England**.

> (1) (Surrey) "When you have seen more of this country, I am afraid you will think you have overrated Hartfield. Surrey is full of beauties." "Oh! yes, I am quite aware of that. It is the garden of England, you know. Surrey is the garden of England." "Yes; but we must not rest our claims on that distinction. Many counties, I believe, are called the garden of England, as well as Surrey." "No I fancy not," replied Mrs. Elton, with a most satisfied smile. "I never heard any county but Surrey called so." Emma was silenced [Jane Austen, *Emma*, 1815].
>
> (2) (Kent) "Yes, sir, Kent's my county, but even in the garden of England they can't grow finer roses than them" [Benjamin Farjeon, *The Sacred Nugget*, 1885].
>
> (3) (Kent) One of her applications was to Gillingham, in Kent, one to Kingston-on-Thames, and one to Swanwick in Derbyshire. Gillingham was such a lovely name and Kent was the Garden of England [D.H. Lawrence, *The Rainbow*, 1915].
>
> (4) (Kent) Kent is the Garden of England, but then what isn't? [Theodora Benson and Betty Askwith, *Muddling Through, or Britain in a Nutshell*, 1936].

(5) (Kent) From this ridge of chalk hills which constitute the north and south Downs we can look down and realise at once why this lovely county of ours is called the "Garden of England" [J.S. Ash in George Bennett, ed., *The Guide and Handbook to Sevenoaks & District*, 1948].

(6) (Kent) Loquacious Mrs Elton, in Jane Austen's *Emma*, will admit no county but Surrey to the title 'Garden of England.' Surrey manages pretty well ... but it has to award the palm to Kent [Alan Jenkins in Hadfield 1980, p. 179].

**Garden of Erin** *see* **Garden of Ireland**

**Garden of Europe, the** *(1) Belgium; (2) Italy.* The name is primarily associated with Italy, famous for the fertility of its soil, the variety of its vegetables, and the general beauty of its countryside. Belgium has these in rather more modest measure.

**Garden of France, the** *Touraine, France.* The historic province is noted for the beauty of its countryside and for the quality and quantity of its agricultural produce, the latter including the grapes of its many vineyards.

(1) *Je suis né et ay esté nourry jeune au jardin de France, c'est Touraine* (I was born and bred in my younger years in the garden of France, to wit, Touraine.) [François Rabelais, *Pantagruel*, 1532, translated by Thomas Urquhart and Peter Motteux, 1653].

(2) Touraine, the 'garden of France,' richest of all these rich provinces [Young, p. 205].

(3) When it comes to healthy eating, nothing beats the food of the Loire Valley. "Here, in the 'Garden of France,' we have everything," says chef Jean-Noël Lumineau [*Sunday Times*, January 9, 2005].

**Garden of Denmark, the** *Fyn, Denmark.* Denmark's second-largest island is mainly a fertile plowland, with much of it given over to horticultural crops. Hence its nickname.

**Garden of Helvetia, the** *Thurgau, Switzerland.* The canton is an agricultural region where cereals and fruit are grown. *See also* **Helvetia**.

**Garden of India, the** *Ayodhya (Oudh), India.* The historic region, now part of Uttar Pradesh state, is noted for its fertility.

**Garden of Ireland, the** *(1) Co. Carlow, Ireland; (2) Co. Wicklow, Ireland.* The adjoining counties, in the east of the republic, are noted for their natural beauty and the fertility of their soil. Wicklow also has many big houses with impressive gardens.

(1) (Wicklow) The Chinese spy satellite which some experts predicted would plunge to earth somewhere in the Garden of Ireland within the next month may now land in Limerick instead [*Sunday Tribune*, February 11, 1996].

(2) (Wicklow) You might also like to join an optional excursion to County Wicklow, celebrated as the "Garden of Ireland," where you can visit the spectacular Powerscourt Gardens [Cruise brochure, 2005].

**Garden of Italy, the** *(1) Campania, Italy; (2) Lombardy, Italy; (3) Sicily, Italy.* The name is primarily associated with Sicily, as an island region long noted for the fertility of its soil, its pleasant climate, and its natural beauty. *Cp.* **Granary of Europe**. But the two other regions also have a fair claim to the title, and Campania is famed for its vineyards.

(Lombardy) I am arriv'd for fruitful Lombardy,
  The pleasant garden of great Italy [William Shakespeare, *The Taming of the Shrew*, 1592].

**Garden of Micronesia, the** *Pohnpei, Micronesia.* The island, one of the largest in the central Pacific, owes its nickname to its fertility

**Garden of Quebec, the** *Eastern Townships, Quebec, Canada.* The region of towns and villages east of Montreal and south of the St. Lawrence is so nicknamed for its scenic countryside.

**Garden of Scotland** see in Appendix 1, p. 269.

**Garden of Skye, the** *Sleat, Scotland.* The parish and peninsula in the southwest of the Isle of Skye is so known for its fertility.

[The Sleat peninsula is] an uncharacteristically fertile area that has earned it the sobriquet "The Garden of Skye" [*The Rough Guide to Scotland*, 1998].

**Garden of South Africa** *see* **Garden Province**

**Garden of South Wales, the** *South Glamorganshire, Wales.* The former county is now largely represented by the fertile Vale of Glamorgan, the justification of its nickname.

**Garden of Spain, the** *(1) Andalusia, Spain; (2) Valencia, Spain.* Andalusia has many richly fertile regions, and Valencia is noted for its intensive cultivation under irrigation, a practice dating from Moorish times. Both regions thus claim the name.

**Garden of Sweden, the** *Blekinge, Sweden.* The county owes its nickname to its intensive cultivation.

**Garden of the Andes, the** *Mendoza, Argentina.* The city is surrounded by a fertile oasis. Hence its nickname.

**Garden of the Argentine, the** *Tucumán, Argentina.* The province derives its nickname from its fertile agricultural land.

**Garden of the Hebrides, the** *Eigg, Scotland.* The privately owned island is so named more for its fine scenery than its fertility.

**Garden of the Pacific, the** *Tahiti, French Polynesia.* The main island of the Society Islands, renowned for its beauty, is covered in dense vegetation and tropical flowers. Hence its well-deserved sobriquet.

**Garden of the Sun, the** *Indonesia (East Indies).* A general nickname for the exotic island country, with its tropical climate, abundant rainfall, and unusually fertile volcanic soil. The name is sometimes applied specifically to Malaysia.

**Garden of the West, the** *(1) Illinois, USA; (2) Kansas, USA.* Both Midwest states have a good claim to the name, Illinois with its rich black soil and Kansas as the nation's former agricultural heartland. *See also* **Garden State.**

> (Illinois) Illinois rejoices in three names: Garden of the West, Sucker State and Prairie State [*Chambers's Journal of Popular Literature*, March 13, 1875].

**Garden of the World, the** *(1) England; (2) Italy; (3) London, England; (4) Midwest, USA; (5) Sri Lanka.* Both England and (to a lesser extent) London have been poetically so named for their scenery as much as their agricultural productivity, whereas Italy and the American Midwest are famed for their fertility, the latter especially in the vast region drained by the Mississippi River and its many tributaries. The island state of Sri Lanka (former Ceylon) is famous for the flora of its forests. The sobriquets are now long dated for England and London, and even outmoded for Sri Lanka, as indicated by "ere while" (i.e. formerly) in quote (1) below.

> (1) (England) Oh Thou, that dear and happy Isle, The Garden of the World ere while [Andrew Marvell, *Upon Appleton House*, c. 1650].
>
> (2) (Italy) And even since, and now, fair Italy! Thou art the garden of the world, the home Of all Art yields, and Nature can decree [Lord Byron, *Childe Harold's Pilgrimage*, 1812].
>
> (3) (Sri Lanka) Promoting foreign destinations, its writers [i.e. of *Cook's Traveller's Gazette* in 1905] used almost every cliché in the tourist lexicon. They specialized in giving spuriously romantic titles to faraway places: Ceylon was 'the Garden of the World'; the Rockies were 'Nature's best picture gallery'; Iceland was the 'tourist's wonderland'; New Zealand was 'the Switzerland of the Southern Hemisphere.' No doubt the hyperbole was harmless, though it was also rather absurd — if Bangkok was the Venice of the East, was Venice the Bangkok of the West? [Piers Brendon, *Thomas Cook: 150 Years of Popular Tourism*, 1991].

**Garden of Wales, the** *Carmarthenshire, Wales.* The southern county (strictly, unitary authority) is largely agricultural and has a varied rural landscape. The rationale behind the label is explained in the quote below.

> The county isn't called the 'Garden of Wales' for nothing. First, there are its magnificent gardens, including of course the National Botanic Garden of Wales... But the title is also inspired by the landscapes in which those gardens are set. From

the rich dairy farming countryside in the west to the rugged moors and hill sheep farms in the east, Carmarthenshire is filled with green spaces [Travel brochure, *Sir Gâr/Carmarthenshire 2005*].

**Garden of West Africa, the** *Kumasi, Ghana.* The nickname of Ghana's second-largest city relates to its many parks and gardens.

**Garden on the Sea, the** *Hsia-men (Amoy), China.* The city and seaport is sometimes so called for its attractive island site.

**Garden Province** or **Garden of South Africa, the** *KwaZulu-Natal, South Africa.* The nickname, also that of the earlier province (originally colony) of Natal, derives from the region's abundant foliage and flora and the natural fertility of its soil.

> (1) The scene is ever green — a common-place for people who live in the 'Garden Colony' [Carel Birkby, *Zulu Journey*, 1936].
>
> (2) Natal is known as the Garden Colony of South Africa because of its beautiful vegetation [Daphne Rooke, *The South African Twins*, 1953].
>
> (3) On account of its fertility it [i.e. Natal] is known as the Garden Province [A.F. Hattersley in *Standard Encyclopaedia of Southern Africa*, 1973].

**Garden Route** see in Appendix 1, p. 269.

**Garden State, the** *(1) Illinois, USA; (2) Kansas, USA; (3) New Jersey, USA; (4) Victoria, Australia.* The name is primarily associated with New Jersey, now a crowded and highly urbanized state but formerly famous for its fertility and noted for its truck farms (market gardens). Illinois and Kansas (*see* **Garden of the West**) have more of a valid claim to the title in modern times. Victoria, although densely populated, is one of Australia's leading agricultural states. *See also* **Cabbage Garden.**

> (1) (Illinois) Verily, Illinois is justly called "The Garden State" [*Daily Morning Chronicle* (Washington, DC), September 29, 1865].
>
> (2) (Kansas) Kansas is often called the Garden State, from the beautiful appearance of rolling prairies and vast cultivated fields [Maximilien Schele De Vere, *Americanisms; The English of the New World*, 1871].
>
> (3) (New Jersey) When the first nip of frost chills the New Jersey air, cooks in the Garden State revive this recipe [*Saturday Evening Post*, November 20, 1948].
>
> (4) (Victoria) Victoria may be the Garden State ... but we all know what you put on gardens [*The Bulletin* (Sydney), September 21, 1982].
>
> (5) (New Jersey) By now I am ensconced at my VIP table with Andrea, Camilla and Carmela... All three are, as in the Tom Waits song, Joyzie Goyls — that is to say they are from the Garden State [*The Times*, March 9, 2005].

**Garment District** see in Appendix 1, p. 269.

**Gas City, the** *Medicine Hat, Alberta, Canada.* The city was founded in 1883 when the Canadian Pacific Railway, drilling for water, found natural gas. Exploitation of the large gas field here thus gave the nickname.

**Gate, the** *Notting Hill Gate, London, England.* A handy short name for the district.

> The Gate boasts two cinemas ... and a number of popular restaurants, cafés and pubs [Carrie Segrave, *The New London Property Guide*, 2003].

**Gate City** *(1) Atlanta, Georgia, USA; (2) Keokuk, Iowa, USA.* As a major port of entry to the USA, Atlanta was so named by Jefferson Davis as occupying the most important position in the lower part of the South from a military point of view. Keokuk, named for an Indian tribal chief (despite the quote below), lies at the foot of the Des Moines River rapids, where it was a natural rest stop for boats ascending the Mississippi.

> (Keokuk) Keokuk, Iowa, is the "Gate City" — a translation, I believe, of its Indian name [*Ladies' Repository*, 1859].

**Gate City of the South, the** *Atlanta, Georgia, USA.* An alternate name for Atlanta as simply the **Gate City**.

> In the Gate City of the South the Confederate Veterans were reuniting [O. Henry, *Roads of Destiny*, 1909].

**Gate City of the West, the** *Pittsburgh, Pennsylvania, USA.* Pittsburgh earned its nickname as an entry point for immigrants heading West after crossing the Alleghenies.

**Gate of Tears, the** *Bab-el-Mandeb, Red Sea.* The English name of the major waterway is a translation of the Arabic, bestowed on the strait for the natural hazards it presented to navigation and the shipwrecks suffered in consequence.

> Like some ill-destined bark that steers
> In silence through the Gate of Tears [Thomas Moore, *Lalla Rookh*, 1817].

**Gates of Hell** see in Appendix 1, p. 269.

**Gateway, the** *St. Louis, Missouri, USA.* St. Louis earns its nickname as the gateway to the Missouri valley and the West. The status is symbolized by the city's major attraction, the spectacular Gateway Arch, erected in 1965 on the banks of the Mississippi, and the Museum of the West below it.

**Gateway of England, the** *(1) Dover, England; (2) Southampton, England.* The Kent and Hampshire ports are two of the main points of arrival and departure in England for passengers from or to France and other countries of continental Europe. *Cp.* **Doorway to Britain.**

> (1) (Dover) Dover, "The Gateway of England," lies in a bay [*Holiday Guide 1952: Area No. 5, South & South East England*].
>
> (2) (Southampton) Giant liners from overseas, passing to and from Southampton, the "Gateway

of England" [*Holiday Guide 1952: Area No. 5, South & South East England*].

**Gateway of India, the** *Mumbai (Bombay), India.* The city and port has long been an ocean gateway to the country. The name is actually that of a Victorian-style arch in the city commemorating the arrival of George V (Emperor of India) and Queen Mary (Empress) in 1911. *See also* **Gateway to India; Urbs Prima in Indis.**

**Gateway of the USA, the** *New York City, USA.* New York has long been the main port of entry for visitors and immigrants to the USA, the latter including the millions who passed through Ellis Island over the period 1892 to 1924.

**Gateway of the West, the** *New York City, USA.* New York acquired this nickname in the 19th century when construction of the Erie Canal provided a passage from the Hudson River to Lake Erie.

**Gateway of the Wye, the** *Ross-on-Wye, England.* The Herefordshire town, above the Wye River, lies on a main through route to Wales.

**Gateway to America, the** *New York City, USA.* An alternate name for the **Gateway of the USA.**

> New York City is both the gateway to North America and its preferred exit to the oceans of the globe [*Britannica*, vol. 24, p. 902].

**Gateway to Bhutan, the** *Phuntsholing, Bhutan.* The town lies at a border crossing to Bhutan from West Bengal, India. Hence its name.

**Gateway to Captain Cook Country, the** *Middlesbrough, England.* Middlesbrough lies close to Captain Cook's birthplace in the nearby Yorkshire village of Marton. Hence the self-promotional name of the otherwise unremarkable industrial town. *See also* **Captain Cook Country** in Appendix 1, p. 269.

**Gateway to Connemara, the** *Galway, Ireland.* The chief town of the county that bears its name, regarded as the unofficial capital of the west of Ireland, stands on a main route to the wild coastal district of Connemara, in the west of the county. Hence its descriptive nickname.

**Gateway to Dovedale, the** *Ashbourne, England.* The Derbyshire town lies at the southern end of the picturesque stretch of the Dove River known as Dovedale.

> Ashbourne is a quaint red-brick town, proudly proclaiming itself the 'Gateway to Dovedale' [Charlie Godfrey-Faussett, *Footprint England*, 2004].

**Gateway to East Friesland, the** *Leer, Germany.* The city so styles itself for its location on a route to the North Sea region in question.

**Gateway to England, the** *Southampton, En-*

*gland.* An alternate description for the major port also known as the **Gateway of England**.

> Proud to be called "The Gateway to England," Southampton is the country's chief passenger port and shipping centre [*Holiday Guide 1952: Area No. 5, South & South East England*].

**Gateway to Europe, the** *(1) Europoort, Netherlands; (2) Hull, England.* The Netherlands port was created in 1958 at the Hook of Holland, the coastal port for Rotterdam, as the terminus for North Sea ferries from the English ports of Harwich and Hull, among others. Hull bears the same nickname, as the city's motto, referring to its role as a major commercial seaport for goods to continental Europe.

**Gateway to Exmoor, the** *Dulverton, England.* The small Somerset town lies on a road leading up to the high moorland area that is Exmoor.

> Set on the southern border of Exmoor, Dulverton delights in the title of "The Gateway to Exmoor" [*Holiday Haunts 1961: Area No. 4, West of England and South and Central Wales*].

**Gateway to Hell, the** *Corrievreckan, Scotland.* The world's second largest whirlpool, between the Hebridean islands of Jura and Scarbo, off the west coast of Scotland, is so nicknamed for its danger to shipping. The name itself means "Brecon's whirlpool."

> This whirlpool, known as Corrievreckan, is a place of extremity, of legendary waters and of monstrous rocks. It is the denizen of a deep subaquatic pit ... known as "The Gateway to Hell" [Peter Ackroyd, review of Bella Bathurst, *The Wreckers, The Times*, April 9, 2005].

**Gateway to India, the** *(1) Khyber Pass, Afghanistan/Pakistan; (2) Mumbai (Bombay), India.* The pass on the border of the named countries has long carried an important eastern route to India. Hence the name. For Mumbai, the name slightly adapts that of its colonial monument known as the **Gateway of India**. *See also* **Urbs Prima in Indis**.

> (1) (Khyber Pass) The most important of the gateways to India is the strongly guarded Khyber Pass, through which conquering armies for centuries have invaded the plains of Hindustan [Jack Tracy, comp. and ed., *The Ultimate Sherlock Holmes Encyclopedia*, 1977].
>
> (2) (Mumbai) And finally, Mumbai. The Gateway to India teems with life, enchanting vistas and memories of the Raj [Travel ad, *The Times Magazine*, June 4, 2005].

**Gateway to Northern Ireland, the** *Newry, Northern Ireland.* As indicated in the quote below, the town lies on a major road and rail route between Dublin and Belfast.

> [Newry is the] predominantly nationalist gateway

to Northern Ireland, just over the border from the Republic [*The Times*, March 15, 2002].

**Gateway to Provence, the** *Sisteron, France.* The town lies on a main route leading south into Provence from Dauphiné. Hence the name.

**Gateway to Scotland, the** *Carlisle, England.* The city lies on a main road route north to Scotland, so justifying its name. (The slogan appeared on a popular railway poster of 1924 depicting St. George on a caparisoned charger.)

**Gateway to Siberia, the** *Omsk, Russia.* The city lies in southwestern Russia in Asia on the Trans-Siberian Railroad, which runs east from here through Siberia on its route from Moscow to Vladivostok. Hence the name.

> The Gateway to Siberia is best seen through the frosty window of a speeding train bearing you to ... Moscow [Adam Russ, *101 Places Not to Visit*, 2005].

**Gateway to South Africa, the** *Cape Town, South Africa.* The seaport city is South Africa's main port of entry. Hence its nickname.

**Gateway to South America, the** *Miami, Florida, USA.* Just one of many sobriquets for the resort city and port, which has long had a close relationship with Latin America. It is equally a gateway to Central America.

> Miami is just 10 minutes away [from Fisher Island]. Given it has become "the gateway to South America, culturally and in business," there is always plenty to do [*Sunday Times*, August 14, 2005].

**Gateway to the Americas, the** *Seville, Spain.* The city and inland port in southern Spain gained its sobriquet as the center for Spanish exploration and commercial exploitation of the New World, with many Spanish emigrants to America sailing from its quays.

> The discovery of the "New World" by Christopher Columbus led to prosperity for Seville, the Spanish gateway to the Americas [*The Times*, August 13, 2005].

**Gateway to the Arctic, the** *Tromsø, Norway.* The northern seaport city lies within the Arctic Circle and is a point of departure for polar expeditions. Hence its nickname.

> It's nicknamed 'Gateway to the Arctic' (which is probably more appropriate than 'Paris of the North,' which was suggested by an apparently myopic German visitor in the early 1900s. Tromsø's great, but Paris is Paris) [*Lonely Planet Norway* 2002].

**Gateway to the Cotswolds, the** *Burford, England.* The picturesque Oxfordshire town lies beside a main route running west from Oxford to the Cotswold Hills, one of England's main tourist attractions.

> Burford has long billed itself as the 'Gateway to

the Cotswolds' [Charlie Godfrey-Faussett, *Footprint England*, 2004].

**Gateway to the Dales, the** *(1) Harrogate, England; (2) Ilkley, England.* The two Yorkshire spa towns, some 13 miles (21 km) apart, are on roads running north to the **Dales** (see in Appendix 1, p. 269), with Ilkley itself actually in Wharfedale. Hence the name.

(Ilkley) Heading into the dales from Leeds on the A65, the charming town of Ilkley is the first of any size that you come to. This allows the town to call itself 'the gateway to the dales' [Charlie Godfrey-Faussett, *Footprint England*, 2005].

**Gateway to the East, the** *(1) Istanbul, Turkey; (2) Marseille, France.* Istanbul lies either side of the Bosporus, partly in Europe (the West) and partly in Asia (the East). It is thus a gateway from one continent to the other, as the Bosporus itself is. The Mediterranean seaport of Marseille is the point of departure for ships sailing east to Italy and on to Asia. The name translates French *la porte de l'Orient.*

(Istanbul) From Istanbul, the "Gateway to the East," enjoy a circumnavigation of the Black Sea [Travel ad, *The Times*, September 25, 2004].

**Gateway to the Fjords, the** *Bergen, Norway.* Norway's second city is a major port on the North Sea coast with fjords to north and south. Hence the nickname.

The delightful old Hanseatic port of Bergen is renowned as "The Gateway to the Fjords" [Travel brochure issued with *The Times*, August 20, 2005].

**Gateway to the Fouta Djalon, the** *Mamou, Guinea.* The town is sometimes known by this name for its location on a main road to the Fouta Djalon plateau, a scenic district in the west of the country.

**Gateway to the Hebrides, the** *Oban, Scotland.* The west coast town is the leading port for ships sailing to the Hebrides. Hence its name.

[Oban] has been described as the Gateway to the Hebrides, to the West Highlands, even the Capital of the Highlands ... and it may well be all these to many people [Macnie/McLaren, p. 214].

**Gateway to the Highlands, the** *Perth, Scotland.* The town lies northwest of Edinburgh on a main route running north to the **Highlands** (see in Appendix 1, p. 269).

As a tourist centre Perth is unrivalled as a 'Gateway to the Highlands' northwards and westwards [Macnie/McLaren, p. 300].

**Gateway to the High Moor, the** *Moretonhampstead, England.* The Devon market town lies on the edge of Dartmoor, the "High Moor" of the title.

**Gateway to the Island, the** *Ryde, England.*

The Isle of Wight resort is one of the points of entry to the **Island** from mainland England.

Known as the "Gateway to the Island," Ryde is famous for its historic pier, vast sandy beach and the Island's oldest carnival [Isle of Wight travel brochure, 2005].

**Gateway to the Lakes, the** *Kendal, England.* The Cumbria town derives its name from its location on a road and railroad (and near a motorway) running up to the **Lakes** (see in Appendix 1, p. 269).

Kendal might be billed as the "Gateway to the Lakes," but it's nearly ten miles from Windermere [*The Rough Guide to England*, 1998].

**Gateway to the Loire Valley, the** *Angers, France.* The city in western France lies on a main route to the scenic Loire valley and its famous châteaux, as mentioned in the quote below. Hence the sobriquet.

Angers is a quintessential French provincial town — a peaceful attractive place that is also the gateway to the Loire Valley with its châteaux and vineyards [*The Times*, July 28, 2005].

**Gateway to the New Forest, the** *Lyndhurst, England.* The Hampshire town lies at the meeting point of main roads from Southampton and the south coast that run through the New Forest. Hence the nickname. *Cp.* **Capital of the New Forest.**

Up the road is the town of Lyndhurst, self-styled "gateway" to the New Forest [*Sunday Times*, May 15, 2005].

**Gateway to the North, the** *(1) Carlisle, England; (2) Edmonton, Alberta, Canada; (3) Watford, England.* Carlisle is so named for its location on a main road to Scotland. Hence its alternate name as the **Gateway to Scotland.** The Canadian provincial capital was formerly so called as an aviation center with flights to the northern regions of the country, though it is now more usually known as the **Oil Capital of Canada.** The nickname of the Hertfordshire town, just northwest of London, ties in with the phrase **North of Watford** (see in Appendix 1, p. 269).

(1) (Carlisle) Carlisle, say the posters, is the Gateway to the North. And for the Englishman it would be difficult to think of a better description of this border town [*Holiday Haunts 1960: Area No. 2, North West England and North Wales*].

 (2) (Watford) Watford would never claim to be glamorous, or exciting, or even particularly political. But Watford, Gateway to the North, with one foot in the metropolis and the other in the countryside, may hold the key to Tory victory [*The Times*, April 12, 2005].

**Gateway to the Outback, the** *Bourke, Australia.* The New South Wales town is on the edge of the Australian outback. *See* **Back o' Bourke** in Appendix 1, p. 269.

**Gateway to the Ozarks, the** *Springfield, Missouri, USA.* The city, a major tourist center, lies on the northern edge of the Ozark Highlands to which it serves as a point of entry.

**Gateway to the Port of London, the** *Gravesend, England.* The Kent town lies on the Thames as a point of entry to the Port of London to the west. It has also long served as the official reception point for distinguished visitors to London.

**Gateway to the Sahara, the** *(1) Erfoud, Morocco; (2) Guelmin, Morocco.* Both towns, in the south of the country close to the Sahara, promote themselves thus.

> (Guelmin) The dusty little town that proclaims itself the 'Gateway to the Sahara' [*Lonely Planet Morocco*, 2001].

**Gateway to the Saxon Switzerland, the** *Pirna, Germany.* The city is so known for its location on a route to the named mountainous region of Saxony.

**Gateway to the South** *(1) Balham, London, England; (2) Louisville, Kentucky, USA.* Kentucky's largest city has long been an entry point to the South. The London district, which arose on the south-running Roman road known as Stane Street, was humorously so named in an American-style "travelogue" recorded by the actor and comedian Peter Sellers in 1958.

> (1) (Balham) In a sense it was a 'gateway to the south' long before Peter Sellers in the 1960s made the place familiar ... with his brilliant depiction of 'Bal-ham, Gateway to the South'! [A.D. Mills, *A Dictionary of London Place-Names*, 2001].
>
> (2) (Balham) The combined efforts of Peter Sellers ('Gateway to the South') and Nikolaus Pevsner ('nothing of interest on Balham Hill except the Odeon') had damned the place into a sort of property limbo [Carrie Segrave, *The New London Property Guide*, 2003].

**Gateway to the Southern Harz, the** *Nordhausen, Germany.* The city derives its nickname from its location at the southern foot of the Harz Mountains.

**Gateway to the Thuringian Forest, the** *Arnstadt, Germany.* The city, south of Erfurt, lies on a route to the wooded mountain range in question.

**Gateway to the West, the** *(1) Cumberland Gap, Tennessee, USA; (2) St. Louis, Missouri, USA; (3) The Narrows, Maryland, USA.* The town of Cumberland Gap, near the pass of this name in the Cumberland Plateau, lies on a westward route. St. Louis lies on a similar route (*see* **Gateway**). The Narrows are so nicknamed because the National Road cuts through the Appalachian plateau here.

**Gateway to Wales, the** *(1) Abergavenny, Wales; (2) Newport, Wales.* The two towns lie on westward routes from England into Wales, Abergavenny on the A40 road and Newport, to the south, on the M4 motorway.

> (Newport) Gateway to Wales since it was the Roman Caerleon, and still the first significant place over the Severn [River] on the M4 [*The Times*, March 15, 2002].

**Gaul** *France.* A poetic name derived from **Gallia** as the Roman name of the ancient country of Europe that extended much more widely than modern France.

> Does haughty Gaul invasion threat?
> Then let the loons beware, Sir,
> There's wooden walls upon our seas,
> And volunteers on shore, Sir [Robert Burns, "Does Haughty Gaul," 1795].

**Gaunt** *Ghent (Gand), Belgium.* A poetic or former English name for the city, familiar from John of Gaunt, Duke of Lancaster (1340–1399), who was born there. (He appears in Shakespeare's *Richard II*, 1597.)

> When captains couragious, whom death could not daunte,
> Did march to the siege of the city of Gaunt ["Mary Ambree," *The Oxford Book of Ballads*, 1910].

**Gay Bay, the** *San Francisco, California, USA.* The nickname refers to San Francisco's sizeable gay community, combining "gay" with the "bay" of San Francisco Bay, on which the city lies.

**Gay Capital of Britain, the** *Brighton, England.* The name refers to the Sussex seaside resort's prominent gay community. *Cp.* **Camptown.**

> Giving Brighton city status bestows the country's blessing on its gay capital and will keep the pink pound rolling in [*The Times*, December 19, 2000].

**Gay Capital of Europe** or **the World, the** *Amsterdam, Netherlands.* The city's legendary libertarian radicalism has made it a Mecca for gays and lesbians from many parts of the world.

> When the editor of one of America's leading gay magazines visited the world's gay capital a fortnight ago, he assumed that he would be safe [*The Times*, May 14, 2005].

**Gay Paree** *Paris, France.* The dated nickname represents French *gai Paris*, "gay Paris," describing the capital in terms of jollity and gaiety, spiced with a soupçon of amorous adventure. *See also* **Paree.**

> (1) There are good young men saving up their money for a beano in "Gay Paree" [Evelyn Waugh, *Labels*, 1930].

(2) The prize: a second honeymoon in — guess where? You've got it — Gay Paree [*The Times*, February 9, 1974].

**GBR, the** *Great Barrier Reef, Australia.* An initialism mainly current among scientists for the famous stretch of coral reefs off the northeast coast of Queensland.

**Geddesburg** *Montreuil, France.* A British army officers' World War I nickname, punning on the USA's Gettysburg, for the Paris suburb, where Sir Eric Geddes, director-general of transportation on the staff of the commander-in-chief of the British army in France, set up his headquarters in 1916.

**Gem City, the** *Dayton, Ohio, USA.* "Gem City" is a common American sobriquet for any distinctive or successful city, and does not necessarily relate to gems in the literal sense. Dayton is one such city, its "gem" being its historic association with aviation.

**Gem of Sunny Somerset, the** *Clevedon, England.* The seaside town has been promoted thus as an attractive holiday resort, while the county has also been dubbed **Smiling Somerset.**

**Gem of the Adriatic** *see* **Hidden Gem of the Adriatic**

**Gem of the Clyde, the** *Largs, Scotland.* The popular resort owes its sobriquet to its pleasant setting on the Firth of Clyde.

Largs, with its two fine bays and background of green hills, is indeed "The Gem of the Clyde" [*Holiday Haunts 1962: Scotland*].

**Gem of the Hebrides, the** *Islay, Scotland.* A nickname for the island of the Inner Hebrides better known as the **Queen of the Hebrides.**

An island whose natural attractions, together with the friendliness of the people, well merit it being called the "Gem of the Hebrides" [*Holiday Haunts 1962: Scotland*].

**Gem of the Karoo, the** *Graaff-Reinet, South Africa.* The Eastern Cape town came to be so named as the center of an important agricultural region in the semidesert region known as the Great Karoo.

**Gem of the Mountains, the** *Idaho, USA.* The name is a variant of Idaho's better known sobriquet as the **Gem State.**

**Gem of the Norfolk Coast, the** *Cromer, England.* The promotional name describes the seaside resort as the best on the local North Sea coast.

Often referred to as the 'Gem of the Norfolk Coast,' this scene [i.e. John Sell Cotman, *Seashore with Boats*] is possibly a ... composition of Cromer beach, where Cotman's wife lived [Tourist map, *A Picture of Britain*, 2005].

**Gem of the Northern World, the** *St. Peters-*

*burg, Russia.* The splendid city in its sparkling setting on the Neva River was so encapsulated by the Russian poet Alexander Pushkin, as in the quote below. *Cp.* **Queen of the North.**

A century — and that city young,
  Gem of the Northern world, amazing,
  From gloomy wood and swamp upsprung,
  Had risen, in pride and splendor blazing
[Alexander Pushkin, *The Bronze Horseman*, 1833, translated by Oliver Elton].

**Gem of the Ocean, the** *England or Britain.* The name describes Britain through a run of song titles relating to America, with "Britannia, the Gem of the Ocean" (1852) a variant of "Columbia, the Gem of the Ocean" (1844) (*see* **Columbia**), attributed to Thomas A'Beckett, itself a variant of "Columbia, the Land of the Brave" (*see* **Land of the Brave**). The eventual title was "Britannia, the Pride of the Ocean."

**Gem of the Sea, the** *Ireland.* A poetic name similar to that of Britain as the **Gem of the Ocean.** The sea is the Irish Sea.

First flower of the earth, and first gem of the sea [Thomas Moore, "Remember Thee!," *Irish Melodies*, 1821].

**Gem of Welsh Villages, the** *Beddgelert, Wales.* An old promotional name for the Welsh village lying in a scenic setting below Snowdon.

**Gem State, the** *Idaho, USA.* The nickname is traditionally said to translate the state's Indian name. But this is now generally seen as a pseudo-Indian invention with no actual meaning, so that the sobriquet is simply one denoting general excellence.

**Gennesaret, Lake (of)** *Lake Tiberias, Israel.* The alternate name of the freshwater lake, occurring once in the New Testament (Luke 5:1), derives from Hebrew *ge*, "valley," and either *netser*, "branch," or *natsor*, "to guard," "to watch."

**Geordieland** *Tyneside, England.* The name derives from Geordie (a pet form of George) as a local nickname for an inhabitant of this northeastern region around Newcastle upon Tyne.

(1) There's a people's culture in Geordieland — it was the last place in England to have its own circuit of music halls [*The Listener*, August 12, 1971].
(2) As soon as something [cultural] comes to London, and it becomes successful, they [i.e. Londoners] claim it as their own. They don't claim it came from Birmingham or Manchester or Geordie-land or wherever. They claim that it's come from London [Judith Holder, *It's Grim Up North*, 2005].

**George Cross Island, the** *Malta.* The George Cross was instituted by George VI in 1940 as an award for heroism displayed by individuals (chiefly civilians) in World War II. In 1942, exceptionally, it was awarded to Malta in recognition of the fortitude of the islanders during bombardment by the Germans. Hence the title.

> Malta has the unique honour of being allowed to use the letters, G.C., after its name [Johnson, p. 159].

**George's Country** *Washington, USA.* A compliment to George Washington, 1st US president, for whom the state was named.

**Georgium Sidus** *South London, England.* A humorous 19th-century nickname adopted from the original name of the planet Uranus, at one time believed to be the furthest from the Earth. The idea was that London south of the Thames River was not part of the "real" London, which lay across the river to the north. (The planet name is Latin for "George's star," denoting its discovery in the reign of George III.)

**German Athens, the** *Saxe-Weimar, Germany.* An old nickname for the duchy, whose capital, Weimar, was long a cultural center.

**German East** *Tanzania.* A colloquial shortening of the name of former German East Africa (later Tanganyika).

> "When George and I were prisoners in German East we had something in common with a vengeance, and that was one shirt" [Francis Brett Young, *The Cage Bird*, 1933].

**Germania** *Germany.* The Latin name of the region of central Europe that is now Germany was adopted for the female figure who formerly represented the nation, rather as **Britannia** represents Britain.

**German Ocean, the** *North Sea.* The historic name of the North Sea, translating Ptolemy's Greek name *Germanikos Okeanos*, was in regular use down to the 20th century. (The *Oxford English Dictionary* actually defines "North Sea" as "The German Ocean.")

> A grey-green expanse of smudgy waters grinning angrily at one with white foam-ridges, and over all a cheerless, unglowing canopy... It isn't for nothing that the North Sea is also called the German Ocean [Joseph Conrad, "Poland Revisited," *Notes on Life and Letters*, 1921].

**German Rome, the** *Salzburg, Austria.* The city derives its nickname from the building activities of its archbishops in the 16th and 17th centuries, when the cathedral and a number of fine palaces arose.

**German Versailles, the** *(1) Kassel (Cassel), Germany; (2) Potsdam, Germany.* The nickname was applicable to both cities before World War II, when many of their fine historic buildings were destroyed by Allied bombing, unlike the royal palace at Versailles, France. Potsdam in particular is noted for its palaces, especially Frederick II's Sans Souci.

**Ghost Town** *Casper, Wyoming, USA.* The name puns on that of Casper, the Friendly Ghost, the cute little ghost who first appeared in a short animated film in 1945 and later in his own comic book. The Wyoming city arose around Fort Caspar [*sic*].

**Giant of West Africa, the** *Nigeria.* Nigeria earned its epithet as the region's largest country and Africa's most populous nation.

**Gib** *Gibraltar.* A colloquial abbreviation for the British colony, more formally known as the **Rock**.

> Gib has very good immigration and customs controls for those entering from outside the EU [*The Times*, August 10, 2004].

**Gibraltar in the Pacific** *Hawaii, USA.* The name of Gibraltar has been adopted for a number of impregnable outposts or defensive sites, like Gibraltar itself. The reference here is to Pearl Harbor, on the island of Oahu.

**Gibraltar of America, the** *(1) Quebec City, Canada; (2) Vicksburg, Mississippi, USA.* For Quebec, the specific reference is to Cape Diamond, the rocky promontory above the St. Lawrence River where the city arose and where a citadel was built. Vicksburg is so named for the fort built by the Spanish on a bluff overlooking the Mississippi.

**Gibraltar of China, the** *Hong Kong, China.* The parallels between the Chinese port and the British colony are enumerated in the quote below, although present-day Hong Kong is hardly "unproductive."

> Just as Gibraltar dominates the entrance to the Mediterranean Sea, so does Hongkong dominate commercially the entrance to the China Seas. Like Gibraltar it is close to the mainland of an alien power, and has similar physical aspects — a rocky height rising abruptly from the sea, with the town at the foot of its slopes. Like Gibraltar too it is almost entirely unproductive [Giles, p. 125].

**Gibraltar of England** or **Wessex, the** *Isle of Portland, England.* The rocky peninsula (rather than actual island) on England's south coast is so nicknamed for its physical profile as a promontory projecting into the English Channel. Thomas Hardy preferred "Wessex" to "England," and in his novels called the peninsula "Isle of Slingers," reviving an ancient name that referred to its inhabitants' mode of defense against invaders.

> (1) This happily styled "Gibraltar of Wessex" [Charles G. Harper, *The Hardy Country*, 1904].
> (2) Sometimes called the Gibraltar of England, Portland is joined to the mainland by a slender isthmus [*Holiday Guide 1952: Area No. 5, South & South East England*].

**Gibraltar of India, the** *Cape Town, South Africa.* The somewhat surprising nickname for the strategically sited seaport city was given by directors of the English East India Company in the late 18th century, when the British fleet sought to occupy it.

**Gibraltar of North America, the** *St. John's, Newfoundland, Canada.* The city was long a strategic settlement, and as such was captured and recaptured several times by France and England. It eventually became British in 1763 and was a naval base in the American Revolution and the War of 1812.

**Gibraltar of the East, the** *Corregidor, Philippines.* The historic fortified island long guarded the entrance to Manila Bay and served as an outpost for the defense of Manila. Hence its sobriquet.

**Gibraltar of the New World, the** *Quebec City, Canada.* An alternate nickname for the Canadian city as the **Gibraltar of America.**

**Gibraltar of the North, the** *(1) Luxembourg; (2) Suomenlinna (Sveaborg), Finland.* The capital city of Luxembourg lies on a rocky height with steep cliffs on each side, suggesting a resemblance to the Rock of Gibraltar. Its advantage lay in its strategic location astride a major military route linking Germanic and Frankish territories. Sveaborg (as its name indicates) arose as a Swedish fortress on islands in the harbor of Helsinki, so equally evokes the comparison.

(Luxembourg) For its unassailability Luxembourg became known as the Gibraltar of the North [Dodd/Donald, p. 475].

**Gibraltar of the North Sea, the** *Heligoland, Germany.* The North Sea island, with its level plateau, was developed by the Germans in the late 19th century into a great naval base, with underground fortifications and coastal batteries. The installations were dismantled after World War I, but then reconstructed by the Nazis in World War II. The island has thus twice justified its sobriquet in modern military history.

**Gibraltar of the Peloponnesus, the** *Corinth, Greece.* The ancient Greek city, long a strategic post in the Peloponnesus, was referred to thus by the English mineralogist and traveler Edward Clarke in *Travels in Various Countries* (1818).

**Gibraltar of the South, the** *Simonstown, South Africa.* The town and port south of Cape Town is so nicknamed for its strategic position on the False Bay shore of the Cape of Good Hope.

**Gibraltar of Wessex** *see* **Gibraltar of England**

**Gin-and-Jag Belt** see in Appendix 1, p. 269.

**Gippoland** *Egypt.* The colloquial name of the country derives from "Gippo" as a slang term for a Gypsy, the people who are erroneously said to have originated in Egypt. The British soldiers who used this nickname in the late 19th and early 20th century probably did so not for the supposed ethnic connection but simply because the country's name sounded like that of the people.

**Gitmo** *Guantánamo, Cuba.* The colloquial abbreviation is widely associated with the US naval base south of the city on Guantánamo Bay (*see* **Pearl Harbor of the Atlantic**).

**Glades, the** *Everglades, Florida, USA.* A common short name for the famous tract of marshland, and for the national park that forms its southern part.

[The Big Cypress National Preserve] is a major player in the Everglades' ecosystem, as the rains that flood the prairies and wetlands here slowly filter down through the 'Glades [*Lonely Planet USA*, 2004].

**Glamarama** *Tamarama Bay, Sydney, Australia.* The resort is so punningly nicknamed for its glamorous image, as described in the quote below.

Tamarama Bay, a deep, narrow beach favoured by the smart set and a hedonistic gay crowd ("Glamarama" to the locals) [*The Rough Guide to Australia*, 2001].

**Glamour Town** *Hollywood, Los Angeles, California, USA.* An obvious nickname for the center of the US motion-picture industry, whose own name is (or was) itself a virtual synonym for "glamour." *Cp.* **Tinseltown.**

**Glasstown** *St Helens, England.* The Merseyside town is the home of the firm of Pilkington, noted flat-glass manufacturers. Hence the nickname.

**Glass Town** *Milton, West Virginia, USA.* The nickname refers to the town's famed glass-manufacturing industry.

**Glasto** *Glastonbury, England.* The abbreviated name relates not so much to the Somerset town itself as to the annual rock festival held nearby. *Cp.* **Glaston.**

(1) The mighty fest that is Glasto is finished [*The Times*, June 30, 2004].
(2) Castle Cary, Glasto's wonderfully obscure rail terminal [*The Times*, June 18, 2005].
(3) [Rock musician] Chris [Martin] also spoke of the band's Glasto show, saying: "Glastonbury's hard to beat" [*The Sun*, July 19, 2005].

**Glaston** *Glastonbury, England.* A local short form of the Somerset town's name, evoking the Medieval Latin *Glastonia*. It matches **Shaston** as a similar name for Shaftesbury in the neighboring county of Dorset, and the two are combined in the old saying: "If the Abbot of Glaston could have married the Abbess of Shaston, the King of England would be the poorer man."

**Glens** see in Appendix 1, p. 269.

**Glesca** or **Glesga** or **Glesgae** or **Glesgie** *Glasgow, Scotland*. A local nickname for the city, reflecting the variable pronunciation of its name. Spellings with *a* for *e* also exist. A "Glesca screwdriver" is a facetious local term for a hammer.

(1) 'They mak' him in the Broomielaw, o' Glasgie cold an' dirt' [Rudyard Kipling, "McAndrew's Hymn," *The Seven Seas*, 1896].

(2) "Heaven seems vera little improvement on Glesga," a good Glasgow man is said to have murmured, after death, to a friend who had predeceased him [C.E. Montague, *The Right Place*, 1924].

(3) The HLI [i.e. Highland Light Infantry] have always been known as 'The Glesca Keelies'—a nickname they cherish with the perverse pride of a dyed-in-the-wool Glaswegian [Tim Carew, *How the Regiments Got Their Nicknames*, 1974].

**Glevum** *Gloucester, England*. The Roman name of the city, which gave its modern name, is preserved in some of its buildings and streets, such as the Glevum Industrial Estate and Glevum Shopping Centre.

**Glitter Gulch** see in Appendix 1, p. 269.

**Glorious Devon** *Devon, England*. The touristic nickname for the West-Country county, with its scenic coastline and popular seaside resorts, derives from the verse quoted below. (Its words were set to music by Edward German in 1905 in a song that still remains popular.) *See also* Appendix 6, p. 325.

When Adam and Eve were dispossessed
  Of the garden hard by Heaven,
  They planted another one down in the West,
  'Twas Devon, glorious Devon! [Harold Boulton, "Glorious Devon," 1902].

**Glorious Goodwood** *Goodwood, England*. The alliterative nickname is that of the horse race run annually since 1801 in a scenic setting on the downs to the north of Goodwood House near Chichester, West Sussex. The name is now more or less official for the July Festival Meeting at Goodwood, which is a glamorous (and thus glorious) conclusion to "The Season," as English aristocrats understand it. The epithet is also sometimes applied to the annual motor race held at Goodwood on the perimeter road of an airforce base from 1948 to 1966 (when it was halted as being too dangerous) and revived as a historic motor show in 1998.

(1) Improvements have been made to meet the requirements of the most enjoyable race-meeting in England, until it has attained the greatest preeminence, and is justly known as "glorious Good-

wood" [John Kent, *Records and Reminiscences of Goodwood*, 1896].

(2) "Glorious Goodwood" in the Sussex downland has one of the loveliest settings of any racecourse [Hadfield 1981, p. 162].

(3) 'Glorious Goodwood' is a phrase uttered in reverence of a quasi-fictional summer upper class idyll. Normally by *Daily Mail* readers from the Rotary Clubs of Surrey [Charlie Godfrey-Faussett, *Footprint England*, 2004].

**Glos** or **Gloucs** *Gloucestershire, England*. A semiofficial abbreviation of the county name, both spellings being pronounced "gloss." *See also* Appendix 6, p. 325.

Gloucs gent, 52, ... seeks patient female, for possible relationship [Personal ad, *Sunday Times*, June 26, 2005].

**Gloster** *Gloucester, England*. The name of the industrial city is spelled thus in certain contexts, notably for the Gloucestershire Regiment, who became known as the "Glorious Glosters" after their successful stand in the Korean War at the Battle of Imjin River (1951).

The Glosters—the City is spelled Gloucester, but the Regiment prefer to be called 'Glosters'—also have the nickname 'The Slashers' [Tim Carew, *How the Regiments Got Their Nicknames*, 1974].

**Gloucs** *see* **Glos**

**Glue Pot, the** *London, England*. An old showmen's nickname for the capital referring to its "attractiveness," or power to draw visitors to its spectacles.

**Gob', les** *Les Gobelins, Paris, France*. A short colloquial name for the district, centering on the famous Gobelin tapestry factory.

**Godge** *Godalming, England*. The colloquial name for the Surrey town is mostly used by students at Charterhouse public school nearby.

**God's Country** *(1) Montana, USA; (2) Oregon, USA*. A general name referring to the states' natural beauty, in each case that of a varied landscape of mountains, plains, valleys, and forests. *See also* **God's Own Country**.

(1) (Montana) 'Montana's my home now—Missoula. You come up there sometime and see God's country' [Jack Kerouac, *On the Road*, 1957].

(2) (Montana) From secluded forests to spacious, wide horizons, Montana has a special allure. Clearly this is 'God's Country' [*Country Magazine*, August/September 1992].

**Godsown** or **Godzone** *(1) Australia; (2) New Zealand*. A shortened form of **God's Own Country**.

**God's Own Country** *(1) Australia; (2) Kerala, India; (3) New Zealand; (4) United States; (5) Yorkshire, England*. The sobriquet is chiefly associated with the United States, which for its original settlers was the "chosen land." Both

Australia and New Zealand were seen similarly, and are now so regarded by their inhabitants, while Kerala is traditionally held to be a model state and Yorkshire a unique county. New Zealand was so named by Richard John Seddon, premier from 1893 to 1906, as indicated in quotes (3) and (7) below. Sir St. Vincent Troubridge, writing about the phrase in *Notes and Queries* of September 26, 1942, quotes from Sir William Craigie's *A Historical Dictionary of American English* (1936–43), which defines it as: "A special part of the U.S. or the country as a whole, viewed nostalgically as almost a paradise." The name is also found without "own," as for **God's Country**.

(1) (New Zealand) I am doing very well here [in Australia] but I would much sooner live on a far smaller salary in 'God's own Country' [Thomas Bracken, *Lays and Lyrics*, 1893].

(2) (USA) But equally I'm hanged if I want to be bullied by it, go to war on behalf of Main Street, be bullied and bullied by the faith that the future is already here in the present, and that all of us must insist ... that this is "God's Country" [Sinclair Lewis, *Main Street*, 1920].

(3) (New Zealand) Richard John Seddon [was] the popularly acclaimed uncrowned king of the land he himself had named 'God's Own Country' [Jean Devanny, *Lenore Divine*, 1926].

(4) (USA) A look at Egypt, then to India, and across to China and Japan, and back through that great sprawling America — God's own country, didn't they call it? [John Galsworthy, *The Silver Spoon*, 1926].

(5) (USA) God's Own Country (Western Division) as opposed to God's Own Country (England) [Ford Madox Ford, *Return to Yesterday*, 1932].

(6) (USA) Over many years of travelling in America and scores of other lands, I have come to the conclusion that God's own country is, by a very wide margin indeed, the most insular nation on earth [Bernard Levin in *The Times*, February 4, 1991].

(7) (New Zealand) The splendid scenery of glaciers, mountains, forests and lakes, the empty beaches, clean air and lush pastures continue to justify the title of 'God's own country,' bestowed by an early prime minister [*RD Places of the World*, p. 490].

(8) (Yorkshire) Yorkshire folk are only half-joking when they talk about living in God's Own Country [*Lonely Planet Great Britain*, 2005].

(9) (Yorkshire) Who cares if the greatest living Yorkshireman is [artist] David Hockney, [writer] Alan Bennett or [cricketer] Geoffrey Boycott? These heroes all choose to live outside God's own country. It's a bit like the world's most famous Scotsman, Sean Connery, living in Spain [Letter to the Editor, *Sunday Times*, October 23, 2005].

**God's Playground** *Poland*. The origin of this sobriquet is explained in the letter from its creator quoted below.

To the Editors: I was delighted to read John Bayley's excellent review of recent Polish writing entitled "In God's Playground" [*NYR*, July 19] and to see that the label of "God's Playground" is now regarded as an original name for "the old *Respublica* in its heyday." I cannot think of a nicer fate for a phrase which I invented myself in 1979 as the subtitle of my history of Poland (*God's Playground: A History of Poland*, Columbia University Press). Kochanowski's similar tag from the 1850s — *Człowiek: Boze Igrzysko* (Mankind: Bauble of the Gods) which I adapted — referred to people in general and not Poland in particular [Norman Davies in *New York Review of Books*, October 25, 1990].

**God's Waiting Room** *(1) Eastbourne, England; (2) Miami Beach, Florida, USA*. The nickname is near-generic for any seaside resort with an elderly population. So it is for the Sussex town and formerly was for the Florida city.

(Miami Beach) It used to be called 'God's Waiting Room.' Even today, if you mention Miami Beach to someone who hasn't been here or read about it lately, they might be able to conjure up a blurry memory of octogenarians mingling poolside while Aunt Sadie implores them to wait half an hour before going into the water [*Lonely Planet Miami*, 1999].

**Godwin Austen** *K2, Pakistan*. The mountain was originally named in 1888 for the British explorer and geographer, Colonel Henry Haversham Godwin-Austen, who made the first maps and descriptions of this region. This remains an alternate name for the peak that is now officially K2, so designated as it is the second in the Karakoram Range and the second highest (after Everest) in the world. It was also the second to be surveyed here.

**Godzone** *see* **Godsown**

**Gogs, the** *Gogmagog Hills, England*. A local abbreviated nickname for the low hills near Cambridge, themselves said to be named for the legendary giant Gogmagog.

**Goldberg's Green** *Golders Green, London, England*. The punning alteration of the district's name refers to its large Jewish population.

**Gold Coast, the** *Onich, Scotland*. The name has been applied to a number of coastal locations and districts, either literally, as in the case of the former name of Ghana, West Africa, so called from the gold discovered there by Portugeuse explorers, or metaphorically, as a place of promise. (*See also* **Gold Coast** in Appendix 1, p. 269.) The growing village of Onish at the mouth of Loch Leven falls into the latter category, as seen from the quote below.

Of late it ... has been favoured by the managers of the new industries as a place to live, hence its newly acquired nickname of 'the gold coast' [Robinson/Millward, p. 483].

**Golden Chersonese, the** *Malay Peninsula.* The sobriquet compares the Malay Peninsula to the ancient Thracian Chersonese, the modern Gallipoli Peninsula. It was "golden" because it promised gold, as outlined in quote (2) below. Chersonese itself is a word of Greek origin meaning simply "peninsula" (literally "land island"). (The first line of the Milton quote refers to Peking as the royal capital of China.)

(1) To Paquin of Sinæan kings, and thence
To Agra and Lahor of Great Mogul,
Down to the golden Chersonese [John Milton, *Paradise Lost*, 1667].
(2) In the early centuries of the Christian era, Malaya was known as far away as Europe. Ptolemy showed it on his early map with the label 'Golden Chersonese.' It spelt gold not only to the Romans but also to the Indians and Chinese, whose traders arrived not long after in search of that most valuable metal [*Lonely Planet Malaysia, Singapore & Brunei*, 1999].

**Golden City, the** *(1) Jaisalmer, India; (2) Johannesburg, South Africa; (3) Kanchipuram, India; (4) San Francisco, California, USA.* Johannesburg and San Francisco are literally associated with gold, the former because gold was discovered on its site in 1886, the latter because gold was unearthed nearby in 1848. Kanchipuram is so known for its many Hindu temples and its status as a sacred city, while Jaisalmer is similarly so nicknamed for its buildings, as described in quote (3) below.

(1) (Johannesburg) Some days ago, at the Golden City, a well-known Secretary was catechising a youthful aspirant for the honoured post of office-boy [*The Journal*, July 14, 1892].
(2) (Johannesburg) I felt like a *goduka* [i.e. migrant mineworker] going to the Golden City for the first time in his life, afraid it may swallow him, afraid he may not return from the dark earth's entrails of gold [Mtutuzeli Matshoba, *Call Me Not a Man*, 1979].
(3) (Jaisalmer) Dubbed the Golden City because of its 99 great bastions and its exquisite mansions, the fortress city of Jaisalmer shimmers above the Thar desert like a mirage [*The Times*, August 20, 2005].

**Golden Gate City, the** *San Francisco, California, USA.* San Francisco lies on the southern shore of the Golden Gate, the strait leading from the Pacific into San Francisco Bay. Hence the descriptive name. *Cp.* **City of the Golden Gate.**

**Golden-Headed City, the** *Moscow, Russia.* The name describes the golden domes of Moscow's many churches and cathedrals, most obviously in the Kremlin. The sobriquet (Russian *zlatoverkhy*, occurring in the works of Pushkin) contrasts with (and complements) the capital's other epithet of **White-Stoned City.**

(1) White-walled and golden-headed,
Beautiful, bizarre,
The pride of all the millions
Ruled by the Russian Tsar [V.E. Marsden, prefatory verse to Wirt Gerrare, *The Story of Moscow*, 1903].
(2) This [i.e. the Kremlin] was the real blood and bones of Russia — of Muscovy, of Pushkin's Golden-Headed Moscow [Lesley Blanch, *Journey into the Mind's Eye*, 1968].

**Golden Land, the** *Australia.* An early nickname for the island continent, or in particular for the state of Victoria, where gold was discovered in 1851. *Cp.* **Land of the Golden Fleece.**

The southern mines sustained the honour of the golden land when the western fields began to fail [*Australian Gold Digger's Monthly Magazine*, February 1852].

**Golden Mile** see in Appendix 1, p. 269.

**Golden Prebend, the** *Swords, Ireland.* The dormitory town for Dublin earned its nickname from its former great wealth from trade, a prebend properly being the shares of the revenue of a cathedral or collegiate church granted to a clergyman, hence generally an income.

**Golden Rock, the** *St. Eustatius, Leeward Islands, West Indies.* The island was so nicknamed for its former lucrative slave trade.

**Golden Sands** *see* **Sunny Beach**

**Golden State, the** *California, USA.* Modern California owes its very existence to the gold discovered at Sutter's Mill in 1848 and to the subsequent gold rush. The state could hardly have any other nickname, although it also refers to the golden California poppies that flower here each summer. *Cp.* **El Dorado State.**

(1) It is now known that the 'golden State' derived its name from a romance whose author invented the name of California for the long-sought El Dorado whose discovery he described [Isaac Taylor, *Names and Their Histories*, 1896].
(2) "California," said its chairman... "the Golden State and the most populous in the nation, cast 91 votes for the next President of the United States, Governor Bryan Roberts" [Fletcher Knebel and Charles W. Bailey, *Convention*, 1964].
(3) Next, we heard about a canning company in Oxnard, California, where the women were not let off the assembly line to relieve themselves, so, naturally, we were off to the Golden State [Michael Moore and Kathleen Glynn, *Adventures in a TV Nation*, 1998].

**Golden Town, the** *Mainz, Germany.* The city and river port became a free city in 1244 and the center of a league of Rhenish towns. This power won it the now historic epithet, also in the form "Golden Mainz."

**Golden Triangle** see in Appendix 1, p. 269.
**Golden Vale** see in Appendix 1, p. 269.

**Golden Vein** *see* **Golden Vale** in Appendix 1, p. 269.

**Golden West** see in Appendix 1, p. 269.

**Gold Purse of Spain, the** *Andalusia, Spain.* The present region was formerly so called as the richest province of the kingdom.

**Goldsmith's Country** see in Appendix 1, p. 269.

**Golf Coast** see in Appendix 1, p. 269.

**Golfsburg** *Wolfsburg, Germany.* The city derives its punning name as the global headquarters of the auto manufacturers Volkswagen, the Golf being one of their most popular models.

**Gomora** *Alexandra, South Africa.* The black township near Johannesburg, formerly notorious for its violence, was nicknamed for the biblical Gomorrah (*see* **Cities of the Plain**).

**Gong, the** *Wollongong, Australia.* A shortened nickname for the New South Wales city.

**Goober State, the** *Georgia, USA.* Georgia is the nation's leading producer of groundnuts (peanuts). Hence the nickname, from "goober" as a Southern word for the nut, itself of African origin.

**Good Town** *see* **Guid Toun**

**Goose, the** or **Goose City** *Tegucigalpa, Honduras.* A nickname based on the spoken form of the first two syllables of the capital city's name.

**Gopher State, the** *Minnesota, USA.* The nickname refers to the gopher, the burrowing rodent found in the state.

Gophers are here such a pest to the farmer that Minnesota has been called the "Gopher State" [J.M. Farrar, *Five Years in Minnesota*, 1880].

**Gossy** *Gosport, England.* The nickname is sailors' slang for the Hampshire town and naval base near Portsmouth.

**Gotham** *(1) Newcastle upon Tyne, England; (2) New York City, USA.* The nickname for New York was coined by Washington Irving as in quote (1) below. He took the name from the English village of Gotham, Nottinghamshire, which features in a folktale called "The Wise Men of Gotham," telling how the villagers feigned stupidity to demonstrate cunning. Newcastle was formerly also so nicknamed from the same source.

(1) (New York) Chap. cix. Of the renowned and antient city of Gotham [Washington Irving, *Salmagundi*, 1807].

(2) (New York) Such things as would strike ... a stranger in our beloved Gotham, and places to which our regular Gothamites are wont to repair [*Fraser's Magazine*, "Sketches of American Society," quoted in E. Cobham Brewer, *A Dictionary of Phrase and Fable*, 1870].

(3) (New York) New York City boasts record low crime rates, a solid economy, rising educational standards, less racial tension and lower and lower levels of illegitimacy and domestic violence. In fact, much of what was once an edgy, terrifying, almost gothic Gotham now seems bathed in near-narcotic calm [*Sunday Times*, August 14, 2005].

**Gothenburg** *Göteborg, Sweden.* The English form of the city's name, rightly suggesting "fort of the Goths," is still sometimes found.

**Goth Town** *Whitby, England.* The North Yorkshire fishing port was the setting for Bram Stoker's classic vampire story *Dracula* (1897), written in a genre popularized by earlier so-called "Gothic" novels. Hence the nickname of the town, which is now visited not only by enthusiasts eager to follow the "Dracula Trail" but twice a year by modern "Goths" in the form of pale-faced, dark-costumed, metallically-decorated devotees of vampires and 1980s Goth rock music.

**Gourmet Capital of Ireland, the** *Kinsale, Ireland.* The Co. Cork port and resort is famous for its restaurants and has an annual gourmet festival.

I feel hungry. I'm heading for the gourmet capital of Ireland — Kinsale [*Sunday Times*, March 13, 2005].

**Gourmetville** *Ludlow, England.* The Shropshire town is noted for its fine food and first-class restaurants. Hence its other nickname of the **Famous Foodie Capital**.

The Merchant House and Hibiscus, two of Ludlow's three Michelin-starred restaurants, are classed among the UK's top ten restaurants... Together with the third, Mr Underhill's, they win Ludlow the nickname "Gourmetville" [*The Times*, June 5, 2004].

**Grace's Country** *Monaco.* The little principality on the Mediterranean coast was so nicknamed following the marriage in 1956 of the US movie actress Grace Kelly to Prince Rainier III of Monaco.

The wedding took place in a blaze of publicity in the cathedral of Monaco. Many Americans, who had never heard of the tiny city-state, began to refer to Monaco as "Grace's country" [Obituary of Prince Rainier III of Monaco, *The Times*, April 7, 2005].

**Grain Coast** see in Appendix 1, p. 269.

**Grainery of Chile, the** *Araucania, Chile.* The region south of the Bío-Bío River is largely agricultural. Hence its nickname, with "grainery" a less common spelling of "granary," as in the entries below.

**Granadaland** see in Appendix 1, p. 269.

**Granary of Aberdeen, the** *Garioch, Scotland.* The lowland district northwest of Aberdeen owes its nickname to the fertility of its soil.

**Granary of Canada, the** *Saskatchewan, Canada.* Although one of the three Prairie Provinces (*see* **Prairie Province**), Saskatchewan has little native prairie. It does have a sizable grain belt, however, and this can justify its nickname.

**Granary of Castile, the** *Tierra de Campos, Spain.* The region of north central Spain is noted for its rich crops of cereals. Hence its nickname.

**Granary of Cuba, the** *Holguín, Cuba.* The city is nicknamed for the fertile region of diversified agriculture in which it lies.

**Granary of Europe, the** *Sicily, Italy.* The old nickname of the island of Sicily stemmed from its rich wheat crop, much of it going to the inhabitants of Rome. *Cp.* **Garden of Italy.**

**Granary of France, the** *Beauce, France.* The major agricultural region, in the Paris Basin, is so nicknamed for its production of wheat.

**Granary of India, the** *Punjab, India.* The state is a noted agricultural region, with wheat its leading crop. Hence the sobriquet.

**Granary of Italy, the** *Apulia (Puglia), Italy.* The region of southeastern Italy is famed for its agricultural produce and especially its grain.

(1) Puglia has long been the granary of Italy, its rich soils producing most of the wheat from which the nation's pasta is made [*Sunday Times*, June 12, 2005].

(2) Puglia — known as "Italy's breadbasket" [*Sunday Times*, November 13, 2005].

**Granary of Kabul, the** *Logar, Afghanistan.* The province is an important agricultural region, so earning its nickname.

**Granary of Lancashire, the** *Fylde, England.* The low coastal plain is a noted agricultural district. Hence its nickname.

**Granary of Mexico, the** *Jalisco, Mexico.* The state owes its sobriquet to its important production of corn and wheat.

**Granary of Portugal, the** *Alentejo, Portugal.* The historic province is famed for its agricultural produce.

Alenteio passes for the Granary of Portugal, by reason of the Corn which it produces [Robert Morden, *Geography Rectified, or A Description of the World*, 1680].

**Granary of Spain, the** *Andalusia, Spain.* An alternate nickname for the **Garden of Spain** or **Gold Purse of Spain.**

**Grand Canyon State, the** *Arizona, USA.* Arizona is famous for the Grand Canyon, the gorge of the Colorado River, regarded as one of the natural wonders of the world. Hence its nickname.

**Grand Dame of the Delta, the** *New Orleans, Louisiana, USA.* A title of honor for the city that lies near the mouth of the Mississippi-Missouri river system.

**Grand Duchy, the** *Luxembourg.* The small European country, on territory claimed by one nation after another, was finally declared an independent grand duchy by the Treaty of London in 1867. It is now the only grand duchy in the world.

The Grand Duchy's government enjoys 30 per cent of its revenues from the finance sector [*Financial Times*, October 18, 2004].

**Grandstand of the Solent, the** *Ryde, England.* The Isle of Wight town and port stands on steep hills, with good views of the Solent, the sea channel separating the island from the English mainland. Hence its sobriquet.

Its nickname, "Grandstand of the Solent," has been well chosen, since no other place can show sea views more lively or more varied [*Holiday Guide 1952: Area No. 5, South & South East England*].

**Grand Strand, the** *Myrtle Beach, South Carolina, USA.* A self-promotional name for the coastal city, the largest seaside resort in the state.

Myrtle Beach styles itself 'the Grand Strand,' but would be better nicknamed the Mall Sprawl [*Sunday Times Travel Magazine*, January 2006].

**Granite City, the** *Aberdeen, Scotland.* The city is so named for the local granite used in many of its public buildings. As "granite" evokes grayness and coldness, in 1997 the city council sought to attract tourists and business by promoting a new title: "Aberdeen, City of Opportunity." But the old sobriquet prevailed.

(1) The "granite city," which inspired a poet to speak of its "glitter of mica" and Lewis Grassic Gibbon of "its shining mail," still deserves those descriptions [Macnie/McLaren, p. 308].

(2) The Granite City, the Flower of Scotland, the Silver City by the Golden Sands... Aberdeen wears its titles with pride [<http://www.agtb.org/aberdeen-scotland.htm>, accessed August 17, 2004].

(3) [Aberdeen's] moniker of 'The Granite City' may conjure up images of a dour, funless sort of town, but nothing could be further from the truth [*Lonely Planet Great Britain*, 2005].

**Granite State, the** *New Hampshire, USA.* The state is so nicknamed from its former repute as an important center of granite quarrying.

(1) I come from New Hampshire, or what we call the Granite state [James Fenimore Cooper, *The Jack o' Lantern*, 1842].

(2) We know, of course, that each of our states is an individual and proud of it. Not content with their names, they take descriptive titles also — the Empire State, the Garden State, the Granite State — titles proudly borne and little given to understatement [John Steinbeck, *Travels with Charley in Search of America*, 1962].

**Granta** *(1) Cam River, England; (2) Cambridge, England.* The local alternate name for the

Cam at Cambridge, representing the river's original name, is also in poetic use for the city itself, especially with regard to its university.

> (Cambridge) Therefore, farewell, old Granta's spires! [Lord Byron, "Granta," *Hours of Idleness*, 1807].

**Grantsville** *Richmond, Virginia, USA.* The state capital owes its sobriquet to General Ulysses S. Grant, commander of the Union armies during the late years of the Civil War, who captured it in 1865 after breaking the Confederate defense.

**Grape Capital of the World, the** *Fresno, California, USA.* The city lies in the San Joaquin Valley, one of the world's major grape-growing centers and heart of the largest wine-growing area of the USA. Hence its nickname. *Cp.* **Grape State.**

**Grape State, the** *California, USA.* The nickname alludes to California's major wine industry, which produces 90 percent of all of the wine made in the United States. *Cp.* **Grape Capital of the World.**

**Grasshopper State, the** *Kansas, USA.* The nickname refers to the Rocky Mountain grasshopper, which wreaks widespread damage to the cereal crops in the state.

**Graveyard of the Atlantic, the** *(1) Cape Hatteras, North Carolina, USA; (2) Sable Island, Nova Scotia, Canada.* Both cape and island derive their name as the scene of many shipwrecks.

**Gravy, the** *Atlantic Ocean.* A nickname common among pilots of the British Royal Air Force, and especially Bomber Command, in World War II. There is a suggestion of "gravyboat" and even of (a watery) "grave." *Cp.* **Graveyard of the Atlantic.**

**Gray City by the Sea, the** *Husum, Germany.* The North Sea city and port was described thus by the German writer Theodor Storm, who was born and is buried there. In his poem "*Die Stadt*" ("The Town") (1870) he addresses it as "*Du graue Stadt am Meer*" and the seaport features in many of his stories.

**Greasepaint Avenue** *Brixton, London, England.* A late 19th-century and early 20th-century nickname for the suburban district at a time when many music-hall artists lived there, with easy access to London's West End theaters.

**Great Australian Outback** *see* **Outback** in Appendix 1, p. 269.

**Great Central State, the** *North Dakota, USA.* The state lies more or less in the middle of the wheat belt. Hence the nickname.

**Great Dismal, the** *District of Columbia, USA.* The nickname has been attributed to

Daniel Webster, who lived in Washington in the early 19th century when the district was damp, dirty, and dreary.

**Great Divide, the** *Rocky Mountains, North America.* The Rockies form the Continental Divide, separating rivers flowing toward the Atlantic in the east from those flowing toward the Pacific in the west. Hence the name. *See also* **Great Divide** in Appendix 1, p. 269.

> I remember as a child reading or hearing the words "The Great Divide" and being stunned by the glorious sound, a proper sound for the granite backbone of a continent [John Steinbeck, *Travels with Charley in Search of America*, 1962].

**Greater Britain** *British Empire.* The byname for the former British Empire denotes a wider scope than Great Britain as the parent country. It also evokes city names such as Greater London and Greater Manchester.

> The main task of Queen Victoria's Navy was ... to act as an organic link between the mother country and "Greater Britain," her increasing territories beyond the seas [*Times Literary Supplement*, February 25, 2005].

**Greater Tasmania** *Fiji.* The sobriquet, mentioned in Jonathan Aitken, *Land of Fortune* (1971), is in use among Tasmanians, referring to Tasmanian emigration to Fiji. The islands were discovered by Abel Tasman (for whom Tasmania is named) in 1643.

**Greatest City in the World, the** *New York City, USA.* A hyperbolic self-promotion which some might view with reservation, including the English writer of the passage quoted below.

> Every time I drove into Manhattan on the Long Island Expressway I would laugh. Here we were entering "The Greatest City in the World," and the road was full of potholes, the verges piled with garbage and the central reservation a line of pre-cast concrete barriers that had been there for five years [*The Times*, June 11, 2005].

**Great Lake, the** *Atlantic Ocean.* A former nickname upgrading the ocean from a lowly **Ditch** or **Pond.**

> I know others that never saw the east side of the great lake [Jared Sparks, ed., *The Life of Gouverneur Morris*, 1832].

**Great Lake State** *see* **Lake State**

**Great Land (of the West), the** *Alaska, USA.* The name is a (partial) translation of the state's Inuit name. The term is appropriate for the largest state in the USA, but also the one with the sparsest population. *Cp.* **Jumbo State.**

> "The great land of the west"—as the word Alayeska translates from the native American Athabascan language [Dodd/Donald, p. 202].

**Great Lone Land, the** *Canada.* The poetic sobriquet comes from the title of a book by the

Irish army officer Sir William Butler, who first went to Canada with his regiment in 1867.

Striking the north Saskatchewan at Carlton, he followed it up to the base of the Rocky Mountains, and then descended it, reaching Fort Garry on 20 Feb. 1871, after a winter journey of 2700 miles. He told the story of this journey ... in 'The Great Lone Land,' which was published in 1872 [*Dictionary of National Biography*].

**Great Nation, the** *England or Britain*. The name was formerly applied to England by the Germans.

The Great Nation. By this name they always designate England, in opposition to the same title self-assumed by the French [S.T. Coleridge, letter to his wife, October 19, 1798].

**Great North** see in Appendix 1, p. 269.

**Great Republic, the** *United States*. A name sometimes applied to the USA as a federal republic.

(1) The Great Republic was the chief foreign threat to the well-being of the British Empire [James Morris, *Pax Britannica*, 1968].

(2) He [i.e. English tourist agent Thomas Cook] told Americans that a million people had made use of his arrangements in Europe and that he would have visited the 'Great Republic' earlier but for its 'disorganization' [Piers Brendon, *Thomas Cook: 150 Years of Popular Tourism*, 1991].

**Great Sea, the** *Mediterranean Sea*. The former name of the sea is now found only in the Bible and in poetry. (In the quote below, it is described as forming the western boundary of the Promised Land. Its location west of Israel caused Hebrew *yam*, "west," to be used to mean "sea," as in Deuteronomy 11:24: "From the river, the river Euphrates, even unto the uttermost sea shall your coast be.")

And as for the western border, ye shall have even the great sea for a border, this shall be your west border [Numbers 34:6].

**Great Smoke, the** *London, England*. An alternate form of the more common nickname **Big Smoke**.

**Great South Land, the** *Australia*. The sobriquet essentially translates the Latin name *Terra Australis*, "southern land," printed on maps by geographers from the 16th century to mark the land mass that they were sure was located in the southern oceans and that would soon be discovered (and named) as Australia.

A new deal for the Australian blacks is coming up fast, and ... public conscience is at last awake to our responsibilities to these ancestral folk of the Great South Land [Frank Clune, *The Fortune Hunters*, 1957].

**Great Weird North, the** *Canada*. A nickname punning on the country better known as the **Great White North**. Canada regards itself as

memorably distinctive from its southern neighbor, not simply a carbon copy.

[Will] Ferguson is a traveller and author of several books on Canada and Japan... For his latest book, he has returned to his native land, the Great Weird North, also known as Canada. "We see things differently," he says [*Sunday Times*, March 27, 2005].

**Great Wen, the** *London, England*. The derogatory nickname was first applied to the British capital by William Cobbett as in quote (1) below, referring to the gradual encroachment of the city into the surrounding countryside, like a growing tumor that could perhaps burst.

(1) But what is to be the fate of the great wen of all? The monster, called by the silly coxcombs of the press, "the metropolis of the empire"? [William Cobbett, *Rural Rides*, 1822].

(2) Let us try to earn the approval of the shade of Cobbett by ignoring the Wen, keeping rather towards the top edge of the [London] Basin [S.P.B. Mais, *The Home Counties*, 1942].

(3) The segments [i.e. postal districts] devised for the delivery of the mail break the great wen ... into a wide spectrum of different villages [Godfrey Smith, *The English Companion*, 1996].

**Great White Continent** *see* **White Continent**

**Great White North, the** *Canada*. A name referring to Canada's vast Arctic and snow-covered territories, giving the overall impression of an entirely northern land (although parts of the country, such as Toronto, are as far south as Italy and the Black Sea).

Is Canada the new Wales? Like its transatlantic cousin, the Great White North has ... largely been overshadowed by its dominant neighbour over the border [*The Times*, September 13, 2005].

**Greenback Belt** see in Appendix 1, p. 269.

**Green City, the** *(1) Freiburg, Germany; (2) London, England*. Freiburg is so nicknamed for its green planning, transport, and environmental policies. (The Green Party has been politically influential in the city.) The British capital gained its sobriquet for its many parks and gardens, one of which is actually called Green Park.

**Green Country** see in Appendix 1, p. 269.

**Green Heart of Austria, the** *Styria (Steiermark), Austria*. The mainly mountainous province derives its nickname from its many pastures, forests, and meadowlands.

The "green heart of Austria" is an appropriate slogan for Styria... Austrians themselves regard the "Green Province" as their favourite holiday region within their own borders [*Insight Guide Austria*, 1998].

**Green Heart of Italy, the** *Umbria, Italy*. The region of central Italy is noted for its farmland and its production of grapes and grain. Hence the nickname, implying an innate growing greenness.

**Green Isle** or **Island, the** *Ireland.* The name refers to Ireland's lush verdure. *Cp.* **Emerald Isle.**

(1) And He, yon Chieftain — strike the proudest tone

Of thy bold harp, green Isle!— the Hero is thine own [Sir Walter Scott, *The Vision of Don Roderick*, 1811].

(2) He loves the Green Isle, and his love is recorded

In hearts which have suffer'd too much to forget [Thomas Moore, "The Prince's Isle," *Irish Melodies*, 1821].

(3) I notice these days that the Green Isle is getting greener [Myles na gCopaleen, *The Best of Myles*, 1968].

**Greenland** *Ireland.* A punning nickname for the **Green Isle** based partly on the real name of Greenland but also hinting at the supposed innocence or naivety ("greenness") of the inhabitants.

**Green Mountain City** *Montpelier, Vermont, USA.* The city derives its nickname as the capital of the **Green Mountain State**.

**Green Mountain State, the** *Vermont, USA.* The sobriquet refers to the Green Mountains that gave the state's French name.

(1) A Mr. Fletcher of Vermont, the only Administration member from the Green Mountain States [*sic*] [*New York Advertiser and Express*, February 7, 1838].

(2) Mello draws heavily on his local knowledge together with news reports and readers' letters in Vermont newspapers such as the *Rutland Herald*: his pride in the Green Mountain State adds an original and often disarming touch to the book [Richard Davenport-Hines, review of Michael Mello, *Legalizing Gay Marriage*, *Times Literary Supplement*, May 20, 2005].

**Green Province** *see* **Green Heart of Austria**

**Green Sea, the** *Persian Gulf.* The rarish nickname alludes to the greenish color of a stretch of water off the Arabian coast.

**Green Valley, the** *Rhondda Valley, Wales.* The nickname for the South Wales valley (in reality two adjacent valleys), popularly identified with the more general **Valleys** (see in Appendix 1, p. 269), derives from its lush meadows before they were smothered by the slag heaps of the coal-mining industry that arose here in the 1860s, peaked in the early 20th century, and finally faded in the 1980s, when greenery began to return. The name owes much to Richard Llewellyn's bestselling novel *How Green Was My Valley* (1939), set here in the second half of the 19th century.

(1) There is a degree of luxuriance in the valley...

The contrast of the meadows, rich and verdant, with mountains the most wild and romantic, surrounding them on every side, is in the highest degree picturesque [Benjamin Heath Malkin, *The Scenery, Antiquities and Biography of South Wales*, 1804].

(2) It was at one time a green and beautiful district [Vaughan-Thomas/Llewellyn, p. 304].

(3) Although best known for their industrial past, the Valleys are green and attractive [*Wales: Where to Stay*, 2005].

**Green Venice** *Marais Poitevin, France.* An occasional nickname (French alliterative *la Venise verte*) for the area of marshland crisscrossed by canals and dykes on the west coast of France to the north of La Rochelle.

(1) The area is sometimes called 'La Venise Verte.' In summer, these canals make a cool green sanctuary, where one may punt for miles under a tunnel of green leaves [Young, p. 235].

(2) Take to the many miles of waterway in the Marais Poitevin — France's 'Green Venice' [Travel ad, *The Times Magazine*, March 26, 2005].

**Gretna Green of the East, the** *Elkton, Maryland, USA.* The Scottish village of Gretna Green, just across the English border, is famous as the place where young couples could marry without the permission of their parents. The nickname refers to the American equivalent. Elkton was the capital of the East Coast for eloping couples, who would be met by taxi off the train, driven to the court for a license, then rushed to one of the "marrying parsons" on Main Street. (In 1938 a law was passed requiring a 48-hour waiting period before marriage.)

**Grey Auld Toon, the** *Hawick, Scotland.* The mill town in southern Scotland is sometimes so dubbed ("gray old town") for its drab-colored buildings. *Cp.* **Auld Grey Town.**

**Grimsby of the West Coast, the** *Fleetwood, England.* The Lancashire seaside resort was formerly noted for its fishing fleets. Hence the comparison with the famous east-coast fishing port of Grimsby.

**Gringolandia** *United States.* A pejorative American Spanish nickname for the USA, based on *gringo*, "foreigner."

**Gringotenango** *Panajachel, Guatemala.* The town on the shore of Lake Atitlán is the site of a large expatriate retirement and resort community, mainly populated by Europeans and North Americans. Hence its nickname among local people, meaning "place of the foreigners," from American Spanish slang *gringo*, "foreigner," and Maya *tenango*, "place." *Cp.* **Gringolandia.**

Dubbed Gringotenango because of its popularity with western tourists, Panajachel stands 100 miles west of Panama City [*Sunday Times*, October 16, 2005].

**Grinnidge** *Greenwich, London, England*. A nickname representing a local (and also national) spoken form of the town's name.

Fred told them that he was undone,
  For his people all went insane,
  And fired the Tower of London,
  And Grinnidge's Naval Fane [W.S. Gilbert, "The King of Canoodle-Dum," *The "Bab" Ballads*, 1869].

**Groperland** *Western Australia, Australia*. The state derives its nickname from the "gropers," more fully known as "sandgropers," the early settlers who sought sustenance in the sand of Western Australia's vast central desert. *Cp.* **Sandgroperland**.

Wild flowers of loveliness, variety and profusion to be found nowhere else on earth but in poor arid Groperland [Xavier Herbert, *Disturbing Element*, 1963].

**Grotty** *Guatemala City, Guatemala*. A disapprobatory English short form of the capital city's name. *Cp.* **Guate**.

There is really no good reason to stay long in Guatemala City, known as *Guate* locally, though foreigners soon dub it 'Grotty' [Natascha Norton and Mark Whatmore, *Cadogan Guides: Central America*, 1993].

**Grotty Groton** *Groton, Connecticut, USA*. A British sailors' alliterative (and cynically critical) nickname for the town and its major submarine base.

**Groundhog State, the** *Mississippi, USA*. A now rare nickname for the state, referring to the formerly abundant groundhogs here.

**Grove, the** *Cedar Grove, New Jersey, USA*. A shortened form of the residential town's name.

**Grove of the Evangelist, the** *St John's Wood, London, England*. A punning alteration of the district's name. *Cp.* **Apostle's Grove.**

**Groyne, The** *La Coruña, Spain*. The old nickname for the seaport city was common among British mariners, who presumably associated the Spanish name with English "groyne" as a type of breakwater.

CORUNNA, or GROYNE, a port-town of Gallicia in Spain [*Encyclopædia Britannica*, 1771].

**G-Town** *Georgetown, Washington, DC, USA*. An initial-based short name for the historic town and present district.

**Guguland** *Philippines*. A derogatory nickname for the island state, based on "gu-gu" (or "goo-goo") as a US slang term for a Filipino, presumably mocking their unintelligible speech.

**Guid Toun, the** *Edinburgh, Scotland*. A Scots nickname ("good town") for the country's capi-

tal. The English form of the name is also used, as in the quote below.

That claim may wrestle blessings down
  On those who fight for The Good Town [Sir Walter Scott, *Marmion*, 1808].

**Guate** *Guatemala City, Guatemala*. A local short form of the capital city's name. *Cp.* **Grotty**.

'*Guate! Guate!*' shout the bus conductors, as you approach, and black clouds blast from revving engines [Natascha Norton and Mark Whatmore, *Cadogan Guides: Central America*, 1993].

**Guinea Pig State, the** *Arkansas, USA*. The state acquired its nickname in the depression of the 1930s, when farmers volunteered to take part in the agricultural experiments proposed by Franklin D. Roosevelt's federal government.

**Guitar Town** *Nashville, Tennessee, USA*. The city gained its nickname as the home of country music.

**Gulf, the** *(1) Gulf of Mexico, North America; (2) Persian Gulf*. The interpretation of the abbreviated name can depend on the speaker's nationality and geographical location. To an American, it usually denotes the Gulf of Mexico. To a Briton, it will normally mean the Persian Gulf, although this arm of the Arabian Sea now appears in many atlases without the adjective. The Gulf War of 1991 reinforced the latter sense.

["The Gulf"] is how broadcasters and recent maps designate the place we all grew up calling the Persian Gulf, now robbed of its distinguishing adjective seemingly in order to placate, or not to offend, Iraq and perhaps other Gulf States. It strikes me as high time the Persian Gulf was given its historic name back. After all, the Gulf of Mexico is so called whatever the USA and possibly other nationalities may think about it [Kingsley Amis, *The King's English*, 1997].

**Gulf City** *New Orleans, Louisiana, USA*. The nickname straightforwardly refers to the city's location inshore from the Gulf of Mexico.

**Gulf Coast** see in Appendix 1, p. 269.

**Gulf Country** see in Appendix 1, p. 269.

**Gulf State, the** *Florida, USA*. The name refers to the Gulf of Mexico by which the state is bounded on the west.

**Gun Crime Capital of England** *see* **Murder Capital of Britain**

**Gunks, the** *Shawangunk Mountains, New York, USA*. The Appalachian range is colloquially known by this abbreviated nickname.

**Gutter** or **Gutter of Australia, the** *Darling River, Australia*. A mock-derisory name for Australia's longest river, hinting at its unpredictable navigability and irregular volume.

(1) 'You're a stranger to this district.' 'Yes, I've come over from The Gutter for a change' [Arthur Upfield, *Winds of Evil*, 1937].

(2) This Darling River, sometimes called the Gutter of Australia [Arthur Upfield, *Madman's Bend*, 1963].

**Guz** *Devonport, England.* A somewhat mysterious nickname for the district of Plymouth, Devon, with its naval dockyard. It is said to be a shortening of "guzzle," referring to the hearty appetite of sailors returning home after a long spell at sea, although another theory derives it from GUZ, the prefix letters of the Devonport Barracks radio call sign.

**Gwalia** *Wales.* The alternate name for Wales dates from medieval times, as a half-Latin, half-Welsh form of *Wallia*, a latinized name used in historical documents. It came into vogue in the 19th century and was adopted by poets, as in *Gwalia Deserta* ("Desert Wales"), a sequence of poems by Idris Davies published in 1938.

Dear Gwalia! I know there are
Towns lovelier than ours [Dylan Thomas, *Under Milk Wood*, 1954].

**Hafnia** *Copenhagen, Denmark.* The Latin name of the capital city, found in poetry, derives from Danish *havn*, "harbor." (It is the "-hagen" of the present name, which overall means "merchants' harbor.")

And [Nelson] launch'd that thunderbolt of war
On Egypt, Hafnia, Trafalgar [Sir Walter Scott, *Marmion*, 1808].

**Haggisland** *Scotland.* A former nickname for the "home of the haggis," referring to the traditional Scottish dish.

**Halicarnassus** *Bodrum, Turkey.* The ancient name of the town is familiar from historical contexts, especially the Mausoleum of Halicarnassus that was one of the Seven Wonders of the Ancient World.

**Hammy** *Hammersmith, London, England.* A colloquial abbreviation of the name of the district, noted for its entertainment, especially at the Hammersmith Odeon theater, renamed the Hammersmith (London) Apollo in 1999.

How to tap up a footballer the Chelsea way: first book the Hammy Odeon [Headline, *The Times*, February 12, 2005].

**Hamp** *Northampton, Massachusetts, USA.* A colloquial abbreviated form of the city's name.

**Hampshire Highlands** see in Appendix 1, p. 269.

**Hampstead-on-Sea** *Southwold, England.* The wealthy Suffolk resort is nicknamed for the fashionable London district as an alternate to its equivalent designation of **Kensington-on-Sea.**

There are no [beach] huts for sale in Southwold in Suffolk, dubbed Hampstead-on-Sea [*Sunday Times*, July 10, 2005].

**Hampstead-on-Wye** *Hay-on-Wye, Wales.* The town just across the English border is so nicknamed for its cultural and intellectual associations, evoking those of the London district of Hampstead. Hay is noted in academic circles not just as the **Town of Books** but for its annual literary festival. (The reference to "green wellies" in the quote below implies a serious interest in rural conservation.)

The Literary Festival at Hay-on-Wye, often labelled Hampstead-on-Wye, is pulling on its green wellies this year [*The Times*, May 20, 2005].

**Hampton** *Southampton, England.* This is the original name of the seaport city, which later added "South" for distinction from Northampton, the county town of Northamptonshire. *Cp.* **Hants.** *See also* Appendix 6, p. 325.

This man
Hath, for a few light crowns, lightly conspir'd,
And sworn unto the practices of France,
To kill us here in Hampton [William Shakespeare, *Henry V*, 1600].

**Hamptons** see in Appendix 1, p. 269.

**Hanging State, the** *Victoria, Australia.* Victoria was the last Australian state to abolish hanging, in 1975, and the nickname applied until that year.

**Hangtown** *Placerville, California, USA.* The city's early inhabitants hanged a number of men as an exercise of frontier justice in the days of the gold rush of the 1850s. Hence the nickname.

**Hanseatic Queen, the** *Lübeck, Germany.* The sobriquet relates to the Hanseatic League, the defensive confederacy of German towns that grew out of the mutual trading treaty between Lübeck and Hamburg. Lübeck became the administrative center of the League in 1358. Hence the title.

**Hants** *Hampshire, England.* The semiofficial name of the county arose as a short form of its medieval spelling as *Hantescire* (in the Domesday Book). *See also* Appendix 6, p. 325. Appreciation of the anonymous limerick quoted below depends on knowledge of this abbreviation for Hampshire and of **Sarum** for Salisbury, Wiltshire, a city not far north of the Hampshire border.

There was a young curate of Salisbury
Whose conduct was all halisbury-scalisbury,
He walked about Hampshire
Without any pampshire
Till his vicar compelled him to walisbury.

**Happiest Place on Earth, the** *Disneyland, Anaheim, California, USA.* A promotional name evoking the delights that await visitors to the famous amusement park.

In 1968 Disneyland had seemed magical... But I was sure that, in the intervening years, rampant commercialism would have changed all that at what Disneyland calls "The Happiest Place on Earth" [*The Times*, August 13, 2005].

**Happy Island, the** *Bermuda.* A self-promotional name for the North Atlantic island colony, and especially the principal island of Main Island.

> A local tourist scene, familiar in "Happy Island" Bermuda, in which the elderly Mark Twain used to read aloud at his holiday home [*Times Literary Supplement*, September 9, 2005].

**Happy Islands, the** *Channel Islands, UK.* A self-promotional name for the islands in the English Channel, popular among vacationers for their sun and "foreign" flavor (they are historically part of Normandy, France) and among residents as a tax haven. The nickname has echoes of **Fortunate Isles**, as the Canary Islands are known, and the two island groups share a common geographical location off the northwest coast of their respective continents, Africa and Europe. *See also* **Hesperides**.

> The "Happy Islands" cannot fail to please the most exacting of tastes [*Holiday Guide 1952: Area No. 5, South & South East England*].

**Happy Valley** *(1) Ruhr, Germany; (2) Vale of Kashmir, India.* The familiar sobriquet for a pleasant or peaceful place owes its origin to Samuel Johnson's *Rasselas* (1759), in which the "province of Abissinia [*sic*] was confined in the Happy Valley, a paradise surrounded by high mountains." The Vale of Kashmir has long been famed for its scenic beauty. In World War II, the name was used ironically by British Royal Air Force pilots for the Ruhr as a region many times bombed. *See* **Crump Dump**.

**Hard Case State, the** *Oregon, USA.* The nickname refers either to the rough life endured by the state's early settlers or, more likely, to the criminal element among them.

**Hardware Village, the** *Birmingham, England.* A former nickname for the city's famed manufacture of hardware goods. *See also* **Village**.

> Birmingham is called "the hardware village" [*The Slang Dictionary*, 1894].

**Hardy Country** see in Appendix 1, p. 269.

**Harrow-on-the-Hill** *Harrow, London, England.* The alliterative name refers to the town's conspicuous hill and the church that crowns it. The name is particularly associated with Harrow School, itself colloquially known as The Hill.

> There are now many Harrows—North, South, West, Etc.—but there is only one Harrow-on-the-Hill. This is the Harrow of the windy ridge and the village street [*Metro-land*, 1932].

**Harry Percy of the Union, the** *South Carolina, USA.* A rare nickname for the state, comparing the stalwartness of its inhabitants to that of the fiery English soldier and horseman Sir Henry Percy, known as Hotspur, who died in a rebellion against Henry IV in the Battle of Shrewsbury (1403).

**Hashbury, the** *Haight-Ashbury, San Francisco, California, USA.* The colloquial name elides the two parts of the full name. It aptly suggests "hash," as if for the gatherings of drug users and flower children for which the district was noted in the 1960s.

> Within The Hashbury circulate more than 25 undercover narcotics agents, who arrest an average of 20 hippies a week, usually for possession of marijuana [*Time*, July 7, 1967].

**Hat, the** *Medicine Hat, Alberta, Canada.* A colloquial shortening of the city's name.

**Hawaii of Asia, the** *Hainan, China.* The island, in the South China Sea, is a popular tourist resort at a latitude identical to that of Hawaii (19°N) and with a matching daytime temperature range of 22°C–27°C (72°F–80°F). Hence the geographically and meteorologically apposite nickname. (The quote below adds a more immediately striking association.)

> The "China's Hawaii" nickname came because it [i.e. Hainan] is on the same latitude as the real Hawaii—and because Chinese and South Korean visitors have a penchant for wearing garish Hawaiian shirts [*The Times*, October 15, 2005].

**Hawaii of Europe, the** *Lanzarote, Spain.* The smallest and easternmost of the Canary Islands, a popular tourist destination, is so nicknamed as offering facilities similar to those of Hawaii, as indicated in the quote below. Both islands are equally noted for their beautiful scenery, ideal climate, and volcanic origin.

> Lanzarote—some surfers call it the Hawaii of Europe [*The Times*, September 18, 2004].

**Hawaii of Japan, the** *Miyazaki, Japan.* The seaport city, a popular tourist and resort center on the island of Kyushu, is so nicknamed for its sunny climate.

**Hawaii of the North, the** *Tiree, Scotland.* The island of the Inner Hebrides has capitalized on its warm sun and windswept sandy beaches to become a Mecca for windsurfers. Hence its comparison with Hawaii.

> [Tiree] is the windsurfing capital of Scotland and is even referred to as 'the Hawaii of the north' [*Lonely Planet Great Britain*, 2005].

**Hawkeye State, the** *Iowa, USA.* The nickname is said to derive either from a fearsome Indian chief known as Hawkeye or from James G. Edwards, editor of the Burlington *Patriot*, nicknamed Old Hawkeye.

> The State of Iowa;—said to be so named after an

Indian chief, who was once a terror to *voyageurs* to its borders [Wheeler, p. 167].

**Hazy Brook** *Hazebrouck, France*. A British soldiers' World War I romantic rendering of the name of the French town in Flanders near the Belgian border, then on the Western Front.

**HCM** *Ho Chi Minh City, Vietnam*. An initialized form of the city's name.

We include 4 nights in Vietnam's premier city, Saigon, officially Ho Chi Minh City ('HCM') [Travel ad, *The Times Magazine*, February 5, 2005].

**Head of Africa, the** *Cape of Good Hope, South Africa*. An old nickname of the well-known cape or headland.

**Head of Goliath, the** *Buenos Aires, Argentina*. The name derives from the title of a book by the Argentine poet and philosopher Ezequiel Martínez Estrada, *La Cabeza de Goliat: Microscopía de Buenos Aires* (1946). The reference is to the capital city's imbalance with regard to the rest of the country, like a big-headed giant with a weak body.

**Heartbeat Country** see in Appendix 1, p. 269.

**Heartbreak Island** *Ellis Island, New York, USA*. The nickname relates to the millions of immigrants who landed at Ellis Island in the period between 1892 and 1924, and who feared they might not be accepted. (In fact more than 98 percent of the prospective immigrants gained entry, most of them within eight hours.) *Cp.* **Island of Tears**.

**Heartland** see in Appendix 1, p. 269.

**Heart of America, the** *Kansas City, Missouri, USA*. As mentioned in the quote below, Kansas City lies almost in the middle of the USA.

Kansas City not only calls itself "The Heart of America" (it is almost the geographical dead centre), but "America's Most Beautiful City." This is a touch of hyperbole [Collinson Owen, *The American Illusion*, 1929].

**Heart of Darkness, the** *Democratic Republic of the Congo*. The sinister name derives from the the title of Joseph Conrad's book, as indicated in the quotes below. At the time of publication (1902), the reference was to the Belgian Congo, the scene of hidden crimes and secret customs. *Cp.* **Dark Continent**.

(1) Some of these journalists comfort themselves with re-reading Conrad's *Heart of Darkness*... It is still the definitive work on what it feels like to be in the Congo [Richard West, *The White Tribes of Africa*, 1965].

(2) "Never forget this [i.e. the Democratic Republic of the Congo] is *Heart of Darkness* country. People do things here just because they can," one female UN employee said, in a reference to Joseph Conrad's novel about the abuses of the former Belgian Congo [*The Times*, December 23, 2004].

**Heart of Dixie, the** *Alabama, USA*. Alabama is in the center of **Dixie** or the **Deep South** (see both in Appendix 1, p. 269). Hence the name.

**Heart of England, the** *(1) Birmingham, England; (2) Warwickshire, England*. Birmingham lies almost in the middle of England and was long in the central county of Warwickshire. (*See also* **Big Heart of England**.) For Warwickshire, the name also alludes to the county's essential "Englishness." In 1973 the name was adopted by the Heart of England (formerly West Midlands) tourist board to designate a broad region of central England.

(1) (Warwickshire) Upon the Midlands now th'industrious Muse doth fall;
That Shire which we the heart of England well may call [Michael Drayton, *Poly-Olbion*, 1612].
(2) (Warwickshire) Our Warwick-shire the Heart of England is [Sir Aston Cokayne, "To William Dugdale," *Small Poems of Divers Sorts*, 1658].
(3) (Warwickshire) It was not accidental that Warwickshire produced the greatest of Englishmen [i.e. William Shakespeare]. "The heart of England," as the county has been called, summed up all that was most purely English in its scenery and associations [Mandell Creighton, *The Story of the English Shires*, 1897].
(4) (Warwickshire) Your Majesty, our friend of many years,
Confirms a triumph now the moment nears:
The lock you have re-opened will set free
The heart of England to the open sea [John Betjeman, "Inland Waterway," 1974; declaimed as Poet Laureate at the opening of a new river lock at Stratford-upon-Avon, Warwickshire, by Queen Elizabeth, the Queen Mother].

**Heart of Kent** see in Appendix 1, p. 269.

**Heart of Midlothian, the** *Edinburgh, Scotland*. The nickname was originally that of the Old Tolbooth, a notorious jail in Edinburgh, itself the capital of the county of Midlothian as well as of Scotland overall. The name then passed by extension to the Old Town in the city. It became familiar as the title of Sir Walter Scott's novel of 1818, which includes an account of the historical storming of the jail in 1736. The Old Tolbooth was demolished in 1817.

The Old Town is ... perched on the ... volcanic stack right in the heart of the city (and Midlothian) [Dodd/Donald, p. 35].

**Heart of Siberia, the** *(1) Irkutsk, Russia; (2) Verkhoyansk, Russia*. Both cities have claimed the title, but Yakutsk is geographically the more central of the two.

(Verkhoyansk) Loyal Russians call Verkhoyansk the heart of Siberia. Political exiles have another name for the place also commencing with the letter H, which I leave to the reader's imagination [Harry de Windt, *From Paris to New York by Land*, 1904].

**Heart of Texas** see in Appendix 1, p. 269.

**Heart of the Chang Jiang, the** *Wuhan, China*. The nickname refers to the city's important transport location in east central China at the junction of the Han River with the Chang Jiang (Yangtze Kiang), China's principal river.

**Heart of the Empire, the** *London, England*. A patriotic title of bygone times for the British capital. (The slogan appeared on a 1939 railway poster depicting a mounted guardsman.)

**Heavenly Kingdom, the** *Sichuan, China*. The nickname of China's second-largest province properly relates to the Sichuan Basin, the Chinese name for which is Tien Fu Chih Kuo, "Heaven on Earth," referring to the region's fertile soil and abundant mineral and forestry resources. *See also* **Rice Bowl of China**.

> We cruise from the 'Queen of the Orient,' Shanghai, to the 'Heavenly Kingdom' of Sichuan [Travel brochure issued with *Sunday Times*, August 14, 2005].

**Heavenly Trio** see in Appendix 1, p. 269.

**Heaven's Reflex** *Killarney, Ireland*. The poetic name implies that Killarney, Co. Kerry, one of the most famous (and commercialized) of Ireland's tourist resorts, with its romantic lakes and mountain scenery, is an earthly reflection of heaven. More prosaically, its lakes reflect the sky (otherwise heaven).

> (1) Angels fold their wings and rest
>   In that Eden of the west,
>   Beauty's home, Killarney,
>   Heaven's reflex, Killarney [Edmund Falconer, *Inishfallen*, 1862].
> (2) [The mountainous country of] Sliabh Luachra has its own beauty — nothing like the so-called Heaven's Reflex or manicured refinement of nearby Killarney, but something more primeval [Donal Hickey, quoted in *Irish Times*, December 29, 1999].

**Hebudes** *Hebrides, Scotland*. The Latin form of the islands' name was preserved in poetry. (The present name is said to have arisen through a miscopying of the *u* as *ri*.)

> Far from Hebudes, dark with rain,
>   To eastern Lodon's fertile plain [Sir Walter Scott, *Marmion*, 1808].

**Heel of Italy, the** *Apulia (Puglia), Italy*. As it appears on the map, the region represents the "heel" of the "boot" that is Italy, as distinct from the **Toe of Italy**. *See also* **Leg of Italy** in Appendix 1, p. 269.

> Puglia is out on a limb. It's the heel of Italy, and has always been at the end of the line [*Sunday Times*, March 27, 2005].

**Helen of the West, the** *St. Lucia, West Indies*. A name that is a nice classical personalization, from Helen of Troy, renowned for her beauty.

The "West" is the West Indies. The title appears in the second verse of the country's national anthem, as quoted below, written by Charles Jesse (1897–1985) and first adopted in 1967.

> Gone the times when nations battled
>   For this 'Helen of the West.'

**Hellas** *Greece*. The classical Greek name of Greece was adopted for poetic use.

> (1) *Hellas* [P.B. Shelley, title of lyrical drama, 1821].
> (2) Gods of Hellas, gods of Hellas,
>   Can ye listen in your silence? [Elizabeth Barrett Browning, "The Dead Pan," 1844].
> (3) O Hellas! Hellas! in thine hour of pride,
>   Thy day of might, remember him who died [Oscar Wilde, "Ravenna," 1878].

**Hellespont** *Dardanelles, Turkey*. The classical name of the strait between Europe and Asia survives in poetry and literary use. It derives from Greek *Hellespontos*, "Helle's sea," alluding to Helle, in Greek mythology the daughter of King Athamas, who fell from a ram into its waters when fleeing her father and cruel stepmother with her brother Phrixus.

> (1) That's on some shallow story of deep love,
>   How young Leander cross'd the Hellespont [William Shakespeare, *Two Gentlemen of Verona*, c.1592].
> (2) Leander who was nightly wont
>   (What maid will not the tale remember?)
>   To cross thy stream, broad Hellespont! [Lord Byron, "Written after Swimming from Sestos to Abydos," 1810].

**Hell Hole of the Pacific, the** *Russell, New Zealand*. The North Island town and port, originally a shore station for whalers, was so nicknamed for its lawlessness.

**Hell Hole of the South Pacific, the** *St Helena Island, Australia*. The Queensland island, off the mouth of the Brisbane River, acquired its nickname in its days as a prison island. The last inmate left in 1933.

**Hell's Corner** see in Appendix 1, p. 269.

**Hell's Hundred Acres** see in Appendix 1, p. 269.

**Hell's Kitchen** see in Appendix 1, p. 269.

**Hellstinky** *Helsinki, Finland*. A disapprobatory punning nickname for the Finnish capital devised by its younger residents.

> For some of the city's teenagers ... Helsinki is small and too provincial: "Hell-stinky," some of them call it [Dodd/Donald, p. 372].

**Hell with the Lid Off** *Pittsburgh, Pennsylvania, USA*. Pittsburgh was so infamously known in its heyday as the **Steel City**. *Cp.* **Big Smoky**.

**Helvetia** *Switzerland*. The Latin name of the federal republic survives not only in poetry but also in official use, as on postage stamps, in order to avoid partiality between the country's four official languages, French, German, Italian, and Romansh, which name Switzerland respectively as *Suisse*, *Schweiz*, *Svizzera*, and *Svizra*. The Roman name is from the Helvetii, the former people here.

> See from the ashes of Helvetia's pile
> The whitened skull of old Servetus smile! [Oliver Wendell Holmes, *A Rhymed Lesson (Urania)*, 1846].

**Hemel** *Hemel Hempstead, England*. A local short name for the Hertfordshire town. (Hemel, the Old English name of the district, meaning "broken country," was later added to Hempstead, the original name of the town.)

> I live in Harrow, which merges into Watford, which merges into Hemel, which merges into St Albans [*The Times*, September 3, 2004].

**Hemp State, the** *Kentucky, USA*. Hemp was formerly one of the state's principal crops.

**Henge, the** *Stonehenge, England*. The short name of Stonehenge, adopted generically in the 20th century to designate similar ancient "hanging" monuments elsewhere in the country, one being nearby Woodhenge, discovered in 1925, where there was an equivalent timber structure. *Cp.* **Stones**.

> Residents ... have complained that the Henge, for all its fame, failed to bring revenue into the region [*The Times*, December 18, 2004].

**Hermit Kingdom** or **Nation** or **Land, the** *Korea*. Following centuries of domination by China, involving several invasions, Korea adopted a policy of isolation from foreign contact by closing its frontiers. Hence the sobriquet, which remained valid until the country's virtual annexation by Japan from the 1890s until 1945. As mentioned in quote (2) below, the name today retains its relevance for North Korea.

> (1) The Rajin-Sonbong free trade zone along the Chinese border is sponsored by the United Nations in an effort to energise economic reforms in the country dubbed "the Hermit Kingdom" [*The Times*, November 13, 2004].
> (2) When Britain signed a treaty of friendship and commerce with undivided Korea in 1884, the remote East Asian country was known as the Hermit Kingdom. Today North Korea ... is still largely isolated [*The Times*, December 1, 2004].

**Hernia Bay** *Herne Bay, England*. A humorous punning name for the Kent coast resort.

> Because of its large number of retired folk, "drab and moribund" Herne Bay in Kent is often called Hernia Bay [*The Rough Guide to England*, quoted in *The Times*, March 16, 2004].

**Hero City** *Santiago de Cuba, Cuba*. The city gained its title after 1953, when Fidel Castro led a band of revolutionaries in an attack on the Moncada army barracks in his struggle against the dictator Fulgencio Batista.

**Heroin Capital of America, the** *Harlem, New York City, USA*. The predominantly black neighborhood was so nicknamed from the 1940s for its many heroin addicts. Until it was closed by the police, the source for the drug was the so-called "Heroin Supermarket" on Eighth Street between 116th and 117th streets.

**Herring Pond, the** *Atlantic Ocean*. A humorous name for the great ocean, in which herrings are a common catch. *Cp.* **Pond**.

> I'le send an account of the wonders I meet on the Great Herring-Pond [John Dunton, *Letters Written from New England*, 1686].

**Herring Town, the** *Great Yarmouth, England*. The Norfolk port and resort was long famous for its herring-fishing industry until stocks were exhausted in the 1960s. Hence the former nickname.

> Rather more than four miles north of the Herring Town we come to the ruins of Caister Castle [E.S. Symes, *The Story of the East Country*, n.d. (*c.*1910)].

**Herriot Country** see in Appendix 1, p. 269.

**Herts** *Hertfordshire, England*. A semiofficial abbreviated name for the county, adopted to form part of the name of the modern administrative district and political constituency of Hertsmere. *See also* Appendix 6, p. 325.

> Herts male, 40, ... seeks outgoing friendly female for lasting relationship [Personal ad, *Sunday Times*, June 26, 2005].

**Hesperia** *(1) Italy; (2) Spain*. The classical name was applied by the Greeks to Italy and the Romans to Spain, each being a "western" land, like the **Hesperides**. (Italy is west of Greece and Spain is west of Italy.) Hence "Hesperian" as a poetic term for Italian or Spanish, as in the quote for **Adria**.

**Hesperides, the** *(1) Canary Islands, Spain; (2) Cape Verde*. For the Canaries, the classical name is a poetic synonym for the **Fortunate Isles**. It represents the plural form of Greek *hesperos*, "western," implying "daughters of the west," referring to the daughters of Hesperus in Greek mythology, who guarded the garden of golden apples in the Islands of the Blessed. An alternate tradition identified the islands with those of Cape Verde, in the Atlantic to the west of West Africa.

> (Cape Verde) 7 Iles of Cape de Verde ... some thinke, these were the Hesperides, so famous for the garden of golden Apples [Sir Thomas Herbert, *A Relation of Some Yeares Travaile Begunne Anno 1626, into Afrique and the Greater Asia*, 1636].

**Heteropolis** *Los Angeles, California, USA*. A Greek-based name meaning "different city," referring to the diversity of ethnic groups, lifestyles, and languages in Los Angeles. The name was used in Charles Jencks's 1993 book so titled, a study of the city and its distinctive characteristics.

**Hibernia** *Ireland*. The Roman name of Ireland survives in poetic and commercial use. (In origin it has the same source as the poetic name **Erin**, influenced by Latin *hibernus*, "wintry.")

> (1) While in Hibernia's fields the labouring swain
> Shall pass the plough o'er skulls of warriors slain
> [John Hughes, "The House of Nassau," 1702].
> (2) For who would leave, unbrib'd, Hibernia's Land,
> Or change the rocks of Scotland for the Strand?
> [Samuel Johnson, "London: A Poem," 1738].

**Hibernian Archipelago, the** *British Isles*. A cumbersome name proposed by Irish nationalists in place of the familiar British one, which geographically (but not politically) includes the island of Ireland. *See also* **Hibernia**.

> As our national confidence soared, at times it seemed as if the term 'the British Isles' might be replaced as 'the Hibernian Archipelago' [*Sunday Tribune*, January 2, 2000].

**Hidden Gem of the Adriatic, the** *Montenegro*. A wry promotional name for the former region of Yugoslavia, north of Albania.

> "Our biggest problem is that many of our fellow Europeans cannot even find Montenegro on a map. For us, to be 'the hidden gem of the Adriatic' ... is not enough" [*The Times*, July 10, 2004].

**Hidden Island** *see* **Lost Island**

**Hielands** see in Appendix 1, p. 269.

**Hierusalem** *Jerusalem, Israel*. An anglicized form of *Hierosoluma*, the Greek name of Jerusalem, taken to mean "holy city of Solomon," as if from Greek *hieros*, "holy," and the name of King Solomon, who in the 10th century BC built the walls of the city and founded his famous temple here, as described in 1 Kings 6. (The status of Jerusalem as a **Holy City** is genuine enough, and its Arabic name is *al-Quds*, "the holy one.") As with the real name, the reference may be either literally to the capital of the ancient kingdom of Israel (the present Israeli capital) or metaphorically to heaven. *Cp.* **Salem**.

> (1) Then peaceably thy painefull pilgrimage
> To yonder same *Hierusalem* shall bend [Edmund Spenser, *The Faerie Queene*, 1590].
> (2) Hierusalem, my happy home,
> When shall I come to thee?
> When shall my sorrows have an end,
> Thy joys when shall I see? [Anonymous hymn, *c.* 1600].

**Highbrowville** *Boston, Massachusetts, USA*. The nickname alludes colloquially to Boston's cultural heritage, as the **Athens of America**.

**Highest Town in Europe, the** *Briançon, France*. The Alpine town, on a steep slope above the Durance and Guisane rivers, consists of the modern Sainte-Catherine district, at an altitude of 3,950 ft (1,204 m), and of the walled old town at an even loftier elevation of 4,350 ft (1,326 m). Hence the proud promotional name.

**Highlands** see in Appendix 1, p. 269.

**High-Tech Capital of the Philippines, the** *Makati, Philippines*. The city has earned its modern nickname as a business and technology center.

**High Water** *Great Falls, Montana, USA*. The nickname refers to the nearby Great Falls of the Missouri that gave the city its name.

**Hill, the** *(1) Forest Hill, London, England; (2) Notting Hill, London, England; (3) Sierra Nevada, California, USA; (4) Washington, DC, USA*. Both London districts are familiarly known thus to local people. The California mountain range is colloquially so nicknamed by way of a humorous belittlement. For Washington, the hill is Capitol Hill, the location of the US Capitol, where the Congress of the United States holds session. The name came to refer to Congress itself and so to the city as a whole.

> (1) (Sierra Nevada) "No kid is a road-kid until he has gone over 'the hill'"—such was the law of the The Road I heard expounded in Sacramento... 'The hill,' by the way, was the Sierra Nevadas" [Jack London, *The Road*, 1907].
> (2) (Forest Hill) This is a canny time to consider the Hill, with transport once more the key [Carrie Segrave, *The New London Property Guide*, 2003].
> (3) (Notting Hill) Handsome Victorian terraces and paired villas characterize the area ... from the crescents and rows at the Hill's top ... to the newly fashionable ... roads down the Hill and in North Kensington [Carrie Segrave, *The New London Property Guide*, 2003].

**Hip City** *Cleveland, Ohio, USA*. The colloquial name arose among the city's young black population.

**Hippy Isle, the** *Papa Stour, Scotland*. The Shetland island was so nicknamed in the 1970s when a collection of motley settlers arrived in response to an advertised bid to halt the declining population. There may also be a pun on "happy isle" or "happy island," as for **Happy Island**.

> Papa Stour was briefly dubbed "the hippie isle," but it wasn't long before some newcomers moved on [*The Rough Guide to Scotland*, 1998].

**Hispania** *Spain*. The Latin name for Spain survived into modern times in poetic use.

> No horrid crags, nor mountains dark and tall,
> Rise like the rocks that part Hispania's land from Gaul [Lord Byron, *Childe Harold's Pilgrimage*, 1812].

**Hitler's Canary** *Denmark.* A disparaging nickname given by the British to the Scandinavian country in World War II when it was favored with relatively mild treatment by the occupying German powers. The author of the quote below adopted the name for the title of a 2005 children's book describing the experiences of her Danish family during the war.

> There might be those in Britain who sneered and referred to the small Scandinavian state as "Hitler's Canary," but they had no idea of the bravery an entire nation was soon to show [Sandi Toksvig in *The Times*, July 6, 2005].

**Hog and Hominy State, the** *Tennessee, USA.* The once derisory nickname refers to the state's traditional diet of pork and maize, regarded as cheap or at best plain and simple food.

**Hog Butcher for the World, the** *Chicago, Illinois, USA.* Chicago was formerly famous for its meatpacking industry. *Cp.* **Porkopolis**. The epithet derives from the Carl Sandburg lines in quote (1) below.

> (1) Hog Butcher for the World,
> Tool Maker, Stacker of Wheat,
> Player with Railroads and the Nation's Freight Handler;
> Stormy, husky, brawling,
> City of the Big Shoulders [Carl Sandburg, "Chicago," 1916].
> (2) No more is Chicago the hog butcher of the world, nor is Pittsburgh its forge, nor Detroit a tourist attraction [Nicholas van Hoffman, "America's Plastic Decade," *The Spectator*, January 5, 1980].
> (3) Bubbly Creek ... is a legacy of Chicago's role as 'hog butcher for the world' [*Lonely Planet USA*, 2004].

**Hogen Mogen** *The Netherlands.* The former nickname is a humorous corruption of Dutch *Hoogmogenheiden*, literally "High Mightinesses," the title of the former States General.

> I have sent him for a Token
> To your Low-Country Hogen-Mogen [Samuel Butler, *Hudibras*, 1678].

**Hoglandia** *Hampshire, England.* A rarish nickname for the southern county, from the derogatory (or simply facetious) term for its native folk as "Hampshire hogs," itself from a local noted breed of hog.

> There are three sorts of Hampshire hog, and they have given the county the subsidiary name of *Hoglandia*. One, the inhabitant of the county. Two, the less domestic animal from whose frequency the inhabitant gets his name... And three, the dish [John Rayner, *The Shell Guide to Hampshire*, 1937].

**Hogopolis** *see* **Porkopolis**

**Hogs Norton** *Hook Norton, England.* The Oxfordshire village was proverbial for the stupidity of its inhabitants, and its name was humorously altered as here. One popular saying referred to "Hogs Norton, where pigs play on the organ," and the corrupted name was revived in the 20th century for a BBC radio series in which the former stage comedian Gillie Potter delivered reports of the goings-on in the mythical village of Hogsnorton.

> "You were born at Hogs-Norton." This is a Village properly called Hoch-Norton, whose inhabitants (it seems formerly) were so rustical in their behaviour, that boorish and clownish people are said [to be] born at *Hogs*-Norton [Thomas Fuller, *The History of the Worthies of England*, 1662].

**Hogtown** *Toronto, Ontario, Canada.* The provincial capital's nickname does not denote a meatpacking center, as for Cincinnati as **Porkopolis**, but refers to the supposed materialistic greed of the city's inhabitants.

> Once known as boring old Hogtown, Canada's largest city is now the most happening hub in the country [*Sunday Times*, June 19, 2005].

**Hole, the** *Bilbao, Spain.* The largest city in the Basque Country derives its local nickname from Basque *botxo*, "hole," referring to its location between hills on either side of the Nervión River (Ría de Bilbao).

> This is a hole with attitude: hang around for an evening and you'll find yourself immersed in a whirlwind of frenetic partying [*Lonely Planet Spain*, 2003].

**Hole with the Mint, the** *Llantrisant, Wales.* A punning name for the undistinguished South Wales village, to which the Royal Mint moved from London in 1967. The name, bestowed by mint employees, is a wry reversal of the advertising tag for Polo Mints, "the mint with the hole." *Cp.* **Polomint City**.

**Holland** *The Netherlands.* The name is popularly used for the European state. Historically, Holland was a country of the Holy Roman Empire, now represented by the provinces of North Holland and South Holland in the Netherlands.

**Holland of America, the** *Louisiana, USA.* The state was so nicknamed for its numerous canals and dams, like those for which the European country is famous.

**Hollyweed** *Hollywood, Los Angeles, California, USA.* A prankish alteration of the movie capital's name, referring to the lenient marijuana laws of the 1970s. *Cp.* **Hollyweird**.

**Hollyweird** *Hollywood, Los Angeles, California, USA.* A punning name referring to the movie capital's perceived freakish image. *Cp.* **Hollyweed**.

**Hollywood East** *Washington, DC, USA.* The capital city of the USA was so dubbed during President Ronald Reagan's tenure of office in the

1980s, the quip alluding to his former role as an actor in various Hollywood B-movies. The nickname has also been applied to the **Hamptons** (see in Appendix 1, p. 269).

**Hollywood North** *Toronto, Ontario, Canada.* Canada's largest city earned its nickname as a center of the motion-picture industry. The Ciniplex Odeon Carlton movie-theater chain has its head office here and the city holds a prestigious international film festival annually.

> The city has been called Hollywood North — you may well wander unexpectedly into a movie shoot [*Lonely Planet Canada*, 2002].

**Hollywood of the North, the** *Muskoka, Ontario, Canada.* The lakeside resort district derives its nickname from the movie stars and moviemakers who have a home here. Muskoka is not far north of Toronto, **Hollywood North**.

> Known as the "Hollywood of the North," Muskoka is an exclusive playground north of Toronto favoured by the likes of Goldie Hawn, Dustin Hoffman and Steven Spielberg [Realtors' ad, *Sunday Times*, July 24, 2005].

**Holy City, the** *(1) Adelaide, Australia; (2) Allahabad, India; (3) Cuzco, Peru; (4) Fez, Morocco; (5) Jerusalem, Israel; (6) Kiev, Ukraine; (7) Macao, China; (8) Mecca, Saudi Arabia; (9) Medina, Saudi Arabia; (10) Moscow, Russia; (11) Palestine, Texas, USA; (12) Ravenna, Italy; (13) Varanasi (Benares), India.* All of the named cities are noted religious centers, or famed for their many places of worship. (Adelaide is also known as the **City of Churches**.) Allahabad has long been sacred to Hindu pilgrims. Cuzco was capital of the Inca empire, and known as the **City of the Sun**. Fez is one of the sacred cities of Islam. Jerusalem is sacred to Christians, Jews, and Muslims, and thus a place of pilgrimage. In 988, Kiev became the seat of the metropolitan of Russian Christianity. Macao became a center of Roman Catholicism, as described in quote (5) below. Mecca and Medina are the two holiest cities of Islam. In 1326, Moscow became the seat of the metropolitan of the Russian Orthodox Church. Palestine gained the nickname for the **Holy Land** after which it is named. Ravenna, former capital of the Western Roman Empire, is famed for its many early Christian monuments, such as the Byzantine church of San Vitale, dating from the 6th century. Varanasi is the holy city of the Hindus. *Cp.* **Sacred City**.

> (1) (Jerusalem) The rest of the people also cast lots, to bring one of ten to dwell in Jerusalem the holy city [Nehemiah 1:11].
> (2) (Jerusalem) Then the devil taketh him up into the holy city, and setteth him on a pinnacle of the temple [Matthew 4:5].

> (3) (Jerusalem) The Pilgrims ... make their way as well as they can to the Holy City [A.W. Kingslake, *Eothen*, 1844].
> (4) (Ravenna) O how my heart with boyish passion burned,
> When far away across the sedge and mere
> I saw that Holy City rising clear,
> Crowned with her crown of towers! [Oscar Wilde, "Ravenna," 1878].
> (5) (Macao) [The title was] bestowed in 1585 upon the city of Macao by the Portuguese settlers residing there. Above the entrance to the Senate House may still be seen — "*Cidade do Nome de Deus — não ha outra mais leal*," i.e., "City of the Name of God — there is not another more loyal" [Giles, p. 123].
> (6) (Adelaide) There is not another city in the whole of the Commonwealth that can boast such a large and variegated collection of canines than can Adelaide... It is time someone took a hand in ridding the Holy City of one of its chief pests [*Truth* (Sydney), May 2, 1909].
> (7) (Moscow) [Every Russian] regards Moscow as the sacred centre of the Empire; and, indeed, it is often called the "Holy City" [L. Edna Walker, *Peeps at Many Lands: Russia*, 1912].
> (8) (Kiev) Kieff is not only the Holy City of Russia ... but the principal town of Little Russia the Blessed [W. Barnes Steveni, *Things Seen in Russia*, 1914].

**Holy Island** *Lindisfarne, England.* The Northumberland island is an ancient monastic site, attracting many pilgrims. (The name is an alternate, without "the.")

> Lindisfarne, an isle on the coast of Northumberland, was called Holy Island, from the sanctity of its ancient monastery, and from its having been the episcopal seat of the see of Durham during the early ages of British Christianity [Sir Walter Scott, explanatory note to phrase "St. Cuthbert's Holy Isle" in *Marmion*, 1808].

**Holy Island, the** *(1) Guernsey, Channel Islands, UK; (2) Ireland.* Guernsey came to be so nicknamed for its many monks, and Ireland for its many saints. Hence the latter's alternate name of **Isle of Saints**. *See also* **Sacred Isle**.

**Holy Land, the** *(1) Palestine or Israel; (2) Tasmania, Australia.* Palestine, or more narrowly Canaan or Judah, is the scene of the biblical narrative relating to Jews (Old Testament) and Christians (New Testament). The name is regularly used in modern Christian contexts and also by travel companies arranging tours (pilgrimages) to biblical sites in Israel. The sobriquet is no longer current for the island state of Tasmania.

> (1) (Judah) And the Lord shall inherit Judah his portion in the holy land [Zechariah 2:12].
> (2) (Canaan) The land of repromission [i.e. the promised land], that men call the Holy Land [John Mandeville, *The Book of John Mandeville*, c.1360].

(3) (Palestine) I'll make a visit to the Holy Land,
To wash this blood off from my guilty hand
[William Shakespeare, *Richard II*, 1597].

(4) (Palestine) From Paneas, the fount of Jordan's flood,
To Beërsaba, where the Holy Land
Borders on Egypt and the Arabian shore [John Milton, *Paradise Lost*, 1667].

(5) (Palestine) The faded palm-branch in his hand
Show'd pilgrim from the Holy Land [Sir Walter Scott, *Marmion*, 1808].

(6) (Tasmania) In the rouse-abouts' hut ... they always spoke of the Cabbage Garden as 'Port Phillip', of the Holy Land as 'tother side [*The Bulletin* (Sydney), October 5, 1889].

(7) (Israel) Here we are in the holy land of Israel—a Mecca for tourists [David Vine, *Superstars*, TV program, quoted in *Private Eye*, February 29, 1980].

(8) (Israel) Such a nice name—the Holy Land—for a place with more evil acts per square mile than the VIP room at Satan's annual marshmallow roast [Michael Moore, *Stupid White Men*, 2001].

**Holy Land of Mountain Adventure, the** *Alps.* The Alps are generally regarded as a "Mecca" for climbers.

**Holy Mother of the Russias** or **Russians, the** *Moscow, Russia.* Moscow has been the seat of the metropolitan of the Russian Orthodox Church since medieval times. *See also* **Holy City**.

Holy Moscow, so reverently and affectionately regarded by the orthodox as the Mother of the Church [Wirt Gerrare, *The Story of Moscow*, 1903].

**Holy State, the** *South Australia, Australia.* The state is sometimes so nicknamed by virtue of its capital city, Adelaide, as the **Holy City**.

**Home** *England or Britain.* The nostalgic by-name became widely current in colonial times, typically among Britons in India and Australia. It was the American J.H. Payne, however, who popularized the concept of "home" in his opera *Clari, or, The Maid of Milan* (1823), with its well-known song "Home, sweet home," which included the sentiment, "There's no place like home."

(1) Home always means England; nobody calls India home [*Letters from Madras During the Years 1836–39, by A Lady* (Julia C. Maitland), 1843].

(2) The fervent New Zealand nationalist ... has contempt for the sentimentalist who still talks of Britain as 'Home' [Shadbolt, p. 72].

(3) 'A condition that's giving us a bad name throughout the world, and particularly at Home.' 'You mean Britain?' 'Of course.' 'But you're Australian born.' 'To me Britain is spiritual home' [Xavier Herbert, *Poor Fellow My Country*, 1975].

(4) "The Old Country!" Buffy said. They were still standing but would have risen if they had been sitting down. "To Home. Here's to Home.

Down the hatch. The Old Country!" "The Queen!" Buffy was inspired. "God bless the Queen" [Elizabeth Jolley, *The Sugar Mother*, 1988].

**Home Counties** see in Appendix 1, p. 269.

**Home for Fallen Buildings, the** *Portmeirion, Wales.* The coastal resort in western Wales was built in an exotic Italianate style in the 1920s by the eccentric Welsh architect Clough Williams-Ellis, who physically imported architectural features from buildings threatened with demolition in both Britain and continental Europe. Hence the sobriquet, which also punningly hints at "fallen" in the moral sense. *See also* **Xanadu of Wales**.

Portmeirion has been called the last nobleman's folly, a Welsh Xanadu, and a home for fallen buildings [Vaughan-Thomas/Llewellyn, p. 298].

**Home for Lost Frogs, the** *(1) England or Britain; (2) London, England.* The nickname puns on "home for lost dogs," referring to Britain's generally damp climate.

**Homely Hertfordshire** *Hertfordshire, England.* A nickname for the large residential county near London that is one of the **Home Counties** (see in Appendix 1, p. 269).

[Croxley Green] is a typical village green of "homely Hertfordshire" [*Metro-land*, 1932].

**Home of Baseball, the** *Cooperstown, New York, USA.* The residential village is popularly believed to be the site of the origin of the sport of baseball in 1839, and the National Baseball Hall of Fame and Museum is here.

**Home of Beauty and the Beast, the** *Hughenden, Australia.* The Queensland town so dubs itself for the nearby Porcupine Gorge National Park (the "Beauty") and the replica skeleton of one of the largest and most complete dinosaur skeletons found in Australia (the "Beast"), on show in the Flinders Discovery Centre here.

**Home of British Military Aviation, the** *Farnborough, England.* The Hampshire town, famous for its air shows, gained its nickname as the headquarters of the UK Defence Evaluation and Research Agency (until 1995 familiar as the Royal Aircraft Establishment). The base arose in 1862 as a location for testing balloons for military use.

Just as [nearby] Aldershot is known as the 'Home of the British Army,' so Farnborough is the 'Home of British military aviation' [Donough O'Brien, *Fame by Chance*, 2003].

**Home of Dr. Pepper, the** *Waco, Texas, USA.* The well-known Dr. Pepper flavor was first blended in Waco in 1885. Hence the sobriquet.

**Home of Horseracing, the** *Newmarket, England.* The Suffolk town is the center of English horseracing and the home of the Jockey Club, with two racecourses. Hence the title.

**Home of Lost Causes, the** *Oxford, England.* The sobriquet derives from Matthew Arnold's dictum in quote (1) below, criticizing the university city's self-indulgence and its reluctance to engage with the contemporary world.

> (1) Beautiful city! so venerable, so lovely, so un-ravaged by the fierce intellectual life of our century, so serene! ... Home of lost causes, and forsaken beliefs, and unpopular names, and impossible loyalties! [Matthew Arnold, *Essays in Criticism*, 1865].
>
> (2) Oxford has often been called "the home of lost causes," or, as Mr. Cram puts it, "of causes not lost but gone before" [*Times Literary Supplement*, August 7, 1914].
>
> (3) Oxford — better known as the home of lost causes — has a fair claim also to being the home of the English language [Melvyn Bragg in *Sunday Times*, April 17, 2005].

**Home of Mother Nature, the** *Ireland.* A touristic tag designed to tempt the tourist to explore the country's rural charms.

> Once described as "the Home of Mother Nature," Ireland is a land of wide-open spaces and natural beauty [Travel brochure issued with *The Times*, May 21, 2005].

**Home of Presidents and First Ladies, the** *Midland, Texas, USA.* The city is notably connected with the Bush family. George Bush, Sr., came here in 1948, George W. Bush, Jr., grew up here (and started an oil business here in the mid–1970s), his wife Laura Bush married here, and her father is buried here.

**Home of Santa Claus, the** *Lapland, Europe.* The north Scandinavian region, above the Arctic Circle, has come to be popularly regarded as the home of Santa Claus and his reindeer, as described in quote (1) below. Enterprising travel companies organize seasonal trips there accordingly, and especially to the city of Rovaniemi in northern Finland, the site of "Santa Claus's Workshop."

> (1) The idea that Santa's workshop existed in Lapland ... is a relatively new addition. [Artist Thomas] Nast had depicted him [in *Harper's Weekly*] as living at the North Pole, but ... in 1925 his 'home' was moved to Lapland in Finland, which is conveniently filled with grazing reindeer [Donough O'Brien, *Fame by Chance*, 2003].
>
> (2) Come bring the whole family with us on one of our great-value day breaks or two-day breaks by air to Lapland, the home of Santa Claus [Travel ad, *The Times*, September 15, 2005].
>
> (3) December will see more than 60,000 Brits ... visiting one of a dozen or so winter resorts, in Finland and Sweden, where Santa has his true home [*Sunday Times*, October 16, 2005].

**Home of the Blues, the** *St. Louis, Missouri,*

*USA.* The blues, as the folk music of American blacks, did not originate exclusively in St. Louis, and it was Chicago that played the greatest role in the development of urban blues. However, the city certainly fostered the style, and music legends such as Chuck Berry, Tina Turner, and Miles Davis made their debuts here. There is thus some justification for the sobriquet.

**Home of the Brave, the** *United States.* The name is a phrase from the national anthem and similar verse, as quoted below. "Home of the brave" can be taken to mean not just a land of brave men but the homeland of the brave as the American-Indian warrior. (This latter sense of "brave" dates from 1800 in English and was adopted from *brave* as used by the French in North America.) *Cp.* **Land of the Brave.**

> (1) 'Tis the star-spangled banner; O long may it wave
> O'er the land of the free, and the home of the brave! [Francis Scott Key, "The Star-Spangled Banner," 1814].
>
> (2) O Columbia, the gem of the ocean,
> The home of the brave and the free [David T. Shaw, attrib., "Columbia, the Land of the Brave," 1843].

**Home of the British Army, the** *Aldershot, England.* The Hampshire town was founded as a military camp in 1855 and has a closer connection with the army than any other British town. Hence the nickname. *Cp.* **Shot.**

> The self-proclaimed 'Home of the British Army' [Sam Jordison and Dan Kieran, eds., *The Idler Book of Crap Towns II*, 2004].

**Home of the Carnival, the** *Bridgwater, England.* The Somerset town is nicknamed for the carnival that it holds annually on the Thursday nearest to November 5, Guy Fawkes Night (Bonfire Night).

**Home of the Cheeseburger, the** *Denver, Colorado, USA.* The nickname derives from the invention of the cheeseburger in Denver in the 1930s.

**Home of the Gnome, the** *Neasden, London, England.* The name is bound up with the collection of characters created by the satirical magazine *Private Eye*, founded in 1961. Lord Gnome is the name of the magazine's absentee proprietor (based on an amalgam of real press barons), who supposedly lives in Neasden, a London suburb remarkable for its ordinariness, where the magazine was originally printed. The name is said to have been created by the poet John Betjeman, as mentioned in the quote below.

> Why are we all beastly to Neasden?
> Just because it lacks spires and dome?
> Or is it the curse of John Betjeman

Who christened it Home of the Gnome? [*The Times*, May 11, 1991].

**Home of the Seven-Day Weekend, the** *Las Vegas, Nevada, USA.* The slogan implies that the **Gambling Capital of the World** is a place where life is "all play and no work."

The grinning cowboy on the billboard above their heads says it all: "Las Vegas, home of the seven-day weekend" [*The Times*, July 17, 2004].

**Home of the Tubular Bandage, the** *Oldham, England.* A much-mocked former promotional name for the Merseyside town.

**Homestead State** *Oklahoma, USA.* The historic nickname refers to the fact that much of the state was settled by homesteaders under the Homestead Act of 1862. (The "-homa" in the state's name is an incidental bonus.)

**Home to All-Weather Shopping, the** *Woking, England.* A promotional name referring to the Surrey town's main enclosed shopping precinct, the Peacocks Shopping Centre, near the railroad station.

The first thing you will notice when you leave Woking train station is a sign that reads: 'Welcome to Woking, Home to All-Weather Shopping' [Sam Jordison and Dan Kieran, eds., *The Idler Book of Crap Towns II*, 2004].

**Homicide City** *New York City, USA.* The name dates from 1972, when a then all-time high of 1,757 murders in the city were reported to the police.

**Honest Toun, the** *Musselburgh, Scotland.* The nickname relates to 1332, when the people of Musselburgh cared for the dying regent of Scotland, Sir Thomas Randolph, 1st earl of Moray, without thought of any reward.

**Honey Island** *see* **Isle of Honey**

**Honeymooners' Capital, the** *Niagara Falls, New York, USA.* The city is traditionally visited by honeymooners, who throw coins into the waters of the famous falls for luck.

**Honkers** *Hong Kong, China.* The colloquial name for the region dates from the 1920s, when it was adopted by British army personnel serving in the Far East and by upper-class expatriates working in the former British crown colony. The name has the characteristic "Oxford -er" ending that was adopted (often with an added -s) in the late 19th century by Oxford university students for local places, as "Adders" for Addison's Walk, "Jaggers" for Jesus College.

Page called Danang 'Dangers,' with a hard g. In a war where people quite seriously referred to Hong Kong as 'Hongers' [*sic*] and spoke of running over Pnompers [i.e. Pnompenh, Cambodia] to interview Sukie [i.e. President Sukarno of Indonesia], a British correspondent named Don Wise made

up a Vietnam itinerary: Canters, Saigers, Nharters, Quinners, Pleikers, Quangers, Dangers and Hyoo-beside-the-sea [Michael Herr, *Dispatches*, 1977].

**Hookers' Beat** see in Appendix 1, p. 269.

**Hoop Pole State, the** *Indiana, USA.* The name refers to the hoop poles at one time used in the state for making baskets.

**Hoosier State, the** *Indiana, USA.* The origin of the state's nickname is much disputed. As well as the source offered in quote (1) below, the following have been suggested: (1) Pioneers greeted visitors at the doors of their log cabins by calling out "Who's 'ere?"; (2) A Louisville contractor called Samuel Hoosier preferred hiring Indiana men; (3) Frontiersmen fighting in early taverns might bite off an opponent's ear, so that a settler would find it on the floor and ask "Whose ear?"; (4) Ohio River boatmen were vicious fighters and were nicknamed "hussars" because they fought like those Hungarian soldiers (or else "hushers," as in the quote, because they could "hush" any opponent); (5) The term evolved from French *houssières*, "bushy places"; (6) It is a form of English dialect *hoose*, "roundworm," a parasite causing disease in cattle; (7) It is a form of a supposed Indian word *hoosa*, "maize"; (8) It represents *huzza*, a shout of early settlers; (9) It represents *hoozer*, a southern dialect word for something especially large.

(1) [The name's] application to the people of Indiana is thus accounted for by ... *The Providence Journal*: "The boatmen of Indiana were formerly as rude and as primitive a set as could well belong to a civilised country, and they were often in the habit of displaying their pugilistic acomplishments upon the Levee at New Orleans. Upon a certain occasion there, one of these rustic professors of the 'noble art' very adroitly and successfully practised the 'fancy' upon several individuals at one time. Being himself not a native of this Western world, in the exuberance of his exaltation he sprang up, exclaiming, in foreign accent, 'I'm a *hoosier*! I'm a *hoosier*!' Some of the New Orleans papers reported the case, and afterwards transferred the corruption of the epithet 'husher' (*hoosier*) to all the boatmen from Indiana, and from thence to all her citizens" [Wagner 1893, p. 34].

(2) Life does strange things to human beings. Charles T. Alston had been raised in a small farming community in Indiana, and here he was, a specialist in geography, ethnography, and allied branches of learning, helping to decide the destinies of men in lands whose very names were unknown to the people of Hoosier State [Upton Sinclair, *World's End*, 1940].

(3) Everybody in America knows that Indiana is the Hoosier State, but nobody now seems to know what a Hoosier is or ever was [Bill Bryson, *Mother Tongue: The English Language*, 1990].

**Hop Out** *Hopoutre, Belgium*. A British soldiers' World War I rendering of the placename. Hopoutre was then a suburb of Poperinge, just across the French border.

**Horicon** *Lake George, New York, USA*. The former name of the lake was said to be that of an Indian tribe. It was actually applied to it by James Fenimore Cooper in his novel *The Last of the Mohicans* (1826), set during the French and Indian siege of Fort William Henry on Lake George in 1757.

**Hornets' Nest, the** *Charlotte, North Carolina, USA*. The nickname dates from the Civil War, when Charlotte was the center of opposition to the Union forces. The name is said to have been given by the British general Charles Cornwallis, who dubbed the city a "hornets' nest of rebellion" during his brief occupation of it in 1780.

**Hot Lanta** or **Hotlanta** *Atlanta, Georgia, USA*. The punning name refers to the city's high temperature, both literally and metaphorically, in the latter case with regard to racial tension and conflict. (Martin Luther King, Jr., was born and is buried here.)

**Hot Town** *Atlanta, Georgia, USA*. A nickname on the lines of **Hot Lanta**.

**Hot Water State, the** *Arkansas, USA*. The name refers to the state's many thermal springs, especially in the region of Hot Springs.

**Housman Country** see in Appendix 1, p. 269.

**Hove Actually** *Hove, England*. The East Sussex residential town and seaside resort just west of Brighton is sometimes so called by local people, alluding to the exchange: "Do you live in Brighton?" "No, I live in Hove actually." Hove is regarded by its inhabitants as a more desirable and peaceful place to live than nearby brash and bustling Brighton, with which, even so, it officially shares city status as Brighton and Hove, a title that seems to rank it as just an adjunct. The nickname nicely echoes the 2003 movie title *Love Actually*.

I know Brighton and "Hove Actually" pretty well, having lived in the town and set up my first enterprise there [Restaurateur Oliver Peyton in *The Times Magazine*, November 27, 2004].

**H-Town** *(1) Harrisburg, Pennsylvania, USA; (2) Houston, Texas, USA*. A name formed from the initial of the respective cities' names.

**Hub, the** *(1) Boston, Massachusetts, USA; (2) Stoughton, Wisconsin, USA*. Any place regarding itself as important, or actually being so, could call itself "the hub" or "the hub of the universe." Boston came to be so called from quote (1) below, where the description originally applied to the statehouse, although the name could equally apply to a cultural center, as Boston is. It also so happens that roads enter Boston from different directions, resembling the spokes of a wheel, centering at the hub. Stoughton is so nicknamed because wagons and hubs for wagon wheels were once made there.

(1) (Boston) Boston State-House is the hub of the solar system. You couldn't pry that out of a Boston man, if you had the tire of all creation straightened out for a crow-bar [Oliver Wendell Holmes, *The Autocrat of the Breakfast-Table*, 1858].

(2) (Boston) Take one of our great centers of culture; take the hub of the Universe, take Boston [Upton Sinclair, *The Brass Check*, 1919].

(3) (Boston) Around 1840 something happened to Boston and surrounding New England. It became the "hub," the forcing ground of ideas, the centre of American intellectual independence [Malcolm Bradbury, ed., *The Atlas of Literature*, 1996].

(4) (Boston) In the middle of a lecture on early nineteenth-century Boston ... a student with a puzzled look raised her hand and asked the instructor: "What is this 'Hub' you keep talking about?" [Thomas H. O'Connor, *Boston A to Z*, 2000].

**Hub City** *Lubbock, Texas, USA*. Located at the intersection of several main highways, the city justifies its nickname as the commercial hub of the South Plains.

**Hub of the Pacific, the** *Auckland, New Zealand*. In the 1950s, New Zealand's largest city began to attract thousands of Polynesian Islanders, drawn by prospects of work and education. Hence its factually-based sobriquet.

**Huffington-on-the-Puffington** *London, England*. The name relates both to "huff and puff" as a term of pretentious reference and to the Greek writer Arianna Huffington, nicknamed Huffington-Puffington, who relocated to London. The phrase could also imply a city that is "huffing and puffing" to keep up with the rest of the Western world, and especially the United States.

"I've always wanted to live in Huffington-on-the-Puffington and smoke a pipe," jokes [US actor Nathan] Lane of his temporary London home and a West End stage debut that seems to have surprised him most of all [*The Times*, November 8, 2004].

**Huggermugger Metropolis of Cloak-and-Dagger Conspirators, the** *Mexico City, Mexico*. A deliberately overblown nickname for the capital city, designed to reflect the lengths to which foreign intelligence agencies go to infiltrate other organizations.

**Hump, the** *(1) Himalayas; (2) Rocky Moun-*

*tains.* The nickname for both great mountain ranges is a mock belittlement, as if denoting a minor protuberance to be negotiated by land or air. The nickname for the Himalayas was current among aircraft pilots in World War II, especially those flying the hazardous route when carrying supplies from Assam to Kunming for the relief and support of China.

(1) (Rockies) There ain't a kid like him this side of the Hump — nor t'other side either [*Saturday Evening Post*, April 4, 1914].

(2) (Himalayas) They're flying it over "The Hump" — the towering Himalayas between India and China [*Time*, June 26, 1944].

**Hungarian Rome, the** *Eger, Hungary.* The city is so nicknamed for the many churches built here from the 18th century.

**Hunland** *Germany.* The name was used in World War I not only for Germany itself but for any territory occupied by the Germans. The term "Hun" for a German dates from the years immediately preceding World War I and was vigorously revived in World War II.

**Hunts** *Huntingdonshire, England.* A semi-official abbreviated name for the former county, absorbed into Cambridgeshire in 1974. *See also* Appendix 6, p. 325.

**Hut, the** *Terre Haute, Indiana, USA.* The colloquial form of the city's name represents the second word, pronounced "hote" or "hut."

**Hydaspes** *Jhelum River, India/Pakistan.* The ancient Greek name of the river, a tributary of the Indus, has been preserved in poetry.

(1) As when a vulture, on Imaus bred,...
...flies toward the springs
Of Ganges or Hydaspes, Indian streams [John Milton, *Paradise Lost*, 1667].

(2) In midmost Ind, beside Hydaspes cool,
There stood, or hover'd, tremulous in the air,
A faery city [John Keats, *The Cap and Bells*, 1819].

**Hymietown** *New York City, USA.* The nickname alludes to New York's large Jewish population, from Hymie, a colloquial term for a Jew (from the common Jewish name Hyman). *Cp.* **Jew York.**

The headline on the newspaper said HARLEM MOB CHASES MAYOR. The words were so big, they took up the entire page. Up above, in smaller letters, it said '*Go Back Down to Hymietown!*' [Tom Wolfe, *The Bonfire of the Vanities*, 1987].

**Hyrcania** *Gorgan, Iran.* The classical name of the former Iranian province, bordering the Caspian Sea (*Hyrcanum Mare*), is preserved in literary use.

But you are more inhuman, more inexorable, —
O! ten times more, than tigers of Hyrcania [William Shakespeare, *Henry VI, Part 3*, 1595].

**Iberia** *Spain.* The name is used poetically for Spain, although in modern terms the Iberian Peninsula includes both Spain and Portugal. It is thus equivalent to the Roman **Hispania**. *See also* **Lusitania**. (The name should not be confused with the ancient region of Iberia corresponding to the eastern part of present-day Georgia.)

Launched with Iberia's pilot from the steep,
To worlds unknown, and isles beyond the deep [Thomas Campbell, *The Pleasures of Hope*, 1799].

**Iberia's Tuscany** *Oeste, Portugal.* A touristic name for the western region of Portugal, comparing it to the famous Italian region, as described in the quote below. *See also* **Iberia**.

Portugal's Oeste region has been described by many as 'Iberia's Tuscany.' With a landscape of rolling hills, patchworked with ancient vineyards and a richness of local heritage and culture, it's easy to see why [Travel ad, *The Times*, July 15, 2005].

**Iceberg, the** *Anchorage, Alaska, USA.* A suitable nickname for the seaport city in the cold northern state.

**Iceberg Alley** *Labrador Sea, North Atlantic.* The sea between Labrador, Canada, and Greenland is so nicknamed for its many icebergs.

We were out in Iceberg Alley, riding among the great towers of ice that had ripped themselves off the flanks of Greenland [*Sunday Times*, January 30, 2005].

**Icebox of the Nation** or **the United States, the** *International Falls, Minnesota, USA.* The town is so nicknamed for frequently recording the coldest temperature readings for the USA (except Alaska) in daily weather reports.

**I-Down** *Idaho, USA.* A nickname punningly contrasting with that of **I-Up**.

**Ierne** *Ireland.* A variant of the more familiar folk name **Erin**, preserved mainly in poetry. *Cp.* **Hibernia**.

From her wilds Ierne sent
The sweetest lyrist of her saddest wrong [P.B. Shelley, *Adonaïs*, 1821].

**Igloo, the** *Minneapolis, Minnesota, USA.* Minneapolis is one of the coldest cities in the USA, with a chance of snow anytime between November and April. Hence the nickname

**Iladelph** *Philadelphia, Pennsylvania, USA.* An eccentric short form of the city's name, obtained by dropping its first and last two letters.

**Ilion** *see* **Ilium**

**Ilium** or **Ilion** *Troy, Turkey.* An alternate name for the ancient city, preserved in poetry. Ilium is the Latin form, Ilion the Greek.

(1) The armipotent Mars, of lances the almighty, Gave Hector a gift, the heir of Ilion [William Shakespeare, *Love's Labour's Lost*, 1598].

(2) Was this the face that launched a thousand ships,
And burnt the topless towers of Ilium? [Christopher Marlowe, *Doctor Faustus*, 1604].
(3) Royal Maud
From the throng'd towers of Lincoln hath look'd down,
Like Pallas from the walls of Ilion [John Keats, *King Stephen*, 1819].
(4) Like that strange song I heard Apollo sing,
While Ilion like a mist rose into towers [Alfred, Lord Tennyson, "Tithonus," 1864].

**Imperial City, the** *(1) Hue, Vietnam; (2) Rome, Italy; (3) Toledo, Spain* . The former imperial capital of Annam was famed for its royal buildings, many of which, including the Temple of Heaven, were severely damaged in the 1968 Tet Offensive of the Vietnam War. Rome was so titled as the capital city of the Roman Empire. Toledo became the Visigothic capital of Spain in the 6th century, the capital of New Castile in the 11th century, and finally the capital of the united kingdoms of León and Castile until 1560, when Philip II moved the seat to Madrid. The name (Spanish *la ciudad imperial*) is still current. *See also* **City of the Three Cultures.**

(1) (Rome) But thou, imperial City! that hast stood
In greatness once, in sackcloth now and tears,
A mighty name, for evil or for good [Matthew Arnold, "Alaric at Rome," 1840].
(2) (Hue) He was looking at the black napalm blasts and the wreckage along the wall. 'Looks like the Imperial City's had the schnitz,' he said [Michael Herr, *Dispatches*, 1977].

**Imperial Triangle** see in Appendix 1, p. 269.

**Ind** *India*. A poetic abbreviation of the country's name, dating from medieval times, when it was regularly found in this form. When qualified by "east" or "west," as in quote (3) below, the reference is to the East Indies (i.e. the Far East) or the West Indies. The name is usually pronounced as "binned" but poetically could equally be as "bind."

(1) And sclendre wyves, feble as in bataille,
Beth egre as is a tygre yond in Inde [Geoffrey Chaucer, "The Clerk's Tale," *Canterbury Tales*, c.1386].
(2) This sayd north parte is callyd Europa
And this south parte callyd affrica
This eest parte is callyd ynde
But this newe landes founde lately
Ben callyd america [John Rastell, *A new iuterlude* [sic] *and a mery of the nature of the .iiij. elements*, 1520].
(3) From the east to western Ind,
No jewel is like Rosalind [William Shakespeare, *As You Like It*, c. 1600].
(4) High on a throne of royal state, which far
Outshone the wealth of Ormus and of Ind [John Milton, *Paradise Lost*, 1667].

(5) An idol foreign to Assyria's worship,
Who conquer'd this same golden realm of Ind [Lord Byron, *Sardanapalus*, 1821].

**Indian Capital of America, the** *Gallup, New Mexico, USA*. The city, located between the Navajo and Zuni Indian reservations, is the area headquarters of the Bureau of Indian Affairs and the venue of the annual Intertribal Indian Ceremonial. Hence the nickname, competing with that of the **Indian Capital of the Nation.**

**Indian Capital of the Nation, the** *Anadarko, Oklahoma, USA*. The Apache, Delaware, and Wichita tribes have their headquarters in Anadarko, and the National Hall of Fame for Famous American Indians is here. The town also holds the annual American Indian Exposition. Nearby is Indian City, USA, comprising seven authentic Native American villages. Hence the nickname, vying with that of the **Indian Capital of America.**

**Indo** *Indonesia*. A mainly Australian abbreviation for the island country, with the common Australian -o already present in the name.

**Indy** *(1) India; (2) Indianapolis, Indiana, USA*. India was sometimes so known from the 16th century to the 19th. (The plural form of the name is still regularly found for the Indies.) For Indianapolis, the name is a colloquial short form of the city's name, familiar from the "Indy 500," the auto race held annually there.

**In-ger-land** *England*. A representation of "England" as chanted trisyllabically by supporters of the home side at an international sports contest, such as a rugby football match between England and one of the other countries in the Six Nations Championship (Scotland, Wales, Ireland, France, or Italy).

This is not England they are celebrating. It is the empty-headed parish of In-ger-land, populated by noisy show-offs [*The Times*, June 11, 2004].

**Inglan** *England*. A West Indian pronunciation of "England."

(1) Inglan is a bitch dere's no escapin' it
Inglan is a bitch dere's no runnin' way fram it [Linton Kwesi Johnson, *Inglan Is a Bitch*, 1980].
(2) Inglan is a bitch, as Linton Kwesi Johnson pointedly observed; but she a bitch who bring people together [*Times Literary Supplement*, July 16, 2004].
(3) They get their first glimpse of our coast as the Windrush brings them from the Caribbean and hail it with the sweetest of Paul Joseph's many hummable songs: "Big time, Inglan, Inglan, we are coming" [Review of black musical *The Big Life*, *The Times*, February 25, 2005].

**Innisfail** *Ireland*. The poetic name, traditionally interpreted as "isle of destiny," in fact derives from Irish *inis*, "island," and either *fáil*, the genitive of *fál*, "wall," "enclosure," referring to the "wall" of mountains that surrounds the central plain of Ireland, or *Fáil*, the genitive of *Fál*, the stone at Tara, Co. Meath, associated with the high kings of Ireland. A similar but less common name of Ireland is *Críocha Fáil*, "territories of Fál," from the plural of *críoch*, "region," "territory."

> (1) Oh! once the harp of Innisfail
> Was strung full high to notes of gladness;
> But yet it often told a tale
> Of more prevailing sadness [Thomas Campbell, "O'Connor's Child," 1810].
> (2) Adieu!— the snowy sail
> Swells her bosom to the gale,
> And our bark from Innisfail
> Bounds away [Richard D'Alton Williams, "Adieu to Innisfail," 1842].

**Inniskilling** *Enniskillen, Northern Ireland.* The altered form of the name is traditionally used for the army regiment known as the Inniskillings, raised for the defense of the Co. Fermanagh town in 1689.

**In Pin, the** *Inaccessible Pinnacle, Scotland.* The rocky peak on the island of Skye is so familiarly dubbed by those attempting to scale it.

**Insular Peninsula, the** *Cronulla, Australia.* The New South Wales town and resort, south of Sydney, is locally so nicknamed as it is cut off from most of the city by two bridges.

**Insula Sanctorum** *see* **Isle of Saints**

**Insurance City, the** *Hartford, Connecticut, USA.* Hartford is so named as a world-famous insurance center. Some of the largest insurance companies in the USA are located in Connecticut.

**Iodine State, the** *South Carolina, USA.* The nickname refers to the iodine found as a natural resource in the state's vegetation.

**Iona of the East, the** *Inchcolm, Scotland.* The island of Inchcolm, in the Firth of Forth, has the remains of an abbey dedicated to St. Columba, who resided here in the 6th century, as he did on Iona, off the west coast of Scotland. Iona is the larger island, however, and was the Christian center of Europe.

> Inchcolm has been described as 'the Iona of the east,' and the name means Columba's isle [Robinson/Millward, p. 390].

**I-O-way** *Iowa, USA.* A local pronunciation of the state's name, as in the "Iowa Corn Song," quoted below.

> We're from I-O-way, I-O-way,
> State of all the land,
> Joy on ev'ry hand,
> We're from I-O-way, I-O-way.
> That's where the tall corn grows [George Hamilton and Ray W. Lockard, "Iowa Corn Song," 1912].

**Irena** *Ireland.* The poetic personification of Ireland happens to be identical with the Latin form of the Greek name Irene, meaning "peace." It is really an equivalent of **Erin**, from the Irish original.

> He now went with him in this new inquest,
> Him for to aide, if aide he chaunst to neede,
> Against that cruell Tyrant, which opprest
> The faire *Irena* with his foule misdeede [Edmund Spenser, *The Faerie Queene*, 1596].

**Irish Alps, the** *Catskill Mountains, New York, USA.* A nickname for a favored leisure and casual labor area among Irish New Yorkers. *Cp.* **Jewish Alps.**

> Jerry is heading for the Catskill Mountains on Memorial Day, the end of May, the Irish Alps [Frank McCourt, *'Tis*, 1999].

**Irish City, the** *Big Bend, Indiana, USA.* The city is so nicknamed for its Irish and Catholic connections, as manifest in the University of Notre Dame, founded in 1842, and educational establishments such as St. Mary's College and Holy Cross (junior) College.

**Irish Free State** *see* **Eire**

**Irish Liverpool, the** *Belfast, Northern Ireland.* A former nickname for the Northern Ireland capital city and seaport.

> They call Belfast the Irish Liverpool. If people are for calling names, it would be better to call it the Irish London at once — the chief city of the kingdom at any rate [W.M. Thackeray, *The Irish Sketch Book*, 1843].

**Irish Rhine, the** *Blackwater River, Ireland.* The comparison does not relate to the size or importance of the Irish river but to the scenic countryside through which it flows, like that of its German counterpart.

**Irish Riviera, the** *Spring Lake, New Jersey, USA.* The upscale residential community near the Atlantic coast was formerly so nicknamed for its Irish families. (St. Catharine's Catholic church here was built by Margaret and Martin Maloney in memory of their 16-year-old daughter Catharine, who died of tuberculosis in 1900. All three are buried in the church.)

**Irish Rome, the** *Armagh, Northern Ireland.* The Irish city assumed its sobriquet on ecclesiastical and geographical grounds, as described in the quote below.

> Armagh has been the site of the Catholic primacy of all Ireland since St Patrick established his church here ... and has rather ambitiously adopted the title the "Irish Rome" for itself— like Rome, it's positioned among seven small hills [*The Rough Guide to Ireland*, 1999].

**Iron City, the** *Pittsburgh, Pennsylvania, USA.* Pittsburgh was a long a center of iron and steel production. Hence the nickname.

**Iron Gate of France, the** *Longwy, France.* The town is historically a well-fortified gateway to France, just south of the Belgian border.

**Iron Mountain State, the** *Missouri, USA.* The nickname derives from the Iron Mountain in the east of the state, a source of iron ore.

**Iron Town, the** *Cleveland, Ohio, USA.* The name refers to the city's noted steel production.

**Irrland** *Ireland.* This was James Joyce's name for his homeland in *Finnegans Wake* (1939), apparently punning on German *irren,* "to wander," "to go astray," and thus the equivalent of English "Errorland." The quote below cites the actual passage.

In *Finnegans Wake,* Joyce speaks through Shem the Penman, who "ran away with hunself and became a farsoonerite, saying he would far sooner muddle through the hash of lentils in Europe than meddle with Irrland's split little pea." And yet, all his life, European Joyce never stopped meddling with Errorland [Justine Beplate, review of Geerts Lernout and Wim Van Mierlo, eds., *The Reception of James Joyce in Europe, Times Literary Supplement,* April 29, 2005].

**Isa, the** *Mount Isa, Australia.* A short colloquial name for the Queensland mining town. For the characteristic prefixed "the" see quote (3) for **Alice.**

(1) All the major settlements ... are mining towns, spaced so far apart that precise names are redundant: Mount Isa becomes "the Isa," Cloncurry "the Curry," Charters Towers "the Towers," as if nowhere else existed [*The Rough Guide to Australia,* 2001].

(2) There are no trendy eateries in the Isa [*Lonely Planet Australia,* 2004].

**Ish** *Ismailia, Egypt.* A former British soldiers' abbreviated name for the town on the Suez Canal.

**Isis** *Thames River, England.* The name is that of the Thames as it flows through Oxford, derived artificially from the second half of its Roman name of *Tamesis.* In the quotes below, Isis is a synonym for Oxford University, and Cam for Cambridge University. (Wordsworth was a Cambridge graduate.)

(1) May you, my Cam and Isis, preach it long! The Right Divine of Kings to govern wrong [Alexander Pope, *The Dunciad,* 1742].

(2) I slight my own beloved Cam, to range Where silver Isis leads my stripling feet [William Wordsworth, "From Oxford, May 30th, 1820"].

**Isla, la** *Isla de la Juventud, Cuba.* A local name ("the island") for the Caribbean island. *Cp.* **Island.**

Cuba's second-largest island after the main island, 'La Isla' (as Cubans know it) is the least populated ... region [*Lonely Planet Cuba,* 2004].

**Island, the** (1) *Isle of Man, British Isles;* (2) *Isle of Wight, England;* (3) *Long Island, New York, USA;* (4) *Robben Island, South Africa.* The name is generic for any familiar island, and is frequently used locally for those named. As applied to the Isle of Wight, the term can also refer to one or other of the prisons Camp Hill and Parkhurst, located on the island. Similarly, Robben Island, in Table Bay, became notorious as a place of detention for political prisoners, otherwise **Mandela University.**

(1) (Isle of Wight) She thinks of nothing but the Isle of Wight, and she calls it *the Island,* as if there were no other island in the world [Jane Austen, *Mansfield Park,* 1814].

(2) (Robben Island) 'Are you a political?' one asked. 'Been to the Island?' said the other. 'Do you know Mandela?' [Gillian Slovo, *Ties of Blood,* 1990].

**Island City, the** *Montreal, Quebec, Canada.* Montreal arose on the island of the same name in the St.Lawrence River. Hence the name.

**Island Coast** see in Appendix 1, p. 269.

**Island for All Seasons, the** *Cyprus.* A nickname designed to attract visitors at any time of the year.

The island for all seasons is famous for the warmth of its Mediterranean sun throughout every season of the year [Cyprus Tourist Office ad, *The Times* (Cyprus Supplement), December 19, 2005].

**Island of a Million Palms, the** *Bahrain.* The nickname of the island country in the Persian Gulf relates not so much directly to its palm trees as to the many freshwater springs that feed them.

**Island of Death, the** *Kahoolawe, Hawaii, USA.* The uninhabited island has served as both a penal colony and a US military bombing range. Hence its blunt byname.

**Island of Eternal Spring, the** *Madeira, Atlantic Ocean.* The Portuguese island is noted for its equable climate, and thanks to its location in the Gulf Stream enjoys temperatures averaging 18°C–24°C (64°F–75°F). Hence the nickname. *Cp.* **Floating Garden of the Atlantic.**

It was a fine introduction to the "island of eternal springtime," where soft winds blow, where the sun is never too hot and the rain never lasts too long [*The Times,* February 19, 2005].

**Island of Hell, the** *Norfolk Island, Australia.* The South Pacific island was in British hands from 1788 to 1855 as a prison colony, where a number of detainees perished. Hence the name. *See also* **Ocean Hell.**

**Island of Memories, the** *Ireland.* A promotional name intended to attract the tourist to the country's many historic sites.

Discover the essence of the Island of Memories. The regional diversity of Ireland and its exceptional history and culture have left a legacy of monuments, settlements and buildings that provide the visitor with a great day out [Travel ad, <http://www.onlinetravel.com/ireland2004/home .asp>, accessed October 17, 2004].

**Island of Saints** *see* **Isle of Saints**

**Island of Sin, the** *Faliraki, Greece.* The resort on the island of Rhodes acquired its pejorative nickname in modern times following scandalous behavior there by (mainly) British tourists, resulting in rape and even murder in 2003.

> The [2003] television series [*Club Reps: The Workers*] was responsible for a 30 per cent rise in bookings to the resort, dubbed the "island of sin" [*The Times*, July 4, 2005].

**Island of Springs, the** *Jamaica, West Indies.* The nickname is an English rendering of the Arawak name, meaning "land of springs." Many short streams flow from the island's mountains.

**Island of Tears, the** *Ellis Island, New York, USA.* The name relates to the often unfeeling admission procedure experienced by immigrants as they passed through the reception center on the island. *Cp.* **Heartbreak Island.**

> [The incomers] were met by generally unsympathetic immigration clerks, inadequate interpreters and aggressive medical examiners, who made the place for many the 'Island of Tears' [Sean McMahon and Jo O'Donoghue, *Brewer's Dictionary of Irish Phrase and Fable*, 2004].

**Island of the Moon, the** *Madagascar, Indian Ocean.* A sobriquet on the same lines as the **Mountains of the Moon.** Madagascar lies to the south of the Comoros.

**Island of 20,000 Saints, the** *Bardsey Island, Wales.* The island off the Lleyn Peninsula is said to be so named for the many monks buried there.

> (1) Following the Battle of Chester in 615, the ousted monks of Bangor-Is-Coed re-established their college on Bardsey, and it may be these brothers and their successors who are the 20,000 saints said to be buried on the island [Booth/Perrott, p. 178].
>
> (2) Walkers on the rugged Pilgrims Trail still make their way out towards the seaward edge of Wales, to cross the sound to Bardsey and puzzle over the mounds and stones of the Island of 20,000 Saints [Christophe Somerville, *Coast: A Celebration of Britain's Coastal Heritage*, 2005].

**Islands, the** *(1) Hawaii, USA; (2) West Indies.* A general local name for the respective island state and island group.

> (West Indies) There were three young African-American men in the class and when one, Ray, complained that he'd been bothered by the police because he was black ... the women from The Islands had no patience with him [Frank McCourt, *'Tis*, 1999].

**Islands of Aloha, the** *Hawaii, USA.* An alternate name for the **Aloha State.**

**Islands** or **Isles of the Blessed** or **Blest, the** *Hebrides, Scotland.* A poetic name for the islands, referring to the islands of classical mythology that were the abode of the blessed dead in the Western Ocean (*see* **Fortunate Isles**). The name is apt for islands located to the west of mainland Scotland (*see* **Western Isles**).

> If you like to tuck into a fish finger after braving the foaming seas of the Minch, then the 'Isles of the Blessed' will spell magic to you [Charles Gore, "Remnants of Scottish Life and Character," in A.S.C. Ross, ed., *What Are U?*, 1969].

**Islands of the Moon, the** *Comoros, Indian Ocean.* The island republic, off the southeast coast of Africa, derives its name from Arabic *kamar*, "moon." This was the Arabs' astronomical name for the Magellanic Clouds, galaxies that to them represented the southern hemisphere. They thus gave the name to all islands in the southern latitudes, including Madagascar. *Cp.* **Mountains of the Moon.**

**Island State, the** *Tasmania, Australia.* An obvious sobriquet for the small state, contrasting it with the mainland states to the north.

> He left Tasmania to take part in the [gold] rushes of the fifties, and was ready to do fight for the Island State [*Huon Times* (Franklin), November 12, 1910].

**Isle of Avalon** *see* **Avalon**

**Isle of Beauty, the** *Corsica, France.* The island is so named (French *l'Île de Beauté*) for its fine mountain scenery.

> Corsica may be known as the *île de beauté*, but driving its tortuous corkscrewing roads ... is white-knuckle stuff [*The Times*, March 19, 2005].

**Isle of Destiny** *see* **Innisfail**

**Isle of Fire, the** *Madagascar, Indian Ocean.* The island has come to be so nicknamed in modern times for the islanders' use of fire to create pastures and rice fields, a procedure that equally results in the widespread destruction of forests and timber. A study of the controversial practice was made by Christian A. Kull in *Isle of Fire: The Political Ecology of Landscape Burning in Madagascar* (2004).

**Isle of Honey, the** *England or Britain.* According to Celtic lore, the island of Britain was at one time full of forests populated by swarms of wild bees. Hence the legendary nickname.

**Isle of Legends, the** *Langkawi, Malaysia.* A touristic nickname alluding to the local lore of the island.

> Beaches whitewashed in royal blood. Giants cursed to become stone. Lakes that get women

pregnant. They don't call Langkawi The Isle of Legends for nothing [Postcard travel ad, 2003].

**Isle of Mist** or **Misty Isle, the** *Skye, Scotland.* The name alludes to the usually damp climate of the island, the largest of the Inner Hebrides.

(1) Nor sleep thy hand by thy side, chief of the Isle of Mist [James Macpherson, *Ossian's Fingal*, 1762].

(2) Only individual experience can convey something of the fascination which emanates from the "Misty Isle" [*Holiday Haunts 1962: Scotland*].

**Isle** or **Island of Saints, the** *Ireland.* St. Patrick is believed to have converted Ireland to Christianity in the early 5th century, after which the island became a stronghold of Celtic Christianity, nurturing a number of ecclesiastics and dispatching missionaries, many of whom were later canonized, to Britain and Western Europe. Hence the name, referring to saints in the mass rather than individually, although including such well-known names as St. Columba, St. Brendan, and St. Brigid. A longer form of the name is "Island of Saints and Scholars," combining sanctity and sagacity.

(1) In the seventh century Ireland was known by the designation of "The Isle of Saints"... Its missionaries laboured with singular success in France, Germany, Switzerland, and Italy, as well as in Great Britain [William Killen, *The Ecclesiastical History of Ireland*, 1875].

(2) It was the Pope's arrival at Dublin Airport ... which truly set the distinctive character of this personal pilgrimage to his 'island of saints' [*The Guardian*, October 1, 1979].

(3) While Ireland may no longer lay claim to the title of 'Island of Saints and Scholars,' the glories of its legendary founders are still remembered and their blessings invoked [*RD Ireland*, p. 236].

**Isles of Nutmeg, the** *Banda Islands, Indonesia.* The chief products of the islands are nutmeg and mace. Hence the descriptive name.

**Isles of the Blessed** *see* **Islands of the Blessed**

**Isolationist Belt** see in Appendix 1, p. 269.

**Istinks** *Hastings, England.* A former promotional respelling of the East Sussex resort's name, designed to aid its pronunciation, as explained in the quote below.

When certain English resorts were being advertised in the Far East ... it was found that the name [of Hastings] ... raised grave difficulties of pronunciation for certain Indian folk. Whereupon [it] ... was amended to "Istinks" [H.G. Stokes, *English Place-Names*, 1948].

**Italia** *Italy.* The Latin name of Italy, adopted in poetry, is also the modern Italian name.

(1) Italia! oh Italia! thou who hast
    The fatal gift of beauty [Lord Byron, *Childe Harold's Pilgrimage*, 1812].

(2) I reached the Alps: the soul within me burned,
    Italia, my Italia, at thy name [Oscar Wilde, "Sonnet on Approaching Italy," *Rosa Mystica*, 1881].

**Italian Riviera** see in Appendix 1, p. 269.

**Italy of America, the** *Arizona, USA.* The nickname refers to the state's fine mountain scenery, evoking that of Italy.

**Italy of England, the** *Torquay, England.* The Devon seaside resort, with its soft air and warm sunshine, was so nicknamed by the 19th-century author and art critic John Ruskin.

**Itchland** *(1) Scotland; (2) Wales.* The former derogatory nickname refers to the supposed bodily uncleanness of the inhabitants of both countries, as well as their raw sexuality. *Cp.* **Louseland; Scratchland.**

(Scotland) So God keep me from Scotland, and all that mangy race,
    For it's a nasty, mangy, lousy, itchy, dirty place [*The Curse of Scotland*, ballad, 18th century].

**I-Up** *Iowa, USA.* A punning name contrasting with that of **I-Down.**

**Ivory Coast, the** *Côte d'Ivoire.* Although the African country has officially adopted the French form of its name, the English form is still widely used, especially by the media. The same goes for the vernacular form in other languages, as German *Elfenbeinküste*, Italian *Costa d'Avorio.*

Since 1986, Côte d'Ivoire has requested that the French form of the country's name be used as the official protocol version in all languages [*Encyclopædia Britannica Book of the Year 2005*].

**Ixta** *Ixtacihuatl, Mexico.* An American and British colloquial short name for the extinct volcano near Mexico City.

**JA** or **Ja** *Jamaica, West Indies.* An initialism or abbreviation of the island state's name.

**Jacaranda City, the** *Tshwane (Pretoria), South Africa.* The nickname alludes to the thousands of jacaranda trees throughout the city.

(1) It's hard to avoid purple prose while jacarandas are still blooming in Johannesburg... Trees in the Jacaranda City bloom two weeks earlier than they do here [*Weekly Mail* (Johannesburg), November 2, 1990].

(2) An optional tour reveals Pretoria, the 'jacaranda city' [Travel ad, *The Times Magazine*, April 30, 2005].

**Jade Sea, the** *Lake Turkana (Rudolf), Kenya/Ethiopia.* The lake is often known by this alternate name for the color of its water.

**Jago** see in Appendix 1, p. 269.

**Jamdung** or **Jam Down** *Jamaica, West Indies.* A West Indian corruption of the island state's name, repesenting "jammed down," referring to the oppression of ordinary Jamaicans by the political bosses.

**Jarrahland** *Western Australia, Australia.* The state derives its nickname from the jarrah, the mahogany gumtree *Eucalyptus marginata,* valued for its hard, durable, reddish-brown wood, which grows in this part of Australia.

**Jax** *Jacksonville, Florida, USA.* A neat local abbreviation of the seaport city's name.

> Jacksonville, in the northeastern corner of Florida and known as "Jax" to locals [*The Times,* January 29, 2005].

**Jayhawk** or **Jayhawker State, the** *Kansas, USA.* The origin of the state nickname is uncertain. Some have traced it to a Colonel Jennison of New York, nicknamed "Gay Yorker," who led a regiment of Kansas Free State men in the period before the Civil War. Others derive it from the "jayhawkers," the irregular troops who combined pillage with guerrilla raids in and around eastern Kansas during the early part of the Civil War, their own nickname perhaps combining the bird names "jay" (for the pillage) and "hawk" (for the raids).

> No one knows for sure ... why Kansans are [called] Jayhawkers (there is no such bird) [Bill Bryson, *Made in America,* 1994].

**Jazz City** *New Orleans, Louisiana, USA.* It was in New Orleans that black musicians formed the first distinctive jazz bands at the turn of the 20th century. Hence the nickname.

**JB** *Johor Bahru, Malaysia.* An initial-based nickname for the capital of the state of Johor.

> JB (as it is known throughout the country) [*Lonely Planet Malaysia, Singapore & Brunei,* 1999].

**J Bay** *Jeffrey's Bay, South Africa.* The Eastern Cape town is so nicknamed by those who know it as one of the best surfing areas in southern Africa.

**Jeans Capital of the World, the** *El Paso, Texas, USA.* Jeans have long played an important part in the city's varied manufactures. Hence the name.

**Jeering Coggeshall** *Coggeshall, England.* The Essex town's epithet honors the Protestant victims of the Catholic queen Mary I ("Bloody Mary"), burned at the stake for heresy and bravely taunting the flames as they met their death.

> Sure I am that no Town in England, of its bigness, afforded more Martyrs in the raign of queen Mary, who did not jeer or jeast with the fire, but seriously suffered themselves to be sacrificed for the testimony of a good conscience [Thomas Fuller, *The History of the Worthies of England,* 1662].

**Jeff City** *Jefferson City, Missouri, USA.* A colloquial shortening and personalization of the city's name.

Amtrak stops in Hermann, Jeff City and Sedalia [*Lonely Planet USA,* 2004].

**Jersey** *New Jersey, USA.* The state's name is usually shortened thus in adjectival use, as for Jersey girl, Jersey justice, Jersey side (but Jersey cows come from the Channel Islands). *See also* **Jersey Blue State.**

**Jersey Blue State, the** *New Jersey, USA.* The state received its nickname either from the blue uniforms worn by troops of the Revolutionary Army or from the so-called "blue laws" (*see* **Blue Law State**).

**Jerusalem of Russia, the** *Kiev, Ukraine.* Kiev is an ancient Christian center, with many religious buildings, and a noted place of pilgrimage, like Jerusalem. Hence the name. (*See also* **Holy City.**)

> Kiev, known as "the Jerusalem of Russia," is a great resort of pilgrims [Karl Baedeker, *Russia,* 1914].

**Jerusalem of Temperance, the** *Preston, England.* The Lancashire city was so nicknamed in the 19th century as a center of the temperance movement. (The word "teetotal" is said to have been coined by a Preston man in 1833.)

**Jerusalem of the North, the** *Valaam, Russia.* The island in the northwest of Lake Ladoga has a famous medieval monastery with a direct religious orientation to Jerusalem and the Holy Land, as explained in the quote below.

> For Orthodox believers, Valaam is a holy isle of saints and hermits, whose shrines echo Christ's Passion in the Holy Land, a "Jerusalem of the North," offering redemption to the sinful and miracles to the faithful... The hundred-odd monks on Valaam maintain their own "time zone," synchronized to Jerusalem and the Holy Land [*The Rough Guide to St Petersburg,* 2004].

**Jerusalem-on-Sea** *Brighton, England.* The nickname of the East Sussex seaside resort derives from the number of Jews who have come to live here in retirement, Jerusalem being the capital of Israel. *Cp.* **New Jerusalem.**

**Jerusalem the Golden** *Jerusalem, Israel.* The epithet is fitting for the Israeli capital, a city dominated by the 7th-century Dome of the Rock, its copper roof gleaming with gold leaf. But the sobriquet is most familiar as the opening words of the hymn by J.M. Neale, published in 1851, in which it is clear that the reference is to heaven. The hymn represents part of Neale's translation of *De Contemptu Mundi,* a 12th-century poem by St. Bernard of Cluny, where the original Latin words are *Urbs Sion aurea,* "Golden city of Zion."

**Jewburg** *Johannesburg, South Africa.* The city's population includes a number of Jewish families. Hence the former derogatory nickname, an alteration of its familiar abbreviated name of **Jo'burg**.

> Johannesburg was writing its nickname 'Jewburg' large over the sands, and the air was thick with broken English [Oliver Walker, *Shapeless Flame*, 1951].

**Jewel in the Baltic Crown, the** *St. Petersburg, Russia*. The former Russian capital, a major cultural center with many architectural treasures and scenic delights, is one of the most striking cities on the Baltic coast. Hence the sobriquet.

> The jewel in the Baltic crown, Russia's most European city was Tsar Peter the Great's "Window on the West" [Travel ad, *The Times*, October 22, 2005].

**Jewel in the Crown, the** *India*. India was long regarded as the prize possession in the British Empire, and the British colonies were generally known as the "jewels of the crown," meaning the royal crown. The name received new life as the title of the British TV drama *The Jewel in the Crown* (1984), based on Paul Scott's *The Raj Quartet*, where the title is that of the first book, published in 1966. *Cp.* **Fairest Jewel in the Imperial Crown**.

> It was in India, "the jewel in the crown," that British imperial experience seemed deepest [Malcolm Bradbury, ed., *The Atlas of Literature*, 1996].

**Jewel in the East, the** *Walthamstow, London, England*. As indicated in the quote below, the grandiose sobriquet was designed to lure the potential housebuyer to the increasingly fashionable district of northeast London.

> 'Walthamstow, the Jewel in the East,' the come-on line used by a property company to tempt investors out to E17, has proved both enticing and in a fair way to being accurate [Carrie Segrave, *The New London Property Guide*, 2003].

**Jewel of Flanders, the** *Bruges, Belgium*. The city was the cradle of Flemish art in medieval times and is famed for its many fine buildings and its important historical associations. It is also a major site of pilgrimage. All of these attributes validate its sobriquet.

**Jewel of the Adriatic, the** *Venice, Italy*. The sobriquet is appropriate for a city with a powerful naval history (*see* **Bride of the Sea**) and a wealth of fine architecture.

**Jewel of the Antilles, the** *Martinique, West Indies*. The name refers to the island's natural beauty in its eastern Caribbean setting.

> On that island where rivers run deep, where the sea sparkling in the sun earns it the name Jewel of the Antilles, the tops of the mountains are bare [Rosa Guy, *My Love, My Love*, 1985].

**Jewel of the Rockies, the** *Lake Louise, Alberta, Canada*. The lake, in Banff National Park,

lies in a small valley amid snow-capped mountains. Hence the nickname, referring to its scenic setting.

**Jewel of the South, the** *New Orleans, Louisiana, USA*. New Orleans earned its sobriquet as a vibrant and colorful city in a dramatic setting between the Mississippi River and Lake Pontchartrain.

> New Orleans, jewel of the South, changes into a toxic wasteland [Headline, *The Times*, September 2, 2005].

**Jewel of the Swiss Riviera, the** *Montreux, Switzerland*. The leading resort on the northeastern shore of Lake Geneva was at one time a meeting place of the rich and famous. Hence its many grand hotels. Hence also its nickname, referring to its pre-eminent position in this attractive lakeside setting.

> Travel in style ... to Montreux, the jewel of the Swiss Riviera, for a relaxing week on the shores of sparkling Lake Geneva [Travel ad, *The Times*, March 26, 2005].

**Jewel of the Weald, the** *Tenterden, England*. The attractive Kent town, with its medieval buildings, is located in the region of southeastern England known as the Weald (and in its own county as the Weald of Kent). Its parish church is known as the "Queen of the Weald." Hence the nickname. *Cp.* **Capital of the Weald**.

> Known as the *Jewel of the Weald*, ... Tenterden is a delightful country town [Heart of Kent Holiday Guide, 2005].

**Jewel of the Windward Islands, the** *St. Lucia, West Indies*. With its twin volcanic peaks and varied scenery, the island is reckoned to be one of the most attractive in the Caribbean. Hence its nickname. *Cp.* **Helen of the West**.

> Few islands in the Caribbean are more beautiful than St. Lucia — the "Jewel of the Windward Islands" [Travel brochure issued with *The Times*, August 20, 2005].

**Jewish Alps, the** *(1) Catskill Mountains, New York, USA; (2) Washington Heights, New York City, USA*. Washington Heights is the home of many successful Jews, while Jewish New Yorkers vacation in the resorts of the Catskills (*see* **Borscht Belt** in Appendix 1, p. 269). Hence the nickname of both "Alps." *Cp.* **Irish Alps**.

> (Catskills) Nowadays, the Catskills are synonymous with the Borscht Belt comedy circuit... But what is less well known is that the Catskills are also referred to as the Jewish Alps [*The Guardian*, January 29, 2005].

**Jew York** *New York City, USA*. The punning nickname refers to the large Jewish population of New York, currently greater than that of any other city in the world. *Cp.* **Hymietown**.

**JFK** *John F. Kennedy International Airport, New York City, USA.* The abbreviated name for the lengthily titled airport, opened in 1948 as Idlewild and renamed in 1963, is universally used. *See also* **LAX.**

BA's Club World offers "supper at JFK" before you leave New York for London [*Sunday Times Magazine*, January 23, 2005].

**Jimtown** *Jamestown, California, USA.* The town gained the colloquial personalization of its name in the 1849 gold rush.

**Jo'burg** or **Joburg** *Johannesburg, South Africa.* The familiar colloquial shortening of the city's rather lengthy name is of military origin and dates from the late 19th century.

(1) His letter proposed my coming to Jo'burg and staying with him on the chance of getting employment [J.H. Drummond, *Diary*, November 15, 1908].

(2) Jo'burg is comparable to no other city [Richard West, *The White Tribes of Africa*, 1965].

(3) Of South Africa's 200 game parks, by far the best known is the Kruger, a short plane hop from Joburg [*Sunday Times*, October 24, 2004].

**Joeys** or **Johies** *Johannesburg, South Africa.* A friendly personalization of the city's name, or of its long-established short form **Jo'burg.**

The spread of Chinese restaurants in Johannesburg is being tentatively followed in our other large cities. In Joeys, you can find traditional Cantonese rooms [*Flying Springbok*, May 1991].

**John Bull** *England or Britain.* A personification of Britain's traditional "bulldog" spirit, dating from the early 18th century, as originally represented by the character so named in John Arbuthnot's collection of pamphlets *The History of John Bull* (1712). The first pamphlet had the full title *Law is a Bottomless Pit. Exemplified in the Case of the Lord Strutt, John Bull, Nicholas Frog and Lewis Baboon: who spent all they had in a Law-suit*, in which "Lord Strutt" represents Philip of Spain, "Nicholas Frog" the Dutch, and "Lewis Baboon" Louis XIV of France.

**Jolly Polly** *Gelibolu, Turkey.* The British soldiers' ironically humorous nickname for **Gallipoli** arose during World War I.

**Joyce's City** *Dublin, Ireland.* The sobriquet stems from James Joyce's novel *Ulysses* (1922), describing a single day in the life of Leopold Bloom in his native Dublin. The name should not be confused with that of Joyce's Country, a mountainous region of Co. Galway, so called after one of the "Tribes of Galway" (*see* **City of the Tribes**).

For most people ... Dublin is still the city through which Leopold Bloom walked on June 16, 1904, and on the anniversary of that day, "Bloomsday," innumerable lovers of Joyce are to be found re-

tracing Bloom's footsteps [David Daiches and John Flower, *Literary Landscapes of the British Isles*, 1979].

**Jozi** *Johannesburg, South Africa.* A short form of the city's name common among Zulu speakers.

Jozi will soon look like Pretoria — where every second mlungu [i.e. white] is in uniform and every darkie knows his place [*City Press*, May 20, 1990].

**Jugland** *Yugoslavia.* A semifacetious name for the country, from "Jug" (pronounced "Yoog") as a nickname for a Yugoslav. (The country's name was also spelled Jugoslavia.) *Cp.* **Yugers.**

**Juice, the** *North Sea.* A colloquial name on the lines of **Gravy**, common among British Royal Air Force pilots. (Gravy is made from the juices of cooking meat.)

**Jumbo State, the** *Texas, USA.* Texas was the largest state in the USA until the admission of Alaska to the Union in 1959. Hence the nickname, from Jumbo, the big circus elephant.

**Junction** see in Appendix 1, p. 269.

**Jurassic Coast** see in Appendix 1, p. 269.

**Juteopolis** *Dundee, Scotland.* In the 19th century, Dundee was Britain's largest manufacturer of jute. The name is thus on the lines of **Cottonopolis.**

Juteopolis, as Dundee became known, flourished on the manufacture of sacking [Robinson/Millward, p. 404].

**J-Ville** *Jacksonville, Florida, USA.* A colloquial abbreviation of the seaport city's name.

**Kal** *Kalgoorlie, Australia.* A local short name for the gold-mining town in Western Australia, now officially Kalgoorlie-Boulder after amalgamating with the latter town in 1989.

Soon sophistication in "Kal" will no longer be regarded as a fully clothed barmaid [*The Rough Guide to Australia*, 2001].

**Kalevala** *Finland.* The poetic name of Finland, meaning "land of heroes" (Finnish *kaleva*, "hero," and *-la*, a suffix denoting place), derives from the national epic compiled in 1849 by Elias Lännrot.

**Kampuchea** *Cambodia.* The indigenous form of the country's name was in official use from 1976 to 1989 and remains current as an alternate in gazetteers and atlases. It was introduced by the Khmer Rouge, the Communist regime then in power, who also gave the country's previous name of Khmer Republic, in official use from 1970 through 1975.

**Kanakaland** *Queensland, Australia.* The state's former nickname derives from Hawaiian *kanaka*, "man," as a term for a Pacific islander employed as a laborer in the sugar and cotton industries of Queensland.

(1) Donald ... reached Port Mackay, the metropolis of Kanakaland [Frank Clune, *The Last of the Australian Explorers*, 1942].

(2) Queensland: *Bananaland, Kanakaland* (now obsolete) and *the Nigger State* (now obsolete) [Sidney Baker, *The Australian Language*, 1945].

**K & A, the** *Kennet and Avon Canal, England.* An abbreviated name for the 100-mile-long canal between Reading and Bristol, in central southern England.

The K&A is itself a kind of secret, so neatly was it squirrelled into the landscape two centuries ago [*Sunday Times*, September 4, 2005].

**Kangarooland** or **Kangaland** or **Kangerland** *Australia.* A nickname derived from the country's distinctive animal. *See also* **Kangaroo Valley**.

(1) Easter Monday ... was signalized among us of Kangaroo Land, in the *usual mode* adopted at seasons of joy [*Monitor* (Sydney), April 20, 1827].

(2) Certain nicknames are given as a matter of course... "Aussy" to Australians or otherwise "we from Kangerland" [Olive Dent, *A V.A.D. in France*, 1917].

**Kangaroo Valley** *Earls Court, London, England.* The district came to be so known in the 1960s from the large number of transient Australian immigrants living there. (There is a real Kangaroo Valley in New South Wales, Australia.) *Cp.* **Bedsit Jungle**.

(1) Londoners call Earl's Court — you can readily imagine the tone of voice — Kangaroo Valley. That's because it's the address of the Australians, the invaders, the temporary, the hit-and-run, cut-and-come-again yahoos, the colonial vagabonds, the loud-mouthed and light-fingered rowdies, the uncouth, irreverent, cock-sure, yankee-ized and so on and so forth so-and-sos [Hal Porter, *The Cats of Venice*, 1965].

(2) Earl's Court was once known as the Polish Corridor, then Kangaroo Valley, after successive waves of transients [Carrie Segrave, *The New London Property Guide*, 2003].

**Kasey** *see* **Casey**

**Kathleen Ní Houlihan** *Ireland.* The name, personifying Ireland as an old woman, is familiar in literature from W.B. Yeats's play so titled (1902), written jointly with Lady Augusta Gregory. There is a tradition of representing Ireland as a woman. Other such names are **Róisín Dubh** and **Shan Van Vocht**.

(1) Oh, Kathleen Ní Houlihan, your road's a thorny way,
And 'tis a faithful soul would walk the flints with you for aye [Ethna Carbery, "The Passing of the Gael," 1902].

(2) If you want to interest him in Ireland, you've got to call the unfortunate island Kathleen ni Hoolihan and pretend she's a little old woman [G.B. Shaw, *John Bull's Other Island*, 1907].

**Kavanagh Country** see in Appendix 1, p. 269.

**Kaw Town** *Kansas City, Missouri, USA.* The city's nickname derives from Kaw as another name for the Kansa, the Indian people who gave the name of Kansas City and the state of Kansas.

**Kay Cee** *see* **KC**

**KB** *Kuala Belait, Brunei.* An initial-derived short name for the town.

'KB' (not to be confused with Kuala Baram on the Sarawak side of the border) [*Lonely Planet Malaysia, Singapore & Brunei*, 1999].

**KC** or **Kay Cee** *Kansas City, Missouri, USA.* The initialism is mostly used for the Missouri city but can also apply to its identically named smaller neighbor across the Kansas River, as in quote (3) below. (Parker was born in Kansas City, Kansas, but as a child moved with his mother to Kansas City, Missouri.) *Cp.* **Casey**.

(1) Then had come Charlie Parker, a kid in his mother's woodshed in Kansas City... Somewhat younger than Lester Young, also from KC [Jack Kerouac, *On the Road*, 1957].

(2) 'Guess what?' 'It's a stolen car.' 'Undoubtedly. But the tags were definitely lifted. Our friends took them off a wrecked De Soto in a K.C. garage' [Truman Capote, *In Cold Blood*, 1965].

(3) [The American Jazz Museum] has displays on key musicians, such as KC Kansas native Charlie Parker [*Lonely Planet USA*, 2004].

**Kelly Country** see in Appendix 1, p. 269.

**Kensington-on-Sea** *(1) Kassiopi, Corfu, Greece; (2) Rock, England; (3) Salcombe, England; (4) Southwold, England.* The London, England, district of Kensington is one of the most fashionable in the capital. Hence the adoption of its name for "high-class" towns or resorts elsewhere. Rock is in Cornwall, Salcombe in Devon, and Southwold in Suffolk. Quote (1) below shows that the name was almost adopted officially for the resort of Westcliff-on-Sea, Essex, now a district of Southend-on-Sea, itself nicknamed **London-by-the-Sea**. *See also* **Hampstead-on-Sea**.

(1) (Westcliff-on-Sea) At the beginning of this Century some local landowners and estate agents [i.e. realtors] sought to re-name Westcliff "Kensington-on-Sea" [Donald Glennie, comp., *Our Town: An Encyclopaedia of Southend-on-Sea*, 1947].

(2) (Kassiopi) This is the colonial capital of the new British invasion... It is perhaps for this reason that Kassiopi has been dubbed Kensington-on-Sea [*The Times*, June 29, 2003].

(3) (Southwold) Ceilings [in the Crown Inn] are elegantly beamed, the walls of the big, laid-back bar are colour-washed and uncluttered — fitting for a town known as Kensington-on-Sea [Alastair Sawday's Special Places to Stay <http://www.specialplacetostay.com/search/display.phpFileD-pub2363> accessed October 13, 2004].

(4) (Rock) Padstow, and, of course, Rock opposite, known as Kensington-on-Sea [Sally Hedgecoe, "Weekend Luxury with Top Service," *Travel-Lady Magazine* <http://www.travellady.com/Issues/Issue60/weekend.htm> accessed October 13, 2004].

(5) (Rock) The village, dubbed Kensington-sur-Mer by locals, is a favourite of the public school set [*The Times* (Travel West Supplement), September 24, 2005].

**Kenso** *Kensington, Sydney, Australia.* A colloquial name for the district and its racecourse, with the typical Australian -o suffix.

**Kernow** *Cornwall, England.* The county's Cornish name, favored by "nationalists" and lovers of the Cornish language.

**Key City, the** *Vicksburg, Mississippi, USA.* The city came to be so nicknamed for its strategic location on the Mississippi River in the Civil War.

**Key of Christendom, the** *Buda, Hungary.* The former town, now incorporated in the Hungarian capital Budapest, was so nicknamed for its strategic location on the Danube between Christian Germany and Muslim Turkey.

**Key of France, the** *St.-Béat, France.* The village was so nicknamed in medieval times for its location on a main route from Spain.

**Key of India, the** *(1) Herat, Afghanistan; (2) London, England.* Herat is so named for its strategic location on the old trade route from Persia to India. London was so named by Benjamin Disraeli, as in the quote below, with reference to the British occupation of Kandahar, Afghanistan, on the same trade route, from 1879 to 1881.

(London) The key of India is London [Benjamin Disraeli, speech in House of Lords, March 5, 1881].

**Key of Russia, the** *Smolensk, Russia.* The fortified city occupies a strategic site on the Dnieper River, where it became an important commercial center on the trade route from the Baltic Sea to Constantinople. It is historically famous for its resistance to the French during Napoleon's invasion of Russia in 1812.

**Key of Spain, the** *Ciudad Rodrigo, Spain.* The town stands on a strategic site in western Spain near the border with Portugal. It was captured by the English in 1706, by the French in 1810, and again by the English in 1812.

**Key of the Gulf, the** *Cuba.* Cuba derives its sobriquet from its strategic position at the entrance to the Gulf of Mexico.

**Key of the Mediterranean, the** *Gibraltar.* Gibraltar derives its byname from its commanding position at the entrance to the Mediterranean. Its coat of arms depicts a castle of three towers from which hangs a key, alluding to this strategic site.

Henry IV, king of Castile ... gave it [i.e. Gibraltar] the arms it still bears, viz. a castle with a key hanging to the gate, alluding to its being the key to the Mediterranean [*Penny Cyclopædia*, 1838].

**Keystone of the South Atlantic Seaboard, the** *South Carolina, USA.* The state of South Carolina is roughly in the shape of a left-skewed triangle, its apex in the Appalachian Mountains, its base on the Atlantic seaboard. As such, it resembles a keystone, the central stone at the summit of an arch that locks the whole together. Hence the name.

**Keystone State, the** *Pennsylvania, USA.* The state is so nicknamed as it was the seventh or central state of the original 13, linking the older states of the Northeast and South with those of the East and Midwest. (As seen on the map, Pennsylvania is the "keystone" of a loose arch of states: New Hampshire, Massachusetts, Connecticut, Rhode Island, New York, New Jersey arcing to it from the north; Delaware, Maryland, Virginia, North Carolina, South Carolina, Georgia arcing from it to the south.) It is also a "key" state historically (the Declaration of Independence was signed at Philadelphia in 1776 and the US Constitution drafted there in 1787) and economically.

Republican aspirants matched strength in the politically important keystone state [*Daily Ardmoreite* (Ardmore, Oklahoma), April 27, 1948].

**Key to the Highlands, the** *Stirling, Scotland.* The historic town occupies a strategic site on the slope of a rocky height above the Forth River at the point where a main road runs north to the Scottish **Highlands** (see in Appendix 1, p. 269). Hence the name.

Centuries of stirring adventure ... centre round this old town, so long the bone of contention as the "natural key to the Highlands and the bulwark of the North" [*Holiday Haunts 1962: Scotland*].

**KI** *Kangaroo Island, Australia.* An initialism of the name of the South Australia island.

There's a freshness in the air of KI that can't fail to lift the spirits [*Sunday Times*, January 16, 2005].

**Kidder** or **Kiddie** *Kidderminster, England.* A shortened local name for the Worcestershire town, especially as used for the distinctive type of carpet made there.

(1) The manufacture of Kidder carpets [Frank Peel, *Spen Valley*, 1893].

(2) Affectionately known to its inhabitants as 'Kiddie' [Harry Soan and John Moore in Speaight, p. 162].

**Kili** *Kilimanjaro, Tanzania.* A short colloquial name used by geographers and others for Africa's highest mountain.

> Climate change has taken care of much of the snow, leading many scientists to predict that by 2020 "Kili" ... will be bald [*The Times*, October 20, 2005].

**Kilvert Country** see in Appendix 1, p. 269.

**King** *King William's Town, South Africa.* An abbreviated name for the former capital of British Kaffraria.

> (1) He was immediately sent on to the hospital at 'King' [F.G. Browning, *Fighting and Farming*, 1880].
> (2) From 'King' the convoy ... will make its way to the Cape via Grahamstown, Port Elizabeth [Mirabel Rogers, *The Black Sash*, 1956].

**King Country** see in Appendix 1, p. 269.

**Kingdom, the** *(1) Fife, Scotland; (2) Co. Kerry, Ireland.* Fife was an actual Pictish kingdom, but Kerry is a "kingdom" only by virtue of the restrictive laws of its former magistracy, which made it a "land apart." The Irish nickname is mainly used in Gaelic sporting contexts as a synonym for the county name.

> (1) (Fife) It is noteworthy that the word 'shire' has been tacked on to the end of the names of Scottish counties — a quite unnecessary Anglicisation, but Fife still proudly prefers to be called by its ancient appellation, "The Kingdom of Fife" [John Hay of Hayfield, comp., *Tartan Tapestry*, 1960].
> (2) (Fife) Fife ... has since long ago been known as the Kingdom of Fife, perhaps because the region is close to Abernethy, an ancient Pictish capital, or perhaps simply because it has long been one of the richest and most self-contained parts of Scotland [John Tomes, *Blue Guide Scotland*, 1992].
> (3) (Kerry) Some Kerrymen say there are only two Kingdoms, the Kingdom of God and the Kingdom of Kerry [*Irish Times*, April 4, 1996].

**Kingdom in the Sky, the** *Lesotho.* The kingdom of Lesotho is a mountainous country with the highest peak in southern Africa (Thabana Ntlenyana). Hence the nickname. *Cp.* **Roof of Africa; Switzerland of Africa.**

**Kingdom of Drought and Stone, the** *Apulia (Puglia), Italy.* The region of southeastern Italy is so nicknamed for its hot, dry climate.

**Kingdom of Heaven, the** *Lundy, England.* The nickname is a nice pun, as the small Devon island at the mouth of the Bristol Channel was bought in 1834 by William Hudson Heaven, who established a "kingdom" here.

**King Harry's Cornwall** see in Appendix 1, p. 269.

**Kingledon** *Wimbledon, London, England.* The former nickname properly applied to the famous Wimbledon tennis courts. It was devised by the *Daily Mirror* with reference to the US ace Billie Jean King after she won the singles championship for the fourth time in 1972. The name blends the player's name with that of the former borough and also punningly suggests "kingdom."

**Kingly River, the** *Congo River, West Africa.* The name denotes a mighty or majestic river, and probably goes back to an indigenous African epithet. As French *Fleuve-Majesté* it occurred in the national anthem of the former Zaïre (now the Democratic Republic of Congo), by Boka Di Mpasi Londi, as quoted below.

> Tricolore, enflamme-nous du feu sacré
> Pour bâtir notre pays toujours plus beau
> Autour d'un "Fleuve Majesté."
> (Tricolor, kindle the sacred fire in us
> To build an even finer country
> Beside a "Kingly River.")

**King of Waters, the** *Amazon River, South America.* A fitting title for one of the world's largest and longest rivers.

**King's City, the** *Copenhagen, Denmark.* The city's sobriquet refers to its royal status since 1443, when it was made capital of the kingdom of Denmark.

**Kingston-on-Railway** *Surbiton, London, England.* The district of Kingston upon Thames arose in the 19th century when Kingston itself refused to accept the railway, which was thus obliged to cut through rising ground to the south. The station opened in 1838 and the new settlement was at first known as Kingston New Town or Kingston-on-Railway. As it was on the main line between London and Southampton it soon grew into a desirable residential neighborhood, and adopted the historic Old English name of the location, meaning "southern grange." Kingston's own station opened in 1863.

**Kirk, the** *Albuquerque, New Mexico, USA.* A colloquial short name formed from the third syllable of the city's regular name.

**Kirkie** *Kirkintilloch, Scotland.* An abbreviated colloquial name for the town near Glasgow. *Cp.* **Kirky.**

**Kirky** *Kirkdale, Liverpool, England.* A local colloquial name for the city district. *Cp.* **Kirkie.**

**Kirrie** *Kirriemuir, Scotland.* A short colloquial form of the town's name.

**Kirton** *Crediton, England.* The local form of the Devon town's name survives in folklore. Quote (1) below relates to the tale of a woman walking from Okehampton to Exeter, a distance of some 25 miles. On reaching Crediton, 8 miles from her journey's end, she saw the town's imposing parish church and took it for the cathedral at "Extra." (In 909 Crediton actually became the county's cathedral "city" and remained as such until the see was transferred to Exeter in 1050.)

(1) That's Extra, as the woman said when she saw Kirton [Devonshire saying, quoted in Brewer, p. 316].

(2) Crediton, or Kirton as it is still frequently called, was once of greater importance than it is to-day [William Crossing, *Folk Rhymes of Devon*, 1911].

**Kissi** *Kissidougou, Guinea.* A short colloquial name for the town.

There's an airport in Kissi, but usually no flights [*Lonely Planet West Africa*, 2002].

**Kitchen of Japan, the** *Osaka, Japan.* The city is famous for its restaurants and the fine variety of dishes they offer. Hence the nickname.

Osaka was always "the kitchen of Japan," a foodies' paradise [Dodd/Donald, p. 223].

**Kite Country** see in Appendix 1, p. 269.

**Kits** *Kitsilano, Vancouver, British Columbia, Canada.* A local abbreviated form of the neighborhood's name.

**Kitz** *Kitzbühel, Austria.* A short name for the resort town and chic winter sports center as used by those who regularly ski there. (Local Alpine skier Toni Sailer, triple winner at the 1956 Winter Olympics, was nicknamed the "Kitz Comet.")

The medieval painted façades and antique store fronts decked with pine wreaths evoke a quaint Yuletide atmosphere in Kitz [*The Times*, December 18, 2004].

**Kiwiland** *New Zealand.* The kiwi is New Zealand's national bird, and New Zealanders, especially sportsmen and women, are colloquially known as Kiwis. Hence the name.

It's not just homegrown celebs such as Sam Neill and Rachel Hunter who choose to hang out in Kiwiland [*The Observer*, April 27, 2003].

**KK** *Kota Kinabalu, Malaysia.* An initial-based name for the capital of the state of Sabah.

(1) KK, as everyone calls it, is a functional sort of place [*Lonely Planet Malaysia, Singapore & Brunei*, 1999].

(2) The city of Kota Kinabalu (or KK as the Malaysians call it) [*The Times*, December 17, 2005].

**KKB** *Kuala Kubu Bharu, Malaysia.* An initial-derived abbreviation of the town's name.

**KL** *Kuala Lumpur, Malaysia.* A regular initial-based abbreviation of the Malaysian capital's name.

(1) Its abbreviation, KL, grants it membership of that select club of cities who need only a few initials for recognition — LA, BA, NYC, DC [Dodd/Donald, p. 264].

(2) The skyscraper-strewn city of Kuala Lumpur, or "KL" as it is commonly known [*The Times*, April 21, 2005].

**Klein-Paris** *Leipzig, Germany.* The nickname, meaning "Little Paris," dates from the 18th century, when Leipzig was noted for its elegance and fashionable French atmosphere. The sobriquet occurs in Part I of Goethe's *Faust* (1808): "*Es ist ein klein Paris, und bildet seine Leute*" ("It is a little Paris, and fashions its people"). *Cp.* **Little Paris**.

In Goethe's *Faust* a character named Frosch calls Leipzig 'a little Paris.' He was wrong — Leipzig is more fun and infinitely less self-important than the Gallic capital [*Lonely Planet Germany*, 2004].

**Klondike** *Orrell, England.* A local adoption of the name of the Canadian gold-bearing region for the district of the Merseyside seaport town of Bootle, at a time when the digging of a large claypit for brickmaking coincided with the opening of a nearby tin-smelting works. The excavation of the one was thus irrationally associated with the metal production of the other.

**Knickerbocker City, the** *New York City, USA.* The nickname alludes to the city's early Dutch settlers, who wore knickerbockers (knee breeches). *See* **Father Knickerbocker**.

**Knightsbridge of the North, the** *(1) Leeds, England; (2) Wilmslow, England.* The nickname compares the Yorkshire city and the Cheshire town with the London district of Knightsbridge, noted for its fashionable shops and stores. For Leeds, the name particularly applies to the Victoria Quarter shopping center, while for Wilmslow the reference is more to the affluence of its shopping-addicted populace, rather than to the stores themselves.

(1) (Leeds) Welcome to the Knightsbridge of the North, a shopping mecca whose counter is just getting longer [*Lonely Planet Great Britain*, 2005].

(2) (Leeds) Leeds really is the place to be seen at the moment. Its trendy Victoria Quarter has been dubbed the 'Knightsbridge of the North' [*Enjoy England Holiday Planner 2005*].

**Knowledge City, the** *Palmerston North, New Zealand.* The city's self-promoting sobriquet refers to its many educational establishments, including a university, as detailed in the quote below.

Palmerston North styles itself the Knowledge City, a tag which is justified by the presence of Massey University (the second-largest in the country), a polytechnic, a college of education, and the private International Pacific College [Nick Hanna, *Explore New Zealand*, 2d ed., 1999].

**Kodak City** *Rochester, New York, USA.* It was in Rochester that George Eastman, inventor of the Kodak camera and film, founded the Eastman Dry Plate Company on State Street in 1880. Hence the nickname.

**Kofifi** *Sophiatown, South Africa.* The nickname for Sophiatown, a black residential area of Johannesburg razed in the 1950s, is apparently based on Sotho *fifi*, as in *lefifi*, "darkness," *sefifi*, "corpse," or *bofifi*, "mourning."

**Königsberg** *Kaliningrad, Russia.* The Russian seaport city is still sometimes referred to by its former German name, as in the quote below. The preservation of the old name may be partly due to the exclave in which the city is located, separated from the parent Russian republic by some 225 miles (360 km).

> The crew ... stopped twice, at Konigsberg and Copenhagen. Yesterday Mr Anisimov and his crew were preparing for the return journey to St Petersburg [*The Times*, August 25, 1992].

**Kop** *Kopaonik, Serbia.* A short name for the mountain range and winter sports resort as used by those who ski there.

> Old skiing hands will remember "Kop," Serbia's leading sports resort, as *the* value destination of the 1970s and 1980s [*The Times*, March 12, 2005].

**Kozzie** *Mt. Kosciusko, Australia.* A short colloquial name for the New South Wales mountain, Australia's highest peak, or for the national park containing it. The full name is pronounced "kozzy-*uss*-ko."

**Krankfurt** *see* **Mainhattan**

**Krautland** *Germany.* The crude nickname is based on "Kraut" as a derogatory term for a German, itself from *Sauerkraut*, "pickled cabbage," supposedly a favorite German food.

> We were doing some biz near Munich ... back to this day in krautland [Robin Cook, *The Crust on its Uppers*, 1962].

**K-Town** *Knoxville, Tennessee, USA.* An initialism from the name of the city.

**LA** *Los Angeles, California, USA.* The familiar abbreviation, not favored locally, has been widely popularized by the many film and TV titles containing it, as *LA Law* (1986–94), *LA Takedown* (1989), *LA Story* (1991), and *LA Confidential* (1997), this last based on James Ellroy's novel *L.A. Confidential* (1990).

> (1) 'Where going?' 'LA.' I loved the way she said 'LA'; I love the way everybody says 'LA' on the Coast; it's their one and only golden town when all is said and done [Jack Kerouac, *On the Road*, 1957].
> (2) From New York City to L.A.,
>   They write, "We must meet up some day..."
> [Vikram Seth, *The Golden Gate*, 1986].
> (3) [Thomas Andersen's movie *Los Angeles Plays Itself*] is perfectly in tune with its subject... While it is a billowy valentine from a protective resident

(he detests the abbreviation LA), it is also a clear-eyed one [*The Times*, November 25, 2004].

**Lacedaemonia** or **Lacedaemon** *Sparta, Greece.* The alternate name of the ancient Greek city is based on that of Laconia, the region of which it was the capital.

> (1) Who through great prowesse and bold hardinesse,
>   From *Lacedæmon* fetcht the fairest Dame,
>   That euer *Greece* did boast, or knight possesse
> [Edmund Spenser, *The Faerie Queene*, 1590].
> (2) To Lacedæmon did my land extend [William Shakespeare, *Timon of Athens*, 1607].

**Ladies' Mile** see in Appendix 1, p. 269.

**Lady of Kingdoms, the** *Babylon, Iraq.* The name derives from the biblical quote (1) below, a prophecy that Babylon would lose its power and no longer be the mistress of many nations. This came about when Babylon was captured by the Persian king Cyrus the Great in the 6th century BC.

> (1) Sit thou silent, and get thee into darkness, O daughter of the Chaldeans: for thou shalt no more be called, The lady of kingdoms [Isaiah 47:5].
> (2) When the curse Heaven keeps for the haughty came over
>   Her merchants rapacious, her rulers unjust,
>   And — a ruin, at last, for the earth-worm to cover —
>   The Lady of Kingdoms lay low in the dust
> [Thomas Moore, "The Parallel," *Irish Melodies*, 1821].

**Lady of the Lakes, the** *Michigan, USA.* The personification refers to the state's location between four of the Great Lakes (*see* **Lake State**). The name evokes the title of Sir Walter Scott's poem *The Lady of the Lake* (1810).

**Lah** *Los Angeles, California, USA.* The short name represents a spoken form of the common abbreviation **LA**. *Cp.* **La-La Land**.

**Lake, the** *Salt Lake City, Utah, USA.* A short colloquial name for the state capital.

**Lake City** *Chicago, Illinois, USA.* The nickname refers to Chicago's location on Lake Michigan.

**Lake County, the** *Co. Westmeath, Ireland.* The nickname is mainly used as a synonym for the county in Gaelic sports reports, as in the quote below. Westmeath has many lakes, including Loughs Ree, Ennell, Owel, and Sheelin.

> While Barney's boys may have been full of optimism against Dublin ... there was no fairytale ending to the Lake County's campaign of the last months [*Westmeath Independent*, June 14, 1996].

**Lake District** see in Appendix 1, p. 269.

**Lake District of Surrey** see in Appendix 1, p. 269.

**Lakehead** *Thunder Bay, Ontario, Canada.*

The city, created in 1970 by the merger of the **Twin Cities** of Fort William and Port Arthur, stands on Thunder Bay, an inlet of northwestern Lake Superior, known as the Lakehead. Hence its alternate name. The quote below relates to the inlet.

It appeared, that a person at the Lake Head, had furnished the York Garrison with 800 bbls. of Flour last year [*Gore Gazette* (Ancaster, Ontario), May 25, 1827].

**Lakeland** see in Appendix 1, p. 269.

**Lakeland by the Sea** *Hornsea, England.* A promotional name for the east-coast seaside resort and adjacent Hornsea Mere, Yorkshire's largest freshwater lake. The name appears on a North Eastern Railway poster of 1911.

**Lakeland's Riviera** *Grange-over-Sands, England.* The Cumbria resort on the banks of the Kent River lies by extensive sands not far from the Lake District (*see* **Lakeland** in Appendix 1, p. 269). Hence its self-promotional name.

This tranquil and charming Edwardian seaside resort is known as "Lakeland's Riviera" [Travel brochure, *Hidden Treasures of Cumbria*, 2005].

**Lake of Shadows, the** *Lough Swilly, Ireland.* The sea inlet in Co. Donegal is poetically so nicknamed for the play of light on its waters.

**Lake of the Four Forest Cantons, the** *Lake Lucerne, Switzerland.* The English name translates the lake's German name of *Vierwaldstätter See*, referring to the four cantons that surround it.

**Lake of the Thousand Lakes, the** *Lake Saimaa, Finland.* Lake Saimaa is the primary lake in Finland's largest lake system. *Cp.* **Land of a Thousand Lakes.**

**Lake or Great Lake State, the** *Michigan, USA.* Michigan lies between four of the five Great Lakes: Lake Superior to the north, Lake Michigan (for which it is named) to the west, Lake Huron to the east, and Lake Erie to the southeast. It also has many inland lakes. Hence the nickname. *Cp.* **Water Wonderland.**

**Lakes** see in Appendix 1, p. 269.

**La-La Land** *Los Angeles, California, USA.* The punning nickname derives partly from the familiar abbreviated **LA** and partly from "la-la land" as a term for a world of "drink, drugs, and dreams," like that supposedly inhabited by actors and entertainers, and in particular Hollywood stars. The name is not used locally.

How come [actress] Nicole [Kidman] has so little influence in LaLa Land? [*The Times Magazine*, June 11, 2005].

**La Lin** *La Línea, Spain.* An abbreviated name for the town just across the border from Gibral-tar, as typically used by members of the British armed forces.

**Lancs** *Lancashire, England.* A semiofficial abbreviation of the county name. *See also* Appendix 6, p. 325.

**Land beneath the Waves, the** *Tiree, Scotland.* The westernmost island of the Inner Hebrides is so nicknamed for its flatness. The sobriquet renders a Gaelic original, as indicated in the quote below.

Tiree is easily the flattest of all the Hebrides, and it had a Gaelic nickname that called it the 'kingdom whose heights are lower than the waves' [Macnie/McLaren, p. 224].

**Land East of the Sun, the** *Siberia, Russia.* A Russian sobriquet for the vast region, which is cold and barren by comparison with European Russia to the west of the Urals.

In the summer, all but the top few feet of this landscape remain frozen in a rock-hard layer of permafrost... Not for nothing have Russians dubbed Siberia "the land east of the sun" [Paul Grogan in *Sunday Times*, June 26, 2005].

**Land God Gave to Cain, the** *Labrador, Canada.* A nickname of biblical origin, from the story in Genesis 4 telling how Cain murdered his brother Abel and was banished by God to a remote land "on the east of Eden." Cain was a tiller of the soil or laborer, the meaning of the placename (from Portuguese *lavrador*).

I am rather inclined to believe that this is the land God gave to Cain [Jacques Cartier, *La Première Relation*, 1534].

**Land o' Burns** see in Appendix 1, p. 269.

**Land of a Million Elephants, the** *Laos.* The name translates the Thai epithet *Lanchang*, from *lan*, "million," and *chang*, "elephant." Elephants have long played a key role in the country's economy, and in 1947 the feudal kingdom adopted a red flag with three white elephants (replaced by the present flag in 1975).

**Land of a Thousand Lakes, the** (1) *Finland;* (2) *Mazuria, Poland.* A partly touristic, partly descriptive name for both the Scandinavian country, which in fact contains around 60,000 lakes, and the region of northeastern Poland, which has over 2,000.

**Land of Black Earth, the** *Ukraine.* The nickname refers to the fertile chernozem (black-earth) soils that occupy around two thirds of the country's area.

Those who care for romance, poetry, and the quaint superstitions of this ... people, should visit the Blessed Land of Little Russia, the Ukraine (the Land of the Black Soil) [W. Barnes Steveni, *Things Seen in Russia*, 1914].

**Land of Bondage, the** *Egypt.* The name is

biblical, referring to the oppression of the Israelites under "a new king over Egypt, which knew not Joseph" (Exodus 1:8). The result was the exodus (departure) of the Israelites from Egypt and their arrival at Mount Sinai.

**Land of Cactus** *see* **Cactus State**

**Land of Cakes, the** *Scotland*. The sobriquet refers to the oatcakes for which Scotland is famous. The name was popularized by Robert Burns, as in quote (3) below. **Cockaigne** is a somewhat similar name.

> (1) If you do not come out of the land of cakes before New Year's day [Sir Robert Moray in *The Lauderdale Papers*, 1669 (1885)].
> (2) Oh soldiers! for your ain dear sakes,
> For Scotland's, *alias* Land o' Cakes [Robert Fergusson, "The King's Birthday in Edinburgh," 1773].
> (3) Hear, Land o' Cakes, and brither Scots,
> Frae Maidenkirk to Johnny Groats [Robert Burns, "On the Late Captain Grose's Peregrinations thro' Scotland," 1789].
> (4) An' fill ye up and toast the cup,
> The land o' cakes for ever [John Imlah, "The Land o' Cakes," song, 1846].

**Land of Castles, the** *Wales*. Some of the grandest castles in Britain are to be found in Wales, as those built for Edward I at Caernarfon, Conwy, and Harlech in the north of the country, a regular draw for tourists.

> Wales, 'the Land of Castles,' enjoys a varied landscape [Travel brochure issued with *The Times*, May 21, 2005)

**Land of Churches, the** *Suffolk, England*. The county of Suffolk has long been famous for its churches, as indicated in the quote below.

> Suffolk has been called the land of churches... In Domesday Book whilst only one church is recorded as existing in Cambridgeshire, and none in Lancashire, Cornwall, or Middlesex, 364 are enumerated in Suffolk [John G. Nall, *Great Yarmouth and Lowestoft*, 1866].

**Land of Columbus, the** *Colombia*. An obvious name for the South American country, named for Christopher Columbus. The name occurs (as Spanish *la tierra de Colón*) in the country's national anthem, which was written by four-times president Rafael Núñez (1825–1894) and officially adopted in 1946.

**Land of Contrasts, the** *Santo Domingo, Dominican Republic*. A touristic name for the country's capital, referring mainly to the city's blend of ancient (fine colonial buildings) and modern (Westward orientation), but also to the extremes between the immense wealth of some of its inhabitants and the grinding poverty of others.

> Few expressions are more overworked by travel writers than 'land of contrasts,' but in the case of Santo Domingo the disparities are so pronounced

that it is transcendentally apt [*Lonely Planet Dominican Republic & Haiti*, 2002].

**Land of Death and Chains, the** *Siberia, Russia*. The nickname is a translation from the Russian original of Maxim Gorky, referring to Siberia as a place of exile.

**Land of Delight Makers, the** *New Mexico, USA*. The name derives from the title of a novel by the Swiss-born archaeologist Adolphe Bandelier, an authority on the early Mexicans. It was first written in German under the title *Die Köshare* ("The Koshare," a Pueblo Indian clown society representing ancestral spirits in rain and fertility ceremonies), and told of the prehistoric Pueblo Indians of New Mexico and their betrayal to the Navajo by their ruling class, the Delight Makers. An English version was published in 1890. *Cp.* **Land of Enchantment**.

**Land of Dreams Come True, the** *Germany*. A touristic promotional name for Nazi Germany in the 1930s.

> [British travel agents Thomas Cook & Son] did not go quite as far as the Poly[technic Touring Association], which advertised Germany with a romantic picture of the Rhine, a Swastika flag and a slogan, 'The Land of Dreams Come True' [Piers Brendon, *Thomas Cook: 150 Years of Popular Tourism*, 1991, quoting R.G. Studd, *The Holiday Story*, 1950].

**Land of Enchantment, the** *New Mexico, USA*. The name is self-promotional, designed to attract tourists to the state's varied landscapes.

> (1) On the license plates in New Mexico it reads: "the Land of Enchantment." And that it is, by God! There's a huge rectangle which embraces parts of four states ... and which is nothing but enchantment, sorcery, illusionismus, phantasmagoria [Henry Miller, *The Air-Conditioned Nightmare*, 1945].
> (2) New Mexico is as much a unique culture as a beautiful place to visit. It's no wonder the state's nickname is 'land of enchantment' [*Lonely Planet USA*, 2004].

**Land of Eternal Spring, the** *Medellín, Colombia*. The city, lying between two mountain ranges, derives its sobriquet from its year-round temperate climate and its perennial profusion of brightly-colored flowers.

> The so-called "land of eternal spring" was for so long shrouded in the daily fear of imminent death [Dodd/Donald, p. 127].

**Land of Fire and Ice, the** *Iceland*. A promotional name for the island nation, referring to its many volcanoes and glaciers.

> Iceland — the "Land of Fire and Ice" is a place of living nature and a land of striking contrasts [Travel ad, *The Times Magazine*, October 16, 2004].

**Land of Flowers, the** *(1) Florida, USA; (2)*

*Valencia, Spain.* Florida's sobriquet is essentially a translation of its name, from Spanish *florida,* "flowering." Valencia, as indicated in the quote below, is noted for its flowering gardens and tree-lined avenues.

(Valencia) The city is full of gardens, romantic 18th-century shrines to bloomers that brought it the folk appellation *"la tierra de las flores,"* the land of flowers [Dodd/Donald, p. 15].

**Land of Fruit and Melons, the** *Kashgar (Kashi), China.* Kashgar, lying in a fertile oasis, is the largest commercial market in central Asia. Wheat, corn, cotton, barley, rice, beans, and fruit are grown, the latter including melons, grapes, peaches, apricots, and cherries. *See also* **Garden of Asia.**

Known as "the Land of Fruit and Melons," the stalls of Kashgar dripped with figs, grapes, apples and apricots [Dodd/Donald, p. 288].

**Land of Gold, the** *California, USA.* The nickname refers to the state's prime and precious asset. *Cp.* **Golden State.**

**Land of Great Privileges** *see* **Land of the White Gloves**

**Land of Heart's Desire, the** *New Mexico, USA.* The sobriquet, implying that the state may satisfy one's innermost longing, quotes the title of W.B. Yeats's 1894 verse drama (*see* **Land of Heart's Desire** in Appendix 1, p. 269).

New Mexico appears to have suffered from the most severe outbreak of narcissism, calling itself at various times the Land of Heart's Desire, the Land of Opportunity, the Land of the Delight Makers and the Land of Enchantment [Bill Bryson, *Made in America,* 1994].

**Land of Hope and Glory** *England or Britain.* The sobriquet derives from the verse quoted below, written at a time of great patriotic pride, when the British Empire was at its peak and comprised 25 percent of the world's population.

Land of Hope and Glory, Mother of the Free [A.C. Benson, "Land of Hope and Glory," written to be sung as the finale to Edward Elgar's *Coronation Ode,* 1902].

**Land of Inverted Order, the** *Australia.* Australia is in the southern hemisphere, so that its seasons are the reverse of those in Europe. Christmas, for example, thus falls in the hottest part of the year. *See also* **Antipodes.**

**Land of Ire, the** *Ireland.* The punning nickname, as an expression of exasperation, was coined by Sir Robert Cecil, Queen Elizabeth I's secretary of state, in a letter of October 8, 1600 to the lord admiral.

**Land of Israel, the** *Palestine.* The Jewish name of Palestine translates Hebrew *eretz Yisrael,* "land of Israel," from the biblical personal name that became that of a people and a nation. The term "land of Israel" occurs several times in the Old Testament, but mostly in Ezekiel, as in the quote below.

I shall bring you into the land of Israel, into the country for the which I lifted up mine hand to give it to your fathers [Ezekiel 20:42].

**Land of Jade, the** *China.* China gained its byname from the jade and jade carving long associated with the country. (The Chinese word for jade, *yù,* is widely used in ceremonious language, so that *yùchéng,* literally "jade result," means "to be so good as to help secure the success of something.")

This [southern] region was particularly famous for its jade work, winning for China its ancient title of 'the Land of Jade' [*Reader's Digest Illustrated History of the World: The Dawn of Civilisation,* 2004].

**Land of Joy, the** *Worms, Germany.* The city is so named in the songs of the medieval Minnesingers, referring to its fine wine.

**Land of La Dolce Vita, the** *Italy. La dolce vita* ("the sweet life") is a phrase synonymous with Italy for many vacationers, second-homers, and travel agents, often with reference to **Chiantishire.** The phrase itself became familiar to English speakers from the Federico Fellini 1960 movie so titled.

(1) There are still plenty of investment opportunities for Britons in the land of La Dolce Vita [*Sunday Times,* August 21, 2005].
(2) It's official — you just can't get enough of La Dolce Vita and have voted Italy your favourite European country for the third time in a row [*Sunday Times Travel Magazine,* January 2006].

**Land of Lamps, the** *Kerala, India.* The state earned its sobriquet for its great variety of indoor and outdoor lamps.

**Land of Liberty, the** *United States.* A historic title for the USA, encapsulating a concept expressed in the Declaration of Independence (1776), according to which all men have a right to "Life, Liberty and the pursuit of Happiness." *Cp.* **Land of the Free.**

My country, 'tis of thee,
Sweet land of liberty,
Of thee I sing [Samuel Francis Smith, "America," 1831].

**Land of Lincoln, the** *Illinois, USA.* The state takes its byname from Abraham Lincoln, 16th president of the USA, who before he became prominent in national politics was a distinguished lawyer in Springfield, Illinois.

**Land of Milk and Honey, the** *(1) Israel; (2) Wisconsin, USA.* The biblical title of Israel, as in the quote below, refers to the **Promised Land,** where there would be rich pastures for the production of milk and a wealth of the flowers on which wild honey bees thrive. It would also be the land where the Israelites would be nourished by God. Wisconsin likewise earned the nickname for its pastures (*see* **America's Dairyland**).

> (Israel) I will bring you up out of the affliction of Egypt ... unto a land flowing with milk and honey [Exodus 3:17].

**Land of Mountains, the** *Austria.* A description of the country from the opening words of its national anthem, as in quote (1) below. With words by Paula von Preradović (1887–1951), it was officially adopted in 1947.

> (1) Land der Berge, Land am Strome,
>   Land der Äcker, Land der Dome,
>   Land der Hämmer, zukunftsreich!
>   (Land of mountains, land on the river [Danube],
>   Land of fields, land of spires,
>   Land of hammers, with a promising future.)
> (2) "Land of Mountains" is the opening line of the country's national anthem and today the people of Austria have even more reason to eulogise their landscapes [*Insight Guide Austria*, 1998].

**Land of My Fathers, the** *Wales.* The name is the title of the Welsh national anthem (*Hen Wlad fy Nhadau*, literally "old land of my fathers"), as in quote (1) below, celebrating the family ties that all true Welshmen feel.

> (1) Mae hen wlad fy nhadau yn annwyl i mi,
>   Gwlad beirdd a chantorion, enwogion o fri.
>   (The land of my fathers is dear unto me,
>   Land where poets and singers are famous and free.) [Evan James, "Hen Wlad fy Nhadau," 1856].
> (2) The land of my fathers. My fathers can have it [Dylan Thomas in *Adam*, December 1953].

**Land of Myrrh, the** *(1) Asseb, Eritrea; (2) Saba (Sheba), Arabia.* Myrrh was exported from the Eritrean region and from the ancient Arabian country, which probably included modern Yemen and is the biblical region of Sheba (1 Kings 10).

**Land of Opportunity, the** *Arkansas, USA.* A promotional name for the state inviting settlers to exploit the natural resources.

**Land of Plenty, the** *South Dakota, USA.* The old promotional name dates from the early 20th century, when each family had over 400 acres of farmland, providing more than enough to feed the state's population at that time.

**Land of Political Exiles, the** *Yakutia, Russia.* A name for the Siberian state to which political nonconformists were traditionally banished.

**Land of Princes** or **Kings, the** *Rajasthan, India.* The state of northwestern India has a nickname that is essentially a rendering of its native name, meaning "abode of the rajahs," these being the Indian princes or kings.

> (1) To get a real flavour of this 'land of princes' we not only visit palaces and forts, we stay in them [Travel brochure issued with *Sunday Times*, August 14, 2005].
> (2) Travel to the Land of Kings, to discover Rajasthan's rich wildlife, history and culture [Travel ad, *The Times Magazine*, October 1, 2005].

**Land of Promise** *see* **Promised Land**

**Land of Religious Assemblies** *see* **Land of the White Gloves**

**Land of Revivals** *see* **Land of the White Gloves**

**Land of Rice and Fish, the** *(1) Hetao, China; (2) Jiangsu (Chiang-tsu), China.* The agricultural region of Hetao, on the banks of the Yellow River, is noted for its rich land, making it comparable to the rich, lower Chian Jiang (Yangtze Kiang) valley in southern China, famous for its marine products. Hence the identical nickname for both regions.

**Land of Roasted Pigs, the** *China.* The nickname derives from Charles Lamb's "A Dissertation upon Roast Pig" in *Essays of Elia* (1823), in which he recounts the discovery by the Chinese of the art of roasting pork.

**Land of Roger Williams, the** *Rhode Island, USA.* The state derives its nickname from its clergyman founder, Roger Williams (*c.*1603–1683), born in London, England, who in 1631 arrived in Massachusetts Bay. He was banished from the bay colony for his doctrines and criticisms, however, and in 1636 laid out Rhode Island's first settlement at Providence, which he named in recognition of "God's merciful providence unto me in my distress."

**Land of Saints (and Scholars), the** *Ireland.* The nickname refers to the missionaries (and scholars) associated with the early Celtic church in the **Isle of Saints**.

> My father upon the Abbey stage, before him a raging crowd:
>   'This Land of Saints,' and then as the applause died out,
>   'Of plaster Saints' [W.B. Yeats, *New Poems*, 1938].

**Land of Sky-Blue Waters, the** *Minnesota, USA.* The nickname alludes to the waters of the many lakes in the **Land of Ten Thousand Lakes**.

**Land of Smiles, the** *Thailand (Siam).* The alternate name of the former Siam derives from Thai *sayam muang yim*, from *syam*, "Siam," *muang*, "land," "town," and *yim*, "smile." The Austrian composer Franz Lehár adopted the title for his opera *Das Land des Lächelns* (1929), but applied it to China.

> "When you're smiling, the whole world smiles

with you," goes the song. In Thailand — "the land of smiles" — it's true [*The Times*, November 3, 2005].

**Land of Song, the** *Wales*. Music has long been important in Welsh culture and especially singing, as in the famous male-voice choirs and the eisteddfodau (festivals of music and poetry). Hence the poetic but accurately descriptive sobriquet, translating Welsh *Gwlad y Gân*.

(1) If Wales has been a land of song, have not the Highlands [of Scotland] also? [George Borrow, *Wild Wales*, 1862].

(2) Croeso i Gymru! Welcome to Wales! The Land of Song is a tourists' dream [<http://icwales. icnetwork.co.uk/yourwales/tourism.tm> accessed February 8, 2005].

**Land of Stars and Stripes, the** *United States*. The name refers to the Stars and Stripes, the flag of the United States, on which the 50 stars stand for the 50 states of the Union and the 13 stripes for the original 13 states.

**Land of Steady Habits, the** *Connecticut, USA*. The nickname refers to the supposed staid and sober way of life of Connecticut's inhabitants, a concept that accords with the state's Puritan background. *Cp.* **Blue Law State**.

**Land of Ten Thousand Lakes, the** *Minnesota, USA*. The nickname refers to the thousands of lakes in the state. The quoted figure is purely promotional, and was included to avoid confusion with Michigan as the **Lake State**.

Minnesota is known as the land of 10,000 lakes, and it offers the intrepid visitor almost as many things to do [*Lonely Planet USA*, 2004].

**Land of the Acronym, the** *South Africa*. As stated in the quote below, South Africa's apartheid policy of the 1950s through 1970s produced a slew of bureaucratic bodies and regulations, many of them in acronymic form. Of the two cited, BOSS is *B*ureau *o*f *S*tate *S*ecurity, and Soweto *So*uth *We*stern *To*wnships.

The language of the apartheid regime ... reduced South Africa to "the land of the acronym": BOSS, Soweto, and so on [*Times Literary Supplement*, September 24, 2004].

**Land of the Beijing Opera, the** *Linqing, China*. The city derives its nickname for its love of the type of opera mentioned. Peking opera (as it is still often known in English) dates from the late 18th century and is recognized as being most representative of the Chinese tradition.

**Land of the Bible, the** *Palestine or Israel*. The name is a synonym for the **Holy Land**, where many of the events in the Bible are set.

**Land of the Big PX** *see* **Big PX**

**Land of the Brave, the** *United States*. The sobriquet lauds a land where a settler or a native-

born may bravely begin a new life. (*Cp.* **Columbia**; **Home of the Brave**.)

(1) Just imagine what happens to Posterity without Columbus...
No land of the Brave and the Free [Ira Gershwin, "Columbus (The Nina, The Pinta, the Santa Maria)," *Where Do We Go from Here?*, 1945].

(2) America is the land of the brave before it is the land of the free [Simon Jenkins, review of Fred Anderson and Andrew Cayton, *The Dominion of War*, *Sunday Times*, July 24, 2005].

**Land of the Broad Acres, the** *Yorkshire, England*. In its original form, Yorkshire was England's largest county, famous for its wide tracts of farmland, its rolling hills and pastoral dales. The nickname is also simply "Broad Acres."

"There's a trip in fra' Leeds, my lad," explained the man from broad acres [*Minister's Gazette of Fashion*, October 1907].

**Land of the Chrysanthemum, the** *Japan*. The chrysanthemum grows profusely in Japan and its 16 petals radiate from the center like the rays of the sun. Hence its adoption as the former badge of the imperial family of the **Land of the Rising Sun**.

One of our most charming painters went recently to the Land of the Chrysanthemum in the foolish hope of seeing the Japanese [Oscar Wilde, "The Decay of Lying," *Intentions*, 1891].

**Land of the Covenant, the** *Canaan, Palestine*. The biblical land of Canaan was given by God to the Israelites according to the terms of an agreement or covenant between them, as in the quote below. *Cp.* **Promised Land**.

And I have also established my covenant with them, to give them the land of Canaan, the land of their pilgrimage, wherein they were strangers [Exodus 6:4].

**Land of the Dakotas, the** *North Dakota, USA*. The state is named for the Dakota Indians who formed its original indigenous population. *See* **Sioux State**.

Among the perennial front runners in this category [of obvious nicknames] we find ... the apt if resplendently self-evident Land of the Dakotas (North Dakota) [Bill Bryson, *Made in America*, 1994].

**Land of the Dragon** or **Thunder Dragon, the** *Bhutan*. The byname of the Himalayan kingdom translates its Tibetan name *Druk-Yul*, referring to the country's totemic beast (*druk* is "dragon"), depicted in scaly splendor on the national flag and mentioned in the opening line of the country's national anthem, as in quote (1) below. The dragon announces its physical presence when thunder is heard in the valleys of Bhutan.

(1) In the Thunder Dragon Kingdom adorned with sandalwood, the protector who guards the

teachings of the dual system, he, the precious and glorious ruler, causes dominion to spread [Translation of first part of national anthem, written by Gyaldun Dasho Thinley Dorji and adopted in 1953].

(2) The Land of the Thunder Dragon, as Bhutan is popularly known, lies at the very heart of the Himalaya [Royal Geographical Society 2006 tours schedule, October 2005].

**Land of the Fish, the** *Newfoundland, Canada*. The Atlantic island was so named by Irish fishermen from the 17th century, referring to the rich grounds off its coast, and especially in the Grand Banks. (The original Irish name was *Talamh an éisc*.)

**Land of the Free, the** *(1) Belize; (2) United States*. For the USA, the name amounts to an alternate for the **Land of Liberty** and occurs in the national anthem, as in quote (1) below. *Cp.* **Land of the Brave**. For Belize, the sobriquet celebrates the country's independence, gained in 1981, and occurs as the opening words of the national anthem, written by Samuel Alfred Haynes (1898–1971), as in quote (3) below.

(1) (USA) 'Tis the star-spangled banner; O long may it wave
O'er the land of the free, and the home of the brave! [Francis Scott Key, "The Star-Spangled Banner," 1814].
(2) (USA) This will remain the land of the free only so long as it is the home of the brave [Elmer Davis, *But We Were Born Free*, 1954].
(3) (Belize) O Land of the Free by the Carib Sea, Our manhood we pledge to thy liberty!
(4) (USA) The land of the free is the world leader in meddling legislation [*Sunday Times*, February 13, 2005].

**Land of the Golden Fleece, the** *Australia*. The nickname relates primarily to the wealth of wool in Australia but also hints at the gold that brought the country's rapid development after its discovery in 1851. The original Golden Fleece was that sought and won by Jason in classical mythology.

**Land of the Golden Hills, the** *California, USA*. The name was given to California by Chinese prospectors at the time of the 1848 gold rush.

**Land of the Leek, the** *Wales*. An occasional nickname given for the country's national plant. *Cp.* **Leekshire**.

**Land of the Little Sticks, the** *Canada*. The nickname comes from Chinook *stik*, "wood," "forest," referring to the subarctic tundra region of Canada, with its stunted vegetation.

**Land of the Long White Cloud, the** *New Zealand*. The sobriquet is said to be the English equivalent of *Aotearoa*, the Maori name for New Zealand, although the interpretation is challenged by some, as presented in quote (1) below.

(1) [Aotearoa is] the old Maori name for New Zealand — 'the long bright world,' popularly mistranslated as 'the land of the long white cloud.' A little sympathetic imagination underlines the accuracy of the first... There is nothing remarkable or distinctive about a long cloud: the tropics have them too [Shadbolt, p. 19].
(2) Ancient Maori pioneers sailed across the South Pacific about 1,000 years ago and named their misty new homeland Aotearoa — land of the long white cloud. And so the name remained, until 1642 when Abel Tasman arrived and changed the name to New Zealand, in honour of his home in The Netherlands. But the ancient name may now return [*The Times*, March 13, 1997].
(3) The Maoris ... called it [i.e. New Zealand] Aotearoa, "the land of the long white cloud," the first indication ... of the presence of the islands being the cloud lying above them [*Eyewitness Travel Guide New Zealand*, 2001].

**Land of the Midnight Sun, the** *(1) Alaska, USA; (2) Norway*. The northern regions of the named lands are within the Arctic Circle, where the sun does not descend below the horizon at night in the summer months and where it is thus still light at midnight. Hence the nickname.

(1) (Norway) This name is often given to Norway, though it could be applied equally well to many other places... You would see it [i.e. the sun] all the day and all the night, even at midnight. For that reason, Norway, or, more correctly, the north of Norway is called the "Land of the Midnight Sun" [Johnson, p. 145].
(2) (Norway) Clients who wanted to escape the 'over-crowded' European countries were introduced to the 'varied charms' of Norway and to the 'Land of the Midnight Sun' [Piers Brendon, *Thomas Cook: 150 Years of Popular Tourism*, 1991, quoting from *The Excursionist*, June 29, 1875].
(3) (Norway) The moniker 'Land of the Midnight Sun' is more than just a promotional slogan for the country, as nearly a third of Norway lies north of the Arctic Circle [*Lonely Planet Norway*, 2002].

**Land of the Morning Calm, the** *Korea*. The name translates *Chosen*, the Japanese name of Korea before its political division into North and South, itself from Korean *Choson*, from *cho*, "morning," and *son*, "calm," "fresh." The implication is of a land nearest to the rising sun. *Cp.* **Land of the Rising Sun**.

**Land of the Nymphs, the** *Ireland*. The nickname refers to the "fairy folk" who have long featured in Irish folklore.

**Land of the Pharaohs, the** *Egypt*. The name applies to the ancient kings of Egypt and the remains of their palaces and other monuments, notably the pyramids that were their royal tombs.

No honeymoon can match a luxurious cruise [on the Nile] with your loved one through the Land of the Pharaohs [Travel ad, *The Times Magazine*, November 20, 2004].

**Land of the Prince Bishops, the** *Co. Durham, England*. A modern official touristic name for the county, referring to the title borne by the bishops of Durham from the 11th through 19th centuries, when they were granted virtually royal status.

**Land of the Red Dragon, the** *Wales*. A proudly promoted title for the Celtic country, from the red dragon (Welsh *Y Ddraig Goch*) that is its heraldic symbol, incorporated in the national flag. According to tradition, the red dragon appeared on a crest borne by King Arthur, whose father, Uther Pendragon, had seen a dragon in the sky foretelling that his son would be king.

> Equally enthralling is the Land of the Red Dragon across the border [Tourist brochure *Chester and Cheshire*, 2006].

**Land of the Rising Sun, the** *Japan*. The sobriquet essentially translates the Japanese name for Japan, which is *Nippon*, from *nichi*, "sun," and *hon*, "origin." The reference is to Japan's eastern situation with regard to China. The meaning is visually presented in the national flag, which is white with a central red "sun disk."

> (1) It is difficult to form an exact picture of the air strength of the land of the Rising Sun [*R.A.F. Journal*, May 2, 1942].
> (2) Nowhere else in the Land of the Rising Sun were so many art treasures collected at this time [as in Kyoto] [Leier, p. 187].

**Land of the Rolling Prairie, the** *Iowa, USA*. The nickname refers to the rolling landscape that occupies the greater part of the state.

**Land of the Rose, the** *England*. The red rose is the national flower of England, and the country is occasionally referred to in this way, just as Scotland is the **Land of the Thistle** and Wales the **Land of the Leek**.

**Land of the Saints, the** *(1) Cornwall, England; (2) Utah, USA*. The English county is so named for its many towns and villages dedicated to Celtic saints. For the US state the name refers to the Church of Jesus Christ of Latter-Day Saints, better known as the Mormons, who in 1847 made their base at Salt Lake City, the state capital.

**Land of the Sky, the** *(1) California, USA; (2) Great Smoky Mountains, USA; (3) North Carolina, USA*. The nickname refers to the mountain peaks in all three regions, although none are probably lofty enough to be considered real "skypiercers."

**Land of the Southern Cross, the** *Australia*. Australia is in the southern hemisphere, where the **Southern Cross** (see in Appendix 7, p. 327) is visible in the night sky. The name was adopted for the Australian flag, on which five of the constellation's brightest stars are represented.

**Land of the Sword, the** *Japan*. The name refers to the prominent role assumed by the sword in the country's history and culture, especially its use by samurai warriors and for harakiri (seppuku), or ritual suicide. *See also* **Land of the Sword** in Appendix 1, p. 269.

**Land of the Thistle, the** *Scotland*. An occasional nickname for the country, referring to the flower that is its national emblem. The Order of the Thistle is the highest Scottish order of knighthood.

**Land of the Thunder Dragon** *see* **Land of the Dragon**

**Land of the White Elephant, the** *Thailand (Siam)*. The name refers to the rare albino elephant that was greatly venerated in Siam. (It was this elephant that the kings of Siam are said to have given as a present to intransigent courtiers, who would then be ruined through the prohibitive cost of maintaining it. Hence "white elephant" as a term for a useless or irksome possession.)

**Land of the White Gloves, the** *Wales*. The name, popular in the 19th century, translates Welsh *Gwlad y Menig Gwynion*, and refers to the custom of presenting judges with white gloves when there were no cases for them to try. The image is of a land where serious crime was unknown. Similar idealistic names were "Land of Great Privileges" (*Gwlad y Breintiau Mawr*), "Land of Religious Assemblies" (*Gwlad y Cymanfaoedd*), and "Land of Revivals" (*Gwlad y Diwygiadau*).

**Land of Three Winters, the** *Finland*. The country at the eastern edge of Western Europe owes its nickname to its long winter season, traditionally divided into autumn winter, high winter, and spring winter.

**Land of Two Rivers, the** *Iraq*. The byname refers to Iraq's two main rivers, the Tigris and the Euphrates. The region between the two is historically famous as Mesopotamia (Greek for "between the rivers"). The name was adopted by Gavin Young and Nik Wheeler as the subtitle of their study of the country and its people, *Iraq: Land of Two Rivers* (1980).

**Land of Tyrconnell, the** *Co. Donegal, Ireland*. The county is sometimes known by this name, referring to the historic territory that covers most of it. Its own name means "Conall's land," for one of the sons of the semilegendary Niall of the Nine Hostages, said to have ruled as High King in the 4th century. The byname appears on a Donegal Railway poster of *c.* 1903.

**Land of Wait-a-While, the** *Kimberley, Australia.* The Kimberley, a sparsely populated region of northwestern Australia, bears the popular name of the tangled shrub *Acacia colletioides*, itself humorously so called because its spiny leaves and thorns impede progress. The name can also be seen as a touristic lure.

> Join us on a visit to Kimberley, the real 'Outback' and an area Australians refer to as 'The Land of Wait A While' [Travel ad, *The Times Magazine*, August 6, 2005].

**Land of Waterfalls, the** *Ingleton, England.* A promotional name for the North Yorkshire village on the Greta River, with its many caves and waterfalls. The byname appeared on railway posters of the 1920s.

**Land of William Penn, the** *Pennsylvania, USA.* The name is that of William Penn (1644–1718), who founded the state by establishing a Quaker colony here in 1682. (The state is actually named for his father, also William Penn.)

**Land of Windmills** see in Appendix 1, p. 269.

**Land of Wisdom, the** *Normandy, France.* The name translates French *le Pays de sapience*, referring to the wise customs of the Norman people, and their skill and judgment in legal matters. (The usual French word for "wisdom" is *sagesse*, and *sapience* more exactly implies "discernment," "judgment.")

**Land o' the Leal, the** *Scotland.* The name, meaning "land of the loyal," properly means heaven, the land of the blessed dead, as in the quote below. But the Scots expression has also been applied to Scotland, notably by the Liberal politician W.E. Gladstone, when campaigning in Midlothian.

> I'm wearin' awa' John
> Like snaw-wreaths in thaw, John,
> I'm wearin' awa'
> To the land o' the leal [Lady Carolina Nairne, "The Land o' the Leal," 1796].

**Land Where the West Begins, the** *Nebraska, USA.* The centrally located state contains river valleys, especially that of the Platte, that have long provided through routes to the West. Today they are mostly followed by railroads.

> We crossed Ohio, the three states beginning with "I," and Nebraska — ah, that first whiff of the West! [Vladimir Nabokov, *Lolita*, 1959].

**Land Without Music, the** *England.* The damning description, popularly attributed to Beethoven, remains of uncertain authorship. It was the title of a book by Oscar A. Schmitz, published at the beginning of World War I, although its subject was not music but England as being a "land without a soul."

> (1) England has been described as "Das Land ohne Musik" ("the land without music"), but this is unjust, for England has a splendid musical history and has been the native land of many excellent composers [Denis Arnold in *The New Oxford Companion to Music*, 1983].
> (2) The Germans used to call us a "land without music." That was never true, though for centuries our standards were lamentable and our leading musical lights imported. Today, few nations can match Britain for musical variety [*The Times*, November 22, 2005].

**Lang Toon, the** *(1) Auchterarder, Scotland; (2) Chirnside, Scotland.* The Scots name, meaning "the long town," describes both villages accurately enough. Auchterarder, near Perth, has a long main street and Chirnside, on a hill between Ayton and Duns, consists of two long streets. *Cp.* **Lang Toun**.

> (Auchterarder) The small village of Auchterarder, known as the "Lang Toon" on account of its long main street [*The Times*, July 6, 2005].

**Lang Toun, the** *Kirkcaldy, Scotland.* The seaside resort first earned its nickname ("the long town") for its lengthy High Street, then for its even longer (and more recent) esplanade, as described in the quotes below.

> (1) Kirkcaldy's name of 'the Lang Toun' derives from its High Street, in which every chain store in Britain seems to be represented [Macnie/McLaren, p. 259].
> (2) [Kirkcaldy] is familiarly known as "The Lang Toun" for its four-mile-long esplanade which stretches the length of the waterfront [*The Rough Guide to Scotland*, 1998].

**Lanzagrotty** *Lanzarote, Spain.* The smallest and easternmost of the Canary Islands, a popular British tourist destination, has been so dubbed for its partly "cheap and cheerful" image, as described in the quotes below.

> (1) These resort towns earned the island its old "Lanzagrotty" tag, specialising in beer and football, loud music and any number of shopping arcades in which to walk off your burger'n'chips [*Sunday Times*, May 8, 2005].
> (2) Lanzarote also boasts Puerto del Carmen which is a bit Blackpool and responsible for the otherwise grossly unfair Lanzagrotty nickname [*The Times*, November 26, 2005].

**Last Frontier, the** *Alaska, USA.* Alaska was the 49th and (at that time) last state to be admitted to the Union, on January 3, 1959. Hence the nickname, which became historically obsolete when Hawaii was admitted as the 50th state on August 21, 1959.

**Last Outpost, the** *(1) Durban, South Africa;*

*(2) KwaZulu-Natal, South Africa.* A light-hearted name for the province, and sometimes also for its city of Durban, referring to the supposed "colonial" outlook of its English-speaking population, as in the days of the British Empire (of which it is thus the "last outpost"). The so-briquet was coined in the early 1970s by the rugby player Tommy Bedford, who claimed the national rugby selectors were biased against Natal players.

(1) They might call his province the Last Outpost of the British Empire, but Mac is no whingeing Pom [*Sunday Times* (Johannesburg), April 1, 1990].

(2) So why come to Durban, the 'Last Outpost'? [*Sunday Nation*, August 8, 1993].

**Las Vegas East** *Atlantic City, New Jersey, USA.* The name promotes the East Coast city, with its many casinos, as an equivalent of the **Gambling Capital of the Far West.**

**Las Vegas in Miniature** *Laughlin, Nevada, USA.* The southernmost town in Nevada began with a couple of casinos in the mid–1980s but by 1996 was third in gambling revenue in the state, with many hotels. Hence the nickname.

Day 7. Time at leisure in Las Vegas before travelling to Laughlin — "Las Vegas in Miniature" — for two nights [Travel brochure issued with *The Times*, August 20, 2005].

**Las Vegas of the North, the** *Blackpool, England.* The Lancashire coastal resort came by its nickname at the turn of the 21st century, when plans were announced to update its traditional seaside entertainments with four huge casinos. Quote (2) below compares the northern resort with the southern one of Bognor Regis.

(1) Blackpool's hopes of reinventing itself as the "Las Vegas of the North" have had wide publicity [*The Times*, August 7, 2004].

(2) In reality, Blackpool is better described as the Bognor Regis of the North than the Vegas of the North [Charlie Godfrey-Faussett, *Footprint England*, 2004].

**Latin** see in Appendix 1, p. 269.

**Latin Quarter** see in Appendix 1, p. 269.

**Lavender Lake** *Gowanus Canal, New York, USA.* The industrial canal in Brooklyn was so nicknamed ironically for its pollution.

**Lawlands** see in Appendix 1, p. 269.

**LAX** *Los Angeles, California, USA.* The abbreviation is properly the code for Los Angeles International Airport, but can also be used for the city itself, as can other such codes. Most of the codes are based on the name of the city where the airport is located, but some derive from the airport itself, as **JFK** and **ORD** (O'Hare International Airport, Chicago.)

(1) "Bill? Hello?" I'm saying. "Bill? What are you

doing? ... Sitting there with a headset on, looking like you belong in the air traffic controllers' room at LAX?" [Bret Easton Ellis, *Glamorama*, 1998].

(2) JFK, LAX, ORD, MIA, RDU, BOS, DFW... Most people tend not to speak in code, so to translate, that's New York, Los Angeles, Chicago, Miami, Raleigh/Durham, Boston and Dallas/Fort Worth. But it doesn't matter what the IATA, sorry, the International Air Transport Association calls them, does it? It's the fact that you have to get there that's important [American Airlines ad, *The Times*, September 20, 2005].

(3) Depending on your route, a flight to an alternative airport in metro L.A. may cost less than a flight to LAX [*Fodor's Los Angeles 2006*].

**L'derry** *see* **So'ton**

**Lead State, the** *Missouri, USA.* The name refers to Missouri's production of lead, which exceeds that of any other state.

**Leafy Bucks** *see* **Beechy Bucks**

**Leafy Hertfordshire** *Hertfordshire, England.* A common nickname for the county, with its many woods and parks.

(1) Leafy Hertfordshire, as it is referred to by both visitors and settlers [*Welcome to East Anglia*, Summer 2005].

(2) Into leafy Hertfordshire we pass the site of Radlett [*The Times*, September 5, 2005].

**Leafy Warwickshire** *Warwickshire, England.* A traditional nickname for the well-wooded county.

(1) "In Leafy Warwickshire" [Poem title, in Norman Gale, *A Country Music*, 1893].

(2) Writing of the ... county early this century, Dr J. Charles Cox said: ... 'Almost everywhere, it can claim to be well wooded, and from its luxurious hedgerows and the number of its well-grown trees, it has acquired the distinctive title of "Leafy Warwickshire"' [Charles Lines in Hadfield 1980, p. 179].

**Leather and Tanning Capital of the US, the** *Peabody, Massachusetts, USA.* The nickname was once applicable to the Boston suburb, but little of the industry now remains.

**Leatheropolis** *Northampton, England.* The city is noted for its shoe and leather industry. Hence the name, like that of **Cottonopolis**.

The first time the great annual gathering of Churchmen has taken place in Leatheropolis [*Westminster Gazette*, October 2, 1901].

**Le Cap** *Cap-Haïtien, Haiti.* An earlier short local name for the former capital of Haiti. *Cp.* **O'Cap.**

**Leekshire** *Wales.* The nickname treats Wales as the "shire" (region) which has the leek as its official emblem. The association between this plant and the Welsh dates from at least the 16th century, and the custom of wearing the leek on St. David's Day (March 1) is still regularly observed by some.

**Left Coast** see in Appendix 1, p. 269.

**Leghorn** *Livorno, Italy.* This form of the seaport's name was long current among English speakers and is still sometimes found. It probably arose among sailors, who adopted it from *Ligorno,* the local Italian form of the name. It remains in use for the Leghorn as a breed of domestic fowl. (The name evokes an image of a "horn on a leg," and the city happens to be located at the top of the **Leg of Italy** (see in Appendix 1, p. 269). There is no actual geographical "horn" here, however, although there is to the south as the promontory on which Piombino lies.)

(1) What is Leghorn? The meaning and history of the corresponding Italian name, Livorno, may appropriately be left to Italian toponymists, but the establishment of the form Leghorn in English is for Englishmen to explain [Aurousseau, p. 20].

(2) Leghorn is now among the three or four greatest seaports of Italy [Peter Kemp, ed., *The Oxford Companion to Ships and the Sea,* 1976].

(3) Use English forms [of placenames] when they are in common use: Basle, Cologne, Leghorn, Lower Saxony, Lyons, Marseilles, Naples, Nuremberg, Turin [*The Economist Pocket Style Book,* 1987].

(4) Your report ... referred to the northern Italian port of Leghorn. Leghorn? The Italians refer to it as Livorno. It was the illiterate jolly jack tars of another epoch who Anglicised the name, although how one manages to transmute Livorno into Leghorn is not entirely clear [Letter to the Editor, *The Times,* August 2, 1999].

**Leg of Italy** see in Appendix 1, p. 269.

**Legshire** *Isle of Man, British Isles.* A humorous name for the crown dependency, referring to its heraldic device of three legs in armor bent at the knee and joined at the center.

**Leics** *Leicestershire, England.* A semiofficial abbreviation of the county name, but only rarely used in speech (when it might be pronounced "leeks"). *See also* Appendix 6, p. 325.

Leics male, 52, ... seeks attractive female to share good times [Personal ad, *Sunday Times,* June 26, 2005].

**Leningrad** *St. Petersburg, Russia.* The former name of the city and port was official from 1924 (the year of Lenin's death) through 1991 (the year of the demise of Communism), but is not preserved as a battle name as **Stalingrad** is. From 1914 through 1924 the city was known as Petrograd. The old name survives in that of the Leningrad oblast (administrative district) of which St. Petersburg is the capital, and there is still a town named Leningrad in Tajikistan.

In a much repeated Soviet joke, an elderly Russian emigrant applies to reenter his homeland. Under "Place of birth" on the form he writes, "St.

Petersburg." Under "Left the country from?" he enters, "Petrograd." Under "Destination?" he puts, "Leningrad." Finally, under "Where would you like to settle?" he puts, "St. Petersburg" [*Time,* January 27, 1992].

**Leperland** *Queensland, Australia.* The now obsolete nickname refers to the lepers who inhabited the former colony.

He had to cross a creek up Leperland way, which is infested with alligators [*The Worker* (Sydney), August 20, 1898].

**Lettland** *Latvia.* The German name of Latvia was formerly current among English speakers and "Lettish" is still sometimes found as a synonym for "Latvian" with reference to the language, as is "Lett" for a Latvian.

Latvia. Sometimes called Lettland [Johnson, p. 147].

**Levant** see in Appendix 1, p. 269.

**Lewo** *Lewisham, Sydney, Australia.* A colloquial abbreviation of the city suburb name, with the typical Australian -o suffix.

**Liége** *Liège, Belgium.* The name of the city was at one time formerly spelled thus (with an acute accent), as in the quote below, but the grave was officially approved over the acute from 1946.

Liége is situated in a very pretty part of Belgium [Johnson, p. 150].

**Lightning in the Morning** *Laughton en le Morthen, England.* A local punning perversion of the Yorkshire village's name.

**Lima la Horrible** *Lima, Peru.* The Spanish nickname of the Peruvian capital refers to its many undesirable aspects of noise, dirt, gloom, damp, and general depression, all of which adversely affect both permanent residents and the casual visitor. (As in English, Spanish *horrible* means both "ghastly" and "nasty.") A further negative factor gave the city its more common nickname of the **Octopus.**

James Higgins defends Lima from its detractors, who have sullied it with the term "Lima the horrible" [Jason Wilson, review of James Higgins, *Lima, Times Literary Supplement,* November 18, 2005].

**Limestone City, the** *Galway, Ireland.* The capital city of the west of Ireland is so named for the stone used in many of its buildings.

**Limeyland** *England or Britain.* The colloquial term "Limey," first used in the late 19th century by Australians for an English immigrant to their country, was a shortened form of "Lime-juicer," an earlier American term for a British sailor, who drank lime juice on long voyages to guard against possible scurvy.

**Lincs** *Lincolnshire, England.* A semiofficial

abbreviation of the county name. *See also* Appendix 6, p. 325.

**Line, the** *Equator.* The line is that dividing the northern and southern hemispheres, marked as a latitude of 0°. The ceremony of "crossing the Line" may be observed when a ship first crosses the Equator. The Line Islands south of Hawaii are so named as they lie north and south of the Equator.

**Linenopolis** *Belfast, Northern Ireland.* The Northern Ireland capital was formerly one of the word's greatest centers of linen manufacture. Hence its nickname, on the lines of **Cottonopolis**.

> 'Linenopolis' was the name given to Belfast in the great age of linen manufacturing when its Brown and White Linen Halls were the centres of the trade [Brian Lalor, *Blue Guide Ireland,* 2004].

**Lingerie Capital of Latin America, the** *Medellín, Colombia.* The self-promoting name ties in with the city's fashion shows as well as more generally with its reputation as the **Manchester of Colombia**.

**Lion City, the** *Singapore.* The nickname translates the city's Sanskrit name, popularly derived from a legend about a visiting Sumatran prince who saw a strange animal here and took it for a lion.

**Lion of the Sea, the** *Cape of Good Hope, South Africa.* A former nickname of Portuguese origin for the famous cape, referring to its fancied resemblance to a crouching lion.

**Liquid History** *Thames River, England.* The nickname was created by the British Labour leader John Burns, as in quote (1) below, referring to the historic towns through which the river flows, among them Oxford, Windsor, and London.

> (1) Every drop of the Thames is liquid 'istory [John Burns, speaking to an American who had compared the Thames unfavorably to the Mississippi, quoted in *Daily Mail,* January 25, 1943].
> (2) That the Thames is 'liquid history' is a statement so often quoted as to have become a cliché [Ivor Brown in Hadfield 1981, p. 84].

**Little Aberdeen** *Hebburn, England.* The shipbuilding town on the banks of the Tyne River near Gateshead is so nicknamed from the shipyard workers who migrated here from the area around Aberdeen, Scotland.

**Little Barbary** *Wapping, London, England.* The nickname, adopted from the Barbary Coast of North Africa, a haunt of pirates, was current in the 17th and 18th centuries for what was then a rough dockland area of London. *Cp.* **Barbary Coast**.

**Little Beijing** *Chengdu, China.* The city derives its nickname, comparing it to the Chinese capital, by virtue of its long-standing reputation as a cultural center.

**Little Britain** *Brittany, France.* The name of Brittany in northwestern France is directly related to that of Britain. This is because in the 5th century AD Britons inhabiting southern Britain fled here across the English Channel to escape the invading Germanic tribes of Angles, Saxons, and Jutes. Hence Britain's formal name of Great Britain, by contrast with this "Little Britain," as it came to be alternately known. The name is common in legends about King Arthur, as in the ballad cited in quote (2), where the speaker is Sir Gawain, Arthur's nephew.

> (1) The Danes wofully harassed the Land, which caused him to ship himself over into little Britain in France [Thomas Fuller, *The History of the Worthies of England,* 1662].
> (2) 'I'le make mine avow to God,
> And alsoe to the Trinity,
> That I will have yonder faire lady
> To Litle Brittaine with mee' ["King Arthur and King Cornwall," *The Oxford Book of Ballads,* 1910].

**Little Cuba** *Miami, Florida, USA.* The city is so nicknamed for its large Cuban immigrant population. *Cp.* **Cuba of America**.

**Little Dixie** see in Appendix 1, p. 269.

**Little Egypt** *Cairo, Illinois, USA.* The city lies on a tongue of land by the confluence of the Mississippi and Ohio rivers. Hence both its regular geographical name and its nickname, comparing it to the location of the Egyptian capital near the head of the Nile delta. *Cp.* **Egypt**.

**Little England** (1) *Barbados, West Indies;* (2) *Nuwara Eliya, Sri Lanka.* Barbados was claimed for England in the early 17th century, while the resort town of Nuwara Eliya was settled by the British in 1827. Both places thus have an English colonial history, and the physical evidence of this remains today.

> (1) (Barbados) Residents of neighbouring islands often talk about Little England. Barbados does look like it when you arrive and see English-style churches and stately homes, well-behaved, unexcitable, hard-working people [Hunter Davies in *The Times,* July 3, 2004].
> (2) (Barbados) You can be sure of a warm welcome in Barbados, the 'Little England' of the Caribbean [Travel brochure issued with *The Times,* August 20, 2005].
> (3) (Nuwara Eliya) The train stops at Kandy, then continues on to the region known as "Little England," home of tea plantations [*The Times,* November 12, 2005].

**Little England beyond Wales** *Pembrokeshire, Wales.* The name, now regularly used for the southern part of the county, refers to a region that has been mainly English-speaking since the 9th century. It was first applied to the county in the 16th century (as Latin *Anglia Transwallina*) by the English antiquary William Camden.

(1) Pembrokeshire, a county which has acquired the name of a 'Little England beyond Wales' owing to the fact that it is mainly peopled by the descendants of a colony of Flemings settled here by Henry I [Karl Baedeker, *Handbook to Great Britain*, 1890].

(2) Radnorshire has only 655 Welsh speakers ... Pembrokeshire ('Little England beyond Wales') and Breconshire both have about one in five [Ruth Thomas, *South Wales*, 1977].

**Little Gray Lady, the** *Nantucket, Massachusetts, USA.* The nickname is an old sailors' name for the island, referring to its fancied appearance.

**Littlehampton** *Lillehammer, Norway.* A British soldiers' World War II rendering of the town's name, suggested by that of the English seaside resort. (Lillehammer is also a resort, but an inland winter-sports one.)

**Little Holland** *Arnol, Scotland.* The village near the northwest coast of the island of Lewis in the Outer Hebrides is so nicknamed for its many stone dykes.

**Little Italy** see in Appendix 1, p. 269.

**Little Java** *Bali, Indonesia.* Bali lies just east of Java and is popularly regarded as its smaller counterpart.

**Little Jerusalem** *Worms, Germany.* The city derived its nickname from its former Jewish community, reportedly the oldest in Germany.

**Little London** *Göteborg (Gothenburg), Sweden.* The city owes its nickname to the former presence of a large English merchant colony.

A 19th-century vogue for things Britannic led to the city acquiring the nickname "Little London" [Dodd/Donald, p. 434].

**Little London beyond Wales** *Beaumaris, Wales.* The seaside resort arose around the castle built in the 13th century by Edward I with the aim of attracting English settlers. The town has retained an English flavor ever since, its "Englishness" perhaps enhanced by its location in Anglesey, a name popularly interpreted as "island of the English." The nickname echoes that of **Little England beyond Wales**.

**Little Moscow** *(1) Chopwell, England; (2) Finsbury, London, England; (3) Maerdy, Wales, (4) Matun (Khost), Afghanistan.* The former mining villages of Chopwell in northeastern England and Maerdy in South Wales were noted in the 1920s for their Communist associations, as was the former London borough of Finsbury, where Lenin lived and worked. Matun, on the

other hand, was so dubbed in the 1980s because many of the Afghan Marxist leaders came from there.

(1) (Maerdy) Some villages, such as Maerdy in the Rhondda Valley, were known as Little Moscow on account of their political complexion between the World Wars [Meic Stephens, comp. and ed., *The Oxford Companion to the Literature of Wales*, 1986].

(2) (Maerdy) The Communist Party ran the town of Maerdy (nicknamed "Little Moscow" by Fleet Street in the 1930s) for decades [*The Rough Guide to Wales*, 1997].

**Little Mother Moscow** *Moscow, Russia.* As intimated in the quote below, Moscow was long regarded as the royal and religious mainstay of Russia. "Little Mother" (Russian *matushka*) is an affectionate diminutive.

Well may the people call it "Little Mother Moscow," for of all the cities it has been in the past a refuge and a source of strength and consolation to the Russians in their tragic and terrible struggles [W. Barnes Steveni, *Things Seen in Russia*, 1914].

**Little Mother Volga** *Volga River, Russia.* The Volga, more than any other river, is for Russians the maternal mainspring of their land. ("Little" goes with "Mother" as an affectionate diminutive.) *Cp.* **Mother Volga**.

(1) "Mátushka Volga," or "Little Mother Volga," is spoken of in Russia so often and with such affection that it is easy to cherish too high hopes of the attractions of a voyage upon it [Karl Baedeker, *Russia*, 1914].

(2) "Mother Volga" (*Matushka Volga*, as this central artery of the country is affectionately known in folklore and folksong) [Arthur Voyce, *Moscow and the Roots of Russian Culture*, 1964].

**Little Muddy, the** *Yarra River, Australia.* The river, in Victoria state, with the city of Melbourne at its mouth, is so nicknamed for its discolored water. The name itself is perhaps based on **Big Muddy**.

**Little Odessa** *Brighton Beach, New York City, USA.* The neighborhood in southwestern Brooklyn between Manhattan Beach and Coney Island has a large number of immigrants from the former Soviet Union, many of them from the Black Sea resort of Odessa. Hence the name, which was also the title of a 1994 movie set in Brighton Beach, about a hired killer who returns to his Russian-Jewish community here on an assignment.

**Little Paris** *(1) Beirut, Lebanon; (2) Brussels, Belgium; (3) Bucharest, Romania; (4) Milan, Italy.* All of the named places are seen as resembling the French capital in some way, mostly in physical attributes or lifestyle. In the 1950s and 1960s, Beirut was famed for its elegance and luxury, while the capital cities of Brussels and

Bucharest are cultural and commercial centers to match. Brussels and Milan also sport a lively social scene, so likewise claim comparison. *Cp.* **Klein-Paris.**

**Little Poland** *Galicia.* The historic region of southeastern Poland and western Ukraine was known by this name in the 14th century, when it was annexed by Casimir III of Poland.

**Little Raj-by-the-Sea** *Southwold, England.* The Suffolk town and resort was so nicknamed for the Britons who came to settle here in the late 19th and early 20th century after service in the Raj (India under British colonial rule). *Cp.* **Raj on the Med.**

**Little Rhody** *Rhode Island, USA.* The nickname is applied affectionately to the smallest state in the Union.

**Little Rome** *Liverpool, England.* The seaport city's nickname derives from its high proportion of Catholic residents. Liverpool has both an Anglican and a Roman Catholic cathedral.

**Little Rothenburg** *Vellberg, Germany.* The nickname compares the small town with the larger one by virtue of their comparable medieval fortifications.

**Little Russia** *Ukraine.* The name arose in the 17th century, when Ukraine sought independence from the Muscovite realm of "mainstream" Russia. It thus came to be known as "Little Russia" (Russian *Malorossiya*) by comparison with "Great Russia" (*Velikorossiya*). Both names were current until the 20th century.

(1) What would Russia be without Little Russia? It would be England shorn of all that beautiful land south of the Thames, for Little Russia, the Crimea, and the Caucasus are the garden of the Tsar's dominions [W. Barnes Steveni, *Things Seen in Russia*, 1914].

(2) "Little Russia" (or, as it is now called, the Ukraine — literally "Borderland") [Max Hayward, Introduction to Chloe Obolensky, *The Russian Empire*, 1980].

**Little Saigon** *Westminster, California, USA.* The city near Los Angeles came to be so nicknamed for its high concentration of Vietnamese-Americans.

**Little Seoul** *New Malden, London, England.* The former Surrey town, now a district of Kingston upon Thames, derives its nickname from its large number of South Korean residents, Seoul being their capital city. (Information kindly supplied by Jo Healy of neighboring Worcester Park.)

**Little Switzerland** *(1) Church Stretton, England; (2) Dovedale, England.* The name has been given to various places set in a region of hills and valleys, suggesting a miniature Switzerland. The

Shropshire resort town of Church Stretton is set amid hills, one being the nearby Long Mynd, while the stretch of the Dove River valley on the Derbyshire-Staffordshire border lies between steep limestone cliffs. *See also* **Little Switzerland** in Appendix 1, p. 269.

(1) (Church Stretton) This popular spa town, which the Victorians called 'Little Switzerland,' abounds with small shops [Travel brochure, *Shropshire*, 2005].

(2) (Church Stretton) Don't miss the splendours of Little Switzerland — a.k.a. Church Stretton — where there are neither wolves nor avalanches, just fine walking country [Tourist brochure, *Shrewsbury*, 2005].

**Little Tibet** *Ladakh, India/Pakistan.* The region of extreme northern India and extreme northeastern Pakistan, on the border of China, is so nicknamed by India for its ethnological and geographical kinship with Tibet.

Also known as Little Tibet, Ladakh is one of the great centres of Lamaistic Buddhism [*Sunday Times*, February 27, 2005].

**Little Twin, the** *Duluth, Minnesota, USA.* Duluth is a major port on Lake Superior at the mouth of the St. Louis River opposite Superior, Wisconsin, of which it is a "twin." The nickname is humorous, as Duluth is by far the larger city. The two are often jointly referred to as the Twin Ports. *Cp.* **Twin Cities.**

**Little Venice** *Arendal, Norway.* The town and port on Norway's south coast is sometimes so called because its geographical location, with a harbor on a protected sound, is somewhat similar to that of Venice, Italy. *See also* **Little Venice** in Appendix 1, p. 269.

**Lively Experiment State, the** *Rhode Island, USA.* The nickname derives from the state's royal charter of 1663, which undertook to "hold forth a lively experiment ... with a full liberty in religious concernment."

**Liverpool of the Cape** or **of South Africa, the** *Port Elizabeth, South Africa.* The name compares the industrial growth of the seaport city with that of Liverpool, England.

*Liverpool of South Africa. Port Elizabeth is sometimes so designated, but whether the designation is intended to be taken humorously, or as being anticipative, is somewhat uncertain* [Charles Pettman, *Afrikanderisms: A Glossary of South African Colloquial Words and Phrases of Place and Other Names*, 1913].

**Lizard State, the** *Alabama, USA.* The nickname refers to the state's early settlers, who made their homes by lakes and rivers, or in nearby woods, like the lizards that frequented these sites.

**Llanfair PG** *Llanfairpwllgwyngyllgogerychwyrndrobwllllantysiliogogogoch, Wales.* A traditional shortening of the very long name of the Anglesey village, itself a 19th-century humorous embroidering of its original name. (It means "St. Mary's church in the hollow of the white hazel near a rapid whirlpool and the church of St. Tysilio near the red cave.")

**LM** *Maputo, Mozambique*. The initials of Lourenço Marques, as capital of Portuguese East Africa, now Maputo, the capital of Mozambique. The present name was officially adopted in 1976.

> I planned to remain in LM for one week before returning to the Reef [J. Van Der Colff, *Bible Route: Mozambique*, 1976].

**Locombia** *Colombia*. The punning alteration of the country's name is based on "loco" in the sense "crazy," referring to the Colombians' grim search for pleasure amid the violence and corruption.

> This headlong quest for enjoyment amidst the anarchy has created a special kind of energy, the headlong delirium that has given the whole country the nickname of "Locombia" [Dodd/Donald, p. 119].

**LoDo** see in Appendix 1, p. 269.

**Loegria** or **Logres** or **Logris** *England*. The literary name, found chiefly in tales of romantic chivalry, such as those featuring King Arthur, evokes the mythical Locrinus, father of Sabrina (*see* **Sabrina**) and eldest son of Brutus (*see* **Brute's City**), king of Britain. On his father's death, Locrinus became king of Loegria, a name directly related to *Lloegr*, the Welsh name for England, and in turn probably linked to the Ligore, the Celtic people who gave the name of Leicester.

> (1) *Locrine* was left the soueraine Lord of all;
> But *Albanact* had all the Northrene part,
> Which of [i.e. after] himself *Albania* he did call;
> And *Camber* did possesse the Westerne quart,
> Which *Seuerne* [River] now from *Logris* doth depart [i.e. separate] [Edmund Spenser, *The Faerie Queene*, 1590].
> (2) Faëry damsels met in forest wide
> By knights of Logres, or of Lyonesse [John Milton, *Paradise Regained*, 1671].

**London Blizzard** *Leighton Buzzard, England*. A humorous name for the Bedfordshire town formerly current among railroad workers.

**London-by-the-Sea** *(1) Brighton, England; (2) Southend-on-Sea, England*. The name can be applied to any seaside resort popular with Londoners, especially day visitors, but is chiefly associated with the two mentioned, the former in Sussex, the latter in Essex. The name arose in the 19th century. The *Slang Dictionary* (1894) has a related entry "London ordinary" ("ordinary" meaning "eating place"): "The beach at Brighton, where the 'eight-hours-at-the-seaside' excursionists dine in the open-air." *Cp.* **London-on-Sea**.

> (1) (Brighton) Brighton is unfortunately so ill-provided with shade that this 'London-by-the-Sea' has been cynically described as made up of 'wind, glare, and fashion' [Karl Baedeker, *Handbook to Great Britain*, 1890].
> (2) (Southend) Sometimes called London-by-the-Sea, since it is a favourite seaside resort of Londoners [Johnson, p. 230].
> (3) (Brighton) Suddenly the city became host to deviants, dandies and dabblers from the city... A love-nest conveniently close to the capital, London by the sea was born [Dodd/Donald, p. 10].
> (4) (Brighton) Brighton — the hip and happening town nicknamed London-by-the-Sea [*Lonely Planet Great Britain*, 2005].

**Londonderry** *see* **Stroke City**

**Londoner's Garden, the** *Kent, England*. A promotional name for the county used on railway posters. *Cp.* **Garden of England**

**Londonistan** *London, England*. A media nickname for the British capital following the terrorist attack by Muslim extremists on July 7, 2005 (with a further attempted attack on July 21), when the city was seen as a European "hub" of Muslim fundamentalism. The "-stan" refers to Afghanistan (or Pakistan), a Muslim country.

> So entrenched is the British capital as an outpost of the Muslim diaspora, that London is commonly referred to as "Londonistan" — a word used several times in different papers [*The Guardian*, July 12, 2005].

**London of the North, the** *Leeds, England*. A self-promotional name for the northern city, implying that it has more to offer than the manufacturing industries for which it is chiefly noted.

> Yes, Leeds, 'the London of the North' — if you're going on the number of homeless people wandering its streets, perhaps [Sam Jordison and Dan Kieran, eds., *The Idler Book of Crap Towns II*, 2004].

**Londonograd** *London, England*. A nickname for the British capital as a home-from-home for rich Russians, especially from the 1990s. *Cp.* **Moscow-on-Thames**.

> They each have a foot on the "Londonograd" property ladder, though Khloponin's is a base for his daughter while she studies at the London School of Economics [*Sunday Times Magazine*, November 20, 2005].

**London-on-Sea** *Brighton, England*. A variant of the nickname **London-by-the-Sea**. *Cp.* **London-super-Mare**. Quote (1) below evokes the heady hedonism of **Swinging London**.

> (1) Brighton has the world's "hippest beach," according to *GQ* magazine, which has included the resort in its 2003 travel awards. The beach may be shingle, it says, "but on a rocking Friday night

in summer when the local clubs pour out, this is swinging London-on-Sea" [*The Times*, May 5, 2003].

(2) To call it London-on-sea is to understate its individual, laidback charm [*Sunday Times*, June 12, 2005].

(3) The last time I wrote about trying to get a good meal in London-on-Sea, it was difficult to avoid being hard on its restaurants. But now, a year or so later, eating out in Brighton ... no longer sucks [*The Times Magazine*, October 22, 2005].

**London's Country** see in Appendix 1, p. 269.

**London-super-Mare** *Brighton, England*. A variant of the nickname **London-on-Sea**, based on the name of another seaside resort, Weston-super-Mare, on the Bristol Channel, its Latin suffix meaning "on sea."

Like all the larger English watering-places, it [i.e. Hastings, 32 miles from Brighton] is simply a little London *super mare* [Henry James, "An English Winter Watering-Place," 1879, in *Portraits of Places*, 1883].

**London's Washtub** *South Acton, London, England*. The district was at one time so nicknamed for its many laundries. *Cp.* **Soapsuds Island**.

[The] 1870s property was once a big laundry, in the area called Acton Green but nicknamed "London's wash tub" [*Sunday Times*, December 4, 2005].

**London Town** *London, England*. A form of the British capital's name found mainly in ballads and popular songs, as well as more generally in poetry. It emphasizes the city's quintessentially urban nature.

(1) John Gilpin was a citizen
   Of credit and renown,
   A trainband captain eke [i.e. also] was he
   Of famous London town [William Cowper, "John Gilpin," 1783].

(2) A huge, dun cupola, like a foolscap crown
   On a fool's head — and there is London Town [Lord Byron, *Don Juan*, 1823].

(3) A foggy day in London Town
   Had me low and had me down [Ira Gershwin, "A Foggy Day," song, 1937].

(4) Maybe it's because I'm a Londoner
   That I love London Town [Hubert Gregg, "Maybe It's Because I'm a Londoner," song, 1947].

(5) The centuries-old traditions of "London Town" die hard [*Holiday Guide 1952: Area No. 5, South & South East England*].

**Londrix** *London, England*. A former nickname for the British capital, perhaps based on its Spanish name, *Londres* (pronounced "Londriss").

**Lone Mother of Dead Empires, the** *Rome, Italy*. The sobriquet, expressing the past power and glory of Rome, derives from the quote below.

Oh Rome! my country! city of the soul!
   The orphans of the heart must turn to thee,
   Lone mother of dead empires [Lord Byron, *Childe Harold's Pilgrimage*, 1812].

**Lone Star of Civilization, the** *Santa Fe, New Mexico, USA*. The state capital was so nicknamed because for many years after its founding by the Spanish in 1610 it was the sole town in a vast region of desert and mountains.

**Lone Star State, the** *Texas, USA*. The state is so nicknamed for the single star on its flag, representing its independence from Mexico in 1836 as the Republic of Texas.

(1) The lone star of Texas shall continue to wave proudly in the air as long as one brave Texan remains to defend it [Willim P. Dewees, *Letters from an Early Settler in Texas*, 1843].

(2) Two experts from Texas are using Cork as a base... [This is] appropriate, since co Cork has always had some of the aggressive independence of the lone star state [*The Times* (Ireland Supplement), September 21, 1971].

(3) Welcome to Texas, and the incomparable three dishes of the Lone Star State: venison, chilli con carne and rattlesnake [Alistair Cooke, *Letter from America*, "Christmas in Vermont," December 31, 1976 (2004)].

**Long** *Longdon, England*. The Staffordshire village is so known locally, as instanced in the folk rhyme quoted below.

The stoutest beggar that goes by the way,
   Can't beg through Long on a midsummer's day [William Hazlitt, *English Proverbs*, 1869].

**Long Island** or **Isle, the** *(1) Harris and Lewis, Scotland; (2) Outer Hebrides, Scotland*. The descriptive nickname is appropriate in each case, as Harris and Lewis are a single island in the Outer Hebrides, of which they form the northern and larger part, and the group as a whole consists of a string of islands extending for some 130 miles (209 km) from northeast to southwest in what is essentially one long island broken into several smaller ones.

(1) (Outer Hebrides) When I lived in the island of Barra I always put "Outer Hebrides" on my notepaper because the word "Hebrides" has for me a magic... However, it is true that the Outer Hebrides are also called the Outer Isles, the Western Isles and the Long Island, though the last should strictly be only Lewis and Harris [Compton Mackenzie in John Hay of Hayfield, comp., *Tartan Tapestry*, 1960].

(2) (Outer Hebrides) These are often called, as a group, 'The Long Isle' [Booth/Perrott, p. 38].

**Long Town** *London, England*. A former nickname for the British capital, perhaps evolving as a form of **London Town**.

**Loo, the** *(1) Borroloola, Australia; (2) Woolloomooloo, Sydney, Australia*. A short name for

Northern Territory town and the rough, working-class district of the New South Wales capital. For the characteristic prefixed "the" see quote (3) for **Alice**.

> (Borroloola) By the turn of 1900, just a handful of whites remained in "The 'Loo" [*The Rough Guide to Australia*, 2001].

**Loop** see in Appendix 1, p. 269.

**Loretto of Austria, the** *Mariazell, Austria.* The town's proper name means "Mary's cell," referring to the medieval image of the Virgin Mary in the Gnaden Church, an equivalent of that at Loreto, Italy. Both towns are important places of pilgrimage.

**Loretto of Switzerland, the** *Einsiedeln, Switzerland.* The town contains a famous image of the Virgin Mary, an equivalent of that at Loreto, Italy. Both towns are noted places of pilgrimage. *Cp.* **Loretto of Austria**.

**Lorna Doone Country** see in Appendix 1, p. 269.

**Los** *Los Angeles, California, USA.* A colloquial name formed by adopting the first word of the city's name (Spanish for "the").

**Los Anchorage** *Anchorage, Alaska, USA.* The seaport city's nickname is a punning adaptation of that of Los Angeles.

**Losantiville** *Cincinnati, USA.* The original name of the city, laid out in 1788, still sometimes serves as a nickname, perhaps partly by virtue of its quirky composition. (It comprises *L*, the initial of *Licking Creek*, *os*, Latin for "mouth," *anti*, Greek for "opposite," and *ville*, French for "town," so that it was the "town opposite the mouth of Licking Creek.") The present name was adopted in 1790.

**Lost City of the Incas, the** *Machu Picchu, Peru.* The ancient Inca city, now a major tourist draw, was "lost" in the Andes until it was discovered by the US explorer Hiram Bingham in 1911. Below lies the Urubamba River, the **Sacred Valley of the Incas**.

> Take a spectacular train ride through the Andes to Machu Picchu, the 'Lost City of the Incas' [Travel ad, *The Times Magazine*, November 27, 2004].

**Lost** or **Hidden Island, the** *Cephalonia, Greece.* The Ionian island is so called because "it was only by chance that those who visited it could find it again" (Brewer, p. 566).

**Lost Wages** *Las Vegas, Nevada, USA.* A wry pun on the gambling city's name.

> Vegas, Lost Wages, the greatest Gonzo city in the world [Dodd/Donald, p. 191].

**Lotusland** *Los Angeles, California, USA.* The nickname somewhat resembles the city's actual name, but really denotes a "land of lotus eaters,"

like the Lotophagi of Greek legend, who on eating the lotus entered a state of luxurious languor. Los Angeles is thus cast as a land of indolence.

**Lou** or **Lou'** *St. Louis, Missouri, USA.* An affectionate shortening and personalization of the city's name.

**Lourdes of Wales, the** *Holywell, Wales.* The North Wales town earns its nickname (and its real name) by virtue of its healing well, dedicated to St. Winifred. The well is hallowed by Catholics, as famously is the French resort of Lourdes in southern France, a prime place of pilgrimage for the sick.

> For thirteen hundred years a place of pilgrimage, Holywell ... comes billed as "The Lourdes of Wales," though it doesn't really warrant such a comparison [*The Rough Guide to Wales*, 1997].

**Louseland** *Scotland.* A former derogatory name similar to **Itchland**, implying a country infested with vermin (or one whose inhabitants are such).

**Lousy** *Lahoussoye, France.* A British soldiers' World War I version of the name of the village near Amiens.

**Lousy Anne** *Louisiana, USA.* A mock-derogatory punning name for the state. *Cp.* **Lucy Anna**.

**Loveliest Town in England** *see* **Most Beautiful Town in England**

**Loveliest Village in the North, the** *Linton, England.* The Yorkshire village, also known as Linton-in-Craven, was awarded its title in 1949 as the result of a national newspaper contest. The poetic description is still largely valid.

**Loveliest Village on the Plains, the** *Auburn, Alabama, USA.* The city is so nicknamed after the poetic line quoted below, which gave its regular name, as well as those of many other US towns named Auburn. (The hamlet of the poem was long identified as Lissoy, Co. Westmeath, Ireland, where the poet spent his childhood, but it is now believed to be a composite depiction. It is not the English coastal village of Auburn, Yorkshire, which was gradually eroded by the sea from the 18th century, so is now itself a "deserted village.")

> Sweet Auburn, loveliest village of the plain [Oliver Goldsmith, *The Deserted Village*, 1770].

**Low Countries** see in Appendix 1, p. 269.

**Lower 48, the** *United States.* The name relates to the 48 states of the continental USA excluding Alaska, so called as lying south of ("lower than") the latter. (Before Alaska and Hawaii became states in 1959, these 48 were the *only* states of the USA.)

People arrive steadily. And people go. They go from Anchorage and Fairbanks [in Alaska]... Some, of course, are interested only in a year or two's work, then to return with saved high wages to the Lower Forty-eight [*New Yorker*, June 20, 1977].

**Lowlands** see in Appendix 1, p. 269.

**Loyalist City, the** *Saint John, New Brunswick, Canada*. The city is so known for the United Empire Loyalists, or settlers from republican America loyal to Britain, who settled here in 1783.

**L'pool** *see* **So'ton**

**Lubberland** *London, England*. The name of a legendary "land of laziness" came to be applied to London in the same way as **Cockaigne**. Just as the transference of "Cockaigne" to the capital city was probably influenced by "Cockney," so "Lubberland" may have been influenced by **Lud's Town**.

**Lucky Country, the** *Australia*. The name denotes a "land of opportunity" where there are prospects and potential. It came from the ironic title of Donald Horne's critique of Australian society, *The Lucky Country* (1964), as in quote (1) below. The name was adopted by Rosa Cappiello for her Italian novel *Paesa Fortunata* (1981), published in English in 1985, as an account of the migrant experience of a group of women. Quote (3) refers to the so-called "£10 Poms" of the 1960s.

(1) Australia is a lucky country run mainly by second-rate people who share its luck [Donald Horne, *The Lucky Country*, 1964].

(2) We take it for granted that this is the Lucky Country, ignoring the fact that when Donald Horne titled his book he was writing in acid [Kit Denton, *Walk Around My Cluttered Mind*, 1968].

(3) Thousands of ... Britons each paid £10 to travel to the so-called Lucky Country, enticed by the promise of good weather, cheap housing and the guarantee of a well-paid blue collar job [*The Times*, November 23, 2004].

(4) Not one to suffer fools gladly, he bristled ... at questions from generations of younger journalists like: "So, are we still the lucky country?" [Obituary of Donald Horne, *The Times*, September 16, 2005].

**Lucy Anna** *Louisiana, USA*. A pleasantly punning nickname for the state on the lines of **Lousy Anne**.

**Ludslow** *Ludlow, England*. The Shropshire town was the first in Britain to be awarded "Slow City" status by Cittaslow, an Italian organization campaigning for towns with a slower and calmer way of life than in the bustling, jostling cities. Hence the punning name. As **Gourmetville**, Ludlow is also associated with "slow food" (the opposite of "fast food"), as described in quote (2) below.

(1) Many of the people who do buy in to "Ludslow" are elderly outsiders selling up from the rat race and seeking a quiet backwater [*The Times*, April 16, 2004].

(2) The Slow Food Movement was born from Italian journalist Carlo Petrini's frustration at finding his local eateries being replaced by corporate fast-food chains. Today, it holds no stronger foothold in Britain than in Ludlow, the first town in Britain to be awarded 'Slow City' status [Tourist brochure *Taste England*, 2005].

**Lud's Town** *London, England*. The literary name derives from Lud, a legendary king of Britain, who was said to have given the name of London (and also of Ludgate Hill, one of its central streets, named for the Lud Gate that he supposedly built in 66 BC).

The fam'd Cassibelan, who was once at point —
O giglot fortune! — to master Cæsar's sword,
Made Lud's town with rejoicing-fires bright
[William Shakespeare, *Cymbeline*, c.1609].

**Lumber State, the** *Maine, USA*. Maine is famed for its forests, which cover some two thirds of the state. Hence the nickname, referring to the timber harvest on which many of Maine's manufacturing industries depend.

**Lunnon** or **Lunnun** *London, England*. A spelling of the city's name intended to represent Cockney or working-class speech. At one time, as shown in quote (2) below, the name was regularly pronounced thus in smart circles. In quote (4), "sarf" is Cockney "south."

(1) And Gowler he answered sadly,
"Oh, mine is a doleful tale!
They've treated me werry badly
In Lunnon, from where I hail" [W.S. Gilbert, "The King of Canoodle-Dum," *The "Bab" Ballads*, 1869].

(2) In the early part of this [i.e. 19th] century it was the correct thing to say 'Lunnon.' At that time young people practised to say it, and studied to fortify thermselves against the vulgarism of saying *London* literally [John Earle, *The Philology of the English Tongue*, 1892].

(3) The ladies ... easily relapsed into a phonetic system representing the pronunciation which they shared with families of less 'edjication' in 'Lunnon' or the country [Ernest Weekley, *Adjectives—And Other Words*, 1930].

(4) The member of the "sarf Lunnun" Callaghan clan judged ... to have become most like an aristocrat ... was little Tiffany, the Eliza Doolittle of the family [*The Times*, December 17, 2004].

**Lusitania** *Portugal*. The Latin name of Portugal, adopted in poetry, derives from the Lusitani, the people who originally inhabited the region.

(1) And raised fair Lusitania's fallen shield,

And gave new edge to Lusitania's sword [Sir Walter Scott, *The Vision of Don Roderick*, 1811].
(2) Where Lusitania and her Sister [i.e. Spain] meet,
Deem ye what bounds the rival realms divide? [Lord Byron, *Childe Harold's Pilgrimage*, 1812].

**Lutetia** *Paris, France.* The poetic name for the French capital is its ancient Roman name, deriving from Gaulish *luto*, "mud," "marsh," referring to the low-lying land by the Seine River. The French form of the name is *Lutèce*.

**Lynn** *King's Lynn, England.* A local name for the Norfolk town and port that was formerly more widely current than now.

(1) But whither shall we then?
To Lynn, my lord; and ship from thence to Flanders [William Shakespeare, *Henry VI, Part 3*, 1595].
(2) Two stern-faced men set out from Lynn, Through the cold and heavy mist [Thomas Hood, "The Dream of Eugene Aram," 1829].
(3) Since we came back to London, we have discovered (sheepishly) that Lynn, as they call it for short, has for years been famous among English intellectuals [Ruth McKenney and Richard Bransten, *Here's England*, 1955].
(4) Before it became royal property it was called Bishop's Lynn. Nowadays the town is usually known simply as Lynn [Hadfield 1981, p. 411].

**M1, the** *Rajang River, Borneo, Malaysia.* The nickname, borrowed from the M1, Britain's main motorway, was adopted by British troops in the Borneo Campaign (1961–5) for the chief river of central Sarawak.

A hovercraft saved a woman's life after a difficult birth in a midnight dash up the "M1"—the great Rejang river that is the only highway in an anarchy of peaks and jungle completely devoid of road or rail in central Sarawak [Dennis Bloodworth, *An Eye for the Dragon*, 1975].

**M4 Corridor** see in Appendix 1, p. 269.
**Ma** *see* **Ma State**
**Macc** *Macclesfield, England.* An abbreviated name of the Cheshire town favored by local people.

John Howarth, a retired builder, ... said: "It's gone upmarket, but lost a lot of atmosphere. I'm 60, but when I were courting my wife Delia there were five cinemas in Macc" [*The Times*, November 8, 2004].

**Macedon** *Macedonia, Greece.* A poetic form of the ancient kingdom's name.

(1) I think Alexander the Great was born in Macedon: his father was called Philip of Macedon, as I take it [William Shakespeare, *Henry V*, 1600].
(2) Prince Alexander, Philip's peerless son, Who carried the great war from Macedon Into the Soudan's realm [Matthew Arnold, *Tristram and Iseult*, 1852].

**Mack City** *Allentown, Pennsylvania, USA.* The city is so nicknamed for Mack Trucks, Inc., founded there in the early 20th century as the Mack Brothers Motor Car Co. and based there ever since.

**Madchester** *Manchester, England.* The punning alteration of the city's name became current in the 1980s and 1990s, referring to Manchester's lively rock music scene. It also implied an indulgence in MDMA (methylene-dioxymethamphetamine), the drug more familiar as Ecstasy. The name was generally popularized by a 1990 TV documentary, *Madchester: Sound of the North*, about the rise of the Manchester music scene. (Two leading bands of the time were the Stone Roses and the Happy Mondays.) *Cp.* **Museumchester**.

(1) The explosion of the Madchester scene [was] in 1989 when the Stone Roses, 808 State and Happy Mondays all made it into the charts [*DJ*, July 6, 1995].
(2) Led by the Stone Roses, the Happy Mondays and a revitalized New Order, Sadchester became Madchester [Dodd/Donald, p. 27].
(3) Manchester's reputation is best represented by the almost mythological nightlife that for a brief, crazy time earned the city the moniker 'Madchester' [*Lonely Planet Great Britain*, 2005].
(4) Yes, it really lives up to its nickname. From the real-life footballers' wives to the jungle ravers, everybody out at night in Madchester seems to be totally trollied [i.e. drunk or drugged] [*Sunday Times*, June 12, 2005].

**Madeira of the Gulf of Guinea, the** *Bioko, Equatorial Guinea.* The nickname for the former **Fernando Po** was quoted by Richard Burton in *Wanderings in West Africa* (1863). Madeira is an island group off the coast of northwestern Africa, just as Bioko lies off the coast of West Africa.

**Madras** *Chennai, India.* The capital of Tamil Nadu state, long familiar as Madras, officially adopted its Tamil name in 1996, although the old form continued to appear in media reports for some time after. Both names are short forms. Madras was originally Madraspatnam, "Madras town," while Chennai is properly Chennapatnam, "Chenna's town," after a Telugu chief.

Madras, India's fourth largest city, is changing its name to Chennai... British tour operators, however, will be sticking with Madras for the moment to avoid confusion. Even the Indian tourist board in London was reluctant to change. "I think eventually we will accept it as Chennai—but we don't mind what anybody else does," said a spokesman [*Sunday Times*, July 21, 1996].

**Mad Town** *Madison, Wisconsin, USA.* A punning abbreviation of the state capital's name.
**Maeotis** *Sea of Azov.* The sea between Russia

and Ukraine was often described by classical writers as a lake or marsh, probably because of its shallowness. Hence its fuller name *Palus Maeotis* (Latin *palus*, "marsh"). The name was adopted for later poetic use. Pontus in quote (1) below is the Black Sea. For the river in quote (2), *see* **Tanais**.

(1) Sea he had searched and land
From Eden over Pontus, and the Pool
Maeotis, up beyond the river Ob [John Milton, *Paradise Lost*, 1667].
(2) Lo! where Mæotis sleeps, and hardly flows
The freezing Tanais thro' a waste of snows [Alexander Pope, *The Dunciad*, 1728].

**Mafeking** *Mafikeng, South Africa*. The earlier form of the name became widely known in the Boer War when the besieged garrison of British troops in the town was relieved in 1900. The displays of unruly public rejoicing that followed this "Relief of Mafeking" produced a verb "to maffick," meaning "to indulge in an exuberant national celebration." The old name remains in historical references.

**Magic City, the** *(1) Birmingham, Alabama, USA; (2) Leadville, Colorado, USA*. Birmingham is said to be so called either because it developed rapidly ("like magic") with the expansion of the railroad, or because its population soon recovered after a cholera outbreak. Leadville was so nicknamed for its unexpected rich deposits of gold and silver.

(Leadville) Leadville, Colorado, was the largest mining town in the Rocky Mountains. The hills around the 'Magic City' were a rich source of gold and silver [Edward Platt, *Leadville*, 2000].

**Magic Isle, the** *Maui, Hawaii, USA*. A promotional name designed to attract tourists to the natural charms of Hawaii's second-largest island.

Snap the waterfalls of Maui, known as 'The Magic Isle' [Travel ad, *The Times*, January 15, 2005].

**Magic Parallelogram** see in Appendix 1, p. 269.

**Magic Valley, the** *Rio Grande Valley, Texas, USA*. The region near the mouth of the Rio Grande known as the Rio Grande Valley is so nicknamed for its abundant production of citrus fruits and vegetables.

**Magnolia State, the** *Mississippi, USA*. The state is so nicknamed for the magnolias that grow in the coastal regions bordering the Gulf of Mexico. The magnolia was proclaimed the state's official emblem in 1938.

**Maiden, the** *Maiden Castle, England*. Britain's largest Iron Age hill fort, near Dorchester, Dorset, is colloquially so known. Its name implies that it is impregnable (*cp.* **Maiden City**),

although it was actually besieged and captured by the Romans in AD 43.

(1) A visit to the County Museum [in Dorchester] will add much to the interest of 'the Maiden' [Geoffrey Boumphrey in Speaight, p. 66].
(2) Perhaps fog is the best thing for a first visit to the Maiden [Julian Cope, *The Modern Antiquarian*, 1998].

**Maiden City, the** *(1) Londonderry (Derry), Northern Ireland; (2) Tournai, Belgium; (3) Venice, Italy*. A maiden city or castle is one that is impregnable, i.e. it is not taken and remains a "virgin." Londonderry is so called because it withstood many sieges, notably that of the army of James II in 1689, when it held out for 105 days. Tournai, first the fortified capital of a Roman province, then a seat of the Merovingian kings of Austrasia, was destroyed by the Normans in 881. The great Venetian Republic, long powerful in Europe, gradually lost its possessions from the 15th century and was finally dissolved in 1797. See also **Maiden Town**.

(1) (Tournai) Tournay ... at that time termed the Maiden Citie [John Wheeler, *A Treatise of Commerce*, 1601].
(2) (Venice) Venice, the eldest Child of Liberty.
She was a maiden City, bright and free;
No guile seduced, no force could violate,
And, when she took unto herself a Mate,
She must espouse the everlasting Sea [William Wordsworth, "On the Extinction of the Venetian Republic," *Poems Dedicated to National Independence and Liberty*, 1802].
(3) (Londonderry) And even those whose faith and historical background might beget a different set of emotions, could never find it in their hearts to grudge the grand old Maiden City its well-earned and most glorious fame [Richard Hayward, *Ulster and the City of Belfast*, 1950].

**Maiden Town, the** *(1) Abbeville, France; (2) Edinburgh, Scotland; (3) Magdeburg, Germany*. The sobriquet is most closely connected with the Scottish capital, which is said to have been so named from a tale that the maiden daughters of a Pictish king took refuge in Edinburgh Castle during a civil war. In the writings of the 12th-century chronicler Geoffrey of Monmouth, Edinburgh Castle is referred to as *Castrum Puellarum*, "Maiden Castle," as in quotes (2) and (4) below. As with **Maiden City**, however, the title more usually refers to an impregnable town or castle, one that remains "inviolate." The name of Magdeburg, if interpreted literally, actually means "maiden castle," and the city enjoyed an unsullied status until 1631, when it was sacked and burned during the Thirty Years' War, as mentioned in quote (1). Abbeville, as indicated in quote (3), has long been a well-preserved town.

(1) (Magdeburg) Victorie forsook him for ever since he ransacked the maiden town of Magdenburg [John Taylor (the "Water Poet"), *The Suddaine Turne of Fortunes Wheele*, 1631].

(2) (Edinburgh) The Castle of Edinburgh was formerly call'd *castrum puellarum, i.e.* the Maiden castle, because, as some say, the Kings of the Picts kept their daughters in it while unmarry'd [Thomas Hearne, *Reliquiae Bodleianae*, 1703].

(3) (Abbeville) [Abbeville] is called *The maiden town*, because it was never taken by an enemy [Thomas Nugent, *The Grand Tour; or, A Journey through the Netherlands, Germany, Italy, and France*, 1756].

(4) (Edinburgh) The Pictish maidens of the blood-royal were kept in Edinburgh castle, thence called *Castrum Puellarum*. "A childish legend," said Oldbuck... "It was called the Maiden Castle ... because it resisted every attack, and women never do" [Sir Walter Scott, *The Antiquary*, 1816].

(5) (Edinburgh) Your hearts are stout and true;
So bide ye in the Maiden Town,
While others fight for you [W.E. Aytoun, "Edinburgh After Flodden," *Lays of the Scottish Cavaliers*, 1849].

**Mainhattan** *Frankfurt, Germany.* Frankfurt am Main is a leading financial center, with a stock exchange dating from the 16th century. It is also the place from which the Rothschild family started its banking empire. Hence not only this name, punning on the business buildings of Manhattan, but the alternate nicknames of Bankfurt, punning on that of the city, and Chicago on the Main (German, *Chicago am Main*), referring to the equivalent buildings of Chicago. A more sinister sobriquet is Krankfurt (German *krank*, "sick"), referring to the city's ill repute as a center of trade in sex (prostitutes) and illegal drugs (junkies), a side elaborated in quote (5) below.

(1) Skyscrapers (most of them banking headquarters) sprouted all over Frankfurt; the town was dubbed "Mainhattan" and "Bankfurt" [Gale Wiley in *International Herald Tribune*, February 6, 1979].

(2) They call it 'Bankfurt' and 'Krankfurt' and 'Mainhattan' and more [*Lonely Planet Germany*, 2004].

(3) This is "Bankfurt"—a ... city unashamedly designed around the pursuit of money... Its Tetris skyline leads some to call it "Mainhattan" [Dodd/ Donald, p. 456].

(4) Its [i.e. Frankfurt's] current attempt to promote itself as "Mainhattan," based both on the river that it is built on and its self-professed similarities to the heart of NYC, has been about as successful as the introduction of a smoking gallery on the Hindenburg [Adam Russ, *101 Places Not to Visit*, 2005].

(5) Krankfurt. Auch Mainhattan, Bankfurt oder G'stankfurt genannt. Einzige deutsche Stadt mit Dippemess. Sitz des Hessischen Kaninchenzüch-

tervereins. Murat Özcan & Dragan Bosic wurden hier geboren. Döner, Sushi, Fallafel, Lahmacun, Doughnuts and Cabanossi kommen von hier. Es ist diese Mischung aus Subkultur, Abscheu, Armseligkeit, Siechtum, Kleinstadtcharme and Provinzialität, die den Geiz Frankfurts ausmacht. Und daran kann leider auch di relative Nähe zu Offenbach nichts ändern... Ha, Ha, Ha ... Das Imperium schlägt zurück! (Krankfurt. Also called Mainhattan, Bankfurt or Stankfurt. Only German town with the Dippemess [funfair]. Home of the Hessian Rabbit Breeders Union. Murat Özcan and Dragan Bosic were born here. Kebabs, sushi, falafel, lahmacun, and cabanossi come from here. It is this mix of subculture, repugnance, wretchedness, debilitation, small-town charm, and provinciality that makes up Frankfurt's meanness. And unfortunately the relative proximity to Offenbach cannot change any of that... Ha, ha, ha ... The empire strikes back!) [<http://www.assoziations-blaster.de/info/krankfurt.html> accessed August 27, 2005].

**Mainland, the** *(1) Australia; (2) England or Britain; (3) North Island, New Zealand; (4) South Island, New Zealand.* The name is used for any "main land" as seen from a lesser one, as an island or peninsula. Australia is thus so called from the point of view of Tasmania; England or Britain are so seen from Ireland or from the Scottish islands; North Island, New Zealand, is so viewed from South Island, and vice versa. The largest islands of both the Orkney and the Shetland Islands in northern Scotland are officially named Mainland for this reason.

(1) (Australia) They are tied to Australia—"the mainland," they call it... "The mainland" is an object of suspicion, envy, and dislike [Thomas Wood, *Cobbers*, 1934].

(2) (South Island) Greater numbers of adventurous North Islanders than ever before have crossed the seas this summer to the "mainland" [*Weekly News* (Auckland), February 10, 1965].

(3) (Britain) The Shetlanders ... were happy in their independence from the 'mainland'—for indeed they had their own Mainland and were largely self-contained [Macnie/McLaren, p. 445].

(4) (England) Catholics and Protestants look alike ... but there are ways to tell them apart. For example, Protestants ... are likely to refer to England as "the Mainland" [Sean Kelly and Rosemary Rogers, *How to Be Irish*, 2000].

**Mainland State, the** *Alaska, USA.* The nickname is that of a state that is part of mainland America (*see* **Mainland**) although geographically isolated from it.

**Main Street of Russia, the** *Volga River, Russia.* Western Russia's principal waterway is navigable over most of its length and combines with its tributaries to carry both freight and passenger traffic. Hence its deserved description.

Here is a wonderful opportunity to travel along

'the main street of Russia,' an apt title for the mighty Volga River as she snakes her way through the Russian heartland, from the Caspian Sea to Moscow [Travel ad, *The Times*, October 1, 2005].

**Mairsy Dopes (and Dozy Dopes)** *Merseyside, England.* A local nickname for the region (and former county) centering on Liverpool, based on the popular novelty song by Milton Drake, Al Hoffman, and Jerry Livingston, "Mairzy Doats and Dozy Doats" (1944). (The words disguise "Mares eat oats and does eat oats.") The spelling of the name, which reflects the local pronunciation of "Mersey," is liable to vary.

**Makesicko City** *Mexico City, Mexico.* A wry pun on the name of the Mexican capital, referring to its ambient pollution.

(1) This sprawling metropolis ... has been nicknamed Makesicko City because of its infamous health hazards, including high levels of air and water pollution [*Sunday Times Magazine*, March 20, 2005].
  (2) A place the size of Make-Sicko city is bound to produce at least one artist of note [Adam Russ, *101 Places Not to Visit*, 2005].

**Maliboo-boo** *Malibu, California, USA.* A playful pun on the name of the coastal community. *Cp.* **Bu.**

**Mallows** *St.-Malo, France.* A former version of the French seaport's name, found mainly in English maritime writings.

The captain's boy brought me four barrels of Mallows oysters which Captain Tatnell had sent me from Murlace [i.e. Morlaix] [Samuel Pepys, *Diary*, May 21, 1660].

**Manc** or **Mancs** *Manchester, England.* A local shortening of the city's name, on more or less the same lines as **Winch.** (The form of the name as "Manc" rather than "Manch" was influenced by "Mancunian" meaning both "native or inhabitant of Manchester" and, adjectivally, "belonging to Manchester.")

(1) Parts of Manc are no-go ruins despite Salford Quays [Jonathan Meades in *The Times*, November 6, 2004].
  (2) He's got a little round head as well, and a Manc accent [Ricky Gervais in *Four*, 2004].
  (3) You can make it to Mancs from most places in the UK in time for lunch [*Sunday Times* (Northwest England Supplement), September 11, 2005].

**Manche, la** *English Channel.* Insular England gradually became aware of its broader basis after joining the European Community in 1973 and the French name of the English Channel, separating Britain from the **Continent**, was increasingly heard instead of the familiar English name. Most European countries have long used a form of the French name, meaning "the sleeve" (*see* **Sleeve**), as Italian *La Manica*, Spanish *La Mancha*, and German *Ärmelkanal* (from *Ärmel*, "sleeve"), so it made sense for the British to follow suit, especially in business circles. *See also* **Channel.**

(1) Before you cross La Manche, transfer your bank account [*The Times*, April 14, 2005].
  (2) The Channel Tunnel is doing quite well out of it [i.e. the reduction in sea travel]—the number of journeys under la Manche were up 8 per cent [*The Times*, September 27, 2005].

**Manchester of America, the** *Lowell, Massachusetts, USA.* The former nickname refers to the cotton mills for which both cities are noted. *Cp.* **City of Spindles.**

**Manchester of Belgium, the** *Ghent (Gand), Belgium.* The former nickname refers to the commercial city's manufactures of linen, cotton, leather goods, and engines, like those of its English counterpart.

**Manchester of Colombia, the** *Medellín, Colombia.* The nickname refers to the city's textile mills and clothing factories, like those of its English equivalent. *Cp.* **Lingerie Capital of Latin America.**

**Manchester of France, the** *Lyon, France.* The former name compares the textile manufactures of both cities. In the case of Lyon this was silk, while for Manchester it was cotton.

Lyons is the Manchester of France; filled with a manufacturing, money-getting tribe, who wear their hearts in their purses [Henry Matthews, *The Diary of an Invalid*, 1820].

**Manchester of Japan, the** *Osaka, Japan.* The seaport city is a major manufacturing center, as is its English equivalent.

**Manchester of Prussia, the** *Elberfeld, Germany.* Elberfeld, as the central section of Wuppertal, is a noted manufacturing center, as is the English city with which it is compared.

**Manchester of Spain, the** *Barcelona, Spain.* Both Barcelona and Manchester have important textile manufactures, among other industries. Hence the former nickname. *Cp.* **Manchester of the Mediterranean.**

**Manchester of the Mediterranean, the** *Barcelona, Spain.* The alliterative nickname casts the comparison with the English manufacturing city wider than its national reputation as the **Manchester of Spain.**

In my late father's copy of *The Children's Encyclopaedia* [issued fortnightly 1908–10] Barcelona was described as "the Manchester of the Mediterranean" [*The Times*, 17 January 2004].

**Mancs** *see* **Manc**

**Mancunium** *Manchester, England.* The miscopied form of the city's Roman name (properly *Mamucium*) gave "Mancunian" to mean "of Manchester." A native of Manchester is thus a Mancunian, who may well speak with a Mancunian accent. *Cp.* **Manc.**

**Mandela University** *Robben Island, South Africa.* The nickname refers not so much to the island as to its infamous prison, formerly used for the detention of political prisoners, including African National Congress leader Nelson Mandela, who four years after his release in 1990 became South Africa's first black president. See the quotes below for the "university" reference.

(1) Despite the hardships, Robben Island became known as 'Mandela University' to younger inmates because of the lessons in politics that Mandela taught them [*Time*, July 22, 1991].
(2) As restrictions on studying were eased, Robben Island became known ... as the University. In truth, it was known as Mandela University [*New York Review of Books*, February 2, 1995].

**Mangrove Coast** see in Appendix 1, p. 269.

**Manhattan of the Middle Ages, the** *Antwerp, Belgium.* The name refers to the city's former role as Europe's main commercial and financial center.

As the "Manhattan of the Middle Ages" Antwerp was wealthier in the sixteenth century than any other European city [Leier, p. 46].

**Manhattan of West Africa, the** *Abidjan, Côte d'Ivoire.* The former Ivorian capital is so nicknamed not only for its modern skyscrapers but also as the financial center of French-speaking West Africa. *See also* **Pearl of the Lagoon.**

**Manhattan-on-Sea** *Dubai, United Arab Emirates.* The buildings of the capital city and principal port of the United Arab Emirates, where most of the Emirates' banks and insurance companies are based, include many skyscrapers, producing a cityscape like that of Manhattan. Hence the nickname. *Cp.* **Mainhattan.**

The latest plans are part of the transformation of Dubai from a fishing village to Manhattan-on-Sea [*Sunday Times*, January 2, 2005].

**Mansionville** *Prestbury, England.* The pretentious style of many of its homes and buildings earned the Cheshire village this nickname from residents of the neighboring town of Bollington.

**Manxland** *Isle of Man, British Isles.* An alternate name for the island, from "Manx" as the adjectival form of "Man." (The "-x" represents the Old Scandinavian equivalent of Old English "-ish" in "English," etc.)

[Douglas] is Manxland's natural centre for excursions to places of interest within the island [*Holi-*

*day Haunts 1960: Area No. 2, North West England and North Wales*].

**Maoriland** *New Zealand.* The name refers to the Maoris who form New Zealand's indigenous population (today less than 15 percent of the total). *See also* **King Country** in Appendix 1, p. 269.

(1) I prepared to make my *entrée* into Maori land in a proper and dignified manner [Frederick Edward Maning, *Old New Zealand*, 1863].
(2) *The King Country; Or, Explorations in New Zealand, A Narrative of 600 Miles of Travel through Maoriland* [J.H. Kerry-Nicholls, book title, 1884].

**Maple City, the** *(1) Adrian, Michigan, USA; (2) Ogdensburg, New York, USA.* Both cities are nicknamed for the maples that are their shade trees.

**Maple Sugar State, the** *Vermont, USA.* Vermont is noted for its production of maple sugar and syrup, and the sugar maple is the state tree. Hence the nickname.

**Marble City, the** *Kilkenny, Ireland.* The town is so nicknamed for the locally quarried limestone, which develops a deep black shine when polished.

It's known as the marble city, but Kilkenny may face the prospect of becoming a mere town... The marble town? Doesn't quite have the same ring to it [*Irish Times*, May 24, 2000].

**Marches** see in Appendix 1, p. 269.

**Mardi Gras City** *New Orleans, Louisiana, USA.* The city is famous for the Mardi Gras celebrations held on the day before Ash Wednesday as the culmination of the winter carnival season. Hence the nickname. *Cp.* **City Care Forgot.**

**Marianne** *France.* A personification of the French Republic in the form of a lightly-dressed young woman wearing a Phrygian cap. Her figure appears on French coins and stamps and her bust is found in every town hall. She first appeared at the time of the Revolution and her figure remained anonymous until 1969, when the authorities decided to base her on Brigitte Bardot, then aged 35. In 1984 she was succeeded in this role by another actress, Catherine Deneuve, then 41, who in turn handed on the torch in 1999 to Laetitia Casta, a 21-year-old Corsican model.

(1) Nor will Marianne be in a position to act the vindictive hostess this time... France and Britain had their chance of making a world peace in 1918, and they muffed it [H.G. Wells, *Babes in the Darkling Wood*, 1940].
(2) Marianne can still throw impressive tantrums, and France remains fundamentally revolutionary [*The Times*, September 1, 2005].

**Marienbad** *Mariánskě Lázne, Czech Republic.* The German name of the fashionable spa town is familiar to many from the acclaimed 1961 movie *Last Year at Marienbad*. The name in both languages means "Mary's springs."

**Maritzburg** *Pietermaritzburg, South Africa*. A shortening of the city's lengthy name, achieved by dropping the first name of one of the two Afrikaner leaders that it commemorates, Pieter Retief (1780–1838) and Gerrit Maritz (1798–1839).

> We British shortened the name to 'Maritzburg,' and pronounced it in English fashion [Alan Paton, *Towards the Mountain*, 1980].

**Market Jew** *Marazion, England*. The alternate name of the Cornish coastal town, originally that of an adjacent place, derives from Cornish words meaning "Thursday market," whereas the name of Marazion itself means "little market." The present form of the alternate name, preserved in that of Market Jew Street in the nearby much larger town of Penzance, became popularly associated with Jews, who are said to have been banished to Cornwall by Roman emperors to work in the local tin mines. Not surprisingly, the name Marazion similarly became associated with **Zion**. The alternate name was formerly more common than the regular name, presumably because the latter place, as a "little market," was the less important of the two.

> Then a town among us, too, which we call Market Jew, but the old name was Market Zion, that means the Bitterness of Zion, they tell me; and bitter work it was for them no doubt, poor souls! [Charles Kingsley, *Yeast*, 1851].

**Marmalade Country, the** *Scotland*. A nickname originating in the music halls from a familiar Scottish product, one famous make being Keiller's "Dundee" Marmalade, dating from the late 18th century.

**Marrowbone** *Marylebone, London, England*. A former corruption of the district's name. In the days when it was still a village, the diarist Samuel Pepys recorded a visit to "a pretty place called Marrowbone" (May 7, 1668).

**Marsh** see in Appendix 1, p. 269.

**Marsh City, the** *St. Petersburg, Russia*. The former nickname for Russia's second-largest city refers to the low-lying site intersected by streams at the eastern end of the Gulf of Finland where Peter the Great founded it in 1703.

> Peter's "lofty thoughts" for a city to be built "on the mossy, marshy banks" facing the Gulf of Finland began to be realized in 1703 [Patricia Barnes, *The Children of Theatre Street*, 1978].

**Marsiale** *Marseille, France*. A colloquial corruption of the seaport city's name as current among French speakers.

**Marvellous Melbourne** *Melbourne, Australia*. The Victoria state capital gained its sobriquet in the 1880s, when it was a center of the gold rush and enjoyed great wealth from the surrounding goldfields. The phrase was popularized by the journalist George Augustus Sala, as in quote (1) below.

> (1) It was on the 17th of March in the present year of grace, 1885, that I made my first entrance, shortly before high noon, into Marvellous Melbourne [George Augustus Sala, "The Land of the Golden Fleece," in *The Argus* (Melbourne), August 8, 1885].
>
> (2) Visitors to the colony of Victoria in the 1880s were awed and dazzled by the astonishing progress of the city. They began to call it "Marvellous Melbourne" [Michael Cannon, *The Land Boomers*, 1966].
>
> (3) The establishment of the University of Melbourne (1853), the Melbourne Public Library (1856), and the forerunner of the National Gallery of Victoria (1861) were manifestations of "Marvellous Melbourne's" confidence [*Britannica*, vol. 14, p. 484].

**Marvelous City, the** *Rio de Janeiro, Brazil*. The former Brazilian capital earned its Portuguese nickname for the natural beauty of its beaches and of its peaks, ridges, and hills, these last all partly covered in tropical forests.

> (1) The tour culminates in the 'cidade maravilhosa,' Rio de Janeiro [Travel ad, *The Times Magazine*, November 27, 2004].
>
> (2) Bornay was not born in the "marvellous city" but in the hill town of Novo Friburgo, in upstate Rio [Obituary of Rio carnival costume designer Clóvis Bornay, *The Times*, October 15, 2005].
>
> (3) Rio, known as "the Marvelous City," is the entrance gate to a State that has a lot to offer [Rio Convention & Visitors Bureau ad, *Sunday Times*, December 4, 2005].

**Masate** *Mazatenango, Guatemala*. A local short form of the town's name, in both speech and writing.

> The next large town is Mazatenango (*Masate* in conversation and on the bus windows) [Natascha Norton and Mark Whatmore, *Cadogan Guides: Central America*, 1993].

**Mascot** *Kingsford Smith Airport, Sydney, Australia*. Sydney's main airport is commonly referred to by the name of the suburb where it is located, near Botany Bay, New South Wales.

**Ma State, the** or **Ma** *New South Wales, Australia*. New South Wales is Australia's oldest state. It is thus the "mother state" or "ma state." The Cabbage Gardeners in quote (2) below come from the **Cabbage Garden**.

> (1) Strange how the importing mania clings to the Ma State [*The Bulletin* (Sydney), January 18, 1906].
>
> (2) The Cabbage Gardeners will have to be

licked outright if Ma is to have a hope [*The Bulletin* (Sydney), January 24, 1934].

**Matterhorn of Africa, the** *Spitzkoppe, Namibia.* The mountain is so nicknamed for its shape, like that of the European original.

**Maub, la** *Maubert, Paris, France.* A short colloquial name for the district centering on the place Maubert, in the Latin Quarter. *Cp.* **Mocobo.**

**Maxfield** *Macclesfield, England.* A former spelling of the Cheshire town's name, familiar from the saying "Maxfield measure, heap and thrutch," i.e. full measure. This form of the name also gave the surname Maxfield.

**Maximum City** *New York City, USA.* A nickname for the **City that Has Everything**, promoted by the title of Michael Pye's book *Maximum City: A Biography of New York* (1991).

**Mazurian Venice, the** *Mikolajki, Poland.* The town is a noted yachting and water-sports center in Mazuria, the **Land of a Thousand Lakes.** Hence its touristic nickname.

**Mecca** *New York City, USA.* The name of the birthplace of Muhammad in Saudi Arabia, the chief place of Muslim pilgrimage, is sometimes applied to New York as a city that many aspire to visit.

**Med, the** *Mediterranean Sea.* A colloquial abbreviation of the lengthy name among sailors and sunseekers, denoting not simply the sea itself but the coastal regions around it.

(1) We went all round the Med., Capri, Istanbul, Gib [Gillian Freeman, *The Liberty Man*, 1955].
(2) The best way to find your personal outpost on the Med is to walk the coast [*The Times*, May 14, 2005].

**Medallo** *Medellín, Colombia.* A local variant of the city's name.

Medallo, as it is affectionately known to locals [Dodd/Donald, p. 127].

**Mediterranean of the New World, the** *Caribbean Sea.* The New World Caribbean and Old World Mediterranean can be equated for their touristic popularity and favorable climatic conditions. There is also something of a geographical similarity, if one regards the Caribbean as bounded by the West Indies on the north and east, South America on the south, and Central America on the west, and the Mediterranean as enclosed by Europe on the west and north, Asia on the east, and Africa on the south. The two seas are even approximate in area, with the Caribbean at around 1,065,000 square miles (2,754,000 square km), and the Mediterranean at around 970,000 square miles (2,512,000 square km). *Cp.* **American Mediterranean.**

The Caribbean has been described as Europe's other sea, the Mediterranean of the New World [V.S. Naipaul, *The Middle Passage*, 1962].

**Megacity** see in Appendix 1, p. 269.

**Megalopolis** *(1) Los Angeles, California, USA; (2) Tokyo, Japan.* The Greek name, meaning "big city," has been applied as a nickname to a number of cities that have grown to a huge size, like the two mentioned. It was the proper name of more than one ancient Greek city, such as Megalopolis, Arcadia, founded in the 4th century BC as a fortress against Sparta from the inhabitants of around 40 existing towns. *See also* **Megalopolis** in Appendix 1, p. 269.

**Mel** *Melbourne, Australia.* A colloquial short form of the city's name. *Cp.* **Syd.**

The city [i.e. Adelaide] does not come in for the same attention as her siblings Mel and Syd [Dodd/Donald, p. 219].

**Melita** or **Melite** *Malta.* The classical name of the Mediterranean island is found in both the Bible and later literature, as in the quotes below.

(1) And when they were escaped, then they knew that the island was called Melita [Acts 28:1].
(2) To fabulous Solyma, and the Ætnean Isle, Ortygia, Melite, and Calypso's Rock [P.B. Shelley, *Œdipus Tyrannus; or, Swellfoot the Tyrant*, 1820].

**Melting Pot, the** *(1) New York City, USA; (2) United States.* The name applies to any place of mixed peoples or races. New York was so called because it was the place where immigrants from many lands entered the country to blend as a new nation. The term was first used in this sense as in quote (1) below. *Cp.* **City of the World.**

(1) (USA) America is God's Crucible, the great Melting-Pot where all the races of Europe are melting and re-forming! [Israel Zangwill, *The Melting Pot*, 1908].
(2) (New York) New York isn't a melting pot, it's a boiling pot [Thomas E. Dewey, quoted in John Gunther, *Inside U.S.A.*, 1947].
(3) (New York) It used to be said that New York City was a melting pot. It never was, and it isn't today [Mayor Ed Koch, quoted in Alistair Cooke, *Letter from America*, "Mayor Koch at Work," August 12, 1988 (2004)].

**Merrimuck** *Merrimack River, USA.* A punning alteration of the river's name, referring to the former pollution of the Merrimack's waters by the textile mills that lined its banks.

**Merry England** *England.* A nostalgic, ironic, or simply conventional name for England, used by many who are unaware that "merry" here meant "pleasant," as in quotes (1) and (2) below, not "joyous," "festive,"as now. Edward German's operetta *Merrie England* (1902), set in Elizabethan times, aimed to capture the spirit of the earlier sense, which was also that of "the merry month of May" and even originally "merry Christmas." In the 20th century the title came to be used ironically, with "Merry" often in the "Olde Englishe" spelling "Merrie."

(1) Saint *George* of mery England, the signe of victoree [Edmund Spenser, *The Faerie Queene*, 1590].

(2) Then call'd a halt, and made a stand,
And cried, "St. George, for merry England!" [Sir Walter Scott, *The Lay of the Last Minstrel*, 1805].

(3) England was merry England, when
Old Christmas brought his sports again [Sir Walter Scott, *Marmion*, 1808].

(4) They called Thee MERRY ENGLAND, in old time;
A happy people won for thee that name
With envy heard in many a distant clime;
And, spite of change, for me thou keep'st the same
Endearing title [William Wordsworth, "They called Thee MERRY ENGLAND," *Yarrow Revisited, and Other Poems*, 1835].

(5) The war was over, democracy saved, and here was Merrie England [J.B. Priestley, *Bright Day*, 1946].

(6) The point about Merrie England is that it was about the most un–Merrie period in our history [Kingsley Amis, *Lucky Jim*, 1954].

(7) [Thorpeness] was built ... in the 1920s by Glencairn Stuart Ogilvie, an eccentric Scot who set out to re-create the spirit of merrie olde Englande [*Sunday Times*, August 1, 2004].

**Merry Wakefield** *Wakefield, England.* The adjective as applied to the Yorkshire town bears not so much its original sense of "pleasant," as for **Merry England**, as the modern meaning "happy," "joyful." The epithet has been attributed to the legendary character George-a'-Green, the merry pinder (poundkeeper) of Wakefield, mentioned in quotes (1) and (2) below.

(1) My friend, this is the towne of merry Wakefield [Robert Greene, attrib., *George-a'-Green*, 1599].

(2) The first whereof that I intend to show,
Is merry *Wakefield* and her *Pindar* too [Richard Brathwaite, *A Strappado for the Devil*, 1615].

(3) What peculiar cause of mirth this Town hath shown above others I doe not know [Thomas Fuller, *The History of the Worthies of England*, 1662].

(4) Round Wakefield's merry May-pole now,
The maids may twine the summer bough [Sir Walter Scott, *The Lord of the Isles*, 1815].

**Merthyr** *Merthyr Tydfil, Wales.* The name of the town north of Cardiff is frequently shortened thus, especially locally.

**Mesopotamia** *Belgravia, London, England.* The former nickname for the London district worked on two levels. Geographically, it compared the area by the Westbourne River with the region between the Tigris and Euphrates in Iraq. Racially, the district was so dubbed as the home of a number of newly rich Jews. *Cp.* **New Jerusalem**. Mesopotamia (which literally means "between the rivers") is also the nickname of an area of Oxford between the Cherwell River and one of its branches.

A house in Great Adullam Street, Macpelah Square, in that district of London whilom known as "Mesopotamia" [Edmund H. Yates, *Broken to Harness: A Story of English Domestic Life*, 1864].

**Mespot** or **Messpot** or **Messup** *Mesopotamia, Iraq.* A British soldiers' World War I nickname for the region, which at the time was in fact something of a metaphorical "messpot" or "messup." The punning alteration would have come naturally to army men, for whom the word "mess" was familiar in everyday contexts.

Mr. Whipple ... had gone off and joined the army and had done his bit in Mespot [C.S. Forester, *The Ship*, 1943].

**Metroland** see in Appendix 1, p. 269.

**Metrollops, the** *London, England.* A former humorous corruption of **Metropolis** alluding to the capital's "ladies of pleasure."

**Metropolis, the** *London, England.* A byname of the British capital, as the "mother city" (the literal sense of the Greek word).

(1) To the METROPOLIS of GREAT BRITAIN. The most renowned and late flourishing City of London [John Dryden, dedication, *Annus Mirabilis*, 1667].

(2) LONDON ... the Metropolis of *Great-Britain* [Nathan Bailey, *An Universal Etymological English Dictionary*, 1721].

(3) *The metropolis*, often somewhat pompously used for 'London.' Also, in recent use, occasionally applied to London as a whole, in contradistinction to *the City* [*Oxford English Dictionary*, 1884–1933].

(4) Situated in the heart of the country, yet within easy reach of the Metropolis [Realtor's ad, *Metro-land*, 1932].

(5) The walk by Ridge Hill [in Hertfordshire] is the most agreeable country stroll near the Metropolis; I have known country-lovers pent in the town on urgent tasks come all across the city for its healing and refreshment [S.P.B. Mais, *The Home Counties*, 1942].

**Metropolis of Dissent, the** *Leicester, England.* The city was famous in the 19th century for its many Protestant places of worship, including seven Baptist chapels.

Leicester was an ideal place from which to run temperance excursions. Leicester was also 'the metropolis of Dissent' [Piers Brendon, *Thomas Cook: 150 Years of Popular Tourism*, 1991, quoting A. Temple Patterson, *Radical Leicester*, 1954].

**Metropolis of Golf, the** *St Andrews, Scotland.* The nickname refers to the historic town as the home of the Ancient and Royal Golf Club, one of the governing organizations of golf.

**Metropolis of the Cotswolds** *see* **Capital of the Cotswolds**

**Metropolis of the Empire, the** *London, England.* An extension of the capital's title **Metropolis** to the borders of the former British Empire.

> But what is to be the fate of the great wen of all? The monster, called…"the metropolis of the empire?" [William Cobbett, *Rural Rides*, 1822].

**Metro Toronto** see in Appendix 1, p. 269.

**Mex** *Mexico City, Mexico.* An easy abbreviation of the capital city's name.

> 'What we'll do is, we'll go back to Mex, sell the car, and maybe I can get a garage job' [Truman Capote, *In Cold Blood*, 1965].

**Mexico** *see* **El Paso**

**Mezzogiorno** see in Appendix 1, p. 269.

**Mia** *Miami, Florida, USA.* A colloquial shortening of the city's name.

**Miami of the North, the** *Buffalo, New York, USA.* Despite its harsh winters, the city is so nicknamed for its warm and sunny summer weather.

**Middle, the** *South Island, New Zealand.* The island is so named as lying between North Island and Stewart Island.

> The North Island of New Zealand has its western coastline and so has tiny Stewart Island, but there is, as every New Zealander knows, only one West Coast, and that is in the 'Middle,' or South Island [Shadbolt, p. 225].

**Middle America** see in Appendix 1, p. 269.

**Middle Britain** see in Appendix 1, p. 269.

**Middle East** see in Appendix 1, p. 269.

**Middle England** see in Appendix 1, p. 269.

**Middle Kingdom, the** *China.* The name, translating Chinese *zhōngguó*, "middle country" (from *zhōng*, "middle," and *guó*, "country"), dates from around 1000 BC, when the Zhou people here, unaware of any civilizations elsewhere in the world, believed they occupied the center of the earth. A similar name is *zhōnghuá*, "middle flower," from *zhōng*, "middle," and *huá*, "magnificent," "flourishing." The official name of China today is thus *zhōnghuá rénmín gònghéguó*, literally "middle magnificent people's republican country." *Cp.* **Flowery Kingdom**.

> (1) [It is] generally believed that China is situated at the centre of the earth, surrounded by the Four Seas, beyond which lie a number of small islands inhabited by the red-haired barbarians who come to the Middle Kingdom to trade [Giles, p. 179].
>
> (2) When the Chinese described their land as the "Middle Kingdom," they weren't just expressing a world view with China's vast domains at the centre, but a cosmological one, in which the Forbidden City was designed and positioned to be

the focal point, not just of a vast empire but of the entire universe [*The Times Magazine*, October 22, 2005].

**Middle of England, the** *Meriden, England.* The former Warwickshire village claims to be located in the exact center of England, as marked by an old cross here. The sobriquet may owe something to the real name, which suggests "meridian" (but which actually means "pleasant valley," literally "merry dene").

**Midi** see in Appendix 1, p. 269.

**Midland** see in Appendix 1, p. 269.

**Midland Metropolis, the** *Birmingham, England.* The sobriquet sees Britain's second city as a regional equivalent of London, the **Metropolis** that is the nation's first city. *Cp.* **Capital of the Midlands**.

> Birmingham was so entitled because it was the largest town, and has more inhabitants than any town in the centre of England. To use a Yankeeism, it is "the hub" of the Kingdom… If London is the Metropolis of all that is effete and aristocratic, Birmingham has the moving-power of all that is progressive, recuperative and advancing [Walter Showell, *Dictionary of Birmingham*, 1885].

**Midlands** see in Appendix 1, p. 269.

**Midland Sea, the** *Mediterranean Sea.* A poetic name for the sea, translating its Latin-based name.

> (1) His task and mine alike are nearly done;
>   Yet once more let us look upon the sea;
>   The midland ocean breaks on him and me [Lord Byron, *Childe Harold's Pilgrimage*, 1812].
>   (2) Not by those hoary Indian hills,
>   Not by this gracious Midland sea
>   Whose floor to-night sweet moonshine fills,
>   Should our graves be! [Matthew Arnold, "A Southern Night," 1861].

**Midtown** see in Appendix 1, p. 269.

**Midwest** see in Appendix 1, p. 269.

**Mighty Brahmaputra, the** *Brahmaputra River, Bangladesh.* The adjective is a stock epithet for the great river, which rises in Tibet, then flows east and south to join the Ganges in Bangladesh.

> "It may be a cliché," remarked one of our passengers, looking at the broad sweep of muddy river in front of us, … "but it really is the mighty Brahmaputra" [*The Times*, November 6, 2004].

**Mile High City, the** *Denver, Colorado, USA.* Denver earns its nickname from its location at an altitude of 5,280 ft (1,609 m), the exact length of a mile.

> The 'Mile High City' shows little of its erstwhile cow-town days [*Lonely Planet USA*, 2004].

**Milesian Republic, the** *Ireland.* The nickname derives from the legendary warrior Milesius, whose two sons, Heber and Amergin, are said to have conquered Ireland in the 13th century BC.

**Milky Way, the** *Val di Susa, Italy.* The winter sports area in northwestern Italy is so nicknamed for its snowy roads and routes. The astronomical name (see in Appendix 7, p. 327) translates Italian *Via Lattea,* itself of a type with the Latin names of famous Roman roads in Italy, as the *Via Appia* (Appian Way), *Via Aurelia* (Aurelian Way), *Via Flaminia* (Flaminian Way), and *Via Latina* (Latin Way).

**Mill City** *Minneapolis, Minnesota, USA.* Minnesota was long famous for its flour and dairy industry (*see* **Bread and Butter State**), while from the 1880s to around 1920 Minneapolis produced more flour than any other city in the world. Flour is no longer produced in Minneapolis, although several major milling companies are still based here.

**Millionaires' Village** *Overstrand, England.* The Norfolk coastal resort attracted many rich and famous people in the early 19th century. Hence the nickname.

**Millpond, the** *Atlantic Ocean.* The humorous name, supposedly implying a smooth crossing, was often applied to the sea route from Britain to North America. *Cp.* **Pond.**

And now, while Minna Wroe was waiting at table in Regent's Park, ... how was our other friend Hiram Winthrop employing his time beyond the millpond? [Grant Allen, *Babylon,* 1885].

**Mining State, the** *Nevada, USA.* The state is so named as one of the richest mineral regions in the USA. The copper that was originally mined has now been replaced by gold as a more commercially valuable mineral.

**Mini State, the** *Rhode Island, USA.* The state is so nicknamed as the smallest in the USA. *Cp.* **Little Rhody.**

**Minnesnowta** *Minnesota, USA.* A local punning nickname for the state, where some parts have continuous snow cover for at least three months, with snow known to fall even as late as May.

**Minnie** or **Minny** *Minneapolis, Minnesota, USA.* A colloquial personalization of the city's name.

'Minny' is brash and bustling [*Lonely Planet USA,* 2004].

**Minnie Apple** or **Mini-Apple, the** *Minneapolis, Minnesota, USA.* A name punning on the city's real name but also implying a smaller-sized **Big Apple.**

(1) Minneapolis has ... more theatres and dance companies per capita than New York City. Small wonder they call it the Minnie Apple! [Dodd/Donald, p. 171].

(2) Look for events at the following venues (all in 'Mini-Apple' unless otherwise noted) [*Lonely Planet USA,* 2004].

**Miracle Strip** see in Appendix 1, p. 269.

**Miss** *Mississippi, USA.* A colloquial name for the state, from its standard abbreviated form. The University of Mississippi at Oxford is regularly known as "Ole Miss."

**Mistake on the Lake, the** *Cleveland, Ohio, USA.* The name refers to the incident in 1969 when an oilslick on the Cuyahoga River caught fire, resulting in damaging pollution. *See* **Burning River City.**

The tag "The Mistake on the Lake" looked like it would be hard to shake off [Dodd/Donald, p. 149].

**Mist Belt** see in Appendix 1, p. 269.

**Mistress of the Adriatic, the** *Venice, Italy.* The name refers to the city's former commercial status as a center of trade between Europe and the East. *Cp.* **Queen of the Adriatic.**

**Mistress of the Seas, the** *Britain.* The nickname alludes to Britain's former naval supremacy.

(1) In the War of 1812, our navy, still in its infancy, ... boldly entered the lists with the Mistress of the Seas, and bore away the palm from many a gallant encounter [Edward Everett, *Orations and Speeches on Various Occasions,* 1853–68].

(2) It is the year of grace 1850 ... Britain is the mistress of the seas, the empire upon which the sun never sets [Webster Tarpley, "Palmerston's London During the 1850's — A Tour of the Human Multicultural Zoo," *The Executive Intelligence Review,* April 15, 1994].

**Mistress of the World, the** *Rome, Italy.* The sobriquet has long been associated with ancient Rome, as the grandest, richest, and most populous of cities, deferred to by all others, and in its day the capital of a powerful empire.

Rome now is mistress of the whole
  World, sea and land, to either pole [Ben Jonson, *Catiline his Conspiracy,* 1611].

**Misty Isle** *see* **Isle of Mist**

**Mizzoo, the** *Missouri River, USA.* A colloquial nickname based on the pronunciation of the river's name.

**MK** *Milton Keynes, England.* An initialism from the name of one of Britain's best-known New Towns.

Volvos with 'I♥MK' stickers, driving around and around the roundabouts [Sam Jordison and Dan Kieran, eds., *The Idler Book of Crap Towns II,* 2004].

**Mlungustan** *South Africa.* A satirical name for "white" South Africa during the apartheid era. It was coined by *Drum* magazine, as in the quote below, and derives from Khosa *mlungu,* "white person," suffixed by "-stan," from "bantustan," the (derogatory) term for a black homeland, itself from the name of Pakistan. *Cp.* **Londonistan.** ("Pluralstan" in the quote comes from "plural" as a term for a black person, from the Department of Plural Relations and Development, a former name for the Department of Bantu Affairs.)

> Mlungustan is Mlungustan. Pluralstan is Pluralstan ... and never the twain shall meet [*Drum*, July 24, 1985].

**Mo** *Missouri, USA.* An adoption of the official state abbreviation, found in the (regular) names of Mobridge, South Dakota, on the Missouri River, and Moville, Iowa, near this river, as well as in the nickname "Mighty Mo" for the battleship USS *Missouri*, flagship of the US Pacific Fleet in World War II.

**Moa's Ark** *New Zealand.* The punning name refers to the numerous species of flightless bird that have evolved in the country's isolated environment. (The moa is now extinct, but the kiwi, takahe, and other flightless species are extant.) The nickname was created by British naturalist David Bellamy.

**Mo' Bay** *Montego Bay, Jamaica.* An abbreviation of the seaport and resort's name, as popularly used among visitors.

**Mobtown** *(1) Baltimore, Maryland, USA; (2) Cicero, Illinois, USA.* Baltimore was formerly so nicknamed for the lawless element that prevailed here during the Civil War. Cicero came by its sobriquet from its reputation for civic corruption after 1924, when Al Capone moved here and organized gunmen to control an election.

**Mob Town** *Mobile, Alabama, USA.* A nickname based on the city's real name.

**Mockingbird State, the** *Florida, USA.* The state is nicknamed for the bird, found not only in Florida but elsewhere in the USA.

**Mocobo, la** *Maubert, Paris, France.* A colloquial argot name for the district centering on the place Maubert, in the Latin Quarter. *Cp.* **Maub.**

**Model City of Tomorrow, the** *Saigon South, Vietnam.* The development zone of Ho Chi Minh City is planned as the capital's new center. Hence its promotional name.

**Model County, the** *Co. Wexford, Ireland.* The county is so nicknamed for its progressive farming methods and for Ireland's first agricultural school, established in the mid–1850s. The name is mainly used in reports of Gaelic sports event, and especially hurling.

> Model county greets return of hurling victors [Headline, *Irish Times*, September 3, 1996].

**Model Settlement, the** *Shanghai, China.* As stated in the quote below, the seaport city was formerly so nicknamed for its efficient administration. On one occasion Shanghai was described in Parliament by the Duke of Somerset as a "sink of iniquity," leading the English Chinese scholar and traveler E.C. Baber to quip in a letter to the *North-China Herald*: "I am not burning to return to the Model Sink."

> Often called the "Model Settlement," in allusion to its efficient municipal administration [Giles, p. 253].

**Model Sink** *see* **Model Settlement**

**Modern Athens, the** *(1) Boston, Massachusetts, USA; (2) Edinburgh, Scotland; (3) Weimar, Germany.* The nickname of all three cities views them as cultural centers on a par with ancient Athens. Boston is also known as the **Athens of America**, Edinburgh as the **Athens of the North**, and Weimar as the **Athens of Germany**.

> (1) (Edinburgh) It was about this time that the foolish phrase "The Modern Athens" began to be applied to the capital of Scotland, a sarcasm, or a piece of affected flattery, when used in a moral sense; but just enough if meant only as a comparison of the physical features of the two places [Lord Henry Thomas Cockburn, *Memorials of His Time, c.*1815 (1856)].
> (2) (Edinburgh) I think our Modern Athens much obliged to me for having established such an extensive manufacture [Sir Walter Scott, Introductory Epistle, *The Fortunes of Nigel*, 1822].
> (3) (Edinburgh) Pompous the boast, and yet a truth it speaks
> A "modern Athens,"—fit for modern Greeks [James Hannay in *The Edinburgh Courant*, November 10, 1860].

**Modern Babylon, the** *London, England.* London was formerly so nicknamed for its opulence and decadence, like that of the biblical city. *Cp.* **Babylon.**

> (1) I proceeded to London... Months passed away, and I was still a wanderer upon the streets of the modern Babylon [J.M. Wilson, *Tales of the Borders*, 1835].
> (2) London is a modern Babylon [Benjamin Disraeli, *Tancred*, 1847].
> (3) In bidding adieu to the modern Babylon, ... Mrs Micawber and myself cannot disguise from our minds that we part ... with an individual linked by strong associations to the altar of our domestic life [Charles Dickens, *David Copperfield*, 1850].
> (4) London has been called "The Modern Babylon"—but not lately [Cecil Hunt, *Talk of the Town*, 1951].

**Modern Face of Gas, the** *Roma, Australia.* The Queensland town promotes itself thus for its natural gas and oil deposits. Its commercial natural gas field, discovered in 1960, was the first in Australia.

**Modern Mother of Presidents, the** *Ohio, USA.* The nickname was in vogue for the state in the 1920s and 1930s, when it was realized that seven US presidents had been born in Ohio: Ulysses S. Grant, Rutherford B. Hayes, James A. Garfield, Benjamin Harrison, William McKinley, William Howard Taft, and Warren G. Harding. Like Virginia, Ohio is also known as the **Mother of Presidents.**

(1) Ohio may claim to take rank with Virginia as a "mother of Presidents" [*Chicago Record*, March 8, 1897].

(2) Ohio is the mother of Presidents, and Taft is one of her sons [*Chicago Daily News*, April 21, 1948].

**Mohammed's Paradise** *Nicaragua.* As indicated in the quote below, the country was so nicknamed by the Spanish for its natural beauty.

The country is so pleasing to the eye, and so abounding in all things necessary, that the Spaniards call it Mohamed's paradise [Thomas Gage, *The English-American*, 1648].

**Moleps** *Molepolole, Botswana.* A friendly (and practicable) shortening of the town's name.

**Mombers** *Mombasa, Kenya.* The nickname for the city and port was given by British sailors, using the "Oxford -er," as for **Honkers.** (The ending of the actual name virtually invites this.)

**Momo** *Detroit, Michigan, USA.* A colloquial name for the city, duplicating the first syllable of **Motor City** or **Motown.**

**Mona** *(1) Anglesey, Wales; (2) Isle of Man, British Isles.* The Roman name of Anglesey is directly related to its Welsh name of Môn. The classical name of both islands is found in literature.

(1) (Anglesey) Nor on the shaggy top of Mona high,
Nor yet where Deva spreads her wisard stream [John Milton, *Lycidas*, 1638].

(2) (Anglesey) The Roman Mona is the Mona Lisa of islands [Christopher Wordsworth in *Observer Colour Magazine*, August 24, 1980].

**Mon & Brec, the** *Monmouthshire and Brecon Canal, Wales.* A friendly short name for the former industrial canal running between Brecon and Pontypool.

The Monmouthshire and Brecon Canal, completed in 1812, ... failed to meet its makers' commercial expectations. Today the 'Mon & Brec' wiggles for 35 miles, mostly through the Brecon Beacons National Park [Simon Calder in *A View of Wales*, Spring/Summer, 2005].

**Monarch of British Mountains, the** *Ben Nevis, Scotland.* Britain's highest mountain is so nicknamed in a North British Railway poster of *c.* 1921. The name may have been adopted from that of Mont Blanc as the **Monarch of Mountains.**

**Monarch of Mountains, the** *Mont Blanc, France.* The distinctive mountain is the highest peak of the Alps. Hence its nickname. (The French name it simply "white mountain.")

Mont Blanc is the monarch of mountains;
They crown'd him long ago
On a throne of rocks, in a robe of clouds,
With a diadem of snow [Lord Byron, *Manfred*, 1817].

**Monkey Britain** *Monchy-Breton, France.* A British soldiers' World War I version of the name of the village in northern France.

[The] village of Monchy-Breton (known, of course, as Monkey Britain), near St-Pol [Edmund Blunden, *Undertones of War*, 1928].

**Monkey City** or **Town** *Montgomery, Alabama, USA.* A colloquial name for the state capital, based on its real name.

**Monkey State, the** *Tennessee, USA.* The nickname refers to the so-called "Monkey Trial" of 1925, in which a Dayton, Tennessee, high-school teacher, John T. Scopes, was charged with violating the state law by teaching the Darwinian theory of evolution (which essentially states that man descended from monkeys).

**Monte** *Monte Carlo, Monaco.* A familiar name for the fashionable resort, with its world-famous casino and auto rally.

(1) After her extraordinary luck at Monte, ... she had lost all her winnings the following night at the Cannes Casino [Paul de Ketcheva, *Confessions of a Croupier*, 1928].

(2) A bicycle is never a cycle or bike, any more than Monte Carlo is Monte [Guy Egmont, *The Art of Egmontese*, 1961].

(3) 'We love it here. *Just* adore it. Though, of course, it's very *diff*erent from our other life. The life we've always known. Paris and Rome. Monte. London' [Truman Capote, *In Cold Blood*, 1965].

**Montmartre on the Mississippi** *New Orleans, Louisiana, USA.* The nickname is a reminder of the city's French origins, comparing it with the district of Paris, France, that is noted for its liveliness and colorfulness. *Cp.* **Mardi Gras City.**

**Montparno** *Montparnasse, Paris, France.* A short colloquial name for the Left-Bank district and its boulevard du Montparnasse.

**Montpellier of England, the** *Bury St Edmunds, England.* The cathedral town of Suffolk, with its many beautiful buildings, came to be compared in the 18th century with the handsome French city of Montpellier, set in a fertile plain near the Mediterranean. The English town was formerly familiar as **St. Edmundsbury.**

(2) From St. Edmundsbury to Thetford I had been accompanied by a clergyman... He said St. Edmundsbury had been called "The Montpellier

of England," from its fine air, and dry soil [Joseph Farington, *Diary*, August 16, 1812].

(3) The Montpelier [*sic*] of England [Edward D. Clarke, *Travels in Various Countries of Europe, Asia, and Africa*, 1810–23].

**Montpellier of Surrey, the** *New Malden, London, England*. The former decayed Surrey town was transformed in the 19th century into a thriving and presentable community, as described in the quote below. The comparison is with the historic French city of Montpellier, a popular tourist center near the Mediterranean.

Due to the energy and drive of its inhabitants, the town was drained, good roads were laid out, churches and solid houses were built, so that, in time, the place became known as 'The Montpelier [*sic*] of Surrey' [Weinreb/Hibbert, p. 557].

**Mont Valo** *Mont Valérien, France*. A colloquial short name for the hill near Paris, the site of a memorial to French citizens shot by Germans during World War II.

**Monument** or **Monumental City, the** *Baltimore, Maryland, USA*. The nickname alludes to the city's many monuments, especially the Washington Monument (1829), the first to be erected to George Washington.

(1) Baltimore is the 'Monument City,' from the great battle monument, and several others of note, within its limits [*Life Illustrated*, May 31, 1856].

(2) What, in that sad event, would not have been the fate of the Monumental City, of Harrisburg, of Philadelphia, of Washington, the Capital of the Union, each and every one of which would have lain at the mercy of the enemy? [Edward Everett, "Gettysburg Oration," November 19, 1863].

(3) Baltimore has been known for years as the 'Monument City,' and some of these monuments are in reality works of art [*Springfield Weekly Republican* (Springfield, Massachusetts), March 8, 1906].

(4) "The Monumental City" is the nation's second largest seaport [*Business Week*, September 24, 1949].

**Monumental State, the** *Maryland, USA*. The state derives its nickname from its largest city, Baltimore, the **Monument City**.

**Moon's Backside, the** *Brasília, Brazil*. A nickname given the Brazilian capital from its modern, "moonscape" appearance.

**Morea** *Peloponnese, Greece*. The medieval name of the peninsula survives in later literature.

Slow sinks, more lovely ere his race be run,
  Along Morea's hills the setting sun [Lord Byron, *The Corsair*, 1814].

**Moreal** *Montreal, Quebec, Canada*. A spelling of the city's name that reflects the pronunciation of its French form as Montréal.

**Mormon City, the** *Salt Lake City, Utah, USA*. Salt Lake City is the home of the Mormons (Church of Jesus Christ of Latter-Day Saints). Hence the nickname. *Cp.* **City of the Saints**.

We got to the Mormon City all beat out [John H. Beadle, *Western Wilds, and the Men Who Redeem Them*, 1878].

**Mormondom** *United States*. A former name for the USA, seen, mainly by Europeans, as the home of the Mormons.

(1) We also wish ... to see once more the Americans at home, and to learn from actual observation the social conditions of those who have left old England ... for the vaunted new world of Mormondom [English tourist agent Thomas Cook in *The Excursionist*, September 21, 1872].

(2) All that part of Mormondom south of the rim of the Great Basin is called Dixie [John H. Beadle, *The Undeveloped West; or, Five Years in the Territories*, 1873].

**Mormon State, the** *Utah, USA*. The state is so nicknamed for its capital, Salt Lake City, the **Mormon City**. *See also* **Deseret State**.

Utah, otherwise The Mormon State, is called by the Mormons themselves Deseret [Wagner 1893, p. 35].

**Moscow-on-Thames** *Hampstead, London, England*. The name is used not only for the fashionable district of Hampstead, where a number of wealthy immigrant Russians have settled, but for similar London communities, as those mentioned in the quote below, even if none of them is actually on the Thames River.

[The New White Russian] lives ... in Moscow-on-Thames (St John's Wood, Hampstead, Mayfair) [*The Times Magazine*, July 24, 2004].

**Moses Mountain** *Mount Sinai, Egypt*. A popular touristic name for the biblical mountain where God is said to have given the Ten Commandments to Moses (Exodus 3:1).

The terrible tale of the excursion to "Moses Mountain" (as Mount Sinai is called in the lowest-common-denominator excursion lingo) [*Sunday Times*, January 23, 2005].

**Mosquito State, the** *New Jersey, USA*. The state was formerly so nicknamed from the swarms of mosquitoes that at one time plagued its coastal regions.

We get the scornful title, the *Mosquito State*, because we seem to have our share of these industrious and bloodthirsty insects [Quoted in G.E. Shankle, *American Nicknames*, 1937].

**Most Aristocratic Café in Europe, the** *Spa, Belgium*. The fashionable resort gained its nickname from the various European royal and noble families who came to visit its mineral springs.

**Most Beautiful City in Europe, the** *Budapest, Hungary*. A subjective nickname for a city that, as first seen, could indeed have a fair claim to the title.

> I had heard Budapest described as the most beautiful city in Europe. It is strange and dramatic, to be sure, but there is something rather barbaric about it [Edmund Wilson, *Europe Without Baedeker*, new ed., 1967].

**Most Beautiful Fjord in the World, the** *Geirangerfjord, Norway.* The hyperbolically subjective sobriquet is to an extent justified, since in 2005 the western fjord was awarded world heritage site status for its outstanding natural beauty.

> We thought we'd seen everything until we arrived at Geirangerfjord, dubbed "the most beautiful fjord in the world" [Travel ad, *The Times Magazine*, September 10, 2005].

**Most Beautiful or Loveliest Town in England, the** *Ludlow, England.* The historic Shropshire town is noted for its huge craggy castle, imposing parish church, and impressive array of black-and-white half-timbered buildings, all spread over a low hill.

> (1) Ludlow is one of the most picturesque towns in the Midlands, if not in England [*The Rough Guide to England*, 1998].
> (2) No one is sure who first called Ludlow "the most beautiful town in England." Or who decided it was "the most English of market towns." But it would be hard to argue with them [*The Times*, June 5, 2004].
> (3) For all its renown as a foodie's paradise, let us not forget its other title: "the loveliest town in England" [Shropshire travel brochure, 2005].

**Most Christian Kingdom, the** *France.* A nickname that is not easy to quantify, but to which France can lay a good claim, ever since Clovis I, traditional founder of the French monarchy, was converted to Christianity by his wife St. Clotilda in 493.

**Most English City Outside England, the** *Christchurch, New Zealand.* The South Island city was founded in 1851 by the Canterbury Association as a Church of England settlement and is traditionally regarded as typically English, both in its outward appearance and in the conservative (or "imperial") outlook of certain of its inhabitants.

> (1) In spring ... the city still echoes and honours the homeland of its pioneer fathers. Its Englishness may be a matter for dispute, but its reputation as a garden city is not [Shadbolt, p. 262].
> (2) Often described as 'the most English City outside England,' Christchurch is a wonderful city [Travel ad, *Sunday Times Magazine*, July 3, 2005].

**Motel City** *Breezewood, Pennsylvania, USA.* Breezewood, at a state highway junction between Pittsburgh and Harrisburg, with exit south to Baltimore and Washington, is noted for its many motels. Hence the obvious nickname.

**Mother and Mistress of All Cities, the** *Paris, France.* The capital city was so described in an anonymous French eulogy of the early 14th century.

**Mother City, the** *Cape Town, South Africa.* Cape Town is the oldest city in South Africa and was the first point of settlement by people from Europe. Hence the sobriquet.

> (1) Those who believe that the Mother City still has its best days to come, are equally assured that ... fair women and brave men will never be lacking to grace and guard the Cape Town yet to be [Herbert Tucker, *Our Beautiful Peninsula*, 1913].
> (2) A tourist in the heart of Cape Town, South Africa's "Mother City," will perhaps not notice the extent of changes to the place [*The Times* (South Africa Supplement), February 16, 2005].

**Mother England** *England.* A personalization of England as the maternal ancestor of the English. *Cp.* **Motherland.**

> (1) "What horse is that?" said I to a very old fellow... "The best in mother England," said the very old man [George Borrow, *Lavengro*, 1851].
> (2) Young men were expected ... to die for their country, for the myth of Mother England [Maureen Duffy, *England*, 2001].

**Mother-in-Law of the Navy, the** *Norfolk, Virginia, USA.* The city and port, headquarters of the US Atlantic Fleet, is so nicknamed because the Norfolk Navy Yard, Portsmouth, lies directly opposite it on the south side of the Elizabeth River.

**Mother Ireland** *Ireland.* A personalization of Ireland as the maternal ancestor of the Irish. *Cp.* **Mother England.** For the reference to Rosaleen in the quote below, *see* **Róisín Dubh.**

> Countries are either mothers or fathers ... Ireland has always been a woman, a womb, a cave, a cow, a Rosaleen, a sow, a bride, a harlot, and, of course, the gaunt Hag of Beare [Edna O'Brien, *Mother Ireland*, 1976].

**Motherland, the** *England or Britain.* The name could obviously apply to any native land, but particularly came to be used in colonial times for England or Britain, the homeland of the British Empire. *Cp.* **Fatherland.**

> (1) Land of our Birth, our faith, our pride,
> For whose dear sake our fathers died;
> Oh, Motherland, we pledge to thee
> Head, heart, and hand through the years to be!
> [Rudyard Kipling, "The Children's Song," *Puck of Pook's Hill*, 1906].
> (2) England is both a real place ... and an imagined icon, almost, indeed, a person as embodied in 'motherland.' Where other nations speak of a male state, a fatherland, ours, like France, is always female [Maureen Duffy, *England*, 2001].

**Mother of All Cities, the** *Córdoba, Spain.* The historic city derives its sobriquet from its early origin by comparison with the capital, Madrid, which dates only from the 10th century. It was probably Carthaginian in origin and flourished under the Romans in the 2d century BC. However, the cities of Barcelona and Granada are equally ancient and probably even older.

> Visitors may rush to Madrid, Barcelona and Granada; but this, as the locals would have it, is the mother of all cities [Dodd/Donald, p. 46].

**Mother of All Nations, the** *Germany.* An old sobriquet for Germany, denoting its assumed superiority over other lands and races. The country is more usually regarded as the **Fatherland**.

> Germany is the Queene of all other Provinces, the Eagle of all Kingdomes, and the Mother of all Nations [Thomas Coryat, *Crudities*, 1611].

**Mother of Books, the** *Alexandria, Egypt.* The nickname alludes to the city's famous library, the greatest of ancient times, which was partly destroyed by fire in the 1st century BC and entirely gone by the 4th century AD. The sobriquet is a typical Arabic concept, with "mother" in the sense "ultimate example."

**Mother of Cities, the** *Balkh, Afghanistan.* The city is so nicknamed for its antiquity, as if the oldest and greatest of all others. The English phrase translates Arabic *umm al-bulud*, with "mother" as for the **Mother of Books**.

**Mother of Colonies, the** *England or Britain.* The nickname refers to England as the engenderer and nurturer of the British Empire, in its day the largest in the world, comprising around 25 percent of the world's population. *See* **Colonies** in Appendix 1, p. 269.

> The Mother of Colonies has a wonderful gift for alienating the affection of her own household by neglect [Rudyard Kipling, *From Tideway to Tideway*, 1892].

**Mother of Diets, the** *Worms, Germany.* The city derived its nickname as the historic seat of a large number of imperial diets, notably the Diet of Worms (1521), at which the religious reformer Martin Luther made his defense.

**Mother of Missouri Counties, the** *Howard County, Missouri, USA.* The county is so nicknamed for its original large size and for the fact that many other counties were formed from it.

**Mother of Parliaments, the** *England.* The sobriquet is sometimes taken to refer to the English Parliament itself, as being the first of its kind. It properly refers to England, as being the first country to achieve a parliament that was both independent and more powerful than the monarch. The phrase stems from the politician John Bright, as in quote (1) below.

> (1) England is the mother of parliaments [John Bright, speech at Birmingham, January 18, 1865].
> (2) The early date at which the principle of self-government was established in England, the steady growth of the principle, the absence of civil dissension, and the preservation in the midst of change of so much of the old organization, have given its constitution a great influence over the ideas of politicians in other countries. This fact is expressed in the proverbial phrase — "England is the mother of parliaments" [*Encyclopædia Britannica*, 1910].
> (3) A fierce controversy was under way over the question of self-government for Ireland, the Ulstermen were swearing they would never be ruled by Catholics, and Sir Edward Carson was organizing an army and threatening civil war. In short, the Mother of Parliaments was hardly setting the best of examples to her children all over the world [Upton Sinclair, *World's End*, 1940].

**Mother of Presidents, the** *(1) Ohio, USA; (2) Virginia, USA.* Virginia is so nicknamed as the birthplace of eight US presidents, including four of the first five: George Washington, Thomas Jefferson, James Madison, James Monroe, William Henry Harrison, John Tyler, Zachary Taylor, and Woodrow Wilson. For the name as applied to Ohio, *see* **Modern Mother of Presidents**.

> (1) (Virginia) James Monroe ... was born in Va., the mother of Presidents [Adiel Sherwood, *A Gazetteer of the State of Georgia*, 1827].
> (2) (Virginia) Virginia concluded not to indorse any candidate. The "Mother of Presidents" is a trifle particular [*New York Herald Tribune*, June 12, 1904].

**Mother of Rivers, the** *New Hampshire, USA.* All of the chief New England rivers rise in the mountains of New Hampshire. Hence the nickname. *Cp.* **Father of Rivers**.

**Mother of Russian Towns** or **Cities, the** *Kiev, Ukraine.* The Ukrainian capital came by its sobriquet as one of the oldest and most prominent cities in Europe, dating from the 8th century AD.

> (1) According to legend, Kiev, "the mother of all the towns of Russia," was founded by three brothers [Karl Baedeker, *Russia*, 1914].
> (2) The mother of all Russian cities deserves more than a place in the frozen food section of a supermarket [Dodd/Donald, p. 358].
> (3) The golden age of Kiev, 'Mother of Russian Cities,' was during the eleventh century [Travel ad, *The Times Magazine*, June 4, 2005].

**Mother of Sevenoaks, the** *Otford, England.* The Kent village near Sevenoaks is locally so nicknamed as being older than that town, with a name recorded at least 300 years earlier (first in the 8th century).

> Otford, which I have heard described as the "Mother of Sevenoaks," obviously because it has

such an ancient past [J.S. Ash in George Bennett, ed., *The Guide and Handbook to Sevenoaks & District*, 1948].

**Mother of Southwestern Statesmen, the** *Tennessee, USA.* The state has been the home of a number of noted US statesmen, among them Andrew Jackson, James K. Polk, and Andrew Johnson (although not the birthplace of any of these).

**Mother of States, the** *(1) Connecticut, USA; (2) Virginia, USA.* Virginia has two good claims to the sobriquet. First, it was here that the first permanent English settlement in North America was founded, at Jamestown, in 1607. Second, all or part of eight other states were formed from territory originally claimed by Virginia: West Virginia, Kentucky, Illinois, Indiana, Michigan, Minnesota, Ohio, and Wisconsin. Connecticut also claims the title as one of the original 13 states.

(1) (Virginia) Virginia has been the mother of states [William A. Caruthers, *The Kentuckian in New York*, 1834].
(2) (Connecticut) To thee, Mother of States! to thee, good old Connecticut, do our praises most belong [*Yale Literary Magazine*, 1838].

**Mother of the Midlands, the** *Lichfield, England.* The sobriquet of the Staffordshire city properly applies to its cathedral, itself nicknamed "the Ladies of the Vale" for its three slender spires. The name then passed generally to the town.

**Mother of the Navy, the** *Hastings, England.* The former port of the present East Sussex seaside resort earned its sobriquet as the chief of the **Cinque Ports** (see in Appendix 1, p. 269).

This famous Cinque Port has been described as "the mother of the Navy" [*Holiday Guide 1952: Area No. 5, South & South East England*].

**Mother of the Potteries, the** *Burslem, England.* The Staffordshire town, one of the five of the **Potteries**, is sometimes so nicknamed, as the birthplace of the potter Josiah Wedgwood.

**Mother of the World, the** *Cairo, Egypt.* The sobriquet of the Egyptian capital is of Arabic origin on the lines of Alexandria as **Mother of Books**, so that it is an ancient city and predominant in its local world. The quote below appears to refer to the *Arabian Nights*.

The Jewish Physician, in the story of the Humpback, calls Cairo "The Mother of the World" [Stanley Lane-Poole, *Cairo*, 1892].

**Mother of Wales, the** *Anglesey, Wales.* The island off the coast of northwestern Wales was long noted for its fertility, "feeding" the rest of the land. As indicated in the quotes below, the name translates the original Welsh. In personal

terms, the nickname was familiar as that of Catrin of Berain (*c.*1534–1591), the granddaughter of an illegitimate son of Henry VII, who was born in Anglesey and who was connected by descent and marriage with many leading families of North Wales.

(1) The island has long been considered agriculturally important, leading the mainland Welsh to give it the name *Mam Cymru*, or Mother of Wales [Adam Russ, *101 Places Not to Visit*, 2005].
(2) Back in medieval times when it was known as Môn Mam Cymru, 'Anglesey, Mother of Wales,' the island's farms were a vital bread basket [Mark Porter in *A View of Wales*, Spring/Summer, 2005].

**Mother Russia** *Russia.* A traditional personalization of Russia as the genetrix and ancestrix of all Russians. Quote (2) below, heading a report on the Beslan school siege, in which many mothers lost their children, would surely have been more effective with "her" for "its."

(1) Came as quite a shock to them when they realised we weren't doing it all for Mother Russia [Patrick Ruell, *Red Christmas*, 1972].
(2) Tears for the living and the dead as Mother Russia vents its grief [Headline, *Sunday Times*, September 5, 2004].
(3) Mother Russia has been blessed with numerous vast rivers, lakes and inland seas [Travel ad, *The Times Magazine*, September 10, 2005].

**Mother Volga** *Volga River, Russia.* A variant of the nickname **Little Mother Volga**.

**Motopolis** *Oxford, England.* The sobriquet for the university city was apparently created by the British poet and writer on architecture John Betjeman, as in the quote below, referring not only to the traffic that (still) clogs the center of the city but to the automobile works at Cowley, just outside Oxford. (In the quote, Christminster is Thomas Hardy's fictional name for Oxford.)

Evening in Oxford was the romantic time. The bells would ring for evening chapel from all the colleges... Now, though the bells ring, you cannot hear them above the motor-bicycles and gearchanging... Christminster is no longer a rival to the University, and the University is no longer a rival to Motopolis [John Betjeman, *An Oxford University Chest*, 1938].

**Motor City** *(1) Coventry, England; (2) Detroit, Michigan, USA.* A fairly formal sobriquet for the more familiar American **Motown**. The city of Coventry, as the **Detroit of Britain**, was the center of the nation's motor industry until the 1980s.

(Detroit) The Motor City remains a culturally rich region [*Lonely Planet USA*, 2004)

**Motorway City of the Seventies, the** *(1) Leeds, England; (2) Rotherham, England.* Both

Yorkshire cities claimed this title in the 1970s, and Leeds was still claiming it on mailing shots at the start of the 1980s. The M1 motorway runs just east of Leeds and, to the south, just west of Rotherham.

**Motown** *Detroit, Michigan, USA.* The nickname, an abbreviation of "Motor Town," refers to the city's famed auto manufacturing, dating from 1899. The name became familiar from the record label Tamla Motown, launched in 1960 by Berry Gordy, Jr., and from the music of its black artists.

> Detroit may be Motown, but in recent years it's been rap and techno that have pushed the city to the forefront of the music scene [*Lonely Planet USA*, 2004].

**Mound City, the** *St. Louis, Missouri, USA.* The nickname refers to the ancient artificial mounds on the site where the city arose in the late 18th century.

> On the western bank of the Mississippi ... stands the large town of St. Louis, poetically known as the "Mound City" [Mayne Reid, *The Hunters' Feast*, 1855].

**Mount, the** *(1) Montreal, Quebec, Canada; (2) Mount Isa, Australia.* The Canadian city gained an English shortening of its originally French name, from the "royal mount" on which it arose. The Australian mining town, in western Queensland, has come to be known by a simple shortening of its name. *Cp.* **Isa.**

**Mountain City, the** *Altoona, Pennsylvania, USA.* The city lies on the slopes of the Allegheny Mountains. Hence the nickname, which may also tie in with the real name, if this is based on Latin *altus*, "high." But some, as in the quote below, reject the connection, on the grounds that the town's name has a quite different origin.

> Although Altoona ... is known as "the Mountain City," its name has no direct or indirect etymological relation to the Latin adjective *altus*, signifying "elevated, lofty" [A. Howry Espenshade, *Pennsylvania Place Names*, 1925].

**Mountains of the Moon, the** *Ruwenzori, Africa.* The mountain group, on the border between Uganda and the Democratic Republic of the Congo, was so described in the 2d century AD by the geographer Ptolemy, referring to its misty peaks, like those seen on the Moon. It is possible the name is connected with the **Islands of the Moon**, as the Ruwenzori are not too far from the Comoros and Madagascar, off the southeast coast of Africa.

**Mountain State, the** *(1) Montana, USA; (2) West Virginia, USA.* The name is obvious for Montana, as its Spanish name implies, while hilly, rugged West Virginia is the highest of any

US state east of the Mississippi River. (Its Latin motto is *Montani semper liberi*, "Mountaineers always freemen.")

**Mount of Gore, the** *Balkan Mountains, Bulgaria.* A poetic rendering of the range's classical name Haemus, as if from Greek *haima*, "blood."

> Doth thy fierce soul still deplore
> The ancient rout by the Cilician hills,
> And that curst treachery on the Mount of Gore?
> [Matthew Arnold, *Empedocles on Etna*, 1852].

**Moviedom** or **Movieland** or **Movieville** *Hollywood, Los Angeles, California, USA.* An obvious nickname for the major center of the US motion-picture industry. *Cp.* **Filmdom.**

**Mr. Whiskers** *United States.* The name relates to **Uncle Sam**, a cartoon personification of the United States in the form of a man with long white hair and chin whiskers wearing a tall hat and a swallow-tailed coat. (Some may see a more homely association with Samuel Whiskers, the rat in the children's stories by Beatrix Potter.)

**Muchty** *Auchtermuchty, Scotland.* The name of the Fife town is (understandably) abbreviated thus in local use.

> Auchtermuchty, a 'joke' name among visitors and map-readers because of its spelling and pronunciation, is sensibly cut down to 'Muchty' locally, leaving only one 'ch' to be mastered [Macnie/McLaren, p. 245].

**Mudcat State, the** *Mississippi, USA.* The state is nicknamed for the catfish found in its swamps and muddy river reaches.

> Mississippi is occasionally spoken of humorously as the *Mudcat State*, the inhabitants being quite generally known as Mud-cats [Maximilien Schele De Vere, *Americanisms; The English of the New World*, 1871].

**Muddle East** see in Appendix 1, p. 269.

**Mud Island** *Southend-on-Sea, England.* A Londoners' former nickname for the Essex seaside resort, from the muddy foreshore of the Thames estuary there.

**Mudland** *Guyana.* A West Indian nickname for the South American republic, from its muddy Atlantic coast.

**Muesli Hill** *Muswell Hill, London, England.* The district of north London was so punningly nicknamed in the 1980s as the home of professional families and media folk, with their supposedly faddish addiction to muesli.

**Mukden** *Shenyang, China.* The traditional name of the former capital of the Manchu empire became familiar from the so-called "Mukden Incident" of 1931, in which an explosion on a nearby railroad served as a pretext for a Japanese invasion of the city and then the rest of

Manchuria. In 1950 the city reverted to its original Chinese name.

**Municon Valley** see in Appendix 1, p. 269.

**Murder Capital of America, the** *Washington, DC, USA.* The state capital has been so nicknamed for its high number of homicides. Other cities given the title include Birmingham (Alabama), Dallas (Texas), and Houston (Texas).

A frequent winner of the hotly contested title of Murder Capital USA [Adam Russ, *101 Places Not to Visit*, 2005].

**Murder Capital of Britain, the** *Nottingham, England.* The city experienced a gradual increase in gun crime and fatal shootings from the 1980s, mostly in connection with drug dealing. Hence the undesirable sobriquet.

(1) "Nottingham is the murder capital of the UK at the moment," he told a reception [in Saudi Arabia] for the Queen's birthday [*The Times*, April 22, 2005].
(2) Nottingham, the "gun crime capital of England," is the least secure university town in the country [*The Times*, August 17, 2005].
(3) Correction. A brief report incorrectly referred to Nottingham as the gun crime capital of England and the least-secure university town with a third of students being victims of muggings (University crime, August 17). In fact, the first description is untrue, the second was based on statistics for the whole of Nottinghamshire, not just the city, and the third was a national statistic [*The Times*, August 25, 2005].
(4) Nottingham next, rapidly gaining a reputation as England's capital of drink-fuelled street crime [*The Times*, September 5, 2005].

**Murder Capital of the World, the** *South Africa.* South Africa gained its sobriquet (more usually applied to a city) as a nation with one of the world's highest crime rates.

Every day [South African] newspapers are full of the gruesome details of the rapes and murders that earn the country the title of "murder capital of the world" [*The Times*, August 5, 2005].

**Murph, the** *Ballymurphy, Belfast, Northern Ireland.* A local colloquial abbreviated name for the district of west Belfast.

**Murphyland** *Ireland.* The former nickname was mainly in American use from the mid–19th century to World War II. Murphy is a common Irish surname.

**Muscovy** *Russia.* The historic and literary name, from that of the Russian capital, originally applied to the principality founded in the 13th century, with the fortified settlement of Moscow at its center.

Sea-sick, I think, coming from Muscovy [William Shakespeare, *Love's Labour's Lost*, 1598].

**Museumchester** *Manchester, England.* The city is noted for its many museums, such as the Manchester Museum, Museum of Science and Industry, City Art Gallery, and Pumphouse People's History Museum. *Cp.* **Madchester**.

**Museum City, the** *Novgorod, Russia.* The city, one of the oldest in Russia, received its nickname from its many fine architectural monuments, including a kremlin and a large number of cathedrals and churches.

**Museumland** see in Appendix 1, p. 269.

**Mushroomopolis** *Kansas City, Missouri, USA.* The nickname refers to the rapid growth of the city's suburban areas in the 1970s and 1980s.

**Music City USA** *Nashville, Tennessee, USA.* Nashville is famed worldwide for its music industry and in particular for its country music, popularized from the 1920s by the Grand Ole Opry music show (*see* **Country Music Capital of the World**).

(1) The state capital of Tennessee, Nashville is often called 'Music City USA,' and with good reason [Phil Hardy and Dave Laing, *Encyclopedia of Rock*, 1987].
(2) Nashville, Tennessee — nicknamed Music City USA, regarded as the heart and soul of American music [*The Times*, January 1, 2005].

**Muskrat State, the** *Delaware, USA.* The former nickname worked on two levels. First, muskrats indeed form part of the state's wildlife populace. Second, Delaware is the nation's second smallest state, giving rise to a standing joke that only muskrats would have enough space to breed in it.

**Musso's Lake** *Mediterranean Sea.* The World War II nickname sprang from Mussolini's abortive attempt to drive the British out of the Mediterranean in 1940, the year that Italy entered the war on Germany's side.

**Mwah-Mwah Land** *Los Angeles, California, USA.* The nickname puns on **La-La Land** by substituting "mwah-mwah" as a verbal representation of a double air kiss, as supposedly exchanged by actors and media people. The city is famed for its entertainment and, through Hollywood, especially for its filmmaking. *See* **Moviedom**.

When they relocated to Los Angeles, they proceeded to stir things up in mwah-mwah land with incendiary live shows [*Sunday Times*, May 2, 2004].

**N1** *Islington, London, England.* A substitution of the postal district designation (north 1) for the neighborhood's name.

So what about N1? It's central, and full of interesting, slightly seedy Georgian houses ... but for a generation now Islington has been progressively gentrified [Godfrey Smith, *The English Companion*, 1996].

**Nail City** *Wheeling, West Virginia, USA.* A former nickname for the city, referring to its nail factories.

**'Nam** or **Nam** *Vietnam.* The abbreviated form of the country's name, widely current among US troops during the later stages of the Vietnam War (1955–75), is still in use, mostly in a military context.

(1) "Nam" or "The Nam" is widely used by U.S. troops to refer to Vietnam [*Time*, May 2, 1969].

(2) Four Americans caught in Vietnam... The GIs become buddies in Germany... Now in "Nam" they hope their camaraderie will be closer still [*Publishers Weekly*, December 30, 1974].

(3) It was perfectly correct to be here where the fighting would be the worst, where you wouldn't have half of what you needed, where it was colder than Nam ever got [Michael Herr, *Dispatches*, 1977].

(4) Sometimes it's like 'Nam in the playgrounds of Primrose Hill, as all the helicopter parents hover [*The Times Magazine*, November 5, 2005].

**Nameless City, the** *Rome, Italy.* Ancient Rome was said to have an earlier mysterious name that would bring death to anyone who spoke it. According to Greek writers such as Aristotle and Theophrastus, this name was *Valentia*, deriving from Latin *valens, valentis*, "strong," and translated into Greek as *Rōmē*, from *rōmē*, "strength," to give the present form of the name.

(1) Thus the true Name of Rome was kept conceal'd,
To shun the Spells, and Sorceries of those
Who durst her Infant Majesty [Prince James] oppose [John Dryden, *Britannia Rediviva*, 1668. A footnote runs: *Some Authors say, that the true name of* Rome *was kept a secret;* ne hostes incantamentis Deos elicerent (lest the enemy evoke the Gods by their incantations)].

(2) They [i.e. certain local names and nicknames] are all inferior, I think, to the one sacred and proverbial name which belonged to Rome. They take many words to convey one idea. In one word, the secret qualifying name of the ancient city, many ideas found expression,—*Valentia!* [John Doran, quoted in Wheeler, p. 256].

**Nantoche** *Nanterre, France.* A colloquial (French argot) name for the city, now a northwestern suburb of Paris.

**Nap** or **Nap Town** *Indianapolis, Indiana, USA.* A colloquial shortening of the city's name, based on its stressed syllable.

**Naples of England, the** *Weymouth, England.* A promotional name for the formerly fashionable Dorset seaside resort, which stands on a bay, as does the Italian city.

Weymouth styles itself— or others style it —"the Naples of England," but no one has ever yet found Naples returning the compliment and call-

ing itself "the Weymouth of Italy" [Charles G. Harper, *The Hardy Country*, 1904].

**Naples of the North, the** *(1) Grange-over-Sands, England; (2) Llandudno, Wales.* A somewhat overblown promotional name for both seaside resorts, comparing their respective locations on a broad bay (the English town lies on Morecambe Bay, the Welsh on Conwy Bay) with that of the Italian seaport city on the Bay of Naples.

**Naplus** *Indianapolis, Indiana, USA.* A colloquial form of the city's name, based on its second half. *Cp.* **Nap.**

**Nappy Valley** see in Appendix 1, p. 269.

**Nap Town** *see* **Nap**

**Narrow Seas** see in Appendix 1, p. 269.

**Nastyville** *Nashville, Tennessee, USA.* A punning nickname based on the real name, alluding to the city's less attractive aspects, which became more noticeable following the golden age of its fame as **Music City**.

**Nation of Gentlemen, a** *Scotland.* A nickname given to Scotland by George IV, referring to the royal welcome he was accorded during his visit to the country in 1822 following his coronation.

**Nation of Shopkeepers, a** *England or Britain.* A contemptuous sobriquet for England, as a nation whose chief concern is commerce. It was popularized by Napoleon as in quote (2) below, following Adam Smith's use of the term as in quote (1).

(1) To found a great empire for the sole purpose of raising up a people of customers, may at first sight appear a project fit only for a nation of shopkeepers [Adam Smith, *Inquiry into the Nature and Causes of the Wealth of Nations*, 1776].

(2) England is a nation of shopkeepers [Napoleon I, quoted in Barry E. O'Meara, *Napoleon in Exile*, 1822].

(3) They spoke of the English as a nation of shopkeepers and had no doubt in their minds that as artists, men of science and philosophers, they were greatly superior [W. Somerset Maugham, *The Summing Up*, 1938].

**Nation's First Commuter Suburb, the** *Brooklyn Heights, New York City, USA.* The neighborhood in northwestern Brooklyn was so nicknamed by the Brooklyn Historical Society after the subway opened in 1908, making it easier for its residents to work elsewhere.

**Nation's Most Corrupt State, the** *Rhode Island, USA.* The nickname was current at the turn of the 20th century, referring to the corruption then rife in the state.

**Native America** *Oklahoma, USA.* The state's subtle title relates both to its natural beauty and to its sizable Native American population, the largest in the country.

**Natty** *Cincinnati, Ohio, USA.* A friendly shortening (and slight respelling) of the city's name.

**Natural State, the** *(1) Arkansas, USA; (2) Tasmania, Australia.* The nickname, punning on "natural state" as a term for a realm of nature, refers to Arkansas's scenic mountains, rivers, and forests, such as the Ozarks, and the natural springs of Hot Springs National Park. Australia's island state has a similar unspoiled landscape.

> (1) (Arkansas) Unnatural attractions include sites associated with Bill Clinton, civil rights history and quirky hillbilly culture [*Lonely Planet USA*, 2004].
>
> (2) (Tasmania) This delicious, full-flavoured cheese has come all the way from Australia's wild and wonderful 'Natural State'— the breathtaking island of Tasmania [*Somerfield Magazine*, August 2005].

**Nature Island of the Caribbean, the** *Dominica, West Indies.* The nickname refers to the mountains, forests, and rivers that dominate the island.

> The tourist slogan is not mere hyperbole: "The Nature Island of the Caribbean" lives up to its billing [*Sunday Times*, October 17, 2004].

**Nature's Venice** see in Appendix 1, p. 269.

**Navel of Ireland, the** *Birr, Ireland.* The Co. Offaly town is almost at the geographical center of Ireland. Hence the ancient nickname, also recorded in its Latin form *Umbilicus Hiberniae.*

**Navel of Sicily, the** *Enna, Italy.* The city and resort lies on a high plateau almost in the center of the island of Sicily. Hence its nickname.

**Navel of the Nation, the** *Kansas, USA.* The state derives its nickname from its geographical situation almost in the center of the continental USA.

**Navel of the World, the** *(1) Easter Island, South Pacific; (2) Jerusalem, Israel.* The island's nickname translates its Polynesian name *te pita o te henua,* referring to its location in the middle of the ocean. Jerusalem was so known in medieval times, and was shown at the center of the world in some maps. The title has a biblical basis: "This is Jerusalem: I have set it in the midst of the nations and countries that are round about her" (Ezekiel 5:5).

**N'Awlins** or **Nawlins** *New Orleans, Louisiana, USA.* The altered form of the city's name represents its casual pronunciation by many of its inhabitants, especially black musicians.

> (1) The older he gets, the deeper Dr John buries himself in the music and mythology of his beloved New Orleans. His new album offers a guided tour of the rich "N'Awlins" tradition, from ragtime to gris gris [*The Times*, June 11, 2004].
>
> (2) "How mad is this?" my sister said. "Who builds a city on a swamp six feet below sea level?" Then, in an authentic N'Awlins drawl, she added: "It really didn't ought to be here" [*The Times*, September 2, 2005].
>
> (3) Syrupy tributes to Nawlins from writers who couldn't tell a housing project from a science project [*The Times*, September 6, 2005].

**NB** *New Brighton, England.* A local short name for the Merseyside coastal resort, a district of Wallasey.

**NB** *see* **North Britain**

**Near East** see in Appendix 1, p. 269.

**Needle Park** see in Appendix 1, p. 269.

**Negroland** see in Appendix 1, p. 269.

**Nether World, the** *London, England.* The name for the British capital comes from the title of George Gissing's 1889 novel about London's slum life, a gloomy study telling how industrialization has condemned the working classes to life in a hell from which there is no escape. *Cp.* **Abyss** in Appendix 1, p. 269.

**Neulin** *Berlin, Germany.* A former term for the German capital combining German *neu,* "new," and the second half of the city's name. It was used by planners in the 1920s and 1930s, but history had other ideas.

**Neuneu** or **Neuneuille** *Neuilly-sur-Seine, France.* A colloquial name for the wealthy northwestern suburb of Paris.

**Neurope** *Europe.* An abbreviation of "new Europe," applied to the continent as it stood after World War I, with the emergence of new countries such as Yugoslavia and the Baltic States. The term was mainly current among stamp collectors.

> Many stamp issues are now credited to Neurope ... a considerable number being purely speculative or created to raise funds for depleted treasuries [B.W.H. Poole and Willard O. Wylie, *The Standard Philatelic Dictionary,* c.1923].

**Neutral Ground** *Westchester County, New York, USA.* The county came to be so called during the War of Independence, when it was an area of divided allegiances.

**Never Never** see in Appendix 1, p. 269.

**New Amsterdam** *New York City, USA.* The original name of New York was given by Dutch settlers in the mid–1620s. It fell into disuse when the British defeated the Dutch in 1664 but is still familiar in a historical context.

**New Athens, the** *Paris, France.* The French capital was so titled in the 18th century, when first famed as the **City of Light**.

> Enlightenment Paris had been — as Louis-

Sébastien Mercier, journalist, dramatist and observer of Parisan mores, put it — 'the capital of light,' 'the centre of the republic of letters,' the 'New Athens' [Colin Jones, *France*, 2004].

**New Brasilia, the** *Newcastle upon Tyne, England*. The northeastern city was promoted under this name in the 1960s, the comparison being with the tailor-made Brazilian capital, then still under construction. The slogan, created by the city's council leader, T. Dan Smith, is quoted in John Ardagh, *A Tale of Five Cities* (1979).

[T. Dan Smith] was the unveiler of a £200-million plan to make Newcastle the "Brasilia of the North" [Obituary of T. Dan Smith, *The Times*, July 28, 1993].

**New England of the West, the** *Minnesota, USA*. The state earned the nickname for the New England Yankees who were its first settlers.

**Newfie** *Newfoundland, Canada*. A friendly abbreviation of the island's rather lengthy name.

Nobody in Newfie ... underestimates Joey Smallwood's abilities as a propagandist [*Globe and Mail* (Toronto), January 29, 1965].

**New France** *Canada*. The old name of Canada, still valid in historical contexts, dates from the time of the first claim of land here by Jacques Cartier in 1534, and more formally from 1627, when the Company of the Hundred Associates was founded. The name remained current until the territory was ceded to the English in 1763.

**Newhaven** *Le Havre, France*. The French port, its name meaning "the harbor," was known as Newhaven by English speakers for some time after its foundation in 1517. It so happens that Le Havre lies across the English Channel due south of the English port of Newhaven, East Sussex, although the English port arose as a "new harbor" only in the 1580s.

**New Hebrides** *Vanuatu*. The name given to the Pacific islands by Captain Cook in 1774 remained in informal use long after the republic adopted its present indigenous name in 1980.

French law, language and culture persist in every continent — from Canada to the New Hebrides, from Indo-China to French Guiana, from the Ivory Coast to the Lebanon [Nick Yapp and Michel Syrett, *The Xenophobe's Guide to the French*, 1993].

**New Jerusalem, the** *(1) Belgravia, London, England; (2) Salt Lake City, Utah, USA*. The London district derives its nickname from the wealthy Jews who bought houses there. *Cp.* **Jerusalem-on-Sea**. Salt Lake City was a "new

Jerusalem" for the Mormon immigrants who flocked to the city after its foundation in 1848.

**Newk** or **Newky** *Newcastle upon Tyne, England*. A colloquial local abbreviation of the northeastern city's name. ("Newky Broon" in the quote below is Newcastle Brown Ale.) *See also* **Toon**.

If it's not frem the Toon, hoo can ye caal it Newky Broon? [Headline, *The Times*, March 2, 2004].

**Newmarket of France, the** *Chantilly, France*. The town in northern France is a noted horseracing center, as is Newmarket, England, the **Home of Horseracing**. Hence its nickname.

**New-Reared Troy** *see* **Troynovant**

**New Sarum** *see* **Sarum**

**New South** *New South Wales, Australia*. An occasional abbreviated form of the state name.

(1) I took a turn in New South, and tried Tassy [i.e. Tasmania] and New Zealand [*The Bulletin* (Sydney), December 17, 1892].

(2) In New South you just hauled off and spread the troublesome bloke on the floor [John G. Brandon, *Th' Big City*, 1931].

**New Spain** *Mexico*. The colonial name of Mexico was current for almost three centuries, from 1535 to 1821, and is still found in historical references.

**New World, the** *North and South America*. The term for the Western Hemisphere was first used by the Italian geographer Pietro Martire (Peter Martyr) d'Anghiera (1457–1526) in his *De orbe novo* ("On the New World") published posthumously in 1530, in which he gives the first account of the discovery of America.

The English valiant attempts in searching almost all the corners of the vaste and new world of America [Title page of Richard Hakluyt, *The Principall Navigations, Voiages and Discoveries of the English Nation*, 1589].

**New York, New York** *New York City, USA*. The name is administratively and postally correct for New York City in New York State, but the duplicated name caught on for the city alone as a kind of emphatic designation ("so good they named it twice," runs the quip).

New York, New York, — a helluva town,
The Bronx is up but the Battery's down,
And people ride in a hole in the groun';
New York, New York, — It's a helluva town
[Betty Comden and Adolph Green, "New York, New York," *On the Town*, 1944].

**New York of the Tropics, the** *Abidjan, Côte d'Ivoire*. The nickname refers to the modern American-style skyline of the former Ivorian capital, as indicated in the quote below. *Cp.* **Manhattan of West Africa**.

Abidjan's downtown skyscrapers have led to the

city being frequently described as the New York of the tropics (although its lakeside setting suggests Chicago even more strongly) [Dodd/Donald, p. 43].

**Next Parish to America, the** *Aran Islands, Ireland.* A former nickname for the Co. Galway island group, off the west coast of Ireland.

**Nic** *Nicaragua.* A colloquial short form of the country's name, as chiefly used by US visitors.

**Nice of the North, the** *(1) Dinard, France; (2) Folkestone, England; (3) Wiesbaden, Germany.* Dinard, a stylish resort with grand villas on the Brittany coast, is a worthy counterpart to the famous Mediterranean seaport city. The English seaside town of Folkestone, Kent, owes its sobriquet to the feature mentioned in quote (1) below. The German city of Wiesbaden, on the banks of the Rhine at the foot of the Taunus Mountains, became a fashionable spa in the 18th and 19th centuries, its hot saline springs and warm climate drawing many famous visitors. In their own way, all three thus merit comparison with the leading resort of the French Riviera.

(1) (Folkestone) Folkestone, which in another book I have called the Nice of the North, because of its magnificent sea-front [Richard Church in Hadfield 1981, p. 133].
(2) (Wiesbaden) Numerous poetic descriptions have been bestowed upon Wiesbaden during its glorious past, such as 'Emperor's City,' 'Nice of the North,' 'World Spa' or 'City of Festivals and Wine' [Hildebrand Diehl, mayor of Wiesbaden, 'Welcome to Wiesbaden' <http://www.germany-travel-mart.de/pages/intro_wiesbaden_e.htm> accessed November 17, 2005].

**Nick the Bear** *Russia.* A former nickname of Russia (*see* **Bear**), personalized with the name of Czar Nicholas II.

**Nidaros** *Trondheim, Norway.* The name of the seaport and former Norwegian capital was current in medieval times and again for a period in 1930, when it was rejected by local people in favor of its present name, earlier spelled Trondhjem. It remains as an alternate name, notably for Nidaros Cathedral, Scandinavia's largest medieval building, and translates as "estuary of the Nid River."

(1) In 1929, the name of the town was changed to Nidaros; but many of the war communiques of 1940–1 spoke of Trondheim, which seems to show that the old name is still used [Johnson, p. 249].
(2) Listen to Trondheimers talk about their city, and you may wonder whether they're all referring to the same place [*Lonely Planet Norway*, 2002].

**Nineteen Suburbs in Search of a Metropolis** *Los Angeles, California, USA.* The name, quoted by H.L. Menken in *Americana* (1925), refers to the city's sprawling layout and appar-

ently focusless nature. *Cp.* **Seventy-Two Suburbs in Search of a City.**

**Niobe of Nations, the** *Rome, Italy.* The sobriquet springs from the quote below. Byron so named Rome because of its lost empire (*see* **Capital of the Vanished World**). Niobe, a daughter of Tantalus in Greek mythology, lost her children when she boasted of having more and better children than Leto.

The Niobe of nations! there she stands,
  Childless and crownless, in her voiceless woe
[Lord Byron, *Childe Harold's Pilgrimage*, 1818].

**Nippon** *Japan.* The alternate name of Japan is actually the country's Japanese name, from *nichi*, "sun," and *hon*, "origin." *Cp.* **Land of the Rising Sun.** The Western form of the name represents the Chinese pronunciation of the two Japanese pictograms, pronounced approximately "Jipen."

(1) This Empire is by the Europeans call'd *Japan.* The Natives give it several names and characters. The most common, and most frequently us'd in their writings and conversation, is *Nipon*, which is sometimes in a more elegant manner, and particular to this Nation, pronounc'd Nifon... It signifies, *the foundation of the Sun* [J.G. Scheuchzer, translating E. Kæmpfer, *History of Japan*, 1727].
(2) The sons of Nippon had become aware that their destiny was to establish a New Order in the East [*R.A.F. Journal*, June 13, 1942].

**Nizam's Dominions, the** *Hyderabad, India.* The former sobriquet referred to the nizam named in the quote below. ("Nizam," meaning literally "regulator," was the title of the prince of the state of Hyderabad down to 1950.)

[Nizam-ul-Mulk Asaf Jah] was independent sovereign of a large territory in the Deccan, with his residence at Hyderabad, and with dominions in a general way corresponding to those still held by his descendant [Henry Yule and A.C. Burnell, *Hobson-Jobson*, 1886].

**NJ** *New Jersey, USA.* A common initialism of the state's name.

Himself a native of New Jersey ... [Zach Braff] plays a small-time actor, Andrew Largeman, who now lives in Los Angeles, but has to return home to NJ for the first time in nine years when his mother dies [Review of movie *Garden State*, *Sunday Times*, December 12, 2004].

**NO** *New Orleans, Lousiana, USA.* An initialized abbreviation of the city's name. *Cp.* **NOLA.**

The tourists were not apparently coming to colorful and picturesque old NO to gorge themselves upon Paradise products [John Kennedy Toole, *A Confederacy of Dunces*, 1980].

**Noble Belgium** *Belgium.* A stock description of the country, from the opening words of its national anthem, *La Brabançonne*, as quoted below. It was originally written during the 1830 revolution, but the present version was written in 1860 with words by Prime Minister Charles Rogier.

> Noble Belgique à jamais terre chérie, à toi nos cœurs, à toi nos bras.
> (Noble Belgium, forever a dear land, to you our hearts, to you our arms.)

**No Cool** *Northern California, USA.* The punning nickname for the northern part of the state describes its self-perceived image, as against laid-back **So Cool**. An alternate abbreviated name is NorCal.

**Nodding Hull** *Notting Hill, London, England.* The nickname apparently plays on the district's supposedly sedate and somnolent ambience.

**Noddytown** *Cumbernauld, Scotland.* The New Town near Glasgow, designated in 1955, is so nicknamed for its small, boxlike houses, like those in Toyland, the home of Noddy, the little pixie in the children's stories by Enid Blyton. The name also echoes the second part of the town's real name.

**NoHo** see in Appendix 1, p. 269.

**NOLA** *New Orleans, Louisiana, USA.* A nickname formed from the combined abbreviations of city name (*see* **NO**) and state name.

> New Orleans, known as "The Big Easy" or NOLA [*The Times*, September 1, 2005].

**NoLita** see in Appendix 1, p. 269.

**No Man's Land** see in Appendix 1, p. 269.

**Noo York** or **Noo Yawk** or **Noo Yoik** *New York City, USA.* Three of the many modified spellings of the city's name designed to reflect its (supposed) pronunciation by New Yorkers or by Americans from elsewhere in the USA.

> (1) Nearly all th' most foolish people in th' country an minny iv th' wisest goes to Noo York [Finley Peter Dunne, *Mr. Dooley's Opinions*, 1901].
> (2) 'Want to be with you as much as possible, m'boy, and besides it's so durned cold in this New Yawk' [Jack Kerouac, *On the Road*, 1957].
> (3) "Noo Yoik is not as dangerous as they say," said my cabbie as he careered through... Manhattan [*Sunday Times*, November 7, 2004].
> (4) The five American contestants include ... a very "Noo Yawk" girl named Maria [*The Times*, August 13, 2005].

**NorCal** *see* **No Cool**

**Norfolk Broads** *see* **Broads** in Appendix 1, p. 269.

**Noroway** or **Norroway** *Norway.* A poetic name of the country, as in the quotes below.

> (1) 'To Noroway, to Noroway,
> To Noroway o'er the faem [i.e. foam];
> The king's daughter o' Noroway,

> 'Tis thou must bring her hame' ["Sir Patrick Spens," *The Oxford Book of Ballads*, 1910].
> (2) My plaid awa', my plaid awa',
> And o'er the hill and far awa';
> And far awa' to Norrowa',
> My plaid shall not be blown awa'! ["Lady Isabel and the Elf-Knight," *The Oxford Book of Ballads*, 1910].

**Norseland** *Norway.* An occasional literary name for the Norse country.

> Have we not broken Wales and Norseland? [Alfred, Lord Tennyson, *Harold*, 1877].

**North, the** *Northern Ireland.* A name used in the Republic of Ireland for Northern Ireland, as part of the UK. *Cp.* **South.** *See also* **Black North** and, in Appendix 1, p. 269, **North.**

> (1) I don't want to be trapped between the North and the South, Toome and Limerick [Frank McCourt, *'Tis*, 1999].
> (2) Catholics in the North are, if possible, more reserved than their coreligionists in Eire [Sean Kelly and Rosemary Rogers, *How to Be Irish*, 2000].

**Northants** *Northamptonshire, England.* A semiofficial abbreviation of the county name. *Cp.* **Hants.** *See also* Appendix 6, p. 325.

**North Britain** *Scotland.* The designation for Scotland was mainly current in the 18th and 19th centuries but is still encountered in some contexts. The abbreviation NB (taken by some to mean North of the Border) was written in the postal addresses of places in Scotland. *Cp.* **South Britain.**

> (1) The reviewers of North Britain, in common with the other inhabitants of the Scottish metropolis, enjoy some advantages, unknown, it is believed, to their southern brethren [*Edinburgh Review*, quoted in Wheeler, p. 261].
> (2) N.B. North Britain, i.e. Scotland... Not much used, nor liked, by the Scottish people [Eric Partridge, *A Dictionary of Abbreviations*, 1942].
> (3) [Robert Louis Stevenson's argument was with] the starchy complacency of Victorian conformity which threatened to downgrade Edinburgh into the capital of "North Britain" — a term he came to detest [Malcolm Bradbury, ed., *The Atlas of Literature*, 1996].

**North Country** see in Appendix 1, p. 269.

**Northern Athens, the** *(1) Belfast, Northern Ireland; (2) Edinburgh, Scotland.* An alternate sobriquet for the two capital cities. (*See* **Athens of the North.**)

**Northern Bear** *see* **Bear**

**Northern Giant, the** *Russia.* An epithet presenting the country as a fearsome force to be reckoned with. *See also* **Bear.**

> It is no small delight to the lovers of truth, freedom, and England, to see that the Northern Giant has, by dint of too much *finesse*, suffered his

once-willing prey to slip through his hands [*Edinburgh Review*, quoted in Wheeler, p. 261].

**Northern Palmyra** *see* **Palmyra of the North**

**Northern Reserve, the** *Heilongjiang, China.* The northeastern province derives its nickname from its great potential for agriculture.

**Northern Riviera, the** *Doncaster, England.* A self-promotional name for the Yorkshire town, designed to downgrade its industrial image and upscale its favorable geographical location in the lee of the Pennine Hills on the Don River (although some actual distance from the sea, the normal prerequisite for a "riviera").

**Northern Sochi, the** *Svetlogorsk, Russia.* The Baltic seaside resort derives its nickname from its (much warmer and sunnier) Black Sea counterpart.

**Northern Territories** see in Appendix 1, p. 269.

**North Ken** *North Kensington, London, England.* The shortened form of the district name matches that of the better-known **South Ken**.

North Kensington ('North Ken' to everyone) ... remains delightfully mixed in every sense [Carrie Segrave, *The New London Property Guide*, 2003].

**Northland** see in Appendix 1, p. 269.

**North of the Tweed** *Scotland.* The dated expression denotes the part of Britain to the north of the Tweed. (The term is not strictly accurate, for although the river forms the border between the two lands for much of its course, it rises in Scotland and enters the North Sea at Berwick-upon-Tweed in England.)

Sometimes the phrase 'North of the Tweed' is used by southern writers to describe Scotland [Macnie/McLaren, p. 112].

**North of Watford** see in Appendix 1, p. 269.

**North Star State, the** *Minnesota, USA.* Minnesota was at one time the northernmost state in the Union, and the state seal and flag bear the French motto "*L'Étoile du Nord*" ("the north star"), chosen by Minnesota's first governor, Henry Hastings Sibley. (The French phrase is said to be one of the few he knew.)

In the North Star State here, we rejoice in having a Grand Master, who knows no such word as fail [*American Odd Fellow*, 1862].

**Northumbria** *Northumberland, England.* The name of the historic Anglo-Saxon kingdom is sometimes used for that of the present county, although the latter now occupies a much smaller area. (It is, however, the official name of the local Northumbria police force.) Quote (2) below shows a converse error, with the county name used for that of the larger region. *Cp.* **Cumberland.**

(1) A parachutist plunged to his death during a jump near Chathill, Northumbria [*Sunday Times*, November 26, 2000].
(2) Correction. The references to Northumberland in Simon Jenkins's column yesterday should have read Northumbria, the region which embraces the counties of Northumberland and Durham [*The Times*, June 8, 2002].

**North Van** *North Vancouver, British Columbia, Canada.* A colloquially abbreviated name for the suburb of Vancouver.

North Van's beautiful sculpt themselves on the beaches of residential Kitsilano, while South Van's bohemians muse ... under the bridge on Granville Island [Dodd/Donald, p. 201)

**Norvic** *Norwich, England.* An abbreviated form of Latin *Norvicensis*, "of Norwich," as used for his official signature by the bishop of Norwich and also as a commercial name (as that of the Norvic Shoe Company).

**Nor'west** see in Appendix 1, p. 269.

**Nottamun Town** *Nottingham, England.* A colloquial local form of the city's name, popularized by the lines quoted below.

In Nottamun Town not a soul would look up,
  Not a soul would look up, not a soul would look down,
  Not a soul would look up, not a soul would look down,
  To tell me the way to Nottamun Town [Anonymous rhyme].

**Notting Hill of South London, the** *Deptford, London, England.* A realtor's promotional name for the former Kent town and Thameside naval dockyard, comparing it with the fashionable west London district of Notting Hill.

The prize for optimism ... goes to the [estate] agents who described Deptford as 'The Notting Hill of South London' [Carrie Segrave, *The New London Property Guide*, 2003].

**Notts** *Nottinghamshire, England.* A semi-official abbreviation of the county name, in both written and spoken form, familiar in sport for both the Notts County cricket club and Notts County football club. (The name of the county capital, Nottingham, is usually abbreviated as "Nottm" in written form.) *See also* Appendix 6, p. 325.

He announced his intentions to do something special on his 50th birthday and ... scored 164 for Notts v Worcester [Peter Matthews, *The Guinness International Who's Who of Sport*, 1993].

**Notty** *Nottingham, England.* A colloquial abbreviation of the city's name, used mainly by local university students.

**Nova Zembla** *Novaya Zemlya, Russia.* The name of the two large islands in the Arctic Ocean was long spelled thus, with *b* inserted for ease of pronunciation (as happened with the name of

Wimbledon). The *Oxford English Dictionary* defines the rare adjective "Zemblan" as "belonging to Nova Zembla."

> Such buxom chief shall lead his host
>   From India's fires to Zembla's frost [Sir Walter Scott, *Marmion*, 1808].

**Nowhere City, the** *Los Angeles, California, USA.* The name comes from Alison Lurie's 1999 novel so titled, exploring the responses of two newcomers to the city.

**NSW** *New South Wales, Australia.* An initialism of the state's name.

> (1) Justice ministers in Victoria and NSW, said yesterday they were considering ... changes [*Sunday Australian*, August 8, 1971].
> (2) NSW is the popular gateway for most visitors to Australia [*Lonely Planet Australia*, 2004].

**NT, the** *Northern Territory, Australia.* An initialism of the territory's name.

> Pascal Tremblay ... said that crocodile attacks in the Northern Territory ... help to raise the profile of the region... He said: "It's free publicity. The NT gets in the news. Bookings increase" [*The Times*, November 13, 2004].

**NTH** *Newtownhamilton, Northern Ireland.* A practical abbreviation of the lengthy name of the Co. Armagh village, as mostly used among members of the British armed forces.

> Soldiers consider it [i.e. Newtownhamilton] the "softest" posting in South Armagh and some joke that the acronym NTH stands for "No Terrorists Here" [Toby Harnden, *Bandit Country*, 1999].

**Nueva York** *New York City, USA.* The Spanish form of the city's name, ostensibly used by English speakers to refer to New York's large Hispanic population, is really little more than an affected alternate.

**Nuremberg** *Nürnberg, Germany.* The English form of the city's name is still current and is regularly used to refer to the post–World War II Nuremberg Trials.

> (1) Nuremberg or 'Nürnberg' as the Germans call it [Donough O'Brien, *Fame by Chance*, 2003].
> (2) While other German cities sweep their Third Reich history under the carpet, Nuremberg is rebranding itself as a place determined to face up to its past [*The Times*, December 26, 2005].

**Nutmeg State, the** *Connecticut, USA.* As implied in quote (1) below, the nickname derives from the tale that early settlers in Connecticut carved wooden nutmegs and cunningly sold them as the genuine article.

> (1) *Nutmeg State*, a name given to the State of Connecticut, in allusion to the story that wooden nutmegs are there manufactured for exportation [John R. Bartlett, *Dictionary of Americanisms*, 2d ed., 1859].
> (2) "You pick out a book that may keep her from being lonely, and write something in it, so she can

remember you when you marry an oil princess in Connecticut." "There isn't any oil in Connecticut, Rick." "Well, nutmegs then. Your father says it's called the Nutmeg State" [Upton Sinclair, *World's End*, 1940].

**NW1** *Camden Town, London, England.* A substitution of the postal district designation (northwest 1) for the name of the neighborhood, in the late 1960s and early 1970s regarded as intellectually modish and satirized as such.

> (1) Who could have littered the *Times* with bye-lines and signed columns and a woman's page so close to NW1's heart? [*The Listener*, November 30, 1967].
> (2) I did a series on television with sketches about this area, N.W.1, of which I am a part, and so in a sense it was making fun of myself. But it pinpointed something and since then N.W.1 has been used as a catchphrase to indicate Sunday supplement trendiness which people now find rather suspect [Alan Bennett in David Nathan, *The Laughtermakers*, 1971].
> (3) NW1 or Camden Town is Stringalong territory, though you have to be over a certain age to remember this trendy family created by [cartoonist] Mark Boxer [Godfrey Smith, *The English Companion*, 1996].
> (4) His most popular creations were Simon and Joanna String-Along—an awful upper-middle-class trendy couple from London's NW1 district based on characters from Alan Bennett's BBC series *On the Margin*. They first appeared in the strip 'Life and Times in NW1' in the *Listener* in August 1967 [Mark Bryant, *Dictionary of Twentieth-Century British Cartoonists and Caricaturists*, 2000].

**NW3** *Hampstead, London, England.* A fairly common substitution of the postal district designation for the name of the fashionable London neighborhood.

> (1) Living with him was his beautiful companion, a Madame de Bargeton of N.W.3, something of a Madame Verdurin also [*The Listener*, May 27, 1965].
> (2) Hampstead (for that is NW3 under another name) is still *sympathique*, but very, very pricey [Godfrey Smith, *The English Companion*, 1996].
> (3) So the Hampstead Heath swimming ponds have been saved... What a triumph for the oppressed masses of London NW3 [*The Times*, December 20, 2004].

**NW8** *St John's Wood, London, England.* A postal district designation for the fashionable region, on the lines of **NW3**.

> It is inconceivable that there is any crossover between the residents of NW8 and the hordes who swarm through the nearby yet unconnected world of the touristic streets around Madame Tussaud's [Jonathan Meades in *The Times Magazine*, July 31, 2004].

**NW11** *Golders Green, London, England.* A

postal district designation for the fashionable residential district, noted for its large Jewish population (and more recently Japanese). The designation also applies to the older part of neighboring Hampstead Garden Suburb, as in the quote below. (The newer part is N2.)

> The houses, particularly in the Old Suburb or NW11 area, really are 'full of character' [Carrie Segrave, *The New London Property Guide*, 2003].

**NY** *New York City, USA.* A fairly common colloquial abbreviation of the city's name, adopted from that of the state. *Cp.* **NYC.**

> You have a brain that could really grow and flower here in NY [John Kennedy Toole, *A Confederacy of Dunces*, 1980].

**NYC** *New York City, USA.* A fairly common colloquial abbreviation of the city's full formal name.

> (1) It's brash, it's sexy, it's brilliant. It's NYC [*Lonely Planet USA*, 2004].
> (2) Writers penned in NYC, then schlepped to the studios in LA [*The Times Magazine*, January 22, 2005].

**NZ** *New Zealand.* A colloquial initialism of the country's name. *Cp.* **Enzed.**

> Combine Oz with NZ and fly on to Queenstown [*Sunday Times*, April 24, 2005].

**Oaktown** *Oakland, California, USA.* A chiefly black alteration of the city's name.

**OB** *Oak Bluffs, Massachusetts, USA.* A familiar abbreviation for the town on Martha's Vineyard.

> After the sun sets, OB is the Vineyard's playground [*Lonely Planet USA*, 2004].

**OC** *Ocean City, Maryland, USA.* A common initialism for the popular Atlantic coast resort.

> OC is all about the beach [*Lonely Planet USA*, 2004].

**OC, the** *Orange County, California, USA.* The initialism became familiar as the title of the TV show named in the quotes below, about the relationships between family members and teenagers in a wealthy, harbor-front community in southern California, where Orange County is effectively an urbanized extension of Los Angeles. One of the local newspapers is the *OC Weekly.*

> (1) I've got some family who live in Orange County, and the girls there are quite like the girls in the show, *The OC*, about their make-up [*The Times Magazine*, June 18, 2005].
> (2) Orange County's 31 cities are diverse, multicultural places, and some come with a claim to hipness, thanks to Fox's *The O.C.* [*Fodor's Los Angeles 2006*].

**O'Cap** *Cap-Haïtien, Haiti.* A local colloquial name for Haiti's former capital city. *Cp.* **Le Cap.**

**Ocean Gateway, the** *Le Havre, France.* A

translation of French *la Porte Océane* as a nickname for one of France's leading commercial seaports.

**Ocean Hell, the** *Norfolk Island, Australia.* An old nickname for the South Pacific island, in the days when it was a British penal colony.

> (1) We designated it for the first time 'the Ocean Hell' [*Britannia* (Hobart), April 4, 1850].
> (2) Norfolk Island, known as 'The Ocean Hell' and 'Earthly Paradise' [J.G. Pattison, *'Battler's' Tales of Early Rockhampton*, 1939].

**Ocean Island** *Banaba, Kiribati.* An alternate name for the Pacific island.

**Ocean State, the** *Rhode Island, USA.* A touristic name adopted by the state for its location bordering the Atlantic Ocean.

**Ocean Villas** *Auchonvillers, France.* A British soldiers' World War I version of the name of the village near Albert. *Cp.* **Funky Villas.**

**O-City** *Oklahoma City, Oklahoma, USA.* An initial-based nickname for the state capital. *Cp.* **O-Town.**

**Octopus, the** *Lima, Peru.* The nickname, translating Spanish *el Pulpo*, refers to the growing sprawl of the Peruvian capital, whose other undesirable aspects are encapsulated in its sobriquet **Lima la Horrible.**

**Officers' Mess, the** *Mull, Scotland.* The second-largest island of the Inner Hebrides, off the west coast of Scotland, has a population that decreased sharply in the 19th century but that then stabilized, albeit at a lower figure, when the original native islanders were replaced by settlers from elsewhere in Britain. Hence the (half-punning) nickname for this new "elite," which includes seasonal tourists.

> The locals refer to the incomers as 'White Settlers' and sometimes refer to the island as 'The Officers' Mess' [Newton, p. 149].

**Oggyland** *Cornwall, England.* The nickname derives from the "tiddy oggy," or Cornish pasty, for which the county is famous. (The origin of the dish's name is uncertain, although "tiddy" may be "tidbit.") For the reference to "Guzz" in the quote below, *see* **Guz.**

> [Cornwall is] the home of the tiddy-oggy, beloved of the Janners [i.e. West Countrymen] in depot at Guzz [Wilfred Granville, *A Dictionary of Sailors' Slang*, 1962].

**OH-10** *Ohio, USA.* A wry alteration of the state name, with its third and fourth letters turned into the figure 10.

**O-HI-O, the** *Ohio River, USA.* A comic pronunciation of the river's name, popularized by the song quoted below.

> "Down by the O-HI-O" [Abe Olman and Jack Yellen, song title, 1922].

**Oil Capital of Canada, the** *Edmonton, Alberta, Canada*. The provincial capital, formerly familiar as the **Gateway to the North**, came to be known by its present name from the 1970s following the exploitation of Alberta's resources of natural gas and crude oil.

**Oil Capital of the World, the** *Tulsa, Oklahoma, USA*. Tulsa gained its nickname as a major center of the nation's petroleum industry, although the refining side of its functions began to decline from the mid–20th century.

**OK** *Oklahoma, USA*. The state zip code was long punningly adopted for license plates reading "Oklahoma is OK."

**OKC** *Oklahoma City, USA*. A common abbreviation of the state capital's name.

In 2003 OKC got a new convention center [*Lonely Planet USA*, 2004].

**Okie** *Oklahoma City, USA*. A diminutive nickname for both the state and its capital, as well as for a resident of either.

**Old Big Strong** *Mississippi River, USA*. One of many powerful nicknames for the great river.

**Old Colony State, the** *Massachusetts, USA*. The name refers to the original Plymouth Colony founded by the Pilgrim Fathers in 1620.

In the Old Colony days, in Plymouth the land of the Pilgrims [H.W. Longfellow, *The Courtship of Miles Standish*, 1858].

**Old Country, the** *(1) England or Britain; (2) Ireland*. The name is applied to the given homeland as seen from the point of view of those who have left it to settle elsewhere, as in the United States or Australia. *Cp.* **Old England**

(1) (England) The barn-doors about the farms (in imitation of a similar custom in the 'old country') were decorated by the brushes and tails of ... the Dingo [George Bennett, *Wanderings in New South Wales*, 1834].

(2) (Ireland) Loudly declaiming ... about the injustice done to "the ould counthry," and forcibly giving vent to his views upon "Home Rule" [J. Dodsworth Brayshaw, *Slum Silhouettes*, 1898].

(3) (England) "By golly," Babbitt droned, "wouldn't be so bad to go over to the Old Country and take a squint at all these ruins and the place where Shakespeare was born" [Sinclair Lewis, *Babbitt*, 1922].

(4) (England) In 1877, twenty-five years after he had sailed from Liverpool for Victoria, Christison left Australia to visit the Old Country [Mary Montgomerie Bennett, *Christison of Lammermoor*, 1927].

(5) (England) "The Old Country!" Buffy said. They were still standing but would have risen if they had been sitting down. "To Home. Here's to Home. Down the hatch. The Old Country!" "The Queen!" Buffy was inspired. "God bless the Queen" [Elizabeth Jolley, *The Sugar Mother*, 1988].

(6) (Ireland) You're an Irishman that wants to see his mother in the Old Country and you're a teacher killing himself in a vocational high school [Frank McCourt, *'Tis*, 1999].

**Old Dart, the** *England or Britain*. The nickname, used mainly in Australia and New Zealand, is a corruption of "old dirt," meaning a settler's or immigrant's native soil. *Cp.* **Old Sod.**

(1) News has been received from London, of this extraordinary match, which excited exceeding interest amongst the sporting fraternity in the Old Dart [Pierce Egan, *Book of Sports and Mirror of Life*, 1832].

(2) He was from England... He is one of the sort who return to the old dart and say that fruit-growing here is a failure [*Quiz* (Adelaide), November 18, 1892].

(3) Joshua Medley had had a dispute with his father in England and when he came out to Australia he decided to forget his relatives in the "Old Dart" [Dymphna Cusack, *Caddie, The Story of a Barmaid*, 1953].

**Old Dirigo State, the** *Maine, USA*. The nickname comes from the state motto, Latin *Dirigo*, "I steer (the ship)."

**Old Dominion, the** *Virginia, USA*. The state is usually regarded as being so named for its loyalty to the exiled Charles II during the Puritan Commonwealth, although the origin in quote (2) below has also been mooted.

(1) What means the Old Dominion? Hath she forgot the day
When o'er her conquered valleys swept the Briton's steel array? [John Greenleaf Whittier, "Massachusetts to Virginia," 1843].

(2) In Captain John Smith's "History of Virginia," edition of 1629, there is a map of the settlement of Virginia, which, at that time, included New England, as well as every other part of the British settlements in America. He there calls our present Virginia "Ould Virginia," — the word *old* being so spelt at that time, — in contradistinction to the New England colony, which is called "New Virginia." Here, then, we have the word "ould," the distinctive word of the title. Now, we know, that, from the settlement of the colony to the Revolution, every act of parliament, every letter of the king to the governor, always designated Virginia as the "Colony and Dominion" of Virginia. Here is found the other word; and the change in common talk from "Ould Virginia" to "Old Dominion" was easy, imperceptible, and almost inevitable [*Virginia Historical Magazine*, quoted in Wheeler, p. 266].

(3) Virginia, the Old Dominion State, unanimously cast all 30 of its votes for a great fighter, Charles B. Manchester [Fletcher Knebel and Charles W. Bailey, *Convention*, 1964].

**Old England** *England*. A former or literary name for England as the **Old Country** and as distinguished from New England in the USA.

In later usage the term gained a nostalgic ring. The bogus archaic spelling "olde" (as in "olde-worlde") is sometimes used, as in quote (3) below.

(1) Oh! the roast beef of England,
   And old England's roast beef! [Henry Fielding, *Grub Street Opera*, 1731].
(2) 'Still my heart is so sad, that I wish myself back in Old England.
   You will say it is wrong, but I cannot help it: I almost
   Wish myself back in Old England, I feel so lonely and wretched' [H.W. Longfellow, *The Courtship of Miles Standish*, 1858].
(3) Medieval man was incapable of stopping the plague from racing through the teeming alleys of Olde England [*The Times*, September 14, 2005].

**Oldest City in the United States, the** *St. Augustine, Florida, USA.* The factually correct byname refers to the founding of the town in 1565 by the Spanish explorer Pedro Menéndez de Avilés.

I am stopping for two or three days at the "oldest city in America" [Henry James, letter to Edmund Gosse, February 18, 1905].

**Oldest Inhabited Town in England, the** *Abingdon, England.* The Oxfordshire (originally Berkshire) town justifies its sobriquet by its long history, growing up around a Benedictine abbey founded in 676.

**Oldest Town in Britain, the** *Colchester, England.* The Essex town claims its unique title as a settlement dating back to the 5th century BC. Before the Roman invasion it was the capital city of the Celtic chieftain Cunobelinus (Shakespeare's Cymbeline), and, as Camulodunum, it was the earliest Roman town in Britain, captured by the emperor Claudius in AD 44. *See also* **Camelot.**

**Old Father Thames** *Thames River, England.* England's best-known river is so named for its ancient living presence and its perceived engenderment of the country's capital. *Cp.* **Father Thames.** The personalization was popularized by the song in quote (2) below.

(1) In that blest moment from his oozy bed
   Old Father Thames advanced his reverend head [Alexander Pope, "Windsor Forest," 1704].
(2) High in the hills, down in the dales,
   Happy and fancy free,
   Old Father Thames keeps rolling along,
   Down to the mighty sea [Raymond Wallace and Betsy O'Hogan, "Old Father Thames," 1933].
(3) "Old Father Thames" allows for a third system of travel much appreciated by [London] sightseers, namely the water-bus service [*Holiday Haunts 1960: Area No. 2, North West England and North Wales*].
(4) I hoped that the Environment Agency would ... not be drawn into such an exercise of power as

to destroy the extraordinary beauty that Old Father Thames still unquestionably has [*The Times*, September 27, 2004].

**Old Home Town, the** *Cairo, Egypt.* A nickname given to the Egyptian capital by soldiers of the Eighth Army in World War II.

**Old Line State, the** *Maryland, USA.* In early colonial days, the state was the dividing line between the Crown land grants of Lord Baltimore and those of William Penn. The boundary between Maryland and Pennsylvania was later fixed as the Mason-Dixon Line.

**Old Man River** *Mississippi River, USA.* The nickname for the Mississippi personalizes the river as an ancient engendering force, like that of **Old Father Thames.**

Ol' man river, dat ol' man river,
   He must know sumpin', but don't say nothin',
   He jus' keeps rollin',
   He jus' keeps rollin' along [Oscar Hammerstein II, "Ol' Man River," *Show Boat*, 1927].

**Old Man with the Whiskers, the** *United States.* A personalization of the USA referring to the traditional representation of **Uncle Sam.** *Cp.* **Mr. Whiskers.**

**Old Muddy** *(1) Mississippi River, USA; (2) Missouri River, USA.* A variant of the more familiar nickname **Big Muddy** for each river, with "Old" intended affectionately.

**Old North State, the** *North Carolina, USA.* An affectionate nickname for the state, from its geographical location with regard to South Carolina.

**Old Oak, the** *London, England.* The nickname for the capital is Cockney rhyming slang for "the **Smoke.**" The Old Oak is a familiar pub name.

**Old Pueblo, the** *Tucson, Arizona, USA.* The nickname serves as a reminder that Tucson is the oldest city in Arizona, founded as a Spanish mission on a site near the present city in 1700.

The "Old Pueblo" has lived under four flags [*Britannica*, vol. 12, p. 27].

**Old Reekie** *see* **Auld Reekie**

**Old or Ould or Auld Sod, the** *Ireland.* The nickname can be affectionate, meaning "old earth" (*cp.* **Old Dart**), or derogatory, evoking "old sod" as a term for an annoying person or thing. Both "Ould" and "Auld" represent the Irish pronunciation of the adjective. *See also* **Old Country.**

(1) The mere suspicion that the landlord wished to get rid of them has driven many an Irish family far away from the 'old sod' [Charles Kickham, *Knocknagow*, 1879].
(2) From the moment I had first set foot on the Ould Sod I had yearned to pick up a typical sam-

ple of the local crafts [S.J. Perelman, *Baby, It's Cold Inside*, 1970].

(3) The old pattern — emigrants returning to the Auld Sod to mark Paddy's Day — was now reversed. "Ireland is so rich now that we come over here [to New York] to celebrate properly" [*Independent on Sunday*, March 19, 2000].

(4) We note that the clientele seem to be elderly, all rather alike in their appearance, and a bit familiar — of course, they're Boston Irish! Here for a vacation on the old sod with a bit of literature thrown in [Mark Doty in *Mortification*, 2003].

**Old Virginny** *Virginia, USA.* The colloquially affectionate form of the name relates to the original state of Virginia before the creation of West Virginia from its western counties in 1861. "Old" is sometimes omitted.

(1) "Virginny's black daughter" [Elias Howe, *Ethiopian Glee Book*, song title, 1849].

(2) He was from old Virginny — from what, he said, they call the *Pan-handle* [*Porter's Spirit of the Times*, November 8, 1856].

(3) Carry me back to old Virginny,
That's where the cotton and the corn and taters grow [James A. Bland, "Carry Me Back to Old Virginny," 1875].

**Old World, the** *Europe.* The name relates historically to the **New World**, and thus refers to Europe, or the Eastern Hemisphere, as a land known before the discovery of America. The term has a scientific application in the designation of Old World monkeys, found in Asia and Africa, and distinct from the New World monkeys of Central and South America.

(1) [The founding of Harvard] ensured our intellectual independence of the Old World [James Russell Lowell, *Works*, 1886].

(2) A glance at the map shows that very few rivers of the Old World flow into the Atlantic, compared with the number that do so of the New World [Johnson, p. 32].

**Ol' Man River** *see* **Old Man River**

**One-Eyed City, the** *Birkenhead, England.* A disparaging nickname for the Cheshire town and port, mostly used among residents of nearby Liverpool. It is said to be short for "the one-eyed city of undiscovered crime," referring to Birkenhead's inadequate police force at a time when the town was still growing. Local people have other explanations for the name, including the following: (1) It depicts Birkenhead as looking only in the direction of Liverpool, and so denotes the town's inferiority to that city; (2) Local shipyard workers had lost an eye when catching red-hot rivet ends; (3) The "one eye" is the nearby Mersey Tunnel, taking the road to Liverpool; (4) Liverpool city slickers looked over their shoulder with one eye at their inferior neighbors; (5) Only one illuminated clock in

Birkenhead was visible from Liverpool at night; (6) The term "one-eyed" denotes the stupidity or insignificance of the town's residents.

**000 City, the** *Council Bluffs, Iowa, USA.* The city is said to have been so nicknamed by an Omaha mayor for its casinos and sex shops, the three zeros denoting a gambling win or an unspecified adult novelty.

**Ooty** *Udagamandalam (Ootacamund), India.* A former colloquial abbreviation of the name of the colonial hill station (*see* **Queen of Hill Stations**). It was also dubbed "Snooty Ooty" for the supposed snobbishness of its residents.

**Opiumland** see in Appendix 1, p. 269.

**Orange State, the** *Florida, USA.* The state is so nicknamed for its citrus fruit production.

**Orcades** *Orkney Islands, Scotland.* The Roman name of the island group has been preserved in literary use.

(1) Ask where's the North? at York, 'tis on the Tweed;
In Scotland, at the Orcades [Alexander Pope, *An Essay on Man*, 1734].

(2) From Tweed to the Orcades was her domain [*Robert Burns*, "Caledonia," 1791].

(3) Harold was born where restless seas
Howl round the storm-swept Orcades [Sir Walter Scott, *The Lay of the Last Minstrel*, 1805].

**Orchard of England, the** *Herefordshire, England.* The county is famed for its fruit, and especially for its apple orchards (*see* **Cider Country**).

Described as the 'orchard of England,' Herefordshire (and indeed Worcestershire) produces dessert and cooking apples, plums, damsons, pears and cherries for the markets of the region [Robin Whiteman, *The Heart of England*, 1992].

**Orchard of Ireland, the** *Co. Armagh, Northern Ireland.* The county is the fruit-growing center of Northern Ireland. Hence the nickname.

This [i.e. Co. Armagh] is the Orchard of Ireland, but it is also the centre of mythical Ireland [*RD Ireland*, p. 300].

**Orient** see in Appendix 1, p. 269.

**Original Paradise, the** *Sri Lanka.* A name used both by the island state's native inhabitants and by world tourist companies to describe what is claimed to be the first "earthly Eden." The sense is chiefly spiritual, rather than agricultural, and the mountain of Adam's Peak in the center of the island is sacred to Hindus, Buddhists, and Muslims. *See also* **Garden of the World**.

The Sri Lankans themselves look forward to welcoming guests old and new to their 'original paradise' [Travel brochure issued with *Sunday Times*, August 14, 2005].

**Orleans** *New Orleans, Louisiana, USA.* A

shortening of the city's name, making it closer to the French *Orléans* from which it originated.

**Orstralia** or **Orstralier** *Australia*. A humorous respelling of the country's name, as it is said to be pronounced by Australians.

(1) All the bush in wide Orstralia can't compare with Shepherd's Bush! [Norman Campbell, *The Dinky-Di Soldier*, 1918].

(2) Lord, I don't know what Orstralier is comin' to [Douglas Stewart and Nancy Keesing, eds., *Australian Bush Ballads*, 1955].

**Ostrich-Feather Capital of the World, the** *Oudtshoorn, South Africa*. The town was the world's leading producer of ostrich feathers in the late 19th century.

**Other Place, the** *Cambridge, England*. As is clear from the quotes below, the belittling name for the home city of one of England's two oldest universities, both dating from the 12th century, originated in Oxford. Cambridge has long been traditionally regarded as the "lesser" of the two, as is evident from the pairing "Oxford and Cambridge" (not "Cambridge and Oxford"), and as is apparently implied by *Baedeker's Great Britain* (1890), which advises: "Oxford is on the whole more attractive than Cambridge to the ordinary visitor, who should therefore visit Cambridge first, or omit it altogether if he cannot visit both." In modern times, however, tourists have been drawn more to Cambridge, with its beautiful "Backs" (college gardens), than to industrial Oxford.

(1) This City which being the other University of England, the other eie [i.e. eye], the other strong-staie ... standeth upon the river *Cam* [William Camden, *Britannia*, 1586, translated by Philemon Holland, 1610].

(2) "The Other Town" could best be visited by night [Christopher Isherwood, *Lions and Shadows*, 1938].

(3) The other place is quieter than Oxford, and to some disinterested eyes more beautiful [Godfrey Smith, *The English Companion*, 1996].

(4) Smaller and prettier than Oxford (referred to here as 'the other place'), Cambridge is undeniably a university town [*Lonely Planet Great Britain*, 2005].

**Other Side, the** *England*. The nickname for England is valid for any country or (former) colony separated from it by a natural barrier, such as Ireland or Australia. *See also* **Other Side** in Appendix 1, p. 269.

(1) Five years on the 'other side' had given me a love for Australia [A.R. Grant, *Memories of Parliament*, 1937].

(2) It would not be considered funny to say: 'I have been staying with friends on the other side,' meaning 'I have been staying with friends in England.' To substitute 'the other side' for England

suggests that ... the speaker is giving recognition to a ripple of dissension over the waters of the Irish Sea and St George's Channel [Alison Larminie, "U-Irish," in Alan S.C. Ross, ed., *What Are U?*, 1969].

**O-Town** *(1) Omaha, Nebraska, USA; (2) Orlando, Florida, USA*. An initial-based nickname for the cities. *Cp.* **O-City**.

**Ouaga** *Ouagadougou, Burkina Faso*. A convenient short form of the capital city's name.

"Ouaga," as the place has become known to film fans and returning visitors [Dodd/Donald, p. 21].

**Ould Sod** *see* **Old Sod**

**Our Lady of the Snows** *Canada*. Canada was so dubbed by Rudyard Kipling in a poem on the 1897 Canadian Preferential Tariff, as quoted below. The name is properly that of a Catholic liturgical feast originating in a legend about a 4th-century Roman couple to whom the Virgin Mary appeared in a dream, instructed them to build the Basilica of St. Mary Major, and caused a miraculous midsummer snowfall.

A Nation spoke to a Nation,
 A Throne sent word to a Throne:
'Daughter am I in my mother's house,
 But mistress in my own.
The gates are mine to open,
 As the gates are mine to close,
And I abide by my Mother's House,'
 Said our Lady of the Snows [Rudyard Kipling, "Our Lady of the Snows," 1898].

**Outback** see in Appendix 1, p. 269.

**Outer Mongolia** *Mongolia*. The name, used generally to represent any remote place, contrasts with Inner Mongolia, now a region of northern China. The two territories have been separate entities since the 17th century, although geographically Outer Mongolia is now usually named as just Mongolia.

Outer Mongolia ... is such *terra incognita* that Tibet is practically Coney Island by comparison [John Gunther, *Inside Asia*, 1939].

**Outremer** see in Appendix 1, p. 269.

**Out-Yonder State, the** *California, USA*. The state has been so nicknamed as the furthest and remotest from the East Coast.

California, The Out-Yonder State [Ishmael Reed, *The Last Days of Louisiana Red*, 1974].

**Oven of Spain, the** *Seville, Spain*. The city is in one of the hottest regions of Spain. Hence the nickname, of Spanish origin.

**Owlsville** *London, England*. A former nickname for the British capital, as a place of late-night revelry and petty crime. *Cp.* **City of the Midnight Sun**.

**Oxenford** *Oxford, England*. A poetic or former English name for the city, still found in this form as a family name, as for the English playwright John Oxenford (1812–1877).

(1) A Clerk there was of Oxenford also,
That unto logyk hadde longe ago [Geoffrey Chaucer, "The Prologue," *The Canterbury Tales*, *c.* 1387].

(2) Away rode the Abbot all sad at that word,
And he rode to Cambridge, and Oxenford ["King John and the Abbot of Canterbury," *The Oxford Book of Ballads*, 1910].

**Oxford or Cambridge of the North, the** *St Andrews, Scotland*. The name equates Scotland's oldest university town with one or other (or even both) of England's oldest universities.

It's often referred to in tourist literature as "the Oxford or Cambridge of the North" and, like Cambridge, by and large St Andrews *is* its university [*The Rough Guide to Scotland*, 1998].

**Oxford and Cambridge of India, the** *Poona (Pune), India*. The city, in Maharashtra state, was so dubbed by Prime Minister Nehru for its reputation as a major cultural and educational center, with a university, a famed oriental research institute, and many bookshops.

Poona ... is often called the Oxford of the East [*The Times*, October 20, 2005].

**Oxon** *(1) Oxford, England; (2) Oxfordshire, England*. The name is most commonly used as a semiofficial short form for the county. It comes from *Oxonia*, a latinized form of *Oxenford*, the earlier form of the city's name, and is also used for an academic title relating to Oxford university, as "MA, Oxon." As a short form of Latin *Oxoniensis*, "of Oxford," it is the official signature of the bishop of Oxford. *See also* Appendix 6, p. 325.

(Oxfordshire) The golden triangle, the weekender fairyland where Oxon cocktails with Gloucs and Wilts [*The Times*, November 12, 2004].

**Oyster State, the** *Maryland, USA*. The state is so nicknamed for the oyster fisheries on Chesapeake Bay.

**Oz** *Australia*. The nickname is both a representation of the first syllable of "Australia" and, probably, an adoption of the name of Oz, the magical country of L. Frank Baum's children's novel *The Wonderful Wizard of Oz* (1900). The name became familiar from the "alternative" magazine *Oz*, originally appearing in Sydney in 1963 but subsequently published in London, England.

(1) If you're an English Aborigine wanting to migrate to Oz — it's stiff cheese! [Barry Humphries, *Bazza Comes Into His Own*, 1979].

(2) Combine Oz with NZ and fly on to Queenstown [*Sunday Times*, April 24, 2005].

**Ozark State, the** *Missouri, USA*. The nickname derives from the Ozark Mountains that are

one of the state's most popular tourist attractions.

**PA** *Prince Albert, Saskatchewan, Canada*. An initialism of the city's name.

**Pacific Rim** see in Appendix 1, p. 269.

**Paddo** *Paddington, Sydney, Australia*. A colloquial shortened name for the city suburb, with the characteristic Australian -o suffix, as in **Kenso**.

**Paddyland** *Ireland*. A former nickname based on Paddy (Patrick) as a traditional name for an Irishman. *Cp.* **Patland**.

Paddy's land, "ould Ireland" [*The Slang Dictionary*, 1894].

**Paddy's Milestone** *Ailsa Craig, Scotland*. The rocky island off the west coast of Scotland serves as a landmark on the sea route from Glasgow to Ireland (*see* **Paddyland**). Hence its nickname.

Ailsa Craig ... has been known to generations of Glaswegians as 'Paddy's Milestone' due to its position about half-way between Glasgow and Belfast [Newton, p. 173].

**Padstein** *Padstow, England*. The Cornish resort derives the punning version of its name from the restaurateur and seafood specialist Rick Stein, who owns several commercial premises in the town.

TV chef Rick Stein has the place pretty much sewn up — the town is often known these days by its alternative name of 'Pad-stein' [*Lonely Planet Great Britain*, 2005].

**Padstow of the North, the** *Ilkley, England*. The Yorkshire spa town has gained prestige for its designer shops and gourmet restaurants, suggesting a comparison with the southern seaside resort, itself nicknamed **Padstein**.

Ilkley ... is suddenly hip and fast gaining a reputation among the chattering classes as the Padstow of the North [*The Times*, September 3, 2005].

**Pak** *Pakistan*. A short name for the country, whose residents are colloquially known as "Pakis" in Britain.

**Palm Beach of Britain, the** *Poole, England*. A promotional name for the Dorset seaside resort and its fashionable district of Sandbanks.

Marketed as the 'Palm Beach of Britain,' Europe's largest natural harbour plays host to B-list celebs [*Lonely Planet Great Britain*, 2005].

**Palmetto City, the** *Charleston, South Carolina, USA*. The nickname refers to the palmetto trees lining the streets of the seaport city.

**Palmetto State, the** *South Carolina, USA*. South Carolina is so nicknamed for the palmetto tree on its flag. The tree is found throughout the state, but is especially abundant in its coastal regions.

Officials of the U.S. Justice Department firmly rejected a disputed reapportionment plan Thursday for the S.C. House of Representatives charging that it could deny equal voting rights to blacks in the Palmetto State [*The State* (Columbia, South Carolina), February 15, 1974].

**Palm Forest of Europe, the** *Elche, Spain.* The city in southeastern Spain is surrounded by an extensive grove of date palms, the only grove of its kind in Europe, and this gave the unique sobriquet.

**Palmyra of the Deccan, the** *Bijapur, India.* The historic city is so nicknamed for its many old notable remains, suggesting a resemblance to the ancient Syrian city of Palmyra.

**Palmyra of the North** or **Northern Palmyra, the** *St. Petersburg, Russia.* An occasional nickname for the northern city, comparing its status and imposing buildings with those of the important ancient city of Palmyra in Syria.

In 1710 he [i.e. Peter the Great] issued an *Ukaz* to the effect that 40,000 workmen should be sent to the "Northern Palmyra" [W. Barnes Steveni, *Things Seen in Russia*, 1914].

**Paname** *Paris, France.* A French argot form of the capital city's name. *Cp.* **Pantruche.**

**Panhandle State, the** *(1) Idaho, USA; (2) West Virginia, USA.* Both states have the rough shape of a pan with a handle, the latter in each case being a narrowing section. In Idaho, the "panhandle" runs north between Washington and Montana, while West Virginia actually has two such sections, one knifing northward between Ohio and Pennsylvania, the other projecting eastward between Maryland and Virginia. Hence the name.

We will wrap the flag of our fathers around the "Pan Handle" of Virginia, and upset the entire dish of Old Dominion Secession [*Vanity Fair* (New York), May 25, 1861].

**Pantown** *Moreton, England.* A local name for the Merseyside district of Wallasey, now a modern community but at one time a virtual shantytown, full of tents and trailers that were littered with pots and pans.

**Pantruche** *Paris, France.* A French argot form of the capital city's name. *Cp.* **Paname.**

**Papal City, the** *Rome, Italy.* The city is not only the present capital of Italy but the historic capital of the Papal States and the site of the Vatican, the palace and official residence of the Pope. Hence the sobriquet.

**Paper City** *Holyoke, Massachusetts, USA.* The nickname refers to the high-quality paper produced by the city's mills.

**Papermaking Town, the** *Penicuik, Scotland.* A now mostly historic nickname for the town south of Edinburgh, from the days when it was noted for its paper mills.

Its standing as the 'Papermaking Town' suffered a severe blow in 1975, when its last big mill was closed as the result of a big-business merger [Macnie/McLaren, p. 150].

**Paradise of England, the** *(Vale of ) Taunton Deane, England.* The nickname relates to the fertile plain of Taunton Deane, Somerset, noted for its natural beauty, as described in quote (2) below, which relates to a local proverb: "Where should I be born else than in Taunton Deane."

(1) I was once in Somersetshire, about a place neere Tanton, called Tandeane... You speake of the Paradice of England [John Norden, *The Surveyors Dialogue*, 1607].
  (2) This is a parcel of ground round about Taunton, very pleasant and populous... The peasantry therein ... are so highly conceited of their good country ... that they deem it a disparagement to be born in any other place; as if it were eminently all England [Thomas Fuller, *The History of the Worthies of England*, 1662].

**Paradise of Exiles, the** *Italy.* The nickname originally related to the many foreign rentiers in Italy, who profited from the properties they leased to others. In essence the situation still applies today. *Cp.* **Chiantishire.**

**Paradise of Fife, the** *Saline, Scotland.* The village near Dunfermline was at one time praised for its natural charm. As described in the quote below, it has long lost its claim to the idyllic sobriquet.

Though a nice-looking place, it can scarcely be entitled to this epithet, seeing that it lies at a considerable height above sea level, that during winter it is a cold and remote locality, and that the harvest here is generally a fortnight or three weeks behind that of the districts on the shores of the Forth [David Beveridge, *Between the Ochils and the Forth*, 1888].

**Paradise of Italy, the** *Naples, Italy.* The seaport city has good claim to the title, if only from its picturesque site on hills around the scenically striking Bay of Naples.

(1) Naples, the Paradise of Italy,
  As that is of earth [John Fletcher and Philip Massinger, *The Double Marriage, c.* 1621].
  (2) Although John Fletcher ... called Naples "the Paradise of Italy," there would appear to be no historical reason why this of all the world's noble cities should be singled out for the saying "See Naples and die" [Cecil Hunt, *Talk of the Town*, 1951].

**Paradise of the Pacific, the** *Hawaii, USA.* The islands rightly deserve the alliterative title for their mild climate, lush foliage and bright flora, palm-fringed coral beaches with rolling white surf, and lofty cloud-covered peaks, combining to give both visitor and resident a natural environment of breathtaking beauty.

> In due course he [i.e. US tourist agent E.M. Jenkins] fostered new resorts, from Bermuda in the east to islands like Hawaii ('Paradise of the Pacific') in the west [Piers Brendon, *Thomas Cook: 150 Years of Popular Tourism*, 1991].

**Paradise of Wales, the** *Powys, Wales*. The historic kingdom and modern county that succeeded it (although not corresponding exactly to the medieval territory) occupy one of the most picturesque parts of Wales, between the mountains of the north and valleys of the south.

> (1) "Pywys Paradwys Cymry." That is, "Powis is the Paradise of Wales." This Proverb referreth to Teliessen [i.e. the 6th-century poet Taliesin] the Author thereof, at what time Powis had far larger bounds than at this day [Thomas Fuller, *The History of the Worthies of England*, 1662].
>
> (2) Montgomeryshire was once part of the old Welsh kingdom of Powys and its inhabitants have long boasted of it as "Powys Paradwys Cymru" (Powys, the Paradise of Wales) [*Holiday Haunts 1961: Area No. 4, West of England and South and Central Wales*].

**Paradise on Earth** *see* **Earthly Paradise**

**Paree** *Paris, France*. An English colloquial rendering of the French pronunciation of the name of the French capital, especially when qualified as **Gay Paree**.

> (1) "Walk in, gentlemen, and see the collection ... which beats the Zoological Gardens all holler, and can't be come over by the Gardens des Plantys in Par-*ee*!" [Francis Alexander Durivage, *Stray Subjects*, 1848].
>
> (2) The major ... revived recollections of an old visit to "Paree" [Mrs. George de Horne Vaizey, *Pixie O'Shaughnessy*, 1903].
>
> (3) "That's What Makes Paris Paree" [Sammy Cahn and Vernon Duke, song title, sung by Doris Day in movie *April in Paris*, 1952].

**Paris of Africa, the** *Conakry, Guinea*. The sobriquet was valid for the capital city in its heyday as one of colonial France's major ports in West Africa.

**Paris of America, the** *(1) Annapolis, Maryland, USA; (2) New Orleans, Louisiana, USA*. The sobriquet for both cities is as much for promotion as for any real comparison or identity with the capital of France, although for New Orleans there is of course a historic French link.

**Paris of Eastern Europe, the** *Bucharest, Romania*. A more specific nickname for the capital city than the more common **Paris of the East**.

**Paris of Germany, the** *Munich, Germany*. The Bavarian capital city gained its nickname as a noted cultural and artistic center with a wealth of spectacular architecture, evoking the French capital.

It is Munich, the 'Paris of Germany,' that is Bavaria's heart and soul [*Lonely Planet Germany*, 2004].

**Paris of Japan, the** *Osaka, Japan*. The city and port was at one time so known, presumably for its culture rather than its architecture or any obvious French connection.

**Paris of Latin America** *see* **Paris of the South**.

**Paris of Siberia, the** *Irkutsk, Russia*. The city seems to have been so nicknamed generally for its aristocratic associations.

> (1) Visit Irkutsk, the "Paris of Siberia," where wooden buildings built by Russian aristocrats and Polish intellectuals are tastefully decorated [Travel ad, *The Times*, July 10, 2004].
>
> (2) Paris would seem to have a relative in every part of the world; but the one in the heart of Siberia is perhaps its least known [Dodd/Donald, p. 259].

**Paris of South America** *see* **Paris of the South**

**Paris of Spain, the** *Barcelona, Spain*. The nickname was bestowed on the city by Hans Christian Andersen during a visit in 1862, mainly for its cultural connections.

**Paris of the Amazon, the** *Manaus, Brazil*. The city, on the Rio Negro above its junction with the Amazon, was so nicknamed in the 19th century when it gained great wealth as the world's sole supplier of rubber.

**Paris of the Ancient World, the** *Ma'rib, Yemen*. The town and historic site has been so nicknamed for its cultural associations.

**Paris of the Antilles, the** *Cap-Haïtien, Haiti*. The city was founded by the French in 1670, originally as Cap Français, and received its nickname at that time as the capital of what was then the colony of Saint-Domingue.

**Paris of the Balkans, the** *Bucharest, Romania*. The Romanian capital is so nicknamed both for its social life and for its early 20th-century architecture and city planning, modeled on that of Paris, France. *Cp.* **Paris of the East**.

> Carr: Bucharest.
> Tzara: Oh, yes. Yes. The Paris of the Balkans...
> Carr: Silly place to put it, really [Tom Stoppard, *Travesties*, 1975].

**Paris of the Belgians, the** *Brussels, Belgium*. The sobriquet is valid for the Belgian capital, which like Paris grew up around a river island, was favored by aristocracy, and was noted for the luxury and gaiety of its social scene.

> Brussels is the Paris of the Belgians and wants a little fire and Brimstone [Robert Southey, letter to Miss Barker, October 1, 1815].

**Paris of the Desert, the** *Marzuq, Libya*. The

town earned its former nickname by virtue of its local importance as a trading center.

**Paris of the East, the** *(1) Bucharest, Romania; (2) Budapest, Hungary; (3) Ho Chi Minh City, Vietnam; (4) Prague, Czech Republic; (5) Shanghai, China; (6) Warsaw, Poland.* Bucharest and Warsaw gained the nickname for their former gaiety and lively entertainment, as well as their Parisian-style culture and architecture. Budapest and Prague are both noted for their wealth of palaces, villas, and churches. Shanghai is famed for its exuberant and exotic appeal, not always to its advantage, as testified by a former nickname, **Whore of the Orient.** Ho Chi Minh City has a direct Parisian connection as the former French colonial city of Saigon. Shanghai was also the **Pearl of the East** and Saigon the **Pearl of the Orient.** *See also* **Paris of the Middle East.**

(1) (Ho Chi Minh City) Beautiful for once and once only, just past dawn flying towards the centre of the city... In that space, at that hour, you could see what people had seen forty years before, Paris of the East, Pearl of the Orient, long open avenues lined and bowered over by trees running into spacious parks, precisioned scale [Michael Herr, *Dispatches*, 1977)

(2) (Warsaw) He dreamt that one day Warsaw would regain the title it conferred on itself in the interwar years when he grew up: "the Paris of the East" [*The Times*, April 29, 2004].

(3) (Shanghai) The Peace Hotel ... is an art deco reminder of Shanghai's jazz age as the "Paris of the East" [Dodd/Donald, p. 232].

(4) (Budapest) Budapest really does deserve its accolade 'Paris of the East' [Travel brochure issued with *Sunday Times*, February 13, 2005].

**Paris of the Middle East** or **East** or **Orient, the** *Beirut, Lebanon.* The sobriquet has a social reference, as in the 1960s Beirut was famed for its nightlife.

(1) Beautiful people, wild parties — the Paris of the Middle East is back [*Sunday Times*, October 17, 2004].

(2) Beirut was dubbed "Paris of the Orient" before the 1975–90 civil war [*The Times*, May 7, 2005].

(3) Beirut's reputation as the Paris of the Middle East is well earned — unfortunately the Paris in question is the Nazi-occupied city of 1940–4 [Adam Russ, *101 Places Not to Visit*, 2005].

(4) Nearly all my memories of childhood holidays involve the Middle East... We'd go on trips all over the region ... and take in Beirut, which really was the Paris of the East before the troubles started [Andy Serkis in *Sunday Times*, December 11, 2005].

**Paris of the North, the** *(1) Copenhagen, Denmark; (2) Southport, England; (3) Tromsø, Norway.* The Danish capital came to be so known for its general charm and elegance. The English

town near Liverpool, a planned resort of the early 19th century, qualifies for the sobriquet by virtue of its pleasing layout and handsome buildings, especially those on tree-lined Lord Street, its central thoroughfare. The Norwegian seaport city dates from medieval times and has grown into an important cultural and academic center. *Cp.* **Playground of the North.**

(1) (Southport) The Paris of the North is a delightful Victorian resort [*Enjoy England Holiday Planner 2005*].

(2) (Tromsø) With its bustling riverside cafés, Tromsø has been called the "Paris of the North" [Travel ad, *The Times Magazine*, September 10, 2005].

(3) (Southport) [Southport is the] most select of Lancashire seaside resorts. Once known as "The Paris of the North," it has a gracious main street that reputedly inspired the Champs-Elysées [*The Times*, November 12, 2005].

**Paris of the Orient, the** *Hanoi, Vietnam.* The Vietnamese capital was long under French control and has retained something of a Parisian appearance in its buildings and tree-lined boulevards. The nickname is otherwise hardly valid today, however. *See also* **Paris of the Middle East.**

The city's restored Opera House is a miniature version of Charles Garnier's Opéra National in Paris (Hanoi's nickname was "the Paris of the Orient") [Dodd/Donald, p. 255].

**Paris of the South** or **Latin America** or **South America, the** *Buenos Aires, Argentina.* The Spanish colonial origin of the Argentine capital has given it much in common with stylish European cities such as Paris, and its traditional architecture is similar to that of late 19th-century France. Hence the sobriquet. *See also* **BA without the LA.**

(1) If you have limited time in South America ... B.A.'s the place to go. And if you're solely in pursuit of the best restaurants, the biggest monuments, the grandest boulevards and the chicest people, then the "Paris of the South" is your spot [Josh Schonwald, "The Full Montevideo," *Washington Post*, April 9, 2000].

(2) The Paris of South America is a heady blend of Latin exotica and awfully European familiarity [*Sunday Times*, February 13, 2005].

**Paris of the Subcontinent, the** *Lahore, Pakistan.* Pakistan's second-largest city was long under British ownership and acquired a European character which it has to some extent retained. Its nickname is hardly valid today, however, despite its fine architecture and generally impressive appearance. *See also* **Subcontinent.**

**Paris of the West, the** *Dawson (City), Yukon Territory, Canada.* The town earned its sobriquet in the late 19th century, when it was at the peak of its fame and size following the Klondike gold rush. *Cp.* **City of Gold**.

**Paris of the Western Hemisphere, the** *Havana, Cuba*. As the quote below implies, the Cuban capital may have once merited its sobriquet, partly for its atttractive location and layout, partly for its commercial and cultural prominence, but it scarcely deserves such an overblown epithet in modern terms.

> Its claim to be "the Paris of the western hemisphere" is to some extent borne out in its lay-out and disposition. Rather, one should say, to *have* been the Paris [Sacheverell Sitwell, *Golden Wall and Mirador*, 1961].

**Paris of West Africa, the** *Abidjan, Côte d'Ivoire*. The former Ivorian capital is so nicknamed for its French colonial past. *See also* **Pearl of the Lagoon**.

> Abidjan ... is decidedly dog-eared these days, no longer justifying such monikers as 'Paris of West Africa' [*Lonely Planet West Africa*, 2002].

**Paris on the Lake** *Chicago, Illinois, USA*. An occasional nickname for the city on Lake Michigan, referring to its civilized amenities and perceived stylishness, especially in the world of fashion.

> (1) Chicago's shopping scene is unmatched. Call it Paris on the Lake. The Milan of the Midwest. Whichever way, this is one city with a downtown that's big on dress-up [*Time Out*: Introduction to Chicago: Shops and Services <http://www.timeout.com/chicago/shops/> accessed May 20, 2005].
>
> (2) What defines Chicago style? Once dubbed "Paris on the Lake," Chicago is an eight-hour flight from London [*The Times*, May 20, 2005].

**Paris without the Jet Lag** *Montreal, Quebec, Canada*. A mainly American sobriquet for the city, with its French history and predominantly French-speaking population.

**Parnassus of Japan, the** *Mt. Fuji (Fujiyama), Japan*. The sacred mountain has won its sobriquet as an oriental equivalent to ancient Greece's Mount Parnassus, sacred to Apollo and the Muses.

**Parra** *Parramatta, Sydney, Australia*. A short name for the city, now a suburb of Sydney.

**Parthenon of Prehistory, the** *Lascaux, France*. The somewhat presumptuous nickname works on a creative level by comparing the French caves, with their famous display of prehistoric paintings, to the Greek temple of the goddess Athena on the hill of the Acropolis at Athens, an outstanding exemplar of Doric architecture.

> Lascaux is the Parthenon of prehistory [Cyril Connolly, "Dordogne," *Ideas and Places*, 1953].

**Parthenope** *Naples, Italy*. The poetic name of the seaport city is that of the ancient Greek colony near which it was founded. Hence its present name, from the Greek for "new city." (Hospital reformer Florence Nightingale was born in Florence, Italy; her older sister, Parthenope, was born in Naples.)

> (1) Æolia and Elysium, and thy shores,
> Parthenope, which now, alas! are free! (P.B. Shelley, *Œdipus Tyrannus; or, Swellfoot the Tyrant*, 1820].
>
> (2) Or let me loiter, soothed with what is given,
> Nor asking more, on that delicious Bay,
> Parthenope's Domain — Virgilian haunt [William Wordsworth, "Musings near Aquapendente," *Memorials of a Tour in Italy*, 1837].

**Party Capital of the World, the** *Ibiza, Spain*. The third-largest island of the Balearic group, in the western Mediterranean, has long been a popular tourist resort and has latterly become a focus of uninhibited, alcohol-fired, drug-fueled, sex-driven partying by the young.

> Ibiza, the party capital of the world, the sun-bleached home of house music and, more recently, the scene of a thousand drunken ... horror shows [*The Times*, August 20, 2005].

**Pass the Doughnuts** *Pasadena, California, USA*. A colloquial name punning on the city's real name.

**Patland** *Ireland*. A former nickname of the same origin as **Paddyland**, from Patrick (pet name Pat).

**Patrie, la** *France*. A patriotic French title for France, from Latin *patria*, "fatherland." *See also* **Fatherland**.

> Allons enfants de la Patrie,
> Le jour de gloire est arrivé.
> (Arise, children of the fatherland,
> The day of glory has come.) [Claude-Joseph Rouget de l'Isle, "La Marseillaise," 1792].

**P'boro** *see* **So'ton**

**PE** *Port Elizabeth, South Africa*. An initialized abbreviation of the seaport city's name.

> (1) I can't sit straight up all night in a coat waiting! Think what I should look like tomorrow at P.E. station! [Iris Vaughan, *These Were my Yesterdays*, 1966].
>
> (2) Six years ago, he was unemployed; about 45 per cent in PE, as it's known, are [*The Times*, November 13, 2004].
>
> (3) Garden Routers often miss a trick here, heading straight to "PE" airport and back to Cape Town [*Sunday Times* (South Africa Supplement), March 15, 2005].

**Peaceful Isle, the** *Fuerteventura, Canary Islands*. The second-largest of the Canary Islands has come to be so named (and commercially promoted) for its tranquil setting.

> Fuerteventura, universally known as "The Peaceful Isle" of the Canary Islands [Travel ad, *Sunday Times*, September 25, 2005].

**Peace Garden State, the** *North Dakota, USA.* The nickname refers to the International Peace Garden, a park on the border between North Dakota, USA, and Manitoba, Canada, established in 1932 as a symbol of friendship between the United States and Canada. In 1956 the North Dakota Motor Vehicle Department placed the name on license plates, and it was formally adopted by state legislature in 1957. The name could equally be taken to describe North Dakota, a rural, agricultural, and sparsely populated state, as a "garden of peace."

**Peach State, the** *Georgia, USA.* The nickname refers to the peaches grown in the state, especially along the Atlantic coast. It may also be taken to imply that Georgia is a "peach of a state."

(1) "Everything Is Peaches Down in Georgia" [Milton Ager, song title, 1918].

(2) Georgia was nicknamed *The Peach State* in 1939 because "peaches have been an important product of Georgia since the middle of the sixteenth century" [G.E. Shankle, *State Names*, rev. ed., 1941].

(3) With out-of-state tourists flocking to Jimmy Carter's home town in Plains, Georgia, officials are looking for ways to lure the visitors to the peach state's other attractions [*South Wales Echo*, November 26, 1976].

**Peanut State, the** *Georgia, USA.* Georgia is the nation's top producer of peanuts. Hence the nickname.

**Pearl City of the South, the** *Hyderabad, India.* The city derives its nickname from its famed handicraft industry, including gold and pearl jewelry.

**Pearl Coast** see in Appendix 1, p. 269.

**Pearl Harbor of the Atlantic, the** *Guantánamo Bay, Cuba.* The Caribbean Sea inlet is a training center for ships of the US Atlantic fleet and has extensive naval installations. Hence the name, comparing the site with Pearl Harbor, Hawaii, where the US naval station is connected with the Pacific Ocean. *See also* **Gitmo.**

**Pearl of Africa, the** *Uganda.* The country owes its sobriquet not only to its mountains, lakes, and forests, richly fertile land, and favorable climate, but in modern times also to its significant economic potential. The phrase occurs in the third stanza of the country's national anthem, as in quote (1) below, written by George Wilberforce Karoma and adopted on gaining independence in 1962.

(1) Oh Uganda! the land that feeds us
   By sun and fertile soil grown,
   For our own dear land
   We'll always stand,
   The Pearl of Africa's Crown.

(2) Long ago, in colonial days, British statesman Winston Churchill ... described Uganda [in *My African Journey*, 1908] as 'the pearl of Africa.' Then, the description was not unmerited [*RD Places of the World*, p. 690].

(3) Winston Churchill described Uganda as the "Pearl of Africa," and it is hard to take issue with that. It is beautiful — a lush, fertile landscape of rolling hills, tea and banana plantations, wetlands and ... Lake Victoria [*The Times*, December 24, 2005].

**Pearl of Arabia, the** *Sana, Yemen.* The Yemeni capital can justify its valued sobriquet by virtue of its ancient history, its imposing physical presence, and its importance as a commercial and cultural center.

Unesco has done its best to ensure the heritage of this "pearl of Arabia" is protected [Leier, p. 147].

**Pearl of France, the** *Menton, France.* The town and resort on the French Riviera near the Italian border lies below an amphitheater of mountains in a setting of subtropical plants and lemon and olive trees. Hence its sobriquet.

Often called the "pearl of France," Menton was a haunt of aristocracy in the 19th century, and still has ornate *belle époque* gardens [*The Times* (Hidden France Supplement), May 14, 2005].

**Pearl of Kent, the** *Whitstable, England.* The Kent seaside resort, famous for its oysters, is so nicknamed for its old houses and attractive setting.

Compared with Margate, Broadstairs and Ramsgate, Whitstable has more of a remote, unspoilt charm, which may be why it's known as the 'Pearl of Kent' [*Lonely Planet Great Britain*, 2005].

**Pearl of Lake Ladoga, the** *Valaam, Russia.* The picturesque island, with its famous medieval monastery, is the largest of its group in the northwestern part of Europe's largest lake.

**Pearl of Lake Neusiedler, the** *Podersdorf am See, Austria.* The tourist resort, Austria's largest campsite, claims pride of place on Lake Neusiedler in the east of the country.

**Pearl of the Adriatic, the** *Dubrovnik, Croatia.* The ancient seaport city owes its nickname, first popularized by Byron, to its imposing site and appearance.

(1) Like a fiery flower the "Pearl of the Adriatic" sits in a cerulean sea, protected by massive fortified walls, with beautiful Italianate architecture [Leier, p. 37].

(2) The 1,000-year old city of Dubrovnik, Byron's "pearl of the Adriatic," has been fully restored after its savage pounding in the early 1990s [*Sunday Times*, February 13, 2005].

**Pearl of the Antilles, the** *Cuba.* Cuba derives its nickname from its size as the largest island of the Greater Antilles, its rich production of sugar, fish, citrus fruits, and tobacco, its fine harbors, its picturesquely varied scenery, and its strategic geographical position at the entrance to the Gulf of Mexico.

**Pearl of the Balkans, the** *Lake Ohrid, Macedonia.* The deepest lake in the Balkans, long noted for its beauty, suffered touristically as a result of the Yugoslavian civil war of the 1990s. Its old sobriquet thus fell into abeyance.

> Once upon a time, Lake Ohrid ... was known as the pearl of the Balkans — people flew in from Dubrovnik in their thousands to complete one of the region's classic twin-centre holidays. Not any more [*Sunday Times*, July 24, 2004].

**Pearl of the Chilterns, the** *Wendover, England.* The Buckinghamshire town, with its old inns and timbered cottages, derives its nickname from its attractive location on the edge of the Chiltern Hills.

> Wendover is the pearl of the Chilterns. Its setting is perfect [*Metro-land*, 1932].

**Pearl of the Desert, the** *(1) Ghadames, Libya; (2) Timbuktu, Mali.* Ghadames deserves its nickname as a town set in a fertile oasis in the Sahara, with hot springs. Timbuktu, on the other hand, on the edge of the Sahara, has hardly justified its sobriquet since its decline in the late 16th century.

**Pearl of the Dolomites, the** *Cortina d'Ampezzo, Italy.* The noted ski resort, site of the 1956 Winter Olympics, owes its name to its prime location in the heart of the Dolomites.

> Known as "the Pearl of the Dolomites," Cortina d'Ampezzo ... has ranked among Europe's top mountain resorts since skiing became fashionable in the Twenties [*The Times*, October 28, 2004].

**Pearl of the East, the** *(1) Damascus, Syria; (2) Shanghai, China.* The Syrian capital, believed to be the world's oldest city, justifies its sobriquet by its location alone beteween desert and mountains on the edge of an oasis near beautiful gardens and groves. Its Great Mosque and other buildings complement its charm, and its reputation is enhanced by its status as a major trading center. As implied in the quote below, Shanghai has long held a spell over Westerners, who quickly succumbed to its gaudy glamor and (often through personal experience) expensive eroticism. *Cp.* **Whore of the Orient.**

> (Shanghai) Western labels are piling into high-tech, high-rise Shanghai... But as designer style takes over, will the city once known as the 'pearl of the east' forget its romantic, exotic past? [*Financial Times*, October 16, 2004].

**Pearl of the Lagoon, the** *Abidjan, Côte d'Ivoire.* The former Ivorian capital derives its nickname from its commercial and cultural importance and its location as a port on Ébrié Lagoon.

For Europeans it is the Paris and for North Americans the Manhattan of West Africa. However, inhabitants and those who know it call it the "Pearl of the Lagoon" [Leier, p. 202].

**Pearl of the Orient, the** *(1) Damascus, Syria; (2) Gibara, Cuba; (3) Ho Chi Minh City, Vietnam; (4) Macao, China; (5) Manila, Philippines; (6) Penang, Malaysia.* This is the commonest of the "Pearl" nicknames, popularized by its association with "pearl of orient" as a term for an orient (or oriental) pearl, meaning one from the Indian seas, as distrinct from one of lesser beauty or value found in the European mussel. For Damascus, the term equates with **Pearl of the East.** For Gibara, the phrase refers to its pleasant site in eastern Cuba. Ho Chi Minh City, familiar in its French colonial days as Saigon, was noted for its oriental beauty. Macao earned the name more generally as a Portuguese colonial province, while Manila and Penang are famed for their wealth, as noted in quote (3) below.

> (1) (Macao) On the basis of an overnight sojourn, I can report that I found the Pearl of the Orient slightly less exciting than a rainy Sunday evening in Rochester [S.J. Perelman, *Westward Ha!*, 1948].
>
> (2) (Gibara) Its beauty prompted several pseudonyms — "Encanto Eden" (Enchanted Eden), "Perla del Oriente" (Pearl of the Orient), and, from sailors approaching the bay and dazzled by its whitewashed houses, "La Villa Blanca" [*The Rough Guide to Cuba*, 2003].
>
> (3) (Penang) As you fly over the ... island, its green, hilly terrain contrasted against the azure sea, you wonder whether emerald might be a better description — until you realise that the name refers to the island's prosperity [*The Times*, March 31, 2004].
>
> (4) (Damascus) Damascus in the twenty-first century is a city of two million and once again a "pearl of the Orient" [Leier, p. 142].

**Pearl of the Pacific, the** *(1) Acapulco, Mexico; (2) Mazatlán, Mexico; (3) Valparaíso, Chile.* Acapulco and Mazatlán vie for their their respective sobriquets as popular tourist destinations on one of the world's most beautiful coasts, with Acapulco having the social and scenic edge, as indicated by the quote below. Valparaíso (its name meaning "valley of paradise") occupies a similar idyllic site by the same ocean.

> (Acapulco) For three decades, the "Pearl of the Pacific," the "Queen of the Mexican Riviera" was a magnet for Hollywood stars, presidents, dictators and royalty [*The Times* (Mexico Supplement), November 17, 2005].

**Pearl of the Pyrenees, the** *Bagnères-de-Luchon, France.* The summer and winter resort is so nicknamed for its picturesque setting in the central Pyrenees.

**Pearl of the Renaissance, the** *Florence, Italy.* Although dating from Roman times, most of the city was created during the Renaissance period of the 14th through 16th centuries, as is especially evident in its church architecture. Hence the nickname.

> After breakfast we have a guided walking tour of Florence, 'pearl of the Renaissance,' a superb and beautiful city [Travel brochure issued with *The Times*, July 9, 2005].

**Pearl of the South, the** *Cienfuegos, Cuba.* The city and port acquired its nickname for its attractive location on Cuba's south coast.

**Pearl of the Thaya Valley, the** *Raabs an der Thaya, Austria.* The town derives its nickname from its scenic setting in the valley of the Thaya River.

**Pearl of the Vienna Woods, the** *Neulengbach, Austria.* The township deserves its nickname for its well-preserved Renaissance architecture and its attractive location between two mountains on the western fringe of the Vienna Woods.

**Pearl of the Vogtland, the** *Greiz, Germany.* The former capital of the principality of Reuss is set in a wooded valley enclosed by forest-covered hills in the old district known as the Vogtland. Hence the nickname.

**Pearl of the Wachau, the** *Dürnstein, Austria.* The medieval town is so nicknamed for its picturesque setting in the Wachau, a section of the valley of the Danube to the west of Vienna.

**Pearl of the West, the** *Guadalajara, Mexico.* The name, translating Spanish *Perla del Occidente*, refers to the former colonial city's generally charming appearance. It is "West" because it is in the western hemisphere (as distinct from Guadalajara in Spain, after which it is named, in the eastern hemisphere).

**Pearl of the West Indies, the** *Cuba.* The name is a broader recognition of Cuba's special attributes, more locally praised as **Pearl of the Antilles**.

**Pearl of Venezuela, the** *Margarita Island, Venezuela.* The Caribbean island, a popular tourist resort, is nicknamed both for its natural beauty and, more pragmatically, for its important pearl-fishing industry. Hence its name, Spanish for "pearl."

> Next came Margarita Island. After a romantic stroll along an unspoilt beach, I could see why it's called the "Pearl of Venezuela" [Travel ad, *Sunday Times Magazine*, September 18, 2005].

**Peg, the** *Winnipeg, Manitoba, Canada.* A colloquial abbreviation of the city's name, at first mainly used by vagrants.

**Peking** *Beijing, China.* A long-familiar form of the name of the Chinese capital, representing an anglicized form of the Wade-Giles romanization *Pei-ching*, as distinct from the now generally used Pinyin form. The older form is still found in some tourist literature, as in quote (2) below, and remains regularly current for derivatives, as the examples in quote (3).

> (1) Use the English (Wade-Giles, not Pinyin) style for Canton, China, Chou En-lai, Mao Tse-tung, Mongolia, Nanking, Peking, Shanghai [*The Times English Style and Usage*, 1992].
> (2) I say "Beijing" when speaking Mandarin and "Bak-geng" when speaking Cantonese, but "Peking" when speaking English [Respondent in "Questions Answered" column, *The Times*, January 28, 2003].
> (3) [Use] Peking only in phrases such as Peking duck or Peking man. The city is now Beijing [*The Times Style and Usage Guide*, 2003].
> (4) Day 5. Flight to Peking for a three night stay [Travel brochure issued with *The Times*, August 20, 2005].

**Pelican State, the** *Louisiana, USA.* The brown pelican was once commonly found on the Gulf Coast but is now an endangered bird. It remains as the state symbol of Louisiana and gave the familiar nickname.

> A well-known writer in the Pelican State writes us a good thing from one of his little folks [*Harper's Magazine*, May 1859].

**Peninsula, the** *(1) Cape Peninsula, South Africa; (2) Iberian Peninsula (Spain and Portugal).* Just two examples of the name used for any local or well-known peninsula. The name of the Iberian Peninsula is preserved unqualified in the title of the Peninsular War of 1808–14, when the French were opposed by British, Spanish, and Portuguese forces.

> (1) (Spain and Portugal) My thoughts are anxiously turned to the Peninsula [Sir Walter Scott, letter to Miss Joanna Baillie, April 4, 1812].
> (2) (Cape Peninsula) The Peninsula is entirely cut off from the mainland by a sandy isthmus, the Cape Flats [M. Nathan, *South Africa from Within*, 1926].

**Peninsular State, the** *Florida, USA.* An obvious descriptive name for the state, which occupies a peninsula between the Gulf of Mexico and the Atlantic Ocean.

**Pennsy** *Pennsylvania, USA.* A colloquial abbreviation of the state name, the final -sy evoking a diminutive. The name came to be particularly associated with the Pennsylvania Railroad.

> 'And think, Sal, when we get to Pennsy we'll start hearing that gone Eastern bop on the disc jockeys' [Jack Kerouac, *On the Road*, 1957].

**Pennsylvania of the West** *Missouri, USA.* The nickname emphasizes the similarity between the states in their mining industry and in the large number of foreign immigrants in each, especially Germans.

**Pennycomequick** *Falmouth, England.* The alternate name for the Cornish resort and port was current in the latter half of the 17th century, and is still found elsewhere in England as a field name. The name means what it says, as an equivalent of "get rich quick," applied to a fertile or promising location, but the initial Pen- has led to a bogus Cornish interpretation, as in the quote below.

> A Cornish derivation, supposedly meaning 'head of the valley creek,' is sometimes given ... but there are several good reasons why that derivation cannot possibly be right, and anyway the phrase does not mean that, nor anything else, in Cornish [O.J. Padel, *Cornish Place-Names*, 1988].

**People's Republic of Berkeley, the** *Berkeley, California, USA.* The half-humorous, half-serious radical title dates from the days of anti–Vietnam protests by students of the University of California at Berkeley in the 1960s.

> Its unofficial moniker, the 'People's Republic of Berkeley,' was originally meant as a red-baiting disparagement but has instead been embraced as a rallying cry [*Lonely Planet USA*, 2004].

**People's Republic of Cork, the** *Cork, Ireland.* Ireland's second city has played a central role in the country's Republican history (*see* **Rebel County**) and its people regard themselves as inhabitants of the true capital. Hence the Soviet-style sobriquet.

> "The People's Republic of Cork" has always been the spiritual capital of Ireland [*The Times*, November 6, 2004].

**People's Republic of Santa Monica, the** *Santa Monica, California, USA.* The oceanside resort, a district of Los Angeles, derives its local nickname from its efficient provision of public amenities, as outlined in the quote below.

> Santa Monica ... is known to the rest of Los Angeles as the People's Republic of Santa Monica, because of its infamously liberal politics... The buses run on clean fuel, the libraries and swimming pools regularly win awards, and the local school sytem is one of the few where the middle classes happily send their children [*Sunday Times*, February 27, 2005].

**Perfidious Albion** *England.* The concept of England as treacherous in international affairs is said to have been first expressed by the French preacher Jacques-Bénigne Bossuet (1627–1704) in his first sermon on the Circumcision, quoted in volume 11 of the *Œuvres de Bossuet* (1816) as follows: "*L'Angleterre, ah, la perfide Angleterre, que le rempart de ses mers rendait inaccessible aux Romains, la foi du Sauveur y est abordée*" ("En-

gland, ah, faithless England, which the protection afforded by its seas rendered inaccessible to the Romans, the faith of the Savior spread even there"). The present form of the phrase is first recorded in the poem "L'Ère des Français" (1793) by the Marquis de Ximénèz Augustin in his *Poésies Révolutionnaires et contre-révolutionnaires* (1821): "*Attaquons dans ses eaux / La perfide Albion!*" ("Let us attack perfidious Albion in her own waters!") (*see* **Albion**). The phrase was later popularly ascribed to Napoleon.

> (1) We always go through these stages of being beastly to our friends because we are frightened of our enemies. It is this that has earned us the reputation of *perfide Albion* [Harold Nicolson, *Diary*, January 2, 1947].
> (2) [General de Gaulle] felt it to be essential ... that he should maintain a proud and haughty demeanour towards "perfidious Albion" [*The Observer*, May 18, 1958].
> (3) The phrase "*la perfide Angleterre*," later to become "*perfide Albion*," may have been coined by Jacques Bénigne Bossuet in a sermon on New Year's Day, 1654 [Richard Mayne, *The Europeans*, 1972].

**Perfume City, the** *Salalah, Oman.* The town and port on the Arabian Sea is noted for its trade in frankincense. Hence the name.

> Known as the "Perfume City of Arabia," it is one of the few places on Earth where the trees that produce frankincense grow [Travel brochure issued with *The Times*, August 20, 2005].

**Perfumed Isle, the** *Nosy Bé, Madagascar.* The island off the northwestern shore of Madagascar gained its nickname from its production of sugar and oils for perfumery. *Cp.* **Scented Isle**.

> Rounding the coast of Madagascar to the "Perfumed Isle" of Nosy Bé [Travel ad, *The Times*, July 17, 2004].

**Perfume Islands, the** *Comoros.* The islands are so nicknamed for the ylang-ylang oil produced there.

**Persia** *Iran.* The former name of the kingdom of Iran was used for centuries until 1935, when the government requested that the country be named Iran instead of Persia. The old name was so familiar from history and literature, however, that it persisted for some time after this date and is still current geographically in adjectival form for the Persian Gulf (*see* **Gulf**) as well as for such nongeographical designations as Persian carpets, Persian cats, and Persian powder.

> I am bound
> To Persia, and want guilders for my voyage
> [William Shakespeare, *The Comedy of Errors, c.* 1594].

**Peter** *see* **Piter**

**Peterbore** *Peterborough, England.* A wry pun

on the name of the East Anglian city, regarded by some as dull and dreary.

> "Friends of ours have moved to Sevenoaks." "You might as well move to Peterbore" [*The Times*, April 27, 2004].

**Petersburg** *St. Petersburg, Russia.* A name for the city that omits the saint but preserves the name of its founder, Peter the Great.

> (1) Suppose him then at Petersburgh; suppose That pleasant capital of painted snows [Lord Byron, *Don Juan*, 1823].
> (2) The ballet in Petersburg is rightly claimed to be the finest in Europe [W. Barnes Steveni, *Things Seen in Russia*, 1914].

**Petrified City, the** *el-Ashmunain, Egypt.* The ancient city, also known as Hermopolis Magna, is so nicknamed from its necropolis of Tuna el-Gebel, where there are statues of men, women, children, and animals, which according to local legend were at one time alive but were mysteriously changed into stone.

**Petrograd** *see* **Leningrad**

**PG** *Punta Gorda, Belize.* A common initialism of the seaport town's name.

> P.G. never gets many visitors [Natascha Norton and Mark Whatmore, *Cadogan Guides: Central America*, 1993].

**Pharian Fields, the** *Egypt.* The poetic name of Egypt comes from Pharos, the former island off its coast on which there was a famous lighthouse.

> And past from Pharian fields to Canaan land Led by the strength of the Almighties hand [John Milton, *Paraphrase on Psalm 114*, 1624].

**Philly** or **Phillie** *Philadelphia, Pennsylvania, USA.* A colloquial shortening (and quasi-personalization) of the city's name.

> (1) Draw up a chair 'thatch,' I'll tell you a story, That happened in 'Philly' some twenty years since [William DeVere, *Tramp Poems of the West*, 1891].
> (2) After a while, Kitty murmured something to Cappy, and he held her close, answering, "We'll just have to wait till we pull into Philly, honey" [*Rogue*, May 1961].
> (3) Philly often gets brushed aside as a worthy city destination because NYC ... steals the limelight [*Lonely Planet USA*, 2004].

**Philosophers' Corner** see in Appendix 1, p. 269.

**Phils, the** *Philippines.* A colloquial short form of the island republic's name, used mostly by vacationing visitors.

**Phoenix City** *Chicago, Illinois, USA.* The city was so nicknamed by preacher and reformer Henry Ward Beecher following its rapid recovery from the great fire of 1871.

**Pickle Capital of Arkansas, the** *Atkins, Arkansas, USA.* The town derives its nickname from its prominent production of pickles and peppers.

**Pictland** see in Appendix 1, p. 269.

**Pie and Cake County, the** *Yorkshire, England.* A former nickname for the county, referring to the food traditionally doled out to vagrants. *Cp.* **Bread and Cheese County.**

**Pig Island** *New Zealand.* The country was so nicknamed by Australians for the large number of wild pigs in its rural regions. They were the descendants of the pigs originally brought by Captain Cook.

> Another guy got black-mailed into taking a sheila half-way around Pig Island [*New Zealand Listener*, December 21, 1970].

**Pile O'Bones** *Regina, Saskatchewan, Canada.* The city originated as a hunters' camp and was known by this name for the heaps of bones remaining after the skinning and cutting of buffalo. The name persisted as a nickname.

**Pillars of Heaven, the** *Atlas Mountains, North Africa.* The sobriquet, given by the Moors, is an equivalent of the actual name of the mountains, from the mythical giant Atlas, who held up the sky. The name is an old phrase found in the Bible: "The pillars of heaven tremble and are astonished at his reproof" (Job 26:11).

**Pillars of Hercules, the** *(Rock of) Gibraltar, Europe, and Jebel Musa, Africa.* The two promontories at the eastern end of the Strait of Gibraltar, poetically known as **Abyla** and **Calpe**, are fabled to have been set up by Hercules as a memorial in his travels to seize the cattle of Geryon. Hence their name.

**Pineapple State, The** *Hawaii, USA.* Hawaii deserves its nickname as a leading producer of pineapples.

**Pine Tree State, the** *Maine, USA.* Much of the state is covered with forests of pine, spruce, and fir, and a pine appears on the state seal.

> The good old Pine-tree state is pretty well represented in this locality [*The Boston Transcript*, 1888].

**Pink City, the** *Jaipur, India.* The city was founded in 1727 by Maharajah Jai Singh II, who ordered the houses to be painted pink to create the impression of red sandstone. They were repainted in 1876 on the occasion of a visit by Prince Albert Edward (the future Edward VII). Hence the sobriquet.

> (1) In the eighteenth century AD, Maharajah Jai Singh decided to lay out his 'pink city' of Jaipur in Rajasthan [John Keay, *India: A History*, 2000].
> (2) Full day excursion to Jaipur, the 'Pink City' and capital of the state of Rajasthan [Travel ad, *The Times Magazine*, January 22, 2005].

**Pink Town, the** *Toulouse, France.* The city

owes its nickname (French *la Ville Rose*) to the local red brick from which many of the houses in its older quarter are built, as described in the quote below.

> Characteristic deep-pink bricks, baked from the alluvial clay of the river, give the medieval city its name of "La Ville Rose" [*Sunday Times*, August 1, 2004].

**Pirate City, the** *Tampa, Florida, USA*. The port city was so nicknamed at a time when the Spanish pirate Gasparilla (died *c.* 1821) had his headquarters here. Tampa holds an annual festival celebrating Gasparilla, and the local football team, the Tampa Bay Buccaneers, are named in his honor.

**Pirate Coast** see in Appendix 1, p. 269.

**Piter** *St. Petersburg, Russia*. A traditional Russian shortening of the city's name, pronounced rather like English "Peter" and sometimes actually anglicized as such. *Cp.* **St. Pete's**.

> "Piter" (as it's affectionately known) [*The Rough Guide to St Petersburg*, 2004].

**Pittsburgh of India, the** *Jamshedpur, India*. The city, also known as **Steel City**, is so nicknamed for its great production of iron and steel.

**Pittsburgh of the South, the** *Birmingham, Alabama, USA*. A mutual comparison between this steel-producing city, named for its English original, and the **Birmingham of America**.

**Pittsy** *Pittsburgh, Pennsylvania, USA*. A colloquial short form of the city's name.

**Pivot City, the** *Geelong, Australia*. The origin of the Victoria city's former nickname is best explained by the quote below.

> The Pivot City is a sobriquet invented by the citizens of Geelong to symbolise it as the point on which the fortunes of the colony would culminate and revolve [William Kelly, *Life in Victoria*, 1859].

**PJ** *Petaling Jaya, Malaysia*. An initial-based short name for the city, established in 1953 as a satellite settlement of Kuala Lumpur, the national capital, and now one of its suburbs.

> Buses to PJ run regularly from the Kelang bus station in KL [*Lonely Planet Malaysia, Singapore & Brunei*, 1999].

**Place of the Sacred Cow, the** *Karur, India*. According to Hindu legend, the god Brahma began the work of creation in Karur. Hence the name, referring to the cow as a sacred animal for Hindus.

**Plain, the** *Salisbury Plain, England*. The extensive tract of chalk upland north of Salisbury in Wiltshire, the setting for Stonehenge, is sometimes known by this shortened name.

> The vast grey-green desert that is 'The Plain' [Hogg, p. 301].

**Plain City of the Queans** or **Queens, the** *Bathurst, Australia*. A joky metathesis of the New South Wales city's prim nickname, **Queen City of the Plains**.

**Plantation State, the** *Rhode Island, USA*. The sobriquet derives from the state's official name as the State of Rhode Island and Providence Plantations, the latter referring to the first settlement at Providence made by the minister Roger Williams in 1636. *See* **Land of Roger Williams**.

**Planter of the Lion, the** *Venice, Italy*. The name is a personification popularized by Byron in the quote below. The words are an English rendering of Italian *Piantaleone*, "Pantaleone," a saint specially favored in Venice, his name being popularly interpreted as *pianta leone*, "plants a lion," referring to the republican standard (and present civic coat of arms), which shows the winged lion of St. Mark, patron of Venice, to whom the city's famous cathedral is dedicated. The lion holds an open book with the Latin words "*PAX TIBI MARCE, EVANGELISTA MEA*" ("Peace to thee, O Mark, my evangelist"). The concept is of a Venetian warrior bearing the banner into battle and "planting" it as an emblem of victory. The saint's name, ultimately the source of "pantaloon" and so of "pants," is really Greek in origin and means "all-merciful."

> In youth she [i.e. Venice] was all glory,— a new Tyre;
>   Her very by-word sprung from victory,
>   The "Planter of the Lion," which through fire
>   And blood she bore o'er subject earth and sea
> [Lord Byron, *Childe Harold's Pilgrimage*, 1812].

**Plate, River** *Río de la Plata, South America*. The traditional English name of the estuary of the Paraná and Uruguay rivers, itself meaning "river of silver." The English name (which fortuitously suggests "silver plate") became familiar from the 1939 Battle of the River Plate between a British cruiser squadron of three ships and the German pocket battleship *Graf Spee* and later from the 1956 movie based on it.

**Platinum Coast** see in Appendix 1, p. 269.

**Playground of England** see in Appendix 1, p. 269.

**Playground of Europe, the** *Switzerland*. Switzerland has long attracted skiers and climbers as well as vacationers who come to visit the spas or indulge themselves at a luxury hotel in the country's spectacular Alpine setting.

**Playground of the Middle West, the** *(1) Indiana, USA; (2) Wisconsin, USA*. Both states have a good claim to the promotional name. Indiana attracts visitors through the mineral springs at West Baden and French Lick, the Wyandotte Cave, one of the largest natural caverns in the USA, and the famous automobile race at Indianapolis. Wisconsin draws vacationers by hosting tourist and recreational activity in its scenic forest and lake country.

**Playground of the Nation, the** *Minnesota, USA.* The state's broad woodlands and innumerable lakes offer scope for a host of recreational and sporting activities, from swimming and boating to camping and fishing. Hence the nickname.

> Like hundreds of others we wish our vacation would never end, and we know now why Minnesota has become the "Playground of the Nation" [A.E. Ford, *My Minnesota*, 1929].

**Playground of the North, the** *New Brighton, England.* The promotional name aims to lure visitors to this popular resort across the Mersey estuary from Liverpool. *Cp.* **Playground of the South**

> Both the "Playground of the North" and the "Paris of the North" are hoping that the ripples of regeneration currently flowing through Liverpool … will reach them [*The Times*, August 7, 2004].

**Playground of the South, the** *Southend-on-Sea, England.* A former promotional name for the popular Essex resort, echoing its real name. *Cp.* **Playground of the North.**

**Plett** *Plettenberg Bay, South Africa.* A colloquial short name for the Western Cape resort and retirement village on the bay of the same name.

> Beyond "Plett," the N2 winds through ancient tracts of eucalypt and pine trees [*Sunday Times* (South Africa Supplement), March 13, 2005].

**Plug Street** *Ploegsteert, Belgium.* A British soldiers' World War I version of the name of the Flemish village near the French border.

**Plymouth of the West, the** *San Diego, California, USA.* San Diego was one of the first European settlements on the West Coast, founded in 1769 by the Franciscan missionary Junípero Serra. Its name pays tribute to Plymouth, Massachusetts, the first permanent settlement in New England, founded by the Pilgrim Fathers in 1620.

**Poacher Country** *Lincolnshire Wolds, England.* A touristic name for the hilly region, from the popular folksong "The Lincolnshire Poacher."

**Poca** or **Pocaloo** *Pocatello, Idaho, USA.* A colloquial short form of the city's name.

**Poets' Corner** see in Appendix 1, p. 269.

**Poet's Country** see in Appendix 1, p. 269.

**Polar Bear Capital of the World, the** *Churchill, Manitoba, Canada.* The seaport city lies on a polar bear migration route and the animals often wander into town. Hence the nickname.

**Polar Star State, the** *Maine, USA.* The state's nickname refers poetically to its geographical position, at the northeastern tip of the USA, on the border with Canada.

**Poldark Country** see in Appendix 1, p. 269.

**Polish Corridor** see in Appendix 1, p. 269.

**Polish Fujiyama, the** *Cisowa Góra, Poland.* The hill in northeastern Poland, near the Lithuanian border, is so nicknamed as the site of pre–Christian sacred rituals. It thus shares an association with the Japanese mountain itself known as the **Parnassus of Japan**.

**Polish Manchester, the** *Łódź, Poland.* The city grew from a small village into a major industrial center in the 19th century, earning a comparison with the English manufacturing capital.

**Political Bellwether, the** *New Hampshire, USA.* It is traditionally in New Hampshire that campaigning begins in the presidential primaries. The state is thus a "bellwether," like the leading sheep in a flock with a bell around its neck.

**Polomint City** *East Kilbride, Scotland.* The New Town near Glasgow, designated in 1947, is so nicknamed for its many roundabouts (rotaries), resembling the named circular mint with its central hole. *Cp.* **Hole with the Mint**.

**Pomfret** *Pontefract, England.* The name of the Yorkshire town was long familiar in this form, and still exists for the Pomfret Gallery here and more generally for the Pomfret (or Pontefract) cakes made in the town. (They are not cakes but a type of round flat licorice candy.)

> Lord Rivers and Lord Grey are sent to Pomfret [William Shakespeare, *Richard III*, c.1592].

**Pomgolia** *England or Britain.* A facetious New Zealand name for the "mother country," blending "Pom" (*see* **Pommyland**) with the name of Mongolia, implying Britain's remoteness, as if **Outer Mongolia**.

**Pommyland** *England or Britain.* As a traditional Australian nickname for a Briton, "Pommy" or "Pom" is a shortening of "pomegranate," itself probably a whimsical alteration of "immigrant."

> (1) It amuses me to hear the way the Pommies run the Australian girls down. They are forgetting that they come out here for their bread and butter, and also good money in hand, more than they got in Pommyland [*Truth* (Sydney), October 1, 1916].
> (2) Sir Robert himself wanted to be a whiskey-taster at the Melbourne show, but ended up as some kind of wharfie [i.e. waterside worker] over

in Pommy Land [Frank Hardy, *Billy Borker Yarns Again*, 1967].

**Pomona** *Mainland, Orkney Islands, Scotland.* On the face of it, the alternate name for the largest island of the Orkneys appears to represent the name of the Roman goddess of fruit trees. But this is hardly appropriate here, and the name probably arose from a medieval mapmaker's error, perhaps in connection with the fruit trees on some other island, real or mythical. *See also* **Mainland.**

**Pompeii of Africa, the** *Asmara, Eritrea.* The capital city is so named because, despite being a base for invasion and a scene of armed conflict, it has been preserved, like Pompeii in Italy, buried under volcanic ash in AD 79.

"Africa's Pompeii" as it has been dubbed [Dodd/Donald, p. 329)

**Pompeii of the Caribbean, the** *Plymouth, Montserrat, West Indies.* The island capital was so nicknamed after it was buried by the eruption of the Soufrière Hills volcano in 1997.

The ruins of Plymouth remain a shockingly vivid testament to the havoc caused by the volcano. The town is a modern-day Pompeii: eerily deserted and still covered in ash [*Sunday Times Magazine*, July 17, 2005].

**Pompeii of the East, the** *Jerash, Jordan.* The ancient city of the Decapolis, also known as Gerasa, is probably the best-preserved Palestinian city of Roman times. Its ruins include a long street with over 100 columns, two theaters, and a triumphal arch. Hence the comparison with the famous city in Italy.

The ancient Graeco-Roman city of Jerash is known as the Pompeii of the East and was built over 2,000 years ago [Travel brochure issued with *Sunday Times*, December 19, 2004].

**Pompey** *Portsmouth, England.* The nickname of the Hampshire city, port, and dockyard is of uncertain origin. Theories to explain it include: (1) It is a corruption of *bom bahia*, the supposed Portuguese origin of the name of **Bombay** (Mumbai), applied to Portsmouth by Portuguese sailors, from a similarity between the Indian port and the English one; (2) It refers to the port's Roman origins, with a reference to the Roman general Pompeius, known in English as Pompey; (3) It evolved from French *pompier*, "fireman," a nickname given to local soldiers when they were assigned the demeaning task of lining a marchpast, a duty enacted by members of the Paris Fire Brigade; (4) It derives from the captured French ship *Pompée*, which played a key role in the 1797 Spithead naval mutiny. Whatever the actual source, the name probably arose as naval jargon. It was early also the nickname

of Portsmouth football club, as in quote (1) below.

(1) Wilkie, amid tremendous cheering from the Pompey lads, won the toss, and played with the wind in their favour [*Evening News*, December 9, 1899].

(2) An old roadman [said]: "There's been a lot of unemployment in Pompey and Southampton" [*The Observer*, March 22, 1959].

(3) Lloyd's [of London] had gone to unusually imaginative lengths to pay homage to another national institution — Lord Nelson. And to pay homage, moreover, on the very date, 200 years ago, when he sailed from Pompey in *Victory* for his last meeting with destiny [*The Times*, September 19, 2005].

**Pond, the** *Atlantic Ocean.* The nickname humorously trivializes one of the world's greatest oceans. The name is often qualified, as **Big Pond, Herring Pond, Millpond.** *Cp.* **Puddle.**

Great Britain has been our greatest ally through wars and other international disasters. However, not one bit of news has come through about assistance from our friends across the Pond [Letter to the Editor, *The Times*, September 2, 2005].

**Pontic Sea, the** *Black Sea.* The poetic name derives from Greek *pontos*, "sea." *Cp.* **Propontis.**

Like to the Pontick sea,
Whose icy current and compulsive course
Ne'er feels retiring ebb, but keeps due on
To the Propontic and the Hellespont [William Shakespeare, *Othello*, 1604].

**Ponty** *(1) Pontypool, Wales; (2) Pontypridd, Wales.* A local colloquial name for both towns, handily formed from the first half of their names, which happens to end with a diminutive-type -y suffix.

**Pool, the** *Liverpool, England.* A local colloquial name for the Merseyside city and port, where the original "pool" was a former tidal creek. Quote (3) below is worded in Scouse, the local dialect. *See* **Scouseland.**

(1) Liverpool is the pool of life [Carl Jung, quoted in Dodd/Donald, p. 31].

(2) His origins: a street of back-to-backs ... off the Scotland Road ... the toughest part of the Pool to grow up in [Peter Driscoll, *The Wilby Conspiracy*, 1972].

(3) Ar Alf sez darrevry Scouse Big'ead's brood special fer d'Pool, like. ("Our Alf says that every Scouse Bighead [beer] is brewed specially for Liverpool.") [Beer ad, *The Observer*, August 8, 1976].

**Poor Man's Palm Beach, the** *St. Petersburg, Florida, USA.* The nickname implies that the winter resort is an inferior version of the summer one.

Another nickname for the town is the Poor Man's Palm Beach [Ring Lardner in *The Cosmopolitan*, July 1924].

**Poor Man's Paradise, the** *San Francisco, Cal-*

*ifornia, USA.* The name suggests that the city has affordable pleasures and delights for everyone, the least expensive being one's pure presence there.

**Popo** *Popocatépetl, Mexico.* A short colloquial name in American and British use for the volcano south of Mexico City. A variant form from the 1930s was "Popeye."

**Poppy Alley** see in Appendix 1, p. 269.

**Poppyland** see in Appendix 1, p. 269.

**Pork City** *see* **Porkopolis**

**Porkies, the** *Porcupine Mountains, Michigan, USA.* A friendly nickname for the mountains in northern Michigan and for the Porcupine Mountains Wilderness State Park there.

**Porkopolis** or **Hogopolis** *(1) Chicago, Illinois, USA; (2) Cincinnati, Ohio, USA.* Both cities earned their 19th-century nickname as renowned porkpacking centers. The name itself is on the lines of **Cottonopolis**. *Cp.* **Hog Butcher for the World**.

(1) (Cincinnati) Cincinnati, the "Porkopolis" of the Union [William M. Punshon, 1868, in Frederic W. Macdonald, *Life of William Morley Punshon*, 1887].

(2) (Chicago) She has reached the position of the porkopolis of the world [*Chicago Times*, April 16, 1881].

(3) (Cincinnati) The many meatpacking plants earned Cincinnati the nickname 'Porkopolis' and provided enough leftover lard for Messrs Procter & Gamble to become one of the world's largest soap makers [*Lonely Planet USA*, 2004].

**Pornography Capital of the World, the** *San Fernando Valley, California, USA.* The valley has been so dubbed as a center of the porno video industry. Over 95 percent of all such videos in the USA are said to be made here. *Cp.* **World Capital of the Adult Entertainment Industry**.

Raised in the San Fernando Valley in California— "the pornography capital of the world"—[US singer Ambrosia] Parsley was surrounded by a colourful family [*The Times*, April 9, 2005].

**Porta Gutta** *Port Augusta, Australia.* A caustically punning name for the South Australia seaport town, referring to its seedy side, as outlined in the quote below.

Unkindly dubbed "Porta Gutta" by Adelaide's smart set, who paint dire pictures of a town rife with petty crime [*The Rough Guide to Australia*, 2001].

**Port Arthur** *Lüshun, China.* The original name of the seaport derives from a British naval officer, Lieutenant William C. Arthur, who in August 1856, during the Second Opium War, towed a damaged British warship into the natural harbor here to effect repairs. His name caught on, and was adopted by the Russians when they

leased the port in 1898. In 1905 it was captured by the Japanese, who renamed it Ryojun, but reverted to Russian control in 1945, when it became a joint Sino-Soviet base. The Russians left in 1955, after which the Chinese name officially prevailed, although the traditional English name is still current.

**Portingale** *Portugal.* An old poetic name for the seafaring country, probably from Middle French *portingallais* (modern *portugais*), "Portuguese." The suggestion of "port in gale" must have helped.

(1) With "Tu mi chamas's" from Portingale
To soothe our ears, lest Italy should fail [Lord Byron, *Don Juan*, 1824].

(2) God! let never soe old a man
Marry soe young a wife
As did old Robin of Portingale! ["Old Robin of Portingale," *The Oxford Book of Ballads*, 1910].

**Port Nick** *Port Nicholson, New Zealand.* A handy shortening and part-personalization of the name of the harbor, on which the New Zealand capital of Wellington lies.

[The name was] abbreviated to 'Port Nick' early, and to 'Poneke' by the Maoris [Shadbolt, p. 196].

**Port of Big Ships, the** *Port Hedland, Australia.* A self-promotional name for the Western Australia commercial port.

Labelling itself rather clumsily "The Port of Big Ships," it's an iron and salt port [*The Rough Guide to Australia*, 2001].

**Port o' Missing Men, the** *San Francisco, California, USA.* The nickname refers to the seaport city's potential for hiding a fugitive, either because he could lose himself among the cosmopolitan populace or because he could escape on board one of the ships docked here.

**Porto Rico** *Puerto Rico, West Indies.* The former name of the island state (meaning "rich port") remained current for some time after it was officially changed in 1932.

In 1898, Spain and the United States went to war and the U.S. won, with the result that the U.S. annexed Porto Rico [Johnson, p. 202].

**Portuguese Paradise, the** *Sintra (Cintra), Portugal.* The city and resort, rapturously described by Portuguese and foreign writers, the latter including Byron (as in the quote below), is noted for its commanding site on a mountain amid orange groves and vineyards. Hence the entirely apt nickname.

Lo! Cintra's glorious Eden intervenes
In variegated maze of mount and glen [Lord Byron, *Childe Harold's Pilgrimage*, 1812].

**Poshopolis** *Beverly Hills, Los Angeles, California, USA.* A humorous nickname of the **Cottonopolis** type, describing the city's prestige as a place of wealth, luxury, and fame.

**Poshtershire** *Gloucestershire, England.* A punning nickname based on that of the county, given for its upper-class sporting and social connections, as instanced in the quote below.

> During the summer plenty of young aristocrats mingle like meerkats at Cirencester Park for the polo competitions. No wonder the county has been dubbed "Poshtershire" [*The Times*, August 6, 2004].

**Potch** *Potchefstroom, South Africa.* A colloquial short form of the North-West Province town's name.

> Potch this week admitted a coloured student to its classrooms [*Sunday Times* (Johannesburg), March 19, 1978].

**Pothole City** *Charleston, West Virginia, USA.* The state capital is not the only city to be so nicknamed for its poor highway maintenance.

**Pothole County, the** *Co. Cavan, Ireland.* Owing to the friable nature of the soil, many of the county's roads are liable to subsidence, and thus readily form potholes. Hence the occasional nickname.

**Pot Smugglers' Paradise** see in Appendix 1, p. 269.

**Potteries, the** *Stoke-on-Trent, England.* The Staffordshire district, famed for its production of china and earthenware, comprises Stoke-on-Trent and the surrounding towns that are now included in the city but that were formerly separate and jointly known as the **Five Towns**. (A local nickname for the region is "the Pisseries," from "pisspot," for the sanitaryware made there.) *See also* **Creative County**.

> (1) This [railway] line takes us into the heart of the Potteries [Karl Baedeker, *Handbook to Great Britain*, 1890].
> (2) Neither Waterford Wedgwood nor Royal Doulton ... have managed to escape the relentless downward spiral that has gripped the Potteries since Asia reclaimed its trade [*The Times*, October 22, 2004].
> (3) Stoke-on-Trent, well known throughout the world for its fine china, is affectionately known as "The Potteries" [Travel brochure, *Staffordshire*, 2005].

**Pozzy** *Pozières, France.* A nickname used by British and Australian soldiers for the village near Albert, northern France, a scene of fierce fighting in World War I.

**PR** *Puerto Rico, West Indies.* An initialism of the island state's name.

> The pull of NY is such that there are allegedly more Puerto Ricans there than in PR itself [Dodd/Donald, p. 99].

**Prairie Province, the** *Manitoba, Canada.* Manitoba is the easternmost of the three Prairie Provinces, the other two being Saskatchewan and Alberta. Hence the nickname, given as the first province of the three to be established.

> *The Prairie Province: Sketches of Travel from Lake Ontario to Lake Winnipeg* [J.C. Hamilton, book title, 1876].

**Prairie State, the** *Illinois, USA.* Much of the state is covered by flat prairies, so that the nickname is entirely appropriate.

> (1) Federal Coon Whiggery extinct in the Prairie State! [Headline, *People's Advocate* (Carrollton, Illinois), August 6, 1842].
> (2) Illinois, the "Prairie State," then proved that she was as rich in her patriotism as in her soil and exhaustless resources [Orville J. Victor, *History of the Southern Rebellion*, 1861].

**Premier County, the** *Co. Tipperary, Ireland.* The nickname, chiefly found in Gaelic sports reports, as in the quote below, is sometimes said to refer to the county's prominent Butler family. More realistically, it could denote its agricultural prosperity, as the region of the **Golden Vale** (see in Appendix 1, p. 269).

> '99 leader still stokes the Premier County fire [Headline, *Sunday Tribune*, September 3, 2000)

**Premier State, the** *New South Wales, Australia.* New South Wales, discovered and named in 1770 by Captain Cook, was the first Australian colony to be established by the British. Hence the name.

**President's Playground, the** *Cape May, New Jersey, USA.* The city, one of the nation's oldest beach resorts, is so nicknamed because US presidents Lincoln, Grant, Arthur, Buchanan, Hayes, and Benjamin Harrison vacationed here.

**Prettiest Town in the South Pacific, the** *Madang, Papua New Guinea.* The town earned its nickname by virtue of its parks and waterways.

**Prettiest Village in the Lake District, the** *Hawkshead, England.* The picturesque Cumbria village, with its old cottages and narrow courtyards, is a fair contender for the unique title. *See* **Lake District** in Appendix 1, p. 269.

> Hawkshead is often trumpeted as the 'prettiest village in the Lake District,' a claim that could well be justified thanks to the measures that have been taken to keep it that way [Charlie Godfrey-Faussett, *Footprint England*, 2004].

**Prettiest Village in Yorkshire, the** *Thornton-le-Dale, England.* The title claimed by the North Yorkshire village is epitomized by a picture-perfect thatched cottage near the parish church, said to be the most photographed house in England. The right to the unique claim has been disputed by some, as in quote (2) below.

> (1) It is the tourist heart along the stream that earns Thornton Dale [*sic*] its reputation as the loveliest village in Yorkshire [Hadfield 1980, p. 338].

(2) The village of Thornton-le-Dale would have you believe it's the 'prettiest village in Yorkshire.' Unfortunately, that's just not the case [Charlie Godfrey-Faussett, *Footprint England*, 2004].

**Pride of the North, the** *Newcastle upon Tyne, England.* A local nickname for the northeastern city and port.

Newcastletonians also call it 'The Pride of the North' [Partridge 1984, p. 179].

**Pride of the Ocean** *see* **Gem of the Ocean**

**Pride of the West, the** *Cincinnati, Ohio, USA.* A former nickname for the city on the lines of **Queen of the West**.

**Principality, the** *Wales.* Wales was made an English principality in 1284, and Edward II, who was born that year, was created the first Prince of Wales by his father, Edward I, in 1301. The eldest son of the British monarch has borne the title ever since. Prince Charles, eldest son of Queen Elizabeth II, was given the title in 1958. *Cp.* **Duchy**.

(1) Of your fashionable sea-bathing resorts, the Principality boasts a pair — Tenby and Aberystwith [Frederic E. Gretton, *Memory's Harkback through Half-a-Century 1850–58*, 1889].
(2) The Principality, a land of 8,000 square miles, 2.0 million people and a lot of sheep [*The Times*, October 6, 2004].

**Prom, the** *Wilsons Promontory, Australia.* A colloquial short name for the cape in southern Victoria, and in particular for the well-known national park established there.

Victoria's most popular national park, "The Prom" boasts some superb coastal scenery and bushwalks [*The Rough Guide to Australia*, 2001].

**Promised Land, the** *(1) Canaan; (2) Palestine.* The name refers to the land that God promised to Abraham and his descendants, as described in the Bible: "For all the land which thou seest, to thee will I give it, and to thy seed for ever" (Genesis 13:15). The land itself was Canaan, later known as Palestine, which the Israelites occupied and gradually conquered. In general terms, the name denotes any desired place, and in particular heaven. Quote (3) below is based on words in *The Excursionist* of May 3, 1867.

(1) By faith he [i.e. Abraham] sojourned in the land of promise, as in a strange country [Hebrews 11:9].
(2) Over Mount Sion, and, though that were large,
Over the Promised Land to God so dear [John Milton, *Paradise Lost*, 1667].
(3) [English tourist agent Thomas] Cook had found it impossible to obtain much definite information about Palestine which was, the dragoman indicated, more a land of promises than the

Promised Land [Piers Brendon, *Thomas Cook: 150 Years of Popular Tourism*, 1991].

**Propontis** or **Propontic Sea** *Sea of Marmara, Turkey.* The classical name of the sea between Europe and Asia, preserved in poetry, derives from Greek *pro*, "before," and *pontos*, "sea," the latter meaning the Black Sea, with which it connects through the Bosporus. *Cp.* **Pontic Sea**. (The Symplegades in the quote below are two rocks at the entrance to the Bosporus said to close in on ships passing between them.)

Where the narrowing Symplegades whitened the straits of Propontis with spray [A.C. Swinburne, *Atalanta in Calydon*, 1865].

**Prostitution Capital of the South, the** *New Orleans, Louisiana, USA.* A former nickname for the city, of obvious origin.

**Protestant Rome, the** *Geneva, Switzerland.* The French theologian John Calvin made the city the intellectual center of Protestant Europe in the 16th century. Hence its sobriquet, comparing it to Rome as the center of Catholicism. The epithet is now historical, as just over half of the city's inhabitants are Roman Catholic. *Cp.* **Athens of Switzerland**.

During the period of religious persecution the "Protestant Rome" became a city of refuge into which flowed a constant stream of emigration from France [*The Spectator*, January 27, 1912].

**Protestant Vatican of the South, the** *Nashville, Tennessee, USA.* Nashville is a noted religious center and the national headquarters of a number of boards and agencies of the United Methodist Church. Hence the name, comparing the city to the Vatican as the headquarters of Catholicism.

**Proud Preston** *Preston, England.* A historic alliterative name for the Lancashire city for the vaunting self-awareness of its better-educated citizens.

(1) The Town ... is full of Gentlemen, Attorneys, Proctors, and Notaries... The People are gay here, though not perhaps the richer for that; but it has on this Account obtained the name of Proud Preston [Daniel Defoe, *A Tour Thro' the Whole Island of Great Britain*, 1724–6].
(2) Wilfred ... was slain at Proud Preston, in Lancashire, on the day that General Carpenter attacked the barricades [Sir Walter Scott, *Rob Roy*, 1818].
(3) The old lines ... are, 'Proud Preston, Poor people, High church, And low steeple' [*Notes and Queries*, 1852].

**Province, the** *Northern Ireland.* The title, used mainly by Protestants and the media, refers to the territory's historic origins as part of the former Irish province of Ulster.

The most secret military unit serving in Northern

Ireland is to be pulled out of the Province and posted to Iraq [*The Times*, April 18, 2005].

**Province of Brick, the** *London, England.* The British capital was so named by the French writer Madame de Staël (1766–1817), who lived in Argyll Street after being banished from France by Napoleon.

**Provinces** see in Appendix 1, p. 269.

**Provo** *Providenciales, Turks and Caicos Islands, West Indies.* A short colloquial name for the island, with its luxury resorts.

**P-Town** *(1) Philadelphia, Pennsylvania, USA; (2) Provincetown, Massachusetts, USA.* An initialized abbreviation for the city and the resort town.

(Provincetown) "P-Town"— the "gayest" town in America [*The Times*, May 17, 2004].

**Puddle, the** *Atlantic Ocean.* A humorous diminutive for the great ocean, especially in phrases such as "this side of the puddle" or "across the puddle." *Cp.* **Pond.**

For many years the American company ... have made fine enlarging frames (masking frames this side of the puddle) both for retail distribution and for exclusive use by Simmon-Emegs [*SLR Camera*, August 1978].

**Puke State, the** *Missouri, USA.* The state is said to take its former nickname from the "Pikes," or white migratory workers from Pike County, Missouri, although it may well come from "puke" as a term for an obnoxious person (from the word in its sense "to vomit"), as a derogatory nickname for a native of Missouri given by a resident of neighboring Illinois.

**Pumpkinshire** *Boston, Massachusetts, USA.* An old nickname for the state capital, dating from the 18th century and referring to the pumpkins grown and eaten there.

**Punta** *Punta del Este, Uruguay.* A short colloquial name for one of the most popular beach resorts in South America.

"Punta" is a rather rudely proportioned peninsula in the corner of the country [*Sunday Times*, March 27, 2005].

**Puritan City, the** *Boston, Massachusetts, USA.* Boston was settled in 1630 by Puritan Englishmen of the Massachusetts Bay Company and for the first 50 years of its existence was a self-governing Puritan community. Hence the sobriquet. *Cp.* **Puritan State.**

**Puritan State, the** *Massachusetts, USA.* The nickname stems from the Massachusetts Bay Colony, one of the original English settlements in the present state, settled in 1630 by a group of around 1,000 Puritan refugees from England. *Cp.* **Puritan City.**

**Purple Land, the** *Uruguay.* In 1811, Uruguay became involved in the wars of independence in the Spanish American colonies, bringing years of bloodshed and depredation that finally brought independence in 1828 but that were followed by a civil war lasting from 1839 to 1851. Hence the name.

I will call my book *The Purple Land*; for what more suitable name can one find for a country so stained with the blood of her children? [W.H. Hudson, *The Purple Land*, 1885].

**PWV** see in Appendix 1, p. 269.

**Quad Cities** see in Appendix 1, p. 269.

**Quake City** *San Francisco, California, USA.* The seaport city has suffered serious earthquakes resulting from its location in the vicinity of the San Andreas Fault, especially in 1906 and 1989. Hence the name. *See also* **Shaky City.**

**Quaker City, the** *Philadelphia, Pennsylvania, USA.* The city was laid out in 1682 by the English Quaker reformer William Penn as a colony of refuge for the peaceable Quakers. Hence the nickname. *Cp.* **Quaker State.**

The First Troop, Philadelphia City Cavalry ... celebrated its 200th anniversary on November 15th, 1974, the night we flew into the "Quaker City" [*Country Life*, January 2, 1975].

**Quaker State, the** *Pennsylvania, USA.* The state dates from 1682, when William Penn founded Philadelphia (*see* **Quaker City**) as a haven of religious tolerance for his fellow Quakers. Hence the nickname.

Five nicknames are given to the State of Pennsylvania; namely, the *Coal State*, the *Keystone State*, the *Oil State*, the *Quaker State*, and the *Steel State* [G.E. Shankle, *State Names*, 1934].

**Quaky Isles, the** *New Zealand.* The nickname refers to the many earthquakes and earth tremors experienced in New Zealand.

**Quarter, the** *French Quarter, New Orleans, Louisiana, USA.* A short name for the city district, also known as the Vieux Carré (French, "Old Square"), with its distinctive Spanish-French architecture.

'There may be a few costumes. That's what's so wonderful about New Orleans. You can masquerade and Mardi Gras all year round if you want to. Really, sometimes the Quarter is like one big costume ball' [John Kennedy Toole, *The Confederacy of Dunces*, 1980].

**Quartier** *see* **Latin Quarter** in Appendix 1, p. 269.

**Queen Above All Other Cities, the** *Paris, France.* The burgeoning French capital was so dubbed by the theologian and chronicler St. Abbo of Fleury as early as the 9th century.

**Queen City, the** *(1) Charlotte, North Carolina, USA; (2) Cincinnati, Ohio, USA.* Charlotte's title derives from its proper name, given in honor of Princess Charlotte Sophia of Mecklenburg-Strelitz, queen of George III. Cincinnati was so nicknamed for its commercial supremacy. *Cp.* **Queen of the West.**

**Queen City of the Lakes, the** *(1) Buffalo, New York, USA; (2) Chicago, Illinois, USA* . The nicknames of both cities relate to their position and importance. Buffalo is on Lake Erie, Chicago on Lake Michigan.

**Queen City of the Mississippi, the** *St. Louis, Missouri, USA.* The nickname refers to the city's size and commercial importance as the nation's second-largest river port.

**Queen City of the Mountains, the** *Knoxville, Tennessee, USA.* The name relates to the city's importance as a trade and shipping center and to its prime site on the Tennessee River in the Great Smoky Mountains, surrounded by mountains and lakes.

**Queen City of the Pacific** *see* **Queen of the Pacific**

**Queen City of the Plains, the** *(1) Bathurst, Australia; (2) Denver, Colorado, USA; (3) Regina, Saskatchewan, Canada.* Each city has "queen" status in its respective state and province, and each lies in or near a region of plains. Bathurst, New South Wales, was founded in a region originally known as Bathurst Plains (*see also* **Plain City of the Queans**), while Regina is the distribution and service center for one of the world's largest wheat-growing plains (*cp.* **Granary of Canada**). The first reference in quote (2) below is to Denver as the **Mile High City.**

(1) (Denver) So much for my feeling toward the Queen City of the plains and peaks [Walt Whitman, *Specimen Days and Collect,* 1882].

(2) (Denver) First-timers in Denver are often surprised that the city is not perched in the mountains... In fact it sits on flat plains — hence its other, and less well known nickname, the Queen City of the Plains [Dodd/Donald, p. 185].

**Queen City of the South, the** *(1) Cebu, Philippines; (2) Sydney, Australia.* Cebu owes its nickname to its commercial and industrial importance in the southern half of the Philippines. Sydney, in southeastern Australia, is capital of New South Wales and a major commercial and manufacturing center. Hence the nicknames of both cities.

**Queen City of the West, the** *(1) Bath, England; (2) Wilcannia, Australia.* The English city derives its nickname from its status as a fashionable spa and the splendor of its Georgian architecture. The Australian town, in New South Wales, was formerly so titled as a major port on

the Darling River, from which produce was transported down to Adelaide.

(Bath) A fierce defence of the "Queen City Of The West" against the ravages of speculators when Bath was threatened with wholesale redevelopment [Video ad, *The Times,* August 7, 2004].

**Queen City of the World, the** *Paris, France.* The French capital was so titled by Napoleon III in the 1850s and 1860s, at the time when Baron Haussmann was implementing his radical improvements (*see* **Capital of Progress**).

**Queen City of Vermont, the** *Burlington, Vermont, USA.* Vermont's largest city was accorded its sobriquet both for its size and importance and for its picturesque location on a hillside sloping towards Lake Champlain and the Adirondacks, with the Green Mountains to the east.

**Queen o' a' the Borders** *see* **Queen o' the Borders**

**Queen of American Watering Places, the** *Monterey, California, USA.* A former touristic name for the resort city.

The Hotel del Monte, a 'veritable paradise' set in vast, beautifully landscaped grounds at Monterey, 'Queen of American Watering Places' [Piers Brendon, *Thomas Cook: 150 Years of Popular Tourism,* 1991, quoting from *The Excursionist,* November 1888].

**Queen of British India, the** *Lahore, Pakistan.* The city came under British rule in 1849 and was so nicknamed as the capital of the imperial Punjab. It passed to Pakistan in 1947 and remains the capital of the province of Punjab.

**Queen of Cities, the** *(1) Baghdad, Iraq; (2) Rome, Italy.* Both capital cities deserve their nickname for their historic cultural, religious, and commercial importance.

**Queen of Floods, the** *Mississippi River, USA.* The former nickname refers both to the great river's ever-rolling stream and to the frequency with which it overflows its banks and levees, especially in spring.

Through a vast uncultivated territory coursed the Queen of Floods and her many tributaries [Opening words of newspaper article, 1832, quoted in Hendrickson, p. 598].

**Queen of Idaho Ghost Towns, the** *Silver City, Idaho, USA.* As the name of the present village implies, there was a silver boom here. As the nickname indicates, little of the original settlement remains (some 70 buildings in all).

**Queen of Hill Stations, the** *Udagamandalam, India.* The resort and tourist center in the Nilgiri Hills, at one time also familiar as Ootacamund (*see* **Ooty**), was so nicknamed as the colonial summer capital of the former state of Madras.

**Queen of the Adriatic, the** *Venice, Italy.* The sobriquet essentially equates to that of **Jewel of the Adriatic**. *See also* **Bride of the Sea.**

> What a funny old city this Queen of the Adriatic is! Narrow streets, vast, gloomy marble palaces ... and all partly submerged [Mark Twain, *The Innocents Abroad*, 1869].

**Queen of the Antilles** *see* **Pearl of the Antilles**

**Queen of the Brittany Resorts, the** *Dinard, France.* With its grand Victorian villas and its fine natural setting, the seaside resort has long been visited by the rich, and is still favored by an international clientèle. *Cp.* **Nice of the North.**

> Set in impressive rock scenery, by emerald seas and golden sands ... opposite St-Malo, Dinard lives up to its title of 'Queen of the Brittany Resorts' [Young, p. 168].

**Queen of the Coast, the** *Scarborough, England.* A nickname for the seaside resort formerly known as the **Queen of Watering Places.**

**Queen of the Cotswolds, the** *Painswick, England.* The stone-built Gloucestershire town, set in the Cotswold Hills, is famed for its beautiful old cottages and medieval inns. Hence its fair claim to its royal title.

> The 'Queen of the Cotswolds,' Painswick is a rare delight [*Lonely Planet Great Britain*, 2005].

**Queen of the Danube, the** *Budapest, Hungary.* The Hungarian capital has good claim to its former title as it evolved from the merger of two royal towns, Buda and Pest, on either side of the Danube.

> Day 4. Depart Prague and transfer to Budapest, known as the "Queen of the Danube" [Travel brochure issued with *Sunday Times*, December 11, 2005].

**Queen of the Dekkan, the** *Poona (Pune), India.* The cultural capital of the Maratha people, in Maharashtra state, is a major educational and cultural center, with a university and many historic and religious monuments. Hence the city's sobriquet, from its location in the Dekkan, India's great southern peninsula.

**Queen of the Earth, the** *Rome, Italy.* A status name similar to **Mistress of the World** or **Queen of Cities.**

> "The city which thou seest no other deem
> Than great and glorious Rome, queen of the earth" [John Milton, *Paradise Regained*, 1671].

**Queen of the East, the** *(1) Antakya, Turkey; (2) Jakarta, Indonesia.* The former capital of Syria, familiar under the name Antioch, was long celebrated as one of the supreme cities of the Middle East, while the Indonesian capital, founded in the 17th century as **Batavia**, was a major trade center of the Far East. Hence their well-deserved titles.

**Queen of the Eastern Archipelago, the** *Java, Indonesia.* Java merits its royal title as one of the most naturally beautiful and fertile islands of the Malay Archipelago (or Eastern Archipelago, as it was formerly known).

**Queen of the English Riviera, the** *Torquay, England.* The Devon resort lies at the heart of the **English Riviera** (see in Appendix 1, p. 269).

> Visit Torquay, the Queen of the English Rivieras [*sic*], this year [*Holiday Haunts 1961: Area No. 4, West of England and South and Central Wales*].

**Queen of the Hebrides, the** *Islay, Scotland.* The southernmost island of the Inner Hebrides is sometimes so known for its varied landscape and rich agricultural potential.

> Islaymen still believe that their island is the 'Queen of the Hebrides' [Booth/Perrott, p. 107]

**Queen of the Lakes, the** *Ullswater, England.* The second-largest lake in the Lake District is generally regarded as the most beautiful. Hence its justifiable sobriquet.

**Queen of the London Suburbs** *see* **Queen of the Suburbs**

**Queen of the Mexican Riviera, the** *Acapulco, Mexico.* The seaport city and international resort on the Pacific coast is famed for its favorable climate and fine beaches, like those of the French Riviera. *See also* **Pearl of the Pacific.**

**Queen of the Midlands, the** *Nottingham, England.* The Industrial Revolution of the early 19th century raised the profile of the city from an agrarian community to a prosperous manufacturing center. Hence the sobriquet.

> The awful truth is that the 'Queen of the Midlands' has been on a life-support machine since the 1980s [Sam Jordison and Dan Kieran, eds., *The Idler Book of Crap Towns II*, 2004].

**Queen of the Mississippi Valley, the** *St. Louis, Missouri, USA.* The name refers to the city and port's prime position on the Mississippi River below its confluence with the Missouri. *Cp.* **Queen City of the Mississippi.**

**Queen of the North, the** *(1) Edinburgh, Scotland; (2) St. Petersburg, Russia.* The Scottish capital has been so dubbed, especially in poetic use, with reference to its importance and its dominant presence. The same goes for the Russian city, better known as the **Venice of the North**. Quote (2) below refers to the Scottish poet Thomas Campbell.

> (1) (Edinburgh) Still, as of yore, Queen of the North!
> Still canst thou send thy children forth [Sir Walter Scott, *Marmion*, 1808].
> (2) (Edinburgh) My ingenious and valued

friend, Mr. Thomas Campbell, proposed to celebrate Edinburgh under the epithet here borrowed. But the "Queen of the North" has not been so fortunate as to receive from so eminent a pen the proposed distinction [Sir Walter Scott, explanatory note to phrase "Caledonia's Queen," *Marmion*, 1808].

(3) (St. Petersburg) There it was ... the "Queen of the North" standing proudly on the shores of the Neva and the Neva's many confluents and those canals dug by Czar Peter to make it look like another Amsterdam [Vladimir Nabokov, *Bagazh*, 1975].

**Queen of the North Isles, the** *Westray, Scotland.* The westernmost island of the northern group of Orkney Islands is sometimes so named for its varied landscape and for the panoramic view of the other islands from its highest point.

**Queen of the Orient, the** *Shanghai, China.* An alternate nickname for the city and port more commonly known as the **Pearl of the East**.

We cruise from the 'Queen of the Orient,' Shanghai, to the 'Heavenly Kingdom' of Sichuan [Travel brochure issued with *Sunday Times*, August 14, 2005].

**Queen of the Pacific, the** *San Francisco, California, USA.* The sobriquet describes the seaport city's dominant status on the Pacific seaboard.

(1) Local prejudice ... and proverbial procrastination ... unite to keep "Chinatown" practically a sealed book to the better-class denizens of the Queen City of the Pacific [*Harper's Magazine*, December 1880].

(2) For almost nine weeks, the shattered city, known not only as the "Queen of the Pacific," but as the "queen of larceny" as well, entered into a period of benign brotherhood [Howard Fast, *The Immigrants*, 1977].

**Queen of the Rinns, the** *Port Charlotte, Scotland.* The coastal village on the island of Islay, in the Inner Hebrides, is sometimes so nicknamed for its attractive appearance, as indicated in the quote below. It lies on the peninsula known as the Rinns of Islay, where "Rinns" represents a Celtic word meaning "promontory."

Port Charlotte, a pretty village of neat pastel-painted houses, known as the 'Queen of the Rinns' [Booth/Perrott, p. 106].

**Queen of the Scottish Peaks, the** *Ben Loyal, Scotland.* The mountain in the far north of Scotland is sometimes so nicknamed for its elegant appearance.

**Queen of the Sea, the** *Tyre, Lebanon.* Ancient Tyre (modern Sour) was accorded this sobriquet as being, next to Sidon, the oldest and most important seaport city in Phoenicia.

**Queen of the Seas, the** *Venice, Italy.* The nickname equates to that of **Queen of the Adriatic**. The sobriquet is familiar in art as the title of Tintoretto's 16th-century allegorical painting *Venice as Queen of the Seas.*

**Queen of the South, the** *(1) Dumfries, Scotland; (2) New Orleans, Louisiana, USA.* Dumfries is so named from its key location in southwestern Scotland, at the center of a web of roads leading east to England, west to Galloway, and north to Glasgow. The title gave the name of the Scottish football club Queen of the South, based in Dumfries and founded in 1919. New Orleans merits its sobriquet as a unique, majestically dominant city of the South. *Cp.* **Pearl of the South**.

(New Orleans) How *could* the Yankees have injured ... New Orleans, the Queen City, so completely [Mignon Eberhart, *Bayou Road*, 1979].

**Queen of the South Coast, the** *Bournemouth, England.* The formerly gentle, genteel seaside resort, long favored by invalids and retirees, gained this nickname in the 19th century.

**Queen of the Suburbs** or **London Suburbs, the** *(1) Ealing, London, England; (2) Surbiton, London, England.* The respective sobriquets of the west London borough and southwest London residential district date from the late 19th century. For Surbiton, there may have been a subconscious association between the actual name of the place and "suburban."

(1) (Ealing) In the 1870s and 1880s house building transformed Ealing into what the publicists of the 1890s termed the 'Queen of the Suburbs,' famed for its healthy environment, modern accommodation and good amenities [Weinreb/Hibbert, p. 254].

(2) (Surbiton) It became a very fashionable and desirable residential neighbourhood, earning itself the name 'Queen of the London Suburbs' [Weinreb/Hibbert, p. 870].

(3) (Ealing) In an early exercise in brand-building, Ealing invented the soubriquet 'Queen of Suburbs' as a signal of its policy to stay resolutely middle class [Carrie Segrave, *The New London Property Guide*, 2003].

**Queen of the West, the** *(1) Cincinnati, Ohio, USA; (2) England; (3) Ireland.* The commendatory sobriquets are mainly familiar from poetry, especially for Cincinnati by Longfellow as in quote (4) below. The titles themselves imply a natural beauty rather than a preeminence resulting from human achievement. In the case of Ireland, the westernmost land of the British Isles, the sobriquet has a popular link with the country's alternate name of **Eire**, at one time supposedly derived from Irish *iarthar*, "western." In quote (1), the poem title is Irish for "my darling" (literally "vein of my heart"). In quote (4) the "Beautiful River" is the Ohio.

(1) (Ireland) Dear Erin, how sweetly thy green
bosom rises!
An emerald set in the ring of the sea.
Each blade of thy meadows my faithful heart
prizes,
Thou queen of the west, the world's cushla ma-
chree [John Philpot Curran, "Cushla ma-Chree,"
late 18th century].
(2) (England) Hail England, dear England, true
Queen of the West
With thy fair swelling bosom and ever-green vest
[Leigh Hunt, "National Song," *The Examiner*,
June 25, 1815].
(3) (Cincinnati) I should prefer Cincinnati as a
residence... The "Queen of the West" is en-
throned in a region of wonderful and inex-
haustible beauty [Harriet Martineau, *Retrospect of
Western Travel*, 1838].
(4) (Cincinnati) And this Song of the Vine,
This greeting of mine,
The winds and the birds shall deliver
To the Queen of the West,
In her garlands dressed,
On the banks of the Beautiful River [H.W.
Longfellow, "Catawba Wine," *Birds of Passage*,
c.1857].

**Queen o' the Borders** or **o' a' the Borders,
the** *Hawick, Scotland*. The largest town in the
Scottish Borders region has long been noted for
its independent spirit, which alone justifies its
nickname. The feminine label may also bear on
its former repute as a "women's town," so called
for the predominance of women workers in its
hosiery mills.

**Queen of Watering Places, the** *(1) Brighton,
England; (2) Eastbourne, England; (3) Scarborough, England; (4) Torquay, England*. All four
seaside resorts, the first two in East Sussex, the
third in North Yorkshire, the fourth in Devon,
have claimed the title, and all enjoyed a fashionable clientèle in the 19th century. Eastbourne
was also known as the Empress of Watering
Places.

(1) (Torquay) It contests with Brighton and Scarborough the title of Queen of English watering-
places [Karl Baedeker, *Handbook to Great Britain*,
1890].
(2) (Scarborough) If Scarborough can lay claim
to the title of 'Queen of the Northern Watering
Places,' then Brighton is its obvious parallel for
the south coast [Robinson/Millward, p. 97].
(3) (Eastbourne) Titles such as 'Queen of Watering Places' or 'the Gentlemen's resort built by
Gentlemen' were now showered on the town
[Robinson/Millward, p. 309].
(4) (Scarborough) "Scarborough, Queen Of Watering Places" was one of those awkward half slogan, half factually-descriptive handles that the
*National Geographic* magazine does so well
[Michael Palin, Introduction, *Happy Holidays:
The Golden Age of Railway Posters*, 1987].
(5) (Eastbourne) Look out for the original

bathing machine outside the Langham Hotel, a
reminder of the days when Eastbourne was
known as the 'Empress of Watering Places' [Travel
brochure *Eastbourne 2005*].

**Queen State, the** *Maryland, USA*. The sobriquet refers to the origin of the state's name in
that of Queen Henrietta Maria, wife of Charles I.

**Quiet Village, the** *Venice, Los Angeles, California, USA*. Black residents of Los Angeles devised this name for the relatively peaceful suburban area. Perhaps intendedly, the nickname
suggests a smaller version of the **Silent City**.

**Railroad City, the** *(1) Indianapolis, Indiana,
USA; (2) Topeka, Kansas, USA*. Both state capitals earned their nickname as major railroad centers, in the case of Topeka as headquarters of the
Atchison, Topeka and Santa Fe Railway.

**Rainbow Nation, the** *South Africa*. South
Africa is a multiracial country, with peoples of
different skin colors. Hence the nickname, not
universally favored.

(1) The Rainbow Nation had a surprise for the
folks at Birmingham... South Africa won the critical doubles rubber in the Davis Cup promotion
decider [*Sunday Times*, September 26, 1999].
(2) The new regime ... had nothing much in the
way of a national story to celebrate the triumph of
what some like to call the "Rainbow Nation,"
other than the long struggle ... against white oppression and exploitation [Adam Ashforth, review
of R.W. Johnson, *South Africa, Times Literary
Supplement*, January 14, 2005].

**Rainbow of Cuba, the** *Soroa, Cuba*. The resort region near Havana is so nicknamed for its
heavy rainfall and resulting lush growth of trees
and flowers, as well as the rainbows themselves.

**Raj on the Med, the** *Santa Eulalia, Ibiza,
Spain*. As explained in the quote below, the
Mediterranean resort is so nicknamed for the
Britons who came to live here following service
in the Raj (India under British colonial rule).

In the early 1950s, the town of Santa Eulalia became known as the "Raj on the Med" because of
the large number of former colonial-service Brits
who settled there [*Sunday Times*, June 6, 2004].

**Ramshackle Empire, the** *Austria-Hungary*.
The former monarchy was so described by Winston Churchill after the outbreak of World War
I. Its ultimatum to Serbia after the assassination
of Archduke Francis Fedinand on June 28, 1914,
precipitated the war, and it collapsed at the end
of it.

**Rand, the** *Witwatersrand, South Africa*. A
shortening of the name of the goldfield district
near Johannesburg, in itself meaning "bank,"
"border." The abbreviation gave the name of the
basic South African monetary unit, adopted in
1961. *Cp.* **Reef**.

I'ld bet you ten thousand pounds to a farthing ... that before twenty years are gone, there'll be a quarter of a million people living on the Rand [Francis Brett Young, *The City of Gold*, 1939].

**Rangoon** *Yangon, Myanmar.* The former familiar name of the country's capital is still current, although in 1989 the government requested that the official name, a transliteration reflecting the name's Burmese pronunciation, be adopted by other countries.

Rangoon, the British-built city on the Bay of Bengal, which has been the capital since independence in 1948 [*The Times*, November 8, 2005].

**Rapid** *Rapid City, South Dakota, USA.* A colloquial short form of the city's name.

**Real Spain, the** *Spain.* The Spain that is far removed from the artificiality of the crowded tourist resorts. Spain is the favorite destination of British vacationers, and the phrase is used by travel companies as an enticement to explore those parts of Spain that normally remain untouched by such visitors. (The name has an incidental suggestion of Spanish *real*, "royal," as in the name of the famed Spanish football team Real Madrid. Spain is, after all, a monarchy.)

(1) The Costa Brava ... is also known as 'The Gateway to Spain,' but those who treat it as such, hurtling down the A17 autopista in search of 'the real Spain' further south, miss out on the best bit of all [*Sunday Telegraph*, July 10, 1994].
(2) It's out there somewhere — taunting us, tantalising us, flitting into view, then fading into the distance. The "real Spain"... We know this dream is real because, every now and again, we find it — and we fall in love with it [*Sunday Times*, July 17, 2005].
(3) Holiday in Real Spain. Attractive villa in Andalucian pinewood... Close to Cadiz, Jerez, Seville, beaches [Ad, *Times Literary Supplement*, October 14, 2005].

**Rebel Capital, the** *Philadelphia, Pennsylvania, USA.* The name was given by the British when the city became the American capital in 1777.

**Rebel County, the** *Co. Cork, Ireland.* The nickname is generally believed to have originated during the Anglo-Irish War of 1919–21, when the center of the city of Cork was burned. More probably, it has a historical basis, referring to the execution in 1499 of the mayor of Cork (*see* **People's Republic of Cork**) and his son together with Perkin Warbeck, pretender to the English throne. The name is mainly used in commentaries of Gaelic sports.

**Red Bologna** *Bologna, Italy.* As described in the quote below, the nickname relates both to the red tiles of the city's roofs and to its leftwing local government.

[The name] reminds one of the tile-clad roofs and the color of the houses but also recalls that venerable Bologna has been governed by the left for more than fifty years [Leier, p. 34].

**Redbrick City, the** *Belfast, Northern Ireland.* The name relates to the rows of redbrick houses built in the city during the 19th century to cater for the rising working population.

**Red Capital, the** *Moscow, Soviet Union.* The nickname referred to Moscow as the capital of the Soviet Union (*see* **Russia**), the **Red Empire**. (Moscow's famous Red Square is so named from Russian *krasny* in its original sense "beautiful," not in its current sense "red," and there is no socialist connection.)

The Red Capital in winter is a silent place [Robert Byron, *First Russia, then Tibet*, 1933].

**Red Centre** see in Appendix 1, p. 269.

**Red China** *China.* A former name for China as a Communist state (officially the People's Republic of China, proclaimed by the Communists on October 1, 1949). The Communists were already a strong force in China by the 1930s.

(1) *Red China* [Translated title of work by Mao Tse-tung, 1934].
(2) There has been perhaps no greater mystery among nations, no more confused an epic, than the story of Red China [Edgar Snow, *Red Star over China*, 1937].
(3) The entry permit into what we used to call 'Red China' is stamped on your passport [*The Listener*, June 8, 1978].

**Red City, the** *Marrakesh, Morocco.* The city came by its nickname through its buildings and ramparts of red beaten clay. *Cp.* **Rose City**.

**Red Clydeside** *Clydeside, Scotland.* The name refers to the militant socialist trade-union and political activity in the named industrial region along the lower length of the Clyde River, west of Glasgow. The sobriquet particularly applied to the period between the two world wars and for many was synonymous with the city itself.

(1) It was largely as a result of political activities that the west of Scotland labour movement began to acquire the reputation of 'red Clydeside' [David Daiches, ed., *The New Companion to Scottish Culture*, 1993].
(2) The term 'Red Clydeside' is more than a generally accepted description of some important events; it is a concept over which commentators on 20th-century Scotland still divide, on politically revealing grounds as well as those of historical interpretation [Terry Brotherstone in Michael Lynch, ed., *The Oxford Companion to Scottish History*, 2001].
(3) A stop at Revolution is a chance to examine the Communist history of the city once known as Red Clydeside, where in 1919 the red flag was

raised in George Square [*The Times* (Scotland Supplement), September 10, 2005].

**Red Empire, the** *Soviet Union*. The former Soviet Union (*see* **Russia**) gained its byname from the conventional color of communism, itself associated with the blood shed in revolutionary combat. The "empire" was not only the union of the 15 republics comprising the USSR but the countries that the Soviet powers had already won over politically and that they aimed to enfold in their already extensive domain. *Cp.* **Evil Empire.**

> There are still hundreds of writers in gaol all over the Red Empire, not to mention Franco's or Salazar's prisons [*The Spectator*, June 6, 1958].

**Red Grave, the** *Sierra Leone*. The nickname refers to the dominant red color of the soil in Sierra Leone, and to the swamps there where British colonizers died of malaria in the 19th century. *Cp.* **White Man's Grave.**

> (1) The "Red Grave," as this portion of the great cemetery of the Anglo-Saxon race is called [Richard F. Burton, *Wanderings in West Africa*, 1863].
> (2) But how stand the facts at the white man's Red Grave? [Richard F. Burton, *To the Gold Coast for Gold*, 1883].

**Redland** *Soviet Union*. An alternate name for the **Red Empire.**

> (1) If Redland have got a finger in the pie then that part of the world could be warmish [John Gardner, *Amber Nine*, 1966].
> (2) 'You can imagine who the first suspects are?' Bond could. 'Redland' [Christopher Wood, *James Bond*, 1977].

**Red Menace, the** *Soviet Union*. Although primarily referring to the political or military threat seen as emanating from the Soviet Union, the name by extension came to be applied to the country itself.

> (1) Once the election is over ... we shall quietly lay aside our witch hunting, put the Red Menace in cold storage [J.F. Carter, *What We Are About to Receive*, 1932].
> (2) [William] Joyce saw himself as a patriotic Englishman, who believed Britain should have made common cause with Germany against the "Red Menace" [Tristan Quinn, review of Nigel Farndale, *Haw-Haw*, Times Literary Supplement, September 2, 2005].

**Redneck Riviera** see in Appendix 1, p. 269.

**Red Peril, the** *Soviet Union*. A less common designation of the **Red Menace.** *Cp.* **Yellow Peril.**

> We have to guard against the Red Peril on our borders [*The Observer*, December 4, 1927].

**Redriff** *Rotherhithe, London, England*. The former name of the Thames-side district is preserved in the name of Redriff Road there.

> Mr. *Gulliver* growing weary of the Concourse of curious People coming to him at his House in *Redriff*, made a small Purchase of Land ... near *Newark*, in *Nottinghamshire* [Jonathan Swift, *Gulliver's Travels*, 1726].

**Red Rose County, the** *Lancashire, England*. The northern county derives its nickname from the 15th-century Wars of the Roses, between the dynasties of Lancaster, represented by a red rose, and York, represented by a white rose.

> (1) The Red Rose county provides within its boundaries the most remarkable contrasts [Frank Singleton and Alan Brack in Speaight, p. 257].
> (2) Further details of the delights of the Red Rose County are available from www.lancashire-tourism.com [Tourist brochure, *Lytham, St Annes-on-Sea and the Fylde Countryside*, 2005].

**Red Sea Riviera** see in Appendix 1, p. 269.

**Red Vienna** *Vienna, Austria*. The Austrian capital was so known from the end of World War I to 1934, when the (Marxist) Social Democrats had an absolute majority in the city council.

**Reef, the** *Witwatersrand, South Africa*. The colloquial name of the goldfield district near Johannesburg relates to "reef" in the geological sense of a rock that surrounds a lode or vein. *Cp.* **Rand.**

> In proportion to population, there are twenty times as many murders on the Reef than in the U.S.A [*Drum*, October 6, 1951].

**Reek, the** *Croagh Patrick, Ireland*. The Co. Mayo mountain, on which St. Patrick is said to have fasted, derives its nickname from a local form of "rick," the English word translating Croagh (Irish *cruach*).

> From our drawing-room windows one had a perfect view of the Reek [*The Irish Rosary*, May 1930].

**Reekie** *see* **Auld Reekie**

**Reeks, the** *Macgillycuddy's Reeks, Ireland*. A familiar short name for the mountain range in Co. Kerry. "Reeks" is a form of English "ricks," in the sense "ridges,"as for the **Reek.**

> The ridge of the Reeks springs up suddenly, a wall of rock, from the plains of Kerry [D.D.C.P. Mould, *Peter's Boat*, 1959].

**Regno, the** *Naples, Italy*. The name, pronounced "Rainyo," is Italian for "kingdom," and was formerly used to distinguish Naples from other Italian states.

> Are our wiser heads leaning towards alliance with the Pope and the Regno, or are they rather inclining their ears to the orators of France and Milan? [George Eliot, *Romola*, 1863].

**Reindeerland** *Belfast, Northern Ireland*. The city adopts this name postally in the period before Christmas, when its mail sorting office receives (and replies to) letters from children to

Santa Claus. The quote below is part of an interview with Royal Mail letter administrator Lucy Granet.

[LG:] Any letter addressed to Santa will get to us eventually but it's best to send them to Santa Claus, Santa's Grotto, Reindeerland, SAN TA1. [Interviewer:] Reindeerland — now there's a new spin on Belfast! [LG:] It is Reindeerland at that time of year — very cold and snowy. That's part of the whole magic of it — Belfast can transform itself and I am part of that [*The Times Magazine*, December 18, 2004].

**Remotest Island in the World, the** *Tristan da Cunha, South Atlantic*. The British-owned island group consists of six small islands, of which Tristan da Cunha is the largest. Four of the islands are uninhabited. The group lies about midway between southern Africa and South America, giving substance to the sobriquet.

Tristan da Cunha has been called the loneliest islands in the World, as a ship calls there only about once a year [Johnson, p. 249].

**Renaissance City, the** *Glasgow, Scotland*. Glasgow adopted this title for itself following its dramatic transformation in the late 20th century from a stolidly prosperous Victorian city (albeit with a long history) to a vibrant modern community. This "renaissance" won it the title of Cultural Capital of Europe in 1990.

Modern Glasgow sometimes likes to call itself the Renaissance City. And deservedly [John Tomes, *Blue Guide Scotland*, 1992].

**Republic, the** *Ireland*. A short designation of the Republic of Ireland, distinguishing it from Northern Ireland. See quote at **Eire**.

**Republic of Samsung, the** *South Korea*. The country has been so nicknamed for the dominant presence of the electronics company Samsung, founded in what is now South Korea in 1938.

Given the group's power and influence, and its clear proclivity for wielding it, some Korean media have dubbed their country "the Republic of Samsung" [*The Times*, November 29, 2005].

**Repulsive Bay** *Repulse Bay, Hong Kong, China*. A punning name for the beach area, as used by those unenamored of its charms.

**Rheims** *Reims, France*. The old spelling of the city's name with an inorganic "h" is still sometimes found among English speakers and in British newspapers, especially when pronounced "Reems."

(1) This young scholar, that has been long studying at Rheims [William Shakespeare, *The Taming of the Shrew*, c. 1592].
(2) "The Jackdaw of Rheims" [R.H. Barham, title, *The Ingoldsby Legends*, 1840].
(3) Reims. Often spelt Rheims [Johnson, p. 207].
(4) The Via Francigena [pilgrim route] runs

from Canterbury through Calais, Rheims, Besançon and Lausanne [*The Times*, November 14, 2005].

**Rhine of America, the** *Hudson River, New York, USA*. The nickname refers to the river's topography, notably the mountains and forests along its course and the fine scenery through which it passes.

**Rhine of Maoriland, the** *Wanganui River, New Zealand*. The scenic North Island river, also known as the "Rhine of New Zealand," flows through a region which was the original home of the Maoris. Hence the name. *See also* **Maoriland**.

(1) [The city of Wanganui is the] starting point for 130-mile jet-boat journeys up [the] 'Rhine of New Zealand' [Shadbolt, p. 160].
(2) This former boatsman's house has views of the "Rhine of Maoriland" [*The Times*, September 24, 2005].

**Rhine of New Zealand** *see* **Rhine of Maoriland**

**Rhos** *Rhosllanerchrugog, Wales*. The abbreviated name is occasionally (and understandably) used for the name of the town near Wrexham. (As such, it should not be confused with the seaside resort of Rhos-on-Sea.)

**Rice Bowl of China, the** *Sichuan, China*. The province is China's leading rice producer. *See also* **Heavenly Kingdom**.

**Rice Capital of Louisiana** or **the World, the** *Crowley, Louisiana, USA*. The nickname proclaims the town's prestige in rice production.

**Rice State, the** *South Carolina, USA*. The state is now better known for its tobacco and soybean production than its rice, but the nickname was formerly valid.

**Richest Hill on Earth, the** *Butte, Montana, USA*. The city's economy has been dominated by the mining industry since settlement began in the 1860s, with copper the former main product, but also zinc, silver, gold, and lead. Hence the nickname, which puns on the literal meaning of the placename (from French *butte*, "hill").

**Richest Square Mile on Earth, the** *Central City, Colorado, USA*. The town earned its nickname following a major discovery of gold in the 1850s.

Central City is an old mining town that was once called the Richest Square Mile in the World [Jack Kerouac, *On the Road*, 1957].

**Ricky** *Rickmansworth, England*. A local abbreviated personalization of the Hertfordshire town's rather lengthy name.

**Rifle City** *Springfield, Massachusetts, USA*. The city derived its nickname from the firearms manufactured here. The Springfield rifle was in regular use with the US Army for most of the period from 1873 to 1936.

**Ringing Island, the** *(1) Avignon, France; (2) England.* For Avignon, the name translates French *l'Île sonnante*, found in Book V of Rabelais' *Gargantua and Pantagruel*, as in quote (1) below, although it has been suggested that the reference is to Rome, not papal Avignon. Either way, it refers to the ringing of church bells, as can be seen from both quotes. (Avignon is hardly on an island, although many of its numerous churches and chapels are in a bend of the Rhône River.)

(1) (Avignon) Our pilot told us that it was the Ringing Island, and indeed we heard a kind of a confused and often repeated noise ... not unlike the sound of great, middle-sized, and little bells, rung all at once, as it is customary at Paris, Tours, Gergeau, Nantes, and elsewhere, on high holidays [François Rabelais, *Gargantua and Pantagruel*, Book V, 1562, translated by Thomas Urquhart and Peter Motteux, 1653].

(2) (England) "England is the ringing island." Thus it is commonly call'd by Foreigners, as having greater, moe, and more tuneable [i.e. tuneful] Bells than any one Country in Christendom [Thomas Fuller, *The History of the Worthies of England*, 1662].

**Rio** *Rio de Janeiro, Brazil.* A common short form of the seaport city's name.

(1) It is hard for man to make any city worthy of such surroundings as Nature has given to Rio [James Bryce, *South America*, 1912].

(2) Rio's is undisputedly the biggest and most flamboyant carnival in the world [Dodd/Donald, p. 85].

**Rip Van Winkledom** *Catskill Mountains, New York, USA.* The mountains were formerly so nicknamed as the place where the good-for-nothing Rip Van Winkle fell asleep for 20 years, as told in Washington Irving's *Sketch Book* (1819–20).

A Cyclist's Visit to Rip Van Winkledom [Heading, *Outing*, April 1892].

**River, the** *Thames River, England.* Just as residents in any town usually refer to the local river, whatever its name, as "the river," so the Thames, as the river on which London stands, is often denoted by the generic.

People nowadays call the Thames 'the River' [Eilert Ekwall, *English River-Names*, 1928].

**River City** *(1) Memphis, Tennessee, USA; (2) San Antonio, Texas, USA.* Memphis derives its nickname from its location on the Mississippi River. San Antonio lies at the source of this name, but here the nickname alludes more specifically to the River Walk, which follows the river as it winds its way through the city's downtown.

(San Antonio) The city's eminently walkable downtown holds ... Riverwalk, the gentrified renovation of a once-seedy flood-control canal. It's this feature that has given San Antonio the nickname River City [*Lonely Planet USA*, 2004].

**River of Swans, the** *Potomac River, USA.* The nickname alludes to the swans found on some stretches of the river.

**Riviera di Levante** *see* **Italian Riviera** in Appendix 1, p. 269.

**Riviera di Ponente** *see* **Italian Riviera** in Appendix 1, p. 269.

**Roaring Forties** see in Appendix 1, p. 269.

**Rock, the** *(1) Alcatraz, California, USA; (2) Corregidor, Philippines; (3) Gibraltar; (4) Little Rock, Arkansas, USA.* The byname refers in each case to the physical rock at the place in question. Alcatraz is a rocky island in San Francisco Bay. Corregidor, known also as **Gibraltar of the East**, is a rocky island at the entrance to Manila Bay. The town of Gibraltar lies at the foot of the Rock of Gibraltar, a rocky peninsula in the southern part of Spain. Little Rock, for which the nickname is a short form, arose by a rocky formation on the Arkansas River.

(1) (Gibraltar) They [i.e. the English] call it "The Rock," a nickname it appropriately shares with Alcatraz [Kenneth Tynan, "The Rising Costa del Sol," *Tynan Right and Left*, 1967].

(2) (Gibraltar) Gibraltar's year-long celebrations of 300 years of British sovereignty are ending on a momentous note. Spain's anger over the anniversary festivities and its own claims to sovereignty over the Rock have been put aside [*The Times*, December 15, 2004].

(3) (Alcatraz) Alcatraz means "gannet" or "pelican" in Spanish, and ... was named by the Spanish explorer Juan Manuel de Ayala as he sailed into San Francisco Bay for the first time in 1775. "The Rock" was used as a fortress from 1850 and became a prison in 1933 [*The Times*, September 15, 2005].

(4) (Gibraltar) When it comes to shopping, 'The Rock' is in a class of its own [Gibraltar Tourist Board ad, *The Times Magazine*, October 1, 2005].

**Rockbroker Belt** see in Appendix 1, p. 269.

**Rock City** *Little Rock, Arkansas, USA.* A straightforward byname for the city. *Cp.* **Rock**.

**Rocket City** *Huntsville, Alabama, USA.* The city is a major center for US space research. Hence the nickname.

**Rockies, the** *Rocky Mountains, North America.* A common byname for the great mountain system, turning an adjective into a plural noun.

If you want to see scenery see the Rockies [American gold prospector to Lafcadio Hearn, quoted in letter to Elizabeth Bisland, July 1887].

**Rocky** *Rockhampton, Australia.* A colloquial

short name for the Queensland city and river port.

**Rodeo Town** *Cheyenne, Wyoming, USA.* The state capital is famous for its annual Frontier Days rodeo, one of the oldest and largest in America.

**Rodings** see in Appendix 1, p. 269.

**Róisín Dubh** *Ireland.* The personification of Ireland is Irish for "Dark Little Rose," the subject of a famous poem by James Clarence Mangan, as in quote (1) below (where he renders the name as Rosaleen), based on Sir Samuel Ferguson's literal translation of the Gaelic original, published in the *Dublin University Magazine* (1834). In this, the poet meets a beautiful fairy woman who identifies herself as Ireland. *Cp.* **Kathleen Ní Houlihan.**

(1) O, My Dark Rosaleen,
  Do not sigh, do not weep! [James Clarence Mangan, "My Dark Rosaleen," 1846].
  (2) The ship's name also proved contentious. The [Defense] Minister departed from the recommended shortlist supplied to him from the Naval Service and chose *Róisín Dubh*, symbolising Ireland [*Irish Times*, October 28, 2000].

**Romanesque Museum**, the *Zamora, Spain.* The city earned its nickname (Spanish *el museo románico*) for its many medieval churches, crowned by its Romanesque cathedral.

**Rome of France, the** *Nîmes, France.* The city has an impressive number of well-preserved Roman buildings, including a perfect Roman arena. Hence its deserved nickname.

**Rome of the North, the** *(1) Bremen, Germany; (2) Cologne, Germany; (3) Salzburg, Austria.* Bremen was so nicknamed because after its foundation by Charlemagne in 787 it became a base for missionary activity in northern Europe. Cologne was a Roman garrison in the 1st century BC and was made a Roman colony in AD 50 by the Emperor Claudius. It is thus of pure Roman origin, and even its name is Roman, from Latin *colonia*, "colony." Salzburg's sobriquet is an alternate form of its designation as the **German Rome.**

**Rome of the West, the** *Aachen (Aix-la-Chapelle), Germany.* The city is of Roman origin, with Roman baths, and was the capital of the Carolingian empire of Charlemagne, just as Rome was the capital of the Roman empire. Hence the name.

**Romeville** or **Rumville** *London, England.* The old nickname of the British capital derives from "rum" in its now obsolete slang sense of "excellent," itself perhaps from the name of Rome as a city of grandeur and glory.

**Roof of Africa, the** *(1) Kilimanjaro, Tanza-*nia; *(2) Lesotho.* The central peak of the Tanzanian volcanic massif, Kibo, is the highest point in Africa, while Lesotho has Thabana Ntlenyana, the highest peak in southern Africa. Hence the nicknames. *Cp.* **Kingdom in the Sky; Switzerland of Africa.**

(1) (Lesotho) 'If we go to Lesotho, maybe we can live in the mountains,' Rose said. 'They call it the Roof of Africa, don't they?' [Jenny Hobbs, *Thoughts in a Makeshift Mortuary*, 1989].
  (2) (Kilimanjaro) Conditions on the mountain, known as the "roof of Africa," have been described as a shambles [*The Times*, February 19, 2005].

**Roof of Arabia, the** *Yemen.* The country has the highest mountains in the Arabian peninsula. Hence its nickname.

**Roof of Australia, the** *Snowy Mountains, Australia.* As indicated in the quote below, the name is not entirely apt for the New South Wales range.

Compared to the high mountain ranges of other countries, the "roof of Australia" is relatively low and, despite the name, the flattened mountaintops lie below the line of permanent snow [*The Rough Guide to Australia*, 2001].

**Roof of Norway, the** *Hardangerfjell, Norway.* The nickname applies both to the lofty mountain mass in southwestern Norway, rising to 6,153 ft (1,875 m), and to the massive Hardangerjøkel glacier located here.

You may also have the chance to take a scenic flight over the Hardangerfjord and view the mighty Hardangerfjojokulen [*sic*] Glacier — also known as the "Roof of Norway" [Cruise brochure, 2005].

**Roof of the World, the** *(1) Pamirs, Tajikistan; (2) Tibet, China.* The Pamirs merit their lofty name by virtue of their peaks, many of which rise to more than 20,000 ft (6,100 m), the two highest being Communism Peak and Lenin Peak. Tibet, to the southeast, is also a contender for the title, as are the Himalayas. The name itself is of local origin, translating Wakhani *bam-i-dunya.*

(Pamirs) We were now about to cross the famous "Bam-i-dunya," "The Roof of the World," under which name the elevated region of the hitherto comparatively unknown Pamir tracts had long appeared in our maps [T.E. Gordon, *The Roof of the World, being the Narrative of a Journey over the High Plateau of Tibet to the Russian Frontier and the Oxus Sources on Pamir*, 1876].

**Rose City, the** *(1) Madison, New Jersey, USA; (2) Marrakesh, Morocco; (3) Portland, Oregon, USA.* The nickname can have different meanings. Madison is a rose-growing center. Marrakesh is so known for the reddish color of its buildings. (Hence its alternate name of **Red**

City.) Portland holds an annual Rose Festival. *Cp.* **Pink Town.**

(Marrakesh) Marrakech is known as "the rose city," after the russet colour of its architecture [*Imagine*, Summer 2004].

**Roseland** see in Appendix 1, p. 269.

**Rose-red City, the** *Petra, Jordan.* The famous ruined city, a stronghold (or even the capital) of the biblical Edomites, derives its epithet from quote (1) below, in allusion to the rose, crimson, and purple sandstone out of which its temples and tombs are carved.

(1) Match me such marvel, save in Eastern clime,—
A rose-red city — half as old as Time! [John William Burgon, *Petra*, 1845].
(2) A classic combination of the "rose-red" city of Petra, St. Catherine's Monastery and Aqaba [Travel ad, *Sunday Times Magazine*, June 13, 2004].

**Rotten Apple, the** *Harlem, New York, USA.* A nickname that saw Harlem as the rotten part of the **Big Apple**, referring to the district's crime, ethnic conflict, and social problems, especially in the latter half of the 20th century.

**Rotto** *Rottnest Island, Australia.* A short colloquial name for the island off Fremantle, Western Australia, with the typical Australian -o suffix, as for **Kenso.**

**Roughest Place in the World, the** *Skagway, Alaska, USA.* The gold-rush town of the 1890s was notorious for its lawlessness. Hence the nickname.

[Mascot Saloon] is now a museum devoted to Skagway's heyday as the 'roughest place in the world' [*Lonely Planet USA*, 2004].

**Roughrider State, the** *North Dakota, USA.* The state adopted its promotional name in the 1960s and 1970s, with reference to the Roughriders, or members of the 1st Volunteer Cavalry in the Spanish-American War. The force, recruited by Theodore Roosevelt, included several North Dakota cowboys.

**Round City, the** *Baghdad, Iraq.* The Iraqi capital was founded in the 8th century under the name Madinat as-Salam, "City of Peace." Its byname refers to the original manner of its construction, within circular walls and centering on the caliph's palace. The circular form was later erased by the city's expansion.

**Royal Berkshire** *Berkshire, England.* The historic county, split in 1998 into six unitary authorities, was so officially designated for its royal connections at Eton and Windsor (*see* **Royal Borough**).

**Royal Borough, the** *Kensington, London, England.* There are three English boroughs so titled

for their royal connection, the other two being Kingston upon Thames, London, and Windsor, Berkshire. (Kensington was the birthplace of Queen Victoria, whose youth was spent at Kensington Palace.) The title alone usually denotes Kensington (from 1965 Kensington and Chelsea). The rank is conferred by the sovereign, as described in quote (1) below, where the title was granted by Edward VII, Victoria's eldest son, in the year of his mother's death. *Cp.* **Royal Burgh.**

(1) The King has been pleased to direct Letters Patent to be passed ... granting the title "Royal" to the Metropolitan Borough of Kensington, and ordaining and declaring that the said Borough shall henceforth be called and styled the "Royal Borough of Kensington" [*London Gazette*, November 19, 1901].
(2) Grim concrete council blocks scar the landscape... You're still in the Royal Borough, though it's hard to tell [Carrie Segrave, *The New London Property Guide*, 2003].

**Royal Burgh, the** *Edinburgh, Scotland.* There are 66 royal burghs in Scotland, so titled as they derive their charter direct from the crown. The title alone is usually taken to refer to the Scottish capital, Edinburgh, a royal burgh since the 12th century. ("Burgh" is the Scottish form of "borough.") *Cp.* **Royal Borough.**

**Royal City, the** *Abomey, Benin.* The town is sometimes so called as the former capital of the kingdom of Abomey.

**Royal County, the** *Co. Meath, Ireland.* The county is so titled since it contains Tara, the historic seat of Irish kings. The name is mostly used in the context of Gaelic sports commentaries.

Back in the 1950s and early 1960s, a government resettlement programme introduced farmers from the west to available land in Meath. Since then, there have been little pockets of the Royal County which are forever Mayo [*Irish Times*, September 12, 1996].

**Royal Deeside** see in Appendix 1, p. 269.

**Royal Troon** *Troon, Scotland.* The name properly applies to the golf course at the westcoast resort rather than to the town itself. The course was established in 1878 and gained the royal prefix in its centennial year. Other towns with championship golf courses also bear the epithet, as Royal Birkdale and Royal Lytham & St Annes on the northwest coast of England. All three are venues for the men's British Open Golf Championship. *See also* **Golf Coast** in Appendix 1, p. 269.

**RSA, the** *South Africa.* A common initialism of the country's formal name as the Republic of South Africa. *Cp.* **SA.**

(1) The need for a single comprehensive and authoritative work of reference on the RSA has long

been experienced [*South African Panorama*, November 1974].

(2) 19-year-old Daniela Di Paolo, of Durban, was crowned Miss RSA at a glittering function in Cape Town on Saturday night [*Rand Daily Mail*, April 13, 1981].

**RTP** *Research Triangle Park, North Carolina, USA*. A local initialism for the research and business park, itself so named for its location in the triangle formed by Raleigh, Durham, and Chapel Hill. *See also* **Triad** in Appendix 1, p. 269.

**Rubber City** *Akron, Ohio, USA*. The city gained fame as the center of the nation's rubber and tire manufacturing industry. Hence the descriptive name.

**Ruhr of Central America, the** *El Salvador*. The country is so nicknamed as it is more highly industrialized than its Central American neighbors. The Ruhr is one of Germany's main manufacturing centers and was formerly one of the greatest industrial complexes in the world.

El Salvador is known affectionately as the Ruhr of Central America, but I can't believe the Ruhr is anything like so exciting [Nicholas Wollaston, *Red Rumba*, 1962].

**Ruin** *Rouen, France*. A British soldiers' World War I alteration of the name of the Normandy city, perhaps suggested by its use as a base for the treatment of venereal diseases.

**Rumville** *see* **Romeville**

**Rupert** *Prince Rupert, British Columbia, Canada*. A short name regularly used locally for the city and port.

**Russet Sleat of the Bonnie Women** *Sleat, Scotland*. The parish and peninsula in the southwest of the Isle of Skye has several nicknames, of which this is one of the best known. *See also* **Garden of Skye.**

Sleat has been variously named by her children and others; Sleibhte riabhach nam ban boidheach, russet Sleat of the bonnie women; Mnathan Sleibhte, Sleat wives (worth having); Sleibhte nam bradan, Sleat of the salmon; and a questionable characteristic is Ceilidh nam ban Sleibhteach, the gossiping of the Sleat women [Alexander Robert Forbes, *Place-Names of Skye*, 1923].

**Russia** *Soviet Union*. The name of the country as now geographically and politically applicable was popularly used for the Soviet Union (Union of Soviet Socialist Republics, USSR) during its period of existence from 1922 to 1991 and in particular for the Russian Soviet Federative Socialist Republic (RSFSR), the largest of the 15 socialist republics that comprised this union.

**Russian America** *Alaska, USA*. A historic name for the territory during the period when it was claimed by Russia, who in 1867 ceded it to the USA (*see* **Seward's Folly**). The name is still sometimes found, and as a sobriquet gives the state a special cachet. (Several Russian place-names remain in Alaska.)

**Russkiland** *Russia*. A nickname based on Russian *russky*, "(a) Russian," especially current during the country's period as the Soviet Union.

A.E.F. Siberia ... en route to Russki-land [*American Legion Weekly*, March 12, 1920].

**Rust Belt** see in Appendix 1, p. 269.

**SA** *(1) South Africa; (2) South Australia, Australia*. An initialism of the country's and state's respective names.

(1) (South Africa) *You* [magazine] tells all about the love affair that shocked SA [Ad on Radio Algoa, September 22, 1993].

(2) (South Africa) Never use the abbreviation SA, even in headlines [*The Times Style and Usage Guide*, 2003].

**Sabrina** *Severn River, Wales*. Britain's longest river, rising in Wales and flowing into the Bristol Channel, between Wales and England, is poetically known by its Roman name, that of the virgin daughter of Locrinus (see **Loegria**), who personifies the Severn and dwells in its waters.

(1) Sabrina fair,
Listen where thou art sitting
Under the glassy, cool, translucent wave [John Milton, *Comus*, 1637].

(2) The Romans came up short against Sabrina Fair; they stood a long time pondering its 'rough water brown' [Maurice Wiggin in Hadfield 1981, p. 73].

**Sac** *Sacramento, California, USA*. A shortened form of the city's name. *Cp.* **Sacto**.

**Sacred City, the** *Lhasa, Tibet*. The capital city has long been the religious center of Tibet. Hence its sobriquet.

The Tibetans having made up their minds to prevent us going to the Sacred City peaceably [*Shanghai Courier*, November 1877].

**Sacred Isle** or **Island, the** *(1) Mt. Athos, Greece; (2) Eynhallow, Orkney Islands, Scotland; (3) Guernsey, Channel Islands, UK; (4) Ireland; (5) Scattery, Ireland*. All of the named places are holy to Christians. Mt. Athos, known to the Greek Orthodox Church as Hagion Oros ("holy mountain"), is on a peninsula rather than an actual island. Eynhallow, with a Scandinavian name meaning "holy isle," is a small islet with the faint remains of a medieval monastery. The island of Guernsey was noted for its monks, just as Ireland was famed for its many saints. Scattery Island, Co. Clare, has the remains of a 6th-century monastery. Guernsey and Ireland are also known as **Holy Island**.

(Scattery) "Oh! haste and leave this sacred isle,

Unholy bark, ere morning smile" [Thomas Moore, "St. Senanus and the Lady," *Irish Melodies*, 1821].

**Sacred Valley of the Incas, the** *Urubamba Valley, Peru*. The valley of the Urubamba River contains Inca ruins and lies below Machu Picchu, the **Lost City of the Incas**. Hence the sobriquet.

Day 4. Drive along the scenic Urubamba Valley, the so-called "Sacred Valley of the Incas," to Pisac [Travel ad, *The Times Magazine*, October 22, 2005].

**Sacto** *Sacramento, California, USA*. An abbreviated form of the city's name. *Cp.* **Sac.**

**Sadchester** *see* **Madchester**

**Safari Capital of the World, the** *Nairobi, Kenya*. The Kenyan capital has long been a center from which white Europeans embark on a safari, or animal-watching expedition, and Nairobi National Park is a large game park nearby. The sobriquet occurs in John Gunther, *Inside Africa* (1955).

**Sagebrush State, the** *(1) Nevada, USA; (2) Wyoming, USA*. Nevada is so nicknamed for the sagebrush (*Artemisia tridentata*) that flourishes in the higher regions of its arid and rugged terrain. The name was also formerly given to Wyoming.

(Nevada) Sagebrush, Silver and Battle Born State are nicknames for Nevada, first explored by the Spaniards in 1776 [*Billings* (Montana) *Gazette*, June 20, 1976].

**Saigon** *Ho Chi Minh City, Vietnam*. The former capital of South Vietnam was officially renamed for the deceased leader of the Vietnamese Communists after it was taken by North Vietnam in 1975. Yet the old and simpler name lives on, both locally and popularly (*see* **HCM**). It even occurs officially (*see* **Model City of Tomorrow**).

(1) Three years, how quick they moved —
Look how the world's improved.
Saigon, that queen of sin,
Re-named for Ho Chi Minh! [Alain Boublil, *Miss Saigon*, 1989].
(2) Saigon is like all the other great modern cities of the world. It's the mess left over from people getting rich [P.J. O'Rourke, *Give War a Chance*, 1992].
(3) Saigon, which has been named Ho Chi Minh City since 1975, but is still called Saigon by its inhabitants [Leier, p. 170].

**Sailboard Capital of the World, the** *Hood River County, Oregon, USA*. Sailboarding became a popular sport in the county thanks to the steady winds that blow through the Hood River Gorge.

**Sailor City** *Norfolk, Virginia, USA*. The city

and port of entry acquired its nickname as a major shipbuilding center and, with Portsmouth, as the headquarters of the US Atlantic Fleet.

**St. Barts** or **St. Barths** *St.-Barthélemy, Guadeloupe, West Indies*. A common colloquial abbreviation of the fashionable resort island's name.

(1) The buzz ... is in St Barths, the island with the best food and the most hair-raising airport approach [*Debrett's Society*, Summer 2004].
(2) St Barts in the French Caribbean thinks of itself as understated and chic [*The Times*, December 18, 2004].

**St. Botolph's Town** *Boston, England*. The name of the Lincolnshire town is popularly derived from St. Botolph, to whom the parish church is dedicated. But the Botolph in question may actually have been the name of the original Anglo-Saxon landowner here.

St. Botolph's Town! Hither across the plains
And fens of Lincolnshire, in garb austere,
There came a Saxon monk, and founded here
A Priory [H.W. Longfellow, "Boston," *A Book of Sonnets*, 1876].

**St. Brew** *St. Louis, Missouri, USA*. Blacks favor this nickname for the city, referring to its beer production (with perhaps also a pun on the jazz classic "St. Louis Blues").

**St. Edmundsbury** *Bury St Edmunds, England*. The former name of the Suffolk town is still officially current for the local administrative district and today is also present in the dedication of St Edmundsbury Cathedral. The names are identical, but with the elements transposed. *Cp.* **Bury.**

(1) Lords, I will meet him at Saint Edmundsbury [William Shakespeare, *King John*, c. 1596].
(2) St. Edmund's Bury, or Bury St. Edmund's, or simply Bury [William Pulleyn, *The Etymological Compendium*, 3d ed., revised and improved by Merton A. Thoms, 1853].

**Saint-Ger** *St.-Germain-des-Prés, Paris, France*. A colloquial short form of the name of the Left-Bank district, with its famous boulevard St.-Germain, centering on the ancient church of St.-Germain-des-Prés.

**St. Jo** or **St. Joe** *St. Joseph, Missouri, USA*. A colloquial short form of the city's name.

(1) Saint Jo, Buchanan County,
Is leagues and leagues away;
And I sit in the gloom of this rented room,
And pine to be there to-day [Eugene Field, "Lover's Lane, St. Jo," *A Second Book of Western Verse*, 1892].
(2) In 1860 the first Pony Express carried messages from 'St Jo' 1900 miles west to California [*Lonely Planet USA*, 2004].

**St. Looie** *St. Louis, Missouri, USA*. A colloquial respelling of the city's name.

**St. Pancras of East Africa, the** *Nairobi, Kenya.* The Kenyan capital arose around the railhead that arrived here in 1899. Hence its former touristic nickname, referring to St Pancras mainline station in London, England, the terminus of the Midland Railway, with trains to and from the north of England.

It was a journey up the Nile to Khartoum, south to Lake Victoria, and then on to Nairobi (the 'St Pancras of East Africa') and Mombasa by the new Uganda Railway [Piers Brendon, *Thomas Cook: 150 Years of Popular Tourism*, 1991, quoting *Cook's Traveller's Gazette*, December 10, 1903].

**St. Pete's** *St. Petersburg, Russia.* An English speaker's colloquial abbreviation of the city's name.

Moscow and St Pete's may steal the tourist limelight but Kiev is the Jerusalem of Russia [Dodd/Donald, p. 358].

**St. Reatham** *Streatham, London, England.* A mock "sanctification" of the district's name. Streatham is mostly fashionable but has some neglected commercialized areas.

(1) Streatham is still a bit grotty. Tell your friends you have moved to St Reatham instead [*The Times*, December 5, 2003].

(2) Sleepy Streatham — aka "St Reatham" in south London [*Sunday Times*, April 24, 2005].

**St. Trop** *St.-Tropez, France.* An abbreviation of the chic Mediterranean resort's name favored by those who frequent it.

(1) St Tropez is pronounced as spelt, but preferably St Trop [Guy Egmont, *The Art of Egmontese*, 1961].

(2) Ibiza may be a riot and only a short hop away, St Trop is glamorous and New York a buzz, but none of these places can match the rude variety of Britain after dark [*Sunday Times*, June 12, 2005].

**St. Tropez of Greece, the** *Hydra, Greece.* The Aegean island has attracted a number of celebrity residents, as noted in the quote below, while its tourist facilities have led to a comparison with France's St.-Tropez (*see* **St. Trop**).

Now the likes of [singer and poet] Leonard Cohen have homes in "Greece's St Tropez" [*Sunday Times*, August 8, 2004].

**St. Tropez of the Adriatic, the** *Budva, Montenegro.* The popularity and favorable climate of the town and summer bathing resort invites a (modest) comparison with the stylish French seaside center.

The pretty beach resort of Budva, nicknamed the Saint Tropez of the Adriatic [*The Times*, September 9, 2005].

**St. Tropez of Tunisia, the** *Hammamet, Tunisia.* The popular resort has a character and style similar to those of the fashionable French town. The comparison is apt in a country that is geographically African but historically French.

Known as the 'Tunisian St. Tropez,' with its bustling commercial centre and bohemian atmosphere, Hammamet has grown to be one of Tunisia's largest resorts [Holiday brochure, 2005].

**St. Tropez of Turkey, the** *Bodrum, Turkey.* The seaport city, on the site of the classical **Halicarnassus**, gained its sobriquet at the turn of the 21st century as an increasingly fashionable resort on the lines of its French eponym.

Like Marbella, made famous by the Spanish royal family, the Istanbul in-crowd regularly visits Bodrum, earning it the nickname "Turkey's St Tropez" [*Sunday Times*, December 11, 2005].

**St. Ubes** *Setúbal, Portugal.* The seaport's old name, found in literature, was the creation of English sailors, who took the "Set-" of its real name to be "Saint." The name of the London church of the Holy Sepulchre (St. Sepulchre) was similarly corrupted at one time to "St. Pulchre" or "St. Pulcre."

(1) St. Ubes, a city and port-town of Portugal, situated on a fine bay [*Encyclopædia Britannica*, 1771].

(2) [St. Sepulchre] was misunderstood as St. Pulchre, just as Setubal became St. Ubes and [the Italian mountain] Soracte became San Oracte and San Oreste [A. Smythe Palmer, *The Folk and their Word-Lore*, 1904].

(3) The nautical mind has canonized a new saint, unknown even to the Bollandists, by the change of Setubal into St. Ubes [Isaac Taylor, *Words and Places*, c.1908].

**Sala** *Surakarta, Indonesia.* A local short name for the Javan city. *Cp.* **Yogya.**

**Salem** *Jerusalem, Israel.* A biblical and literary shortening of the city's name, referring either to the capital of historic Israel or to Jerusalem as a synonym for heaven, as in quote (3) below. *Cp.* **Hierusalem.**

(1) And Melchizedek king of Salem brought forth bread and wine [Genesis 14:18].

(2) "Here is a holy Palmer come,
From Salem first, and last from Rome" [Sir Walter Scott, *Marmion*, 1808].

(3) Light's abode, celestial Salem [J.M. Neale, hymn in *Joys and Glories of Paradise*, 1865].

**Sally Booze** *Sailly-Labourse, France.* A British soldiers' World War I corruption of the name of a village in northern France. It combines a homely female name with a regular off-duty activity, evoking a barmaid in a pub.

**Salmon Capital of New Zealand, the** *Rakaia, New Zealand.* The South Island town is so nicknamed for the excellent trout and salmon fishing to be had at various spots in the river for which it is named.

**Salmon Capital of the World, the** *Campbell River, British Columbia, Canada.* The town and port on Vancouver Island is a noted salmon-fishing center. Hence its self-promotional sobriquet.

**Salonica** *Thessaloníki, Greece.* The name is a shortened European form of the seaport city's Roman name, Thessalonica. In 1937 the name was restored to its original form by Greek royal decree.

> Salonica's name is polymorphic. Poised between Europe and Asia, the city in northern Greece has been known as Salonicco, Selanik, Solun, Salonicha and Salonique [Ross Leckie, review of Mark Mazower, *Salonica, City of Ghosts*, *The Times*, October 22, 2005].

**Salop** *Shropshire, England.* The conventional abbreviated form of the county name derives from a late 11th-century Norman spelling of it as *Salopescira*, with *l* for *r*. When this short form was officially adopted as that of the county from 1974 through 1980 it was unpopular with local people, and especially with the European Member of Parliament for what was then Salop and Staffordshire, who discovered when attending debates in continental Europe that French *salope* means "slut." Even so, it is still in general use, and forms the regular adjective Salopian for a native or resident of Shropshire or of Shrewsbury, its county town. The alternate abbreviated form "Shrops" is also sometimes found. *See also* Appendix 6, p. 325.

> Miss Mitford, I believe, would write Shropshire for Salop. The thoughtful student may well prefer to follow the usage on his hostess's notepaper ["Strix" (Peter Fleming), "Posh Lingo," in Nancy Mitford, ed., *Noblesse Oblige*, 1946].

**Salt Lake State, the** *Utah, USA.* The name derives from the Great Salt Lake in the state's northern part, where the state capital, Salt Lake City, is located.

**Salt of the Earth, the** *Kansas, USA.* The nickname refers to the state's large salt reserves.

**Salt Sea, the** *Dead Sea.* The sea, on the boundary between Israel and Jordan, is actually a salt lake (rather than a freshwater one). Hence its biblical name, as in the quote below.

> And those that came down toward the sea of the plain, even the salt sea, failed, and were cut off [Joshua 3:16].

**Samba City** *Gort, Ireland.* The Co. Galway town was nicknamed for the Brazilian dance when meatpackers from Brazil were offered work in 2000 by a local butcher after his Irish employees proved unreliable.

> They call it "Samba City," a place where hundreds of smiling Brazilians dance in the streets ... to the Latin beat of the local disco [*The Times*, January 8, 2005].

**Sampa** *São Paolo, Brazil.* The nickname represents a local pronunciation of the city's Portuguese name.

> (1) It lacks Rio's visual splendour, or the colonial heritage of Salvador, but "Sampa" trumps them both for its dynamism [*The Times*, February 12, 2005].
>
> (2) Sampa, as it is known locally, is the wealthiest city in Brazil [*The Times*, April 14, 2005].

**San Antone** or **Antone** *San Antonio, Texas, USA.* A casual colloquial form of the city's name.

> (1) 'We might as well goof a coupla hours in San Antone' [Jack Kerouac, *On the Road*, 1957].
>
> (2) A motorcycle kid suddenly roared through ... singing, 'Houston, Austin, Fort Worth, Dallas — and sometimes Kansas City — and sometimes old Antone, ah-haaaaa!' [Jack Kerouac, *On the Road*, 1957].

**San Berdoo** *see* **Berdoo**

**Sanctuary of the Gods, the** *Annapurna, Nepal.* The Himalayan massif, with its four peaks, is sacred to Hindus, and its actual name is that of a Hindu goddess.

> Just five days through rhododendron forest from ... Pokhara, the "Sanctuary of the Gods" is a stupendous, inspiring goal [*Sunday Times*, November 7, 2004].

**Sandgroperland** *Western Australia, Australia.* The full form of the nickname **Groperland**, from the early immigrant "Sandgropers" who scraped a living in the deserts of this part of the island continent.

> (1) They do things differently over in Sandgroperland [*Truth* (Sydney), July 12, 1908].
>
> (2) How the swimmers of Sandgroperland attained the standard they reached ... surpasses my understanding [*Referee* (Sydney), February 11, 1920].

**Sand Hill** or **Sandhill State, the** *Arizona, USA.* The nickname refers to the tracts of desert for which the state is well known.

**Sandlapper State, the** *South Carolina, USA.* The name refers to the frugal existence of the early settlers among the sandy ridges of the Sandhills, where they supposedly had to "lap sand" to survive.

**Sandwich Islands, the** *Hawaii, USA.* In 1778 Captain Cook discovered the island group now known as Hawaii and named them in honor of John Montagu, 4th Earl of Sandwich, then first lord of the Admiralty. The name was in regular use, together with the indigenous one, down to the late 19th century and is still occasionally found today. The name and its source remain official for the South Sandwich Islands in the South Atlantic.

> (1) The Sandwich Islands remain my idea of the perfect thing in the matter of tropical islands [Mark Twain, *More Tramps Abroad*, 1897].

(2) Sandwich Islands... As these islands prefer to be known as the Hawaiian Islands, they have been described in this book under that name [Johnson, p. 217].

**Sandy Kitty** *Kansas City, Missouri, USA.* A humorous quasi-spoonerism of the city's name.

**San Fran** *San Francisco, California, USA.* One of many colloquial abbreviations of the city's name.

(1) I wrote long letters to Dean and Carlo... They said they were ready to come join me in San Fran as soon as this-and-that was ready [Jack Kerouac, *On the Road*, 1957].

(2) San Fran's famous musical revue, *Beach Blanket Babylon* [*The Times*, November 5, 2005].

**Sanhattan** *Santiago, Chile.* As indicated in the quote below, the punning name refers to Santiago's many skyscrapers, like those of Manhattan, as well as to the capital city's status as the financial heart of Chile. *Cp.* **Mainhattan.**

Downtown Santiago, known as Sanhattan because of its raft of skyscrapers [Dodd/Donald, p. 107].

**Sansan** see in Appendix 1, p. 269.

**São** *São Paulo, Brazil.* A colloquial short form of the city's name (the equivalent of calling a place "Saint Paul" as simply "Saint").

The Jardims district, São's answer to Beverly Hills [Dodd/Donald, p. 86].

**Sapphire City** *Inverell, Australia.* The New South Wales town lies in a major sapphire-mining area. Hence the name.

**Sarmatia** *Poland.* The poetic name is that of the historic region in this eastern part of Europe, between the Vistula River and the Caspian Sea, itself named for the people known as the Sarmatae.

Oh, bloodiest picture in the book of Time!
Sarmatia fell unwept, without a crime [Thomas Campbell, *The Pleasures of Hope*, 1799].

**Sarnia** *Guernsey, Channel Islands, UK.* The supposed Roman name of the island (actually that of the smaller Herm) has been preserved in poetry and in the anthem of Guernsey, with opening lines as in the quote below.

Sarnia, dear Homeland, Gem of the sea,
Island of beauty, my heart longs for thee [George Deighton, "Sarnia Cherie," 1911].

**Sarum** *Salisbury, England.* The abbreviated form of the Wiltshire city's name apparently combines the first three letters of *Saresbury*, an early form of the name, with the Latin ending *-um*. The name is in regular use for Old Sarum, the Iron Age hill fort and Roman camp nearby where the original city arose, and New Sarum, the formal name of the present city, in the valley below. It is also used in the official signature of the bishop of Salisbury. In ecclesiastical terminology the Sarum use or rite was the order of divine service that was used in the diocese of Salisbury from the 11th century to the Reformation and that for a time was more widely adopted, as described in quote (4) below. Quotes (1) and (2) refer to Salisbury Plain. *See also* **City of the Spire.**

(1) Goose, if I had you upon Sarum plain,
I'd drive ye cackling home to Camelot [William Shakespeare, *King Lear*, c. 1604].

(2) Once among the wilds
Of Sarum's Plain, my youthful spirit was raised [William Wordsworth, *The Prelude*, 1850].

(3) The city is often spoken of as *Sarum*, and the milestones in the district tell motorists how many miles it is to Sarum, not to Salisbury [Johnson, p. 216].

(4) In the later Middle Ages the Sarum Use was increasingly followed ... in other dioceses, and in 1457 stated to be in use in nearly the whole of England, Wales, and Ireland [E.A. Livingstone, ed., *The Oxford Dictionary of the Christian Church*, 1997].

**Saudi** *Saudi Arabia.* The short name, mainly used adjectivally or as a noun for a national, may occur in context. Grammatically, it is the adjectival form of the dynastic name of the country's founder in 1932, Abdul Aziz ibn Sa'ud.

"The real face of Saudi Arabia is not the same as that portrayed in the media in the US and in some UK papers," Prince Sultan adds. "Saudi is a friendly country and Saudis are naturally hospitable and welcoming" [*The Times* (Saudi Arabia Supplement), March 8, 2005].

**Saudi Venezuela** *Venezuela.* As intimated in the quote below, the nickname arose when members of the Organization of Petroleum Exporting Countries (OPEC) met in the Venezuelan capital. Saudi Arabia and Venezuela are two of the organization's original five founder members.

When Caracas was regularly hosting meetings of the OPEC members, the country that the city reigns over was known by jealous and more impoverished neighbours as "Saudi Venezuela" [Dodd/Donald, p. 100].

**Saxon Manchester, the** *Chemnitz, Germany.* The city in western Saxony earned its nickname in the 19th century for its smokestack industries, like those of England's Manchester.

**Saxon Shore** see in Appendix 1, p. 269.

**Saxon Triangle** see in Appendix 1, p. 269.

**Scabby Liz** *Scapa Flow, Orkney Islands, Scotland.* A World War I naval nickname for the large natural anchorage. The name denotes a disenchantment with the place, with the female name Liz substituted for a notional "Flo."

**Scale City** *Toledo, Ohio, USA.* The city gained its nickname for its manufacture of weighing machines.

**Scampi Belt** see in Appendix 1, p. 269.

**Scanderoon** *see* **Alexandretta**

**Scarlet Town** *Reading, England.* The old nickname of the Berkshire town puns on the pronunciation of its name as "Redding." There could also be a more subtle reference to the red bricks manufactured there. (The identification of the name with Reading in the quote below is disputed.)

> In Scarlet town, where I was born,
>   There was a fair maid dwellin',
>   Made every youth cry *Well-a-way!*
> Her name was Barbara Allen ["Barbara Allen's Cruelty," *The Oxford Book of Ballads*, 1910].

**Scarlet Woman** or **Whore, the** *Rome, Italy.* An abusive epithet for the city and thus also, some hold, for the Roman Catholic Church (*see* **Papal City**). The allusion is to the woman seen by St. John in a vision "arrayed in purple and scarlet colour ... drunken with the blood of the saints, and with the blood of the martyrs of Jesus," on whose forehead was written "MYS-TERY, BABYLON THE GREAT, THE MOTHER OF HARLOTS AND ABOMINA-TIONS OF THE EARTH," as described in Revelation 17:1–7. It is likely that Rome was actually "drunken with the blood of the saints" at the time the biblical book was written, in the late 1st century AD, when Christians suffered persecution under Nero following the great fire of AD 64.

**Scented Isle, the** *Corsica, France.* The name, translating French *l'île parfumée,* refers to the powerful scent of the flowers of the *maquis* (brushwood) that grows on the island's lower slopes. *Cp.* **Perfumed Isle.**

> The "Scented Isle" ... was ruled by the Genoese from the Middle Ages until 1768 [Young, p. 437].

**Sceptred Isle, the** *England or Britain.* The sobriquet denotes an island country ruled by a monarch, one of whose symbols of authority is a scepter. The phrase comes from Shakespeare, as in the quote below.

> This royal throne of kings, this scepter'd isle,
>   This earth of majesty, this seat of Mars [William Shakespeare, *Richard II*, 1597].

**Schmaltzburg** *Salzburg, Austria.* The punning name is favored by tourists who regard the city's musical, architectural, and culinary delights and Mozartian memorabilia as distinctly overegged.

> Birthplace of kitsch, Salzburg (or Schmaltzburg) is Mozart's Graceland [Dodd/Donald, p. 426].

**Science Capital of India, the** *Bangalore, India.* The city is not only the home of the Indian Institute of Science and the Raman Research Institute but widely known as the **Silicon Valley of India.** Hence its promotional nickname.

**'Sconset** *Siasconset, Massachusetts, USA.* A local short form of the Nantucket resort's name.

> The NRTA Shuttle ... operates buses to popular beaches and 'Sconset [*Lonely Planet USA*, 2004].

**Scotia** *(1) Ireland; (2) Scotland.* The Latin name remains in poetic use for Scotland and to a lesser extent for Ireland (the home of the original Scots). It also gave the standard name of Nova Scotia, Canada.

> (Scotland) Farewell, old Scotia's bleak domains,
>   Far dearer than the torrid plains
>   Where rich ananas blow! [Robert Burns, "The Farewell," 1786].

**Scotland in Miniature** *Arran, Scotland.* The island in the Firth of Clyde, off the west coast of Scotland, is so nicknamed for the contrast between the jagged mountain peaks in the north and gentle farming landscape in the south, similar to the landscape in the mainland **Highlands** and **Lowlands** (see both in Appendix 1, p. 269), as well as for its great variety of scenery.

> Arran has a much more varied landscape than most of Scotland's islands and in many ways justifies the local Tourist Board's slogan — 'Scotland in Miniature' [Newton, p. 176].

**Scotland's Holiday Isle** *Arran, Scotland.* A self-promotional name for the island off the west coast of Scotland, which has many attractions for the vacationer and casual visitor.

> Arran claims to be 'Scotland's holiday isle,' and indeed there is plenty for the visitor to do [Booth/Perrott, p. 112].

**Scott Country** see in Appendix 1, p. 269.

**Scottish Geneva, the** *Dundee, Scotland.* The town earned its sobriquet not for its geographical resemblance to the Swiss city but because it was a center of the Reformation, as Geneva was.

**Scottish Riviera** see in Appendix 1, p. 269.

**Scottish Sahara, the** *Culbin Forest, Scotland.* The state forest on Scotland's west coast was planted in the 1920s on drifting sand which had buried the original farmland. Hence its former nickname.

**Scouseland** *Liverpool, England.* Native residents of Liverpool and their local dialect are known as "Scouse," an abbreviation of "lobscouse" as a sailor's meal of meat stewed with vegetables and ship's biscuit. Hence the city's nickname.

> Scouseland on the Silver Screen. Made in Liverpool — the 51st State... We looked at some of the movies and tv shows made in Liverpool and found a few Hollywood surprises! ["Where I Live: Liverpool." BBC website <http://www.bbc.co.uk/liverpool/features/2003/07/movielocations/index.shtml> accessed November 16, 2004].

**Scratchland** *Scotland.* A former uncomplimentary nickname for Scotland as land of "lousy" inhabitants. The name partly puns on "Scotch." *Cp.* **Itchland.**

**Scunny** *Scunthorpe, England.* A colloquial name for the North Lincolnshire town, more commonly applied to the local football club, Scunthorpe United.

**Scutari** *(1) Shkodër, Albania; (2) Üsküdar, Turkey.* The identical Italian name of both towns (the latter now a district of Istanbul) is still found in historical contexts. The Turkish town was the base of the British army in the Crimean War and the site of the hospital under the charge of the English nurse Florence Nightingale (the "Lady with the Lamp").

**Seabird Capital of the World, the** *New Zealand.* The country has been so nicknamed for the many species of seabirds that visit or breed along its coasts.

**Sea-Born City, the** *Venice, Italy.* The city's sobriquet was popularized by Byron as in the quote below. *Cp.* **Bride of the Sea.** (It is tempting to see a link between the name of the Italian city and that of Venus, the Roman goddess of love, who in the persona of her Greek alter ego, Aphrodite, was born from the sea. But such an association is not mentioned by Geoffrey Grigson in *The Goddess of Love*, 1976, in which he considers various aspects of the goddess's two names.)

> And at the moment when I fix my story,
> That sea-born city was in all her glory [Lord Byron, *Beppo: A Venetian Story*, 1817].

**Seafood Capital of the Country, the** *Crisfield, Maryland, USA.* The city has been an important center of the seafood industry since the arrival of the railroad in the 1860s. Hence the self-styled nickname.

**Sea-Girt Isle, the** *England or Britain.* Milton's poetic name for Britain, as in quote (3) below, has its Shakespearean antecedents, as can be seen in the first two quotes.

> (1) England, hedg'd in with the main,
> That water-walled bulwark [William Shakespeare, *King John*, 1596].
> (2) England, bound in with the triumphant sea,
> Whose rocky shore beats back the envious siege
> Of watery Neptune [William Shakespeare, *Richard II*, 1597].
> (3) In th' Ocean wide,
> Beyond the Realm of Gaul, a Land there lies,
> Sea-girt it lies [John Milton, "Brutus," *The History of England*, 1670].

**Seán Buí** *England.* The Irish nickname for England is the equivalent of **John Bull**, from *Seán*, "John," and the disparaging word *buí* (literally "yellow," but implying "dirty," "bad"). In literature the name was applied by John O'Cunningham to the followers of William III, as in the quote below.

> They'll accomplish whate'er may in man be.
> Just heaven! They will bring
> Desolation and woe
> On the hosts of the tyrannous Shane Bwee!
> [John O'Cunningham, "The Wild Geese," 1732].

**Sea of Reeds, the** *Red Sea.* The alternate name is the English translation of Hebrew *yam sûp*, referring to a body of water east of the Nile delta, but not the Red Sea as now defined. The similarity between English "red" and "reed" is purely a coincidence. (The Red Sea is often referred to in the Bible as simply "the sea," as in Exodus 14:2, and where in the Pentateuch, or first five books of the Bible, it is named "the Red sea," as in Exodus 10:19, this translates Greek *thalassa eruthra*. In Isaiah 11:15 it is referred to as "the Egyptian sea.")

**Sea of Straw, the** *Tagus River, Spain/Portugal.* Portugal's main river is so nicknamed for the color of its waters as it expands into a lagoon above Lisbon, as described in the quote below.

> From the hilltop near St. George's Castle, the sun often gives the River Tagus the golden reflection that has earned it its name "Mar da Palha," or "Sea of Straw" [Cruise brochure, 2005].

**Seashore Pleasure Ground of America, the** *Atlantic City, New Jersey, USA.* A cumbersomely dated touristic name for the city and seaside resort.

> British tours still went to Canada and the United States, and the firm [of Thomas Cook & Son] puffed places like Atlantic City, 'The Seashore Pleasure Ground of America' [Piers Brendon, *Thomas Cook: 150 Years of Popular Tourism*, 1991].

**Seat of Royalty, the** *Aachen (Aix-la-Chapelle), Germany.* The city is so named as the northern capital of Charlemagne. *Cp.* **Rome of the West.**

**Second Alexandria, the** *Berwick-upon-Tweed, England.* The Northumberland town, long disputed between the Scots and the English, was formerly so nicknamed as Scotland's richest port. The comparison is with Alexandria in Egypt, a center of Hellenistic culture and the site of the greatest library of ancient times.

**Second City, the** *(1) Birmingham, England; (2) Chicago, Illinois, USA.* Both cities are traditionally regarded as second in importance after London and New York, respectively. (Birmingham is also second in population after London, but Chicago is now third in the USA, with Los Angeles in second place.)

> (1) (Chicago) A small village of only 250 people

in 1833, it had exploded and was now the nation's Second City (New York being the First) [Malcolm Bradbury, ed., *The Atlas of Literature*, 1996].

(2) (Chicago) It has been said that Chicago's intelligentsia is hindered by a "second city" mentality and an accompanying tendency toward self-disparagement [*Britannica*, vol. 16, p. 3].

(3) (Chicago) Given all its assertiveness, it's reassuring that Chicago has a sensitive soul, able to be a little prickly about its "Second City" sobriquet [Dodd/Donald, p. 162].

**Second City of the Empire, the** *(1) Birmingham, England; (2) Dublin, Ireland; (3) Glasgow, Scotland; (4) Kolkata (Calcutta), India; (5) Liverpool, England.* The Irish capital was so known when the present Republic of Ireland was part of the British Empire. The Scottish capital was so titled at the turn of the 20th century, when two international exhibitions were held (in 1888 and 1901) to promote the city and its industries to the world. Kolkata was so called in the days of British imperial rule in India. The "First City" was of course London, the **Capital of the World**. Birmingham and Liverpool have claimed the name on rather doubtful grounds, although the former is indubitably the **Second City**.

(1) (Glasgow) At this time Glasgow became "Second City of the Empire"—a curious epithet for a place that today rarely acknowledges second place in anything [*The Rough Guide to Scotland*, 1998].

(2) (Birmingham) Liverpool and Birmingham have recently advanced utterly spurious claims to the title [Cowan, p. 341].

**Second Rome, the** *Istanbul (Constantinople), Turkey.* The epithet is due to Constantine the Great, the first Roman emperor to profess Christianity, who in AD 330 rebuilt Byzantium as his permanent capital and renamed it after himself. The title marked the breach with the old traditions of Rome, and Constantinople became the traditional seat of Eastern Christianity. *Cp.* **Third Rome**.

On May 11, 330 AD the Emperor Constantine resolutely chose Byzantium as his "second Rome" but quickly renamed it Constantinople in his own honor [Leier, p. 40].

**Serendip** or **Serendib** *Sri Lanka.* The poetic name was the one given by Arab traders to the island long known as **Ceylon**. The name itself, a corruption of a Sanskrit word meaning "island of the place of lions," gave English "serendipity" as the term for a chance happy or useful discovery. The word was coined by the writer Horace Walpole, as described by him in quote (1) below.

(1) The discovery I made by a talisman, which Mr. Chute calls the Sortes Walpolianae, by which I find everything I want, à pointe nomméé [*sic*], whenever I dip for it. This discovery, indeed, is almost of that kind which I call "Serendipity," a very expressive word, which, as I have nothing better to tell you, I shall endeavour to explain to you: you will understand it better by the derivation than by the definition. I once read a silly fairy story called "The Three Princes of Serendip."As their Highnesses travelled, they were always making discoveries of things which they were not in quest of [Horace Walpole, letter to Horace Mann, January 28, 1754].

(2) This Solimaun [i.e. Solomon], Serendib had in sway —
And where's Serendib? may some critic say.—
Good lack, mine honest friend, consult the chart,
Scare not my Pegasus before I start! [Sir Walter Scott, *The Search after Happiness*, 1817].

**Serenissima, La** *Venice, Italy.* The Italian epithet means "the most serene," "the sublime," and properly applies to the republic of Venice that existed down to 1866.

(1) In its great days as the capital of an independent republic, it was the abstract concept of Venice as 'the eldest child of Liberty,' inviolate, perfect, 'La Serenissima,' the Most Serene, to which Venetians and their colonial subjects through the eastern Mediterranean were expected to stay loyal [Jonathan Keates, *Venice*, 1994].

(2) The Doges swept around the Venetian lagoon in their gilded barges. Now you can enjoy the same views of La Serenissima from the deck of your own cruiser [*The Times*, April 9, 2005].

(3) Get in the mood for a weekend break in La Serenissima by reading *The Stones of Venice* by John Ruskin [*The Times*, November 26, 2005].

**Sericana** *China.* The poetic name derives from the Seres, an Asian people believed to have inhabited China. Their own name gave (or derived from) Latin *sericum*, "silk," which they were said to have originally made.

But in his way lights on the barren plains
Of Sericana, where Chineses drive
With sails and wind their cany waggons light [John Milton, *Paradise Lost*, 1667].

**Serps, the** *Serpentine, London, England.* A colloquial short name for the long curved lake (hence its full name) in Hyde Park and Kensington Gardens, popular for swimming and boating in summer and skating in winter.

This morning was another normal day — up at 5.45, off to the Serps and swimming as usual with Janie [Serpentine Swimming Club News <http://www.serpentineswimmingclub.com/News%202005.htm> accessed May 20, 2005].

**Seven-Hilled City, the** *Rome, Italy.* The city of Rome was built on (or about) seven hills: Aventine, Caelian, Capitoline, Esquiline, Palatine (where Romulus is traditionally said to have founded the original city), Quirinus, and Viminal. Hence the epithet, recorded as Latin *septi-collis* in the writings of the 4th-century Roman poet Prudentius.

(1) The Goth, the Christian, Time, War, Flood, and Fire,
Have dealt upon the seven-hill'd city's pride [Lord Byron, *Childe Harold's Pilgrimage*, 1812].
(2) Up! up with the lily!
And down with the keys!
In old Rome, the seven-hilly,
We'll revel at ease [Lord Byron, *The Deformed Transformed*, 1824].

**Seven Seas** see in Appendix 1, p. 269.

**Seventy-Two Suburbs in Search of a City** *Los Angeles, California, USA*. A nickname attributed to various sources that refers to the city's shifting, shapeless sprawl. *Cp.* **Nineteen Suburbs in Search of a Metropolis**.

(1) James Gleason, Dorothy Parker, and several other people are credited with calling Los Angeles: Seventy-two suburbs in search of a city. No matter who said it, it's still true [John Walker, ed., *Halliwell's Who's Who in the Movies*, 2003].
(2) When Dorothy Parker described Los Angeles as "72 suburbs in search of a city" a half century or so ago, it was probably true; today the world at large tends to think of Los Angeles as *several* cities [*Fodor's Los Angeles 2006*].

**Seven Worlds of Wonder, the** *Phinda Game Reserve, South Africa*. The nickname, punning on the Seven Wonders of the World, refers to the seven different habitats that have been nurtured in the KwaZulu-Natal reserve, from wetlands to sand forests.

**Severn Sea, the** *Bristol Channel, England/ Wales*. A literary name for the extension of the mouth of the Severn River between England and Wales.

(1) Between Newport and the 'Severn Sea' ... there are curious fens or 'levels' [Ruth Thomas, *South Wales*, 1977].
(2) One may prefer this north-western Somerset, its steep-hilled roads, its cleft valleys, its brows raised over the peculiar Severn Sea [Geoffrey Grigson in Hadfield 1981, p. 275].
(3) Before the arrival of the railways in the 1850s, most of the produce of the Herefordshire countryside was shipped down the Wye [River] to the 'Severn-Sea' [Robin Whiteman, *The Heart of England*, 1992].

**Seward's Folly** or **Icebox** *Alaska, USA*. The early derisory nickname refers to Secretary of State William H. Seward, who negotiated the treaty of 1867 by which Russia ceded Alaska to the USA for $7,200,000.

**Sex Capital of the World, the** *Bangkok, Thailand*. The capital city came by its seamy sobriquet for its commercial sex industry, a lure for many foreign tourists.

**SF** *San Francisco, California, USA*. A fairly common initialism of the city's name. *Cp.* **SFC**.

(1) One year at the University of Wisconsin, then moved to S.F. with her boyfriend, drummer in a rock-band [Brown Meggs, *The Matter of Paradise*, 1975].
(2) What might shift under LA, SF and Santa A? [Cryptic crossword clue, *The Times*, January 15, 2005; anagrammatic answer: San Andreas Fault].

**SFC** *San Francisco, California, USA*. An initialism of "San Francisco City" or of the city's nickname "Sucka Free City" (*see* **Sucka Free**).

**Shakespeare Avon, the** *Avon River, England*. A nickname for the river that rises near Naseby, Northamptonshire, and flows through Stratford-on-Avon, Warwickshire (Shakespeare's birthplace), to enter the Severn near Tewkesbury, Gloucestershire. It is also known as the Upper Avon or Warwick(shire) Avon. Its literary prefix distinguishes it from the Lower Avon or Bristol Avon, which rises at Tetbury, Gloucestershire, and enters the Bristol Channel at Avonmouth, from the East Avon or Wiltshire Avon (or Salisbury Avon or Hampshire Avon), which rises near Devizes, Wiltshire, and flows south through Salisbury in that county and then through Hampshire into Christchurch Harbour, and from the Little Avon or Middle Avon, which rises near Wotton-under-Edge, Gloucestershire, and flows into the Severn near Berkeley in that county. All of these identically named rivers are in southern England and require their respective epithets.

**Shakespeare Country** see in Appendix 1, p. 269.

**Shaky City** *(1) Los Angeles, California, USA; (2) San Francisco, California, USA*. A nickname referring to the earthquakes experienced by both cities. *Cp.* **Quake City**.

**Shaky Isles, the** *New Zealand*. A nickname similar to **Shivery Isles**, referring to the earthquakes occurring in New Zealand.

He came over from the Shaky Isles in his early 30s [*Sunday Telegraph* (Sydney), May 16, 1971].

**Shakyside** *California, USA*. A nickname referring to the earthquakes occurring in the state. *Cp.* **Shaky City**.

**Shakytown** *Los Angeles, California, USA*. A nickname with the same meaning as **Shaky City**.

**Shamrockshire** *Ireland*. The former nickname comes from the plant that is the country's national emblem. Its three leaves are said to have been used by St. Patrick to illustrate the doctrine of the Trinity. (The title of the work quoted below is pseudo–Greek for "Description of the Western Isle.")

Priests in Shambroghshire, they say,
Can women kiss, as well as pray [William Moffet, *Hesperi-Neso-Graphia*, 1716].

**Shangri La** *Camp David, Maryland, USA*. The US presidential retreat in Catoctin National Park has had different names over the years.

When built in 1939 it was called Hi-Catoctin. Franklin Roosevelt later dubbed it Shangri La, for the hidden paradise in James Hilton's novel *Lost Horizon* (1933). Dwight Eisenhower then renamed it Camp David, as now, for his grandson. The name Shangri La is still in use for any "paradise on earth" or hidden retreat. (Hilton's name is mock–Tibetan, although *la* means "pass.")

**Shank End, the** *Cape Peninsula, South Africa.* The nickname denotes the lower extremity or "leg end" of the country. *Cp.* **Top End.**

**Shan Van Vocht, the** *Ireland.* The 18th-century literary name is a personification of Ireland as a poor old woman (Irish *sean bhean bhocht*). It occurs in the ballad quoted below, commemorating the rising of 1798.

> Will Ireland then be free?
> Said the Shan Van Voght [*sic*].
> Yes Ireland shall be free
> From the centre to the sea,
> Hurray for liberty!
> Said the Shan Van Voght [Popular ballad, 1798].

**Shaston** *Shaftesbury, England.* The alternate name of the Dorset town (adopted in his novels by Thomas Hardy) may have resulted from a shortening of the Medieval Latin form *Shaftonia*, with *f* misread as *s*. (The confusion would have been between *f* and the so-called "long *s*," written or printed like italic *f* without the crossbar and occurring in such words as "most" and "west.") *See also* **Glaston.**

> "Shaston," as Mr. Hardy, the milestones, and old chroniclers agree to call it [Charles G. Harper, *The Hardy Country*, 1904].

**Sheba** *Saba, Yemen.* The ancient country that probably included modern Yemen is familiar from the Bible story of the Queen of Sheba's visit to King Solomon (1 Kings 10).

**Sheer Nasty** *Sheerness, England.* A sailors' gloomy nickname for the Kent port, with its former naval dockyard and barracks.

**Sheffield of Germany, the** *Solingen, Germany.* The former nickname refers to the city's reputation as a center of the cutlery industry, like Sheffield in England.

**Shelley's Country** see in Appendix 1, p. 269.

**Shellfare State, the** *Brunei.* The sultanate on the island of Borneo was made rich by oil, and its nickname, punning on "welfare state," derives from the Royal Dutch/Shell Group that has dominated its economy.

> In what is often referred to as the "Shellfare State," housing is subsidised, education is free up to university level, [and] the Government spends $600 a head annually on medical services [*The Times*, March 31, 2004].

**Sherry Triangle** see in Appendix 1, p. 269.

**Shiny, the** *India.* A former British army nickname for the hot country, with its bright sunshine. The reference could equally be to the white man's skin, glistening with sweat. *Cp.* **Sweatipore.**

**Shipwreck Coast** see in Appendix 1, p. 269.

**Shire, the** *Wigtownshire, Scotland.* The historic county was often locally so known, as distinct from neighboring Kirkcudbright. *See* **Stewartry.**

**Shires** see in Appendix 1, p. 269.

**Shivering Mountain, the** *Mam Tor, England.* The Derbyshire hill is so nicknamed for the landslides that continually occur, resulting from the alternate layers of grit and shale that compose its surface. ("Shivering" here means "crumbling," not "trembling," and there are two distinct verbs "shiver" of differing origin. *Cp.* **Shivery Isles.**)

> (1) Mam Tor, the "shivering" mountain (whose shaley rock is always slipping and pushing the road further downhill) [*Holiday Haunts 1960: Area No. 2, North West England and North Wales*].
> (2) Pass behind that strange hill shown on your map as Mam Tor but colloquially known as 'Shivering Mountain.' And for a very good reason. Is it fact, or is it merely an optical illusion, that persuades you as you stand there contemplating it that the north face of Mam Tor is in motion? [Hogg, p. 95].

**Shivery Isles, the** *New Zealand.* The nickname refers to the earthquakes and earth tremors experienced in New Zealand. *Cp.* **Shaky Isles.**

> Maorilanders inform me that shellfish is regarded as a luxury in the Shivery Isles [*The Bulletin* (Sydney), July 18, 1951].

**Shocks** *Chocques, France.* A British soldiers' World War I version of the name of the village in northern France.

**Shoot, the** *Walthamstow, London, England.* The nickname was current in the early years of the 20th century as a short form of "rubbish shoot," referring to the human "trash" who populated this heavily industrialized urban area.

**Shopping Centre of England, the** *Peterborough, England.* The former Cambridgeshire city, now a unitary authority, was long essentially an agricultural market town with a medieval cathedral until it was designated a New Town in 1967, after which it expanded considerably to become an important industrial and commercial center.

> For those visitors with a more modern agenda [than nearby Cambridge], Peterborough is known as England's shopping centre [*Lonely Planet Great Britain*, 2005].

**Shortest River in the World, the** *Roe River, Montana, USA.* The river, near Great Falls, is only 201 feet (61 m) long. Hence its nickname.

**Shot, the** *Aldershot, England.* A late 19th-century soldiers' nickname for the Hampshire town, established as a military camp in 1855 and associated with the British Army more than any other town in Britain.

**Show Me State, the** *Missouri, USA.* The nickname refers to the reputed skepticism and wariness of Missouri people. The familiar catchphrase "I'm from Missouri, you'll have to show me," was popularized by Congressman Willard D. Vandiver (1854–1932), as in quote (1) below.

> (1) I come from a state that raises corn and cotton and cockleburs and Democrats, and frothy eloquence neither convinces nor satisfies me. I am from Missouri. You have got to show me [Willard D. Vandiver, speech at naval banquet, Philadelphia, 1899].
>
> (2) Ex-Lieut.-Gov. Chas. P. Johnson thinks he knows the origin of the extensively-used expression: "I'm from Missouri; you'll have to show me"; at least he can recall its use in Colorado twenty years ago [*Missouri State Tribune* (Jefferson City), December 13, 1900].
>
> (3) *Vicarro:* Just as dark as my arm is!
> *Flora:* You don't have to show me! I'm not from Missouri! [Tennessee Williams, *27 Wagons Full of Cotton*, 1946].
>
> (4) The expression [Show Me State] was coined as an insult by outsiders and was meant to suggest that Missourians were so stupid that they had to be shown how to do everything. The state's inhabitants, however, contrarily took it as a compliment, persuading themselves that it implied a certain shrewd caution on their part [Bill Bryson, *Made in America*, 1994].
>
> (5) There have been many jokes about Missouri's nickname, the 'Show Me State'; it's based on the legendary skepticism, not willful flashers [*Lonely Planet USA*, 2004].

**Show Village of England, the** *Broadway, England.* The Worcestershire village has been so styled for its impressive broad main street (not the one that actually gave its name) lined with well-preserved houses and cottages.

> Not without reason has Broadway been called 'the show village of England' [*AA Book of British Villages*, 1980].

**Shroppie** or **Shroppy, the** *Shropshire Union Canal, England.* The colloquial short form of the name is mainly used by canal-boating enthusiasts. The canal itself connects the Mersey River at Ellesmere Port, Cheshire, with the Staffordshire and Worcestershire Canal at a point near Wolverhampton, a course that traverses Shropshire. *See also* **Canal County.**

> A bit of time spent in quiet contemplation on the "Shroppy" will show more of the county's timeless, unspoiled rural side [*Sunday Times* (Northwest England Supplement), September 11, 2005].

**Shrops** *see* **Salop**

**Siam** *Thailand.* The country's long-familiar name was current until 1939, when it was changed to Thailand by the new Thai premier, Pibul Songgram, who in 1942 concluded an alliance with Japan and declared war on the USA and Britain. In 1944 his government was overthrown by Pridi Phanomyong, who restored the earlier name. In 1948, however, Pibul returned as premier, in turn overthrew Pridi, and brought back the name Thailand. The old name is kept alive by Siamese cats and Siamese twins (and by the 1946 movie *Anna and the King of Siam*).

> (1) In June, 1939, the Siamese Government announced by official decree that the name of Siam would henceforth be Thailand 'in the English language.' Sir John Squire protested against this curious announcement, and wrote: 'When that change was made I asked a Siamese why on earth they had done it. His reply was that they thought the change would please Europe, and particularly England. I said: "Look here, my dear fellow, all Europe since Elizabeth's day has known your country as Siam;..."' Unfortunately, British authorities acquiesced in the change, and the bastard name Thailand has gained currency as a postal name. But that we should renounce our living name 'Siam' in favour of one which the Siamese themselves do not use (they call their country Prathet Thai or Muang Thai) is, I hope, unlikely while English is a living tongue [Aurousseau, pp. 22, 24].
>
> (2) What is the name of our country? Is it Siam or Thailand? How comes it that we are called Siamese? [M.L. Manich Jumsai, "Siam or Thailand, which is right?" in *Sammaggi Sara*, February 1970].

**Sick Man of Europe, the** *Turkey.* The metaphor was current for Ottoman Turkey during its decline in the 19th century. The phrase is said to have originated in a conversation at St. Petersburg between the Russian czar and the British chargé d'affaires as reported in quote (1) below.

> (1) We have on our hands a sick man, a very sick man. It would be a great misfortune, I tell you frankly, if, one of these days, he should happen to die before the necessary arrangements were all made [Nicholas I to Sir George Seymour, January 11, 1853, reported in *Annual Register*, 1853].
>
> (2) Before World War I Turkey was known as the "Sick Man of Europe"; now it is almost a terminal case [Richard Nixon, *The Real War*, 1980].

**Sierra State, the** *California, USA.* The nickname refers to the Sierra Nevada that runs down the eastern part of the state.

**Silent City, the** *(1) Mdina, Malta; (2) Venice, Italy.* The former Maltese capital is a small city enclosed within walls that deaden external sounds. The Italian city is nicknamed for its silent "streets" (canals), which lack the usual noise of vehicles found in other cities.

(Venice) [The name of Venezuela means] "Little Venice," which designation was given to this country owing to the discovery of some Indian villages built upon piles after the manner of the "Silent City" on the Adriatic Sea [Wagner 1892, p. 44].

**Silent Highway, the** *Thames River, England.* The nickname could be applied to any soft-flowing river but caught on for the Thames.

> The Silent Highway has been their travelling route. On the broad ... bosom of Father Thames, they have been borne in swift, grimy little steamboats [G.A. Sala, *Twice Round the Clock*, 1859].

**Silesian Rome, the** *Nysa, Poland.* The city in southern Poland, the former capital of a Silesian principality, was so nicknamed for its many religious houses and its status as a center of Catholic education.

**Silicon Alley** see in Appendix 1, p. 269.

**Silicon Chip Valley of the West Country, The** *Tewkesbury, England.* The name alludes to the many electronics firms that arose around the Gloucestershire town. (For **West Country** see Appendix 1, p. 269.)

> Tewkesbury is still recovering from the recession which hit local aerospace and electronics industries particularly badly — its title "The Silicon Chip Valley of the West Country" rings rather hollow these days [*The Rough Guide to England*, 1998].

**Silicon Fen** *Cambridge, England.* The nickname, based on the original US **Silicon Valley**, alludes to the many electronics firms that have grown up in and around the fenland city of Cambridge, several having links with the university (which has long had a "science" bent as against the "arts" leaning of Oxford). *See also* **Fens** in Appendix 1, p. 269.

> (1) The city and university have been rapidly acquiring a reputation as a high-tech centre of excellence, what locals refer to half-seriously as "Silicon Fen" [*The Rough Guide to England*, 1998].
> (2) Silicon Fen, the nickname given to the area that surrounds and takes in Cambridge [*The Times*, May 6, 2005].
> (3) Although Cambridge's grouping of biotechnology, software and IT companies, known as "Silicon Fen," is considered one of the most important centres for technology in Europe, it is still dwarfed by Silicon Valley in California [*The Times*, September 15, 2005].

**Silicon Glen** *Glenrothes, Scotland.* The nickname, punning both on the New Town's name and on the **Silicon Fen** of Cambridge, refers to the electronics industries that have become established in the area. (The Californian company Hughes Microelectronics has its European base here.)

> The project aims to raise the level of expertise in Silicon Glen [*The Scotsman*, January 12, 1999].

**Silicon Island** *Kyushu, Japan.* Japan's southernmost island is a center of the country's electronics industry. Hence its nickname.

> The economy of Kumamoto Prefecture has been transformed over the past 20 years by the introduction of the semiconductor industry, which has given Kyushu its contemporary nickname of 'silicon island' [Richard Bowring and Peter Kornicki, eds., *The Cambridge Encyclopedia of Japan*, 1993].

**Silicon Valley** *Santa Clara County, California, USA.* The county is the home of the USA's microchip technology industry, in which silicon is used to make the "chips" for microprocessors. Hence the nickname, which has been adopted and adapted in similar regions elsewhere in the world (as in the entries above). The valley is Santa Clara Valley, which runs through the county. A short form of the name is Siva.

> (1) They have turned part of Santa Clara County into "Silicon Valley," the world capital of semiconductor technology [*Fortune*, June 1974].
> (2) In more recent years "Silicon Valley" has grown up along the peninsula from San Francisco through Stanford University to San Jose [*New York Times*, June 22, 1980].
> (3) Silicon Valley's "computer cops" are using the latest high-tech tools to track down the growing number of criminals who plan to kidnap children [*Sunday Correspondent*, April 22, 1990].

**Silicon Valley North** *Ottawa, Ontario, Canada.* The Canadian capital has a large computer and technology workforce. Hence its nickname, based on the US **Silicon Valley** as its southern original.

**Silicon Valley of India, the** *Bangalore, India.* The city earns its nickname as the center of the country's high-tech industries, including computer and electronics industries and the manufacture of watches and telephones. *Cp.* **Science Capital of India.**

**Silk City** *Hangzhou, China.* The city of eastern China is a noted center of silk production. Hence the nickname.

**Silk City of the World, the** *Paterson, New Jersey, USA.* The nickname alludes to the city's booming silk industry of the mid-19th century.

**Silkingrad** *Stevenage, England.* Protesting residents of the Hertfordshire town renamed it thus (as described in the quote below) during a visit in 1946 by Labour planning minister Lewis Silkin in connection with his proposal to make Stevenage Britain's first New Town. The name was based on Russia's (also renamed) **Stalingrad.**

> At the meeting in the town to explain the project he was greeted with cries of 'Gestapo!' 'Dictator!' The tyres of his car were let down and sand put in the petrol tank. The name boards on the railway station were replaced with ones marked 'Silk-

ingrad' [Frank Schaffer, *The New Town Story*, 1970].

**Silk Stocking District** see in Appendix 1, p. 269.

**Silly Suffolk** *Suffolk, England.* The adjective of the alliterative name supposedly refers to the naivety or simple innocence of local people. It may have been suggested by the sheep, a traditionally "silly" animal, for which Suffolk is noted, although some sources, as in' quotes (2) and (3) below, link the sobriquet with "silly" in its original sense of "holy," referring to the county as a **Land of Churches**. *Cp.* **Silly Sussex**.

(1) "Silly Suffolk" and "Essex Calves" are local amenities liberally bestowed on each other by the natives [John G. Nall, *Great Yarmouth and Lowestoft*, 1866].

(2) Perhaps the catch-phrase 'Silly Suffolk' echoes somewhere in the depths of memory? May be so; but the origin of the word dates back to the Anglo-Saxon *selig*, and that word means simple, innocent, blessed. It has, it is true, been used also of Sussex; but it is pre-eminently of Suffolk that the epithet seems so just [Hogg, p. 117].

(3) Suffolk is called Silly Suffolk ... because of its holiness, deduced from its profusion of flint churches erected when it was the wool-basket of Europe because of its Suffolk sheep [Philip Howard in *The Times*, April 1, 2005].

**Silly Sussex** *Sussex, England.* As with **Silly Suffolk**, the historic county (divided into the modern counties of East Sussex and West Sussex) may have a nickname alluding either to its sheep or to its many churches and religious houses. "Seely" is sometimes substituted for "silly" to represent a dialect form of the word, as in the quote below.

What is there about Hawkhurst that is different from these other "hursts," Ticehurst, Wadhurst, and the rest that lie within the confine of "seely" Sussex? [S.P.B. Mais, *The Home Counties*, 1942].

**Silly Sutton** *Sutton, England.* As for **Silly Suffolk**, the adjective of the alliterative sobriquet refers to the supposed naivety of the Norfolk village's inhabitants.

In this district we had ... "Silly Sutton"... Sutton is awarded its ... title from the tradition that its aged natives ... put their hands out of their bedroom windows to feel if it was daylight [*Eastern Evening News* (Norwich), November 15, 1892].

**Silver City, the** *(1) Aberdeen, Scotland; (2) Broken Hill, Australia.* The "silver" in the sobriquet of the Scottish city designates a color, as described in the quote below, whereas in that of the Australian city it is the actual metal. Broken Hill has been a center of zinc and silver mining since 1883 and nearby Silverton, now a ghost town, was a flourishing silver-mining town at that time.

(1) (Broken Hill) The Silver City is the scene of the following story [*Quiz* (Adelaide), May 1, 1891].

(2) (Aberdeen) When the sun shines, the mica in the granite sparkles, hence "Silver City" has become a popular description for Aberdeen [*Baedeker's Scotland*, 3d ed., 1999].

**Silver City by the Sea** or **by the Golden Sands, the** *Aberdeen, Scotland.* The poetic name refers to the coastal location of the city and seaside resort. *Cp.* **Silver City**.

(1) For anyone passing their night and days in The Silver City by the Sea ... it is comparable to passing one's existence in a refrigerator [Lewis Grassic Gibbon, *Scottish Scene*, 1934].

(2) The building of Marischal College was started in 1844 by the famous local architect Archibald Simpson who had a vision of 'a planned silver city by the sea' [Robinson/Millward, p. 410].

(3) Take a bracing walk along the Silver City's "Golden Sands" [*The Times* (Scotland Supplement), September 10, 2005].

**Silver Coast** see in Appendix 1, p. 269.

**Silver Smile, the** *New Orleans, Louisiana, USA.* An occasional literary name for the **Crescent City**, describing the white water of the Mississippi and the curve of the city on its east bank.

The Silver Smile, New Orleans, ringed all around them now that the tug was pushing midriver [Maureen McCoy, *Divining Blood*, 1992].

**Silver State, the** *(1) Colorado, USA; (2) Nevada, USA.* The nickname refers to the mining of silver in both states. The name is now applied less often to Colorado, but is still valid for Nevada, where the famous Comstock Lode yielded a rich deposit of silver in 1859.

(1) (Nevada) The Silver State struck it rich when they elected H.G. Blasdel to the Gubernatorial chair [*Eastern Slope* (Washoe, Nevada), September 15, 1866].

(2) (Colorado) Colorado miners had been looking for gold but silver became of such importance that when the Territory became a state in 1876, it was known as the Silver State and Georgetown was called the Silver Queen [*Trail and Timberline*, May 1946].

**Silver Streak, the** *English Channel.* A former nickname for the narrow stretch of water between England and France.

(1) The silver streak, on the other side of which is dear England [James Payn, *The Mystery of Mirbridge*, 1888].

(2) "The silver streak" can be crossed in little over an hour from Folkestone or Dover [*The Sphere*, March 27, 1909].

**Sin Angeles** *Los Angeles, California, USA.* A Spanish nickname for the city, and especially the barrios of East Los Angeles. The name implies a "city of sin" but more subtly puns on the real name to mean "without angels."

**Sin Capital, the** *Singapore*. A nickname prompted by the seamier side of the sprawling seaport city.

**Sin City** *(1) Chicago, Illinois, USA; (2) Covington, Kentucky, USA; (3) Las Vegas, Nevada, USA*. All three cities have had a reputation for some kind of unlawful or undesirable activity. Chicago was known worldwide for the underground violence during and after the Prohibition era of the 1920s and 1930s, while Las Vegas was notorious for the gangsterism of the 1940s. The latter city's later "adult" appeal, enhanced by Hunter S. Thompson's 1971 classic *Fear and Loathing in Las Vegas*, has prompted targeted tourist publicity, as in quote (2) below. (In 2001 Las Vegas was promoted by its convention center as the city "where you can do what you want, when you want.")

(1) (Chicago) What's going to happen in Chicago? ... All you want to do is run amok in 'Sin City' [Alec Thackeray, *One-Way Ticket*, 1975].

(2) (Las Vegas) In a further attempt to cash in on its sleazy reputation, the Nevada Commission recently ran an advertising campaign promoting Las Vegas as "Sin City" [*The Times*, February 26, 2005].

(3) (Las Vegas) One hundred years ago today, the San Pedro, Los Angeles and Salt Lake Railroad Company held an auction for 1,200 lots of barren sand, where they promised a new town would soon spring up... In fact, they'd just created Sin City. Also known as America's Playground. Also known as the holiday destination that ate the world [*Sunday Times*, May 15, 2005].

(4) (Las Vegas) Sin City has come over all family-friendly of late. Don't be fooled: Vegas is still America's prime den of iniquity. Strip shows, swingers' clubs — not for nothing does the US porn industry hold its version of the Oscars here [*Sunday Times*, September 25, 2005].

**Singapore of the Gulf, the** *Bahrain*. The island country in the Persian Gulf acquired its sobriquet at a time when it was diversifying its economy before its oil supplies ran out. The comparison with Singapore is apt, as both countries are major ports and trade centers and share a geographical similarity.

**Singers** *Singapore*. A British naval nickname for the seaport city, with the "Oxford -er" ending as for **Honkers**.

**Sing Sing** *Ossining, New York, USA*. Sing Sing was originally the regular name of the village that is now Ossining. It was renamed in 1901, however, to avoid too close an association with Sing Sing state prison, built in the 1820s, although in 1969 the latter was officially renamed Ossining Correctional Facility. Even so, the old name is still current for the prison and occasionally even for the community.

**Sinjin's Wood** *St John's Wood, London, England*. The affected "prim" pronunciation of the fashionable district's name puns on "sin" and "gin," two of its erstwhile pleasures, the former involving its prevalent "mistresses."

**Sinkhole of the East, the** *Port Said, Egypt*. The name refers to the seaport city's former reputation for vice and corruption.

**Sink of the Pacific, the** *Thursday Island, Australia*. The Queensland island, northwest of Cape York, was formerly so nicknamed for the great mix of people who passed through it in pearl-fishing days.

**Sinny** *Sydney, Australia*. A representation of the colloquial local pronunciation of the New South Wales capital city's name. It was popularized by A.A. Morrison, who as "Afferbeck Lauder" (i.e. "alphabetical order"), "Professor of Strine" (i.e. "Australian") at the "University of Sinny," published several "papers" on Australian English in the *Sydney Morning Herald* in 1965.

I still felt like an exile in Sydney. I was stranded among people who could not even muster the glottal energy to pronounce the 'd' in the name of their own city [Barry Humphries, *More Please*, 1992].

**Sin Strip** see in Appendix 1, p. 269.

**Sin Valley** *Sun Valley, Idaho, USA*. A punningly reprobatory name for the popular resort.

**Sion** *see* **Zion**

**Sioux, the** *Sioux Falls, South Dakota, USA*. A convenient short form of the city's name.

**Siouxland** *Sioux City, Iowa, USA*. An alternate name for the city, named for a French-Canadian settler, Théophile Bruguier, who arrived here in 1849 with his Sioux Indian wives and their father, Chief War Eagle.

**Sioux State, the** *North Dakota, USA*. The nickname derives from the American Indian people who once populated the plains and prairies of the territory that is now the state of North Dakota.

**Sip, the** *Mississippi, USA*. Blacks have adopted this abbreviation of the state name.

He loaded up the trunk with all his fine clothes and lit' out for "the sip" [*Black Scholar*, January 1971].

**Sister Isle, the** *Ireland*. A former nickname for Ireland, as related to England in the British Isles.

Dublin (where new hotels were built as England's 'Sister Isle ... roused from her Rip Van Winkle sleep') [Piers Brendon, *Thomas Cook: 150 Years of Popular Tourism*, 1991, quoting *The Excursionist*, April 21, 1900].

**Siva** *see* **Silicon Valley**

**Six Counties, the** *Northern Ireland*. The six

counties in question are those constituting Northern Ireland: Antrim, Armagh, Down, Fermanagh, Londonderry, and Tyrone. The name, used by those who disapprove of the state's separate existence, contrasts with the **Twenty-Six Counties** of the Republic of Ireland. *See also* **Thirty-Two Counties.**

(1) The House of Commons contained only Unionist members, who were obviously deeply concerned at the position of affairs while anxious to say nothing which might compromise the position of the Six Counties [C.J.C. Street, *Ireland in 1921*, 1922].

(2) As a part of the United Kingdom, the "Six Counties" were actively involved in the Second World War, whereas the independent "Twenty-six Counties" ... remained neutral [Killanin/Duignan, p. 32].

(3) Do not use the phrase Six Counties [*The Times Style and Usage Guide*, 2003].

**Six Suburbs in Search of a Center** *Oslo, Norway.* The Norwegian capital developed rapidly after World War II and absorbed a number of outlying communities. Hence its nickname. *Cp.* **Seventy-Two Suburbs in Search of a City.**

One of our ambassadors described it to me as "Six Suburbs in Search of a Centre" [R.H. Bruce Lockhart, *My Europe*, 1952].

**Skeggy** *Skegness, England.* A friendly nickname for the popular Lincolnshire seaside resort. It amounts to a genuine personalization, as it happens to represent the name of Skeggi, the Scandinavian landowner who originally gave his name to the place.

'Skeggy' is Lincolnshire's premier seaside resort [Christopher Somerville, *Coast: A Celebration of Britain's Coastal Heritage*, 2005].

**Skeleton Coast** see in Appendix 1, p. 269.

**Skem** *Skelmersdale, England.* A local short name for the New Town, designated in 1951. Together with Speke and **Stockie**, mentioned in the quote below, it is a district of Liverpool.

The door shuts soft. The rain has turned to ice.
 She lifts the arm out of infinity
 in Huyton, and in Skem and Speke and Stockie
*née* Cantril Farm, so good they named it twice [Paul Farley, "The Sleep of Estates," *The Boy from the Chemist Is Here to See You*, 1998].

**Skib** *Skibbereen, Ireland.* A local colloquial name, used also by boating enthusiasts, for the Co. Cork town and port.

**Skid Row on the Sound** *Seattle, Washington, USA.* A nickname for the city on Puget Sound where the original Skid Row (Skid Road) arose near the present Yesler Way. (Logs from a logging camp above town would "skid" down to Henry Yesler's mill here. The area later became a haven for homeless vagrants.)

**Sky City, the** *Acoma, New Mexico, USA.* The pueblo of Acoma Indians is situated at an altitude of *c.*7,000 ft (2,130 m) atop a precipitous butte 357 ft (109 m) high. Hence the understandable nickname.

**Slackers** *Halifax, Nova Scotia, Canada.* A Royal Canadian Navy nickname for the provincial capital in World War II. The name simply puns on the city's proper name, and does not specifically imply slackness.

**Slackerville** *Austin, Texas, USA.* The state capital gained its nickname following release of the 1991 movie *Slackers*, set in Austin, in which young fun-loving misfits confide to camera their reasons for avoiding work as they wander through the city's streets and coffee shops.

**Slate Capital of Wales, the** *Blaenau Ffestiniog, Wales.* The North Wales town was formerly a center of the slate-mining industry.

**Slave Coast** see in Appendix 1, p. 269.

**Slave States** see in Appendix 1, p. 269.

**SLC** *Salt Lake City, Utah, USA.* A frequently found abbreviated form of the state capital's name.

Salt Lake City (often abbreviated as SLC) [*Lonely Planet USA*, 2004].

**Sleeping Warrior, the** *Arran, Scotland.* The nickname of the island in the Firth of Clyde refers to its profile when seen from the mainland, which resembles a recumbent knight on his tomb.

The profile of the 'Sleeping Warrior' of Arran as seen from the Clyde coast is unforgettable [Newton, p. 170].

**Sleepy Hollow** *(1) Nelson, New Zealand; (2) Pietermaritzburg, South Africa.* The name for any quiet provincial place or one with a soporific atmosphere, as the two cities named here, derives from Washington Irving's "The Legend of Sleepy Hollow" in *The Sketch Book* (1820), where he writes: "This sequestered glen has long been known by the name of Sleepy Hollow, and its rustic lads are called the Sleepy Hollow boys."

(Pietermaritzburg) Party-time in the Sleepy Hollow. It's party time in Pietermaritzburg, and the Natal capital seems hell-bent on shrugging off its "Sleepy Hollow" tag... Cynics had better note — "Sleepy Hollow" is wide awake [*Natal on Saturday*, January 8, 1990].

**Sleepy Suffolk** *Suffolk, England.* The eastern county came by its epithet as an essentially peaceful, pastoral region of England.

Suffolk is an odd county. Famously known for being 'sleepy,' the arrival in recent years of large numbers of commuters ... has livened up the area considerably [Charlie Godfrey-Faussett, *Footprint England*, 2004].

**Sleeve, the** *English Channel.* The former nickname translated the French name *la Manche* (*see* **Manche**) for the English Channel, from its shape, with the Strait of Dover as the "cuff."

> He learned that a Frenchman had aeroplaned the Sleeve [*Daily Chronicle*, August 14, 1909].

**SLO** *San Luis Obispo, California, USA.* A colloquial initialism of the city's name.

> SLO's attractions cluster around Mission Plaza [*Lonely Planet USA*, 2004].

**Slot, the** *New Georgia Sound, Solomon Islands.* A nickname of American origin for the passage, used by the Japanese in World War II as a supply route for the reinforcement of Guadalcanal.

**Slovak Rome, the** *Trnava, Slovakia.* A center of Slovak Catholicism in medieval times, the city is so nicknamed for its many churches and monasteries, and particularly its Gothic cathedral.

**Slowbart** *Hobart, Australia.* The punning nickname refers to the relatively leisurely way of life in the Tasmanian capital, as compared to most other Australian cities. For the Parramatta description in the quote below, *see* **Sleepy Hollow**.

> [The Sydney suburb of] Parramatta has always been regarded as a Sleepy Hollow — sleepier than Slowbart [*Truth* (Sydney), September 24, 1905].

**Slow Town** *Detroit, Michigan, USA.* A nickname formerly current among vagrants, who saw the city as unpromising or "slow."

**Slumabad** *Islamabad, Pakistan.* An uncomplimentary nickname for the Pakistani capital, as used by United Nations personnel. *Cp.* **Slumopolis**.

**Slumopolis** *London, England.* A 19th-century nickname for the British capital, referring to its many slum districts, especially in the East End.

**Slush** *Sleaford, England.* The somewhat sequestered Lincolnshire town was so nicknamed by Royal Air Force personnel stationed locally. (The town is actually named for the Slea River here, its own name meaning "muddy." The nickname thus rings reasonably true.)

**Smallbany** *Albany, New York, USA.* A local nickname for the state capital, referring to its perceived lack of cultural charisma.

**Small Wonder, the** *Delaware, USA.* The state is so nicknamed for its small size but economic importance. *Cp.* **Diamond State**.

**Smart State, the** *Queensland, Australia.* A slogan promoting the state as fashionable, businesslike, and technologically advanced.

> Coming to work in Queensland won't just help you get over the winter blues... Make a smart

move to Queensland and escape the common cold. Queensland the Smart State [Government ad, *The Times*, September 22, 2005].

**Smellbourne** or **Smellburn** *Melbourne, Australia.* The derogatory punning name of the Victoria capital has a factual basis, referring to the city's crude method of disposing of its sewage by simply dumping it in the Yarra River. The name was coined by the Sydney *Bulletin* in the late 19th century.

> (1) My trip to Melbourne — Smelbourne the *Bulletin* calls it, and rightly [Arthur J. Vogan, *The Black Police; A Story of Modern Australia*, 1890].
>
> (2) There has been a rumpus lately in the good old Sydney town,
> All the "Holy Joes" of Smellbourne wear the mourning garb and gown [*Truth* (Sydney), October 27, 1907].
>
> (3) Beaches? *Beaches?* In Smellburn? [Nina Pulliam, *I Traveled a Lonely Land*, 1955].

**Smiling Coast** see in Appendix 1, p. 269.

**Smiling Somerset** *Somerset, England.* A promotional name for the West-Country coastal county, as formerly found in railroad literature.

> (1) [The city of] Wells [is] in the heart of "Smiling Somerset" [*Holiday Haunts 1961: Area No. 4, West of England and South and Central Wales*].
>
> (2) If your preferences were occidental you could 'Go Great Western!,' where more alliteration awaited you in 'Smiling Somerset' [Michael Palin, Introduction, *Happy Holidays: The Golden Age of Railway Posters*, 1987].

**Smoke, the** *London, England.* A common nickname still current for the British capital, referring to the pall of smoke that hung over it before the clean-air legislation of the 1950s. *Cp.* **Big Smoke**; **Great Smoke**.

> (1) The metropolis is by no means so smoky as Sheffield, Birmingham, &c.; yet country-people, when going to London, frequently say they are on their way to the SMOKE; and Londoners, when leaving for the country, say they are going out of the SMOKE [*The Slang Dictionary*, 1894].
>
> (2) A Northerner by birth, she had spent 24 years in London... But she had had enough of The Smoke. It was time to come home [*The Times*, October 22, 2004].

**Smoky City, the** *Pittsburgh, Pennsylvania, USA.* The city was formerly so nicknamed for its severe air and water pollution, the former caused by the volumes of smoke issuing from the bituminous coal used in the steel industry.

**Smoky Sea, the** *Bering Sea, Russia/USA.* The sea between Siberia and Alaska has been poetically so named for its smoky-gray color.

> Now this is the law of the Muscovite, that he proves with shot and steel,
> When you come by his isles in the Smoky Sea you must not take the seal [Rudyard Kipling, "The Rhyme of the Three Sealers," 1893].

**Smuggler's Alley** *St. Lawrence River, USA.* A nickname used in the period of Prohibition, when liquor was channeled into the USA via the named river.

**Smyrna** *Izmir, Turkey.* The ancient name of the seaport city remains familiar from biblical and historical contexts.

Send it unto the seven churches which are in Asia; unto Ephesus, and unto Smyrna, and unto Pergamos, and unto Thyatira, and unto Sardis, and unto Philadelphia, and unto Laodicea [Revelation 1:11].

**Snellens** *St Helens, England.* A local form (more often spoken than written) of the name of the Merseyside industrial town.

**Snoek Town** *Cape Town, South Africa.* The city was formerly the center of the snoek (barracouta) fishing and processing industry.

**Snooty Ooty** *see* **Ooty**

**Snor City** *Tshwane (Pretoria), South Africa.* The nickname derives from Afrikaans *snor,* "mustache," referring to the many males in the city who supposedly sport mustaches. (In the quote below, "total on*snort*" puns on "total onslaught," the topical term for the perceived campaign by foreign countries and left-wing movements against South Africa's Nationalist government. For the second nickname, *see* **Spark Plug Country**.)

Other aliases are Snor City (there's a "total on*snort*" of moustachioed men), and Spark Plug (NGK) Country [*Cosmopolitan,* December 1987].

**Snotty Bash** *Knotty Ash, Liverpool, England.* A local (mock) derisory corruption of the district name, especially as used by residents of the neighboring town of Bootle.

**Snowbelt** see in Appendix 1, p. 269.

**Snowdon's Arm** *Lleyn Peninsula, Wales.* The peninsula dividing Caernarfon Bay from Cardigan Bay, on the west coast of Wales, is so nicknamed as if extending from the "shoulder" of the mountain of Snowdon, to the northeast.

**Snowies, the** *Snowy Mountains, Australia.* A friendly name for the mountain range, which forms part of the Great Dividing Range in New South Wales and Victoria.

**Soapsuds Island** *South Acton, London, England.* The nickname referred to the many laundries that existed in the district in the 19th century, the foam from which frothed in Stamford Brook (now piped). *Cp.* **London's Washtub**.

**Soapville** *Port Sunlight, England.* A local nickname for the Merseyside industrial village, founded in 1888 as a residential estate for workers at the nearby soap factory, manufacturers of Sunlight Soap.

**SoBe** *South Beach, Miami, Florida, USA.* An abbreviated form of the resort district's name.

(1) SoBe (the inevitable contraction of 'South Beach') [*Lonely Planet Miami,* 1999].

(2) In SoBe, stay on or near the beach. It'll cost more, but it is worth it [*Sunday Times,* November 21, 2004].

(3) Ocean Drive, or Ocean as it's known here in SoBe [*Sunday Times,* July 31, 2005].

**SoCal** *Southern California, USA.* A colloquial short name for the southern part of the state, especially the coastal region centering on Los Angeles.

(1) The beach towns of Ocean Beach, Mission Beach and Pacific Beach all epitomize the laid-back SoCal lifestyle [*Lonely Planet USA,* 2004].

(2) How do you survive and conquer SoCal freeway driving if you're not a native? [*Fodor's Los Angeles 2006*].

**Social Laboratory of the World, the** *New Zealand.* The sobriquet was applied to the country in the 1930s, when the Labour government abandoned its idealistic socialist theories in favor of a pragmatic policy of welfare and credit-reform proposals.

By 1935 Labour was the dominant political force, had become the Government, and was able to introduce a full welfare state. This was the period ... when New Zealand was called "the social laboratory of the world" [*Times Literary Supplement,* June 11, 2004].

**So Cool** *Southern California, USA.* A punning nickname for the southern part of the state, especially the coastal region centering on Los Angeles, describing its self-perceived laid-back image. A more common abbreviated name is **SoCal**. *Cp.* **No Cool**.

**Sodom** *London, England.* A 19th-century literary nickname for the British capital as a supposed den of vice, after Sodom, the biblical city whose wickedness and destruction is recorded in Genesis 18–19.

**Sodom-by-Sea** *(1) Hollywood, Los Angeles, California, USA; (2) New Orleans, Louisiana, USA.* The name can refer to any coastal resort regarded as corrupt or decadent, especially by the puritanical. Hollywood was notorious for its many reputed illicit liaisons, while New Orleans is regarded by some as a sink of depravity, as described in quote (1) below. *Cp.* **Sodom**.

(1) (New Orleans) 'Is it the part of the police department to harass me when this city is the flagrant vice capital of the civilized world?' ... 'This city is famous for its gamblers, prostitutes, exhibitionists, anti–Christs, alcoholics, sodomites, drug addicts, fetishists, onanists, pornographers, frauds, jades, litterbugs, and lesbians, all of whom are only too well protected by graft' [John Kennedy Toole, *A Confederacy of Dunces,* 1980].

(2) (Hollywood) The legendary film city —
sometimes referred to as Sodom-by-the-Sea —
seems far from glamorous to the casual visitor
[John Walker, ed., *Halliwell's Who's Who in the
Movies*, 2003].

(3) (New Orleans) Some Bible-thumpers will be
hailing divine retribution for decades of decadence, as Sodom-by-Sea is swamped [*The Times*,
September 2, 2005].

**Sodom of India, the** *Hyderabad, India.* The
city was formerly accorded the sobriquet for the
supposed depravity of its inhabitants.

**Sodom-on-the-Liffey** *Dublin, Ireland.* A derisory sobriquet for the Irish capital (on the
Liffey River), for its supposed profligacy. The
name was mainly used by residents of Liverpool
and surrounding Merseyside, England, with its
sizable Irish population.

**Soft South** see in Appendix 1, p. 269.

**SoHo** see in Appendix 1, p. 269.

**Soho-on-Thames** *Maidenhead, England.*
The Berkshire town and fashionable riverside resort gained its nickname in the 1930s as a popular venue for extramarital liaisons among the
"bright young things" of the day. The district of
Soho, London, was at one time noted for its
prostitutes.

The town became known as "Soho-on-Thames,"
notorious for the depravity of the "roadhouse set"
[*Sunday Times Magazine*, August 28, 2005].

**Solar City** *see* **City of the Sun**

**Solid South** see in Appendix 1, p. 269.

**SoMa** see in Appendix 1, p. 269.

**Somerset with Vines** *Burgundy, France.* A
nickname for the wine-growing region as viewed
through the eyes of the nostalgic British, comparing its beautiful countryside and historic
towns with those of the English county.

With a landscape described as "Somerset with
vines," Burgundy is a treasure-trove of medieval
architecture [Celia Brayfield, "Hidden Treasure,"
*The Times*, May 6, 2005].

**Soo, the** *(1) Sault Sainte Marie, Michigan,
USA; (2) Sault Sainte Marie, Ontario, Canada.*
The two cities, opposite each another at the falls
on St. Mary's River, are known by the same byname, representing the pronunciation of the first
word of the name (which means "falls").

**Sooner State, the** *Oklahoma, USA.* The
name derives from the eager homesteaders who
staked claims in the future Oklahoma Territory
before (sooner than) the US government officially opened the former Native American lands
to settlers at noon on April 22, 1889.

(1) Oklahoma uses on its road signs a phrase
which I first heard in Kansas and never again except in the Sooner State [*New Yorker*, October 14,
1939].

(2) That's right: the Sooner State is named for
law-breakers [*Lonely Planet USA*, 2004].

**Sooside** see in Appendix 1, p. 269.

**So'ton** or **Soton** *Southampton, England.* A
regular abbreviation of the Hampshire seaport
city's name, used mainly in written or printed
form (e.g. in road signs, press ads). Similar forms
for other towns and cities are B'ham (Birmingham), B'head (Birkenhead), B'mouth (Bournemouth), L'pool (Liverpool), L'derry (Londonderry), P'boro (Peterborough). Southampton is
also sometimes S'ton.

Holiday Inn [Hotel] So'ton [Ad, *The Times*, February 7, 2005].

**Soul City** or **Soulville** *Harlem, New York
City, USA.* The predominantly black neighborhood is traditionally regarded as one of the
homes of soul music in the 1960s.

[Harry] Lesser descended ... into Soul City
by himself [Bernard Malamud, *The Tenants*,
1971].

**Soul of Mexico, the** *Michoacán, Mexico.* The
touristic name promotes the southwestern state,
bordering the Pacific, as encapsulating the quintessence of the country.

A three-hour bus journey takes you to the heart
of Michoacán, the "soul of Mexico," as the tourist
guides dub it [*The Times*, May 28, 2005].

**Sourdough State, the** *Alaska, USA.* The state
is so nicknamed for the "sourdoughs," or gold
prospectors in Alaska in the latter half of the 19th
century. They were themselves so called from
their practice of saving a lump of sour (unleav-
ened) dough for use as leaven when baking bread
in the winter.

**South, the** *Ireland.* The name refers to the
Republic of Ireland from the point of view of
Northern Ireland. *Cp.* **North**. *See also* **South** in
Appendix 1, p. 269.

In Northern Ireland one has a wide choice of
names for the rest of the island: the Twenty-six
Counties, the Free State, Southern Ireland, the
South, Eire and the Republic of Ireland [Dervla
Murphy, *A Place Apart*, 1978].

**South Britain** *England.* A now uncommon
designation of England (and usually including
Wales) as lying south of the border with Scotland. *Cp.* **North Britain**.

**South Chelsea** *Battersea, London, England.*
A realtor's former name for the district south of
the Thames, adopted from the fashionable district of Chelsea on the north side of the river in
place of the real name, which is associated with
the long-derelict Battersea Power Station (and
has overtones of "battered").

Battersea. Gone are the days when estate agents
tried to promote it as "South Chelsea." Battersea,

these days, is allowed to be itself [*Sunday Times*, January 30, 2005].

**South Country** see in Appendix 1, p. 269.

**South East** see in Appendix 1, p. 269.

**Southern Gateway of New England, the** *Rhode Island, USA*. The state is the southernmost in New England, so that the main routes to the other New England states pass through it. Hence the nickname.

**Southie** *South Boston, Boston, Massachusetts, USA*. A colloquial name for the city's southern district, as described in the quote below.

"Southie" is a popular name for the predominantly Irish American, working-class neighborhood of South Boston, situated on a peninusla across the channel from downtown Boston [Thomas H. O'Connor, *Boston A to Z*, 2000].

**South Ken** *South Kensington, London, England*. A popular short form of the name of the fashionable district. Quote (1) below, however, refers to the Natural History Museum, in South Kensington. *Cp.* **North Ken**.

(1) If we get away with this we might start on the South Ken. There's a large-size model of a flea there I've always had my eye on [Margery Allingham, *Sweet Danger*, 1933].

(2) Some Middle-Eastern families still remain in neighbouring South Ken, as it is known, but it is no longer the 'Saudi Ken' of the 1970s [Carrie Segrave, *The New London Property Guide*, 2003].

**South Sea, the** *Pacific Ocean*. The name is said to have been given in 1513 by the Spanish explorer Vasco Núñez de Balboa, as described in quote (3) below. (Keats referred to this exploit in his poem "On First Looking into Chapman's Homer" but confused Balboa with Hernán Cortés: "Or like stout Cortez when with eagle eyes / He stared at the Pacific — and all his men / Looked at each other with a wild surmise —/ Silent, upon a peak in Darien.") The name is also used in the plural, as in quote (4) below, to refer to the South Pacific.

(1) [The Pacific] was called south-sea, because the Spaniards crossed the isthmus of Darien [i.e. the present Isthmus of Panama] from north to south, when they first discovered it: though it is properly the Western ocean, with regard to America [*Encyclopædia Britannica*, 1771].

(2) The Pacific ... is also called the South Sea, because vessels sailing from Europe can only enter it after a long southerly course [*Penny Cyclopædia of the Society for the Diffusion of Useful Knowledge*, 1840].

(3) [Balboa] arrived, on the 29th of September, at a mountain, from the summit of which, *looking south*, he beheld the boundless expanse of the ocean stretched out before him, while the northern portion was shut out from his view. He named it, therefore, *Mar del Sur*, or the South Sea [Wheeler, p. 349].

(4) This voyage tells the story of Polynesia and uncovers its history and legends as we sail through the South Seas [Travel ad, *The Times*, July 9, 2005].

**South Slav Athens, the** *Dubrovnik, Croatia*. The seaport city acquired its nickname from the flourishing of art and literature that occurred there from the 15th through 17th centuries.

**South Van** *see* **North Van**

**South West** *Namibia*. A shortening of the name of the country when it was known as South West Africa.

A small collection of semi-precious stones from South West [André P. Brink, *Rumours of Rain*, 1978].

**Sovietland** *Soviet Union*. A rarish alternate name for the former Soviet Union. *Cp.* **Russkiland**.

Romanov would crack down on the mishmash of more than 100 government ministries and independent agencies that create confusion in Sovietland [*Detroit Free Press*, March 5, 1978].

**Soviet Riviera** *see* **Crimean Riviera** in Appendix 1, p. 269.

**Soviet Union** *see* **Russia**

**Sowhereto** *Soweto, South Africa*. A punning alteration of the name of the black residential complex near Johannesburg.

They shouldn't call this place Soweto! ... They should call it 'Sowhereto.' I don't know where I'm going, that's for sure [P.C. Venter, *Soweto, Shadow City*, 1977].

**SP** *Sungai Petani, Malaysia*. A local abbreviated name for the town.

Known locally as SP, the acronym gives Sungai Petani an air of importance it doesn't deserve [*Lonely Planet Malaysia, Singapore & Brunei*, 1999].

**Space City** *Houston, Texas, USA*. The city has been a center of space research and travel since the 1960s. Hence the nickname. *See also* **Astrodome City**.

**Space Coast** see in Appendix 1, p. 269.

**Spaceship City** *Huntsville, Alabama, USA*. The city is so nicknamed as a major center of US space research.

**Spade Town** *Lurgan, Northern Ireland*. The Co. Armagh town is so punningly nicknamed from Irish *lorgán spáid*, "spade handle," as if from the placename. There is also a reference to the phrase "to have a face like a Lurgan spade," meaning "to look miserable."

**Spanish Harlem** *El Barrio, New York City, USA*. The name for the neighborhood on the East Side of Manhattan is justified in so far as the first word refers to its Spanish-speaking Puerto Rican population, while the second word locates it within East Harlem. Otherwise El Barrio (Spanish for "the district") has little connection with Harlem in the broader sense.

**Spanish Main, the** *Caribbean Sea.* The name was originally given by English colonists to the northern mainland of South America, along the coast of the former Spanish colonies of Colombia and Venezuela. It was then wrongly taken to apply to the Caribbean, as the sea off this coast, as if it were a main sea or ocean, although it is actually an arm of the Atlantic. The name became popular among writers of pirate fiction.

(1) Then up and spake an old Sailòr,
  Had sailed the Spanish Main [H.W. Longfellow, "The Wreck of the Hesperus," 1839].
  (2) Under which diabolical ensign he was carrying me and little Em'ly to the Spanish Main to be drowned [Charles Dickens, *David Copperfield*, 1850].

**Spanish State, the** *New Mexico, USA.* Spanish settlement began in New Mexico in the late 16th century, and Spanish-Americans (Spanish settlers who intermarried with Indians) formed the majority of the population until the 1940s. The Spanish influence in New Mexico is thus still evident, and gave the nickname.

**Spa of the Seven Hills, the** *Clevedon, England.* The Somerset town and resort is centered on hills near the estuary of the Severn River. Hence its nickname, which reflects its actual name (meaning "hill of the cliffs").

**Spark Plug Country** *Tshwane (Pretoria), South Africa.* Punning on the Japanese spark plug company NGK, the nickname derives from NGK as the initials of *Nederduitse Gereformeerde Kerk* (Dutch Reformed Church), the largest church of South African whites.

**Speck, the** *Tasmania, Australia.* The name refers to the small size of the island state compared to the five much larger mainland states. *Cp.* **Fly Speck.**

N.S.W., V., Q., S.A., W.A. and the Speck [*The Bulletin* (Sydney), June 11, 1930].

**Spice Island, the** *(1) Grenada, West Indies; (2) Zanzibar, East Africa.* The names refer to Grenada's production of nutmeg (also cloves and mace) and to Zanzibar as a major producer of cloves. The byname is sometimes used in the plural for the latter, as geographically the former British protectorate is an archipelago, comprising Zanzibar, Pemba, and adjacent small islands.

(1) (Zanzibar) After visiting the 'Spice Island' of Zanzibar, your final port of call is Mesali [Travel ad, *The Times*, January 22, 2005].
  (2) (Grenada) It was this thought and its ramifications for tsunami-hit Asia which brought me to Grenada, six months on, to see how the spice island was coping [*The Times*, April 23, 2005].
  (3) (Grenada) The rich aroma of cinnamon, nutmeg and cloves hovers over the fertile volcanic hills of Grenada, renowned as the "Spice Island" [Travel brochure issued with *The Times*, August 20, 2005].
  (4) (Zanzibar) Spice islands in turmoil as troops fire at election protesters [Headline, *The Times*, November 2, 2005].

**Spice Islands, the** *Maluku (Moluccas), Indonesia.* The islands were formerly major producers of spices, especially nutmegs, mace, and cloves. Hence the name, still sometimes found.

(1) Malaysia ... includes ... Sumatra, Java, Borneo, and Celebes, and the Moluccas or Spice Islands [*Cassell's Popular Educator*, 1890].
  (2) Moluccas. A group of islands sometimes spoken of as the Spice Islands [Johnson, p. 168].

**Spinach Capital of the World, the** *(1) Alma, Arkansas, USA; (2) Crystal City, Texas, USA.* Both towns are noted for their vegetable canneries and both boast a statue of the cartoon character Popeye, who turns into a superhero whenever he eats a can of spinach.

**Spindle City** *see* **City of Spindles**

**Spires** *Speyer, Germany.* The alternate English name of the city, misleadingly suggesting the spires of its churches, is famous historically for the Diet of Spires (1529), at which Lutheran protests at the Catholic decree to end toleration of Lutherans in Catholic districts gave rise to the term "Protestant."

**Spoke** *Spokane, Washington, USA.* A casual abbreviation of the city's name.

**Sport City** *Shreveport, Louisiana, USA.* The nickname is not so much an allusion to the city's recreational facilities as a pun on its actual name in abbreviated form (as if "S-port").

**Sportsman's Paradise** *Louisiana, USA.* The promotional name alludes to the state's many amenities for hunting and fishing.

**Springs, the** *Palm Springs, California, USA.* A short local name for the resort city.

Locals call it "the Springs." And it's tiny, a city in name only [*The Times*, October 7, 2005].

**Spruce** or **Spruceland** or **Sprucia** *Prussia, Germany.* Former English names for the historic German state, which itself gave the name of the *spruce* (originally *spruce fir*), a tree that grows abundantly here. The initial *S-* is not organic.

(1) For the Hollanders ... are compelled to fetch ... their hoopes and Barrell-boords out of Norway and Sprucia [Tobias Gentleman, *England's Way to Win Wealth, and to Employ Ships and Mariners*, 1614].
  (2) They busied themselves in defending of Christendome, ... as the Teutonick order defended Spruceland against the Tartarian [Thomas Fuller, *The Historie of the Holy Warre*, 1639].

(3) On the east and north corner of Germany lyeth a country called Prussia, in English Pruthen or Spruce [Archbishop George Abbot, *A Briefe Description of the Whole Worlde*, 1656].

**Spruce Capital of the World, the** *Prince George, British Columbia, Canada.* The city has a major timber industry, especially in the cutting and milling of spruce trees.

**Spud Island** *Prince Edward Island, Canada.* The nickname alludes to the province's famous potatoes.

**Spud State, the** *Idaho, USA.* The nickname refers to the potatoes for which the state is noted. *Cp.* **Famous Potatoes.**

**Spud Town** or **City** *Boise, Idaho, USA.* The city derives its nickname not so much for the potatoes it produces as those of the **Spud State** of which it is the capital.

**Square Mile, the** *(City of) London, England.* The nickname applies to the central and oldest part of the British capital, where the nation's business and financial activities are centered. The area of the original walled city of London is approximately 1 square mile. Hence the name. *See also* **City.**

The Square Mile, as London's financial district is known [*Financial Times*, October 8, 2004].

**Squatter State, the** *Kansas, USA .* The nickname refers to the period before the Civil War, when proslavery and antislavery groups vied with one another to rush the greater number of settlers into the territory. These were thus the "squatters" who gave the name.

It [i.e. Kansas] appears occasionally as Squatter State, from the pertinacity with which the squatter-sovereignty was discussed there [Maximilien Schele De Vere, *Americanisms; The English of the New World*, 1871].

**S'side** *Summerside, Prince Edward Island, Canada.* A colloquial local short name for the town and summer resort.

**Stab City** *Limerick, Ireland.* The Co. Limerick city gained the nickname from its reputation for violence.

(1) But any negativity stemming from [Frank McCourt's novel] *Angela's Ashes* is benign compared to the "Stab City" nickname, which appears to stem from Christmas 1982, when there were three unconnected murders in Limerick [*Irish Times*, January 29, 2000].
(2) The sobriquet 'Stab City' causes embarrassment and shame to the city's mostly law-abiding inhabitants [Sean McMahon and Jo O'Donoghue, *Brewer's Dictionary of Irish Phrase and Fable*, 2004].

**Staffs** *Staffordshire, England.* A semiofficial abbreviation of the county name. *See also* Appendix 6, p. 325.

**Stag City** *Hartford, Connecticut, USA.* The name plays on the state capital's real name (adopted from that of Hertford, England, which means "hart ford").

**Stalingrad** *Volgograd, Russia.* The city, originally called Tsaritsyn, was renamed in 1925 for Stalin, and this name became memorable from the Battle of Stalingrad in 1942. Stalin himself then fell from favor, and in 1961 the city was again renamed as now (for the Volga River on which it lies). But the earlier name carries the greater weight and comes first to mind in any reference to the city. At the turn of the 21st century there was a strong lobby for a return to the historic name.

**Stamboul** *Istanbul, Turkey.* The archaic or poetic form of the city's name became familiar from Graham Greene's novel *Stamboul Train* (1932), about events on the Orient Express running to the former Turkish capital. (The present form of the name was officially adopted in 1930). The name of Istanbul in some languages is similar to the earlier form, as Russian *Stambul.*

And Afric's coast and Calpe's adverse height,
  And Stamboul's minarets must greet my sight
[Lord Byron, *English Bards and Scotch Reviewers*, 1809].

**Star City** *Lincoln, Nebraska, USA.* The nickname refers specifically to the city's planetarium but can also be understood to describe its "star" status as state capital and its generally "bright and shining" image.

**Start, the** *London, England.* The British capital was formerly so nicknamed by vagrants because it was the starting point of their journey around the country.

(1) All the "regular bang-up fakes" are manufactured in the "Start" (metropolis) [Henry Mayhew, *London Labour and the London Poor*, 1851].
(2) "The Start," London,— the great starting-point for beggars and tramps. This is a term also used by many of superior station to those mentioned [*The Slang Dictionary*, 1894].

**Stasiland** *East Germany.* The name refers to the Stasi, or East German secret police, abolished in 1990. (It is an abbreviation of *Staatssicherheitsdienst*, "state security service"). The nickname, perhaps influenced by "Swaziland," was the title of a 2003 book of memoirs by Anna Funder.

**State, the** *Ireland.* The name, as used for the Republic of Ireland, derives from its former title of Irish Free State (*see* **Eire**).

Now, ironically, children from "the State"—as the Republic is called — are coming to Cashel community hall [in Northern Ireland] for Irish dancing classes [Theresa Judge in *Irish Times*, March 12, 1999].

**State of Excitement, the** *Western Australia, Australia.* A punning promotional name, suggesting the many attractions to be found in the state.

**States, the** *(1) South Africa; (2) United States.* The common short name for the USA was adopted by South African soldiers serving abroad to mean "home." (The name of the former Orange Free State may have played its part here.)

(1) (USA) And Delia Dobbs, the lecturer from 'the States'
Upon the 'Woman's Question' [Elizabeth Barrett Browning, *Aurora Leigh*, 1857].
(2) (USA) To the States or any one of them, or any city of the States,
*Resist much, obey little* [Walt Whitman, *Leaves of Grass*, "To the States," 1860].
(3) (South Africa) They are reluctant to talk, far preferring to tell you what they'll do when they get back to the States — as everyone from the most wet-behind-the-ears private to the rugged and weatherbeaten commanding officer, calls South Africa [*Fair Lady*, November 14, 1984].

**Stateside** *United States.* The name has "-side" in the sense "land," "region," as in "countryside," but is popularly understood by the British to denote a nation on the west side of the Atlantic. The term is used only adjectivally or adverbially, i.e., one would not say "in (the) Stateside." The designation first became widely used in World War II.

(1) "Stateside" is a mighty popular word out here [in Guam] because a service man going "stateside" is going home [*The Sun* (Baltimore), March 12, 1945].
(2) The kids keep up with the latest Stateside fad [*Encounter*, February 1960].

**State that Forgot, the** *South Carolina, USA.* The name comes from the title of William Watts Ball's book *The State that Forgot: South Carolina's Surrender to Democracy* (1932), a reactionary white view of the state's supposed abnegation of its political principles.

**Steak and Kidney** *Sydney, Australia.* An old rhyming slang nickname for the New South Wales capital, from the pudding or pie so called, itself known in rhyming slang (and also a partial spoonerism) as "Kate and Sidney."

**Steel Capital of England** or **Britain, the** *Sheffield, England.* The city was famous for cutlery as early as the 14th century. The steel products for which it later became noted date from 1740, when Benjamin Huntsman invented the crucible process.

**Steel Capital on Grassland, the** *Baotou, China.* The city is so nicknamed for its large iron and steel complex, raised in the 1950s in a former agricultural region.

**Steel City, the** *(1) Bethlehem, Pennsylvania, USA; (2) Jamshedpur, India; (3) Newcastle, Australia ; (4) Pittsburgh, Pennsylvania, USA; (5) Wollongong, Australia.* All of the named cities are or were noted for their steel manufacture. Bethlehem's steel industry dates from 1873 and was formerly dominated by the Bethlehem Steel Corporation. Jamshedpur is also known as the **Pittsburgh of India**. Newcastle long had a giant steelworks. Pittsburgh's iron and steel industry was its economic mainstay for over a century. Wollongong has an iron and steel industry dating from 1928. *See also* **Steeltown**.

**Steel City of the Northwest, the** *Jiayuguan, China.* The city, in northwestern Gansu province, is an important iron and steel center. Hence the nickname.

**Steel State, the** *Pennsylvania, USA.* The state could hardly have any other sobriquet with Pittsburgh as its **Steel City**.

**Steeltown** *(1) Bethlehem, Pennsylvania, USA; (2) Hamilton, Ontario, Canada; (3) Magnitogorsk, Russia; (4) Pittsburgh, Pennsylvania, USA.* For Bethlehem and Pittsburgh the name alternates with **Steel City**. Hamilton's steel and iron industry began in the 19th century and became the largest in the country. Magnitogorsk, built in 1929 to exploit the magnetite iron ore of nearby Mt. Magnitnaya ("Magnetic Mountain"), was so dubbed by Stephen Kotkin in his 2002 book *Steeltown, USSR: Soviet Society in the Gorbachev Era.*

**Stewartry, the** *Kirkcudbright, Scotland.* The historic county of Kirkcudbright, also known as Kirkcudbrightshire, was often so designated locally for distinction from the neighboring county of Wigtownshire (*see* **Shire**). A stewartry was governed by a steward appointed by the monarch.

**Stockbroker Belt** see in Appendix 1, p. 269.

**Stockie** *Stockbridge Village, Liverpool, England.* A colloquial local form of the name of the neighborhood, originally known as Cantril Farm. (See the quote at **Skem**.)

**Stokey** *Stoke Newington, London, England.* A friendly nickname for the district.

Developers latched on to the creative types who make a beeline for 'Stokey' [Carrie Segrave, *The New London Property Guide*, 2003].

**S'ton** *see* **So'ton**

**Stonehenge of the North, the** *(1) Arbor Low, England; (2) Thornborough, England.* Arbor Low, an ancient stone circle in the Peak District, Derbyshire, bears some resemblance to the famous stones of Stonehenge, Wiltshire, although its stones are recumbent, not standing. (They may have originally have been erect, but fell because of the shallowness of the holes in which they were originally placed.) The Thornborough Henges in Yorkshire also suggest the layout of the southern original, but lack its stones. *See also* **Henge**.

> (Thornborough) Thornborough — sometimes called "the Stonehenge of the North" although the monuments consist of three huge earthen banked circles without stones [*The Times,* August 24, 2004].

**Stones, the** *Stonehenge, England.* A popular name for the ancient monument in Wiltshire, used mainly by cultists, such as the modern Druids, who gather to celebrate the summer solstice there, but also more generally.

> There are plans for a train to take visitors to the Stones via a series of other points of interest [*The Times,* March 19, 2005].

**Straddie** *North Stradbroke Island, Australia.* A colloquial short name for the island off the coast of southeastern Queensland.

**Strait** or **Straits, the** *Strait of Dover, Europe.* A short name in British use for the narrow stretch of water between Dover, England, and Calais, France, separating Britain from continental Europe.

> (1) To England's cliffs my gaze is turn'd,
>  O'er the blue Strait mine eyes I strain [Matthew Arnold, "Calais Sands," 1867].
> (2) The sea is calm to-night,
>  The tide is full, the moon lies fair
>  Upon the Straits [Matthew Arnold, "Dover Beach," 1867].

**Straits, the** *(1) Straits of Gibraltar; (2) Straits of Malacca.* The short designation applies either to the sea passage connecting the Mediterranean Sea and Atlantic Ocean, between Spain and Africa, with Gibraltar and Ceuta on either side at the eastern end, or to the channel between the southern Malay Peninsula and the island of Sumatra, connecting the Indian Ocean with the South China Sea. The former name came to be applied following Russian expansion to the Black Sea, when the "Straits Question," regarding restrictions on the passage of warships between the Black Sea and the Mediterranean, became a recurrent issue in European diplomacy. In naval parlance, "up the straits" means "in the Mediterranean," as in quote (3) below. The latter name became familiar from the Straits Settlements, the former British crown colony on the south and west coast of the Malay Peninsula, comprising the four trade centers Singapore, Penang, Malacca (Melaka), and Labuan. The name could apply equally to the sea passage or to the settlements themselves, as respectively in quotes (1)

and (2). It survives in the *Straits Times,* the daily newspaper published in Singapore, founded in 1845. *See also* **Strait**.

> (1) (Straits of Malacca) A succession of men-of-war and transports belonging to both nations passed through the Straits. The hospitality of Government House [in Singapore] was tendered to all [Sir Orfeur Cavenagh, *Reminiscences of an Indian Official,* 1884].
> (2) (Straits Settlements) I must always look back with pleasure to my connection with the Straits [Sir Orfeur Cavenagh, *Reminiscences of an Indian Official,* 1884].
> (3) (Straits of Gibraltar) 'Er commander's a werry nice gentleman; 'e was shipmates along o' me in th' *Duncan* up the Straits six year ago ["Taffrail" (Henry Taprell Dorling), *Pincher Martin, O.D.: A Story of the Inner Life of the Royal Navy,* 1916].

**'Stralia** *Australia.* A colloquial shortening of the country's name.

> 'Like 'Stralia?' 'Very much,' I said and was glad I said it [Harold Lewis, *Crow on a Barbed Wire Fence,* 1973].

**Strip, the** *Gaza Strip.* A short name for the territory that is a strip of land on the southeast Mediterranean coast.

> Labour's blueprint for a string of Jewish villages south of Gaza, aimed at sealing off Sinai from the Strip and from Israel [*The Times,* July 22, 1977].

**Stroke City** *Londonderry (Derry), Northern Ireland.* The compromise nickname derives from the stroke (slash) in the city's dual name of Derry/Londonderry, with Derry preferred by Catholics and nationalists (favoring the claims of Ireland to be an independent nation), and Londonderry by Protestants and unionists (favoring the union of Ireland with Britain). The name may have been partly suggested by that of Strokestown in the Republic of Ireland, although the sense there is quite different. It was devised by radio personality Gerry Anderson, as in quote (1) below.

> (1) I ... took to naming the city Derry Stroke Londonderry until ultimately settling for the more natural user-friendly "Stroke City" [Gerry Anderson, *Surviving in Stroke City,* 1999].
> (2) Political correctness amongst local people in Northern Ireland occasionally demands the use of both names, Derry/Londonderry (or in reverse order), leading to the coining of the ironic and double-meaning title, 'Stroke City' [Brian Lalor, *Blue Guide Ireland,* 2004].

**Stubtoe State, the** *Montana, USA.* The nickname refers to the state's steep mountain slopes, where one may stub one's toe.

**Stuka Valley** see in Appendix 1, p. 269.

**Stur** *Sturminster Newton, England.* A local abbreviated form of the Dorset town's name.

**Subcontinent, the** *(1) India; (2) South Africa.* The term, denoting a geographically or politically independent part of a continent, was formerly applied to South Africa, as part of Africa, and is still used for India, as part of Asia, sometimes with an inclusion of Pakistan, Bangladesh, and Sri Lanka. In each case the subcontinent is the southern part of the continent in question, under (Latin *sub*) the main part.

(1) (South Africa) The springbuck ... is the only representative of the gazelle group, which is found in the sub-continent [James Stevenson-Hamilton, *Wild Life in South Africa*, 1947].

(2) (India) Many Indians refused to accept the partition of the sub-continent [Louis Heren, *Growing Up on The Times*, 1978].

(3) (India) The city formerly known as Bombay [i.e. Mumbai] is the most cosmopolitan and diverse on the sub-continent [Travel ad, *The Times Magazine*, May 7, 2005].

**Suburb, the** *Hampstead Garden Suburb, London, England.* A short name for the district created in the early 20th century as a residential area adjoining Hampstead Heath.

The Suburb was once viewed as being inhabited largely by eccentrics [Carrie Segrave, *The New London Property Guide*, 2003].

**Sucka Free** *San Francisco, California, USA.* A nickname favored by young blacks, punning on the city's regular name but also suggesting "sucker" (a gullible person) and "free." *Cp.* **SFC.**

**Sucker State, the** *Illinois, USA.* The origin of the nickname is disputed. Theories to account for it include the following: (1) Local miners went to the mines in the spring and returned in the fall, like the sucker fish in the rivers; (2) Early settlers were duped by land speculators, so were simpletons or "suckers"; (3) Much-needed water was sucked through hollow reeds from the natural artesian wells.

(1) There was a long-haired "hooshier" from Indiana, a couple of smart-looking "suckers" from the southern part of Illinois, a keen-eyed leather-belted "badger" from the mines of Ouisconsin [Footnote for "suckers": So called after the fish of that name, from his going up the river to the mines, and returning at the season when the sucker makes its migrations] [Charles F. Hoffman, *A Winter in the West*, 1833].

(2) Said a Missouri man to a party of Illinois miners on their way home from Galena, "You remind me of *Suckers*: up in the spring spawn, and back again in the fall" [Wagner 1893, p. 32].

**Suffrage State, the** *Wyoming, USA.* Wyoming was the first state to grant full suffrage (voting rights) to women. Hence its alternate nickname **Equality State.**

**Sugar Bowl** see in Appendix 1, p. 269.

**Sugaropolis** *Mackay, Australia.* The nickname is appropriate for the Queensland town and its major sugar industry.

(1) Mackay is today the Sugaropolis of Queensland [*Queensland Handbook of Information*, 1884].

(2) Mackay, the sugaropolis of Australia, and the 'Gateway to the Great Barrier Reef' [*Daily Mercury Centenary Story of Mackay*, 1962].

**Sugar State, the** *Louisiana, USA.* The state earned its nickname from its many sugarcane plantations.

**Sulphur City** *Rotorua, New Zealand.* The North Island city is a noted resort with thermal springs, and the emissions of hydrogen sulfide from the latter provided its nickname.

**Sultan of the Andes, the** *Riobamba, Ecuador.* The nickname denotes the city's importance and prominent position near Mt. Chimborazo in the Andes.

**Summer Capital, the** *Rehoboth Beach, Delaware, USA.* The resort gained its title on the basis that in the summer it is frequented by visitors from Washington, DC, and Baltimore.

**Summer Wine Country** see in Appendix 1, p. 269.

**Sunbelt** see in Appendix 1, p. 269.

**Sun City** *Phoenix, Arizona, USA.* The state capital is so nicknamed for its location in the **Sunbelt** (see in Appendix 1, p. 269). Sun City is also the regular name of a residential suburb of Phoenix. *Cp.* **Valley of the Sun.**

**Sun Coast** see in Appendix 1, p. 269.

**Sunflower State, the** *Kansas, USA.* The sunflower is the state flower of Kansas, and the plant grows there in profusion.

(1) 'Now, when you received parole, it was on condition that you never return to Kansas.' 'The Sunflower State. I cried my eyes out' [Truman Capote, *In Cold Blood*, 1965].

(2) It was a pleasant journey back to the Ranch, flying over the flat, rich lands of Kansas ... sunflowers everywhere, as big as salad plates. You can see why it's called the Sunflower State [Lady Bird Johnson, *A White House Diary*, September 2, 1965 (1970)].

**Sunni Triangle** see in Appendix 1, p. 269.

**Sunny Australia** *Australia.* An official touristic name designed to tempt visitors and settlers to Australia, where the weather is indeed often sunny (and the climate predominantly hot and dry). (Queensland, Australia's second-biggest state, is known as the **Sunshine State.**)

When Cherise Town came [from California] to Melbourne, in the state of Victoria, for study she was a little disappointed that it didn't offer the sort of beach lifestyle that she'd come to expect of Sunny Australia [Transcript of Radio Australia series *Australia Now*, program 1: "Postcard from Down Under," 2005 <http://www.radio

australia.net.au/australia/now/default.htm>
accessed September 13, 2005].

**Sunny Beach** *Slanchev Bryag, Bulgaria.* As
explained in quote (2) below, the name of this
Black Sea resort is regularly translated in British
travel literature. The same goes for Zlatni
Pyasatsi, further up the coast, which is trans-
muted as Golden Sands.

(1) Resorts such as Sunny Beach and Golden
Sands are experiencing a new lease of life [*The
Times,* July 17, 2004].

(2) Those seeking sun, cheap beer and noisy
nightlife will make for Sunny Beach or the
slightly leafier Golden Sands — known respectively
as Slanchev Bryag and Zlatni Pyasatsi to Bulgari-
ans, they have been rebranded under English
names for the British market [*Sunday Times,* August 21, 2005].

**Sunny South** see in Appendix 1, p. 269.

**Sunny Southeast** see in Appendix 1, p. 269.

**Sunny Southsea** *Southsea, England.* A descriptive self-promotion for the popular seaside
suburb of Portsmouth, Hampshire.

The favourite slogan for Southsea is "Sunny
Southsea"... Situated in the centre of the South
Coast, it invariably takes a very high place in the
sunshine records of the country [*Holiday Guide
1952: Area No. 5, South & South East England*].

**Sunny Spain** *Spain.* A common alliterative
name for the country, long favored by the British
for sun, sea, and sport, and at the turn of the 21st
century outranking France as their top vacation
destination.

The same things that attracted Brits in the pioneering days of package tourism still exist: the
people are friendly, the food is good, the wine is
cheap ... and the sun barely stops shining [*Sunday
Times,* January 23, 2005].

**Sunrise Coast** see in Appendix 1, p. 269.

**Sunrise Kingdom, the** *Japan.* An alternate
sobriquet to the more familiar **Land of the Rising Sun**.

Neither opium-smoking nor feet-binding is
known in the Sunrise Kingdom, a fact which
differentiates the inhabitants strongly from the
people of the Middle Kingdom [William Elliot
Griffis, quoted in Giles, p. 271].

**Sunrise Land** see in Appendix 1, p. 269.

**Sunrise Strip** see in Appendix 1, p. 269.

**Sunset Country** see in Appendix 1, p. 269.

**Sunset State, the** *(1) Arizona, USA; (2) Oregon, USA .* Arizona is noted for its spectacular
sunsets, especially in the region of the Grand
Canyon. Oregon lies in the Far West, where the
sun sets. Hence the respective sobriquets.

**Sunshine Coast** see in Appendix 1, p. 269.

**Sunshine Island, the** *Guernsey, Channel Islands, UK.* A promotional name for the second-
biggest island of the group, designed to attract

visitors and vacationers. Guernsey has long been
traditionally favored over Jersey by those seeking
rest and recuperation.

**Sunshine Isle, the** *Isle of Wight, England.*
The island's southern location in the English
Channel brings above-average hours of sunshine.
Hence the self-promotional name.

**Sunshine State, the** *(1) California, USA; (2)
Florida, USA; (3) New Mexico, USA; (4) Queensland, Australia; (5) South Dakota, USA.* The
nickname is most closely associated with Florida,
although the other states have an equally good
claim to the title, as does Queensland in northeastern Australia, which boasts 300 days of sunshine a year. (*See* **Sunshine Coast** in Appendix
1, p. 269.)

(1) (South Dakota) South Dakota is known as
"the Sunshine State," not because it surpasses in
this respect ... states ... in the southwest, but because of the contrast between South Dakota and
the Eastern States and northern European countries from whence most of the persons not born in
South Dakota came [S.S. Visher, *The Geography
of South Dakota,* 1918].

(2) (Florida) Employees ... are happier in The
Sunshine State where living is so pleasant and
healthful [*Time,* March 17, 1947].

(3) (California) And although the Sunshine State
has seen a few fancy sights the citizens of Palm
Springs are in for an extra special treat next week
[*Daily Record* (Glasgow), November 30, 1976].

(4) (Queensland) Small but insistent reminders
of being in the Sunshine State. All those middle-
aged men in safari suits, long socks and shorts
[*The Bulletin* (Sydney), June 12, 1984].

(5) (Florida) South Beach [is] the St Trop of the
Sunshine State [*Sunday Times,* August 7, 2005].

**Superba, La** *Genoa, Italy.* The seaport city
has many fine buildings but its sobriquet chiefly
derives from its splendid situation at the head of
the Gulf of Genoa at the foot of the Apennines.

(1) There is a technical description of the chief
towns in Italy, which those who learn the Italian
grammar are told to get by heart — *Genoa la superba, Bologna la dotta, Ravenna l'antica, Firenze
la bella, Roma la santa* (Genoa the splendid,
Bologna the learned, Ravenna the ancient, Florence the beautiful, Rome the holy) [William Hazlitt, *Notes of a Journey through France and Italy,*
1826].

(2) La Superba is worthy of her name [George
Meredith, letter to his wife, September 15,
1882].

**Superdome City** *New Orleans, Louisiana,
USA.* The city derives its nickname as the site of
the Louisiana Superdome, one of the world's
largest sports arenas.

**Surf City** *Huntington Beach, California,
USA.* The beach resort southeast of Los Angeles
is noted for its fine surf. Hence the nickname,

popularized by (or directly adopted from) the 1963 Jan and Dean hit "Surf City."

Huntington Pier stretches 1,900 feet out to sea, well past the powerful waves that made Huntington Beach America's "Surf City" [*Fodor's Los Angeles 2006*].

**Surf Coast** see in Appendix 1, p. 269.

**Surfers** *Surfers Paradise, Australia*. A short colloquial name for the Queensland seaside resort, with its sand and surf.

Many people migrate to Surfers in search of an easier life [*The Rough Guide to Australia*, 2001].

**Surfing Capital of Britain, the** *Newquay, England*. The Cornish resort attracts surfers from all over the world, and one of its beaches has an international surfing center known as Surf City. Hence its rightful claim to the nickname.

(1) Newquay is the home of surf-riding in Britain [*Holiday Haunts 1961: Area No. 4, West of England and South and Central Wales*].
(2) Newquay is the surfing capital of the United Kingdom [*The Times*, August 9, 2003].

**Surfing Capital of New Zealand, the** *Whangamata, New Zealand*. The North Island resort has one of the country's best surf beaches, famous for the size of the waves. Hence the nickname.

**Sussex by the Sea** *Sussex, England*. The alliterative nickname of the coastal county was made familiar by Rudyard Kipling's verse in quote (1) below, was further popularized by W. Ward-Higg's 1907 musical setting of this, and is now used as a touristic epithet, as in quote (3). (Kipling's lines are based on Psalm 16:7 in the Book of Common Prayer: "The lot is fallen unto me in a fair ground: yea, I have a goodly heritage.")

(1) Each to his choice, and I rejoice
The lot has fallen to me
In a fair ground — in a fair ground —
Yea, Sussex by the sea! [Rudyard Kipling, "Sussex," 1902].
(2) It is small wonder that this county ... has long been known in song and story as 'Sussex-by-the-Sea' [Hogg, p. 231].
(3) Sussex by the Sea offers you 14 miles of beautiful contrasting coastline [Tourist brochure, *Sussex by the Sea*, 2005].

**Sussex Highlands, the** *Ashdown Forest, England*. A former railway company's extravagant promotion of the historic East Sussex forest, now mostly high-lying heathland.

**Suwaneeland** see in Appendix 1, p. 269.

**SW1** *Westminster, London, England*. The postal district designation (southwest 1) carries considerable cachet as that of one of London's most fashionable and influential areas, incorporating St James's and Belgravia.

We can rule out SW1 or Belgravia; home of

American film actors, Arab oil sheiks and, increasingly, Japanese tycoons [Godfrey Smith, *The English Companion*, 1996].

**SW3** *Chelsea, London, England*. The postal district designation has the same cachet of desirability as that of Chelsea itself.

SW3 or Chelsea is now as classy as Hampstead [Godfrey Smith, *The English Companion*, 1996].

**SW7** *South Kensington, London, England*. The postal district designation represents the smart district popularly known as **South Ken**.

Kensington proper (SW7) is now a maze of museums and stuccoed apartments for the well-to-do [Godfrey Smith, *The English Companion*, 1996].

**SW11** *see* **Swone One**

**SW18** *Wandsworth, London, England*. A postal district designation synonymous with the reputable residential area of Wandsworth.

Real, raw life always seems to be somewhere else: in palaces or shantytowns, not among the clipped hedges of SW18 [Marcel Theroux, *The Confessions of Mycroft Holmes: A Paperchase*, 2001].

**SW19** *Wimbledon, London, England*. The postal district designation (southwest 19) is frequently used in media reports as shorthand for the annual international tennis tournament held in Wimbledon at what is officially known as the All England Lawn Tennis and Croquet Club.

With their rivals stricken by injury, ... the Williams sisters can look forward to having things all their own way at SW19 [*Sunday Times*, June 20, 2004].

**Swabby Town** *San Diego, California, USA*. The seaport city is a major naval base, with lots of swabbies (sailors). Hence the nickname.

**Swamps** see in Appendix 1, p. 269.

**Swamp State, the** *South Carolina, USA*. The nickname describes the state's many swamps and rice fields.

**Swan Stream, the** *Perth, Australia*. The nickname relates to the West Australia capital city's location on the Swan River.

**Swartland** see in Appendix 1, p. 269.

**Sweatipore** *India*. A British army officers' former nickname for the hot country, implying "sweaty pore" (or "sweaty paw") as a pun on an Indian placename typically ending in -pore, as Cawnpore (now more accurately spelled Kanpur). *Cp.* **Shiny**.

**Sweetest Place on Earth, the** *Hershey, Pennsylvania, USA*. A punning name for **Chocolate City**.

The ultimate chocolate destination is Hershey, Pennsylvania ("The Sweetest Place on Earth"), home to the famed chocolate bars [*Sunday Times*, July 31, 2005].

**Sweet Sea, the** *Amazon River, South Amer-*

*ica.* An old nickname for the river, referring to its size and fresh water.

> This river ... is called of many the Sweet Sea [Robert Harcourt in Samuel Purchas, *Purchas his Pilgrimes*, 1625].

**Swinging City, the** *London, England.* The British capital came to be so nicknamed in the 1960s, when it was regarded as lively and fashionable. *Cp.* **Swinging London.**

> (1) [*Vogue* editor] Diana Vreeland ... has said simply "London is the most swinging city in the world at the moment" [*Weekend Telegraph*, April 16, 1965].
> (2) London: The Swinging City [Cover caption, *Time*, April 15, 1966].
> (3) By 1966 when *Time* magazine broke the story of "London: The Swinging City" to its readers, Chelsea had arrived ... and the Chelsea girl who wrote to *Time* about the article sounds like one of the Mitford sisters: "As a dolly from the scene, I say cheers for your gear article on the swinging, switched-on city of London and boo to all the American geese who call it humbug" [Rosemary Hill, review of Max Décharné, *King's Road*, *Times Literary Supplement*, December 16, 2005].

**Swinging London** *London, England.* A nickname applied to the British capital in the 1960s, when it was regarded as excitingly fashionable and forward-looking. *Cp.* **Swinging City.**

> (1) The British film industry ... was committed to making zany films about Swinging London [Simon Brett, *Murder Unprompted*, 1982].
> (2) More playful yet were the "target" posters that went on the back of London buses in 1958 — they featured no text ... but essentially implied the imminent arrival of Swinging London [*The Times*, December 14, 2004].

**Switzerland in the Tropics, the** *Jarabacoa, Dominican Republic.* A local promotional name for the town in the Cordillera Central.

> Residents of Jarabacoa like to describe their mountain town as 'Switzerland in the tropics.' While the description is hardly accurate, the town isn't without character [*Lonely Planet Dominican Republic & Haiti*, 2002].

**Switzerland of Africa, the** *Lesotho.* One of several nicknames referring to the kingdom's mountainous terrain, two others being **Kingdom in the Sky** and **Roof of Africa.**

**Switzerland of America, the** *(1) Alaska, USA; (2) Garrett County, Maryland, USA; (3) Maine, USA; (4) New Hampshire, USA; (5) New Jersey, USA; (6) West Virginia, USA.* All of the named regions are to some degree mountainous, such as the White Mountains of New Hampshire or the Appalachians of West Virginia. Garrett County, in the Alleghenies, was so nicknamed by the man for whom the county itself is named, John W. Garrett (1820–1884), president

of the Baltimore and Ohio Railroad, who developed its resort interests.

**Switzerland of Central Asia, the** *Kyrgyzstan.* The sobriquet is a given for a country that is entirely mountainous, with the Tian Shan Range along the Chinese boundary and the Alai Mountains in its southwestern part.

> The Switzerland of Central Asia may be about to erupt [Subheading, *The Times*, March 16, 2005].

**Switzerland of Greece, the** *Evrytania, Greece.* The prefecture is one of the most mountainous in Greece. Hence its nickname.

> Foreigners are just beginning to discover the beauty of Evrytania, the "Switzerland of Greece" [*Sunday Times*, January 30, 2005].

**Switzerland of South America, the** *(1) Bolivia; (2) Ecuador.* Both of the named countries are to some extent mountainous, although as implied in the respective quotes below, there are additional factors for evoking a comparison with Switzerland, a landlocked country popular with both vacationers and convalescents.

> (1) (Bolivia) Bolivia is the Switzerland of South America, a Republic without access to the sea [Julian Duguid, *Green Hell*, 1931].
> (2) (Ecuador) Ecuador is sometimes referred to as the Switzerland of South America. It might have something to do with the ... snow-capped volcanoes... But it is more likely to do with the fact the country ... offers a refreshing and relaxing respite as an island of mellowness [Dodd/Donald, p. 136].

**Switzerland of the Americas, the** *Costa Rica.* The Central American country is noted for its varied mountain scenery. Hence the sobriquet.

> Costa Rica is a small country ... remarkable for its landscapes. Often called the 'Switzerland of the Americas' [Travel ad, *The Times*, November 20, 2004].

**Switzerland of the Arctic, the** *Pangnirtung, Nunavut, Canada.* The Baffin Island town lies below snow-covered mountains.

**Switzerland of the Caribbean, the** *Kenscoff, Haiti.* An appropriate descriptive name for the mountain resort.

**Switzerland of the East, the** *Kashmir, India.* The former princely state in northern India, a territory disputed between India and Pakistan, lies in the Himalayas. Hence its nickname.

> The opening in April of the so-called "peace bus" route, linking the Indian- and Pakistani-administered halves of the region, brought a flood of tourists eager to rediscover the "Switzerland of the East" [*Sunday Times*, July 10, 2005].

**Switzerland of the Southern Hemisphere, the** *New Zealand.* A touristic name current at the turn of the 20th century, referring to the mountains for which the country is noted. See quote (3) at **Garden of the World**.

**Swone One** *Battersea, London, England.* A quirky punning nickname of the 1970s based on the district's postal designation SW11 (as if SW One One). The name is pronounced "Swun wun," like the numeral.

**Syd** *Sydney, Australia.* An abbreviated personalization of the city's name. *Cp.* **Mel.**

**Sydneyside** see in Appendix 1, p. 269.

**Taco Town** *(1) Corpus Christi, Texas, USA; (2) San Jose, California, USA.* Both cities are so derogatorily nicknamed for their Mexican inhabitants, taco being a typical Mexican food.

**Tadpole State, the** *Mississippi, USA.* The nickname is said to refer to the state's early young French settlers, their elders being "frogs" (*see* **Frogland**).

**Taffyland** *Wales.* The pretentious (and potentially offensive) sobriquet derives from "Taffy" as a nickname for a Welshman, representing a supposed Welsh pronunciation of "Davy," a pet form of David (Welsh *Dafydd*), a common Welsh first name (and that of the country's patron saint). *See also* **Taphydom.**

> Does it really help, or is it really humorous, to call the fox "Charles James," a hare "Madam," a nose a "proboscis," and Wales "Taffyland"? [Phrases from book review in *The Times*, quoted in Fowler, p. 547].

**Tahiti of the Caribbean, the** *St. Vincent, West Indies.* The principal island of the state of St. Vincent and the Grenadines is so nicknamed because its fertile soil and luxuriant vegetation evoke those of Tahiti, the **Garden of the Pacific**.

**Taiwan of Nigeria, the** *Aba, Nigeria.* The city is so nicknamed because of its ability to copy technology, as the Taiwanese did.

**Tall Timber Country** see in Appendix 1, p. 269.

**Tanais** *Don River, Russia.* The classical name of the river is preserved in literature. The ancient and modern names are actually related.

> Lo! where Mæotis sleeps, and hardly flows
> The freezing Tanais thro' a waste of snows
> [Alexander Pope, *The Dunciad*, 1728].

**Tangentopoli** *Milan, Italy.* The nickname means "Bribesville,"from Italian *tangente*, "protection money," referring to the corruption scandal involving government ministers, industrialists, and businessmen that began in Milan in 1992. The first main judicial inquiry was held in October 1993 with regard to the Enimont company. It was a sensation and resulted in the suicide of some key figures.

**Tangiers** *Tangier, Morocco.* The seaport city probably acquired the final "s" of its familiar English name by association with Algiers rather than from its ancient Roman name of *Tingis*.

**Tanja** *Tangier, Morocco.* A local short name for the seaport city.

**Taphydom** *Wales.* The former nickname is a variant spelling of "Taffydom" as an equivalent of **Taffyland.**

**Tarheel State, the** *North Carolina, USA.* The nickname, referring to the tar produced in the state, is said to relate specifically to an incident in the Civil War, when North Carolinians failed to hold a certain hill and were mocked by Mississippians for having forgotten to tar their heels that morning.

> A little fellow from North Carolina ... announced to the convention that he was from "the tar-heeled state" [*Scribner's Monthly*, April 1878].

**Tassie** or **Tassy** or **Tazzie** *Tasmania, Australia.* An affectionate nickname for the island state. (The spelling with "zz" represents the pronunciation of the forms with "ss.")

> (1) I took a turn in New South [Wales], and tried Tassy and New Zealand [*The Bulletin* (Sydney), December 17, 1892].
> (2) Today Tassy — as most Victorian cricketers and footballers familiarly term our neighbour over the straits — will send a team into the field [*The Argus* (Melbourne), January 26, 1894].
> (3) Every state has 'em, of course — except Tazzie, that is [Nina Pulliam, *I Traveled a Lonely Land*, 1955].
> (4) 'Would I be right in assuming you're not from around here?' I asked ... 'No, I'm from Tassie. Why?' 'Just wondered.' I whispered to Allan: 'She's from Tasmania' [Bill Bryson, *Down Under*, 2000].
> (5) Born and bred in outback Tazzie, he's an authority on everything [*Sunday Times*, October 31, 2004].

**Tavern of Europe, the** *Paris, France.* The nickname, translating French *le Cabaret de l'Europe*, is said to have been given the French capital by the Prussian diplomat Prince Otto von Bismarck.

**Taxachusetts** *Massachusetts, USA.* A wry pun on the name of the state, referring to the high taxes formerly imposed there.

> Critics are still calling us Taxachusetts. But that's so 1981. A new study ranks the Bay State 47th in the nation for the tax-and-fee burden imposed on residents in 2002 [Andrew J. Manuse in *Boston Herald*, September 9, 2004].

**Tazzie** *see* **Tassie**

**Teagueland** *Ireland.* The former nickname for Ireland is based on the personal name Tadhg (pronounced "Taig"), usually equated with the English name Thaddeus.

**Teapot Capital of North Wales, the** *Conwy,*

*Wales*. The resort town is so dubbed for its "Teapot World," a museum of 1,000 different teapots. (The Welsh for "teapot" is *tebot*, a word often reassuringly found in the early stages of a Welsh language course, in a sentence such as *Mae te yn y tebot*, "There's tea in the teapot.")

**TeeJay** *see* **TJ**

**Tegoose** or **Tegus** *Tegucigalpa, Honduras*. An abbreviated form of the capital city's name. *Cp.* **Goose**.

> Tegus is a pleasant city to spend a day or two [Natascha Norton and Mark Whatmore, *Cadogan Guides: Central America*, 1993].

**Tegwini** *Durban, South Africa*. The colloquial name represents Zulu *eThekwini*, literally "at the bay," referring to the seaport city's location on Natal Bay. In 2005 it was announced that Durban was expected to adopt the Zulu name officially.

> "I have a mind to send to the white people at Tegwini," said the King. "They are my friends, but not this new race. It may be that they will aid me to get rid of these Amabuna" [Bertram Mitford, *The Induna's Wife*, 1898].

**Telecom Valley** see in Appendix 1, p. 269.

**Tenderloin** see in Appendix 1, p. 269.

**10 NA** *Iona, Scotland*. A facetious name for the Hebridean island, much visited by tourists for its holy and royal associations. The name may have originated as a genuine error, as in the exchange below.

> US customer in British bookstore: Do you have a map of Ten en a?
> Bookseller: Ten en a, sir? Where is that?
> US customer: Well, it's a little island off the west coast of Scotland [Quoted in *The Bookseller*, January 17, 2003].

**Tennant, the** *Tennant Creek, Australia*. A short name for Australia's last gold-rush town, in Northern Territory. For the characteristic prefixed "the" see quote (3) for **Alice**.

**Tennyson Country** see in Appendix 1, p. 269.

**Terrapin State, the** *Maryland, USA*. The state derives its nickname from the diamondback terrapins farmed there.

> Maryland has had half a dozen or more nicknames since colonial times, but only *Old Line State* and *Terrapin State* have any remaining vitality today [Benjamin A. Botkin, *A Treasury of Southern Folklore*, 1949].

**Territory, the** *Northern Territory, Australia*. A short name for the territory, which unlike the main administrative regions of Australia is not a fully-fledged state.

> (1) The country on this run is some of the best in the Territory [William Sowden, *The Northern Territory as it Is*, 1882].
> (2) Nearly a quarter of The Territory's inhabi-

tants are Aborigines [*The Rough Guide to Australia*, 2001].

**Terror Town** see in Appendix 1, p. 269.

**Texas of Cuba, the** *Camagüey, Cuba*. Cattle raising has been practiced in the province since early colonial days, occupying half of the arable land. Hence the nickname.

**That Toddlin' Town** *Chicago, Illinois, USA*. The nickname derives from Fred Fisher's song "Chicago," as quoted below.

> Chicago, Chicago
>   That toddlin' town
> Chicago, Chicago
>   I'll show you around [Fred Fisher, "Chicago," 1922].

**Theatreland** see in Appendix 1, p. 269.

**These Islands** *British Isles*. The name is mainly found in Irish use. "These" avoids the political and geographical specific "British." *See also* **Hibernian Archipelago**.

> [Harland & Wolff] is still the largest, most innovative and most successful shipyard in what we like to refer to as "these islands" [John de Courcy Ireland, *Ireland's Maritime Heritage*, 1992].

**Thiefrow** *Heathrow Airport, London, England*. London's main airport owes its nickname to the widespread theft and former lax security experienced here.

**Thief's Athens, the** *Grisons (Graubünden), Switzerland*. The name was applied to the region by a character in Friedrich Schiller's play *Die Räuber* ("The Robbers") (1781). (The speaker's actual words were: "Go to the Grisons, for instance, that is what I call the thief's Athens.") The sobriquet met with the displeasure of the Duke of Württemberg, as related by English critic Thomas de Quincey in the passage quoted below.

> The territory of the Grisons had been called by Spiegelberg, one of the robbers, "The Thief's Athens." Upon this, the magistrates of that country presented a complaint to the duke; and his highness having cited [i.e. summoned] Schiller to his presence, and severely reprimanded him, issued a decree that this dangerous young student should henceforth confine himself to his medical studies [Thomas de Quincey, *Autobiographic Sketches*, 1834–41].

**Thinking Man's Provence, the** *Languedoc, France*. The sobriquet compares the region of south central France to neighboring Provence from a British perspective. Provence was popularized as a desirable region by author Peter Mayle and other British who made it their home. Languedoc earned a more discerning cachet among British writers and artists who settled there, from novelist and poet Lawrence Durrell to writer Christopher Hope, journalist Frank Johnson, and publisher Carmen Callil.

**Third Coast** see in Appendix 1, p. 269.

**Third Reich, the** *Germany.* A historic name for Germany under the Nazi regime from 1933 through 1945. It was "Third" following the Holy Roman Empire (962–1806) and the German Empire (1871–1918). The name is a part-translation of German *drittes Reich*, "third state."

(1) Asked to give some idea of the "Third Reich," Herr Hitler said the old Germany was a State of great honour and of glorious events, but the conception of "the people" was not the central pillar of the structure. The second State had placed democracy and pacifism in the centre. They hoped for the Third Reich, which would have as its keystone the conception of the people and the national idea [*The Times*, September 26, 1930].

(2) One man — Adolf Hitler — was always in the driving seat... Not for nothing was he seen as the incarnation of the Third Reich [Robert Service, review of Richard J. Evans, *The Third Reich in Power, Sunday Times*, December 11, 2005].

**Third Republic, the** *France.* The title is used historically to refer to the eventful period from 1871 to 1940 when France was governed as a republic. (The First Republic, under Robespierre, was from 1792 to 1794. The Second Republic, under Louis-Napoléon Bonaparte, lasted from 1852 to 1870. After World War II, during which there was a collaborationist regime under Marshal Pétain, a Fourth Republic under presidents Vincent Auriol and René Coty ran from 1947 to 1958, when the present Fifth Republic began with Charles de Gaulle as its first president.)

**Third Rome, the** *Moscow, Russia.* The sobriquet alludes to Moscow as the historical inheritor of (Greek) Orthodox Christianity (*see* **Second Rome**) on the marriage in 1472 of Ivan III to Zoë (later Sophia) Palaeologus, niece of the last emperor of Byzantium. The first use of the phrase appears to be in a letter from the Russian monk Philotheus to Grand Duke Vasily (Basil) III (reigned 1505–33).

(1) Moscow became the third Rome, the sole depository of all imperial power and the only receptacle of unsullied Orthodoxy [D.S. Mirsky, *A History of Russian Literature*, 1949].

(2) The idea of Moscow as the "Third Rome" ("and a Fourth there shall not be") was ... formulated by a churchman at the beginning of the sixteenth century [Max Hayward, Introduction to Chloe Obolensky, *The Russian Empire*, 1980].

**Third World** see in Appendix 1, p. 269.

**Thirsty Island** *Thursday Island, Australia.* The Queensland island, northwest of Cape York, earned its punning nickname from its great trade in the sale of liquor to pearl fishers.

The local [Aborigine] tag is *Waiben* or (very loosely) "Thirsty Island"— once a reference to the availability of drinking water and now a laconic

aside on the quantity of beer consumed [*The Rough Guide to Australia*, 2001].

**Thirty-Two Counties, the** *Ireland.* The name is used for the whole island of Ireland, especially by those who favor unity between the **Six Counties** of Northern Ireland and the **Twenty-Six Counties** of the Republic.

**Thoroughbred County, the** *Co. Kildare, Ireland.* The nickname derives from the county's equestrian associations, which include the Curragh, a famous racecourse near Kildare town.

Kildare has adopted the horse as its official logo by assuming a new identity as the "thoroughbred county." The brand image was officially introduced yesterday by the Minister for Finance, Mr McCreevy, at his Straffan home [*Irish Times*, November 16, 1999].

**Three-Story City, the** *Chonchi, Chile.* The town, on Chiloé Island, is built on cliffs overlooking the sea. Hence its nickname.

**Threshold of the Cotswolds, the** *Faringdon, England.* The Oxfordshire (formerly Berkshire) town lies on a road running west to the Cotswold Hills and itself somewhat resembles a Cotswold town, as many of its buildings are made of stone.

Faringdon, the 'threshold of the Cotswolds' and a market town in a pretty position on a limestone ridge [Charlie Godfrey-Faussett, *Footprint England*, 2004].

**Throat between Hubei and Sichuan, the** *Yichang, China.* The city derives its nickname as the last major port on the Chang Jiang (Yangtze Kiang) River in Hubei province before entering Sichuan.

**Thule** *Shetland Islands, Scotland.* The name was applied to the island group by Tacitus in his *Agricola* (AD 98). The islands never actually adopted the name, however, and the Roman historian used it simply to denote the northernmost land of the British Isles. The name Thule (often in the Latin phrase *ultima Thule*) has since been regularly used to denote a remote place, whether real or imaginary.

The archipelago ... used to be regarded as the Ultima Thule of Britain (which it is) but as so remote, so inaccessible, as to be unimportant [Macnie/McLaren, p. 445].

**TI** *Thursday Island, Australia.* A local initialism for the best-known of the many Torres Strait Islands, Queensland.

**Tiflis** *Tbilisi, Georgia.* The Georgian capital was long known by the corrupt Turkish form of its name. It officially adopted the Georgian form on becoming capital of Soviet Georgia in 1936, although the old form is still sometimes found.

**Tiger Bay** *Cardiff Bay, Cardiff, Wales.* The sobriquet of the former dockland area and slum district of the Welsh capital supposedly refers to the "wild" behavior of visiting sailors in local bars and brothels. It is said to derive from a popular song current in the 1870s, and became more widely known through the torch singer Shirley Bassey (the "Tigress of Tiger Bay") and the 1959 movie so titled.

(1) The Cardiff Bay area — the spicier tag of Tiger Bay (immortalized by locally born chanteuse Shirley Bassey) being rarely used these days — comprises two distinct parts [*The Rough Guide to Wales*, 1998].

(2) Now the old dockland of 'Tiger Bay' has been completely regenerated [Hazel Irvine in *A View of Wales*, Spring/Summer, 2005].

**Tight Little Island, the** *Britain.* The nickname derives from the popular song in quote (1) below. See also quote (4) at **Continent.**

(1) Oh! what a snug little island,
A right little, tight little island! [Thomas Dibdin, "The Snug Little Island," 1833].

(2) When you get back to the 'tight little island,' otherwise known as England, I hope you'll be able to give a satisfactory account of the antipodes [*Sydney Punch*, January 25, 1868].

**Timbuctoo** *Timbuktu, Mali.* The old spelling of the town's name became familiar from its use to denote any remote and exotic place. The name is accented on the third syllable or the second, as in quote (1) below.

(1) Though travell'd, I have never had the luck to Trace up those shuffling negroes, Nile or Niger, To that impracticable place Timbuctoo [Lord Byron, *Don Juan*, 1823].

(2) If I were a cassowary
On the plains of Timbuctoo,
I would eat a missionary,
Cassock, band, and hymn-book too [Bishop Samuel Wilberforce, attrib., 19th century].

**Timo** *Timor, Indonesia.* The island some 400 miles (645 km) northwest of Australia was colloquially so called in the 19th century by convicts eager to escape from the mainland.

It is an old legend amongst the more ignorant of the convicts, that Timor, or as they call it "Timo," is easily attainable by land from New South Wales [Alexander Harris, *The Emigrant Family*, 1849].

**Tinopolis** *Llanelli, Wales.* The town near Swansea in South Wales was formerly noted for its tinplate industry. Hence its nickname, of the **Cottonopolis** type. (The name is currently in commercial use as that of a local TV production company.)

**Tinseltown** *Hollywood, Los Angeles, California, USA.* The nickname describes the garish glitter and presumptuous pretense of the movie city in its heyday. It is said to derive from a 1940s comment by musician Oscar Levant: "Strip the

phony tinsel off Hollywood, and you'll find the real tinsel underneath." *Cp.* **Glamour Town.**

(1) You wrote me about checking maybe you could sign on with Les Brown if you decide to depart the Apple and come out here to Tinsel Town [*TV Guide*, September 14, 1974].

(2) British talent takes Tinseltown by storm [Headline, *Daily Telegraph*, March 23, 1999].

(3) Tinseltown continues to be the global capital of movie-making, but because of rising costs many big "Hollywood" movies are actually filmed elsewhere [*The Times Magazine*, October 15, 2005].

**Tip, the** *Cape York Peninsula, Australia.* A nickname for Queensland's (and Australia's) northernmost point. *Cp.* **Top End.**

Tackling the rugged tracks and hectic river crossings on the "Trip to the Tip" is an adventure in itself [*The Rough Guide to Australia*, 2001].

**Title Town** *Green Bay, Wisconsin, USA.* The nickname refers to the Green Bay Packers, the successful professional football team whose stadium is in the city.

**TJ** or **TeeJay** *Tijuana, Mexico.* An initial-derived form of the town's name. *See also* **Aunt Jane.**

TeeJay, as the city is known to young Americans [Dodd/Donald, p. 193].

**T'n'T** or **T&T** *Trinidad and Tobago, West Indies.* A local nickname for the island republic.

In the local patois, there's always time for a B'n'C [i.e. Bacardi and Coke] in T'n'T [Dodd/Donald, p. 96].

**TO** *Toronto, Ontario, Canada.* An abbreviated form of the city's name, regarded either as its first two letters or as the initials of city name and province name. "T dot" is a trendy alternate form.

**Tobacco City** *(1) Durham, North Carolina, USA: (2) Winston-Salem, North Carolina, USA.* Durham owes its sobriquet to the tobacco industry that arose after the Civil War, with James B. Duke as the leading manufacturer. Winston-Salem derives its nickname from the tobacco company founded in 1875 by R.J. Reynolds in what was then just Winston. The manufacture of cigarettes here is still a major industry.

**Tobacco State, the** *(1) Kentucky, USA; (2) Virginia, USA.* The name derives from tobacco as a principal product in both states.

(Virginia) If any state in the U.S.A. can be called the "tobacco state," it is Virginia, which gives its name to Virginia tobacco [Johnson, p. 258].

**Toc** *Tocumwal, Australia.* A short local name for the New South Wales river town.

**Toddlin' Town** *see* **That Toddlin' Town**

**Toe of Italy, the** *Calabria, Italy.* As it appears on the map, the region represents the "toe" of the "boot" that is Italy, as distinct from the **Heel of Italy**. *See also* **Leg of Italy** in Appendix 1, p. 269.

> The advancing Allied armies ... forced themselves northwards from the toe of Italy [Ritchie Perry, *Bishop's Pawn*, 1979].

**Tojoland** *Japan*. The dated nickname derives from the World War II Japanese general and military dictator Hideki Tojo, executed as a war criminal in 1948.

> If 'e ever gets to Tojo-land the Japs will die of fright [*Camp Capers*, August 12, 1943].

**Toon, the** *Newcastle upon Tyne, England*. The city's nickname is a local dialect form of "town." It is also the name of the local football club Newcastle United, whose supporters are known as the Toon Army. *See also* **Newk**.

> (1) Fervent supporters of Newcastle United have made the city the replica shirt capital of the world, dressing children in the black and white of the Toon Army long before they can walk [*The Times*, January 4, 2000].
>
> (2) My inquiry for the location of that Toon pub institution, the Free Trade Inn, drew a blank [*The Times*, March 12, 2005].

**Toothpick State, the** *Arkansas, USA*. The nickname derives from the "toothpick," better known as the bowie knife, carried by early settlers in the state.

**Top End, the** *Northern Territory, Australia*. The nickname can denote either the territory in general or more narrowly the northern ("top") part of it. *Cp.* **Centre**.

> (1) She ... left again for the more ... human regions of the Top End, where at least one could drink fresh water occasionally [Frederick E. Baume, *Tragedy Track*, 1933].
>
> (2) The Northern Territory may be divided into two parts—'The Centre' and the 'Top End.' The Centre has Alice Springs as its 'capital,' or administrative base. In the Top End, Darwin is episcopal headquarters and the home of the Northern Territory's Administrator [Frank Flynn, *The Northern Gateway*, 1963].
>
> (3) We would fly on to Darwin in the Northern Territory—the 'Top End' as it is fondly known to Australians [Bill Bryson, *Down Under*, 2000].

**Top of the World, the** *Colorado, USA*. The state claims its sobriquet by virtue of the fact that it has 52 of the 80 peaks in North America that are 14,000 ft (4,267 m) or higher.

**T or C** *Truth or Consequences, New Mexico, USA*. An almost essential abbreviation of the town's lengthy name.

**Tornado Alley** *Oklahoma City, Oklahoma, USA*. The city derives its nickname from the tornadoes to which its state is subject, with southwestern Oklahoma having the highest tornado incidence per unit area in the USA.

> (1) For some, the twister rekindled memories of the May 9, 1999, tornado that ripped through the Oklahoma City area and killed 44 people. Frances Clark said she hid in the same spot for both tornadoes. "It is Tornado Alley, so you get used to it," she said [*USA Today*, May 9, 2003].
>
> (2) It may be the start of "twister season" in "Tornado Alley" in the Midwest of the United States, but a study ... has found that Britain suffers more tornadoes than any other country of its size [*The Times*, May 7, 2005].

**Toronto the Good** *Toronto, Ontario, Canada*. The provincial capital was formerly so dubbed for its religious restraints and strong antivice laws. The sobriquet began to wane in the 1970s when the city started to gain its present progressive status as the unofficial capital of Canada as a whole.

> It may not be a warm, gregarious city, but it's way better than it was when it was known as Toronto-the-Good [*Lonely Planet Canada*, 2002].

**Torrie** *Torremolinos, Spain*. A colloquial English name for the popular Mediterranean resort.

> 'Torrie' ... is a concrete high-rise jungle [*Lonely Planet Spain*, 2003].

**Tortilla Curtain** see in Appendix 1, p. 269.

**'Tother Side** *see* **Other Side** in Appendix 1, p. 269.

**Tout-Paris, le** *Paris, France*. The expression, first used from the 1820s and meaning literally "the whole of Paris," refers to the mixed social, political, and cultural elite of the French capital.

> (1) "Tout Paris" passed them; but they were none the wiser, and agreed that the show was not a patch on that in Hyde Park during the London season [George du Maurier, *Trilby*, 1894].
>
> (2) It is the talk of le tout Paris in the French business world. Who will be getting the plum job? [*The Times*, January 14, 1982].

**Towers, the** *Charters Towers, Australia*. A short name for the former gold-mining town in eastern Queensland.

**Town** *London, England*. A name used since the 18th century (without "the") for the British capital, in such phrases as "in town," "go up to town," etc. The popular BBC radio program *In Town Tonight*, running from 1933 to 1960, opened with the words: "Once again we silence the roar of London's traffic to bring to the microphone some of the interesting people who are *In Town Tonight*!" *See also* **Country** in Appendix 1, p. 269.

> (1) When he is in Town, he lives in Soho-Square [Richard Steele in *The Spectator*, 1721].
>
> (2) At Richmond ... I set out by myself for town, as London is called *par excellence* [Louis Simond, *A Tour of Great Britain*, 1815].

(3) Never refer to "Town" when you mean London [Guy Egmont, *The Art of Egmontese*, 1961].

**Town, the** *St. Anne, Alderney, Channel Islands, UK.* The designation is natural for the island's sole town.

The principal town is called "The Town" and is situated in the middle of the Island [Johnson, p. 17)

**Town for the Motor Age, a** *Radburn, New Jersey, USA.* The borough thus promoted itself as one of the first US planned communities, started in 1928. The pioneering layout segregated traffic and pedestrians, with culs-de-sac for vehicles one side of a line of houses and footpaths the other.

**Town of a Thousand Eyes, the** *Berat, Albania.* The nickname refers to the many windows in the town's old houses.

**Town of Bells, the** *Nicolet, Quebec, Canada.* The nickname is appropriate for a town that is a major religious center, with a cathedral. *Cp.* **City of Bells.**

**Town of Books, the** *Hay-on-Wye, Wales.* The Welsh border town is famed for its secondhand bookshops. The first opened in 1961, and by the end of the century there were over 20, the largest holding around half a million books.

**Town of Murals, the** *Sheffield, Australia.* The Tasmanian town presents itself thus for its many murals depicting the history of the area.

**Town of Oaks, the** *Stellenbosch, South Africa.* The town is nicknamed for the oak trees that line its streets.

**Town of Roses, the** *Molde, Norway.* The town is so nicknamed for its fine rose gardens. *Cp.* **City of Roses.**

Molde, scenically situated beside the sea, ... calls itself the 'Town of Roses' [*Lonely Planet Norway*, 2002].

**Town of the Four Gates, the** *Neubrandenburg, Germany.* The historic core of the city is ringed by a range of fortifications that include four town gates. Hence the nickname.

**Town of the Four Masters, the** *Donegal, Ireland.* The town in the county of the same name was formerly so nicknamed, for the *Annals of the Four Masters*, a 17th-century record of Ireland's annals, compiled at Donegal Abbey.

**Town of the Seven Towers, the** *Martel, France.* The nickname refers to the towers of the town's medieval ramparts.

**Town of Trees, the** *Cambridge, New Zealand.* The North Island town is so nicknamed for its avenues of elm and oak trees.

**Town that Fooled the British, the** *St. Michaels, Maryland, USA.* The name refers to an incident during the War of 1812. As British ships approached, lights were placed as decoys on trees. The British fired at them, with the result that their cannon balls passed harmlessly over the town.

**Town that Moved Overnight, the** *Hibbing, Minnesota, USA.* In 1917 the city was moved two miles to the south to make room for one of the world's largest open-pit iron mines. Hence its nickname.

**Town that Saved Queensland, the** *Gympie, Australia.* The Queensland town came to be so known for its rich gold deposits, although mining mostly stopped in the 1920s.

**Town that Was Murdered, the** *Jarrow, England.* The Tyneside shipbuilding town came to be so known from the title of Ellen Wilkinson's 1939 book describing the intense poverty that followed the closure in 1933 of the Charles Palmer shipyards. The name of the town is still associated with the desperate hunger march from Jarrow to London in 1936.

**Town Too Tough to Die, the** *Tombstone, Arizona, USA.* The nickname refers to the resolve of the inhabitants to stay on after the town's rich silver mines were flooded in the 1880s.

**Town with the Hole in the Middle, the** *Banbridge, Northern Ireland.* The Co. Down town is so nicknamed because in the 19th century the pavement level of the main street was lowered and the sides joined by a bridge.

**Toyshop of Europe** or **the World, the** *Birmingham, England.* As mentioned in quote (1) below, the sobriquet derives from a speech in the House of Commons on March 26, 1777, by the Irish politician Edmund Burke, during the first reading of a bill to license the theater in Birmingham. The term does not refer to toys in the modern sense but to the trinkets and knicknacks then made in the city, among them cheap jewelry.

(1) It is not easy to trace with accuracy the origin of the numerous branches of trade and manufacture which ... obtained for this place, from the celebrated Mr. Burke, the appropriate designation of the "Toy Shop of Europe" [Samuel Lewis, *A Topographical Dictionary of England*, 1840].
(2) It has long been matter of wonder to intelligent foreigners that the "Toyshop of the World" ("Workshop of the World" would be nearer the mark) has never organised a permanent exhibition of its myriad manufactures [Walter Showell, *Dictionary of Birmingham*, 1885].

**Travellers' Coast** see in Appendix 1, p. 269.

**Treacle Town** *(1) Bristol, England; (2) Macclesfield, England.* For Bristol, the former nickname refers to the city's sugar-refining industry.

For the Cheshire town of Macclesfield, the reference is said to be to an occasion when a cask of treacle was accidentally dropped and split in one of the main streets so that its contents ran in the gutters, allowing the townsfolk to enjoy meals of bread and treacle. But this seems an unlikely origin.

**Treasure State, the** *Montana, USA*. The nickname springs from the state's mining industry. As well as the coal that is one of Montana's main resources, the Rocky Mountains have yielded silver, gold, copper, platinum and other metals.

> A solid century of mining has failed to put much of a dent in the state's gold, silver, copper and coal reserves. So the slogan, "Treasure State," which used to grace Montana license plates, is still appropriate [*Billings* (Montana) *Gazette*, June 20, 1976].

**Treasury of Peru, the** *Andes, South America*. The nickname refers to the wealth of mineral resources afforded by the Andes that cover most of the country, including gold, silver, copper, iron, lead, and zinc.

**Trebizond** *Trabzon, Turkey*. The alternate name of the ancient seaport city is that of the Greek empire which flourished here by the Black Sea in medieval times.

> (1) And all who since, baptized or infidel,
> Jousted in Aspramont, or Montalban,
> Damasco, or Marocco, or Trebisond [John Milton, *Paradise Lost*, 1667].
> (2) When we saw Trebizond lying there in its splendid bay, the sea in front and the hills behind, ... it was like seeing an old dream change its shape, as dreams do [Rose Macaulay, *The Towers of Trebizond*, 1956].

**Treeplanter State, the** *Nebraska, USA*. The origin and motive for the state's official nickname is explained in the legislative declaration quoted below. Arbor Day, as an annual day for planting trees, originated in Nebraska, where the first such day to be set apart for the purpose was April 10, 1872.

> Whereas the State of Nebraska has heretofore in a popular sense been designated by names not in harmony with its history, industry or ambition; and whereas the State of Nebraska is preeminently a tree planting state, Be It Resolved by the Legislature of the State of Nebraska that the State of Nebraska shall hereafter in a popular sense be known and referred to as the Tree Planting State [G.E. Shankle, "Laws of Nebraska," *American Nicknames*, 1895].

**Trent** *Trento, Italy*. The name of the Italian city is familiar historically from the Council of Trent (1543–63), an ecumenical council of the Roman Catholic church, convoked in Trento. The name is confused by some with that of the English river.

**Triad** see in Appendix 1, p. 269.

**Triangle of Death** see in Appendix 1, p. 269.

**TriBeCa** see in Appendix 1, p. 269.

**Trichinopoly** *Tiruchchirappalli, India*. The European form of the city's name appears to have been influenced by Greek *trikhinos*, "of hair," and *polis*, "city," although it is hard to envisage what a "city of hair" would be.

**Tricky Dick's** *San Clemente, California, USA*. President Richard Nixon (nicknamed "Tricky Dicky") maintained a "Western White House" summer residence at San Clemente and this gave the city's sobriquet.

**Trimountain City, the** *Boston, Massachusetts, USA*. The nickname refers to the three hills on the Shawmut Peninsula on which the city was settled in 1630.

**Trinco** *Trincomalee, Sri Lanka*. The short name for the seaport town used among navy personnel, especially in World War II.

**Trini** *Trinidad (and Tobago)*. A local nickname for either the island of Trinidad or the republic as a whole. *Cp.* **T'n'T**.

> My name means nothing to anyone [in Tobago], whereas in cricket-besotted "Trini" it has the celebrity of at least a minor Calypsonian [Cricket correspondent Christopher Martin-Jenkins in *The Times*, April 2, 2005].

**Triple X, the** *Amsterdam, The Netherlands*. The American nickname for the capital city refers to its international Triple X Festival of design, music, and the visual arts.

**Tripsville** *San Francisco, California, USA*. The city was so nicknamed in the 1960s for its drug culture.

**Tri-State Area** see in Appendix 1, p. 269.

**Tropi-Coast** see in Appendix 1, p. 269.

**Troynovant** *London, England*. A former literary name for the British capital, supposedly representing *Troy Novant*, "new Troy," after the ancient Greek city, following the latter's capture and destruction by fire. According to this theory, it was given by the English city's founder, the legendary Trojan Brutus (*see* **Brute's City**). The real source of the name is probably in the Celtic people known as the Trinovantes, whose capital is thought to have been at Chelmsford in Essex.

> (1) For noble *Britons* sprong [i.e. sprang] from *Troians* bold,
> And *Troynouant* was built of old *Troyes* ashes cold [Edmund Spenser, *The Faerie Queene*, 1590].
> (2) What famous off-spring of downe raced [i.e. razed] Troy,
> King Brute the Conqueror of Giants fell,
> Built London first these Mansion Towers of ioy,
> As all the spacious world may witnesse well,
> Euen he it was, whose glory more to vaunt,
> From burned Troy, sur-named this Troynouant

[Richard Johnson, *The Pleasant Conceites of Old Hobson*, 1607].

**Turpentine State, the** *North Carolina, USA.* The nickname refers to the turpentine produced from the state's pine forests.

The danger is, we may stick in the Turpentine State [Mayne Reid, *The Rifle Rangers*, 1850].

**Turquoise Coast** see in Appendix 1, p. 269.

**Turtle Island** *North America.* The origin of the name is explained in the quote below.

Since "Turtle Island" was a label bestowed on North America by indigenous peoples long before the first Europeans arrived, many consider it a more valid name for the continent [Henry Beard and Christopher Cerf, *The Official Politically Correct Dictionary and Handbook*, 1992].

**Twenty-Minute City, the** *Adelaide, Australia.* As indicated in the quote below, the nickname refers to the traffic-friendly roads of the city, enabling the car driver to get from one place to another with little delay.

The ease of commuting in Adelaide has earned it the nickname "the 20-minute city." It was laid out as a grid with very wide streets and a surrounding ring of parklands [*The Times*, June 28, 2004].

**27th County of the Irish Republic, the** *Kilburn, London, England.* The district was formerly so nicknamed for the Irish immigrant workers who settled here, where jobs were more plentiful, after World War II. (The Irish-sounding name may have helped the attraction.) The Republic of Ireland has 26 counties (see the next entry below).

We glide through West Hampstead on the edge of Kilburn, once known as the 27th county of the Irish Republic but now home to a far wider ethnic mix [*The Times*, September 5, 2005].

**Twenty-Six Counties, the** *Ireland.* The somewhat dated sobriquet of the Republic of Ireland, with its 26 counties, contrasts with the **Six Counties** of Northern Ireland. *See also* **Thirty-Two Counties**.

(1) The garage ... belonged to a brother-in-law of one of the Sinn Fein leaders in the Twenty-Six Counties ... O'Hagan explained that, within the IRA, no one talked of the "Irish Republic" by any term other than this [Walter Nelson, *The Minstrel Code*, 1979].

(2) They always come over and take their holidays in the Twenty-Six Counties, but maybe they'll venture to the North this year [Contemporary source, quoted in Terence Patrick Dolan, *A Dictionary of Hiberno-English*, 1998].

**Twickers** *Twickenham, London, England.* The colloquial form of the name, with the "Oxford -er" as for **Honkers**, primarily applies to the famous rugby football stadium here at the headquarters of the Rugby Football Union, but can also apply to the former village itself.

A Twickers crowd is typically in high good humour [Godfrey Smith, *The English Companion*, 1996].

**Twilight Zone** see in Appendix 1, p. 269.

**Twin Cities, the** *(1) Fort William and Port Arthur, Canada; (2) St. Paul and Minneapolis, Minnesota, USA.* The state capital of Minnesota and adjacent Minneapolis together form the Twin Cities metropolitan area. Hence their joint name. In Canada, the two named neighboring towns merged in 1970 to form the city of Thunder Bay, also known as **Lakehead**. There are other pairs of cities so known, whether uniting or not, with each individual city called a **Twin City**. (The latter term can equally apply to a city formed from two others, as Winston-Salem.)

(1) (St. Paul and Minneapolis) The twin cities ... emulate each other in metropolitan airs [*Harper's Magazine*, June 1883].

(2) (Fort William and Port Arthur) *Twin Cities*, when spoken of in Canada, usually refer to Port Arthur and Fort William, neighboring cities and ports in Ontario [John Sandilands, *Western Canadian Dictionary and Phrase-Book*, 1912].

(3) (St. Paul and Minneapolis) Fog and clouds gave the Twin Cities respite from the hot weather for a few hours Thursday morning [*St. Paul Pioneer-Press*, August 12, 1949].

(4) (St. Paul and Minneapolis) Minneapolis and St. Paul ... are nicknamed the Twin Cities. They are divided by the Mississippi River, and united by their belief that the inhabitants of the other side of the river are inferior [Trevor Fishlock, *Americans and Nothing Else*, 1980].

**Twin City** *(1) Fort William, Ontario, Canada; (2) Minneapolis, Minnesota, USA; (3) Port Arthur, Ontario, Canada; (4) St. Paul, Minnesota, USA; (5) Winston-Salem, North Carolina, USA.* Fort William and nearby Port Arthur merged in 1970 to form Thunder Bay, also known as **Lakehead**. St. Paul and adjacent Minneapolis together form the **Twin Cities** metropolitan area. Winston-Salem is so known as the two towns of Winston and Salem unified in 1913.

**Ty** *Teyateyaneng, Botswana.* A common short form of the town's name.

**Tyburnia** see in Appendix 1, p. 269.

**Tykedom** *Yorkshire, England.* The name derives from "tyke" as a nickname for a resident of the county. (The word literally means "dog," and was at first applied opprobriously, but is now proudly accepted.)

At Bradford or Sheffield or some other murky stronghold of Tykedom [*Westminster Gazette*, December 18, 1905].

**Ukers** *United Kingdom.* A colloquial nickname (pronounced "Yewkers") favored mostly by British service personnel posted overseas. It consists of the initials UK and the "Oxford -er" as for **Honkers**.

**Ulster** *Northern Ireland.* Ulster is properly the name of a historic province of nine counties in the northern part of Ireland. Six of the counties (*see* **Six Counties**) are in present-day Northern Ireland, created as a political entity in 1920, for which the province name is now sometimes used instead.

(1) It must be carefully noted that Ulster is not another name for Northern Ireland, though it is often wrongly used as such [Johnson, p. 252].
(2) Army 'to start pulling troops out from Ulster by Christmas' [Headline, *The Times*, October 4, 2004].

**Ultima Thule of Asia, the** *Japan.* The nickname sees Japan as the remotest "unknown" land of Asia, like the Thule that was the northernmost land known to the Romans. *Cp.* **Thule**.

Japan, land of high romance ... the Ultima Thule of Asia [*An Official Guide to Japan*, 1933].

**Uncle Sam** *United States.* This and the nicknames below are based on the cartoon figure of a white-haired, bewhiskered man wearing a tall hat and striped trousers and symbolically representing the United States. His name is popularly said to derive from the nation's initials "U.S." although it is also specifically associated with Samuel Wilson, affectionately known as "Uncle Sam," an army yard inspector of Troy, New York. The goods that he passed to the army in the War of 1812 were stamped "U.S." to denote government property. This origin lacks verification, however. As a personification, "Uncle Sam" can denote either the nation itself or the US government.

**Uncle Sam's Attic** *Alaska, USA.* Alaska is so nicknamed as the remote "upper room" belonging to **Uncle Sam**.

**Uncle Sam's Handkerchief** *Delaware, USA.* The nickname refers to the state as one of the smallest belonging to **Uncle Sam**.

**Uncle Sam's Heel** *Florida, USA.* Florida is the "heel" (in shape and position) of the main body belonging to **Uncle Sam**. Hence the nickname.

**Uncle Sam's Icebox** *Alaska, USA.* The state is generally the coldest belonging to **Uncle Sam**.

**Uncle Sap** *United States.* A punning derogatory nickname of the nation personified by **Uncle Sam**.

**Uncle Sham** *United States.* A black distortion of **Uncle Sam**, coined by the US protest movement to point up the shallowness of those who promoted the "American dream."

**Uncle Sugar** *United States.* The nickname represents the military phonetic alphabet names for the letters "U" and "S," as the initials of the United States (and **Uncle Sam**).

'Hey, man, can you OD on grass?' 'I dunno, baby. Maybe we could get jobs at the Aberdeen Proving Grounds smokin' dope for Uncle Sugar' [Michael Herr, *Dispatches*, 1977].

**Uncle Whiskers** *United States.* A nickname referring to the familiar bewhiskered figure of **Uncle Sam**. *Cp.* **Mr. Whiskers**.

**Un-Hamptons, the** *Sag Harbor, New York, USA.* The resort village and former whaling port is so nicknamed for its accessible, low-key profile by comparison with the high exclusivity of the nearby **Hamptons** (see in Appendix 1, p. 269).

They call this old whaling town the "un-Hamptons," as the residents pride themselves on the friendly, unpretentious atmosphere [*Sunday Times*, March 6, 2005].

**Union, the** *(1) South Africa; (2) United States.* The term was formerly used as a short designation for South Africa before it became a republic in 1961. As applied to the United States, the name was current in the 19th century. (In the latter usage, the name could apply to the Northern States, as distinct from the 11 Southern States, whose attempted secession from the original Union led to the Civil War.)

(1) (USA) It has been my invariable rule to do all for the Union. If any man wants the key of my heart, let him take the key of the Union, and that is the key to my heart [Henry Clay, speech in Norfolk, April 22, 1844].
(2) (South Africa) The words 'the Union' shall be taken to mean the Union of South Africa as constituted under this Act [R.H. Brand, *The Union of South Africa*, 1909].
(3) (South Africa) It is in the interest of the Union that its relations with the German Reich should be severed [Jan Smuts in *Hansard*, September 29, 1939].

**United Queendom, the** *United Kingdom.* The punning name was created by the Gay Britain section of the British tourist authority VisitBritain to promote the UK as a suitable destination for gays and lesbians from abroad.

Referring to the United Queendom of Great Britain, the website asks: "Isn't it time you came out ... to Britain?" [*The Times*, January 7, 2005].

**United States of the Southern Hemisphere, the** *Argentina.* The sobriquet sees Argentina as a sort of southern mirror image of the United States. There are similarities of geography (in the respective latitudes north and south), history (both evolving from Spanish colonial settlements in the 16th century), and government (both are a federal republic), and the economy of each is mainly based on manufacturing and agriculture.

> It is the United States of the Southern Hemisphere [James Bryce, *South America*, 1812].

**Unspoiled Queen, the** *Saba, West Indies.* The island of the Netherlands Antilles presumably came by its sobriquet as a translation of a native name amounting to "Virgin Queen," referring to its "unblemished" nature, thanks to its inaccessibility and ruggedness. It is hardly a major objective on the world tourist map.

**Up North** see in Appendix 1, p. 269.

**Up Over** *Alaska, USA.* Alaska is "up over" most of the continental USA, as Australia is **Down Under** Europe.

**Uptown** see in Appendix 1, p. 269.

**Urbs Prima in Indis** *Mumbai (Bombay), India.* The Latin tag, meaning "the foremost city of India," appears on a plaque by the colonial arch known as the **Gateway of India**. The phrase, with other descriptives, became familiar from lines quoted by Salman Rushdie in the italicized passage below. *See also* **Gateway to India**.

> "O Bombay! *Prima in Indis! Gateway to India! Star of the East with her face to the West!*" [Salman Rushdie, *The Moor's Last Sigh*, 1995].

**Uricon** *Wroxeter, England.* The poetic name of the Shropshire village represents the Roman name *Viroconium* (or *Uriconium*), originally applied to a fort atop the nearby hill known as the Wrekin and then transferred to the Roman fortress built below it, from which the present village evolved.

> To-day the Roman and his trouble
>   Are ashes under Uricon [A.E. Housman, *A Shropshire Lad*, 1896].

**Urinal of the Planets, the** *Ireland.* The former sobriquet is not as crude as it seems, but merely denotes the heavy rainfall for which Ireland is noted, and which it thus collects, as if in a urinal (chamber pot).

> Ireland [is so called] because of its frequent and great Rains ["B.E.," *A New Dictionary Ancient and Modern of the Terms of the Canting Crew, c.*1700].

**US, the** *United States.* A common abbreviation, mostly found in the media.

> The free world has no choice but to depend on the US. But is it up to the job? [*The Times*, November 16, 2004].

**USA, the** *United States.* The regular official abbreviation of the formal full name United States of America.

**US Capital of Cocaine, the** *Jackson Heights, Queens, New York City, USA.* The neighborhood is so nicknamed for the Colombian cocaine dealers said to live here.

**Ushant** *Ouessant, France.* The English form of the French name of the island off Brittany arose among sailors, such as those navigating a course northward to England from the Bay of Biscay.

> We'll rant and we'll roar like true British sailors,
>   We'll rant and we'll roar across the salt seas,
>   Until we strike soundings in the Channel of old England,
>   From Ushant to Scilly 'tis thirty-five leagues ["Spanish Ladies," traditional English sea shanty].

**US of A, the** *United States.* A colloquial form of the formal abbreviation **USA.**

> (1) You'll be told ... that won't be until you're back in the US of A under tight security wraps [Antony Melville-Ross, *Trigger*, 1982].
> (2) All that stands between us and having our hands chopped off for the ... crime of wearing nail varnish ... is the good old US of A [Julie Burchill in *The Times*, November 27, 2004].

**Usona** *United States.* A former proposed abbreviation of the name *United States of North America.* There is a community of this name in California. The name "Usonia" was used by the architect Frank Lloyd Wright for the style of buildings he created in the 1930s, as related in the quote below.

> Wright used [his model of] Broadacre City as a repository of ideal designs; he deemed it the characteristic settlement in the decentralized America that he envisioned, "Usonia" (a name derived partly from "United States of North America") [Anthony Alofsin, "Frank Lloyd Wright," in *American National Biography*, 1999].

**Vacation State, the** or **Vacationland** *Nevada, USA.* The state earns its nickname from its many facilities for vacationers, particularly the rich and reckless, who will be drawn to the gaming casinos and glitzy hotels of Las Vegas and Reno.

**Val** *Val d'Isère, France.* A popular short form of the ski resort's name, generally used by English-speaking skiers.

> While nightlife scores highly in Val, the town is slightly lacking [*The Times*, February 5, 2005].

**Valentine State, the** *Arizona, USA.* The state is so nicknamed because it was admitted into the Union on February 14 (Valentine's Day), 1912.

**Valley, the** *San Fernando Valley, Los Angeles, California, USA.* A short name for the well-known region, the home of the Valley Girls of the 1980s and their Valleyspeak jargon. A humorous corruption of the name is "the Walley."

> Referred to simply as "the Valley," the San Fernando Valley is an expansive area that has metamorphosed from ranchland into a string of populous towns [*Fodor's Los Angeles 2006*].

**Valley of Invention, the** *Ironbridge Gorge, England.* The valley of the Severn River at Ironbridge, Shropshire, is sometimes so named in allusion to the role of the region in the development of the Industrial Revolution in the early years of the 18th century. Entrepreneurs associated with the area include the ironmasters Abraham Darby and John Wilkinson, the former of whom in 1778 cast the iron bridge that gave the town its name, and the civil engineer Thomas Telford, for whom nearby Telford is named.

**Valley of Tears, the** *Glencoe, Scotland*. The sobriquet alludes to the Massacre of Glencoe, when on February 13, 1692, 38 members of the MacDonald clan, including the chief, were treacherously slaughtered by soldiers under Archibald Campbell, 10th earl of Argyll. The name echoes the "vale of tears" that serves as a synonym for the world with all its troubles and sorrows.

> To the Scots the valley ... recalls a tragedy of epic proportions. It is still referred to as the "Valley of Tears" [*Baedeker's Scotland*, 3d ed., 1999].

**Valley of the Racehorse, the** *Lambourn Valley, England*. The nickname of the Berkshire valley alludes chiefly to the racehorses trained there, although the name also reflects that of the nearby Vale of White Horse.

> The approach from London is an exhilarating drive along the Berkshire Downs, through the Lambournes [*sic*] and the "valley of the racehorse" and past ... Ashdown House [*The Times*, October 22, 2004].

**Valley of the Stars, the** *San Fernando Valley, California, USA*. The valley, now partly in Los Angeles, is nicknamed for the many movie stars who settled here, among them Bob Hope, Gene Autry, John Wayne, Charlie Chaplin, Clark Gable, and Carole Lombard.

**Valley of the Sun, the** *Phoenix, Arizona, USA*. The state capital lies in the Salt River Valley, renowned for its rich agricultural produce and its equable climate. Hence the nickname, locally shortened to "the Valley." *Cp.* **Sun City**.

> Phoenix, Arizona, is one of America's hottest destinations in both senses of the word, dubbed the "Valley of the Sun" for its 300 days of sunshine a year and 100-degree temperatures [*Sunday Times*, January 30, 2005].

**Valleys** see in Appendix 1, p. 269.

**Valpo** *(1) Valparaíso, Chile; (2) Valparaiso, Indiana, USA*. A colloquial shortening of the names of both cities, the former mainly in nautical use.

**Vandemonia** *Tasmania, Australia*. The former nickname of the island state, applied to it as a penal colony, puns on its original name of Van Diemen's Land, given by Abel Tasman, its discoverer in 1642, in honor of Anthony Van Diemen, governor of the Dutch East Indies.

There is also a suggestion of *pandemonium*, as noted in quote (1) below. *Cp.* **Demon's Land**.

> (1) The island retained the name [of Van Diemen's Land], bestowed by Tasman in honour of his patron, till 1855, when the name was officially changed to Tasmania, partly in honour of the discoverer, and also because the colonists thought the old name opprobrious, the island, as a penal settlement, having became a pandemonium [Isaac Taylor, *Names and Their Histories*, 1896].
>
> (2) One-sided summings up ... may please the social vampires and political pirates of Vandemonia [*Truth* (Sydney), March 1, 1903].

**Vansterdam** *Vancouver, British Columbia, Canada*. As stated in the quote below, Vancouver has long been regarded as an uninhibited or "progressive" city (like **Swinging London** in its day), especially among drug users. Hence its punning nickname, based on the name of Amsterdam, the Netherlands city noted for its marijuana coffee houses and "magic mushroom" stores.

> Vancouver was always the country's alternative, experimental city... Local government tolerates the mass cultivation of pot, earning it the affectionate sobriquet, Vansterdam [Dodd/Donald, p. 201].

**Vapor City** *Hot Springs, Arkansas, USA*. The nickname refers to the steam from the thermal springs for which the city is noted (and for which it is named).

**Varanasi of the South, the** *Kanchipuram, India*. The city is one of the most sacred towns in India. Hence its nickname, comparing it with Varanasi as one of the holiest cities of the Hindus and the object of regular pilgrimages.

**Vaterland** *see* **Fatherland**

**Vectis** *Isle of Wight, England*. The Roman name of the island, from which its present regular name evolved, is found in various local commercial applications, notably that of the Southern Vectis bus company.

> Buy a Southern Vectis Rover Ticket and go where you please [Ad, Isle of Wight travel brochure, 2005].

**Vegas** *Las Vegas, Nevada, USA*. A common short name for the well-known city.

> A week in Vegas is like stumbling into a Time Warp [Hunter S. Thompson, *Fear and Loathing in Las Vegas*, 1972].

**Vehicle City, the** *Flint, Michigan, USA*. The city is famous for its automobile manufacturing industry, which evolved from the horse-drawn vehicles first produced by the Durant-Dort Carriage Company in the late 19th century. Hence its nickname.

> I come from Flint, Michigan — the Vehicle City, not to be confused with the Motor City [Michael Moore, *Stupid White Men*, 2001].

**Venice of Brazil, the** *Recife, Brazil.* The Italian city of Venice is a popular exemplar for nickname purposes, not only for its buildings, especially its palaces, but especially for its canals. As can be seen from the sobriquets below, it is mainly these that have prompted the comparison. Recife is crisscrossed by canals as well as by the channels of the Capiberibe River.

(1) The city is known as the "Venice of Brazil," but its formal name comes from the beautiful coral reefs that run along the shoreline [Travel brochure issued with *The Times*, August 20, 2005].
(2) The city is known as the "Venice of Brazil" due to its criss-crossing waterways and canals [Cruise brochure, 2005].

**Venice of China or the Orient, the** *Suzhou, China.* The city, famed for its beauty, has many canals crossed by arched bridges. Hence its sobriquet.

**Venice of Honduras, the** *Guanaja, Honduras.* The town, on the island of the same name, is built on stilts. Hence its nickname.

It likes to advertise itself as the 'Venice of Honduras' but the floating houses and resident boats are much more like a floating gypsy camp [Natascha Norton and Mark Whatmore, *Cadogan Guides: Central America*, 1993].

**Venice of Ireland, the** *Cork, Ireland.* Cork's canals are a reminder of the watery island on which the city was originally built. Hence its nickname. Hence also its actual name, from the Irish word meaning "marsh."

(1) We have often heard Cork called the Venice of Ireland, but have never heard Venice called the Cork of Italy [Anon, quoted by John Betjeman in a letter to Michael Rose, September 25, 1955].
(2) There's something Dutch about Cork's canals, something Parisian about its quays, something about the light bouncing off the water that makes Cork (*almost*) the Venice of Ireland [*Sunday Times*, January 9, 2005].

**Venice of Japan, the** *Osaka, Japan.* The city and port merits its nickname by virtue of its location on the deltas of several rivers.

**Venice of Mali, the** *Mopti, Mali.* The town on the Bani River near its confluence with the Niger is sometimes so known for its location on three islands joined by dykes.

**Venice of the Cotswolds, the** *Bourton-on-the-Water, England.* The Gloucestershire town is so nicknamed for its location in the Cotswold Hills on the Windrush River, which flows beside the main street beneath five bridges, evoking Venice.

**Venice of the East, the** *Bangkok, Thailand.* As described in quote (2) below, the capital city and chief port of Thailand, on the delta of the Chao Phraya River, formerly had a network of interconnected canals that served as streets. Hence the comparison with the Italian city.

(1) No doubt the hyperbole [in early tourist promotions] was harmless, through it was rather absurd — if Bangkok was the Venice of the East, was Venice the Bangkok of the West? [Piers Brendon, *Thomas Cook: 150 Years of Popular Tourism*, 1991].
(2) The old royal city of Ratanakosin island was ringed by a system of canals ... this was the "Venice of the East." (Dodd/Donald, p. 266].

**Venice of the North, the** *(1) Amsterdam, Netherlands; (2) Birmingham, England; (3) Bruges, Belgium; (4) Giethoorn, Netherlands; (5) Hamburg, Germany; (6) Manchester, England; (7) Ottawa, Ontario, Canada; (8) St. Petersburg, Russia; (9) Stockholm, Sweden.* All of the named cities are or were associated with their canals. Amsterdam was built on several islands separated by canals and connected by bridges. Birmingham's many historic canals, said to number more than those of Venice, were extensively restored in the late 20th century. (It was a Birmingham man, James Brindley, who masterminded Britain's canal network.) Bruges has not only many canals within the city but a major one connecting it with the port of Zeebrugge. Giethoorn is noted for its canal system. The old town of Hamburg is crossed by several canals. Manchester is famous for the Manchester Ship Canal, linking the city with the Irish Sea. The upper and lower towns of Ottawa are separated by the Rideau Canal. St. Petersburg, on the delta of the Neva River, extends over several islands and is a city of waterways and bridges. Stockholm is similarly sited on a number of islands, and its old town (Gamla Stan) is known as the "city between the bridges." All of these "Venices" lie north of the original one.

(1) (Stockholm) Whoever invented the phrase about Stockholm, which calls it "the Venice of the North," seems to me, upon reflection, to have got things wrong... Venice is queenly, Stockholm is homely [Hilaire Belloc, *Places*, 1942].
(2) (St. Petersburg) For once, the sobriquet is justified. Built on mud and water, St Petersburg is every bit as grandiose, decrepit and vulnerable to flooding as Venice is [*The Rough Guide to St Petersburg*, 2004].
(3) (Bruges) Navigate along the canals and discover why Bruges lays claim to the title of the 'Venice of the North' [Travel ad, *Sunday Times*, January 16, 2005].
(4) (Birmingham) Birmingham's nickname — 'the Venice of the north' — feels a lot more apt at night, when the lights from the city's lively bars and clubs glimmer across the water of the canals [*Lonely Planet Great Britain*, 2005].

**Venice of the Orient** *see* **Venice of China**

**Venice of the South, the** *Tarpon Springs, Florida, USA.* The town is not nicknamed for its canals but because it is bordered on three sides by water.

**Venice of the West, the** *(1) Glasgow, Scotland; (2) Nantes, France; (3) San Antonio, Texas, USA.* The rather inappropriate nickname of Glasgow presumably refers to the Clyde River that has played an important part in the city's history, just as the Loire and its streams have in that of Nantes. San Antonio, on the other hand, has canals winding through its streets.

> (1) (Glasgow) A bird proper, on the shield argent of the city of Glasgow, has been identified with the resuscitated pet [robin] of the patron saint [Kentigern]. The tree on which it is there perched is a commemoration of another of the saint's miracles... Another element in the blazon of the Venice of the West is a fish, laid across the stem of the tree, "in base," as the heralds say [J.H. Burton, *The History of Scotland*, 1867–70].
>
> (2) (Nantes) In the last 50 years many of the river channels that gave Nantes that overused sobriquet "the Venice of the West" have been filled in [Dodd/Donald, p. 22].

**Venice on Land** *Vicenza, Italy.* The nickname refers not to the city's canals but to its many palaces, like those of Venice. (The similarity between the names Venezia and Vicenza may have helped associate the two.)

**Venusberg** *Hörselberge, Germany.* The popular name of the mountains in central Germany derives from the cave in which, according to legend, the goddess Venus lived and where she was visited by the medieval lyric poet Tannhäuser. The story was made familiar by Wagner's opera *Tannhäuser* (1845). (The name is a romantic reinterpretation of the original *Vennsberg,* "mountain in the fens.")

**Vermilion Sea, the** *Gulf of California, Mexico.* The Gulf's former nickname refers to the myriads of minute red-colored organisms it contains.

**Versailles of Morocco, the** *Meknès, Morocco.* The city is so nicknamed for the grand palaces and mosques built in the 17th century by the Alawite sultan Maulay Isma'il, evoking the royal palace of Versailles in France.

> The city of Meknès is known as the Versailles of Morocco. Had the [sultan's] enormous building projects ... survived the ravages of time, then this metaphor might not seem so extravagant [*Lonely Planet Morocco,* 2001].

**Versigo** *Versailles, France.* A French argot name for the city, involving the common device of adding a meaningless ending to a word, or altering its final syllable similarly . Thus *ici,* "here," becomes *icigo,* and *là,* "there," *lago.* On this pattern, *Versailles* becomes *Versigo.*

**Verulamium** *St Albans, England.* The Roman name of the Hertfordshire city is preserved in that of its Verulamium Museum, Verulam [*sic*] Industrial Estate, and Ver River, as well as in the title of Baron Verulam adopted by the philosopher Francis Bacon (1561–1626), who owned land in St Albans.

**Vic Falls** *Victoria Falls, Zimbabwe.* The town near the famous falls of the same name is often known by this shortened nickname.

**Vies, the** *Devizes, England.* A local name for the Wiltshire town, based on the real name (with "De-" becoming "the").

**Village, the** *(1) Barnwell, England; (2) Chicago, Illinois, USA; (3) Dulwich, London, England; (4) Greenwich Village, New York City, USA; (5) London, England.* The nickname is used either colloquially for a major city, or properly for an actual village or suburb whose real name is omitted because the local reference is obvious. For London, the name was mainly current among racing or hunting folk. *See also* **City of Villages.**

> (1) (London) I used to keep a good prad [i.e. horse] here for a bolt to the village [Charles M. Westmacott, *The English Spy*, 1825].
>
> (2) (Barnwell) A Cambridge term for a disreputable suburb of that town, viz., Barnwell, generally styled "the village" [*The Slang Dictionary,* 1894].
>
> (3) (Greenwich Village) We came to the Village without any intention of becoming Villagers. We came because the living was cheap [Malcolm Cowley, *Exile's Return,* 1934].
>
> (4) (Greenwich Village) She had grown up in the Village, on West Ninth Street between Fifth and Sixth [Mary McMullen, *But Nellie Was So Nice,* 1979].
>
> (5) (Greenwich Village) 'I don't mind telling you it cost a fortune. I found it in a dear little shop in the Village.' 'You don't look like you from the country.' 'Oh, my,' the young man sighed ... 'I meant Greenwich Village in New York, sweetie' [John Kennedy Toole, *A Confederacy of Dunces,* 1980].
>
> (6) (Dulwich) They [i.e. Londoners] want their London to be as rural as may be. They proudly retain the name of 'Village' for the oldest parts of their favourite suburbs. To be considered a 'villager' in Hampstead or Highgate, Dulwich or Wimbledon, delights the inhabitants [Ivor Brown in Hadfield 1981, p. 87].
>
> (7) (Greenwich Village) When the *Village Voice* ... began life as a chronicler of Greenwich Village nightlife beginning in 1955, "the Village" really had a dissident, artistic, vibrant voice [*The Rough Guide to New York City,* 2004].

**Village of Palaces, the** *Chelsea, London, England.* The sobriquet was applied to Chelsea in the 16th century, when it really was a village, for its palatial buildings. The Duke of Norfolk, the

Earl of Shrewsbury, Sir Thomas More, and Henry VIII himself, among others, all had fine houses here.

> The beauty of its [i.e. Chelsea's] situation on the Thames, which is wider here than in any other part above London bridge, made it, at an early period, the residence of illustrious persons, whose superb mansions procured for it the appellation of the village of palaces [Samuel Lewis, *A Topographical Dictionary of England*, 1840].

**Village of Roses, the** *Hawkchurch, England.* The Devon village was so nicknamed when in 1878 the Revd. John Going, a rose grower, planted rose trees along the walls of the cottages. *Cp.* **City of Roses.**

**Ville-Lumière** *see* **City of Light**

**Villetouse** *La Villette, Paris, France.* A colloquial (French argot) name for the northeastern quarter of the capital.

**Violet-Crowned City** *see* **City of the Violet Crown**

**Virgin Lands** *see* in Appendix 1, p. 269.

**Virginny** *see* **Old Virginny**

**Volunteer State, the** *Tennessee, USA.* The nickname refers to the unexpectedly large number of Tennessee men who responded to Governor Neill S. Brown's call for volunteers to fight in the Mexican-American War (1847).

> (1) A call for 2,800 volunteers [in the Mexican War] in Tennessee brought out 30,000 men and gave Tennessee its nickname, "The Volunteer State" [*Newsweek*, March 20, 1950].
> (2) There was a spectacular ... murder deep in the hills of Tennessee ... as could only happen in the deepest by-ways of the Volunteer State [*The Guardian*, June 14, 1973].

**V-town** *Vallejo, California, USA.* An initial-based short name of the city.

**W1** *Mayfair, London, England.* The postal district designation (west 1) has the same fashionable cachet as that of the district itself.

> If it's culture shocks you're after, take a taxi ride from W1 to E1 and see how the City takes on the challenge of lunch [*Sunday Times Magazine*, July 17, 2005].

**W2** *Paddington, London, England.* The postal district designation conveys the same combination of seediness and smartness that the district itself does.

> W2 (Paddington) still has some interesting enclaves buried between the kebab and tandoori places [Godfrey Smith, *The English Companion*, 1996].

**W3** *Acton, London, England.* The postal district designation stands in for the name of one of London's main residential districts, with a multitude of houses and apartments of all types.

> The W3 postcode lacks the cachet of its neighbours W4, Chiswick, or W5, Ealing [Carrie Segrave, *The New London Property Guide*, 2003].

**W4** *Chiswick, London, England.* The postal district designation names the respectable residential district of west London, with tree-lined streets and neatly-kept gardens laid out in a great bend of the Thames River.

> No disrespect to Chiswick, but the west London district ... could never be described as rock'n'roll. Becalmed and bourgeois, perhaps... But, last summer, leafy W4 was indeed home to the [US hip-hop band] Black Eyed Peas, as they set about recording Monkey Business [*Sunday Times*, May 15, 2005].

**W8** *Kensington, London, England.* The postal district designation evokes the combination of elegance and opulence that the district name itself possesses in its different forms *Cp.* **Kensington-on-Sea; North Ken; South Ken.** *See also* **Royal Borough; SW7.**

> She had managed to access a customer base of strictly W8, W11, SW3 and SW7-based Bankers' Wives [*The Times*, November 10, 2004].

**W11** *Notting Hill, London, England.* As implied in quote (1) below, the postal district designation implies a distinctive region whose image has changed from the seedy and scruffy to the reputable and respectable.

> (1) [W11] is a postcode which has long possessed a certain mythic cachet. Colin MacInnes's ... [1959] novel, *Absolute Beginners* ... might be said to have invented the area [in which the movies *The L-Shaped Room* (1962), *West Eleven* (1963), and *The Comedy Man* (1964) were set] ... W11 is ... impeccably bourgeois [Jonathan Meades in *The Times Magazine*, July 24, 2004].
> (2) I may no longer have my letters addressed to W11, but Notting Hill is now more than a postal district, it's a state of mind [Politician Michael Gove in *The Times*, October 5, 2005].

**WA** *Western Australia, Australia.* An initialism of the state's name.

> (1) The State shipping service in WA has been made the scapegoat for Government indecision [*Sunday Australian*, August 8, 1971].
> (2) The temperate southwest of WA has been relatively tamed by colonization [*The Rough Guide to Australia*, 2001].

**Wagga** *Wagga Wagga, Australia.* A frequently used short form of the New South Wales city's name (pronounced "wogga").

**Wahoo** *Hawaii, USA.* The nickname is a corruption of *Owhyii*, the original Polynesian name of the island state.

**Walley** *see* **Valley**

**Walrus** *Warlus, France.* A British soldiers' World War I transmutation of the name of the village near Arras.

**Wang** *Wangaratta, Australia.* A short colloquial name for the Victoria town.

> The highway on either side of "Wang" is lined with motels [*The Rough Guide to Australia*, 2001].

**Wansford-in-England** *Wansford, England.* The Cambridgeshire village adds the touristic suffix to its name in certain contexts because of the account related below (where it appears as Wanstead). The Haycock Hotel in Wansford uses the byname in its address and its inn sign depicts the central character, said to have been called Barnaby, on a haystack.

> I lay [i.e. stayed] at the Swan in Wanstead-in-England, being a jest on a man makeing hay fell a sleep on a heap of it and a great storme washed the hay and the man into the River, and carry'd him to the Bridge, where he awoke and knew not where he was, called to the people in the grounds and told them he lived in a place called Wanstead in England, which goes for a jest on the men of Wanstead to this day [Celia Fiennes, *Journeys*, 1698].

**Warden of the Honour of the North, the** *Halifax, Nova Scotia, Canada.* The heavily fortified capital city of Nova Scotia, on the Atlantic Ocean, was intended to be a British naval stronghold comparable to that of France at Louisburg. Hence its sobriquet, described in the lines by Kipling below. (The "guardian prows" are those of the rocky peninsula on which it lies. Its ramparts are "virgin" as the base has never been besieged.)

> Into the mist my guardian prows put forth,
>   Behind the mist my virgin ramparts lie,
>   The Warden of the Honour of the North,
>   Sleepless and veiled am I! [Rudyard Kipling, "The Song of the Cities," 1893].

**Warks** *Warwickshire, England.* A semiofficial abbreviation of the county name, usually pronounced "Worriks." *See also* Appendix 6, p. 325.

**Warm Heart of Africa, the** *Malawi.* A touristic name for the country, referring to its friendly people, attractive scenery, and geographical situation in east central Africa.

**Washer of the Ford, the** *Ireland.* The name is a personification of Ireland in the form of an old woman, as described in quote (2) below. She is said to have appeared at scenes of battle, including those of Magh Rath (637) and Corofin (1318). *Cp.* **Kathleen Ní Houlihan; Shan Van Vocht.**

> (1) "Who are thou, hideous one; and from what curst abode
>   Comest thou thus in open day the hearts of men to freeze;
>   And whose lopp'd heads and severed limbs and bloody vests are these?"
>   "I am the Washer of the Ford," she answered; "and my race

Is of the Tuath de Dannan line of Magi" [Samuel Ferguson, *Congal*, 1865].
> (2) An Irish wraith which seems to be washing clothes in a river, but when the "doomed man" approaches she holds up what she seemed to be washing and it is the phantom of himself with his death wounds from which he is about to suffer [E. Cobham Brewer, *A Dictionary of Phrase and Fable*, 1895].

**Washington's Only Salt Water Resort** *Chesapeake Beach, Maryland, USA.* A promotional name for the residential community on Chesapeake Bay.

**Water, the** *Thames River, England.* The name was formerly used for the Thames in London, especially as a river dividing the city into north and south.

> It is on the Surrey side of the water — a little distance beyond the Marsh-gate [Charles Dickens, *Sketches by "Boz,"* 1836].

**Waterfall Country** *Vale of Neath, Wales.* The valley of the Neath River, flowing down from the mountains of Brecon to the Bristol Channel, is so dubbed touristically for its waterfalls.

> Aptly named 'Waterfall Country,' the Vale of Neath is an ideal location for both walking or a more challenging ramble [Swansea Bay travel brochure, 2005].

**Watergate City** *Washington, DC, USA.* The nickname alludes to the Watergate political scandal of 1972–75, which centered on events at the Watergate, the headquarters of the Democratic National Committee in Washington.

**Watering Place of Kings, the** *Aachen (Aix-la-Chapelle), Germany.* The city and health resort was so known in the 18th and 19th centuries, partly in reference to the 32 German kings who were crowned here. *See also* **Seat of Royalty.**

**Water Village, the** *Kampong Ayer, Brunei.* The residential area of Bandar Seri Begawan, Brunei's capital city, consists entirely of houses built on stilts in the waters of the Brunei River. Hence the nickname, given by British colonialists.

**Water Wonderland, the** *Michigan, USA.* Michigan not only borders on four of the five Great Lakes (*see* **Lake State**) but has around 11,000 inland lakes, a number of which are dotted with islands and ringed with summer cottages. There are also many rivers. Hence the nickname.

**Wayback** see in Appendix 1, p. 269.

**WC1** *Bloomsbury, London, England.* The postal district designation (west central 1) has the same literary and intellectual associations as the name itself. (The Bloomsbury group was a coterie of writers who lived in the area before, during, and after World War I. Leading figures were Virginia Woolf, Leonard Woolf, Lytton Strachey, Clive Bell, Vanessa Bell, Roger Fry, Duncan Grant, Maynard Keynes, E.M. Forster, and David Garnett.)

In 1924 the Woolfs returned to magic WC1, taking a ten year lease at 52 Tavistock Square [Malcolm Bradbury, ed., *The Atlas of Literature*, 1996].

**Weary Titan, the** *British Empire*. The sobriquet refers to the heavy colonial responsibilities shouldered by Britain as a sort of equivalent of Kipling's "white man's burden." The name originated with Matthew Arnold's phrase in quote (1) below. For the title in quote (2), *see* **Dark Continent**.

(1) Yes, we arraign her! but she,
The weary Titan! with deaf
Ears, and labour-dimm'd eyes,
Regarding neither to right
Nor left, goes passively by [Matthew Arnold, "Heine's Grave," 1867].
(2) The weary Titan need not complain too much [James Stewart, *Dawn in the Dark Continent*, 1903].

**Webfoot State, the** *Oregon, USA*. The nickname refers to the state's above-average winter rainfall, especially in the coastal area.

**Wee City, the** *Londonderry (Derry), Northern Ireland*. The nickname comes from the local use of "wee" as an adjective of affection for any familiar object, whether actually small or not, as "a wee bus ticket." Northern Ireland itself is sometimes similarly referred to as "the Wee North" (*see* **North**).

**WeHo** *West Hollywood, Los Angeles, California, USA*. A colloquial short form of the residential suburb's name. Quote (2) below also refers to **BH**.

(1) West Hollywood (WeHo) is the heart of LA's gay and lesbian scene [*Lonely Planet USA*, 2004].
(2) WeHo is all Paris Hilton and BH is all Elizabeth Taylor [*Fodor's Los Angeles 2006*].

**Wellywood** *Wellington, New Zealand*. The capital city is so nicknamed (from a blend of its name with that of Hollywood) as a center of the country's motion-picture industry. *Cp.* **Bollywood**.

**Welsh Brighton** *see* **Aber**
**Welsh California** *see* **Aber**
**Welsh Riviera, the** *Tenby, Wales*. The seaside resort derives its nickname from its extensive sandy beaches.

**Welsh Tyrol, the** *Vale of Llangollen, Wales*. A touristic name for the narrow, picturesque valley of the Dee River in which the Denbighshire town of Llangollen lies, for its fancied resemblance to the Austrian Tirol.

**Wessex** see in Appendix 1, p. 269.
**West** see in Appendix 1, p. 269.
**West Britain** *Ireland*. An ironic nickname for Ireland, regarded as a British colony. *Cp.* **Queen of the West**.

**West Brom** *West Bromwich, England*. The abbreviated name of the town near Birmingham is mainly used as a colloquial name of its football club, West Bromwich Albion, but can also be applied to the town itself.

He said ... 'First game I saw was Fulham versus WBA.' 'WBA?' I thought to myself. 'Oh, he means West Brom' [Judith Holder, *It's Grim Up North*, 2005].

**Westchester** or **West Chester** *Chester, England*. A traditional former name for the Cheshire city, with "West" added to distinguish it from any more easterly "Chester," such as Manchester. (Westchester County, New York, USA, is said to be so named as it lies west of Chester, England.) The old saying "to be sent to West Chester" meant to be banished (by implication to Ireland, being deported from the port here).

(1) Passing through a village only six miles from London last week, I heard a mother saying to a child, "If you are not a good girl I will send you to West Chester" [*Notes and Queries*, 1851].
(2) 'But take thee North Wales and Weschester, The countrye all round about' ["Durham Field," *The Oxford Book of Ballads*, 1910].

**West Coast** see in Appendix 1, p. 269.
**West Country** see in Appendix 1, p. 269.
**West End** see in Appendix 1, p. 269.
**Western Approaches** see in Appendix 1, p. 269.
**Western Babylon** *see* **Babylon**
**Western Isles, the** *Hebrides, Scotland*. The alternate, informal name of the island group denotes their western location with regard to mainland Scotland. The islands are divided into two main groups, Inner Hebrides, nearer the coast, and Outer Hebrides, farther out. The name became specifically attached to the latter, which in 1975 were designated a separate administrative authority under the name, either in its English form or in Gaelic as *Eilean Siar*.

The Western Isles, now correctly so known, are ... no longer just a group of islands described vaguely and romantically as 'the Outer Hebrides' [Macnie/McLaren, p. 421].

**Western Ocean, the** *Atlantic Ocean*. The name, locating the ocean to the west of Europe, is still sometimes found in maritime contexts.

**Western Province** see in Appendix 1, p. 269.
**Westminister** *Westminster, London, England*. The name of the central London borough,

officially the City of Westminster, is sometimes ignorantly or carelessly written or pronounced thus, no doubt by association with the government ministers attending the Houses of Parliament (Palace of Westminster) here.

> Cardinal Cormac Murphy-O'Connor, the Roman Catholic Archbishop of Westminister [*The Times*, December 24, 2005].

**Westralia** *Western Australia, Australia.* A telescoped, telegraphic form of the state's name, as described in quote (3) below. *Cp.* **WA**.

> (1) A Melb. [i.e. Melbourne] timber-merchant formed a syndicate ... to prospect Westralia for gold [*The Bulletin* (Sydney), July 29, 1893].
> (2) All well in Westralia stop [Lyndall Hadow, *Full Cycle and Other Stories*, 1969].
> (3) When cable message were confined to words of ten letters, Westralia was coined as an abbreviation [A.W. Reed, *Place Names of Australia*, 1973].

**West Side** see in Appendix 1, p. 269.

**Wet Coast** see in Appendix 1, p. 269.

**Wheat Capital of the World, the** *Wellington, Kansas, USA.* The hyperbolic nickname is justified in so far as Wellington is in a wheat region.

**Wheat State, the** *(1) Kansas, USA; (2) Minnesota, USA; (3) South Australia, Australia.* All three named states are noted for their wheat production. Kansas is first among the US states in wheat and both Minnesota and South Australia have the cereal as a major crop.

> (Kansas) He had a Friend in the Retail Lumber Business ... and he sent him enough Money to get Home to the Wheat State [Douglas Malloch, *Resawed Fables*, 1911].

**Whigland** *Scotland.* The historic nickname refers to Scotland as a center of Whig politics. (The actual name Whig is of Scottish origin.)

**Whipshire** *Yorkshire, England.* The former name for the northern county could refer to local hunting gentry and their whips. On the other hand it may be a miscopying of "Whigshire," a nickname similar to **Whigland**.

**Whisky** or **Malt Whisky Capital of the World, the** *Dufftown, Scotland.* The northern town is home to seven leading distilleries. Hence its self-promotional name. Locals say: "Rome may be built on seven hills, but Dufftown's built on seven stills."

> (1) [Dufftown] proudly proclaims itself "Malt Whisky Capital of the World," and ... exports more of the stuff than anywhere else in Britain [*The Rough Guide to Scotland*, 1998].
> (2) [Realtor] Genesis Properties ... is marketing seven new homes in the "whisky capital of the world," Dufftown [*The Times*, August 5, 2005].

**Whisky Triangle** see in Appendix 1, p. 269.

**White Africa** see in Appendix 1, p. 269.

**White Australia** *Australia.* A former name for Australia as a society into which immigration of nonwhites is restricted. An immigration act of 1901 incorporated the so-called White Australia Policy, which almost entirely debarred Asiatics, and especially the Chinese, from entering Australia. For the reference in quote (2) below, *see* **Empty North** in Appendix 1, p. 269.

> (1) 'A white Australia is the most sacred article in in the creed of every Australian.' — Premier Reid [*Tocsin* (Melbourne), February 3, 1898].
> (2) *White Australia: Or, The Empty North* [Randolph Bedford, play title, 1909].
> (3) We've got enough on our hands without White Australia rearing its ugly head again, especially now [Robert Macklin, *The White Castle*, 1977].

**White Bride of the Mediterranean, the** *Tripoli, Libya.* The mysterious sobriquet of the Libyan capital seems to allude to a city and port that is "married" to the Mediterranean, rather like Venice as the **Bride of the Sea**.

> Tripoli and its beaches have lost some of the allure that once attracted the cryptic title "White Bride of the Mediterranean" [Dodd/Donald, p. 424].

**White City, the** *(1) Arequipa, Peru; (2) Helsinki, Finland; (3) Tangier, Morocco.* The nickname refers to the light-colored stone from which many of the buildings in the respective cities are constructed. Tangier, moreover, is built on the slopes of a chalky limestone hill.

> (Tangier) Known as the "White City," Tangier flaunts a magnificent bay [Cruise brochure, 2005].

**White Cliffs Country** see in Appendix 1, p. 269.

**White** or **Great White Continent, the** *Antarctica.* The world's fifth-largest continent, centered on the South Pole, is covered by an ice cap. Hence its nickname, adopted in recent years for touristic purposes.

> (1) Now YOU can join the few who have stepped ashore on the White Continent [Travel ad, *The Times Magazine*, July 31, 2004].
> (2) The last few years have seen a dramatic increase in the number of vessels visiting the Great White Continent [Travel ad, *The Times*, January 22, 2005].

**White Elephant, the** *Northern Territory, Australia.* The nickname, sometimes expanded to "White Elephant of South Australia," treats the territory as a burdensome responsibility from the point of view of the southern states.

> (1) The Northern Territory ... the 'White Elephant of South Australia' — to use a term very freely used for the Territory in the colonies [Mrs. D.D. Daly, *The Digging, Squatting, and Pioneering Life*, 1887].
> (2) The Northern Territory ... has often been

called Australia's 'White Elephant' [C.T. Madigan, *Central Australia*, 1936].

**White Highlands** see in Appendix 1, p. 269.

**White Island, the** *Rhodesia*. The nickname was applied to the former African state as a white country amid black. Northern Rhodesia (now Zambia) and Southern Rhodesia (now Zimbabwe) were both British colonies.

**White Isle, the** *Ibiza, Spain*. The Mediterranean island, a popular vacation destination, is so nicknamed for its white beaches and buildings.

Live from Cafe Mambo in San Antonio, on the "White Isle," this launches Radio 1's annual Ibiza weekend [*Sunday Times*, August 1, 2004].

**White Man's Grave, the** *(1) Ghana; (2) Jakarta, Indonesia; (3) Sierra Leone*. The tropical forests of the two African countries harbor diseases and noxious insects that have laid low European explorers and settlers, while Jakarta has also proved insalubrious. Hence the former sobriquet for these places.

(1) (Sierra Leone) [Sierra Leone] bears the terrific and poetic title of the 'White Man's Grave' [F.H. Rankin, *The White Man's Grave*, 1836].

(2) (Sierra Leone) My friends ... said, 'Oh, you can't possibly go there; that's where Sierra Leone is, the white man's grave, you know' [Mary H. Kingsley, *Travels in West Africa*, 1897].

(3) (Ghana) What did it matter if the Gold Coast had been the White Man's Grave ever since Columbus had been there? [Sir William F. Butler, *Autobiography*, 1910].

(4) (Sierra Leone) The colony of Sierra Leone is happily no longer known as "The White Man's Grave" [*Times Literary Supplement*, February 25, 1910].

(5) (Jakarta) So it remained, decimated by cholera and known as the "white man's grave" [Dodd/Donald, p. 250].

**White Man's Land, the** *East Africa*. A former touristic name for the countries of East Africa, especially Kenya, Tanzania, and Uganda, where European colonialism had resulted in a sizeable white population. The name consciously contrasted with (and in a sense complemented) that of the **Dark Continent**.

**White Mountain State, the** *New Hampshire, USA*. The state is sometimes so nicknamed, for the White Mountains in its northern part.

**White Russia** *Belarus*. The name is an English rendering of the Slavonic original, itself of disputed meaning. It has nothing to with the White Russians who opposed the "Red Russians" of Soviet Russia.

**White-Stoned City, the** *Moscow, Russia*. The name, translating the Russian title *Belokamennaya* (from *belo-* "white," and *kamen*, "stone"),

refers to the capital city's many light-stoned buildings. *Cp.* **Golden-Headed City**.

A more beautiful sight than White-stoned Moscow, as seen from the Sparrow Hills, one could hardly imagine! [W. Barnes Steveni, *Things Seen in Russia*, 1914].

**Whore of the Orient** or **the East** or **Asia, the** *Shanghai, China*. As indicated in the quotes below, the seaport city owes its nickname to its disreputable past.

(1) As a city dedicated to the making of money, Shanghai attracted tycoons, gangsters and drifters, and was referred to variously as "The Paradise of Adventurers," "The Paris of the East," and "The Whore of Asia" [*The Contemporary Atlas of China*, 1988].

(2) The city, known as the Whore of the East in the 1920s when she seduced the world's riffraff with her drugs, vice and prostitution, is reborn today as the Big Apple of the East [*Sunday Times Magazine*, January 23, 2005].

**Wicked City, the** *London, England*. The British capital was long notorious as a center of commercial sex. Hence its nickname, adopted by Fergus Linnane for his study *London, the Wicked City: A Thousand Years of Prostitution and Vice* (2003).

**Wide Brown Land, the** *Australia*. The name refers to the continent's wide expanse of hot, sandy desert.

(1) I love a sunburnt country
A land of sweeping plains,
Of ragged mountain ranges,
Of droughts and flooding rains.
I love her far horizons,
I love her jewel-sea
Her beauty and her terror—
The wide brown land for me! [Dorothea Mackellar, "My Country," in *Sydney Mail*, October 21, 1908].

(2) *The Wide Brown Land* [George Mackaness, ed., poetry anthology title, 1934].

(3) Migrants are staying away in droves from the widest and brownest part of this wide, brown land [*The Australian*, May 4, 1973].

(4) [We] could tour the whole land ... the whole of this wide brown land, north and south, east and west [J.M. Coetzee, *Slow Man*, 2005].

**Wide Prospect, the** *Europe*. A poetic name for the continent, based on a popular derivation of its name from Greek *eurys*, "wide," and *opsis*, "view," "prospect."

He much, the old man, who, clearest-soul'd of men,
Saw The Wide Prospect, and the Asian Fen [Matthew Arnold, "To a Friend," 1849].

**Wild Coast** see in Appendix 1, p. 269.

**Wild Continent, the** *Africa*. A nickname sometimes favored by travel companies, especially those arranging safari trips. It refers to the continent's wealth of wildlife (and by implication its supposedly "untamed" peoples, worthy of wonder on the part of curious Western tourists).

**Wilderness City** *District of Columbia, USA.* The former nickname is attributed to Abigail Adams, wife of John Adams, second president of the USA, who lived with her husband in Washington, DC, from 1797 to 1801, when the district was still sparsely inhabited and surrounded by woods.

**Wilderness Coast** see in Appendix 1, p. 269.

**Wild North** see in Appendix 1, p. 269.

**Wild Wales** *Wales.* The traditional alliterative epithet of Britain's smallest land alludes to its many unspoiled regions (broadly, mountains in the north, valleys in the south) as well as to the proudly patriotic, "unbroken" spirit of its people. The phrase was first familiar from the prophetic Welsh verse in quote (1) below and was popularized by George Borrow's *Wild Wales* (1862), an account of a walking tour he made with his wife and stepdaughter in Wales in 1854.

(1) *Eu ner a folant* (Their lord they shall praise).
*Eu hiaith a gadwant* (Their language they shall keep).
*Eu tir a gollant* (Their land they shall lose).
*Ond gwyllt Gwalia* (Except Wild Wales) [Late medieval verse, misattributed by Borrow to Taliesin, 6th century].
(2) The wide valleys of the Severn, the Wye, and the Usk form pathways into Central Wales. But the modern motorist, driving towards the west, sooner or later becomes aware that the hills lie ahead of him barring the horizon. Wild Wales is still very much there [Vaughan-Thomas/ Llewellyn, p. 9].
(3) [TV weather presenter] Helen Willetts blew the cobwebs away on a walking holiday in 'Wild Wales' [*A View of Wales*, Spring/Summer, 2005].

**Wild West** see in Appendix 1, p. 269.

**Wilts** *Wiltshire, England.* A semiofficial abbreviation of the county name. *See also* Appendix 6, p. 325.

There was an old person of Wilts,
Who constantly walked upon stilts;
He wreathed them with lilies, and daffy-down-dillies,
That elegant person of Wilts [Edward Lear, *More Nonsense, Pictures, Rhymes, Botany, Etc.*, 1872].

**Wimby** or **Wimbers** *Wimbledon, London, England.* A colloquial abbreviation of the district name, usually referring to the international tennis tournament (*see* **SW19**). The second form has the "Oxford -er" as for **Honkers**.

**Winander** *Windermere, England.* The poetic name for the largest lake in the Lake District, current well into the 19th century, is close to the Scandinavian personal name that gave the real name, meaning "Vinandr's lake."

(1) Where, undisturbed by winds, Winander sleeps [William Wordsworth, "An Evening Walk," 1787–9].
(2) The Lake and Mountains of Winander — I cannot describe them [John Keats, letter to Tom Keats, June 26, 1818].
(3) Derwent! Winander! Sweetest of all sounds The British tongue e'er utter'd! [W.S. Landor, "Written at Hurstmonceaux, on reading a poem of Wordsworth's," *The Last Fruit off an Old Tree*, 1853].

**Winch** *Winchester, England.* A local shortening of the Hampshire city's name. *Cp.* **Winton**.

Winch is a lovely place. It is one of the four cities I have been to that has 'the oldest pub in England' [Sam Jordison and Dan Kieran, eds., *The Idler Book of Crap Towns II*, 2004].

**Windies, the** *West Indies.* The contracted form of the name of the island group (from W. Indies) is mostly applied to its cricket team, as in the quote below, but can also be used of the islands themselves. The nickname is apt for the islands, where hurricanes frequently occur in the summer season.

Would the West Indies beat England in the first Test match? ... In the cricket match, the "Windies" scraped home in a nail-biting finish [*The Economist*, June 21, 1980].

**Window on Europe, a** *St. Petersburg, Russia.* The phrase is attributed to the city's founder, Peter the Great, who projected a modern, westward-looking city, as distinct from the ancient, eastern-oriented capital, Moscow.

(1) And thus he [i.e. Peter the Great] mused:
"From here, indeed
Shall we strike terror in the Swede;
And here a city, by our labor
Founded, shall gall our haughty neighbor;
'Here cut' — so Nature gives command —
'Your window through on Europe: stand
Firm-footed by the sea, unchanging!'" [Alexander Pushkin, *The Bronze Horseman*, 1833, translated by Oliver Elton].
(2) It was the great Peter ... who planted a city on the Baltic, as, he said, a "window by which the Russians might look out into civilized Europe" [L. Edna Walter, *Peeps at Many Lands: Russia*, 1912].
(3) [Peter the Great] wished to erect, at the mouth of the Nevá, a new capital that could be reached more easily from W. Europe (a 'window towards Europe,' in [Francesco] Algarotti's phrase) [*Baedeker's Russia*, 1914].

**Windsor of the North, the** *Alnwick, England.* The occasional nickname of the Northumberland town properly applies to its medieval castle which, with its later additions, bears a resemblance to Windsor Castle near London.

Described by Victorians as the "Windsor of the North," Alnwick Castle and Gardens combines stunning natural beauty with a fascinating history [Cruise brochure, 2005].

**Windsurfing Capital of the World, the** *Paia, Hawaii, USA.* The old sugar town on Maui is so named for a nearby beach, as explained in the quote below.

> In the 1980s, windsurfers began discovering nearby Hookipa Beach, and Paia was dubbed the 'Windsurfing Capital of the World' [*Lonely Planet USA*, 2004].

**Windy City, the** *(1) Chicago, Illinois, USA; (2) Essaouira, Morocco; (3) Port Elizabeth, South Africa; (4) Wellington, New Zealand.* The nickname is meteorologically apt for all four waterside cities, although in the case of Chicago a derivation is also possible in the blustering claims of early municipal promoters. P.E. Raper, in *A Dictionary of Southern African Place Names* (1987), tells how prevailing winds have caused pine trees on the shore at Port Elizabeth to lean permanently at an angle, while Shadbolt (p. 200) recounts that as long ago as 1850 it was said that a resident of Wellington was easily identified because of the way he always clutched his hat, and that even earlier George Selwyn, first Anglican bishop of New Zealand, had remarked on the breezes that "ventilate" the city, which has the alternate alliterative nickname "Windy Wellington." Essaouira, on the Atlantic coast, adopted the name to advertise itself as a windsurfing center.

> (1) (Chicago) The name of "Windy City," which is sometimes used by village papers in New York and Michigan to designate Chicago, is intended as a tribute to the refreshing lake breezes of the great summer resort of the West, but is an awkward and rather ill-chosen expression and is doubtless misunderstood [*Chicago Tribune*, September 11, 1886].
> (2) (Port Elizabeth) One of Port Elizabeth's best loved restaurants ... offers carefully prepared meals and a cosy atmosphere steeped in the Windy City's past [*Fair Lady*, December 20, 1989].
> (3) (Wellington) The Venturi effect caused by the channelling of air flows through Cook Strait can produce winds of over 100kph whistling through the capital — not for nothing is it known as 'Windy Wellington' [Nick Hanna, *Explore New Zealand*, 2d ed., 1999].
> (4) (Essaouira) Essaouira is ... Morocco's best-known windsurfing centre, and increasingly promotes itself as 'Windy City, Afrika' [*Lonely Planet Morocco*, 2001].
> (5) (Chicago) Chicago was given its nickname by a disgruntled New York journalist who was mocking what he saw as the bombastic claims of Chicago's politicians [Dodd/Donald, p. 208].
> (6) (Wellington) Wellington is the other Windy City [i.e. as against Chicago] [Dodd/Donald, p. 208].
> (7) (Chicago) Home to deep-pan pizza, Al Capone and *ER*, slap bang in the centre of America and right on the shores of Lake Michigan.

> Welcome to the Windy City — Chicago [*The Times*, May 20, 2005].

**Wine and Food Capital of the Cape, the** *Franschhoek, South Africa.* The small town in the Western Cape is set in a region of vineyards and restaurants, the latter complementing the former.

> In the valley below is the former Huguenot village of Franschhoek, often billed as the "wine and food capital of the Cape" [*Sunday Times* (South Africa Supplement), March 13, 2005].

**Wine City** see in Appendix 1, p. 269.

**Wine State, the** *California, USA.* California is by far the largest source of American wine, producing three out of four bottles sold in the USA, so clearly merits its nickname.

**Winterless North, the** *Northland, New Zealand.* The long peninsula running north from Auckland toward the equator earned its nickname for its year-round mild climate. (Many northern regions are associated with cold, wintry conditions, but this one is an exception.)

**Winterpeg** *Winnipeg, Manitoba, Canada.* The nickname punningly alludes to the severe winters sometimes experienced in the city. (In a Canadian pronunciation, there would be little distinction between the spoken forms of the nickname and the real name.) *Cp.* **Peg.**

**Winton** *Winchester, England.* A local form of the Hampshire city's name, adopted (and adapted) by Thomas Hardy for his fictional town of Wintoncester. As an abbreviation of Latin *Wintoniensis*, "of Winchester," it is the official signature of the bishop of Winchester. *Cp.* **Winch.**

> "Winton," as its natives lovingly name it, and as the old milestones ... agree to style it [Charles G. Harper, *The Hardy Country*, 1904].

**Wipers** *Ypres, Belgium.* A British soldiers' World War I attempt to pronounce the name of the Flanders town. Three key battles in the region involved great loss of life, and it is possible the name became subconsciously associated with "wipe (out)."

> A soldier said to an old lady, "So when we got to Wipers —" "*Ypres*," said the old lady. The soldier resumed: "So when we got to Wipers —" "*Ypres*," said the old lady. The soldier heaved a sigh and began again: "So when we got to Wipers —" "*Ypres*," said the old lady. "Cor," said the soldier, "you ain't 'arf got 'iccups" [J.B. Morton (?), quoted in James Agate, *Ego 7*, 1935].

**Witch City** *see* **City of Witches**

**Wizard Stream, the** *Dee River, England/Wales.* The sobriquet, meaning "enchanted river," is first found in Milton, as in the quote for **Deva.** The phrase essentially echoes the river's real name, from a Celtic word meaning "holy one."

**Wolfland** *Ireland*. The nickname, current in the late 17th century, arose from a popular belief that there were an unusually large number of wolves in Ireland. The animal has now long been extinct there.

**Wolverine State, the** *Michigan, USA*. The nickname supposedly refers to the wolverines once present in the state, although there are none there now. The animal name may have been originally applied to an inhabitant of Michigan, regarded as strong and fearless (or cunning and greedy), like the wolverine, and transferred from there to the state.

> Michigan is Lake State or Wolverine State [*Chambers's Journal of Popular Literature*, March 13, 1875].

**Wolvo** *Wolverhampton, England*. A colloquial short form of the name of the West Midlands town. *See also* **Yammyland**.

> While other cities suffered brutal, newsworthy recessions ... Wolvo just got quieter and dirtier [Caitlin Moran in *The Times*, December 19, 2000].

**Wonder City of the Southern Hemisphere, the** *Hokitika, New Zealand*. The town received its highflown sobriquet when it arose as a gold-boom center in the 1860s.

> Local myth-makers called it 'Wonder City of the Southern Hemisphere,' and many vessels jammed its busy port [Shadbolt, p. 236].

**Wonderful Copenhagen** *Copenhagen, Denmark*. A nickname for the capital adopted from the popular song, as in quote (1) below.

> (1) "Wonderful Copenhagen" [Frank Loesser, song title in movie *Hans Christian Andersen*, 1951].
>
> (2) This twee vision of "Wonderful, Wonderful Copenhagen." (Dodd/Donald, p. 429].
>
> (3) To reach the capital, Hans [Christian Andersen] would have caught the ferry to West Zeeland. We're spared that ... and in less than two hours we're arriving in "Wonderful, wonderful Copenhagen..." [*The Times*, April 9, 2005].

**Wonderland of America, the** *Wyoming, USA*. The nickname refers to the state's spectacular mountain scenery, which attracts thousands of visitors annually.

**Wonderland of the World, the** *Egypt*. An apt nickname for the ancient country, with its massive architectural monuments, pyramids, temples, and sculptures.

> That wonderland of the world, Egypt [*Westminster Gazette*, May 24, 1902].

**Wonder of the West, the** *Mont-Saint-Michel, France*. The little island, a fortified rock off the northwest coast of France, is famous for the unique ancient abbey and town on the summit of the rock, as well as for its dramatic site. Hence the sobriquet, with "west" denoting its location both in France and in Europe generally.

> A visit to Mont-Saint-Michel is inevitable, for the building in its wonderful setting, 'the Wonder of the West,' seems to beckon one towards it [*AA Road Book of France*, 1972].

**Wonder State, the** *Arkansas, USA*. The state was officially accorded the promotional nickname in 1923, as described in the quote below. Cynics claim the name was designed to mask the state's relative poverty and lack of development, since it has no immediately obvious "wonders."

> This title is so befitting while the old one "the Bear State" is a misnomer, and leads to a false impression, while "the Wonder State" is accurate and deserving of special recognition. Now therefore, Be It Resolved by the Senate of the State of Arkansas, the House of Representatives concurring, that we accept the name "the Wonder State" given us by this patriotic association which has done much to acquaint the world with Arkansas and its wealth of resources and we hereby specially proclaim that hereafter Arkansas shall be known and styled "The Wonder State" [G.E. Shankle, "Acts of Arkansas," *American Nicknames*, 1923].

**Wool Capital of the World, the** *Hamilton, Australia*. The Victoria town's self-promotional name denotes its location in one of Australia's best sheep-farming regions.

**Woolsery** *Woolfardisworthy, England*. A regular short form of the Devon village's lengthy name, not only in speech but also in writing, as in maps, on local signposts, and even in the media, as in the quote below. (There are actually two Devon villages of the name, the one in question here being near Clovelly.)

> Residents of Woolsery ... threatened to resort to direct action [*The Times*, May 18, 2001].

**Worcs** *Worcestershire, England*. A semiofficial abbreviation of the county name, rarely heard in spoken form (when it might be pronounced as "works"). *See also* Appendix 6, p. 325.

**Workshop of the World** or **Empire, the** *(1) Birmingham, England; (2) England or Britain; (3) Glasgow, Scotland*. Both cities, and Britain itself, were so nicknamed in the 19th and early 20th centuries for their great manufacturing output, a direct consequence of the industrial revolution.

> (1) (England) The Continent will not suffer England to be the workshop of the world [Benjamin Disraeli, speech in House of Commons, March 15, 1838].
>
> (2) (Birmingham) This is the workshop of the world, the birth-spot of the steam engine, and the home of mock jewellery [Walter Showell, *Dictionary of Birmingham*, 1885].

(3) (England) The Great Exhibition of 1851 said it all... The engineering wonders and merchandise on display marked Britain's status as "the workshop of the world" [Malcolm Bradbury, ed., *The Atlas of Literature*, 1996].

(4) (Birmingham) By the mid–19th century ... the 'workshop of the world' exemplified everything that was bad about industrial development [*Lonely Planet Great Britain*, 2005].

**World, the** *(1) Charters Towers, Australia; (2) United States.* The Queensland town was so known for its wealth and diversity as a gold rush town in the latter part of the 19th century. For the United States, the term was current among US military personnel in Vietnam in the 1960s, especially in phrases such as "to go back to the world," meaning to return to the USA after service abroad.

(1) (USA) Back in the World now, and some of us aren't making it [Michael Herr, *Dispatches*, 1977].

(2) (USA) He was due to rotate back to "the world," as it was known, in a few weeks [Weekender Magazine, *Tucson* (Arizona) *Citizen*, April 28, 1979].

(3) (USA) You'll kill boo-coo gooks [i.e. lots of Vietnamese] before you go on back to the World [Dale A. Dye, *Platoon*, 1987].

**World Capital of Literature, the** *Paris, France.* The name refers to the many novels by famous writers published in the French capital in the 19th century (*see* **City of a Thousand Novels**). Its publishing fame actually dates from much earlier, and in the 16th century Paris was printing more titles than any other city in Europe.

**World Capital of the Adult Entertainment Industry, the** *Los Angeles, California, USA.* The city is (in)famous for the production of porno movies and videos, and porno actors such as John Holmes and Linda Lovelace have left their hand- and footprints in the sidewalk outside the former Pussycat (now Tomkat) movie theater. Hence the related (and more direct) sobriquet of **Porno Capital of the World** for the nearby San Fernando Valley.

LA lays claim to the rather dubious title of "World Capital of the Adult Entertainment Industry" [Catherine Gerber, *Los Angeles*, 2004].

**World City, the** *London, England.* The British capital was originally so described for its global importance in the 19th century. Later, the sobriquet was interpreted as a reference to its cultural diversity. Londoners speak more than 300 languages and there are more than 50 ethnic communities of 10,000 people. *Cp.* **World in One City**.

(1) As one historian put it, London was a "world city," at the height of its imperial, industrial and social power [Malcolm Bradbury, ed., *The Atlas of Literature*, 1996].

(2) There is no such thing as London any more. There is a world city in the southeast of England and it is growing all the time [Professor Brendan Nevin, speech at Urban Summit, Birmingham, 2002].

(3) If there's one area of London that epitomizes the 'world city' tag, it is Knightsbridge [Carrie Segrave, *The New London Property Guide*, 2003].

(4) He adds, "London's 'World City' image will be enhanced [by its successful bid to host the 2012 Olympics]" [*Sunday Times*, July 10, 2005].

(5) Among the victims [of the terrorist attack] were Asians, Africans, Americans and Europeans who had chosen to make their home in what the Olympic bid team called "the world in one city" [*The Times*, July 11, 2005].

**World in One City, the** *Liverpool, England.* The Merseyside city adopted this slogan in 2003 in its (successful) campaign to be awarded the title European Capital of Culture 2008. The reference is to the city's cultural diversity. *Cp.* **World City**.

**World's Best City, the** *Nottingham, England.* An intentionally or ironically exaggerated self-promotional name for the city, presumably designed to counter the unwelcome media tag of **Murder Capital of Britain**.

Nottingham is ridiculously over-hyped... A radio station announces every ten minutes that we are in 'The World's Best City' [Sam Jordison and Dan Kieran, eds., *The Idler Book of Crap Towns II*, 2004].

**World's Egg Basket, the** *Petaluma, California, USA.* The city's self-promotional nickname refers to its high-profile poultry industry.

**World's Most Popular Country, the** *France.* A self-promotional nickname inviting even more tourists than already visit the country. The sobriquet sounds sweeter in the original French: "*le pays le plus populaire du monde.*"

So it was back to the "world's most popular country," as France styles itself [*The Times*, January 14, 2005].

**World's Smallest Big City, the** *Aarhus, Denmark.* As stated in the quote below, the seaport city adopted a promotional nickname implying a large and outwardly impersonal city with an intimate and well-defined Old Town section.

The city of Aarhus has rather proudly adopted Peter Ustinov's one-liner as a wryly self-deprecating marketing slogan [Dodd/Donald, p. 449].

**World's Smallest Capital, the** *Nuuk, Greenland.* A factual self-promotional nickname for the town, and qualified as in quote (1) below.

(1) "The world's smallest capital," Greenland's tourist office states, "with all a capital city has to offer" [Dodd/Donald, p. 91].

(2) The world's smallest capital has an ice-free harbour [Travel ad, *The Times*, February 26, 2005].

**World's Wildest Island, the** *Australia*. An airline's promotional name of the 1980s, presumably designed to tempt tourists to a land that is not only socially uninhibited but that possesses an untamed interior.

**Wowserland** *New Zealand*. A nickname from "wowser" as a term for a puritanical or prudish person, especially one opposed to the consumption of alcohol, as a typical New Zealander is or was said to be.

**Writing Desk of the Ruhr, the** *Düsseldorf, Germany*. The city's former nickname, translating German *Schreibtisch des Ruhr*, refers to its civil servants and office workers, as described in the quote below.

> The city's old nickname ... is a reference to a preponderance of accountants and paper-pushers [Dodd/Donald, p. 471].

**Xanadu** *Shangdu, China*. The poetic name of China's imperial summer residence, built in 1260 by Kublai Khan in what is now Inner Mongolia, is familiar from Coleridge's famous poem quoted below.

> In Xanadu did Kubla Khan
> A stately pleasure-dome decree:
> Where Alph, the sacred river, ran
> Through caverns measureless to man
> Down to a sunless sea [S.T. Coleridge, *Kubla Khan*, 1898].

**Xanadu of Wales, the** *Portmeirion, Wales*. The exotic Italianate resort was built in the 1920s by the English architect Clough Williams-Ellis as a "dream village." Hence its name, suggested by the dream-like magnificence and luxury of **Xanadu** as described in Coleridge's well-known poem (quoted above).

**XMG** *Crossmaglen, Northern Ireland*. A British army abbreviation of the name of the Co. Armagh village, in **Bandit Country**.

> For the British soldier, Crossmaglen — known as XMG to the military, and Cross to locals — is a place of hostility, isolation and the constant threat of death [Toby Harnden, *Bandit Country*, 1999].

**Yammyland** *Wolverhampton, England*. The West Midland city's local nickname presumably derives from "yammer," describing folk who like "grumbling and groaning," especially as a way of self-promotion.

> Its advertising campaign ... was just the kind of mumbled, low-key self-aggrandisement that the people of Yammyland go in for themeslves [Caitlin Moran, "Yay for Yammyland," *The Times*, December 19, 2000].

**Yankeedom** or **Yankeedoodledom** *United States*. An alternate form of **Yankeeland**, the longer form from the popular 18th-century song.

(1) The ladies of this house (natives though they be of Yankee-doodle-dom) seem to possess, in a high degree, the power of capturing the aristocracy of England [Philip Hone, *Diary*, May 20, 1845].

(2) He ought to take a steamer direct for Yankeedom; ... they'd make him President at once! [*Blackwood's Magazine*, April 1851].

**Yankeeland** *(1) New England, USA; (2) United States*. An obvious term for a region or land of Yankees or Yanks, whatever the origin of the name. (It may derive from *Janke*, a diminutive of the Dutch personal name *Jan*, "John.")

> (New England) It sounds strangely to hear children bargaining in French on the borders of Yankee-land [Nathaniel Hawthorne, *Passages from the American Note-books*, July 13, 1837 (1883)].

**Yankee Land of the South, the** *Georgia, USA*. The state earned its nickname for the role played by its white population in boosting the economy of the former slave states of the South.

**Yankee Heaven** or **Paradise** *Paris, France*. The nickname of the French capital alludes to Thomas G. Appleton's epigram, "Good Americans, when they die, go to Paris," quoted in Oliver Wendell Holmes, *The Autocrat of the Breakfast Table* (1858), and subsequently, in slightly different form, by Oscar Wilde in *A Woman of No Importance* (1893).

**Yankee State, the** *Ohio, USA*. The state was so nicknamed for its free institutions, and also perhaps for the many New Englanders (*see* **Yankeeland**) who immigrated here.

**Yard** or **the Yard** *Jamaica, West Indies*. The nickname derives from West Indian "yard" meaning "home."

> Alton has been on the hit parade down in Yard ... ever since his first smash hit in 1959 [*New York*, November 4, 1974].

**Yay** or **Yay Area, the** *Oakland, California, USA*. The colloquial local name is a form of "Bay Area," referring to Oakland's location on the east side of San Francisco Bay. San Francisco, on the west side, is similarly **Bay City**.

**Yeats Country** see in Appendix 1, p. 269.

**Yellowhammer State, the** *Alabama, USA*. The state's nickname refers to the yellowish hue of the gray uniforms worn by Confederate soldiers in the Civil War.

**Yellow Peril, the** *Asia*. A name originating in Germany at the turn of the 20th century for the Asian peoples and their lands, or more specifically for the people of China or Japan, so called from their yellowish skin and the fear that they would overrun white people or even the world. *Cp.* **Red Peril**.

> But Japan was Asia, part of the Yellow Peril poised like a descending pendulum above Aus-

tralia's rich, empty, underpopulated pit [Colleen McCullough, *The Thorn Birds*, 1977].

**Yerba Buena** *San Francisco, California, USA.* The former nickname represents the Spanish words for "good grass," referring to the local pasturage. The name survives in that of Yerba Buena Island in San Francisco Bay.

**Yidney** *Sydney, Australia.* The punning but potentially offensive nickname alludes to the city's Jewish population.

**Yidsbury** *Finsbury, London, England.* The punning but offensive nickname refers to the district's Jewish population. *Cp.* **Yidney.**

**Yoga Capital of the World, the** *Rishikesh, India.* The town in north central India lures Western tourists by offering instruction in yoga and through its connection with the Beatles, who met Maharishi Mahesh Yogi here in the 1960s.

The itinerary ... includes ... a stay in an ashram in Rishikesh, self-styled yoga capital of the world [*The Times*, April 9, 2005].

**Yogya** *Yogyakarta, Indonesia.* A local short name for the Javan city. *Cp.* **Sala.**

**York** *New York City, USA.* A straightforward shortened form of the city's name.

New York City, or "York," as the Under World prefers to call it [Josiah Flint, *The World of Graft*, 1901].

**Yorks** *Yorkshire, England.* A semiofficial abbreviation of the county's name. *See also* Appendix 6, p. 325.

**You Beaut Country** *Australia.* The nickname ("beaut" is "beauty") comes from the title of Australian artist John Olsen's series of abstract paintings of bush landscape, *Journey into You Beaut Country* (1961).

**Yugers** *Yugoslavia.* The colloquial abbreviation for the former Yugoslavia has the "Oxford -er," as for **Honkers.**

**Yurrup** or **Yurp** *Europe.* The name represents a supposedly typical American pronunciation of the continent's name.

There are the [American] business men trying to make a better position for themselves at home as experts on Yurrup [Nancy Mitford, *Don't Tell Alfred*, 1960].

**Zedland** see in Appendix 1, p. 269.

**Zenith City of the Unsalted Seas, the** *Duluth, Minnesota, USA.* The city gained its poetic sobriquet as the westernmost port in the Great Lakes–St.Lawrence Seaway Navigation system. The "unsalted seas" are thus the freshwater lakes of the five Great Lakes, the largest body of freshwater in the world.

**Zetland** *Shetland Islands, Scotland.* The alternate name of the island group, surviving in certain official and historical contexts, has "Z-" instead of "Sh-" to represent the medieval letter known as yogh, used to convey the initial sound of the original spelling (recorded as *Haltland* in the early 12th century).

**Zion** or **Sion** *(1) Jerusalem, Israel; (2) Palestine or Israel.* The ancient name of Jerusalem, familiar from the Bible and from Jewish and Christian texts, is of uncertain origin. Proposed meanings include "rock," "stronghold," "dry place," and "running water." In the Bible, it is first mentioned for the Jebusite fortress, as in quote (1) below. King David took the fort from the Jebusites (*see* **City of David**) and its name became subsequently equated with Jerusalem. Related to this is the understanding that the temple mount, Mt. Zion, is a dwelling place of Yahweh, the divine king of Israel. The name can also refer to the inhabitants of Jerusalem or to the whole people of Israel. In this context, it often appears in phrases such as "sons of Zion" or "daughters of Zion." The modern Mt. Zion is a hill south of the southwestern portion of the Old City of Jerusalem. By extension, the name came to stand for the homeland of Jews in what was first Palestine, then (after 1948) Israel. In a transferred sense, Zion can further denote the Christian church or heaven.

(1) (Jerusalem) David took the strong hold of Zion: the same is the city of David [2 Samuel 5:7].
(2) (Jerusalem) Look upon Zion, the city of our solemnities [Isaiah 33:20].
(3) (Jerusalem) By the waters of Babylon we sat down and wept: when we remembered thee, O Sion [Psalm 137:1, Book of Common Prayer, 1662].
(4) (Jerusalem) Glorious things of thee are spoken,
Zion, City of our God! [John Newton, "Zion, or the city of God," *Olney Hymns*, 1779].
(5) (Israel) Loud he sang the psalm of David!
He, a Negro and enslaved,
Sang of Israel's victory,
Sang of Zion, bright and free [H.W. Longfellow, *Poems on Slavery*, 1842].
(6) (Israel) [I wanted] to peel this land of its names, designations, descriptions and dates, Israel, Palestine, Zion, 1917, 1929, 1936, 1948, 1967, 1987, the Jewish state, the Promised Land, the Holy Land, the Land of Splendor [David Grossman, *Sleeping on a Wire*, 1993].

**Zoo City** or **Town** *Kalamazoo, Michigan, USA.* A shortened form of the city's name based on its final syllable.

**Zummerset** or **Zummerzet** *Somerset, England.* A humorous representation of a local pronunciation of the West-Country county's name, with "z" for "s." (An actor's imitation of such an accent is known as "Mummerset," from a blend of "mummer" and the county name.)

(1) Not much is known about Somerset except that it is generally known in comic songs as Zummerset. This is because of local dialect [Theodora Benson and Betty Askwith, *Muddling Through, or Britain in a Nutshell*, 1936].

(2) 'Varmer' for 'farmer,' is a standard part of the actor's repertoire when he wants to sound like a Devon or Zummerzet man [C. Stella Davies and John Levitt, *What's in a Name?*, 1970].

(3) The disputed building? Caroline Barry's farmhouse in Butleigh, a lovely bit o' Zummerset near Glastonbury [*The Times*, September 27, 2004].

# Appendix 1: Regional Nicknames

*Below is a selection of nicknames of regions or districts that are mostly undelimited, as distinct from the secondary names of delimited places with a formal primary name. Their entries thus take a different form from those in the main body of the dictionary, the location being combined with the definition and (where appropriate) origin of the name.*

*In a sense, such names do not strictly conform to the protocol of the dictionary, as by definition they are not secondary. But they do mostly hold the status of a secondary name or nickname and thus properly belong here. (In this connection it is worth recalling that although "nickname" literally means "additional name," from Middle English eke, "addition," the word now often means simply "unofficial name.")*

*The names range from the informal, such as* **Bomb Alley**, *to the near-formal, such as* **Pacific Rim**. *Some of the more formal names gain inclusion in gazetteers, but few actually appear on maps. An exception may be made, however, for the many touristic coastal names (as* **Costa del Sol**), *which are included on some national maps and in certain atlases, such as the* Reader's Digest World Atlas *(2004). The regions themselves vary in size from the extensive, such as the* **Sunbelt**, *to the local, such as* **SoHo**. *Geographically they either center generally on a definable object, such as a city, or extend along a particular border or coast, or have arisen to form an area within an existing district or territory. In a few cases the names denote a region encompassing or linking particular established places, as the* **Cinque Ports**, *the* **Cocktail Isles**, *the* **Four Seas**, *the* **Heavenly Trio**, *or the* **Sunni Triangle**. *Such names often (but not always) have some form of numeral as a descriptive. Names formed as the plural of a regular placename are clearly collective, as the* **Hamptons** *or the* **Rodings**.

*Two groups of places dominate the present category, as can be seen from the entries below. First are the many touristically named coasts, either with English* coast *or with a foreign equivalent, such as French* côte *or Spanish* costa. *The name is designed to attract visitors and thus money. Hence the romantic or "rich" nature of such names, many of which are given for colors or gems. Second are the various "country" names, often that of a famous person associated with the region, such as a writer or artist, or sometimes with a fictional character or setting, familiar to many from a popular novel or television series. Again, such regions readily promote the name for commercial reasons.*

*Aside from these two groups, there are also a number of "belts," typically in North America, where particular crops are grown or distinctive conditions prevail. Examples are Canada's* **Banana Belt** *and America's* **Sunbelt** *and* **Snowbelt**. *Elsewhere, South Africa has its* **Mist Belt**, *while Britain has evolved its own familiar* **Stockbroker Belt**, *among others.*

*Some of the districts or areas in this category have their own alternate names, such as London's* **East End**, *formerly the* **Abyss**, *or the aforementioned* **Stockbroker Belt**, *located in a tract of country also known as the* **Gin-and-Jag Belt**.

**Abbevillage** The name is a condensed form of Abbeville Village, itself devised by estate agents (realtors) in the 1980s for the upscale residential neighborhood around Abbeville Road, Clapham, London, England, as described in the quote below.

"The [radio] series [*Lives in a Landscape*] ... makes a visit to that part of South London known as Abbevillage. You don't know it? Not surprising, really — the *A-Z* has it as nothing more exotic than Abbeville Road, Clapham. But it is an area so moneyed and gentrified that the City types who reside there refer to Clapham itself as "Clarm" [*The Times*, July 23, 2005].

**Abyss, the** A nickname for the **East End** of London, England, current from around the

269

1880s. US author Jack London lived near London's docks for two months in 1902 to investigate living conditions there, publishing the result in *The People of the Abyss* (1903).

**Adrian Bell Country** The name is largely synonymous with the county of Suffolk, England, where the writer and farmer Adrian Bell (1901–1980) lived and worked, as described in the quote below.

> He lived, and wrote about, Suffolk for 60 years in a way that made the countryside live for people who would never see it — and some who did, having made a sort of pilgrimage to what became known as Adrian Bell Country [*The Times*, September 2, 2005].

**Albertopolis** The nickname, dating from the 19th century, was applied to the area of land bought in South Kensington, London, England, by Prince Albert, husband of Queen Victoria, for the purposes of founding a number of institutions and museums (*see* **Museumland**). The prince's name is preserved in the Royal Albert Hall, Victoria and Albert Museum, and Albert Memorial, all here. An alternate name for the region was *Coleville*, for the writer and designer Sir Henry Cole (1808–1882), who planned and largely organized the Great Exhibition of 1851 under the patronage of Prince Albert and who implemented many other of the prince's plans. He was first director of the Victoria and Albert Museum.

> (1) Albertopolis, a facetious appellation given by the Londoners to the Kensington Gore district. Now obsolete [*The Slang Dictionary*, 1894].
>
> (2) "Albertopolis," with its remarkable cluster of museums and colleges, plus the vast Albert Hall, now stands as one of London's most enlightened examples of urban planning [*The Rough Guide to London*, 1997].

**Alphabet City** A pleasant punning name for the area containing Avenues A, B, C, and D in Lower East Side, New York City, USA.

> (1) Avenues A, B, C, and D form a dirty appendage to Manhattan's Lower East Side: these Alphabet Blocks have become Indian country, the land of murder and cocaine [Jerome Charyn, *War Cries Over Avenue C*, 1985].
>
> (2) My favourite place is Avenue A … It runs from Houston to 14th Street and is part of Alphabet City, but on the real Lower East Side [Rock singer Deborah Harry, interviewed in *Sunday Times Magazine*, November 13, 2005].

**Amber Coast, the** The stretch of Baltic coast west of Kaliningrad, northwestern Russia, takes its name from the natural deposits of amber here, the largest in the world. The name happens to match the touristic sobriquets of French coasts such as the *Côte d'Émeraude* ("emerald coast") and *Côte de Jade* ("jade coast") (*see* **Côte d'Azur**).

> Day 9. This afternoon there will be an optional guided walk … to the Amber Coast [Travel ad, *The Times*, October 29, 2005].

**Back o' Bourke, the** A name synonymous with the Australian **Outback**, and especially that typical part of it northwest of the town of Bourke, New South Wales.

> Where the mulga paddocks are wild and wide,
> That's where the pick of the stockmen ride,
> At the Back o' Bourke [*The Bulletin* (Sydney), February 15, 1896].

**Baht 'At Country** A touristic name for the region around the spa town of Ilkley, Yorkshire, England. The words come from a nationally-known dialect song with the repeated refrain: "On Ilkley Moor baht 'at" ("On Ilkley Moor without a hat").

> It infuriates me that the local tourist board promotes the area as "Baht 'At Country." It makes us natives sound like flat-cap-wearing ferret handlers — and it's not even a good song [*The Times*, September 3, 2005].

**Baltics, the** A general short name for the Baltic states of Estonia, Latvia, and Lithuania, which lie by the Baltic Sea.

> The Costas were too close to home, the Baltics too cold in winter [*The Times*, November 25, 2005].

**Balti Triangle, the** The name arose in the 1970s for a region centered on Sparkbrook, Balsall Heath, and Moseley, south of central Birmingham, England, where there are many balti houses, specializing in this Indian dish. The name puns on the **Bermuda Triangle**.

> The sizzling Balti Triangle in cosmopolitan Birmingham [*Enjoy England Holiday Planner 2005*].

**Banana, the** A nickname for the banana-shaped industrialized region encompassing London, England, and Milan, Italy, or else Cardiff, Wales, Birmingham, England, and Milan.

**Banana Belt, the** The name was first applied in the 1960s on Baffin Island, Canada, to mainland North America, regarded as (relatively) warm enough to grow bananas. The term then came to be applied to any popular winter resort area, especially a regularly sunny one.

> Skiers … have cause to thank this southern Catskill Mountain country — often joshingly referred to as "The Banana Belt" [*New York Times*, January 6, 1977].

**Banffshire Riviera, the** A name formerly current for the north-facing coast of the historic county of Banffshire, Scotland, between Fraserburgh and Inverness.

> To explore some of the features of this coastline, the 'Banffshire Riviera,' take the B9031 out of Fraserburgh for Macduff and Banff. 'Riviera' seems hardly the right word to describe a shore

that looks directly into the eye of northerly gales and which turns its back on the sun [Robinson/Millward, pp. 416–7].

**Bangla Town** A name for the district centering on Brick Lane in the East End of London, England, where there are several Bengali and Bangladeshi curry houses and warehouses.

**Barbary Coast, the** The nickname was applied to a coastal district of San Francisco, California, USA, notorious for its prostitution and gambling, especially during the period 1849–1921. The name was adopted from the North African Barbary Coast, a haunt of pirates, infamous for its violence and danger. *See also* **Tenderloin.**

> Telegraph Hill ... once looked down on the Barbary Coast, a neighbourhood alive with gaudy wickedness [*Britannica*, vol. 27, p. 1].

**Battleground Coast, the** A nickname for the west coast of Scotland, where there is a constant battle between sea and land (the sea gradually winning) and where island communities battle to survive in the harsh environment. There have also been real battles here, most of them between the Scots and the English but some between the Scottish clans.

> Memorials to this conflict between man and place can be seen up and down the Battleground Coast [Christopher Somerville, *Coast: A Celebration of Britain's Coastal Heritage*, 2005].

**Bergerac Country** A touristic name for those areas on the island of Jersey, Channel Islands, UK, where the popular TV police drama *Bergerac* (1981–91) was filmed.

**Bermuda Triangle, the** A vaguely triangular area of sea in the North Atlantic, between Bermuda, Florida, and Puerto Rico, where more than 50 ships and 20 airplanes are said to have mysteriously disappeared. The first recorded disappearance was that of Flight 19, the "Lost Patrol," five US Navy Avenger torpedo bombers that vanished on a mission from Fort Lauderdale, Florida, on December 5, 1945. The name was popularized by Charles Berlitz's book *The Bermuda Triangle* (1974). The region is also known as the *Devil's Triangle.*

> (1) Draw a line from Florida to Bermuda, another from Bermuda to Puerto Rico, and a third back to Florida through the Bahamas. Within this area, known as the "Bermuda Triangle," most of the vanishments have occurred [*Argosy*, February 28, 1964].
>
> (2) Ships and planes disappear, time skips a beat, and earthlings board extraterrestrial craft, all in the region known as the Bermuda, or Devil's Triangle [*Collier's Encyclopedia Year Book 1976*, 1975].
>
> (3) There have been about half-a-dozen success-

ful books on the Bermuda Triangle ... Although they all tell basically the same stories, they advocate different solutions [*The Listener*, February 19, 1976].

> (4) Enough mystery remained to feed a ... belief that some terrible force awaits mariners and airmen who venture into a "Devil's triangle" defined by Puerto Rico, Bermuda and Miami [*The Times*, November 25, 2005].

**Between the Commons** *see* **Nappy Valley**

**Beyond the Black Stump** A name for the remote **Outback** of Australia, the "black stump" being a fire-blackened tree stump traditionally used as a marker when giving directions to travelers. The location of the original Black Stump is uncertain. The phrase "this side of the Black Stump" is commonly used to mean "here in this civilized part of the world."

> *Beyond the Black Stump* [Nevil Shute, novel title, 1956].

**Bible Belt, the** A name for those areas of the Southern and Midwestern USA and western Canada where Protestant fundamentalism is widely practiced. Nashville, Tennessee, is generally reckoned to be the capital of the US Bible Belt.

> (1) I'm collecting parsons, Gilbert ... That's why I've been living in Kansas City. It's the centre of the Bible belt [Sinclair Lewis in Gilbert Frankau, *My Unsentimental Journey*, 1926].
>
> (2) A hundred miles west and one would be out of the 'Bible Belt,' that gospel-haunted strip of American territory in which a man must ... take his religion with the straightest of faces [Truman Capote, *In Cold Blood*, 1965].
>
> (3) The boondocks. The sticks. Hicksville. Redneck territory. The red states, the Bible Belt, the heartland, the homeland, the back country, the Big Country. Those parts of America where church attendance is mandatory ... That's the USA I've always wanted to see [*Sunday Times*, August 28, 2005].

**Big Bend, the** An informal name for the curving coast of Florida's northwestern panhandle, USA, known more imaginatively as the **Redneck Riviera.**

**Black Africa** A dated name for the continent of Africa south of the Sahara, predominantly inhabited by (and ruled by) black peoples. *Cp.* **White Africa.**

> (1) Mishka and Nakovalny, whose country was now an Indian Ocean Power, regarded Black Africa as a very promising field for Muscovite missionary work [Arthur Keppel-Jones, *When Smuts Goes*, 1947].
>
> (2) The key to Black Africa lies in the vast territory of Nigeria [*The Observer*, November 2, 1958].

**Black Belt, the** The name has two geographical senses. First, it is the region of the Southern

USA, as defined in quote (1) below, in which blacks outnumber whites. Second, it denoted the prairie lowland region of central Alabama, USA, where the rich soil proved ideal for growing the cotton for which the state is famous (*see* **Cotton State** in Dictionary).

(1) (Southern USA) The Black Belt has a curiously irregular shape. Extending from Virginia across North and South Carolina, Georgia, Alabama, to Mississippi and Southern Louisiana, it stretches a narrow arm across the river and up into southern and central Arkansas [*New York Evening Post*, November 21, 1905].

(2) (Alabama) Called the 'Black Belt,' central Alabama was named for the swath of fertile soil perfect for growing cotton [*Lonely Planet USA*, 2004].

**Black Country, the** The nickname for the industrial region west of Birmingham, England, dates from the early 19th century, when the buildings here were blackened and grimed by the murk of the collieries, blast furnaces, and foundries set up during the Industrial Revolution following exploitation of the South Staffordshire coalfield. As indicated in quote (2) below, the name could equally stem from the coal itself. The negative name is now positively promoted as a touristic draw to the area's "industrial heritage."

(1) By night the Black Country blazes up lurid and red with fires which ... are never extinguished [*Daily Telegraph*, December 12, 1864].

(2) Its name is widely supposed to derive from the soot laid down in its long years of heavy industrial production. It is more likely, though, to have been inspired by the region's thick coal seam. This was in many places only a few feet below the surface, making the soil black [Cowan, p. 34].

(3) The blackness of the Black Country will soon be scrubbed out, and good riddance, most people would say [Germaine Greer in *Sunday Times Magazine*, May 29, 2005].

**Black Harlem** The name was current by the 1920s for the area between 130th and 145th streets and Seventh and Madison avenues in Harlem, New York City, USA, where blacks had first begun to settle in the late 19th century.

**Block, the** A name for the block of streets in Australian cities in which it was fashionable to promenade. In Brisbane, it was the rectangle formed by Queen Street, Edward Street, Elizabeth Street, and Albert Street. In Melbourne it was as described in the quotes below. *See also* **Block** in Appendix 2, p. 307.

(1) 'The Block' is supposed to extend down George-street, from King-street to Hunter-street, round Pitt-street, and up King-street into George-street again [Grosvenor Bunster and Dick Thatcher, eds., *It Runs in the Blood*, 1872].

(2) Challis's mind slipped back to the days when ... he 'did the block' on Saturday mornings. Down George Street and around the Post Office, up Pitt Street, past King Street, and through the Arcade, then back to George Street again [Herbert M. Moran, *Beyond the Hill Lies China*, 1945].

**Blue Banana, the** An alternate name for the region more usually known as the **Banana**.

**Blue Water Paradise, the** A name for the region around Port Stephens, New South Wales, Australia. Its ocean side is popular with vacationers for its good surf and wide sandy beaches.

**BoCoCa** An acronym for the neighborhood also known as South Brooklyn, New York City, which takes in *Bo*erum Hill, *Co*bble Hill, and *Ca*rroll Gardens. The name is mainly used in a culinary context to refer to the district's many Italian restaurants, pastry shops, and the like.

**Bogue, the** A former English name for the Pearl River Delta, China, from Portuguese *boca (do) tigre*, translating its Chinese name *húmén*, "Tiger's Gate" (modern Latin *Bocca Tigris*). The name was probably influenced by English *disembogue*, "to discharge at the mouth."

**Bomb Alley** Southeastern England was so named in World War II for the German flying bombs ("doodlebugs") that flew over the area on their way to London. The name has also been applied to heavily bombed areas elsewhere, as in the quote below. *Cp.* **Hell's Corner**.

The narrow stretch of water between the island of Pantellaria and Sicily, officially known as the Sicilian Channel, but called Bomb Alley by the Navy and Merchant Service [*Hutchinson's Pictorial History of the War*, June 10–September 1, 1942].

**Border Counties, the** A name for (the parts of) the counties lying immediately south and north of the border between the Republic of Ireland and Northern Ireland, namely (to the south) Leitrim, Cavan, and Monaghan, and (to the north) Fermanagh, Tyrone, and Armagh.

The international frontier between the United Kingdom and the Republic of Ireland, which is at the heart of the Border Counties, is a product of Irish people's inability to agree among themselves as to where their loyalties lay [Brian Lalor, *Blue Guide Ireland*, 2004].

**Border Country, the** A name that can obviously apply to any region straddling a national or other border. The name is particularly applicable to two such borders. The first is the lengthy frontier between the USA and Mexico, stretching from the Pacific Ocean to the Gulf of Mexico, and associated with its criminal activities, such as the import to the USA of illegal drugs manufactured "south of the border." The second is that between Scotland and England, where the name usually applies to the area of southern Scotland on the north side of the border, although it can also denote the corresponding area of northern England to the south. The name is often shortened to the Border or the Borders for the Scottish region, and as such was adopted in 1975 for a Scottish administrative region that in 1996 became the unitary authority of Scottish Borders. *See also* **Border Counties**.

(1) (Scotland) O, young Lochinvar is come out of the west,
Through all the wide Border his steed was the best [Sir Walter Scott, *Marmion*, 1808].
(2) (England) A car is a great advantage in the Border Country [Ruth McKenney and Richard Bransten, *Here's England*, 1955].
(3) (Scotland) Although Edinburgh was the scene of [Sir Walter] Scott's professional life, his heart lay in the Border Country [Ian Ousby, *Blue Guide Literary Britain and Ireland*, 1990].

**Borscht Belt, the** A showbiz name for the Jewish resort area in the Catskill Mountains, New York, USA, so called from the popularity of this type of Russian soup among Jews of East European origin.

The Borscht Belt, they call this corridor of kosher kitsch, dotted with holiday bungalow complexes and resort hotels [Howard Jacobson in *Sunday Times*, August 29, 1999].

**Bosnywash** The name for the affluent, densely populated eastern region of the USA is formed from the names of three of its cities: *Bost*on, *New York*, and *Wash*ington. *Cp.* **Chippitts**; **Sansan**.

**Broadland** An alternate name for the **Broads**, officially that of a Norfolk, England, council district.

**Broads, the** The name is that of the network of navigable rivers, marshes, and lakes in Norfolk, England, a "broad" being a lake formed by the broadening out of a river. The region is also known as the Norfolk Broads, although one of the lakes is in neighboring Suffolk.

The Norfolk Broads are in their general character and scenery unlike anything else in England [E.S. Symes, *The Story of the East Country*, n.d. (*c.* 1910)].

**Brontë Country** A regional name for the parts of Yorkshire, England, associated with the sister novelists Charlotte Brontë (1816–1855), Emily Brontë (1818–1848), and Anne Brontë (1820–1849), whose home was the parsonage at Haworth, near Keighley.

(1) Yorkshire had the Brontës, and has the Brontë country. It has [the writer J.B.] Priestley. Even in Yorkshire patience has its limits, and there is no Priestley country [Theodora Benson and Betty Askwith, *Muddling Through, or Britain in a Nutshell*, 1936].

(2) The sign says, finally: HAWORTH. Nothing could look less like a literary shrine ... Then, over a crowded shop, ... there was a sign: HEATHCLIFF IRONMONGERS. "Brontë country!" I cried, much excited [Ruth McKenney and Richard Bransten, *Here's England*, 1955].
(3) No tourist walks with more certain tread than the visitor to Haworth, West Yorkshire ... This is Brontë Country, a landscape of many planes, visited by millions [Malcolm Bradbury, ed., *The Atlas of Literature*, 1996].

**Burns Country** A regional name for the area of southwestern Scotland associated with the poet Robert Burns (1759–1796), who was born here at Alloway, South Ayrshire. *Cp.* **Land o' Burns**.

All the famous beauty spots and places of interest in the West of Scotland, such as the Firth of Clyde, Loch Lomond, the Trossachs, the Burns Country, [etc.] [*Holiday Haunts 1962: Scotland*].

**Cadfael Country** A name for the region around the town of Shrewsbury, Shropshire, England, the setting of the detective stories by Ellis Peters featuring the monk Brother Cadfael (1977–94).

The success of the Cadfael books ... created a tourist boom in Shrewsbury, several spin-off books about Cadfael country, and a TV series *Cadfael* (1994–8) [Mike Ashley, comp., *The Mammoth Encyclopedia of Modern Crime Fiction*, 2002].

**Cajun Country** A name for the region of southern Louisiana, USA, extending from the Mississippi River to the Texas border. It is home to the largest French-speaking minority in the USA, and takes its name from the Cajuns, whose ancestors were exiled by the British in 1755 from **Acadia** (see in Dictionary), of which name their own is a corruption.

**California of Wales, the** The name is sometimes applied to the region north of Barmouth, in western Wales, where gold has been mined since Roman times.

**Cambrian Coast, the** A general name for the west coast of Wales (*see* **Cambria** in Dictionary), especially the coast of Cardigan Bay.

The most northerly of the "Cambrian Coast" resorts are to be found on the Caernarvonshire coast of Cardigan Bay [*Holiday Haunts 1961: Area No. 4, West of England and South and Central Wales*].

**Campo, the** A former English name for the foreign settlement at Ning-po, eastern China. It was set up by the Portuguese in the 16th century, but was later also a base for Dutch and British merchants. The main city lay to the south of the Yung River, but the settlement arose to the north. Hence the name, derived by the Portuguese from *campo*, "open land," but in fact a corruption of *kong po*, a local pronunciation of Chinese *jiāng běi*, "north (of the) river."

**Captain Cook Country** A touristic name for the region of North Yorkshire, England, where the explorer James Cook (1728–1779) was born and spent his childhood years. *See also* **Gateway to Captain Cook Country** in Dictionary.

> Join in the annual celebrations of Cook's life and achievements that take place throughout 'Cook Country' in October [Tourist brochure *Waterside England*, 2005].

**Carport** A portmanteau name for the cities of Cardiff and Newport, in South Wales, and the main auto routes between them (as if a "car-port").

**Catherine Cookson Country** A touristic name for the Tyneside region of northeastern England, where the prolific popular writer of historical fiction and gothic romances Catherine Cookson (1906–1998) lived and worked and where many of her novels are set. (Her fictional town of Fellburn was an amalgam of Felling and Hebburn.)

> [In 1985] South Tyneside Council ... announced plans to celebrate its most famous daughter — by inviting visitors to tour Catherine Cookson Country [Cliff Goodwin, *The Catherine Cookson Companion*, 1999].

**Causeway Coast, the** An alliterative touristic name for the northeast coast of Northern Ireland, the site of the formation of basaltic columns known as the Giant's Causeway.

> The small region ... known locally as 'the Causeway Coast' ... is regarded as an area of particular scenic attraction and interest [Brian Lalor, *Blue Guide Ireland*, 2004].

**Celtic Fringe, the** A potentially belittling name for Wales, Ireland, Cornwall, and the northern part of Scotland, or as more fully defined in quote (1) below, as Celtic lands surrounding England, with their own cultural and sociopolitical characteristics. The phrase is usually attributed to the Scottish prime minister Arthur Balfour (1848–1930).

> (1) Remnants of this ancient European culture survive in the six countries of the "Celtic Fringe"— Scotland, Ireland, Wales, Isle of Man, Cornwall and Brittany [William Kirk, "The Scottish People," in John Hay of Hayfield, comp., *Tartan Tapestry*, 1960].
>
> (2) Most of the islands described in this book are part of the culture province known to tourist officers and Celtic film producers as the Celtic Fringe [Newton, p. 17].
>
> (3) Such geographical snobbery is particularly relevant in Scotland and Wales, often referred to dismissively by the English middle class as the 'Celtic fringe' [Greg Hadfield and Mark Skipworth, *Class*, 1994].

**Centralia** A name (blending "central" and "Australia") that was originally proposed for the colony of South Australia but that is now applied to the region surrounding Alice Springs, Northern Territory, as which it is synonymous with the **Centre**.

**Centre, the** A name for the central portion of Australia, as defined in quote (2) below, also known more specifically as the **Red Centre** and as the **Dead Heart**. *Cp.* **Centralia**.

> (1) In common with all other Australian tribes, those of the Centre have been shut off from contact with other peoples [Walter Spencer and Francis James Gillen, *The Native Tribes of Central Australia*, 1899].
>
> (2) In popular present-day Australian usage 'The Centre' is an area roughly within a radius of 400 to 500 miles from Alice Springs [*Australian Encyclopedia*, 1965].

**Channel Country** A name for the pastoral region of east central Australia, mainly in southwestern Queensland, that is crossed by many stream channels.

> The name 'channel country' is not necessarily the proper name of a geographical area, but a common expression used by outback residents to designate a definite order of geographical features [A.M. Duncan-Kemp, *Where Strange Gods Call*, 1968].

**Château Country, the** A touristic name for the region of west central France, and especially the valley of the Loire River, famous for its many châteaux, which range from medieval fortresses, built for defense, to grand country houses, designed for luxurious living.

> 'Visit the Château Country,' adjure the travel posters. And that, of course, means the châteaux of the Loire [*House and Garden*, March 1963].

**China Clay Country, the** A name for the area around St Austell, Cornwall, England, where china clay is produced. The spectacular white spoil heaps have earned the region the nickname "the Cornish Alps."

> Of all the world's industrial landscapes, this is one of the most beautiful and weird [Hadfield 1981, p. 296].

**Chinatown** A number of large cities have a neighborhood of this name where a Chinese community has settled. One of the best known is on the Lower East Side of Manhattan, New York City, USA, which has the largest Asian community in North America, and there are other Chinatowns in Flushing, Queens, and Sunset Park, Brooklyn. Equally well known is the Chinatown in San Francisco, California, centered on Grant Avenue, while the Chinatown in Boston, Massachusetts, is the third largest in the nation, after San Francisco and New York.

London, England, had a notorious Chinatown in Limehouse, in the **East End**, but today the Chinese community is based in Soho, in the **West End**. There is also a small Chinese community of the name in Amsterdam, Netherlands. Toronto, Canada, has a large Chinatown right in the center of town, and there is a small Chinatown in Ottawa, the Canadian capital. Victoria, British Columbia, has Canada's first Chinatown, now much smaller than in its 1860s heyday. A historic district of Moscow, Russia, near the Kremlin, is called *Kitay-gorod*, as if from Russian *Kitay*, "China," and *gorod*, "town," but the name probably derives from *kita*, a term for a bundle of rods used in building fortifications.

(1) (San Francisco) For filth and wretchedness you must go to Chinatown by night [*Chambers's Journal*, January 19, 1889].

(2) (San Francisco) And oh, that pan-fried chow mein flavoured air that blew into my room from Chinatown, vying with the spaghetti sauces of North Beach, the soft-shell crab of Fisherman's Wharf [Jack Kerouac, *On the Road*, 1957].

(2) (London) Limehouse, "Chinatown" with its secret societies and "opium dens" [Malcolm Bradbury, ed., *The Atlas of Literature*, 1996].

(3) (London) Gerrard Street is the main thoroughfare of Chinatown, focus of London's Chinese community since the 1960s [*Time Out London Guide*, 1997].

(4) (New York) On the surface, Chinatown is prosperous — a "model slum," some have called it — with the lowest crime rate, highest employment, and least juvenile delinquency of any city district [*The Rough Guide to New York City*, 2004].

**Chippitts** The occasional name for the northern industrial region of the USA derives from the names of *Chi*cago and *Pitts*burgh, two cities within it. *Cp.* **Bosnywash**; **Sansan**.

**Chops of the Channel, the** A name for the entrance to the English Channel from the western (Atlantic) end, "chops" meaning "jaws." The Channel gradually narrows from this point. The name is sometimes wrongly (but understandably) taken to refer to the choppy water here. *Cp.* **Western Approaches**.

A squadron of 13 French men of warr sailed from Brest ... to lye in the chops of the Channell [Narcissus Luttrell, *A Brief Historical Relation of State Affairs*, 1692].

**Cinque Ports, the** A collective historical name, from Old French *cink porz*, "five ports," for the five English ports of Dover, Hastings, Hythe, Romney, and Sandwich, in the counties of Kent and Sussex, which in medieval times were granted special privileges by the crown in their defense of the English Channel. Other ports, many of them minor, were added later.

**City of the Blue Mountains, the** A collective name for the towns and villages along the Great Western Highway on a ridge of the Blue Mountains west of Sydney, Australia.

The romantically dubbed "City of the Blue Mountains" [*The Rough Guide to Australia*, 2001].

**Cleckheckmondsedge** A contrived portmanteau name for the former conurbation of *Cleck*heaton, *Heckmond*wike, and Liver*sedge*, south of Bradford, Yorkshire, England.

**Clubland** The **West End** district of London, England, centering on St. James's Street and Pall Mall, has been noted for its high-class shops and gentlemen's clubs since the 18th century. Hence the nickname.

(1) [The club] has developed into its most completely-organized form in London, where, especially in the vicinity of St. James's (colloquially called 'clubland'), are to be found the most perfect types of it [*Oxford English Dictionary*, 1884–1933].

(2) Clubland proper is still and will remain pretty much what it was in the days of Major Pendennis [of W.M. Thackeray's novel *Pendennis* (1848)] [*Pall Mall Gazette*, October 4, 1886].

(3) SET [i.e. selective employment tax] and rising land values in Central London are choking clubland like unwelcome smoke from a cheap cigar [*The Guardian*, April 22, 1970].

**Clydeforth** A name created by the Scottish town planner and educator Sir Patrick Geddes (1854–1932) for the conurbation in central Scotland between the Clyde and Forth rivers.

**Coast, the** The name can apply to any specific coastal district, such as the Coromandel Coast in India, the Pacific coast of North America, the West Coast of Africa, and the West Coast region of South Island, New Zealand. In an American context it usually refers to the **West Coast**.

(1) (India) This term [i.e. "the Coast"] in books of the 18th century means the 'Madras or Coromandel Coast,' and often 'the Madras Presidency' [Henry Yule and A.C. Burnell, *Hobson-Jobson: The Anglo-Indian Dictionary*, 1886].

(2) (Africa) We English when we talk about "the Coast" mean only the Gold Coast, whereas it actually includes Gambia, Sierra Leone and Nigeria [Princess Marie Louise, *Letters from the Gold Coast*, 1926].

(3) (USA) I like the Coast because it comprises California, Oregon, Washington and the contiguous States [*Publishers' Weekly*, February 8, 1930].

(4) (USA) Eyes bent on Frisco and the Coast, we came into El Paso as it got dark [Jack Kerouac, *On the Road*, 1957].

(5) (New Zealand) The West Coast (or simply the Coast) is firmly part of the South Island, yet in affection it belongs to all of New Zealand [Shadbolt, p. 226].

**Cocaine Country** A name for the Chaparé region of Bolivia, northeast of Cochabamba, where cocaine is cultivated for the illegal international market.

**Cocktail Isles, the** A humorous collective name for the three small Scottish islands Eigg, Rum, and Muck, in the Inner Hebrides.

(1) Eigg, Rum and Muck, facetiously known as "The Cocktail Isles" [*Holiday Haunts 1962: Scotland*].

(2) Known as the 'Cocktail Isles,' these three neighbouring islands have widely differing characters [Christopher Somerville, *Coast: A Celebration of Britain's Coastal Heritage*, 2005].

**Coleville** *see* **Albertopolis**

**Colonies, the** A former term for the British colonies, from those that in the 18th century became the United States to those that in the 19th century became constituent members of the British Empire, such as Australia and New Zealand.

Wave upon wave of Scots, Irish, Welsh, Manxmen and Channel Islanders left their homelands and headed for 'The Colonies' [Newton, p. 64].

**Combat Zone, the** A sobriquet for the section of downtown Boston, Massachusetts, USA, long notorious for its prostitutes and latterly for its many forms of adult entertainment, such as strip joints, topless dance palaces, pornographic bookstores, massage parlors, and the like. The name sprang from the presence of the military in the area during World War II.

As many of the strip joints closed down, and as some of the saloons went out of business, the Combat Zone became a center for pornographic bookstores, where people of all ages could be found browsing at all hours of the day or night [Thomas H. O'Connor, *Boston A to Z*, 2000].

**Constable Country** The alliterative name is that of one of the best-known English "countries." It describes the area on the Essex-Suffolk border, and especially the eastern part of Dedham Vale, where the painter John Constable (1776–1837) lived and worked. Quotes (3) and (4) below tell the same story from slightly different angles, while quote (5) reports a disturbing development in the picturesque region.

(1) Since the days of Constable, artists have loved "the Constable country" [E.S. Symes, *The Story of the East Country*, n.d. (*c*. 1910)].

(2) I guess the quintessence of pastoral tranquillity is to be found, in the riparian sense, in Constable Country [Maurice Wiggin in Hadfield 1981, p. 75].

(3) Late in life he [i.e. Constable] was on a coach journey from London when one of his travelling companions used the phrase 'Constable country,' a name which has ever since been used to describe the villages which the artist painted so many times [Hadfield 1981, p. 383].

(4) The story goes that Constable once had the flattering experience of being informed by total strangers on a coach journey through Suffolk: "This is Constable Country" [*Times Literary Supplement*, July 22, 2005].

(5) The tranquillity of East Anglia's "Constable country" was destroyed when flight patterns were changed to accommodate a huge expansion of Stansted airport [*The Times*, December 15, 2005].

**Cook Country** *see* **Captain Cook Country**

**Corn Belt, the** The name is used for the east central United States, a region of major corn production.

(1) Crop reports from the West still continue favorable, though there are some discouraging accounts of the prospects in the "corn belt" [*The Nation* (New York), July 13, 1882].

(2) West of the Appalachians, the fertile Interior Plains became the nation's breadbasket, divided roughly into the northern 'corn belt' and the southern 'cotton belt' [*Lonely Planet USA*, 2004].

**Corner Country, the** An Australian name for the region where the borders of New South Wales, Queensland, and South Australia meet.

In the extreme north-west corner, where the border fences of three states meet — the 'Corner Country' they call it [George Farwell, *A Traveller's Tracks*, 1949].

**Cornish Alps** *see* **China Clay Country**

**Cornish Riviera, the** A touristic name for the south coast of Cornwall, England, especially the shoreline of Mounts Bay. The name is attributed to the Great Western Railway, who in 1904 first ran a new train, soon to be called the Cornish Riviera Express, from London to Falmouth and Penzance, both coastal resorts in Cornwall. *Cp.* **English Riviera**.

(1) 'The Riviera Express' is the title chosen by Mr. J.C. Inglis, the General Manager of the Great Western Railway, as the most apposite name for the Plymouth-Paddington non-stop express [*Railway Magazine*, September 1904].

(2) Falmouth. The Gem of the Cornish Riviera [Ad, *Holiday Haunts 1961: Area No. 4, West of England and South and Central Wales*].

**Costa Alegre** The section of Pacific coast in western Mexico between Puerto Vallarta and Manzanillo has a Spanish name meaning "bright coast."

**Costa Bela** The stretch of south-facing Atlantic coast west of Setúbal in southwestern Portugal has a Portuguese name meaning "beautiful coast."

**Costa Blanca** The section of Mediterranean coast in southeastern Spain between the **Costa del Azahar** and **Costa Cálida** has a Spanish name meaning "white coast," referring to the white sands here.

Moraira is a charming fishing village and considered the jewel of the Costa Blanca [Property ad, *The Times*, November 25, 2005].

**Costa Brava** The section of Mediterranean coast in northeastern Spain between the French border and Barcelona has a Spanish name meaning "wild coast," referring to the rugged seaboard here. *Cp.* **Wild Coast.**

(1) The Costa Brava ... is also known as 'The Gateway to Spain' [*Sunday Telegraph*, July 10, 1994].
(2) The Costa Brava ... ranks with the Costa Blanca and Costa del Sol as one of Spain's three great holiday *costas* [*Lonely Planet Spain*, 2003].
(3) The Costa Brava was the first stretch of the Mediterranean to embrace mass tourism, and, boy, does it show [*Sunday Times*, June 26, 2005].

**Costa Cálida** The section of Mediterranean coast in southeastern Spain southwest of Cartagena has a Spanish name meaning "hot coast," for the generally warm climate here.

**Costa da Morte** *see* **Costa de la Muerte**

**Costa da Prata** The section of Atlantic coast north of Lisbon in western Portugal has a Portuguese name meaning "silver coast," referring to its white sands, which contrast with the golden sands of the **Costa Dourada** further south.

North of Lisbon, Portugal's silver coast — so named for its pristine white beaches facing the Atlantic — is looking to golf to turn its real estate gold [*Sunday Times*, November 6, 2005].

**Costa de la Luz** The section of Atlantic coast in southwestern Spain between the **Costa del Sol** and the Portuguese border has a Spanish name meaning "coast of light," referring to its sparkling sea and the silvery-white sand of its beaches.

**Costa de la Muerte** The section of rocky coast centering on Cape Finisterre in northwestern Spain has a Spanish name meaning "coast of death" for the many ships and lives lost here. A new twist to the name was given by the major ecological disaster here in 2002, when the oil tanker *Prestige* sank west of Vigo, seriously damaging the local fishing villages, shellfish beds, and large seabird population. The region is also known by its Portuguese equivalent name, *Costa da Morte.*

For the Romans this was the edge of the world, for the Celts a place of legend, and for the sailors buffeted by the Atlantic waves a place to fear. Hundreds of shipwrecks litter the seabed, a testimony to the dangers of the rocks hidden beneath the waves and the origins of the name of the region [*The Rough Guide to Spain*, 2004].

**Costa del Azahar** The section of Mediterranean coast in northeastern Spain, between the

Costa Blanca and Costa Dorada, has a Spanish name meaning "orange-blossom coast," referring to the broad expanse of orange groves on the plain here.

**Costa del Bálsamo** The section of Pacific coast in southwestern El Salvador between Acajutla and La Libertad has a Spanish name meaning "balsam coast," for the Peruvian Balsam (*Myloxyron pereirae*) here, a tree that yields balsam as a medicinal resin.

**Costa del Coco** A name for the east coast of the Dominican Republic, where the beaches are lined with coconut trees.

**Costa del Concrete** A punningly derogatory name for the resort region of southern Spain, and especially the **Costa del Sol**, as a coastline blighted by entrepreneurial overdevelopment.

Property agents and developers on the Costa del Concrete ... have been searching for "the new Marbella" because prices in southern Spain have slumped [*Sunday Times*, December 11, 2005].

**Costa del Crime** A facetious alternate name for the Spanish **Costa del Sol**, a region serving as a bolthole for British criminals, who can luxuriate in their ill-gotten gains here while remaining immune from extradition laws.

(1) Life goes on as before for the wanted men on the 40-mile Mediterranean coastal strip from Malaga to Marbella, which has been dubbed the "Costa del Crime" [*Daily Telegraph*, November 30, 1984].
(2) Jack Took ... said he expected that Harry Harris was at that very moment living it up on the Costa del Criminal [*sic*] with Miss Eddon Gurney [Fay Weldon, *The Heart of the Country*, 1987].
(3) The sunny "Costa del Crime" also attracted retired CID officers [*The Independent*, May 15, 1990].

**Costa del Golf** An alternate humorous name for the **Costa del Sol**, a region where there are many golf courses, with over 40 alone between Málaga and Gibraltar.

[Property developers] Sotogrande ... has form for this kind of thing, going back to the very dawn of the transmogrification of the Costa del Sol into the Costa del Golf [*Sunday Times*, October 9, 2005].

**Costa del Sloane** A punning name for the area in and around the seaside resort and surf site of Polzeath, Cornwall, England, so dubbed because popular among the young well-to-do. (The so-called "Sloanes," or "Sloane Rangers," were originally upper-class young women who lived around Sloane Square, London and weekended at fashionable country locations. Their name blends "Sloane" and "Lone Ranger"). *See also* **Chelsea-on-Sea** in Dictionary.

Hundreds of expensively educated teenagers made life hell this summer for residents of Polzeath, on what's become known as Cornwall's "Costa del Sloane" [*The Times*, September 12, 2005].

**Costa del Sludge** *see* **Costa del Sol**

**Costa del Sol** The section of Mediterranean coast east of Gibraltar in southern Spain has a Spanish name meaning "sunny coast." The name is touristic, as described in quote (2) below, although the region is in fact no sunnier than anywhere else on the Spanish coast. A jaundiced variant is "Costa del Sludge," referring to local pollution. *See also* **Costa del Golf**.

(1) This is the Costa del Sol, variously known as the Coca Cola Coast and the Costa Mierda, for which a genteel translation would be the Coast of Dung [Kenneth Tynan, "The Rising Costa del Sol," *Tynan Right and Left*, 1967].

(2) The Costa del Sol was launched as a 1950s development drive for impoverished Andalucía and has succeeded admirably on that score [*Lonely Planet Spain*, 2003].

**Costa Dorada** The section of Mediterranean coast in northeastern Spain, between the **Costa del Azahar** and **Costa Brava**, has a Spanish name meaning "golden coast," referring to the golden sands of the beaches here. (The quote below has the Catalan form of the name.) *Cp.* **Costa Dourada**.

The Costa Daurada offers miles and miles of beaches to delight the whole family [Travel ad, *The Times*, November 12, 2005].

**Costa do Sol** The section of Atlantic coast southwest of Lisbon, Portugal, has a Portuguese name meaning "sunny coast." *Cp.* **Costa del Sol**.

**Costa Dourada** The section of Atlantic coast in southwestern Portugal, between Setúbal and the Sagres, has a Portuguese name meaning "golden coast," for its golden sands. *Cp.* **Costa Dorada**.

**Costa Geriatrica** A humorous pseudo-Spanish name dating from the 1970s for the south coast of England, especially the region around resorts such as Bournemouth, Dorset, and Eastbourne, East Sussex, long noted for their large residential population of retired and elderly people. The name, based on well-known Spanish resort areas such as the **Costa Brava** or **Costa del Sol**, may also be applied to coastal districts elsewhere, as in quote (4) below.

(1) This chilling scene, filmed by a concealed police camera in a British nursing home in East Sussex's costa geriatrica, is the dramatic heart of ... a powerful, candid documentary [*Time*, September 5, 1977].

(2) Affectionately derided for decades as the "Costa Geriatrica," even by the geriatric residents themselves, the Dorset resort [of Bournemouth] must now have more nightclubs than Manhattan [*The Times*, July 29, 1999].

(3) [Eastbourne's] reputation for retired middle-class pensioners waiting for God by the sea has earned it the moniker 'Costa Geriatrica' [Charlie Godfrey-Faussett, *Footprint England*, 2004].

(4) East of Louth [in Lincolnshire], the sea lies about 10 miles away across acres of reclaimed farmland and marshes, lined with the 'costa geriatrica' of the east coast [Charlie Godfrey-Faussett, *Footprint England*, 2004].

(5) Once the undisputed capital of Britain's Costa Geriatrica, Eastbourne is now being rejuvenated by young housebuyers from London and Brighton [*Sunday Times*, October 9, 2005].

**Costa Plástica** A wry Spanish nickname for the region around Almería in southern Spain, where acres of land are covered in plastic sheeting for forced vegetable cultivation.

**Costas, the** A colloquial collective for coastal regions with a name beginning *Costa*, typically in Spain, like those listed above and below. All such names are usually preceded by "the" in English.

Once away from the holiday *costas*, you could be only in Spain [*Lonely Planet Spain*, 2003].

**Costa Smeralda** The stretch of Mediterranean coast in northeastern Sardinia, between the bays of Arzachena and Cugnana, has an Italian name meaning "emerald coast," referring to the bright green color of land and sea here.

Since the Aga Khan bought and developed a stunningly beautiful stretch of coastline on the north east of Sardinia in the 1960s, the Costa Smeralda has been a well-known haunt for the rich and famous [*The Times*, June 3, 2005].

**Costa Verde** There are two coastlines of this name. The section of Atlantic coast in northern Spain, on the Bay of Biscay between Gijón and Bilbao, has a Spanish name meaning "green coast," for its general verdure. The section of Atlantic coast in southeastern Brazil between Rio de Janeiro and Parati has a Portuguese name also meaning "green coast," referring either to the emerald-green sea here, or to the verdure of the rainforest below the Serra do Mar, or to the combined effect of both.

**Côte d'Azur** The "azure coast" of southeastern France, better known to English speakers as the French Riviera, is the stretch of Mediterranean coastline between Cannes and Menton or Cannes and La Spezia, Italy. The name comes from a book on the Riviera by Stephen Liégeard, *La Côte d'Azur* (1887), the color being that of the sea and sky. This is the most familiar of France's coastal names. (*See also* **Telecom Valley**.) Others, with names similarly referring to color or character (and usually preceded by "the" in English), are as follows:

The *Côte d'Albâtre*, "alabaster coast," between

Le Havre and Dieppe; *Côte d'Amour*, "coast of love," on the Atlantic seaboard around La Baule; *Côte d'Argent*, "silver coast," on the Bay of Biscay between the Gironde and the Spanish border; *Côte de Beauté*, "coast of beauty," from La Rochelle to the Gironde on the Bay of Biscay; *Côte d'Émeraude*, "emerald coast," in the region of Dinard and Saint-Malo (*cp*. **Costa Smeralda**); *Côte de Grâce*, "coast of grace," between Trouville-sur-Mer and Honfleur along the southern shore of the Seine estuary (the reference is to the port of Le Havre, originally *Havre-de-Grâce*); *Côte de Granit Rose*, "coast of pink granite," along the coast of northern Brittany; *Côte de Jade*, "jade coast," around the estuary of the Loire; *Côte de Nacre*, "pearl coast," to the west of Le Havre; *Côte d'Opale*, "opal coast," from the mouth of the Somme to the Belgian frontier; *Côte Fleurie*, "flowery coast," between Honfleur and Cabourg; *Côte Lumineuse*, "shining coast," along the Atlantic coast north of La Rochelle; *Côte Sauvage*, "wild coast," along the Atlantic coast of the Quiberon Peninsula (*cp*. **Wild Coast**); *Côte Vermeille*, "vermilion coast," from Collioure to the Spanish border.

**Cotton Belt, the** A name for the former agricultural region of the southeastern USA, where cotton was the main cash crop throughout the 19th century and for much of the 20th. Cotton is still grown here, but it is not the dominant crop.

**Country, the** In England, everywhere outside London, which is **Town** (see in Dictionary).

(1) In the Country, the Gentleman ... vndoeth the Farmer. In London, the Vsurer snatcheth vp the Gentleman [Thomas Nashe, *Christs Teares over Jerusalem*, 1598].

(2) [Southerners] talk about 'the country' ... And while this implies that they're not in London it doesn't usually mean they're in the real countryside, like the Fens or Snowdonia. No, it means they're at their second home a few miles up the motorway in Oxfordshire or Gloucestershire [Judith Holder, *It's Grim Up North*, 2005].

**Cow Country, the** An alternate nickname for the American **Midwest**, famous for its cattle.

**Crimean Riviera, the** The name is used for the resort region centering on Yalta on the south coast of the Crimea, Ukraine. In the Soviet era it was known as the Soviet Riviera.

**Crystal Coast, the** A touristic name for the towns, islands, and other features that make up the southern Outer Banks in North Carolina, USA.

**Cubitopolis** The name was applied in the 19th century to the area of London, England, centered on Pimlico, created by the builder and developer Thomas Cubitt (1788–1855). The name may also imply a pun on "cubit" as a measure of length associated with buildings.

Cubitopolis, an appellation originally given by Londoners to the Warwick and Eccleston Square districts. From the name of the builders [*The Slang Dictionary*, 1894].

**Cuchulainn Country** The name is applied to the southern part of Co. Louth, Ireland, the setting for the legends about Cuchulainn, one of the greatest heroes of Irish mythology, who battled against the invading armies of Queen Maeve.

**Dales, the** If unqualified, the name invariably denotes the Yorkshire Dales, England, a scenic area of North Yorkshire that is now also a national park. As steep-sided valleys among the Pennine Hills, "the dales" are individually named for their rivers, as Airedale, Swaledale, Wensleydale. In a sense, the Dales of northern England correspond to the **Valleys** of South Wales.

Local delicacies are everyone's favourites: lamb from the Dales, honey, cheeses, distinctive beers and authentic Yorkshire Puddings [*Enjoy England Holiday Planner 2005*].

**Dead Heart, the** The name for the central arid region of Australia between Lake Eyre and the Simpson Desert was coined by J.W. Gregory in his book *The Dead Heart of Australia* (1906). It was further popularized by C.T. Madigan in *Crossing the Dead Heart* (1946), an account of the first crossing of the Simpson Desert in 1939. *See also* **Centre**.

**Debatable Land, the** The historical name applied to the region between the Esk and Sark rivers on the border of England and Scotland that was claimed by both countries before the union of 1603. *See also* **Disputed Lands**.

(1) And as we cross'd the Bateable Land,
  When to the English side we held ["Kinmont Willie," *The Oxford Book of Ballads*, 1910].

(2) They used to call this part of the world the "debatable land," and back in the days when England v Scotland meant a lot more than a rugby match, there was no more lawless a spot in either kingdom [*Sunday Times*, April 17, 2005].

**Deep South, the** The southeasternmost part of the USA so known is usually regarded as including Alabama, Georgia, Louisiana, Mississippi, North and South Carolina, and all or part of adjacent states. The name first came into prominence in the 1920s. *Cp*. **South**.

(1) He had thought himself right out of the illusions common to the Deep South [Rebecca West, *The Thinking Reed*, 1938].

(2) The US Deep South, home of rednecks, Scarlett O'Hara and the Ku Klux Klan [*The Times*, August 20, 2005].

**Devil's Triangle** *see* **Bermuda Triangle**

**Diamond Coast, the** A name for the south-west coast of Namibia, where many of the country's diamond mines are (or were) located.

[The cruise will explore] a rarely visited African coast, heading from Cape Town to Walvis Bay, Namibia, past the Diamond Coast [*Sunday Times*, September 18, 2005].

**Dickensland** A former promotional name for the area around the resort of Great Yarmouth, Norfolk, England, which was visited by Charles Dickens and which features in his novel *David Copperfield* (1850). A railway poster of 1914 advertising "restful holidays on quiet waters" shows a railroad running east through **Poppyland** and **Broadland** to Dickensland.

**Dinosaur Coast, the** A name for the stretch of North Sea coast in North Yorkshire, England, between Staithes, north of Whitby, to Filey Brigg, south of Scarborough, where dinosaur footprints have been discovered in the cliffs.

**Dinosaurland** A promotional name for northeastern Utah, USA, where one of the largest dinosaur fossil beds in North America was discovered in 1909. The site is now incorporated in the Dinosaur National Monument.

**Dismal Swamp, the** A local name for the dreary tracts of swampy land in southeastern Virginia and northeastern North Carolina, USA. The name may be extended to "the Great Dismal Swamp" or reduced to simply "the Dismal."

(1) In dark fens of the Dismal Swamp
The hunted Negro lay [H.W. Longfellow, *Poems on Slavery*, 1842].
(2) Along the coast it [i.e. North Carolina] is flat and swampy, one area being given the unattractive name of Dismal Swamp [Johnson, p. 183].

**Disputed Lands, the** A general name for the region of northwestern England centering on Carlisle that was formerly claimed by both England and Scotland. *Cp.* **Debatable Land**.

[Carlisle] is the centre of "the Disputed Lands," where Scots and English fought vicious and bloody battles to establish their footholds [Travel brochure, *Hidden Treasures of Cumbria*, 2005].

**Dixie** or **Dixieland** A nickname for the states of the southeastern USA, especially those which comprised the Confederacy. The origin of the name is disputed. According to some, it refers to Jeremiah Dixon, who with Charles Mason laid down the Mason-Dixon Line as the border between Pennsylvania and Maryland. Others relate it to one Dixie, the owner of land in Manhattan Island, where the name is said to have originally applied at a time when slavery existed in New York. Black slaves then emigrated to the South and took the name with them. Wheeler

(p. 101) quotes the following from a correspondent of the *New Orleans Delta*:

I do not wish to spoil a pretty illusion, but the real truth is, that Dixie is an indigenous Northern negro refrain. It is as common to the writer as the lamp-posts in New York city seventy or seventy-five years ago. It was one of the every-day allusions of boys at that time in all their out-door sports. And no one ever heard of Dixie's land being other than Manhattan Island until recently, when it has been erroneously supposed to refer to the South from its connection with a pathetic negro allegory.

**Docklands** The name covers the extensive business and residential district that arose from the 1980s on the site formerly occupied by the port of London, England, extending for around 6 miles along the banks of the Thames River to the east of the city's center. It has its own distinctive character (and its own light railway) and is essentially a "city within a city."

(1) A new transport system for Docklands was first conceived in the 1960s [*Travelling Light*, guide published by Docklands Light Railway, 1987].
(2) Most people, even most Londoners, have yet to grasp the scale of Docklands, and the speed with which it changed from a crowded, vibrant port ... to a most exciting new city [Carrie Seagrave, *The New London Property Guide*, 2003].

**Down Along** An English dialect term for the **West Country**.

Their faces lighted up at the old pass-word of 'Down-Along'; for whosoever knows Down-Along, and the speech thereof, is at once a friend and a brother [Charles Kingsley, *At Last, A Christmas in the West Indies*, 1871].

**Down East** The name applies both generally to the eastern seacoast districts of New England, USA, and more specifically to the state of Maine. "Down" is said to apply to the downwind course formerly followed by sailing ships here. Quote (1) below relates to Dennis, Massachusetts. *See also* **East Coast**.

(1) "Where the deuce is Dennis?" "Oh, down east" [*Massachusetts Spy*, November 25, 1829].
(2) *Down East*, a general term for Maine and the Maritime Provinces of Canada [Joanna C. Colcord, *Sea Language Comes Ashore*, 1945].
(3) If you want a glimpse of this lost American world, you have to head north. Way north, in fact, to a corner that is referred to throughout the state [of Maine] as Down East [*Sunday Times Travel Magazine*, January 2006].

**Down South** A general term for the southern states of the USA (*see* **South**), or more specifically for a passage there down the Mississippi.

"Taking her down south?" said the man. Haley nodded and smoked on [Harriet Beecher Stowe, *Uncle Tom's Cabin*, 1852].

**Downtown** A general term denoting the more central part of a town or city, especially as a business or commercial district, contrasting with the residential area of **Uptown**. In Los Angeles, Downtown is a discrete neighborhood southeast of Hollywood.

(1) The second ward of the city of New York ... is what is called a down-town ward, a business ward [*Congressional Record*, January 28, 1891].

(2) New Orleans' downtown is the old quarter north of Canal Street [Rudolph P. Blesh, *Shining Trumpets: A History of Jazz*, 1946].

(3) Few LA neighborhoods have as much to offer per square mile as Downtown [*Lonely Planet USA*, 2004].

**Drumlin Belt, the** The name is given to the region of drumlins (small rounded hills) that lie along the southern boundary of Northern Ireland and that essentially mark the border with the Republic of Ireland.

The counties of Louth, Monaghan and Cavan occupy the central part of the 'Drumlin Belt' [*RD Ireland*, p. 69].

**Dukeries, the** The northern part of Sherwood Forest, Nottinghamshire, England, is so known, as comprising the ducal estates of Welbeck, Worksop, Clumber, and Thoresby.

(1) The Dukeries still exist, but they are little more than a geographical expression. Welbeck Abbey is the last of those palaces for which this part of England was formerly famous [*The Standard*, December 8, 1879].

(2) We had supposed the "Dukeries" ... would be fascinating, but alas, they were closed to the public [Ruth McKenney and Richard Bransten, *Here's England*, 1955].

(3) The charm and individuality of Nottinghamshire are in Sherwood Forest and the Dukeries. Neither are what they were [Phil Drabble in Hadfield 1981, p. 592].

**Dumbo** or **DUMBO** An acronymic nickname for the waterfront region of Brooklyn, New York City, USA, located *D*own *U*nder the *M*anhattan-*B*rooklyn Bridge *O*verpass.

An artsy neighborhood known — in typical New York fashion (think SoHo and TriBeCa) — as DUMBO [*The Rough Guide to New York City*, 2004].

**Dust Bowl, the** The designation applied to the section of the Great Plains of the USA that extended over southeastern Colorado, southwestern Kansas (*see* **Dustbowl State** in Dictionary), the panhandles of Texas and Oklahoma, and northeastern New Mexico. The area's grasslands suffered a severe drought in the 1930s and the exposed topsoil was carried off by strong winds, resulting in dust storms. The region had largely recovered by the 1940s. The name is said to have originated in a story written by Associated Press reporter Robert Geiger in April 1935.

**East, the** A general term for the eastern states of the USA, and especially those of New England. There is usually an implied contrast with the **West**.

It was beginning to look like the soft sweet East again; the great dry West was accomplished and done [Jack Kerouac, *On the Road*, 1957].

**East Coast, the** The Atlantic coast of the United States, especially that of the New England states, regarded as relatively conservative by comparison with the enterprising **West Coast**. *See also* **Down East**.

You'll probably be keen to hear that we also fly to that quaint, East Coast backwater they call New York City [American Airlines ad, *The Times*, November 7, 2005].

**East Country, the** A name occasionally used for the eastern part of England, and especially East Anglia (the counties of Norfolk and Suffolk). *Cp.* **West Country**.

The counties with which this book is concerned — Norfolk, Suffolk, and Essex, Hertfordshire and Huntingdonshire, and the fenland shires of Bedford, Cambridge, and Lincoln — are almost destitute of mineral treasures [E.S. Symes, *The Story of the East Country*, n.d. (*c*.1910)].

**East End, the** A name for that part of London, England, to the east of the City of London. It has no clear boundaries but historically connotes the capital's working-class district, the "real" London and home of Cockneys (*see* **Cockneyshire** in Dictionary). Its contrast with the **West End** was formerly as marked as that between work and play. *See also* **E1** in Dictionary.

**Eastern States, the** A general name for the rest of Australia from the point of view of those inhabiting the state of Western Australia.

**East Side, the** A name for the district of New York City that lies on the east side of Manhattan, to the east of Fifth Avenue. It is conventionally divided into the (northern) Upper East Side and (southern) Lower East Side, the latter noted for its large immigrant population. *Cp.* **West Side**.

(1) The original 'Bowery Girl' ... passed at a quick gait peculiar to herself along the Bowery, or through Chatham square — it was the perfection of East Side poetry [James D. MacCabe, *New York by Sunlight and Gaslight*, 1882].

(2) He was born to Italian parents, who brought him in infancy to New York, where he had the usual East Side immigrant upbringing [*Times Literary Supplement*, October 11, 1957].

(3) The high-rise elegance of Park Avenue and the Upper East Side rapidly gives way to the teeming streets of Harlem to the north and to the crowded bohemian existence of the Lower East Side and Greenwich Village to the south [*Britannica*, vol. 24, p. 906].

**E-Boat Alley** A nickname given in World War II to the North Sea convoy route taken by German E-boats (motor torpedo-boats) off the coast of Norfolk and Suffolk, England.

**Edge of the World, the** The name has come to be applied to the remoter Scottish islands. It was the title of a classic 1937 movie set on Foula, westernmost of the Shetland Islands, and was adopted by Charles McLean as the title of his 1977 history of St Kilda, westernmost of the Outer Hebrides, *Island on the Edge of the World*.

The St Kilda bookshop ... has stood as a testament to the extraordinary fascination of this romantic and windswept archipelago at the Edge of the World [Ben Macintyre in *The Times*, August 20, 2005].

**Elie, the** The name is used for the combined resorts of Elie, Fife, Scotland, on the Firth of Forth, and neighboring Earlsferry. The two places were officially united in 1929.

'The Elie' is now a most popular holiday resort, with fine sands and other pleasant attractions [Macnie/McLaren, p. 254].

**Emmerdale Country** A touristic name for the region around the village of Esholt, West Yorkshire, England, where the popular TV drama *Emmerdale* (originally *Emmerdale Farm*) was filmed from 1972 (originally in Arncliffe, North Yorkshire) to the 1990s, when a lookalike film set was used to relieve the village from tourist congestion.

**Empty North, the** A name for the northernmost part of Australia as a sparsely populated region. For the reference in quote (1) below, *see* **White Australia** in Dictionary.

(1) The empty North and the White Australia ideal [Gilbert White, *Thirty Years in Tropical Australia*, 1918].

(2) The trouble is, that taxpayers 'Down South' are not interested in developing our 'Empty North' [Frank Clune, *Roaming around Australia*, 1947].

**English Lakes, the** A former name for the **Lake District**, the national epithet distinguishing these lakes from those in Scotland, Wales, or Ireland. *See also* **Lakes**.

*A Complete Guide to the English Lakes* [Harriet Martineau, book title, 1855].

**English Riviera, the** The coast of Tor Bay, Devon, England, is so nicknamed as a region that to some extent resembles the French Riviera (*see* **Côte d'Azur**). Both are fashionable resort areas and both can boast warm weather. The name was already current in the 1920s, and earlier was extended to the **Cornish Riviera** to the west and the Dorset coast to the east.

(1) Lyme Regis, Dorset. Hotel Alexandra ... The only hotel in its own grounds in the English Riviera [Hotel ad, *Bradshaw's Railway Guide*, April 1910].

(2) 'Why not Cornwall?' said Sam. 'The Riviera of England!' [P.G. Wodehouse, *The Girl on the Boat*, 1922].

(3) Old railway posters used to promote Penzance and the sweep of shore around Mount's Bay [in Cornwall] as the English Riviera [Robinson/Millward, p. 256].

(4) The sheltered east-facing coastline ... has long been dubbed the 'English Riviera.' Although finding any similarities to the Cote d'Azur can test the imagination [Charlie Godfrey-Faussett, *Footprint England*, 2004].

(5) Agatha [Christie] ... was born and spent much of her life on the English Riviera — as Torbay, Torquay, Paignton and Brixham are known [*The Times*, April 30, 2005].

(6) If you want reliable summer heat, then the best place to go is the southwest, in the shelter of Dartmoor — it's not called the English Riviera for nothing [Judith Holder, *It's Grim Up North*, 2005].

**Far East, the** A general term for the countries of eastern and southeastern Asia, including China, Indonesia, Japan, Korea (North and South), Malaysia, the Philippines, and Vietnam. The name contrasts with that of the former **Near East**.

The great conflict which for many months bathed the Far East in blood weakened Russia in Europe [*Quarterly Review*, July 1911].

**Farm Belt, the** The name is that given to the north central region of the United States devoted to commercial farming. In many ways the region coincides with the **Midwest**.

Capitol Hill sources say that a White House meeting with Farm Belt congressmen and state legislators last week turned into something of a donnybrook [*Newsweek*, March 2, 1981].

**Far West, the** A name for the part of the USA to the west of the Mississippi River, or more generally, to the west of the Great Plains, otherwise the region to the west of the **Midwest**.

**Faulkner Country** A name for the region centered on New Albany, Mississippi, USA, birthplace of the novelist William Faulkner (1897–1962).

**Fens** or **Fenlands** or **Fen Country, the** The name is that of the low-lying area in eastern England to the west and south of the Wash, mainly in Cambridgeshire, Norfolk, and Lincolnshire. The area has no specific boundaries and its former watery terrain has altered since the 17th century when much of the marshland was reclaimed and made suitable for farming. Even so, individual named fens remain, such as Deeping Fen and Wicken Fen, the latter a nature reserve, and the region southeast of Peterborough is actually below sea level. The name is formal in that of Fenland, an administrative area in northern Cambridgeshire.

(1) [In spring] the east wind sweeps unopposed across the open plain of the Fenlands, with nothing to break its force or temper its keenness [E.S. Symes, *The Story of the East Country*, n.d. (*c.* 1910)].

(2) When the rain comes down in the Fen Country the broad slow rivers soon overflow their banks [E.S. Symes, *The Story of the East Country*, n.d. (*c.* 1910)].

(3) To live in the Fens is to receive strong doses of reality. The great, flat melancholy of reality; the wide empty space of reality [Graham Swift, *Waterland*, 1983].

(4) Cruise the tranquil waterways of The Fens and enjoy far-reaching views to distant horizons under wide-open skies [*Enjoy England Holiday Planner 2005*].

**Fertile Crescent, the** A name for the region of fertile land, suitable for agriculture and stock-breeding, that extends in an arc from the Mediterranean to the Persian Gulf, or as more precisely defined in quote (1) below. The term, popularized by US historian and Egyptologist James Henry Breasted in his *Outlines of European History* (1914), written with James Harvey Robinson, is sometimes extended to include the Nile valley.

(1) The Crescent stretches from Palestine on the Mediterranean coast up to Syria and eastern Turkey, then down the valleys of the Tigris and Euphrates rivers through modern-day Iraq [*Reader's Digest Illustrated History of the World: The Dawn of Civilisation*, 2004].

(2) From the oldest permanent footprint in the "Fertile Crescent" to the expected urban population in excess of seven billion in 2030, the journey ... is fascinating [Philippe Petit, review of Joel Kotkin, *The City: A Global History*, *The Times*, June 18, 2005].

**Fifty-Three** The latitude 53° north, on which lie the cities of Stoke-on-Trent, England, and Bremen, Germany. It was formerly regarded as hazardous to venture further north than this.

But there's never a law of God or man runs north of Fifty-Three [Rudyard Kipling, "The Rhyme of the Three Sealers," 1896].

**Fitzrovia** The name was adopted before or during World War II for what was regarded at the time as a "Bohemian" area of London, England, centering on Fitzroy Square. It was associated with impoverished writers and artists and with craftsmen such as furniture makers.

(1) After leaving school he emigrated into what he calls Fitzrovia — a world of outsiders, down-and-outs, drunks, sensualists, homosexuals and eccentrics [*Times Literary Supplement*, January 10, 1958].

(2) That pub-crawling area of London that

Tambi [i.e. Ceylonese editor and poet J.M. Tambimuttu] called Fitzrovia, from Fitzroy Square and, more important, the Fitzroy Tavern [*The Guardian*, February 3, 1971].

(3) Fitzrovia ... is an area ignored by most Londoners and tourists, sporting a name that appears on few maps [Ed Glinert, *A Literary Guide to London*, 2000].

(4) There is a push from some people to rebrand Fitzrovia as 'Noho'—North of Soho—but locals reckon Fitzrovia is good enough [Carrie Segrave, *The New London Property Guide*, 2003].

**Five Counties, the** A synonym for East Anglia, England, which in the strict geographical sense means Norfolk and Suffolk but in the wider sense comprises these two counties plus Cambridgeshire, Essex, and Hertfordshire.

**Flatlands, the** A name given to the flat country of East Anglia, England, i.e. the counties of Norfolk and Suffolk, where marsh and forest dominated until relatively recent times.

**Florida's Crown** A nickname for the northernmost part of the Florida peninsula, USA. The name evokes a "floral crown," or garland of flowers.

**Forster Country** A touristic name for the region around the town of Stevenage, Hertfordshire, England, where the writer E.M. Forster (1879–1970) spent his childhood years. His novel *Howards End* (1910) is based on his boyhood home of Rooks Nest House there.

(1) There is special interest in this countryside because part of it is Rooks Nest Farm [*sic*], the Forster Country of *Howards End* [*The Guardian*, October 19, 1960).

(2) Small is beautiful. Never have these words been more apt than when applied to the Forster Country of North Hertfordshire, which adjoins Rooks Nest, childhood home of the writer E.M. Forster [Margaret Ashby, *Forster Country*, 1991].

**Four Seas, the** A composite name for the waters that wash the British Isles, identified individually as the North Sea, Irish Sea, Atlantic Ocean, and English Channel.

He ... was the safest confidant to be found within the four seas [Eliza Lynn Linton, *Paston Carew*, 1886].

**Fourth World** *see* **Third World**
**French Riviera** *see* **Côte d'Azur**
**Frostbelt** *see* **Snowbelt**

**Frozen North, the** A conventionally humorous nickname for the **North** of England, where the climate is generally colder than in the **South**. See also quote at **North**.

When they [i.e. the southerners] gloat about how much better their weather is, then this really gets us mad. 'How's the frozen north?' they say [Judith Holder, *It's Grim Up North*, 2005].

**Garden of Scotland, the** An occasional name

for the fertile valley of northeastern Scotland in which the town of Elgin lies, a short distance inland from the Moray Firth seaboard.

**Garden Route, the** A name for the scenic coastal belt in southern South Africa traversed by the main road and rail route between Cape Town and Port Elizabeth, especially the section between Swellendam and Humansdorp. Quote (2) below mentions a possible alternate origin.

(1) I came into Cape Town through the Garden Route, ... which by rail, as well as by road, has always proved an attractive and absorbing path across the southern peak of Africa [Iris Vaughan, *Last of the Sunlit Years*, 1969].

(2) Named thus because of the beautiful scenery incorporating majestic mountains, indigenous forests, lakes, rivers and mountain passes. It has also been suggested ... that the name is derived from the surname *Gardiner*, an entrepreneur, engineer or railway official during the early stages of the New Cape Central Railway Company [P.E. Raper, *A Dictionary of Southern African Place Names*, 1989].

**Garment District, the** A name for the section of Manhattan, New York City, USA, that became the nation's leading center of garment production. It arose in the late 19th century and was initially concentrated on the Lower East Side. Although for a time it subsequently moved north and west it essentially remained in place a century later.

On Wall Street double-breasted suits and peaked lapels were considered a bit sharp, a bit too Garment District [Tom Wolfe, *The Bonfire of the Vanities*, 1987].

**Gates of Hell, the** A former nickname for the entrance to Macquarie Harbour on the west coast of Tasmania, Australia, in the days when the area was used as a penal colony for Van Dieman's Land (as Tasmania was then known).

**Gin-and-Jag Belt, the** A nickname for the area to the west and south of London corresponding to the **Stockbroker Belt**, whose wealthy residents stock gin for their cocktails and run an expensive Jaguar car. The name is also used of similar regions elsewhere, such as Cheshire.

(1) The 'gin-and-Jag' rebels [Headline, *Sunday Telegraph*, March 16, 1969].

(2) Cheshire is all about conspicuous consumption. The undisputed capital, in short, of the "gin and Jag" culture [*Sunday Times* (Northwest England Supplement), September 11, 2005].

**Glens, the** A colloquial or romantic term for the stream and river valleys of the Scottish **Highlands**, whether on the mainland or on the nearer islands, such as Skye.

If [model] Kate Moss can look divine at Glastonbury, surely I could bring some glam to the Glens? [*The Times*, August 20, 2005].

**Glitter Gulch** The name was gained by the block of buildings around the intersection of Fremont Street and Main Street in downtown Las Vegas, USA, a location formally known as the Casino Center. "Glitter" refers to the neon lights (originally lighted marquee signs) of the casinos themselves, while "gulch" implies the equivalent of a ravine with a deposit of gold.

**Gold Coast, the** The name has been applied to various stretches of sandy coast, especially when seen as fashionable, such as the shore of Lake Michigan north of central Chicago, Illinois, USA, where a number of wealthy and socially prominent people live. Another Gold Coast or **Tropi-Coast** runs between Miami and West Palm Beach in southeast Florida, USA.

(1) (Illinois) Lake Shore Drive north of the Loop emerged as the mainline for society—the Gold Coast, it was soon nicknamed [*Britannica*, vol. 16, p. 7].

(2) (Florida) If you are serious about your tennis, consider the Boca Raton Resort & Club, on the Gold Coast in Palm Beach county [*Sunday Times*, November 27, 2005].

**Golden Mile, the** A name for the rich gold-bearing reef that forms the basis of the Kalgoorlie goldfield in Western Australia. *See also* **Golden Mile** in Appendix 2, p. 307.

(1) 'That'll see you pretty well to the Mile.' 'The Mile?' 'Kalgoorlie. They call it the Golden Mile' [William Hatfield, *Buffalo Jim*, 1938].

**Golden Triangle, the** The name is well known for the area at the meeting point of Myanmar (Burma), Laos, and Thailand, where opium poppies are grown. It is also used for any area of high productivity, social superiority, historic importance, or other distinction, such as the industrial zone extending from England's Midlands to Italy's Gulf of Genoa, or the region between Jaipur, Agra, and Delhi, India, or the wealthy residential district centering on Wilmslow, Cheshire, England, or the commercial heart of Beverly Hills, Los Angeles, California, USA, between Wilshire Boulevard, Santa Monica Boulevard, and Rexford Drive, or the sector of Pittsburgh, Pennsylvania, USA, west of Crosstown Boulevard, or the petrochemical and industrial complex linking Beaumont, Port Arthur, and Orange, Texas, USA, or the business, shopping, and entertainment district of Kuala Lumpur, Malaysia, extending north from its base along Jalan Imbi to its apex at the Petronas Towers.

(1) (Asia) Both the opium and the morphine base almost certainly originated in the so-called "golden triangle" where the opium poppy grows in abundance [*Bangkok Post*, April 22, 1973].

(2) (Kuala Lumpur) Most luxury hotels are found in the Golden Triangle commercial district [*Lonely Planet Malaysia, Singapore & Brunei*, 1999].

(3) (Cheshire) Cheshire's so-called Golden Triangle owes its existence not to mindless materialists but to its better weather and the beautiful countryside unblemished by the industrial revolution [*Sunday Times*, October 31, 1999].

(4) (Los Angeles) The commercial heart of Beverly Hills beats within the so-called Golden Triangle [*Lonely Planet USA*, 2004].

(5) (Pittsburgh) The mystical-sounding Golden Triangle, between the converging Monongahela and Allegheny rivers, is Pittsburgh's downtown [*Lonely Planet USA*, 2004].

(6) (India) The Golden Triangle packs some of the country's most enduring icons and rich experiences into a (relatively) small space and time ... There's Delhi for the Raj, Agra for the Taj [Mahal], and Jaipur for forts, festivals and all the romance of Rajasthan [*Sunday Times*, September 25, 2005].

**Golden Vale** or **Vein, the** Generally taken to refer to the richness of the agricultural land in a wide valley extending through the Irish counties of Tipperary and Limerick, the name in fact derives from the village of Golden here, its own name being an English form of an Irish original meaning "the little fork." The alternate name Golden Vein refers to the rivers that run through the region.

(1) If you stand on the Rock of Cashel, amid the ruins of fifteen centuries of history, you will see around you the most fertile stretch of land in the world, the famous Golden Vale of Tipperary [Tourist brochure, 1939].

(2) "Is it in good heart?" I asked Fanning, the tall tavernkeeper who had in his veins Cromwellian blood, that is the blood of the sour, jar-nosed humbug's troopers who settled in the Golden Vein [Oliver St John Gogarty, *It Isn't This Time of Year At All*, 1954].

(3) This area of green fields, gentle hills, wooded valleys and meandering streams and rivers is known as the Golden Vale [*RD Ireland*, p. 100].

**Golden Vein, the** *see* **Golden Vale**

**Golden West, the** A romantic name for the American **West** as a land of promise and riches, especially gold. The name became familiar from Puccini's 1910 opera *The Girl of the Golden West* (Italian, *La Fanciulla del West*), based on David Belasco's 1905 cowboy melodrama of the same title.

(1) The West had become America's destiny, and "plotting the Golden West" became one of the chief tasks of Americans as they travelled and recorded what lay on or beyond the familiar limits of the wide continent [Malcolm Bradbury, ed., *The Atlas of Literature*, 1996].

(2) Famous names and legendary sights are brought to life on this classic tour of America's

'Golden West' [Travel brochure issued with *The Times*, August 20, 2005].

**Goldsmith's Country** A touristically oriented designation of **Poet's Country** for the area around Lough Ree, Co. Roscommon, Ireland, associated with the youth of the poet and dramatist Oliver Goldsmith (1728–1774).

Most of the buildings associated with Goldsmith have either been replaced or demolished, yet the pretty countryside is evocative of the world which he describes. Road signs in the area indicate the sites of 'Goldsmith Country' [Brian Lalor, *Blue Guide Ireland*, 2004].

**Golf Coast, the** A nickname, punning on **Gulf Coast** or **Gold Coast**, for the coast of the Firth of Clyde, Scotland, southwest of Glasgow, where there are many golf courses. There is also a Golf Coast in Lancashire, England, centering on Lytham St Annes, and another at Southport, near Liverpool, with 27 local courses. *See also* **Royal Troon** in Dictionary.

(1) (Scotland) There are so many golf-courses on the seaside that it's known as the Golf Coast [Jack House in Speaight, p. 352].

(2) (England) Breathe in the sea air on England's Golf Coast [Tourist brochure *Waterside England*, 2005].

(3) (England) Infused in tradition and steeped in golfing distinction, Lytham St Annes is the undisputed Golf Coast [Tourist brochure, *Lytham, St Annes-on-Sea and the Fylde Countryside*, 2005].

**Grain Coast, the** The section of the coast in Liberia, West Africa, between Cape Palmas and the Sierra Leone border, was formerly so known from the local trade in grains of paradise (*Aframomum melegueta*), used as spices and in medicine.

**Granadaland** A name for the area around Manchester, England, served by Granada Television and regarded as brash and affluent.

[The county of Cheshire] is home to Granadaland's rich, famous and garish [*The Times*, June 19, 1999].

**Great Divide, the** A touristic name for the region of South Wales between the rural landscape of the Brecon Beacons and the former industrial **Valleys**. The name is adopted from the **Great Divide** (see in Dictionary) that is the Rocky Mountains.

To be inspired by nature, follow the map west and north, across the Great Divide [Simon Calder in *A View of Wales*, Spring/Summer 2005].

**Great North, the** A name for the northernmost part of Australia. *Cp.* **Empty North**.

The Great North would be so invaluable to the rest of the world that it would be permanently protected from predators [Robert Duffield, *Rogue Bull*, 1979].

**Greenback Belt, the** A nickname for the area

of the Chiltern Hills north of Henley-on-Thames, Oxfordshire, England, where wealthy London commuters have their homes in picturesque villages, as described in the quote below. English banknotes were at one time known as greenbacks, like their American equivalent. *Cp.* **Stockbroker Belt.**

> It's also the greenback belt — the expensive and closely guarded northwestern homeland of the high-salaried London commuter [Charlie Godfrey-Faussett, *Footprint England*, 2004].

**Green Country, the** A name for the well-wooded region of northeastern Oklahoma, USA, centering on the city of Tulsa.

> Seen from the highways, Tulsa's downtown pops out of a sea of oaks that give the area its 'Green Country' nickname [*Lonely Planet USA*, 2004].

**Gulf Coast, the** A short name for the southeast coast of the United States, bordering the Gulf of Mexico. *See also* **Gulf** in Dictionary.

> The Gulf Coast is nothing like the rest of Mississippi and it never has been [*Lonely Planet USA*, 2004].

**Gulf Country, the** A general name for the hinterland of the Gulf of Carpentaria, northeastern Australia.

> When I came to the Gulf Country to take up work ... I was to become a permanent 'Gulfite' [*North Australia Monthly*, December 1963].

**Hampshire Highlands, the** A name for the hilly, eastern region of the English county.

> Basingstoke ... is surrounded by the fine country that has been called the "Hampshire Highlands" [*Holiday Guide 1952: Area No. 5, South & South East England*].

**Hamptons, the** A collective name for the resort villages at the eastern end of Long Island, New York, USA, many of which have "Hampton" in their name, as Bridgehampton, East Hampton, Southampton, and Westhampton, among others. *See also* **Hollywood East.**

> (1) "Oh, Patrick, let's go away this summer," she says wistfully. "Let's go to Edgartown or the Hamptons" [Bret Easton Ellis, *American Psycho*, 1991].
> (2) It's true what people say: the Hamptons really is a paradise for the rich and famous [*Sunday Times*, September 4, 2005].

**Hardy Country** A touristic name for the area of southern England associated with the novels of Thomas Hardy (1840–1928), born at Higher Bockhampton, Dorset. Many of the places appear under fictionalized names, as Anglebury for Wareham, Casterbridge for Dorchester, Port Bredy for Bridport, Shaston for Shaftesbury, all towns in Dorset. Much of the region is in the territory of the historic kingdom of **Wessex**. The name was current in the writer's own lifetime.

> (1) Dorsetshire, the centre of the "Hardy Country," the home of the Wessex Novels, is a land literally flowing with milk and honey [Charles G. Harper, *The Hardy Country*, 1904].
> (2) Immediately opposite the church is one of those snug little Dorset cottages which seem to belong to an age other than our own ... This is, of course, all 'Hardy Country' [Hogg, p. 313].

**Heartbeat Country** A touristic name for the region around the village of Goathland, North Yorkshire, England, scene of the filming of the popular TV drama *Heartbeat* (from 1992), about a former London policeman turned village bobby and his doctor wife.

> (1) There's Heartbeat Country, where you can take a trip ... to the village of Goathland, better known as Aidensfield [Travel guide, *Yorkshire*, 2005].
> (2) [The hotel is] a good base for exploring the smart market town of Pickering, the North York Moors and "*Heartbeat* Country" (not to be confused with nearby "Captain Cook Country" or "Catherine Cookson Country") [*The Times*, November 12, 2005].

**Heartland, the** A term adopted by the English geographer Sir Halford Mackinder for interior Asia and eastern Europe. He saw this region as the strategic center of the "World Island" following the relative decline of sea power as against land power and the economic and industrial development of southern Siberia. He introduced his concept in a 1904 lecture to the Royal Geographical Society, London, entitled "The Geographical Pivot of History." The name is also used as a synonym for the American **Midwest.**

> Taken together, the regions of Arctic and Continental drainage measure nearly a half of Asia and a quarter of Europe ... Let us call this great region the Heartland of the Continent [H.J. Mackinder, *Democratic Ideals and Reality*, 1919].

**Heart of Kent, the** The region of the county of Kent, England, southeast of Tunbridge Wells has been so named by the local tourist board.

**Heart of Texas, the** The region of south central Texas centering on Austin, as described in quote (2) below.

> (1) "Deep in the Heart of Texas" [June Hershey, song title, 1941].
> (2) Here you'll find Austin, the state's capital and music scene epicenter; San Antonio, home of the Alamo; and the Hill Country ... Perhaps you've heard of the Heart of Texas? Well, here it is [*Lonely Planet USA*, 2004].

**Heavenly Trio, the** A nickname for the resorts of Clacton-on-Sea, Frinton-on-Sea, and Walton-on-the-Naze, each differing in character, which run up the coast of Essex, England.

> Essex's neighbouring 'Heavenly Trio': Clacton-on-Sea, the epitome of a ... day-tripper's paradise; Frinton, a byword for genteel exclusivity; and

Walton, the old-fashioned family resort [Christopher Somerville, *Coast: A Celebration of Britain's Coastal Heritage*, 2005].

**Hell's Corner** A World War II name for the triangle of Kent, England, centering on Dover, as the recipient of German bombardment from across the English Channel and the scene of fierce air combat during the Battle of Britain. *Cp.* **Bomb Alley.**

**Hell's Hundred Acres** A 19th-century nickname for **SoHo**, New York City, referring to the slums and sweatshops here.

> SoHo became a seamy industrial and red-light area — cheerfully known as Hell's Hundred Acres [*The Rough Guide to New York City*, 2004].

**Hell's Kitchen** The name was given to a notorious slum area on the West Side of Manhattan, New York City, USA, bounded by 59th Street to the north, 8th Avenue to the east, 42nd Street to the south, and the Hudson River to the west. From 1959 the district was known as Clinton. A possible origin of the name is considered in quote (2) below. *See* **Forty-Deuce** in Appendix 2, p. 307, for one of the names mentioned in quote (1).

> (1) The small circle of Midtown New York surrounding rhe Port Authority Bus Terminal for a radius of half a dozen blocks goes by many names. Tour guides call it the Crossroads of the World. The hookers who work it know it as the stroll. Pimps call it the fast track. Three-card monte players speak of Forty-Deuce. Maps show the neighborhood as Clinton. But to the stagestruck and starstruck it is still Broadway, to tourists it is Times Square, to the old people and derelicts who live off discards from the teeming Ninth Avenue food stalls of Paddy's Market it is more aptly Hell's Kitchen, and to the New York City Police, Vice Squad, and Mayor's Special Task Force on Crime it is simply the Midtown Enforcement Area [Alix Kates Shulman, *On the Stroll*, 1981].
>
> (2) Hell's Kitchen was rumored to be named for a tenement at 54th Street and Tenth Avenue. More commonly, the name has been attributed to a veteran policeman who went by the sobriquet, Dutch Fred the Cop. In response to his young partner's comment ... that the place was hell, Fred reportedly replied, "Hell's a mild climate. This is Hell's kitchen" [*The Rough Guide to New York City*, 2004].
>
> (3) [A French investor] is negotiating for up to six apartments in the new Orion condominium development on 42nd Street ... This is the once notorious "Hell's Kitchen" district [*The Times*, August 5, 2005].

**Herriot Country** A touristic name for the region of North Yorkshire, England, where the veterinary surgeon and writer James Herriot (real name James Alfred Wight) (1916–1995) lived and

worked and where his stories are set. (Askrigg was his fictional town of Darrowby.) As indicated in quote (1) below, the name was largely generated by the popular BBC TV series based on Herriot's books, *All Creatures Great and Small* (1978–90), filmed in the area.

> (1) American tour companies were arranging 'Herriot Country' trips around Askrigg [Hilary Kingsley and Geoff Tibballs, *Box of Delights*, 1989].
>
> (2) There are many attractions in Herriot Country suitable for all the family [Tourist brochure *Herriot Country 2005*].
>
> (3) There's Herriot Country, Emmerdale Country and Brontë Country [Tourist guide, *Yorkshire*, 2005].

**Hielands, the** A Scots form of the name of the **Highlands**, pronounced "Heelants."

> (1) Hie upon Hielands
> And laigh [i.e. low] upon Tay,
> Bonny George Campbell
> Rade out on a day ["Bonny George Campbell," *The Oxford Book of Ballads*, 1910].
>
> (2) Speak weel o' the Hielands, but dwell in the Laigh [i.e. Lowland] [Scottish proverb, quoted in Yapp, p. 408].

**Highlands, the** A general name for the northern part of Scotland, where the terrain is markedly more mountainous than in the **Lowlands** to the south. It has no precise boundary, but is usually said to lie north of a line from Dumbarton on the Firth of Clyde in the west to Stonehaven in the east. It thus approximates to the present administrative region known as Highland. The Highlands are traditionally regarded as the "real" Scotland, and are associated with such well-known Scottish distinctives as Highland dress and Highland games. The name can have official status, as for the Scottish parliamentary region of Highlands and Islands.

> (2) Farewell to the Highlands, farewell to the North,
> The birth-place of valour, the country of worth;
> Wherever I wander, wherever I rove,
> The hills of the Highlands for ever I love [Robert Burns, "My Heart's in the Highlands," 1790].
>
> (2) The Highlands are very reasonably higher than the Lowlands. They are wilder and more inaccessible and heatherier and more haunted by men in kilts. They are really Better and More Romantic, although a persevering number of authors such as Sir Walter Scott and Andrew Lang and John Buchan have fair danged away at the Lowlands trying to bolster them up [Theodora Benson and Betty Askwith, *Muddling Through, or Britain in a Nutshell*, 1936].

**Hollywood East** A nickname for the **Hamptons**, from their many vacationing celebrities, including movie stars. The name contrasts with the regular name of West Hollywood (*see* **WeHo** in Dictionary).

**Home Counties.** The name traditionally designates the counties of southeastern England closest to London, i.e. Surrey, Kent, Essex, and (formerly) Middlesex, although it may also encompass more remote counties, such as Berkshire, Buckinghamshire, and Hertfordshire. They are so called because the gentry had their homes there, close to London. The name can have a disparaging "bourgeois" connotation, as in quote (3) below. *Cp.* **Southeast.**

> (1) The phrase "Home Counties" may give but a vague impression to many, like that still more mysterious expression "The Shires" [S.P.B. Mais, *The Home Counties*, 1942].
>
>  (2) Seventy years ago, the words 'Home Counties' conveyed a picture of undulating countryside, leafy lanes, cheerful cottages,and well-kept big houses ... Today they are more often thought of as mere obstacles which tiresomely separate the city dweller from countrysides farther away [Michael Robbins in Speaight, p. 129].
>
>  (3) "You are so smug! You are so self-satisfied! You, you are so ... so HOME COUNTIES!" she spat [*Sunday Times*, August 1, 2004].

**Hookers' Beat, the** A name for the region of New York City, USA, worked by prostitutes. In the 1960s, it was a clearly defined area of Times Square between 34th and 42nd streets, but subsequently expanded to other parts of the city.

**Housman Country** A touristic name for parts of the English county of Shropshire, the setting of many of the poems of A.E. Housman (1859–1936). Housman was not born in Shropshire, and lived long in London, but he is buried in Ludlow, in the south of the county.

> [Shropshire is] Housman country, of course: the country of A.E. Housman's *The Shropshire Lad* and *Last Poems* [Hogg, p. 144].

**Imperial Triangle, the** A partly historic, partly touristic name for the eastern region of China between the imperial cities of Beijing and Xian and the seaport city of Shanghai.

**Island Coast, the** A colloquial name for the coast of extreme southwest Florida, USA, where there are many islands. *Cp.* **Mangrove Coast.**

**Isolationist Belt, the** A name sometimes used for the American **Midwest**, a region where it is generally felt that the USA should pursue a policy of isolationism.

**Italian Riviera, the** A general name for the coastal region of northwestern Italy, traditionally divided into the *Riviera di Ponente* ("western shore"), west of Genoa, and the *Riviera di Levante* ("eastern shore"), east of Genoa. The name was applied to this riviera (an Italian word) before it was adopted for the French Riviera (*see* **Côte d'Azur**).

**Jago, the** A former name for a district of the **East End**, London, England, lying between Shoreditch and Bethnal Green. It first gained prominence from the title of Arthur Morrison's novel *A Child of the Jago* (1896), set in the area. The origin of the name itself is uncertain.

> She also worked in the East End for a short time, in the district well (or ill) known as the Jago [William Scott Palmer and A.M. Haggard, *Michael Fairless: Her Life and Writings*, 1913].

**Junction, the** The name is used for the area of south London, England, around Clapham Junction railroad station. The local name became more widely known from the title of the BBC TV play *Up the Junction* (1965), as described in the quote below.

> *Up the Junction* focuses on three ... girls who live and work in Battersea and have their fun by heading up the Junction (Clapham Junction) [Jeff Evans, *The Penguin TV Companion*, 2d ed., 2003].

**Jurassic Coast, the** A touristic name for the coast of Lyme Bay in southern England, where important prehistoric remains have been found, mainly in the form of fossils dating from the geological Jurassic period. The name came into prominence after 2001, when the Dorset and East Devon Coast, as it is formally known, was declared a world heritage site.

> (1) The Jurassic Coast ... is considered to be the only place in the world displaying unbroken evidence of 185 million years of evolution [BBC News, December 13, 2001].
>
>  (2) The Dorset and East Devon coast has become known as the 'Jurassic Coast,' a brilliant place to hunt for fossils [Christopher Somerville, *Coast: A Celebration of Britain's Coastal Heritage*, 2005].

**Kavanagh Country** A touristic name for the area around the village of Inniskeen, Co. Monaghan, Ireland, birthplace of the poet Patrick Kavanagh (1904–1967) and the source of much of his writing.

**Kelly Country, the** A name for northeastern Victoria, Australia, where the bushranger and folk hero Ned Kelly (1855–1880) had some of his more notorious brushes with the law.

> A gentleman ... had come through from Sydney, and stayed for a time to have a look at 'the Kelly country' [*The Argus* (Melbourne), November 2, 1880].

**Kilvert Country** A touristic name for the area around the village of Bredwardine, Herefordshire, England, where the diarist Francis Kilvert (1840–1879) was vicar in the final years of his life and where he is buried.

The Kilvert Society ... arranges local gatherings and expeditions and an annual commemorative service in a church of the 'Kilvert Country' [Dorothy Eagle and Hilary Carnell, *The Oxford Illustrated Literary Guide to Great Britain and Ireland*, 1987].

**King Country, the** A name for the central region of North Island, New Zealand, that was allotted to the Maoris under their king and that was thus true **Maoriland** (see in Dictionary). The first king was Te Wherowhero, who began his "reign" in 1858 under the name Potatau I. For the reference in quote (3) below, *see* **Land of the Long White Cloud** in Dictionary.

(1) *The King Country; Or, Explorations in New Zealand, A Narrative of 600 Miles of Travel through Maoriland* [J.H. Kerry-Nicholls, book title, 1884].
   (2) The King Country, or Rohe Potae, was originally a large tract of the western central North Island ... Europeans called the area 'the King Country' because it was here that Tawhiao sought refuge following the Maori Wars [*An Encyclopaedia of New Zealand*, 1966].
   (3) No two adjoining districts in New Zealand could contrast with each other in history and landscape more remarkably ... than Taranaki and the King Country. One name has its beginning in the first human occupation of Aotearoa, the other comes from the Maori-European conflict of the 19th century [Shadbolt, pp. 129–30].

**King Harry's Cornwall** A touristic name for the area of southern Cornwall, England, between the towns of St Austell and Falmouth. It is named for King Harry Passage, a reach of the Fal River south of Truro that is itself said to be named for a former chapel here dedicated to King Henry VI (1421–1471).

**Kite Country** An alliterative touristic name for the region of Mid Wales centering on the town of Rhayader, where the red kite can be spotted.

The rare red kite has made a comeback in the peaceful hills of central Wales. Learn more about this majestic bird of prey and see the kites at feeding time by visiting Kite Country [*A View of Wales*, Spring/Summer, 2005].

**Ladies' Mile, the** A former nickname for the fashionable shopping district in New York City, USA, extending from 14th to 23rd streets between 6th Avenue and Broadway.

**Lake District, the** A popular name for the scenic region of Cumbria, northwestern England, where the main 12 lakes are Bassenthwaite, Buttermere, Coniston Water, Derwentwater, Ennerdale Water, Grasmere, Haweswater, Rydal Water, Thirlmere, Ullswater, Wast Water, and Windermere. *See also* **Lakeland**.

**Lake District of Surrey, the** The name, based on that of England's well-known **Lake District**, was adopted promotionally for the attractive district around the Surrey lakes known as Frensham Great Pond and Frensham Little Pond.

The "Lake District" of Surrey is within 40 miles of London and easily reached by convenient Train Services [Southern Railway poster, 1924].

**Lakeland** An alternate name for the **Lake District**, now mainly found in adjectival use, as Lakeland scenery. Quote (1) below is by one of the three so-called Lake Poets, who had all lived in the Lake District. (The others were Wordsworth and Coleridge.)

(1) Those contests were carried on at a distance from our Lake-land [Robert Southey, *Sir Thomas More*, 1829].
   (2) Lakeland ... includes the largest English lake, Windermere, and the highest English mountain, Scafell Pike [Ruth McKenney and Richard Bransten, *Here's England*, 1955].
   (3) I always say there is no such thing as bad weather in Lakeland, only bad clothing [Hunter Davies, "A fine time in Lakeland," *Sunday Times*, September 19, 2004].

**Lakes, the** A name that when unqualified, at least in Britain, usually refers to the **Lake District**. *Cp.* **English Lakes**.

(1) 'We have not quite determined how far it shall carry us,' said Mr. Gardiner, 'but perhaps to the Lakes' [Jane Austen, *Pride and Prejudice*, 1813].
   (2) When I was at university, long years ago, to go and climb in the Lakes was a serious expedition [Sir Jack Longland in Hadfield 1981, p. 64].
   (3) Mass tourism and, more vitally, television mean that we [British] are as familiar with the Lakes, the Highlands, the Cotswolds, the Fens and the Cornish ports as we are with our own streets [*The Times*, June 20, 2005].

**Land o' Burns, the** A touristic name for southwestern Scotland, otherwise **Burns Country**. There may be an intended pun on "land o' burns," meaning "land of streams." The name appears on a railway poster of 1914 showing a picture of the poet.

**Land of Heart's Desire, the** An alternate name for **Yeats Country**, from the title of the poet's own verse drama, as in quote (1) below. *Cp.* **Land of Heart's Desire** in Dictionary.

(1) Land of Heart's Desire,
   Where beauty has no ebb, decay no flood,
   But joy is wisdom, Time an endless song [W.B. Yeats, *The Land of Heart's Desire*, 1894].
   (2) This [i.e. Co. Sligo] is a land whose images and mythology inspired Ireland's most famous poet, William Butler Yeats, for whom this was 'The Land of Heart's Desire' [*RD Ireland*, p. 268].

**Land of the Sword, the** An English rendering of the Muslim name for all non-Muslim countries, in Arabic *dar al-harb*, literally "territory of war," meaning all countries that have never signed a peace treaty with the Muslims following a war, as distinct from *dar as-sulh*, "territory of peace," meaning those countries that have signed such a treaty.

**Land of Windmills, the** A former nickname for the region of Essex, England, centering on the **Rodings**.

> North is the Roding country, as remote and bucolic as ever, though scarcely now to be described as "the land of windmills" [S.P.B. Mais, *The Home Counties*, 1942].

**Latin, le** A short name used by the French for the **Latin Quarter** of Paris. *Cp.* **Quartier**.

**Latin Quarter, the** The name, translating French *Quartier Latin*, is that of the left-bank region, south of the Seine, in Paris, France, associated since medieval times with the Sorbonne university and with the students who attend it (and who originally spoke Latin).

**Lawlands, the** A Scots form of the name of the **Lowlands**.

> Ye Highlands and ye Lawlands,
>   O where hae ye been? ["The Bonny Earl of Murray," *The Oxford Book of Ballads*, 1910].

**Left Coast, the** The name is sometimes applied to the coast of British Columbia, Canada, for the supposed left-wing leanings of its residents. More generally, it is used of the Pacific coast of North America, as being on the left (west) side of the country, as seen on a map.

**Leg of Italy, the** An occasional name for the peninsula of Italy south of the Lombardy plain, a region which on the map represents the "boot" that terminates in the **Heel of Italy** and **Toe of Italy** (see both in Dictionary).

> [The peninsula is] often described as being shaped like a person's leg, with the island of Sicily opposite the toe. Instead of a bone running down the "leg," there is a mountain range called the Apennines [Johnson, p. 135].

**Levant, the** The historical or literary name for the eastern shores of the Mediterranean, with their islands and neigboring countries, derives from French *levant*, "rising," referring to the rising of the sun in the east. The region covered is less extensive than that of the **Middle East** but more or less corresponds to the former **Near East**.

> (1) LEVANT, a name given to the east part of the Mediterranean sea, bounded by Natolia or the lesser Asia on the north, by Syria and Palestine on the east, by Egypt and Barca on the south, and by the island of Candia and the other part of the Mediterranean on the west [*Encyclopædia Britannica*, 1771].
>   (2) If crusades to the Levant were imperialistic,

they were expressing a form of imperialism very different from the 19th-century variety [Jonathan Riley-Smith, review of film *Kingdom of Heaven*, *The Times*, May 5, 2005].

**Little Dixie** A name for the southern part of Oklahoma, USA, where the lifestyle of the **Deep South** is still maintained. *See* **Dixie**.

**Little Italy** A name for the neighborhood of New York City, USA, bounded roughly by Canal Street, Spring Street, Mulberry Street, and Broadway, where Italian immigrants began to settle in the mid-19th century. *See also* **NoLita**.

**Little Switzerland** A name given to various hilly regions in England, such as that around the village of Selborne, Hampshire, or that surrounding the Devon resorts of Lynton and Lynmouth. The latter has high cliffs and roads similar to mountain passes. *See also* **Little Switzerland** in Dictionary.

**Little Venice** The name is used for any local region of canals and is particularly associated with the picturesque district of west central London, England, centering on the junction of the Regent's Canal with the Paddington Canal. It first became widely current only after World War II, although Robert Browning (who lived in Warwick Crescent here) and Lord Byron had earlier compared the locality to Venice.

> (1) 'Little Venice,' a title more complimentary than exact [Ivor Brown in Hadfield 1981, p. 85].
>   (2) The most coveted homes ... are those nearest to or overlooking the canal: truly a 'Little Venice' [Carrie Segrave, *The New London Property Guide*, 2003].

**LoDo** The acronym of "*Lo*wer *Do*wntown," as the area between Colfax Avenue and Broadway, Denver, Colorado, USA, that is noted for its restaurants and nightlife.

> Most other bars and nightspots are in LoDo [*Lonely Planet USA*, 2004].

**London's Country** A former promotional name for the **Home Counties**.

> This area ... is labelled by geographers The London Basin; writers of brochures often refer to it as London's Country [S.P.B. Mais, *The Home Counties*, 1942].

**Loop, the** The name for downtown Chicago dates from 1897, when a number of elevated lines were joined into an overhead loop of tracks that encircled an area of around 35 blocks.

> Within the Loop circumscribed by Chicago's rackety, elevated railway, the El [Dodd/Donald, p. 162].

**Lorna Doone Country** A literary sobriquet for Exmoor, England, an area of high moorland mainly in Somerset, or more precisely for that part of it described in quote (2) below, as the setting of R.D. Blackmore's best-known novel *Lorna Doone: A Romance of Exmoor* (1869). (One of the combes mentioned in the quote is now known as Doone Valley.)

(1) Exmoor, the "Lorna Doone" Country, reaches away to the shores of the Severn Sea [*Holiday Haunts 1961: Area No. 4, West of England and South and Central Wales*].

(2) There are some picturesque combes [on Exmoor] near the Bristol Channel coast, where the *Lorna Doone* country ... is situated [*Illustrated Road Book of England and Wales*, 1965].

**Low Countries, the** An English equivalent of *Nederland*, the Dutch name of the Netherlands, describing the "lower land" that prevails there. The name denotes a much wider area than that country alone and embraces Belgium and all (or part) of Luxembourg.

Immerse yourself in the cultural and horticultural splendours of the Low Countries on ... journeys through the waterways of the Netherlands and Belgium [Travel ad, *The Times*, September 24, 2005].

**Lowlands, the** A general name for the southern part of Scotland, which is noticeably less mountainous than the **Highlands** to the north. It is much more populous than the Highlands, and most of Scotland's industry is concentrated here.

**M4 Corridor, the** A name for the industrial development along the M4 motorway in Berkshire, England, west of London, where a number of computer-oriented companies became established from the 1970s. *Cp.* **Sunrise Strip**.

West of Reading, Newbury is the next major stop along the congested but prosperous 'M4 corridor' [Charlie Godfrey-Faussett, *Footprint England*, 2004].

**Magic Parallelogram, the** A journalistic nickname current during the so-called "Gilded Age" of the late 19th and early 20th centuries for the area of New York City between 14th and 59th streets and 3rd and 6th avenues, where many social events and functions took place.

**Mangrove Coast, the** A colloquial name for the coast of extreme southwestern Florida, USA, off the Everglades, where there are many mangroves. *See also* **Island Coast**.

**Marches, the** A general name (from a word related to "mark") for the region straddling the border between England and Wales. It is also known as the Welsh Marches or, formerly, the Marcher Country, from the Lords Marchers, who had jurisdiction over this territory.

(1) Breconshire is in the Marcher Country which saw so much fighting between Welsh and English in earlier centuries [*Holiday Haunts 1961: Area No. 4, West of England and South and Central Wales*].

(2) The Marches are squarely off the beaten track ... and in many places time and tourism seem to have passed by unnoticed [*Lonely Planet Great Britain*, 2005].

**Marsh, the** A local name for a region of Lincolnshire, England, not far from the coast, where there was once an extensive marsh. The names of the villages here preserve the reference, as Burgh le Marsh, Gayton-le-Marsh, Maltby le Marsh, and Marsh Chapel.

We traverse a strip of strange, un-English-looking country called in North Lincolnshire "the Marsh" [E.S. Symes, *The Story of the East Country*, n.d. (c. 1910)].

**Megacity, the** A nickname for the six municipalities of Toronto, Ontario, Canada, that combined in 1998 to form a single administrative entity. *See also* **Metro Toronto**.

The five cities surrounding and adjacent to ... Toronto proper amalgamated in 1998. This enlarged Toronto has been dubbed 'the Megacity' [*Lonely Planet Canada*, 2002].

**Megalopolis** The name, from Greek *megalo*, "great," and *polis*, "city," was adopted by the French geographer Jean Gottman for the corridor 600 miles (1,000 km) long between Boston, Massachusetts, USA, and Washington, DC, centered at New York City. In his *Megalopolis: The Urbanized Northeastern Seaboard of the United States* (1961), he defined the area as the "richest, best-educated, best-housed, and best-serviced" urbanized region in the world.

**Metroland** The name arose in the early 20th century for the area northwest of London, England, served by the Metropolitan Railway. It was popularized by *Metro-land*, a guidebook issued by the railway annually from 1925 to 1932, as in quote (1) below.

(1) Metro-land is a country with elastic borders which every visitor can draw for himself, as Stevenson drew his map of Treasure Island [*Metro-land*, 1932].

(2) The houses of Metroland and beechy Bucks dot the landscape [John Betjeman, *An Oxford University Chest*, 1938].

(3) The Metroland vision of Sir John Betjeman, with its 'leafy lanes in Pinner,' has spread throughout Britain [Greg Hadfield and Mark Skipworth, *Class*, 1994].

**Metro Toronto** A short name for Metropolitan Toronto, Ontario, Canada, as the administrative title of the central city and five surrounding municipalities. In 1997 the Toronto legislature voted to combine the six muncipalities into a **Megacity**.

This outstanding offer is good in Metro Toronto only [Ad, *Toronto Daily Star*, September 24, 1970].

**Mezzogiorno, the** A general name for the south of Italy, usually including Sicily and Sardinia. It means "midday," the time when the day is at its hottest in the region. *Cp.* **Midi**.

> An abundance of children characterized the villages and towns of the Mezzogiorno [Alan B. Mountjoy, *The Mezzogiorno*, 1973].

**Middle America** The central and western states of the USA, regarded as representing the typical American citizen, with his conservative views and mostly unadventurous way of life. (This use of the name should not be confused with Middle America as a geographical term for the region between the United States and South America which includes Central America, Mexico, and the West Indies.)

> (1) In the spring of 1949 ... I went to Denver, thinking of settling down there. I saw myself in Middle America, a patriarch [Jack Kerouac, *On the Road*, 1957].
> (2) To call Salina Middle America, however, would not be entirely accurate. "We have some pockets of intolerance," says Whitley Austin, editor of the Salina *Journal*, "but most of the people simply try to be fair" [*Time*, July 13, 1970].
> (3) Like most Californians, he was shocked to actually *see* these people from The Outback. Here was the cop-cream from Middle America [Hunter S. Thompson, *Fear and Loathing in Las Vegas*, 1971].
> (4) How is Joe Paycheck in Middle America supposed to think of himself? [*Harper's Magazine*, June 1998].

**Middle Britain** A more broadly representative equivalent of **Middle England**, and only geographical in the vaguest sense.

> "Middle Britain" is easy to make fun of, but it constitutes most of the nation [*The Times*, September 21, 1999].

**Middle East, the** A somewhat imprecise and unofficial term for the countries of southwestern Asia and northeastern Africa. At one time the term also included Afghanistan, India, Pakistan, and Myanmar (Burma). The name is now taken by many to refer to a region midway between Europe and Asia, the latter being the **Far East**. *See also* **Near East**.

**Middle England** A vaguely geographical term for the middle classes of England outside London and other big cities, regarded as representing a force for political and social conservatism. The designation was adopted from the **Middle America** of the USA.

> While Middle England is in vogue with politicians, research suggests that the traditional values it is seen as espousing may be under threat [*Sunday Times*, October 4, 1998].

**Middle West** *see* **Midwest**

**Midi, the** A general name for the south of France, meaning "midday" and referring to a region where midday is a time of extreme heat and inactivity. *Cp.* **Mezzogiorno**.

> I could not fail to flatter myself, on reaching La Rochelle, that I was already in the Midi [Henry James, *A Little Tour in France*, 1884].

**Midland, the** A term used for the central area of the United States, distinguished for its dialect of American English, and defined (in one source) as in quote (1) below.

> (1) Midland: a belt separating the North from the South and extending from the Atlantic to the Mississippi (including Long Island, New York City and the adjoining counties, New Jersey, Del., all but the northern strip of Penn., the upper prong of West Virginia, southern Ohio, middle Ind., middle Ill., and St. Louis county, Mo.) [*Dialect Notes*, 1896].
> (2) The transition area between the North and the Midland reflects partly the complicated history of the settlement [Hans Kurath, *Studies in Area Linguistics*, 1972].

**Midlands, the** A name used for the central region of England. It has no precise boundaries but is usually reckoned to contain the counties of Leicestershire, Lincolnshire, Northamptonshire, Oxfordshire, Rutland, Staffordshire, and Warwickshire. Its western part formed the historic county of West Midlands (1974–86). There has never been an officially demarcated East Midlands, although its territory mostly coincides with that of the **Shires**.

> (1) The Midlands are hideous enough; but compared to similar regions in the United States, they are comfortable and civilized [Ruth McKenney and Richard Bransten, *Here's England*, 1955].
> (2) Anyone looking to find the 'real' England ... would be hard pressed to name a better region to search than the Midlands [*Lonely Planet Great Britain*, 2005].

**Midtown** The name obviously refers to the central area of a town or city. In New York City the term generally applies to the mainly commercial district north of 34th Street to 59th Street, taking in Times Square, the Empire State Building, and the Broadway theater district.

> In the very middle of mid-town, just off (and even just on) Broadway, the whole street is sometimes used as an open-air loading bay and temporary warehouse [*The Listener*, January 31, 1963].

**Midwest** or **Middle West, the** The name for a region of indefinite boundaries in the north central USA. It is usually regarded as including the area around the Great Lakes and in the upper Mississippi Valley from Ohio on the east to North and South Dakota, Nebraska, and Kansas on the west. *Cp.* **Far West**.

> He was their man, the son and champion of that part of the country that is variously known as the

Midwest, the Heartland, the Farm Belt, the Isolationist Belt, and the Cow Country [Alistair Cooke, *Letter from America*, "The Colonel of the Plains," April 21, 1955 (2004)].

**Miracle Strip, the** A nickname for the upper northwestern coast of Florida, USA, familiar from the Miracle Strip amusement park (closed 2004) at Panama City Beach.

**Mist Belt, the** A name for certain areas in the eastern foothills of the Drakensberg mountains, South Africa, where vegetation is increased and agriculture enhanced by the mist and high humidity that supplement the rainfall.

**Muddle East, the** A British forces' World War II punning nickname for the **Middle East**.

**Municon Valley** An English (or American) nickname for the region around Munich, southern Germany, as a center of the microelectronics industry that developed here after World War II. The obvious analogy is with the USA's **Silicon Valley** (see in Dictionary).

**Museumland** The district of South Kensington, London, England, derives its nickname from the many important museums here, including the Victoria and Albert Museum, Science Museum, and Natural History Museum. *Cp.* **Albertopolis**.

> With the founding of "Museumland," the surrounding area was transformed overnight into one of the most fashionable in town [*The Rough Guide to London*, 1997].

**Nappy Valley** The residential district between Clapham Common and Wandsworth Common in south London, England, is so nicknamed as the home of many families with young children (who wear nappies, or diapers). There is an obvious pun on "Happy Valley."

> (1) [The area] properly called Northcote but now known as 'Between the Commons' (less kindly as Nappy Valley) [Carrie Segrave, *The New London Property Guide*, 2003].
> (2) The houses in "nappy valley" are still selling [*Sunday Times*, September 18, 2005].

**Narrow Seas, the** A dated name for the channels separating Britain from continental Europe and from Ireland, and thus mainly for the English Channel and Irish Sea respectively.

> (1) Warwick is chancellor and the Lord of Calais; Stern Faulconbridge commands the narrow seas [William Shakespeare, *Henry VI, Part 3*, 1595].
> (2) Therefore—to break the rest ye seek,
> The Narrow Seas to clear–
> Hark to the siren's whimpering shriek–
> The driven death is here! [Rudyard Kipling, "Destroyers," 1898].

**Nature's Venice** The name describes the region to the northeast of Kaliningrad, northwestern Russia, where there are many canals, the best-known being the one that links the river port of Polessk with the Neman River delta.

**Near East, the** The eastern end of the Mediterranean and the adjacent countries were known by this name until World War II, while the region covered by Iraq, Iran, and neighboring countries was known as the **Middle East**. During the war, the Royal Air Force created a "Middle East Command" which covered both areas, and this caused a gradual replacement of the name "Middle East" for "Near East." *See also* **Far East; Levant**.

> (1) Usually, the Near East refers to anywhere in the Levant, the Suez Canal and down the Red Sea to Aden [Johnson, p. 93].
> (2) I once waited all day in Court on the chance of being called to make a discouraging statement on the names Near, Middle, and Far East [Aurousseau, p. 69].
> (3) My father always used the term "Near East" until his death in the 1970s. And my wife was taught to use the same term in school in the 1950s [*The Times*, June 22, 2004].

**Needle Park** A name for the intersection of Amsterdam Avenue and Broadway, New York City, USA, where drug users gathered and injected themselves with hypodermic needles.

**Negroland** A rare and now redundant name for what an anonymous *Dictionary of Unusual Words* (1946) defines as "the part of the African continent which is inhabited by negroes."

> Africa south of the Sahara is by no means conterminous with negroland [*Times Literary Supplement*, February 26, 1931].

**Never Never, the** The vast area of northern Australia, imprecisely delimited but generally held to include northwestern Queensland and the Northern Territory, has a name of disputed origin. It may refer to a territory that one "never never" wishes to leave, having settled there, or by contrast one to which one "never never" wishes to return, having visited it. The source of the name in an Aboriginal phrase meaning "unoccupied land" is now generally rejected. Alternate forms of the name are "Never Never Land" and "Never Never Country." A film version of the novel cited in quote (3) below was released under the same title in 1981.

> (1) Queensland some day, and above all the "Never Never land"—as the colonists call all that portion of it which lies north or west of Cape Capricorn—will be among the greatest of England's dependencies [Archibald William Stirling, *The Never Never Land: A Ride in North Queensland*, 1884].
> (2) His father ... made him a present of the old horse and a new pair of blucher boots, and I gave him an old saddle and a coat, and he started for the Never-Never country [Henry Lawson, "Water

Them Geraniums," *Joe Wilson and His Mates*, 1901].

(3) *We of the Never-Never* [Jeannie Gunn, novel title, 1908].

(4) Mataranka ... is a small town, the capital of the tediously hyped "Never Never" country [*The Rough Guide to Australia*, 2001].

**NoHo** The name of the neighborhood in lower Manhattan, New York City, USA, stands for "*north* of *Ho*uston," referring to Houston Street, which bounds it to the south. *Cp.* **SoHo**.

(1) The Newport-New York Jazz Festival may be ... failing to tap the loyal audience that listens to the avant-garde in the lofts of SoHo and NoHo [*New York Times Magazine*, June 12, 1977].

(2) Emerge NYC, at 65 Bleecker Street in the chic NoHo neighbourhood, is the department store as reimagined by a bunch of small-scale fashion and jewellery designers [*The Times Magazine*, October 22, 2005].

**NoLita** A fashionable acronymic name for the district of New York City *no*rth of **Li**ttle I**ta**ly, famous for its expensive designer boutiques, coffeehouses, and cafés.

[The section is] referred to (by realtors and editors determined to label every block in the city) as NoLita [*The Rough Guide to New York City*, 2004].

**No Man's Land** The general name for a piece of unowned land is popularly associated with the territory between opposing lines on the Western Front in World War I where British and German troops met in a friendly exchange of gifts on Christmas Day 1914. The name was applied in medieval times to a plot of ground outside the north wall of London, England, that served as a place of execution. (A Latin record of 1320 tells how "*Quædam domina nomine Juliana ... fuit combusta apud Nonesmanneslond extra Londinius*," i.e. "A certain lady named Juliana ... was burned at No Man's Land outside London.")

Perilous work it is repairing wire in the No Man's Land between trenches [George Adam, *Behind the Scenes at the Front*, 1915].

**Norfolk Broads** *see* **Broads**

**North, the** A term for any northern region, such as (geographically) the **North Country** in England or (politically) Northern Ireland (*see* **North** in Dictionary). In the USA, the name is used for the free states north of the Mason-Dixon line, while more recently it has been applied to the economically and technically advanced countries of the world, which are mostly north of the equator. In Australia, the name is used for the **Great North**. The lines in quote (1) below, written in Edinburgh, relate to Scotland. In each case there is an implied contrast with the

South. *See also* **Up North**, and **Deep North** in Dictionary.

(1) (Scotland) And I forgot the clouded Forth, The gloom that saddens Heaven and Earth, The bitter east, the misty summer And grey metropolis of the North [Alfred, Lord Tennyson, "The Daisy," 1855].

(2) (England) Those of us who live here call it 'the North.' Those of you who live in the South insultingly call it 'the grim north' or 'the frozen north' [Judith Holder, *It's Grim Up North*, 2005].

**North Country, the** A general name for the northern part of England, more usually known as the north of England or simply the **North**. It always includes the historic counties of Lancashire, Yorkshire, Durham, Northumberland, and Cumberland (now absorbed into Cumbria), and sometimes takes in Cheshire, Derbyshire, and Nottinghamshire, or at least the northern parts of these. Its southern limit in the east of England is generally regarded as the Humber River. The name is common in adjectival use, as a North-Country accent or North-Country custom. The name is also used for the northern part of Britain, so equates to Scotland, and especially the **Highlands**, and less commonly for the northern portion of the USA, otherwise the **North**.

(1) (Scotland) Doun cam' the Laird o' Lamington Out frae the North Countrie ["Katharine Johnstone," *The Oxford Book of Ballads*, 1910].

(2) (England) 'I am a harper,' quoth Robin Hood, 'And the best in the north countrey' ["Robin Hood and Alan a Dale," *The Oxford Book of Ballads*, 1910].

(3) (England) You will leave this North Country more conscious, perhaps, of what went to its fashioning than will be the case in any other part of Britain save, may be, the softer limestone ... of the Cotswolds and the iron-hard granite of the West Country [Hogg, p. 91].

(4) (USA) [Born in Duluth, Minnesota, Bob] Dylan hit New York's Greenwich Village folk scene in early 1961 and never looked back, though a few songs do mention 'the North Country' [*Lonely Planet USA*, 2004].

**Northern Territories, the** A nickname for the **Highlands** of Scotland, perhaps based on a blend of Australia's Northern Territory and Canada's Northwestern Territories, with a hint of the old British colonial Northern Territories in West Africa. The name implies a cold, sparsely populated region where life is slow to change and where old values are maintained.

[I have] just returned from the Northern Territories, from a world that time forgot, where people still bake cakes and spontaneously take tea without texting each other beforehand [*The Times Magazine*, November 13, 2004].

**Northland, the** An alternate name for the **Great North** in Australia.

> Back to the great Northland, where he could bury himself in the bush, and forget [Arthur Wright, *The Squatter's Secret*, 1927].

**North of Watford** A sociocultural term denoting the part of England that lies to the north of the Hertfordshire town of Watford, itself on the northwestern edge of London. Anywhere in this region is regarded as relatively unsophisticated by comparison with the capital itself. The term is understood by some, as in quote (3) below, to refer not to the town of Watford but to the Watford Gap, a location on the M1 motorway near Daventry in Northamptonshire. (The "Gap" is the break in the hills here through which pass the motorway, the Roman road known as Watling Street, now followed by the modern A5 road, a railroad, and a canal.)

> (1) It used to matter whether you lived north or south of a line running between the Severn [River] and the Wash. Above the line — 'somewhere north of Watford' — you were the poor relations of those beneath it [Greg Hadfield and Mark Skipworth, *Class*, 1994].
> (2) City types who would not normally dream of venturing north of Watford were yesterday falling over each other in their scramble to join in the excitement and buy a little piece of Knutsford [*The Times*, November 4, 1999].
> (3) I think some people used to say north of Watford because for people living in London that was about as far north as they could reasonably visualize civilization extended to ... So the Watford Gap became the frontier for the wild north [TV actor William Roache in Judith Holder, *It's Grim Up North*, 2005].

**Nor'west** or **North West, the** A general name for the northern part of Western Australia.

> (1) South and West of that is the other large area of stations, mostly sheep and not usually quite a million acres, called the North-West [Caroline Gye, *The Cockney and the Crocodile*, 1962].
> (2) North of Meekatharra a road sign ... welcomes you to the fabled "Nor'west" [*The Rough Guide to Australia*, 2001].

**Opiumland** A name for the opium poppy fields of the **Golden Triangle**, where much of the world's illegal supply of raw opium is produced.

**Orient, the** A poetic name for the countries of the East, and especially the **Far East**, so called because it is the part of the world where the sun rises, from Latin *oriens, orientis*, "rising." *Cp.* **Levant.**

**Other Side** or **'Tother Side, the** In Australian use, a term for any part of the country separated from another by a natural barrier, such as continental Australia from Tasmania, or the eastern states from Western Australia, from which they are largely separated by desert. *See also* **Other Side** in Dictionary.

> (1) I found them all eager for information regarding the 'tother side,' as they call the eastern colonies ["A Special Correspondent," *Transportation*, 1863].
> (2) The West Australian cricketers underwent a terrible collapse on the other side [*Quiz* (Adelaide), April 29, 1892].
> (3) Quite a number went 'over the other side,' as the Australian mainland is rather ambiguously described by Tasmanians [J.R. Skemp, *Memories of Myrtle Bank*, 1952].

**Outback, the** A general name for those mainly inland parts of Australia that are isolated and rural, so called because they are "out in the back country," i.e. to the rear of a settled region or remote from civilization. The term is sometimes expanded as "the great Australian outback" in romanticized literary depictions of life in the region. (This form is reflected in the title of Ernestine Hill's 1937 account of five years' travel in the Outback, *The Great Australian Loneliness*.) The term can also be used of similar regions in other countries, as in quote (3) for **Middle America.** *Cp.* **Dead Heart.**

> (1) "Yes, I'm from out back," said a dark, wiry little man, as he dismounted from his horse at a Queensland frontier-township hotel [J.A. Barry, *Steve Brown's Bunyip*, 1893].
> (2) He describes the Great Outback or Heart as a place where "the drover is driven and the shearer is shorn" [*The Bulletin* (Sydney), September 30, 1972].

**Outremer** The name (French for "beyond the sea") is mostly used in a historical sense for the medieval French crusader states, although it can also serve more generally as a noun equivalent of "overseas," a word that is properly an adverb. (The French use *outre* in this way prefixed to the name of a body of water to denote a particular country, so that *outre-Atlantique*, "beyond the Atlantic," is a synonym for America, *outre-Manche*, "beyond the Channel," means England or Britain, and *outre-Rhin*, "beyond the Rhine," is Germany.)

> (1) I, too, in a certain sense, have been a pilgrim of Outre-Mer; for to my youthful imagination the old world was a kind of Holy Land [H.W. Longfellow, *Outre-Mer*, 1833].
> (2) The gay gallant trappings of life in Outremer hung thinly over anxiety, uncertainty and fear [Sir Steven Runciman, *A History of the Crusades*, 1951–4].

**Pacific Rim** A term for the countries bordering on or located in the Pacific Ocean, especially those in Southeast Asia with rapidly developing economies, such as Malaysia. In its broadest sense, the name can include the shorelines of

Central and South America, while the Pacific Rim National Park Reserve is a top attraction in British Columbia, Canada.

> The stripling Australian National University, in Canberra, now one of the great institutions of the Pacific Rim [*The Connoisseur*, April 1988].

**Pearl Coast, the** A former name for the coast of Venezuela from Cumaná to Trinidad, a pearl-fishing region. The islands off the coast here were known as the Pearl Islands, a name now applied to islands in the Gulf of Panama.

**Philosophers' Corner** A name given to a region of Brixton, south London, England, where the streets are named for philosophers (e.g. Plato Road, Solon Road). *Cp.* **Poets' Corner.**

**Pictland** A mostly historical name for the area of Scotland north of the Forth River, where the Picts were the dominant ethnic group from the end of the Roman period until *c.*900.

> The inhabitants of this district, the Caledonians of Tacitus, were afterwards known by the name of Picts; and from them the country for some centuries was called Pictland [John R. McCulloch, *A Descriptive and Statistical Account of the British Empire*, 1846].

**Pirate Coast, the** A name formerly applied to the area of the present United Arab Emirates, at one time notorious for pirates. (The Qawasim in the quote below were Arab pirates.)

> From fortified bases at Ras al-Khaima and Sharjah, near the Gulf of Hormuz, Qawasim war fleets cruised the Persian Gulf. Due to their continuing assaults, the region from Hormuz to Bahrain became known as the "Pirate Coast" [Jan Rogozinski, *Pirates!*, 1995].

**Platinum Coast, the** A touristic name for both the west coast of Barbados, with its fine, white sand, and for the coast of lower southwest Florida, USA, also called the **Silver Coast.**

**Playground of England, the** A somewhat dated nickname for the popular **Lake District.**

> The Lake District is called "The Playground of England" [Ruth McKenney and Richard Bransten, *Here's England*, 1955].

**Poets' Corner** The nickname is that of an area of Brixton, south London, England, with a grid of streets named for poets (e.g. Chaucer Road, Spenser Road, Milton Road). Poets' Corner is properly the part of Westminster Abbey, London, where there are monuments to many famous poets. (Chaucer is actually buried there.)

**Poet's Country** The name has been given to the region around Ballymahon, Co. Longford, Ireland, associated with the poet and dramatist Oliver Goldsmith (1728–1774). He was born at Pallas, near Ballymahon, and found inspiration for his poem *The Deserted Village* (1770) at Lissoy, in neighboring Co. Westmeath, now called (as in the poem) Auburn (*see* **Loveliest Village on the Plains** in Dictionary). *Cp.* **Goldsmith's Country.**

> This is the ... gentle spread of land that has become known as 'Poet's Country,' where visitors can pay their respects at Goldsmith's birthplace [*RD Ireland*, p. 42].

**Poldark Country** A touristic name for the parts of Cornwall, England, where the TV historical drama *Poldark* (1975–7), based on the novels of Winston Graham, was filmed.

> Perranporth is in the heart of the Poldark country [*The Times* (Travel West Supplement), September 24, 2005].

**Polish Corridor, the** A historical name for the strip of land in northern Poland extending to Gdańsk (formerly Danzig) and the Baltic Sea. Originally so known in World War I, the territory subsequently became the cause of friction between Germany and Poland and was an immediate cause of World War II.

**Poppy Alley** An alternate name for a **Chinatown** neighborhood, presumably from the opium found in such areas.

**Poppyland** The name was given to the area of poppy fields around the seaside resort of Cromer, Norfolk, England, by the author and drama critic Clement Scott, the first of whose "Poppyland Papers" appeared in the *Daily Telegraph* on August 30, 1883. He later dubbed the region "Bungalowland."

> (1) *Vera in Poppyland* ["Vera" (Annie Berlyn), book title, *c.* 1894].
> (2) Beyond Sherringham [*sic*] we pass by way of a lonely moor ... into the neighbourhood of Cromer — the tourist-haunted region called Poppyland [E.S. Symes, *The Story of the East Country*, n.d. (*c.* 1910)].
> (3) Cromer. A seaside resort in Norfolk, in the heart of "Poppyland" [Johnson, p. 81].
> (4) The station [at Sheringham] is the headquarters of the North Norfolk Railway, called 'the Poppy Line' after the plant that thrives in this part of Norfolk [*RD Britain's Coast*, p. 143].

**Pot Smugglers' Paradise** A nickname given to the coastline of Florida, USA, which with its many waterways and beaches is regarded as ideal for smuggling drugs into the country.

**Provinces, the** In England, a name for the whole of the country outside London, especially in the terms of reference of the press or the theater. In hunting, as in quote (1) below, the term usually contrasts with the **Shires.** The term can have connotations of the inferior.

> (1) [G.T.] Whyte-Melville has drawn for his own purpose a very wide distinction between the 'Shires' and the 'Provinces,' and his Provinces are very Provincial indeed [Henry Somerset, Duke of Beaufort, and Mowbray Morris, *Hunting*, 1894].

(2) For the time being he [i.e. actor Ian Richardson] is "in the provinces" [*The Times*, August 22, 2005].

(3) People down south seem to wear their ignorance about the North with pride. They talk of 'the provinces' in a way that relegates us to some sort of undeveloped hinterland [Judith Holder, *It's Grim Up North*, 2005].

**PWV, the** A name for the area around the cities of Johannesburg and Tshwane (Pretoria), South Africa, as an abbreviation of Pretoria-Witwatersrand-Vaal (Triangle). From April through December 1994 the name was official for the province subsequently called Gauteng.

Three bombs explode in PWV [Headline, *Financial Mail*, September 16, 1983].

**Quad Cities, the** An unofficial designation for the group of four USA cities East Moline, Moline, and Rock Island, Illinois, and Davenport, Iowa, the last-named being the largest.

**Quartier, le** A short name used by the French for the **Latin Quarter** of Paris. *Cp.* **Latin**.

**Red Centre, the** A more specific name for the Australian region known as the **Centre**, so called from the reddish color of the iron oxide in the soil and rocks. The name springs from the description in quote (1) below.

(1) The Luritja Country — the south-west portion of Central Australia and contiguous tracts in the adjoining States —... might well be known as the Red Centre. Sand, soil, and most of the rocks are a fiery cinnabar [H.H. Finlayson, *The Red Centre: Man and Beast in the Heart of Australia*, 1935].

(2) Think of Outback Australia and you'll probably imagine the Red Centre [*The Times*, July 23, 2005].

**Redneck Riviera, the** A fun name for the coast of Florida's northwestern panhandle, USA.

**Red Sea Riviera, the** A touristic name for the east coast of Egypt, bordering the Red Sea, and including the Gulf of Suez and Gulf of Aqaba as its northern arms. The principal resort is Sharm el-Sheikh.

(1) Sharm el Sheikh, the "Red Sea Riviera" resort so beloved of the Blairs [i.e. British prime minister Tony Blair and family] [*Sunday Times*, January 23, 2005].

(2) The Red Sea Riviera is a thousand miles of sundrenched shores, fringed with wonderful hotels [Travel ad, *Sunday Times Magazine*, May 22, 2005].

(3) Just after two o'clock this afternoon, two British Airways planes will leave Gatwick on the airline's first direct flights to the Red Sea Riviera: one flying to the resort of Sharm el-Sheikh, the other to Hurghada [*The Times*, October 22, 2005].

**Riviera di Levante** *see* **Italian Riviera**
**Riviera di Ponente** *see* **Italian Riviera**
**Roaring Forties, the** A sailors' name for the region of the South Atlantic between latitudes 40° and 50° south, where the strong west winds whip up the waves. The term also originally applied to the corresponding region of the North Atlantic. As shown in the quote below, the name can also apply to the winds themselves.

In the southern hemisphere the disturbance of the planetary winds is much less; 'Roaring Forties' and the 'Brave West Winds' blow all the year round with considerable force [A.A. Miller, *Climatology*, 1953].

**Rockbroker Belt, the** An updated equivalent of the **Stockbroker Belt** in southeastern England, populated less by stockbrokers than by ageing pop musicians (rockers).

**Rodings, The** A collective name for eight villages in Essex, England, their common name prefixed by a distinguishing identifier: Abbess Roding, Aythorpe Roding, Beauchamp Roding, Berners Roding, High Roding, Leaden Roding, Margaret Roding, and White Roding. The Rodings are one of the best-known such "clusters" in England, although Dorset has two equally impressive groups: *The Tarrants*, embracing Tarrant Crawford, Tarrant Gunville, Tarrant Hinton, Tarrant Keyneston, Tarrant Launceston, Tarrant Monkton, Tarrant Rawston, and Tarrant Rushton, and *The Winterbornes*, encompassing Winterborne Came, Winterborne Clenston, Winterborne Herringston, Winterborne Houghton, Winterborne Kingston, Winterborne Muston, Winterborne Stickland, Winterborne Tomson, Winterborne Whitchurch, and Winterborne Zelston. Other English collectives include the following:

*The Acres* (Castle Acre, South Acre, West Acre), Norfolk; *The Barshams* (East Barsham, North Barsham, West Barsham), Norfolk; *The Belchamps* (Belchamp Otten, Belchamp St Paul, Belchamp Walter), Essex; *The Bradenhams* (East Bradenham, West Bradenham), Norfolk, *The Burnhams* (Burnham Deepdale, Burnham Market, Burnham Norton, Burnham Overy Staithe, Burnham Overy Town, Burnham Sutton; Burnham Thorpe), Norfolk; *The Claydons* (Botolph Claydon, East Claydon, Middle Claydon, Steeple Claydon), Buckinghamshire; *The Creakes* (North Creake, South Creake), Norfolk; *The Dunmows* (Great Dunmow, Little Dunmow), Essex; *The Horsleys* (East Horsley, West Horsley), Surrey; *The Lophams* (North Lopham, South Lopham), Norfolk, *The Maplesteads* (Little Maplestead, Great Maplestead), Essex; *The Matlocks* (Matlock, Matlock Bath), Derbyshire; *The Pulhams* (Pulham Market, Pulham St Mary), Norfolk, *The Snorings* (Great Snoring, Little

Snoring), Norfolk; *The Theydons* (Theydon Bois, Theydon Garnon, Theydon Mount), Essex.

**Roseland** A term for southeastern England outside London, regarded as a desirable place to live. The name dates from the 1980s, and is really an acronym of "*rest of southeast*," but also implies a region where life is relatively "rosy" compared to the rest of the country.

**Royal Deeside** The name is popularly used for the area of Aberdeenshire, Scotland, on the banks of the Dee River around Ballater and Braemar. The British royal family has had a holiday home at Balmoral here since 1848, and members of the family usually attend the annual Highland Games at nearby Braemar. The quote below relates to Queen Victoria and her husband Prince Albert, who first visited the region in 1842.

> Both of them seeking escape from an unhappy childhood, they sought to construct an idyllic Highland haven. This picturesque fantasy began with an impromptu visit during which resident aristocrats struggled to maintain the myth, ... then seems to have grown into a full-blown delusion on Royal Deeside [*The Times*, April 13, 2005].

**Rust Belt, the** The name refers to the declining industrial regions of the American **Midwest** and northeastern states, especially the area around Pittsburgh and other steel-producing cities. Creation of the name is attributed to US politician Walter Mondale as Democratic nominee in the 1984 presidential election.

> (1) Mr Mondale's nightmare is inspired by the once great but now decaying cities of the Frost Belt — or Rust Belt, as he describes the old industrial heartland of the Mid-West and North-East [*The Times*, November 2, 1984].
> (2) In sum, the label "Rust Belt" may have had merit five years ago, but our seven-state service area that we call America's Heartland is primed and ready for the future [AEP (i.e. American Electric Power) report to shareowners, 1989].

**Sansan** An occasional name for the affluent strip of the US West Coast between the cities of *San* Francisco and *San* Diego. Cp. **Bosnywash**; **Chippitts**.

**Saxon Shore, the** A historical name, translating Latin *Litus Saxonicum*, for the coastal network of late Roman forts in southeastern England extending from Norfolk, in the east, to Hampshire, in the south. The forts were intended to repel attacks by Saxons. The name is preserved in the national trail (long-distance walking route) Saxon Shore Way in Kent.

**Saxon Triangle, the** The name is that of the urbanized region of eastern Germany based on the cities of Leipzig, Halle, and Dresden, mostly in Saxony.

**Scampi Belt, the** A former nickname for the area to the west and south of London, England, corresponding approximately to the **Stockbroker Belt** and referring to the scampi that in the 1960s was regarded as a desirable dish by its middle-class residents.

> (1) What about a little schmaltzy restaurant down the King's Road? Or ... maybe further up the [Thames] river in the scampi belt? [Desmond Skirrow, *It Won't Get You Anywhere*, 1966].
> (2) By the 1980s scampi was reserved for the 'basket meal' trade, and such areas should perhaps be renamed the 'fresh pasta belt' or 'sun-dried tomato belt' [Green, p. 1233].

**Scott Country** A regional name for the area of southern Scotland associated with the life and work of the novelist and poet Sir Walter Scott (1771–1832). It centers on Scott's home at Abbotsford, in the **Border Country**, and takes in many of the surrounding valleys.

> The Burgh of Hawick ... is one of the best motoring centres in the Scottish Borders for visiting the "Scott" Country [*Holiday Haunts 1962: Scotland*].

**Scottish Riviera, the** The name has been given both to the coast of Fife, southeastern Scotland, where the city and resort of St Andrews and many of the fishing ports have sandy beaches, and to the coast of the Moray Firth, northeastern Scotland.

> [Forres, on the Moray Firth, is] in Scotland's Sunny Riviera of the North [*Holiday Haunts 1962: Scotland*].

**Seven Seas, the** The name essentially encompasses all the waters that cover the earth, but the "seas" can in fact be enumerated as the seven oceans Arctic, Antarctic, North Atlantic, South Atlantic, North Pacific, South Pacific, and Indian. Cp. **Four Seas**.

> (1) Which of our Coming and Departure heeds
> As the Sev'n Seas should heed a pebble-cast [Edward Fitzgerald, *The Rubáiyát of Omar Khayyám*, 1859].
> (2) Far and far our homes are set round the Seven Seas;
> Woe for us if we forget, we who hold by these! [Rudyard Kipling, "The Flowers," *The Seven Seas*, 1896].

**Shakespeare Country** A touristic name for the region of Warwickshire, England, associated with William Shakespeare (1564–1616), born at Stratford-upon-Avon.

> (1) If you are young and have the time and energy, the Shakespeare country is hallowed ground for bicycle or walking tours [Ruth McKenney and Richard Bransten, *Here's England*, 1955].
> (2) [Leamington Spa is] in the Heart of England at the gateway to glorious Shakespeareland [*Holiday Haunts 1961: Area No. 4, West of England and South and Central Wales*].

(3) Stratford-upon-Avon, birthplace of the bard and epicentre of Shakespeare Country [Charlie Godfrey-Faussett, *Footprint England*, 2004].

(4) Home to the world's most famous playwright and internationally renowned theatres — Shakespeare Country provides a most dramatic landscape in which to explore the legend [Travel brochure, *Shakespeare Country*, 2005].

**Shelley's Country** An occasional name for the region around Horsham, West Sussex, England, where the poet was born in 1792, although living the rest of his short life elsewhere.

> The district in which it [i.e. Horsham] stands is often spoken of as "Shelley's country" [*Holiday Guide 1952: Area No. 5, South & South East England*].

**Sherry Triangle, the** The name is that of the region formed by the three towns of Jerez de la Frontera, Sanlúcar de Barrameda, and Puerto de Santa María, in southern Spain, the only ones to make and mature sherry (so named from the first of these).

**Shipwreck Coast, the** A nickname for the southwest coast of Victoria, Australia, where over 80 ships have foundered.

> This stretch from Moonlight Head to Port Fairy, sometimes referred to as the "Shipwreck Coast," is the most spectacular [*The Rough Guide to Australia*, 2001].

**Shires, the** The name was first applied to the counties of England's **Midlands** with names ending in "-shire" by neighboring counties to the east and south with names not ending thus, i.e. Norfolk, Suffolk, Essex, Middlesex, Kent, Sussex, and Surrey. It then came to apply particularly to Northamptonshire and Leicestershire, famous for their hunts, and so became synonymous with hunting and with hunting circles, meaning the upper classes associated with this sport, together with their conservative views and (generally) Conservative political allegiance. The term "knight of the shire" originally denoted a gentleman representing a shire or county in parliament, but is now applied humorously to a Conservative member for a country constituency (typically in the Shires) who has been knighted for political service.

> (1) The Inhabitants of Kent, to express a person's coming from a great distance ... will say, he comes a great way off, out of the shires [Samuel Pegge, *Anonymiana, c.* 1796].
> (2) "Excuse me, sir: take the liberty of asking whereabouts you generally hunt." "Hunt?" repeated the customer. "Oh! Leicestershire — Northamptonshire — all about there" ... A cloud gathered on the foreman's brow. "The Shires!" he rejoined, with a perplexed air; "that increases our difficulties very much indeed" [G.T. Whyte-Melville, *Market Harborough; or, How Mr. Sawyer Went to the Shires*, 1861].

(3) Geographically defined the Shires are limited to three counties, Leicestershire, Rutlandshire, and Northamptonshire. But a geographical definition will not serve. A considerable part of the Belvoir country is, for instance, in Lincolnshire. Now to hunt with that famous pack is most certainly to hunt in the Shires; to hunt with the Burton, the Blankney, or the Brocklesby, which also wage war with the foxes of Lincolnshire, is not [Henry Somerset, Duke of Beaufort, and Mowbray Morris, *Hunting*, 1894].

(4) Within living memory the folk of Norfolk and Suffolk have looked upon immigrants from 'the shires' or the rest of England as being akin to foreigners [Richard Muir in Hadfield 1980, p. 113].

**Silicon Alley** A nickname for a section of Lower Manhattan, New York City, where there are many electronics firms. The name is an easy pun on **Silicon Valley** (see in Dictionary).

**Silk Stocking District** or **Quarter, the** A nickname for the Upper East Side of Manhattan, New York City, USA, denoting its wealthy residents (perceived as wearing silk stockings).

**Silver Coast, the** A nickname for the coast of lower southwest Florida, USA.

**Sin Strip, the** A nickname for the hedonistic North Beach area of San Francisco, California, USA, birthplace of the Beat movement. On Broadway, touts and neon signs lure visitors into the clubs, where a tradition of nude dancing has been preserved from the 1960s.

**Skeleton Coast, the** The Atlantic seaboard of northwestern Namibia extending south from Cape Fria to Cape Cross is so known from the animal detritus strewn along its shore.

> It was only here [at Cape Fria] that we realised how aptly named the Skeleton Coast is, since it is littered with the bleached bones of whales and seals and men. The ocean off Namibia was once full of whales, but the men who hunted them were lured to their deaths by the treacherous Atlantic fogs. One hundred years later, the wooden ribs of their ships now mingle with the ribs of the whales they pursued [Isabel Wolff, "Seasoned by the Sun," *The Times Magazine*, June 5, 1993].

**Slave Coast** The region along the Bight of Benin in West Africa was so known because it was from here that African slaves were deported to other countries from around 1500 to the late 19th century.

> Benin ... has the Slave Coast on the west [*Encyclopædia Britannica*, 1778].

**Slave States, the** A blanket term for those states of the US **South** in which domestic slavery was legal before the Civil War, namely Delaware, Maryland, Virginia, North and South Carolina, Georgia, Florida, Alabama, Mississippi, Louisiana, Texas, Arkansas, Missouri, Kentucky, and Tennessee.

(1) Buffaloe robes ... will be found of much use in the slave states, as a cheap and comfortable bedding for negroes [Henry M. Brackenridge, *Views of Louisiana*, 1812].

(2) The total white population of the slave states in 1860 was 8,098,000 (black, 4,204,000) [Hugh Brogan, *Longman History of the United States of America*, 1985].

**Smiling Coast, the** A touristic name for the short Atlantic coast of The Gambia, West Africa.

Kartong is at the remote southern end of The Gambia, at the mouth of the River Allahein ... It is a far cry from the hotels along the so-called "Smiling Coast," near Banjul, the capital [*The Times*, July 2, 2005].

**Snowbelt, the** The name is used for the northern region of the continental USA, from east to west, where heavy snowfalls are likely. An alternate name is Frostbelt. The name was based on that of the **Sunbelt**.

(1) Snowbelt representatives contended ... that their region was being shortchanged. They said that the formulas were originally drawn when the Sunbelt was poor and the Snowbelt was rich [*New York Times*, September 28, 1977].

(2) The arbitrary antithesis between "Sunbelt" and "Frostbelt" is a crutch that has crippled understanding of cities and their problems, and should be eschewed [*Harper's*, December 1978].

**Soft South, the** A conventional semihumorous nickname for the **South** of England and its inhabitants, regarded as privileged and pampered by those living in the **North**, where life can be (and for many was long) hard and heavy.

(1) Bring back the rope! Your pal in the soft south! Henry Root [Close of spoof letter by "Henry Root" (William Donaldson) to James Anderton, chief constable of Greater Manchester, in *The Henry Root Letters*, 1980].

(2) The age old perception of the 'soft south' and the 'tough north' certainly seems to hold true for pet owners in the UK [<http://www.petplan.co.uk/about/press/southwest2005.asp> accessed December 10, 2005].

**SoHo** The name of the neighborhood in Lower Manhattan, New York City, dates from the 1960s and stands for "*so*uth of *Ho*uston (Street)," the latter bounding it to the north. The name may owe something to the district of Soho in London, England. *Cp.* **NoHo.**

(1) A tour of SoHo, the bustling neighborhood in downtown Manhattan, is a must for visitors who want a firsthand look at New York's famous art community [*New York Times*, July 9, 1976].

(2) SoHo — short in New York Cool for *So*uth of *Ho*uston [*The Rough Guide to New York City*, 2004].

**Solid South, the** A particularized reference for the **South** of the USA, as a politically united region, where the white electorate votes unanimously for the Democratic Party. The phrase is attributed to the Confederate ranger John Singleton Mosby, as in quote (1) below.

(1) We must recognize the solid South as the core of the Democratic party ... The solid South is the Southern Confederacy seeking domination of the United States through the machinery of the Democratic party [John S. Mosby, letter in *Harper's Weekly*, August 26, 1876].

(2) It is possible for the GOP [i.e. Grand Old Party, or Republican Party] to revitalize itself by becoming the necessary counterweight to the newly reconstituted Solid South [*Chicago Tribune*, October 2, 1977].

**SoMa** A handy acronym for "*so*uth of *Ma*rket," as the extensive district south of Market Street in downtown San Francisco, California, USA.

South of Market, or SoMa, refers to a vast area that includes ... a plethora of hot clubs and nightspots [*Lonely Planet USA*, 2004].

**Sooside, the** A Scots form of "South Side,"as a name designating the area of Glasgow to the south of the Clyde River.

**South, the** A general term for the US **Slave States** that in many ways equates to the **Deep South** or **Solid South**. More recently the name has also been used for the less-developed nations of the world, which are mainly in the southern hemisphere. The name gained favor from the mid-1970s as another designation for the **Third World**, a term which to some could imply "third-rate." In Britain, the South may also be the **South Country**. All three senses contrast implicitly with the **North**. *See also* **South** in Dictionary.

**South Country, the** A not very common general name for the southern counties of England, more usually known as simply "the south of England." It is actually quite limited in area, since it normally excludes the **Home Counties**, the **South East**, and the southern counties that are felt to be part of the **West Country**. This leaves a core of Hampshire, Dorset, and Wiltshire, with maybe a further restriction to just the eastern parts of the last two. Quote (3) below has a fuller definition, by the author of the topographical book in quote (1).

(1) *The South Country* [Edward Thomas, book title, 1909].

(2) When I am living in the Midlands
That are sodden and unkind,
I light my lamp in the evening:
My work is left behind;
And the great hills of the South Country
Come back into my mind [Hilaire Belloc, "The South Country," 1910].

(3) Thomas's England, the England of rolling hills, village greens and hedgerows is what he called The South Country. When he explained

what he meant by the term, he spoke of it as being below the Thames and the Severn and east of Exmoor: it included Kent, Sussex, Surrey, Hampshire, Berkshire, Wiltshire, Dorset and part of Somerset [Jeremy Paxman, *The English*, 1998].

**South East, the** A term for the southeastern counties of England, including Surrey and Kent (in the **Home Counties**) and also Sussex, but not seen as embracing London (which although in southeastern England is regarded as "distinct" from any geographical region).

(1) A look at some non-broadcast music events taking place in London and the South East [*Radio Times*, November 28, 1968].

(2) Where is this "South East," and by what scholarly or popular authority is it so defined? Traditionally, I would say, it is Kent, Surrey and Sussex, but certainly not Hampshire or some other counties corralled under its borrowed name, whose historic links are firmly westward with the rest of Wessex [Letter to the Editor, *The Times*, September 5, 2005].

**Soviet Riviera** *see* **Crimean Riviera**

**Space Coast, the** A nickname for the east coast of Florida, USA, around Melbourne and Cocoa Beach, south of Cape Canaveral, the site of the Kennedy Space Center.

As the aerospace industry moved into Florida near the end of the decade [i.e. the 1950s], an entire 'Space Coast' was created around Cape Canaveral [*Lonely Planet Miami*, 1999].

**Stockbroker Belt, the** A term for the prosperous residential region in the **Home Counties** to the west and south of London, England, from which stockbrokers and other professional people commute to the **City**. There are similar regions elsewhere, notably in Cheshire. *See also* **Scampi Belt**.

(1) The area on the London side of Basingstoke [in Hampshire] has long been commuter territory and in part 'stockbroker belt' [John Arlott in Hadfield 1981, p. 197].

(2) The list ... identifies many prosperous enclaves dotted around the country: Macclesfield and its environs, in the heart of the Cheshire stockbroker belt, are among an élite few outside the southeast [Greg Hadfield and Mark Skipworth, *Class*, 1994].

(3) Henk Huffener's house, off the Guildford-Dorking road, is not merely in the Surrey stockbroker belt — it is at its very buckle [*The Times*, March 1, 1999].

(4) Old Amersham's getting its first boutique coaching inn, don't you know. Marlow and Henley already have theirs. The [Buckinghamshire] stockbroker belt, you see, is ... being populated by the gilded youth *de nos jours*: young professionals with loadsamoney who've had it with London but aren't quite ready for the pipe and slippers [*The Guardian Weekend*, October 15, 2005].

(5) [A] £2.5 million home in the Cheshire stockbroker belt [*The Times*, December 10, 2005].

**Stuka Valley** A name used by British troops in World War II for the plain around Suq al Khamis in northwestern Tunisia, an area often attacked by German Stuka dive bombers.

**Sugar Bowl, the** A name applied to any region of sugarcane production, especially the part of southern Louisiana, USA, better known as **Cajun Country**.

**Summer Wine Country** A touristic name for the region around the town of Holmfirth, West Yorkshire, England, the setting of the popular TV sitcom *Last of the Summer Wine* (1973–2000), about three Yorkshire retirees.

The streets of Holmfirth, and the surrounding moors, have become instantly familiar as Summer Wine Country [Tourist guide, *Yorkshire*, 2005].

**Sunbelt, the** As applied to the southern and southwestern states of the USA, the name denotes a region that is generally warmer and drier than elsewhere. It also implies a high standard of living, a rapid population growth, and generally conservative attitudes. The term was coined in 1969 by US writer Kevin F. Phillips, who based it on existing "belt" names.

(1) In California and Florida, both part of the Sunbelt, unemployment has been higher than the national average [*New York Times*, January 9, 1977].

(2) That growth of small towns is unevenly distributed from region to region but national in scope: it is highest in the Sun Belt states of the West and South, lowest in the Middle West, but steady and substantial even in the Northeast, where the big cities are losing population [*Newsweek*, July 6, 1981].

**Sun Coast, the** A popular name for the coast in the Tampa Bay area of Florida, USA.

**Sunni Triangle, the** A name for the area of Iraq between Baghdad, Ramadi, and Tikrit (Saddam Hussein's hometown), inhabited mainly by Sunni Muslims. The region was a center of armed insurgency following Saddam's overthrow in 2003. *See also* **Triangle of Death**.

Whether or not the [Black Watch] regiment's redployment will have them operating in an area southwest of Baghdad or helping control exits and entrances around Fallujah as US forces mount a full-scale offensive, their duties inside the Sunni triangle will see the level of danger they face accelerate daily [*Sunday Herald* (Glasgow), October 24, 2004].

**Sunny South, the** An occasional name for the southern states of the USA and a touristic name for the south of England (*see* **South Country**). The latter name was popularized by the London & North Western and London, Brighton & South Coast railways, who used it for a through train between Liverpool, Manchester, and Brighton first run in 1905. *Cp.* **Sunbelt**.

(1) (USA) The wish of his heart should always be, peace and prosperity to the "Sunny South" [*Spirit of the Times* (New York), April 18, 1846].

(2) (USA) Eric, the redbird ... flew by, fat 'n' sassy from a sojourn in the sunny South [*Chicago Tribune*, March 11, 1950].

(3) (England) It was in 1904 that the 'Sunny South' idea first took shape [Cecil J. Allen, *Titled Trains of Great Britain*, 1983].

**Sunny Southeast, the** A promotional name for the southeast of Ireland, especially southern Co. Wicklow and most of Co. Wexford. The coastal region has the highest average temperatures in the country and the lowest rainfall.

**Sunrise Coast, the** A touristic name for the North Sea coast of northern Suffolk, England, where the resorts face the rising sun. *Cp.* **Sunrise Land**.

The Sunrise Coast — where Broadland meets the sea [Travel ad, *Enjoy England Holiday Planner 2005*].

**Sunrise Land** A former popular name for East Anglia, England. *Cp.* **Sunrise Coast**.

*Sunrise-Land: Rambles in Eastern England* [Annie Berlyn, book title, 1894].

**Sunrise Strip, the** A former promotional name for the Thames valley between London and Bristol, England, where a number of computer-oriented "sunrise" industries became established from the 1970s. *Cp.* **M4 Corridor**.

**Sunset Country, the** The name is used for certain western areas of the eastern states of Australia, especially New South Wales and Victoria, but also parts of Queensland.

(1) During my divagations through the Sunset-country stations, I frequently found that the shearers and co. were decently housed [*The Bulletin* (Sydney), May 7, 1908].

(2) To the southwest is the evocatively named Sunset Country, with nothing but gnarled mallee scrub, red sand and pink salt lakes [*The Rough Guide to Australia*, 2001].

**Sunshine Coast, the** The name is used for various coastal areas where the sunshine is above average. In Canada, it describes the region between Horseshoe Bay and Lund, British Columbia, where there is a higher annual sunshine record than elsewhere on the mainland. In England, it applies to the Essex coast, where resorts such as Clacton, Frinton, and Harwich enjoy a low rainfall and an average of 8 hours of sun daily during the summer. (In Australia, Sunshine Coast is the regular name for the Queensland coast north of the Gold Coast.)

**Surf Coast, the** A nickname for the middle east coast of Florida, USA, where there is good surfing.

**Suwaneeland** An informal name for the basin of the Suwanee River, Florida, USA.

**Swamps, the** A black nickname for the Sunnydale projects in the southern part of San Francisco, California, USA.

**Swartland, the** A name, formerly also spelled Zwartland, for the wheat-growing area centered on Malmesbury, Western Cape province, South Africa. The name, Afrikaans for "black country," refers to the dark soil here, and before 1829 was official for the region.

(1) The district of Malmesbury, near the Mother City, is to this day known as 'Zwartland' to crowds of South Africans [Eric Rosenthal, *Old-Time Survivals in South Africa*, 1936].

(2) Because of better feed, better fertilizers, and better calculation, the grainlands of the Swartland are producing more organic matter than can be incorporated into the soil between sowing seasons [*Cape Times*, April 19, 1972].

**Sydneyside** The name denotes either the Australian state of New South Wales, with capital Sydney, especially as seen from South Australia, to the west, or just the city and its environs. A Sydneysider is someone from Sydney, or New South Wales, or even Australia as a whole.

(1) My name's Dick Marston, Sydney-side native [Rolf Boldrewood, *Robbery under Arms*, 1888].

(2) A barber [in a sheep-shearing contest] ... who comes from Sydneyside, I think, put up, on the last day, the respectable total of 304 [*The Bulletin* (Sydney), October 22, 1914].

**Tall Timber Country, the** A name for the grand forests of southwestern Western Australia.

The brooding, primeval karri forests of the so-called Tall Timber Country are one of WA's greatest natural sights [*The Rough Guide to Australia*, 2001].

**Telecom Valley** An alternate name for the Côte d'Azur, as the location of several French and foreign telecommunications companies. The name is based on the USA's **Silicon Valley** (see in Dictionary).

**Tenderloin** A name given to a nightclub district in Manhattan, New York City, USA, in the 1880s. As "tenderloin" is the term for the tenderest or juiciest part of a loin of beef or pork, the name probably refers to the extortionate payments made to the police for protecting illegitimate businesses in the area. Such "graft" was thus the "juicy part" of the service. (According to Chapman, p. 434, the specific source of the name was the remark of a New York City police captain who, when assigned to the area, remarked that he had always eaten chuck steak but would now eat tenderloin.) Reformers dubbed the district "Satan's Circus." The name was later used for similar districts of vice and corruption in other cities, such as San Francisco's **Barbary Coast**.

(San Francisco) Marylou had been around these people — not far from the Tenderloin — and a grey-faced hotel clerk let us have a room on credit [Jack Kerouac, *On the Road*, 1957].

**Tennyson Country** A name for the western extremity of the Isle of Wight, England, where the poet lived for some time from 1853 at Farringford House, near Freshwater.

The "Tennyson Country" lies on the western side of the Island [*Holiday Guide 1952: Area No. 5, South & South East England*].

**Terror Town** The name has been applied to Chicago's South Side for its terrorist gangs.

Chicago's Southside, an area known as "Terror Town" because of the gangs [Alex Danchev, review of Phil Rees, *Dining with Terrorists*, *Times Literary Supplement*, April 22, 2005].

**Theatreland** A virtual synonym for the **West End** of London, England, where many theaters are located. The designation is said to have first appeared in the *Daily Chronicle* of December 28, 1905.

(1) Piccadilly Circus and Leicester Square, the centre of "theatreland" [*Holiday Guide 1952: Area No. 5, South & South East England*].

(2) Theatreland will also be enhanced by the temporary residence of the Royal Court Theatre ... at two West End theatres [*Time Out London Guide*, 1997].

**Third Coast, the** A local nickname for the Gulf of Mexico coast centering on Houston, Texas, USA, which is "third" (south) after the Atlantic **East Coast** and Pacific **West Coast**.

(1) Houston — the Third Coast as it presumptuously calls itself [Deyan Sudjic, *The Hundred-Mile City*, 1992].

(2) America's 'Third Coast,' as folks there like to call it, is home to one of the country's most diverse cities [i.e. Houston] [*Lonely Planet USA*, 2004].

**Third World, the** The name for the developing countries of Asia, Africa, and Latin America translates French *tiers monde*, a term used by French commentators in the 1950s as against the first world of capitalism and second world of Communism. There is now also a Fourth World, as a term for the poorest and most underdeveloped countries and peoples of the Third World. *See also* **South**.

**Tortilla Curtain, the** A nickname for the USA-Mexico border from San Diego, Florida, to El Paso, Texas, from the popular Mexican dish. *See also* **Twilight Zone**.

**Travellers' Coast, the** A popular name for the west coast of Britain from Fishguard, Wales, to Birkenhead, England, where many ports and harbors are famed for their historic departures and arrivals, from explorers and seafarers to refugees and emigrants.

Many of the journeys associated with the Travellers' Coast had the region itself as their destination [Christopher Somerville, *Coast: A Celebration of Britain's Coastal Heritage*, 2005].

**Triad, the** A local name for the triangular grouping of Winston-Salem, Greensboro, and High Point, North Carolina, USA. The name is a response to the Research Triangle Park that is the area's better-known neighbor to the southeast (*see* **RTP** in Dictionary).

**Triangle of Death, the** An emotive name for the region of Iraq south of Baghdad also known as the **Sunni Triangle**, an area of armed insurgency following the overthrow of Saddam Hussein in 2003.

(1) Chaos Inside The Triangle of Death [Headline, *Sunday Herald* (Glasgow), October 24, 2004].

(2) Don't go to any of the hot spots in the west, the north and the east. The south is relatively safe but the road to it goes through the Triangle of Death [*The Times*, October 15, 2005].

**TriBeCa** The neighborhood in lower Manhattan, New York City, USA, was named by real-estate developers in the 1970s as an acronym for "*tri*angle *be*low *Ca*nal (Street)."

The name TriBeCa is a semiotic construct, and also the mid-Seventies invention of an entrepreneurial realtor who thought the name was better suited to the neighborhood's increasing trendiness than its former moniker, Washington Market [*The Rough Guide to New York City*, 2004].

**Tri-State Area, the** A name for the metropolitan area of New York City, which extends east from New York into the neighboring state of Connecticut and is linked to urban areas of New Jersey, on the west side of the Hudson River.

A tri-state transportation committee is carrying out a survey ... of New York, New Jersey, and Connecticut [*The Times*, January 15, 1963].

**Tropi-Coast, the** A punning nickname for the **Gold Coast** of southeastern Florida, USA, which climatically lies in the tropical zone.

**Turquoise Coast, the** The southwest coast of Turkey is so known for its blue-green water.

The "Turquoise Coast" of Turkey is without doubt one of the most stunning stretches of the Mediterranean [Travel brochure issued with *The Times*, August 12, 2004].

**Twilight Zone, the** A nickname for the USA-Mexico border, a region of "shady" deals. *See also* **Border Country**.

**Tyburnia** The name was formerly used for the district of London, England, between Marble Arch and Lancaster Gate, north of Hyde Park, as described in quote (3) below. Tyburn itself, named for a stream here, was a notorious place of public execution until 1783.

(1) Tyburn still gives a name to the white streets and squares of *Tyburnia*, which are wholly devoid of interest or beauty [Augustus J.C. Hare, *Walks in London*, 1878].

(2) Tyburnia, known more prosaically today as the Hyde Park Estate, though attempts to revive the name persist [Weinreb/Hibbert, p. 47].

(3) The [Hyde Park] Estate owes its character to its long-time landlords, the Church Commissioners. Once, the Bishop of London owned nearly all of Paddington. At the start of the 19th century the Bishop's architect built an elegant Regency estate of squares and crescents — and called it, rather inauspiciously, Tyburnia [Carrie Segrave, *The New London Property Guide*, 2003].

**Up North** A term used for a place or region in the **North Country** of England, especially as viewed by a southerner or Londoner. The term is sometimes humorously spelled or pronounced "Oop North" (especially in the catchphrase "It's grim oop north") to imitate a northern or specifically Yorkshire accent. *See also* **North**.

The way people speak 'up North' is very finely differentiated [Charlie Godfrey-Faussett, *Footprint England*, 2004].

**Uptown** The term generally denotes the residential or prosperous part of a city, which often lies above its **Midtown** area. In New York City it lies north of 59th Street and comprises the Upper East Side and Upper West Side, with Central Park between them. *Cp.* **Downtown**.

**Valleys, the** The name has come to apply to the valleys of the many rivers of South Wales, and especially the Rhondda, that flow generally southeast from the Brecon Beacons toward the Bristol Channel, a region formerly associated with coal and steel mines and with strict Sabbatarianism. *See also* **Green Valley** in Dictionary.

(1) Here, in Glamorganshire and Monmouthshire, you come to the extraordinary landscape of the "Valleys" [Vaughan-Thomas/Llewellyn, p. 11].

(2) All three cities [i.e. Cardiff, Newport, and Swansea] grew as ports, mainly exporting millions of tons of coal and iron from the Valleys, where fiercely proud industrial communities were built up in the thin strips of land between the mountains [*The Rough Guide to Wales*, 1997].

**Virgin Lands, the** A term used for the region of previously uncultivated land in the former Soviet Union, especially in western Siberia and Kazakhstan. An ongoing attempt to reclaim such land for grain production was made from 1954. The term translates Russian *tselina*, from the root of *tselyj*, "whole."

(1) New state farms were to be set up at once mainly in Kazakhstan and western Siberia, where there were said to be many millions of acres of virgin or neglected, but fertile, land [*Britannica Book of the Year*, 1955].

(2) Recently, Soviet efforts have been concentrat-

ing on developing the "virgin lands" of northern Kazakhstan [Michael T. Florinsky, ed., *McGraw-Hill Encyclopedia of Russia and the Soviet Union*, 1962].

**Wayback, the** An Australian synonym for the **Outback**, as in Sarah Musgrave's account of pioneering life in New South Wales, *The Wayback* (1926).

The station is built on a stony rise on the western bank of the Newcastle and like most stock stations in the 'wayback' there has been no attempt made to improve the appearance of the surroundings [Francis James Gillen, *Diary*, October 5, 1901 (1968)].

**Wessex** The historic name of the ancient Anglo-Saxon kingdom in southern Britain has been preserved for this region, and in particular the **West Country**, thanks to the writer Thomas Hardy, who deliberately reintroduced it for the setting for most of his novels. The name does not normally appear on maps or in gazetteers but lives on in the titles of government agencies, such as Wessex Water, and a wide range of commercial businesses.

Most remarkable of all, perhaps, is the continuing and ever-increasing use of the name Wessex throughout southwestern England and the resulting invocation, implicit yet automatic, both of Hardy himself and of that profoundly imagined world he indelibly projected onto the landscape of an entire region [Malcolm Bradbury, ed., *The Atlas of Literature*, 1996].

**West, the** A general term for the western states of the USA, often traditionally divided into the **Midwest** and **Far West**. There is usually an implied contrast with the **East**.

I thought all the wilderness of America was in the West till the Ghost of the Susquehanna showed me different. No, there is a wilderness in the East [Jack Kerouac, *On the Road*, 1957].

**West Coast, the** A general name for the Atlantic coast of the United States, and especially that of California, regarded as relatively "exotic" by comparison with the staider **East Coast**.

(1) Our position here on the West Coast has been and still is a peculiar one [*California Courier* (San Francisco), December 2, 1850].

(2) I sit on the old broken-down river pier watching the long, long skies over New York and sense all that raw land that rolls in one unbelievable huge bulge over to the West Coast [Jack Kerouac, *On the Road*, 1957].

(3) We're the lifeline, the West Coast, San Francisco [Howard Fast, *The Immigrants*, 1977].

(4) In the Hamptons, your hairdo also pinpoints with astounding accuracy whether you're West Coast or East Coast [*Sunday Times*, September 4, 2005].

**West Country, the** A blanket name for the southwestern counties of England, always including Somerset, Devon, and Cornwall and sometimes also Wiltshire and Dorset, or at least the western parts of these. Everywhere west of a line between Bristol and Bournemouth could be generally said to be in the West Country, or "west of England," as it is also called. *See also* **Wessex; Wild West.**

> Once the lovely range known as the Quantock Hills lies behind you, you are truly in the West Country [Hogg, p. 321].

**West End, the** A name for the region to the west of central London, England. It has no precise boundaries, but encompasses the capital's fashionable stores, theaters (*see* **Theatreland**), clubs (*see* **Clubland**) and hotels. Its contrast with the **East End** is traditionally as great as that between rich and poor. *See also* **W1** in Dictionary.

> Its [i.e. London's] smart West End displayed the grandeur of a proud and wealthy nation, its middle class suburbs spread apace, its East End was a jungle of poverty [Malcolm Bradbury, ed., *The Atlas of Literature*, 1996].

**Western Approaches, the** A mainly maritime name for the area of sea immediately to the west of the British Isles, and especially for the western end of the English Channel. The name became generally familiar to the British in World War II, if only from the popular movie *Western Approaches* (1946), a fictional account of how torpedoed merchantmen in the Atlantic were used by a U-boat as a decoy.

> Sometimes homeward-bound convoys would be routed away from the Western Approaches, the Bay of Biscay, and the English Channel [*Mariner's Mirror*, 1976].

**Western Province, the** An informal name for the western districts of the historic Cape Colony, South Africa, for the equivalent districts of the Cape Province that succeeded it, and for part of the Western Cape province that was formed from the Cape Province in 1994. The name was adopted by sports teams representing these districts.

> (1) Wild mustard is known by this name [i.e. ramenas] in the Western Province [Charles Pettman, *Africanderisms: A Glossary of South African Colloquial Words and Phrases and of Place and Other Names*, 1913].
> (2) Western Province finally put things together and whipped up a handsome victory yesterday [*Sunday Times* (Johannesburg), July 31, 1994].

**West Side, the** A name for the district of New York City that lies on the west (Hudson River) side of Manhattan. It is conventionally divided into the (northern) Upper West Side and (southern) Lower West Side. *Cp.* **East Side.**

> (1) As our friend entered the door a well-known 'West side' operator made his bid [*Harper's Magazine*, July 1858].

(2) *West Side Story* [Arthur Laurents and Stephen Sondheim, title of musical, 1957].

**Wet Coast, the** A humorous name for Canada's West Coast, especially in the region around Vancouver, notorious for its heavy rainfall.

**Whisky Triangle, the** A name for the area of northeastern Scotland corresponding approximately to Strathspey (or Speyside). It extends from just north of Craigellachie down south toward Tomintoul and east to Huntly and contains more whisky distilleries than anywhere else in Scotland, including famous brands such as Glenlivet and Glenfiddich.

**White Africa** A mainly dated name for the parts of Africa inhabited (and ruled) by whites, meaning mostly eastern and southern Africa and especially South Africa. *Cp.* **Black Africa.**

> The armies and police forces of White Africa [Alan Williams, *Gentleman Traitor*, 1974].

**White Cliffs Country** A promotional name for the coastal region centering on Dover, Kent, England, the location of the "White Cliffs of Dover," popularized by Nat Burton's 1941 song of this title, especially as sung by Vera Lynn as a patriotic morale booster in World War II.

> Exhilarating, exciting activities are based throughout the beautiful unspoilt coast and countryside of White Cliffs Country [Travel brochure *White Cliffs Country*, 2005].

**White Highlands, the** A former name for the hilly region of western Kenya reserved for European settlers, for the most part Britons. *Cp.* **White Africa.**

> (1) In East Africa the settlers' principal anxiety was that Indians would permeate the relatively small area suitable for colonisation — the 'white highlands' [Elspeth Huxley, *White Man's Country: Lord Delamere and the Making of Kenya*, 1935].
> (2) The reservation of the White Highlands for Europeans prevented the process of expansion by which the more populous tribes would normally have found relief from congestion [William Malcolm Hailey, *An African Survey*, rev. ed., 1956].
> (3) Soil erosion had been one of the great settler obsessions. The battle against it had become part and parcel of the battle for civilisation, providing a powerful argument for the preservation of the status quo in the 'White' Highlands [Shivadhar Naipaul, *North of South*, 1978].

**Wild Coast, the** The section of the Atlantic seaboard in southeastern South Africa between the mouths of the Great Kei and Mtamvuna rivers is so named for its rugged terrain and for the rocky outcrops and reefs extending into the sea, the latter a constant hazard to mariners.

> Just after 4:30 on the morning of August 4, 1782, the *Grosvenor*, East Indiaman, homeward bound, fully laden with goods and passengers, ran

aground during a storm on the Wild Coast of south-east Africa [James Kelly, review of Stephen Taylor, *The Caliban Shore*, *Times Literary Supplement*, August 6, 2004].

**Wilderness Coast, the** The name of the coast of Croajingolong National Park, southeastern Victoria, Australia, which like many such parks is an area of protected wilderness.

Within the park, foothills cloaked in warm temperate rainforest drop down to the unspoilt "Wilderness Coast" [*The Rough Guide to Australia*, 2001].

**Wild North, the** A conventionally humorous nickname for the **North** of England, where to dwellers in the **Soft South** the country is wild and untamed and the people brusque and blunt. See quote (3) at **North of Watford**.

**Wild West, the** In the USA, a name for the American **West** during its lawless frontier period. Although it was the white desperadoes and cattle rustlers who were "wild," the epithet served to tarnish the whole region as a rough and uncivilized wasteland. In Britain, the name is applied colloquially to the **West Country**, where there can be rough weather both on land and along the coasts, and where salt, wind, and rain can make farming difficult and harvests hazardous.

(1) (USA) Has he [i.e. US author Bret Harte] continued to distil and dilute the Wild West because the public would only take him as wild and Western? [Henry James in *Literature*, April 30, 1898].

(2) (USA) Only to the white man was nature a "wilderness" and only to him was the land "infested" with "wild" animals and "savage" people ... When the very animals of the forest began fleeing from his approach, then it was for us the

"Wild West" began [Luther Standing Bear, *The Land of the Spotted Eagle*, 1933].

(3) (England) Britain's south-western corner ... has been the country's natural summertime playground for the best part of 200 years ... But that's only half the story out here in the Wild West, where the toe-tip of the British Isles pokes out into the Atlantic Ocean [Christopher Somerville, *Coast: A Celebration of Britain's Coastal Heritage*, 2005].

(4) (USA) Combine a stay in America's fabled Wild West with a visit to the stunning Grand Canyon [Travel brochure issued with *Sunday Times*, December 11, 2005].

**Wine City** A nickname given by residents of Glasgow, Scotland, to the Clydeside towns of Greenock and Port Glasgow, to the west, frequented by "winos" (drinkers of cheap wine).

**Yeats Country** A name for Co. Sligo, Ireland, and especially its western part, associated with the Irish poet W.B. Yeats (1865–1939), who came to love this region of northwestern Ireland. Although born in Dublin, and dying in France, he is buried here in the cemetery of the Protestant church at Drumcliff, "under bare Ben Bulben's head" (as he himself wrote). *See also* **Land of Heart's Desire**.

More recently, the rise in reputation of W.B.'s brother, the painter Jack B. Yeats, ... has led to the phrase 'the Yeats country' being broadened to accommodate the painter as well as the poet [Brian Lalor, *Blue Guide Ireland*, 2004].

**Zedland** A humorous nickname for England's **West Country**, where "z" is substituted in local speech for "s" (or soft "c") in such words as "summer" and "cider," "zed" being American "zee." (*Cp.* **Zummerset** in Dictionary.)

# Appendix 2: Road and Street Nicknames

*Below is a selection of more than 200 road and street nicknames. Where the nickname does not apply to the whole length of the road, the real or official name is preceded by "(part of )."*

*In American usage, it is common to omit "Street" or other generic word from a street name, as instanced by* **Madison** *and* **Sunset** *below as just two typical examples of many. British English does not normally shorten a street name thus, or if it does, prefixes the name with "the" as for* **Broad** *and* **High** *below.*

**Alex** *Alexanderplatz, Berlin, Germany.* A colloquial shortening of the central square's name.

**Avenue, the** *Broadway, New York City, USA.* A former nickname for the famous street.

**Avenue of the Americas, the** *Sixth Avenue, New York City, USA.* Although often thought of as a nickname, this is actually the *official* name of the street, bestowed in the 1940s to honor the countries of Central and South America. In practice it is rarely used, and the original prosaic name is usually preferred.

> (1) Most streets and avenues [in New York City] have a number, rather than a name, but a few have both — Sixth Ave, for example, is also known as Avenue of the Americas [*Lonely Planet USA*, 2004].
>
> (2) No New Yorker ever calls it thus: the guidebooks and maps labor the convention, but the only manifestations of the tag are lamppost flags of Central and South American countries [*The Rough Guide to New York City*, 2004].

**Avenue of the Arts, the** *(part of ) Broad Street, Philadelphia, Pennsylvania, USA.* The stretch of Broad Street south of City Hall is so nicknamed for its theaters and other entertainment venues.

**Bank Row** *(part of ) Montague Street, New York City, USA.* The eastern end of Montague Street is so nicknamed as Brooklyn's business center.

**Bankruptcy Avenue** or **Row** *Westbourne Grove, London, England.* The now fashionable road was so nicknamed in the mid–19th century, for its many impoverished residents.

> Westbourne Grove is now positively chi-chi. This was not always so: it was known in the 1860s as 'bankruptcy avenue' [Carrie Segrave, *The New London Property Guide*, 2003].

**Barracka** or **Barrackah** *Barrack Street, Cork, Ireland.* The local nickname for the street is formed with the same pet suffix as for **Pana**.

**Bays** or **Baze, the** *Bayswater Road, London, England.* A short colloquial name for the street formerly notorious as a pickup point for prostitutes.

**Big Red with the Long Green Stem, the** *(part of ) 7th Avenue, New York City, USA.* A former black nickname for the section of Seventh Avenue between the 130s and 140s, the center of Harlem nightlife in the 1940s and 1950s. "Big Red" refers to the **Big Apple** (see in Dictionary); the "Long Green Stem" is the street where money is made. *See also* **Big Stem**.

**Big Stem, the** *Broadway, New York City, USA.* The famous street is regarded as the stem of the **Big Apple** (see in Dictionary).

> Mr. Charles Gillett, the president of the New York Convention & Visitors Bureau, Inc., spoke ... on ... the value of the image of New York as "the Big Apple"... It was his organization that plucked the term from the jazz lingo of the twenties... The phrase in the jazz world, he said, had been "playing the Big Stem in the Big Apple"— the Big Stem being Broadway. (Another saying that we subsequently picked up from a dictionary of slang was "There are many apples on the tree, but New York is the big apple.") [*New Yorker*, August 6, 1984].

**Block, the** *(part of ) Collins Street, Melbourne, Australia.* The name was used for the stretch of Collins Street between Swanston Street and Elizabeth Street on which it was fashionable to promenade. *See also* **Block** in Appendix 1, p. 269.

> (1) A certain portion of Collins Street, lined by the best drapers' and jewellers' shops ... is known

as 'The Block,' and is the daily resort of the belles and beaux ["A Resident," *Glimpses of Life in Victoria*, 1872].

(2) We sell more buttons on the Block on Saturday morning than at any other time [*Melbourne University Magazine*, October 14, 1928].

**Bond Street of East Anglia, the** *Connaught Avenue, Frinton-on-Sea, England.* A former sobriquet for the Essex resort's main shopping street, comparing it to London's fashionably expensive Bond Street.

**Booksellers' Row** *Holywell Street, London, England.* A former nickname for the street (which no longer exists), referring euphemistically to the sellers of pornographic literature who had their premises there.

**Boul' Mich', le** *Boulevard Saint-Michel, Paris, France.* A short name for the Left Bank street, used chiefly by the students who frequent its cafés.

In Paris, you soon learn to know where you are in relation to the Champs-Elysées, the Louvre, the Boul' Mich' [Ruth McKenney and Richard Bransten, *Here's England*, 1955].

**Broad, the** *Broad Street, Oxford, England.* A shortening of the name of one of the city's main streets, used mostly by university people.

**Brighton Deck** *King's Road and Marine Parade, Brighton, England.* The broad railed sidewalk running the length of the seafront at the East Sussex resort is so nicknamed for its resemblance to the deck of a passenger liner.

There is plenty of room for everybody on "Brighton Deck," as the promenade is often called [*Holiday Guide 1952: Area No. 5, South & South East England*].

**B-Way** or **B'way** *Broadway, New York City, USA.* An abbreviated name for the famous street.

**Cally, the** *Caledonian Road, London, England.* A short colloquial name for the main street in the northern part of the capital city.

**Canal** *Canal Street, New Orleans, Louisiana, USA.* A short colloquial name for the city's main street, running along the uptown side of the French Quarter to the Mississippi ferry.

We wheeled through the sultry old light of Algiers, back on the ferry, back towards the mudsplashed, crabbed old ships across the river, back on Canal, and out [Jack Kerouac, *On the Road*, 1957].

**Caravan Alley** *M5, England.* A nickname for the motorway heading south for the **West Country** (see in Appendix 1, p. 269), on which caravans (trailers) often experience delays, especially in the summer months.

Regular users jokingly refer to the stretch of the M5 as Britain's largest caravan park during peak summer months [*The Times*, November 2, 2005].

**Cat Street** *Catte Street, Oxford, England.* The street running between High Street and Broad Street was earlier Cat Street. In the 19th century, this name was changed to St Catherine's Street when it was assumed that "Cat" was short for the saint's name. The name "Cat Street" persisted, however, and was taken as a colloquialism. In 1930 the original name was restored, but in the medieval spelling "Catte."

**Champs, les** *Champs-Élysées, Paris, France.* A handy short form of the name of the French capital's main thoroughfare. (The name means "the Elysian Fields," so the abbreviation is simply "the Fields.")

**Chicago's Red Square** *Haymarket Square, Chicago, Illinois, USA.* The former square, off Randolph Street, was the site of the so-called Haymarket Riot of May 4, 1886, a socialist protest rally that ended in the deaths of 11 people. Hence the nickname. The protest had began on May 1 with a one-day strike in support of the eight-hour movement, and it was these events that led to the marking of May 1 as International Labor Day. *Cp.* **New York's Red Square.**

**China Street** *Bow Street, London, England.* A former nickname for the central street, from its proximity to the market at Covent Garden, where China oranges were sold. (China oranges, i.e. ordinary oranges, were so called as they originally came from China. Hence *Apfelsine*, literally "apple of China," as the standard German word for an orange.)

**Concrete Collar, the** *Queensway, Birmingham, England.* A nickname for the inner ring road created in the 1960s by Sir Herbert Manzoni, city engineer of Birmingham. An eastern section of the road is known as Ringway.

**Corn, the** *Cornmarket, Oxford, England.* A shortening of the name of one of the city's main streets, used mostly by university people. *Cp.* **Broad; High.** (The comic verse quoted below, penned by an Oxford classics scholar, treats "Motor Bus" as pseudo-Latin, with case endings accordingly. The last two lines of the excerpt thus mean: "Fear of the motor bus fills me in the Cornmarket and High Street!")

What is this that roareth thus?
Can it be a Motor Bus?
Yes, the smell and hideous hum
Indicat Motorem Bum!
Implet in the Corn and High
Terror me Motoris Bi! [A.D. Godley, letter to C.R.L. Fletcher, January 10, 1914].

**Crossroads of the World, the** *Times Square, New York City, USA.* The sobriquet alludes to the visitors from all countries who pass through the square, now a center of international tourism.

Chelsea and Gramercy Park offer diverse attractions before one reaches Times Square, the "Crossroads of the World," recently transformed from a sleazy strip to a centre of tourism [*Britannica*, vol. 24, p. 906].

**Deuce** *see* **Forty-Deuce**

**Diamond District, the** *(part of) 47th Street, New York City, USA.* The section of the street between Fifth Avenue and Sixth Avenue is so nicknamed for its mass of jewelry shops.

**Dilly, the** *Piccadilly, London, England.* A short colloquial name for the street formerly notorious for its prostitutes, who when working the area were said to be "on the Dilly."

**Dirty Half-Mile, the** *King's Cross Road, Sydney, Australia.* The road is so locally nicknamed for its "rough and tough" reputation.

**Distressway, the** *(part of) John F. Fitzgerald Expressway, Boston, Massachusetts, USA.* The punning nickname refers to the serious backups along the expressway experienced by traffic coming up from the South Shore.

**Doctor's Row** *(part of) Eighth Street, New York City, USA.* The nickname was current in the 1960s for the stretch of 8th Street in Brooklyn, New York City, between Grand Army Plaza and 1st Street, where professional people came to live in the newly renovated row houses.

**Dream Street** *(part of) 47th Street, New York City, USA.* The section of 47th Street between 6th and 7th Avenues was so nicknamed by US writer Damon Runyon as the site of the Palace Theatre, the pinnacle of American vaudeville.

**Eat Street** *(part of) Nicollet Avenue, Minneapolis, Minnesota, USA.* The section of the street between 14th and 29th streets is so nicknamed for its many restaurants, including several ethnic eateries.

**Eisenhower Platz** *Grosvenor Square, London, England.* The square where the US embassy is situated (*see* **Little America**) was so known in World War II when many of its buildings were occupied by the headquarters of the US military forces in Europe, which were under the command of General Dwight D. Eisenhower.

**Embassy Row** *(part of) Massachusetts Avenue, Washington, DC, USA.* The nickname applies to the avenue's central section, which is lined with the embassies and legations of many foreign countries.

**Europe's Loveliest Street** *High Street, Oxford, England.* The city's main street runs between university colleges in a great curve from the central crossroads at Carfax down to Magdalen Bridge over the Thames River.

High Street itself, a majestic curve of colleges, 'Europe's loveliest street' [Martyn Skinner and Geoffrey Boumphrey in Speaight, p. 146].

**Extraterrestrial Highway, the** *Highway 375, Nevada, USA.* The highway runs near a top secret area of Nellis Air Force Base, supposedly a holding base for captured UFOs. Hence the nickname.

**Fashion Avenue** *7th Avenue, New York City, USA.* The street is the traditional center of the New York garment industry. Hence its nickname. Hence also "Seventh Avenue" as a synonym for that industry and its former alternate nickname of "Garment Center."

**Forty-Deuce** *(part of) 42nd Street, New York City, USA.* The nickname, shortened as "the Deuce," puns on the numerical name of the street, whose middle section, between 7th and 8th Avenues, was the center of New York's tourism, nightlife, and vice.

**Front Line, the** *Railton Road, London, England.* The street in Brixton, south London, was so nicknamed in the 1980s at a time of racial tension, with clashes between police and warring groups of black and white residents.

**Garden, the** *Hatton Garden, London, England.* The street is famous as the center of the city's diamond and jewelry business, and the short name refers to it as such. (The name could also denote Covent Garden market or theater.)

The cut stones are chiefly sold to the large dealers in the 'Garden' [*Tit Bits*, May 29, 1890].

**Garment Center** *see* **Fashion Avenue**.

**Gateway to the West, the** *A30, England.* A touristic name for the main road from London to Cornwall and the **West Country** (see in Appendix 1, p. 269).

By the time we hit the dreaded A30, "gateway to the west," our fate was sealed [*The Times*, August 22, 2005].

**Gay White Way, the** *Broadway, New York City, USA.* A former alternate name for the **Great White Way**, with "gay" in its traditional sense of "bright and cheerful."

This is the Gay White Way, the top of the world with no roof and not even a crack or a hole under your feet to fall through and say it's a lie [Henry Miller, *Tropic of Capricorn*, 1939].

**Gold Coast, the** *(part of) Prospect Park West, New York City, USA.* The nickname was formerly given with reference to the many fine residences in the stretch of Prospect Park West, Brooklyn, from Grand Army Plaza to 1st Street.

**Golden Mile, the** *(1) Belgrave Road, Leicester, England; (2) Promenade, Blackpool, England; (3)*

*Queen Street, Auckland, New Zealand; (4) University Road, Belfast, Northern Ireland.* The name can apply to any road or street noted for its cultural or consumer-based attractions. England's most famous Golden Mile is the Lancashire resort's mile-long coastal road, so named for its glittering delights, all involving the expenditure of "gold" (money), as enumerated in quote (1) below. Leicester's Golden Mile is quite different, as a street famous for its Indian and vegetarian restaurants. The epithet here suggests the golden rice that accompanies many curry dishes or even the golden color of the dishes themselves. Auckland's Golden Mile has the commercial attractions mentioned in quote (2), while Belfast's Golden Mile, in the Queen's University quarter, contains most of the city's art galleries, restaurants, and cultural institutions. *See also* **Golden Mile** in Appendix 1, p. 269.

(1) (Promenade) Blackpool is the archetypal British seaside resort, its "Golden Mile" of piers, fortune-tellers, amusement arcades, tram and donkey rides, fish-and-chip shops, candyfloss stalls, fun pubs and bingo halls making no concessions to anything but low-brow fun-seeking of the finest kind [*The Rough Guide to England*, 1998].
(2) (Queen Street) Queen Street, long known as Auckland's "golden mile," is a major entertainment and shopping area [*Eyewitness Travel Guide New Zealand*, 2001].
(3) (Belgrave Road) The shopkeepers and restaurateurs of the city's Belgrave Road, or 'Golden Mile,' have created a vibrant streak of Indian life [Charlie Godfrey-Faussett, *Footprint England*, 2004].
(4) (Promenade) The Golden Mile still exerts its seedy charm [Christopher Somerville, *Coast: A Celebration of Britain's Coastal Heritage*, 2005].

**GP** *Great Portland Street, London, England.* The initialism was used in the 1930s by auto traders at the car mart in this central street (which they also referred to as simply "The Street").

Great Portland Street — "The Street" one and only and unmistakable; "G.P." — the street of perdition [Richard Blaker, *Night-Shift*, 1934].

**Granite Mile, the** *Union Street, Aberdeen, Scotland.* The street runs through the heart of the **Granite City** (see in Dictionary). Hence its name.

**Great White Way, the** *Broadway, New York City, USA.* The nickname refers to the street's brilliant illumination, especially the electric signs used for advertising and on theater fronts. It was adopted from *The Great White Way* (1901), the title of a tale of adventure at the South Pole by Albert Bigelow Paine, and was originally prompted by the heavy snowfall in New York in the novel's year of publication.

(1) Eight weeks since we left Chicago, three shows to the bad, and still a thousand miles from the Great White Way [George V. Hobart, *Go to It*, 1908].
(2) Ever since the 1890s Broadway has reigned as the "Great White Way," the major theatrical centre of the country [*Britannica*, vol. 24, p. 912].

**Grove, the** *Ladbroke Grove, London, England.* A colloquial shortening of the name of the central North Kensington street.

**Gut, the** *Strait Street, Valletta, Malta.* A sailors' nickname for the street, a formerly notorious red-light district. The word has a generic sense for a narrow lane, in this case one winding downhill in the old part of the city.

**High, the** *High Street, Oxford, England.* A shortening of the name of the city's main thoroughfare, used chiefly by university people.

(1) It is still pleasant to see fewer foreign visitors pacing the High with guide books [C.S. Lewis, *Letters*, May 10, 1921 (1966)].
(2) Not so long ago, the High, as it's known, was jammed solid from dawn to dusk with traffic [*Sunday Times*, March 6, 2005].

**Hippest Street in the World, the** *King's Road, Chelsea, London, England.* Chelsea's main thoroughfare gained fame (or notoriety) as a leading light in the commercial counterculture of the 1960s, in what was known as **Swinging London** (see in Dictionary). Hence its nickname, adopted for the subtitle of Max Décharné's 2005 history of the street: *King's Road: The Rise and Fall of the Hippest Street in the World.*

**Hungry Mile, the** *(part of) Sussex Street, Sydney, Australia.* The street was so nicknamed in the 1930s for the unemployed wharf laborers who tramped it looking for work.

**Incandescent District** or **Belt, the** *Broadway, New York City, USA.* The former nickname, said to have been coined by columnist Walter Winchell, refers to the bright lights of the **Great White Way.** *Cp.* **Mazda Lane.**

**Ink Line, the** *Fleet Street, London, England.* A former London cabbies' nickname for the street in the days when it was the center of the newspaper industry. There is a pun on "incline," as the street leads directly to Ludgate Hill.

**International Avenue** *First Avenue, New York City, USA.* An occasional nickname for the street, where the United Nations complex is located.

**Kö, die** *Königsallee, Düsseldorf, Germany.* A short colloquial name for the city's main commercial street. Two shopping arcades here are the Kö-Galerie and Kö-Karree, opened in 1985.

**KP** *King's Parade, Cambridge, England.* An initialism of the central street's name, as commonly current among university students.

**Ladies' Mile, the** *Rotten Row, London, England.* The alternate name of the riding and carriage road in Hyde Park is first recorded in Mary Elizabeth Braddon's novel *The Lady's Mile* (1866).

**Lane, the** *(1) Chancery Lane, London, England; (2) Drury Lane, London, England; (3) Petticoat Lane, London, England.* The short name is used for any well-known street called "Lane" in London. For Chancery Lane the reference would be to the legal institutions there, for Drury Lane to the theater so named (properly the Theatre Royal), for **Petticoat Lane** to the popular market.

> (1) (Chancery Lane) The 'Lane' (as Chancery Lane is familiarly called) [*Chambers's Journal*, February 18, 1865].
>
> (2) (Petticoat Lane) Friday is the day for buying flowers in the Lane [Maisie Birmingham, *You Can Help Me*, 1974].

**Leadville** *Western Avenue, London, England.* The name for the stretch of the A40 motorway as it leads west out of London toward Oxford comes from a study of the people who live beside it, as quoted below. The name refers to the pollution from the leaded petrol of the cars that endlessly stream along the road, and was suggested to the author of the study by one of the residents he interviewed.

> [When] I told him I was writing a book about Western Avenue, he responded enthusiastically. 'I call it Leadville,' he said, as we stood on his doorstep. 'You can put that in your book... Me and my mate did a survey — we reckon eighty million cars pass this house every year' [Edward Platt, *Leadville: A Biography of the A40*, 2000].

**Lex Ave** *Lexington Avenue, New York City, USA.* A common abbreviated form of the central street's name.

> If I make good in the lecture, I might one day end up speaking at the Lex. Ave 'Y' [John Kennedy Toole, *The Confederacy of Dunces*, 1980].

**Little America** *Grosvenor Square, London, England.* The square has been associated with the United States since John Adams, first US minister to Britain, occupied No. 9 in the 1780s. The US embassy is on the west side of the square while in the center stands a statue of President Franklin D. Roosevelt. *See also* **Eisenhower Platz.**

**Little Lebanon** *Edgware Road, London, England.* The road running north from central London to Edgware is so nicknamed for its many Middle Eastern restaurants.

**Loneliest Road in America, the** *Highway 50, Nevada, USA.* The highway, running across Nevada from Utah to California, is often near-empty. Hence the nickname, with an alternate form as "the Loneliest Highway in the World."

> 'The loneliest road in America' crosses picturesque Great Basin terrain ... and towns are few [*Lonely Planet USA*, 2004].

**Mad Ave** *Madison Avenue, New York City, USA.* The abbreviated street name is often used in connection with advertising or public relations, as "Mad Ave hype." (The suggestion of "mad" is fortuitously apt in this usage.)

**Madison** *Madison Avenue, New York City, USA.* A regular short form of the major street's name. *Cp.* **Park.**

> (1) From 72nd and Madison I called Alison's doorman [Bret Easton Ellis, *Glamorama*, 1998].
>
> (2) Madison's most interesting sites come in a four-block strip above 53rd Street [*The Rough Guide to New York City*, 2005].

**Magnificent Mile, the** *(part of) Michigan Avenue, Chicago, Illinois, USA.* The name is that of the northern half of the city's main commercial street.

> North of the river along Michigan Avenue is "the Magnificent Mile" — Chicago's answer to New York City's Fifth Avenue in commercial elegance [*Britannica*, vol. 16, p. 1].

**Main, the** *Boulevard St. Laurent, Montreal, Canada.* The street plays a key role in dividing the city's eastern and western halves, so that any street running right across is suffixed "Ouest" ("West") in the western half and "Est" ("East") in the eastern, such as Rue St. Antoine Ouest and Rue St. Antoine Est.

**Main Stem, the** *125th Street, Harlem, New York City, USA.* The nickname is that of the district's main thoroughfare.

**Main Street of America, the** *Route 66, USA.* The nickname is that of America's most famous highway, running for 2,500 miles from Chicago to Los Angeles. Route 66 was designated in 1926 and decommissioned in 1985.

> Route 66, once the 'Main Street of America,' is a nostalgic driving tour [*Lonely Planet USA*, 2004].

**Mazda Lane** *Broadway, New York City, USA.* The nickname referred to the bright lights of the **Great White Way**, from the Mazda make of lamp. The name was coined by columnist Walter Winchell. *Cp.* **Incandescent District.**

**Millionaires' Row** *(1) The Bishops Avenue, London, England; (2) Kensington Palace Gardens, London, England.* The Bishops Avenue, in Hampstead Garden Suburb, is so nicknamed for its wealthy residents, many of them Middle-

Eastern royals. The better-known Kensington Palace Gardens is so dubbed for its opulent mansions, most of them now occupied by embassies.

(1) (Kensington Palace Gardens) Charles drove off past the park, the Broad Walk, and Millionaire's [*sic*] Row [John Guthrie, *Is This What I Wanted?*, 1950].

(2) (The Bishops Avenue) Even as long ago as the 1930s, The Bishops Avenue was nicknamed "millionaires' row"... Tycoons built houses there to confirm their status [*Sunday Times*, May 22, 2005].

(3) (The Bishops Avenue) The Bishops Avenue is celebrated ... as "Millionaires' Row." It is the street where those with a great deal of money ... congregate to construct immortality symbols [*The Times*, August 9, 2005].

(4) (Kensington Palace Gardens) [The Royal Borough of Kensington and Chelsea] includes Kensington Palace Gardens or "Millionaires Row," where houses sell for up to £70 million [*The Times*, November 14, 2005].

**Minnesota Strip, the** *(part of) Eight Avenue, New York City, USA*. The section of Eighth Avenue in Times Square has been so nicknamed for the Minnesota runaways working as prostitutes here.

**Miracle Mile, the** *(part of) Wilshire Boulevard, Los Angeles, California, USA*. A nickname for the central stretch of the street with its trendsetting shops, fashion houses, and expensive hotels, restaurants, and nightclubs. It was LA's first shopping district outside of downtown, designed in 1921 by developer A.W. Ross to be a "Fifth Avenue of the West."

**Moke Street** *Lightbody Street, Liverpool, England*. A local name for the street in the days when it was regularly used by carthorses.

**Money Street** *Old Ropery, Liverpool, England*. A neatly punning local name for the small street, as if "money for old rope."

**Mother Road, the** *Route 66, USA*. An alternate nickname for the **Main Street of America**, as the nation's former prime artery. The name was made famous by John Steinbeck's novel *The Grapes of Wrath* (1939.

(1) Route 66 between Oklahoma's two biggest cities is the country's longest remaining continuous stretch of the Mother Road [*Lonely Planet USA*, 2004].

(2) John Steinbeck's humanity is better sensed on derelict Route 66, the "Mother Road," than in Cannery Row's tourist tat [Bel Mooney in *The Times*, August 6, 2005].

**Mouffe, la** *rue Mouffetard, Paris, France*. A short colloquial name for the street and the district around it.

**Museum Mile** *(part of) Fifth Avenue, New York City, USA*. The section of Fifth Avenue above 57th Street is so nicknamed for its many museums, including the Metropolitan Museum of Art and Museum of the City of New York.

**New York's Red Square** *Union Square, New York City, USA*. The square earned its Soviet-style nickname from the political protests and mass demonstrations held here in the 1920s to 1940s. Political groups based in the neighborhood included the Communist and Socialist parties, while Tammany Hall, the executive committee of the Democratic Party, moved into a new building on the square's northeast corner in 1929.

**Pana** or **Panah** *Patrick Street, Cork, Ireland*. A colloquial name for the city's main street, based on a short form of its proper name with a local suffix of endearment, as described in the quote below. *Cp.* **Barracca**.

I relish the oddities that show in their vocabulary and positively rejoice when I hear the suffix "ah" which the Cork idiom tends to add to certain words so that Patrick Street becomes *Panah*, Barrack Street *Barrackah*, Farranferris *Farranah* [Tom McElligott, *Six O'Clock All Over Cork*, 1992].

**Park** *Park Lane, New York City, USA*. A regular short name of the major street. *Cp.* **Madison**.

(1) Down on Park, between 79th and 80th, is a black Jeep [Bret Easton Ellis, *Glamorama*, 1998].

(2) The streets which zigzag between the main drags of Madison and Park have attractions of their own [*The Rough Guide to New York City*, 2004].

**PCH, the** *Pacific Coast Highway (Highway 1), California, USA*. An abbreviated name for the scenic route along the California coast between Sonoma County and San Diego.

Avoid driving to Malibu in the rush hour, when traffic along the PCH moves at a snail's pace [*Fodor's Los Angeles 2006*].

**Petticoat Lane** *Middlesex Street, London, England*. The East End street, noted for its Sunday morning market, was officially renamed around 1830 but is popularly known by its original name, deriving from the old-clothes market here.

The man who had been given the licence had described the street as "Petticoat Lane." Section 21 (1) required that the particular street must be named, and Petticoat Lane has become Middlesex Street [*Police Review*, November 17, 1972].

**Piccy** *Piccadilly, London, England*. A short colloquial form of the name of the commercially central street.

**Pill Avenue** *Harley Street, London, England*. A London cabbies' nickname for the street renowned for its medical specialists.

**Processional Street of America, the** *Pennsyl-*

*vania Avenue, Washington, DC, USA.* The central street, running between the White House and the Capitol, is regarded as the USA's main thoroughfare. Its nickname thus refers to the processions that pass along it on important occasions, such as the inauguration of a new president or a visit by a head of state.

**Prom, the** *Promenade, Cheltenham, England.* A colloquial abbreviation of the name of a central street in the Gloucestershire town.

Cheltenham's Promenade was levelled to be 'the Prom,' but Parabola Road did not become 'the Prab' [Ivor Brown, *Words on the Level*, 1973].

**Quincampe, la** *rue Quincampoix, Paris, France.* A colloquial short form of the central street's name.

**Restaurant Row** *(part of) West 46th Street, New York City, USA.* The name relates to the block of eateries between Eighth Avenue and Ninth Avenue here.

**Ride, the** *Rotten Row, London, England.* A short name for the famous track for horseriders in Hyde Park. *Cp.* **Row.**

Onward we moved, and reach'd the Ride
   Where gaily flows the human tide [Matthew Arnold, "Epilogue to Lessing's Laocoön," 1867].

**Road, the** *Charing Cross Road, London, England.* The casual form of the name was long current among bibliophiles and owners of the second-hand bookshops for which the street is famous.

**Road to Ruin, the** *A303, England.* The main road known more positively as the **Sunshine Route** is so punningly nicknamed because its frequent delays cause friction among the families driving down it.

**Rothschild Row** *(part of) Piccadilly, London, England.* The western end of Piccadilly was so formerly nicknamed for the many members of the Rothschild banking family who lived here. The name was based on Rotten Row (*see* **Row**).

**Row, the** *(1) Goldsmith's Row, London, England; (2) Paternoster Row, London, England; . 3) Rotten Row, London, England.* A short name for each of the named streets, Paternoster Row being a center of bookselling and publishing, and Rotten Row a sandy track in Hyde Park reserved for horseriders. ("Long. and Co." in the quote below is the publishing house of Longman and Co., in which Owen Rees, Thomas Hurst, and Cosmo Orme were the "Co." to Thomas Norton Longman. In 1811 Thomas Brown joined the business, and in 1824 Bevis Green, giving the firm's full title as Longman, Hurst, Rees, Orme, Brown, and Green.)

(Paternoster Row) The last edition see, by Long and Co.,

Rees, Hurst, and Orme, our fathers in the Row [Sir Walter Scott, *The Search after Happiness*, 1817].

**Royal Mile, the** *Castlehill, Lawnmarket, High Street, and Canongate, Edinburgh, Scotland.* The street so known, almost exactly a mile in length, consists of the four successive streets named above, which run from Edinburgh Castle to Holyroodhouse. The name is popularly associated with the Scottish kings who rode from one of these royal buildings to the other, but although the route is ancient, the name itself is first found only in 1901, when it appears (in quotes) in W.M. Gilbert's *Edinburgh in the Nineteenth Century.* It was further popularized as the title of a guidebook by Robert T. Skinner published in 1920.

To walk down the Royal Mile is to walk through much of the history of Scotland [Macnie/ McLaren, p. 123].

**Sébasto, le** *boulevard de Sébastopol, Paris, France.* A colloquial shortened form of the central street's name. *Cp.* **Topol.**

**St Old's** *St Aldate's, Oxford, England.* A nickname for one of the city's oldest streets, current among university students. The name is historically correct, as the street name actually means "old gate," and no saint is involved.

**Spaghetti Junction** *Gravelly Hill Interchange, England.* The nickname graphically describes the complex interlacing of flyovers at the point where the M6 motorway links with the A38 and A5127 north of Birmingham. The interchange straddles three canals, two rivers, and a main railway line. The term dates from the 1970s.

**Stagville** *Santa Monica Boulevard, West Hollywood, California, USA.* The street is so nicknamed for its many pornographic shops and massage parlors, from "stag" as a word for a lusty male.

**Street, the** *(1) Fleet Street, London, England; (2) Great Portland Street, London, England; (3) Madison Avenue, New York City, USA; (4) Wall Street, New York City, USA.* Fleet Street was so known in the days when it was the home of the newspaper industry (*see* **Street of Ink**), while Great Portland Street was so called by auto traders (*see* **GP**). Madison Avenue, long associated with fashionable shops and residences, became identified with the US advertising industry, while Wall Street is the location of New York Stock Exchange and synonymous with high finance.

(1) (Wall Street) "The Street" begins to play a larger and larger part in the financial world, owing to the enormous amounts of American capital it holds and of foreign capital it distributes [*The Nation*, August 16, 1883].

(2) (Fleet Street) A year ago he was coming back as Editor to the Street [*News Chronicle*, February 11, 1932].

(3) (Fleet Street) The Street isn't the best place to come looking for a job at the moment [Laurence Meynell, *Virgin Luck*, 1963].

**Street of Ink, the** *Fleet Street, London, England*. A nickname for the street that until the 1980s was the center of the newspaper industry.

It has been called "The Street of Adventure" and "The Street of Ink" [Cecil Hunt, *Talk of the Town*, 1951].

**Street of Shame, the** *Fleet Street, London, England*. The nickname refers to the scandalous and sensational stories printed in the newspapers that formerly had their offices on the street. *See also* **Street of Ink**.

These days the "Street of Ink" or "Street of Shame," as it used to be known, is no more [*The Rough Guide to London*, 1997].

**Strip, the** *(1) (part of) Broadway, San Francisco, California, USA; (2) (part of) Las Vegas Boulevard, Las Vegas, Nevada, USA; (3) Sunset Strip, Los Angeles, California, USA*. The best-known "strip" is that of Las Vegas, the four-mile section of Las Vegas Boulevard that is the city's commercial center, with an array of luxury hotels, casinos, and nightclubs. The San Francisco "strip" is as in quote (1) below. For Los Angeles, *see* **Sunset Strip**.

(1) (Broadway) In San Francisco, Broadway is 'the strip,' a combination of Macdougal Street in Greenwich Village and strip row on 'East Bal'more' in Baltimore. It is about four blocks long, an agreeably goofy row of skin-show nightclubs ... and 'colorful' bars with names like Burp Hollow [Tom Wolfe, "The Put-Together Girl," *The Pump House Gang*, 1968].

(2) (Las Vegas Boulevard) On a trip from Chicago to L.A., he got curious about Vegas and decided to have a look at it. Just passing through, strolling along and digging the sights on the Strip [Hunter S. Thompson, *Fear and Loathing in Las Vegas*, 1971].

(3) (Las Vegas Boulevard) Nothing on earth prepares you for the Strip, the throbbing spine of Las Vegas [*The Times*, June 17, 2005].

(4) (Sunset Strip) It's easier to navigate the Strip by day; cruising and valet gridlock are typical at night [*Fodor's Los Angeles 2006*].

**Suckie** *Sauchihall Street, Glasgow, Scotland*. A short familiar name for the city's best-known street. A local phrase runs "up Suckie, doon Buckie, an alang Argyle," denoting an ideal afternoon's shopping (or window-shopping) perambulation up Sauchihall Street, down Buchanan Street, and along Argyle Street.

**Sunset** *Sunset Boulevard, Los Angeles, California, USA*. A short colloquial name for the familiar street. In quote (1) below, Sunset and Vine,

at the intersection of Sunset Boulevard and Vine Street, is now a luxury high-rise apartment and shopping complex. A little to the north, Hollywood and Vine, at the corner of Hollywood Boulevard and Vine Street, is a world-famous intersection associated with movie stars.

(1) We went to Hollywood to try to work in the drugstore at Sunset and Vine. Now there was a corner! [Jack Kerouac, *On the Road*, 1957].

(2) Continue on Sunset as it snakes past the lush estates of Beverly Hills and Bel Air [*Fodor's Los Angeles 2006*].

**Sunset Strip, the** *(part of) Sunset Boulevard, Los Angeles, California, USA*. The name is that of the original **Strip**, a one-mile section of the 21-mile-long Sunset Boulevard that subsequently came to be associated with the drug users, derelicts, and other subculture and counterculture individuals who frequented it.

(1) This huge red Chevy convertible we'd just rented off a lot on the Sunset Strip [Hunter S. Thompson, *Fear and Loathing in Las Vegas*, 1971].

(2) Sunset Strip has been a haven of hedonism since Prohibition days [Catherine Gerber, *Los Angeles*, 2004].

(3) Turn left and you'll soon be in the middle of the nightclubs and giant billboards of the fabled Sunset Strip [*Fodor's Los Angeles 2006*].

**Sunshine Route, the** *A303, England*. The main road from Basingstoke, Hampshire, takes Londoners down to the beaches of the **West Country** (see in Appendix 1, p. 269). Hence its nickname. *See also* **Road to Ruin**.

**Swing Street** *52nd Street, New York City, USA*. The street was so nicknamed in the 1930s and 1940s for its many jazz clubs, especially between 5th and 6th avenues.

**That Great Street** *State Street, Chicago, Illinois, USA*. The street, running vertically through the city center, was famed as a lively commercial hub.

On State Street, that great street
 I just wanna say
 They do things
 They don't do on Broadway, say [Fred Fisher, song "Chicago," 1922].

**Tin Pan Alley** *(1) Denmark Street, London, England; (2) 28th Street, New York City, USA*. The name originated in New York, where many of the music publishers had their offices around Union Square before moving in the 1890s to 28th Street. The nickname is generally attributed to US composer Monroe H. Rosenfeld, who when preparing an article on popular music for the *New York Herald* is said have headed it "Tin Pan Alley" on hearing the strains of a tinny piano from Harry Von Tilzer's office on that same street. In due course the nickname was also applied to London's equivalent, a small street off Charing Cross Road.

> (28th Street) Down Twenty-eighth Street, which is known as "Tin Pan Alley," a dozen music publishing houses grind out new song "hits" daily [*Busy Man's Magazine* (Toronto), January 1909].

**Tolerance Street** *Nevsky Prospekt, St. Petersburg, Russia.* The city's main street was so nicknamed in prerevolutionary times for the many non–Orthodox denominations that were permitted to build their churches here. The name translates Russian *ulitsa terpimosti*, "street of tolerance."

**Topol, le** *boulevard de Sébastopol, Paris, France.* A colloquial shortened form of the central street's name. *Cp.* **Sébasto**.

**Track, the** *(part of) Stuart Highway, Australia.* A colloquial name for the section of Northern Territory highway between Darwin and Alice Springs.

> (1) Another turn-out had started just before him — a family wagonette from 'up the track' [R.B. Plowman, *The Boundary Rider*, 1935].
>
> (2) Now calling for expressions of interest from performers including those 'down the track.' 'We want to cover the whole of the NT' [*Northern Territory News* (Darwin), September 10, 1984].
>
> (3) Even car drivers tend to press on down the Track before something breaks or wears out [*The Rough Guide to Australia*, 2001].

**Turl, the** *Turl Street, Oxford, England.* A shortening of the name of one of the city's streets, used mainly by university people. (The abbreviated form is etymologically justifiable, as the street was named for the *turl* or twirling gate here, whereas the **Broad** and the **High** take their adjectival names from the streets.)

**Upper Parly** *Upper Parliament Street, Liverpool, England.* A local colloquial form of the street's name, familiar from the children's tongue-twister: "I'll chase a pup up Upper Parly."

**Vaseline, rue de** *Warmoesstraat, Amsterdam, Netherlands.* The central street derives its nickname from its location in the city's gay quarter. (The term is used elsewhere, as Vaseline Heights for the gay focus of Portland, Oregon, USA, and Vaseline Valley for a section of Oxford Street, Sydney, Australia, the city's gay center.)

> Greased-up, black-capped leather boys clink down the Warmoesstraat (dubbed "La Rue de Vaseline") [*Time Out Amsterdam Guide*, 1998].

**Voxey, the** *Vauxhall Road, Liverpool, England.* A local name for the road that leads north from central Liverpool to the district of Vauxhall.

**Whorehouse Row** *South Akard Street, Dallas, Texas, USA.* A nickname used by taxi drivers, for the brothels located on the street.

**World's Crookedest Street, the** *Lombard Street, San Francisco, California, USA.* A touristic name for the short street with its sharp bends, as described in the quote below.

> [Lombard Street] is just a 100-yard or so stretch of downhill road where a 19th-century property developer decided he'd had enough of all this straight-up-and-down business and indulged in a fit of zigzagging [*Sunday Times*, July 24, 2005].

**X-Way, the** *John F. Fitzgerald Expressway, Boston, Massachusetts, USA.* A local colloquial name for the expressway. *See also* **Distressway**.

> The "X-Way," as some residents called it [Thomas H. O'Connor, *Boston A to Z*, 2000].

# Appendix 3: Romany Names of Places

*The Romany (Gypsy) names of places below, all but one in the British Isles, are listed by George Borrow in his* Romano Lavo-Lil: Word-Book of the Romany *(1874). A literal translation of the Romany name is given in square brackets and a gloss on this follows the identified place. References to Dictionary entries are given where appropriate. Gav is "town," tem is "country," engro is "fellow," and eskey is an adjectival suffix. An alphabetical index to the 39 names follows.*

**Baulo-mengreskey tem** [Swineherds' country] Hampshire, a county famous for its hogs. *See* **Hoglandia** in Dictionary.

**Bitcheno padlengreskey tem** [Transported fellows' country] Botany Bay, Australia's first penal colony. (*Bitcheno* is "sent," *padlo* is "across.")

**Bokra-mengreskey tem** [Shepherds' country] Sussex, a county noted for its sheep. *See* **Silly Sussex** in Dictionary.

**Bori-congriken gav** [Great church town] York, a city famous for its minster or cathedral, with other churches of note.

**Boro-rukeneskey gav** [Great tree town] Fairlop, a village, now a district of London, famous for a great oak tree, under which a fair was held.

**Boro-gueroneskey tem** [Big fellows' country] Northumberland, a county noted for its sturdy wrestlers.

**Chohawniskey tem** [Witches' country] Lancashire, a county historically associated with witches. Two notable witch trials were held in Pendle Forest in 1612 and 1633.

**Choko-mengreskey gav** [Shoemakers' town] Northampton, a city still famous for its manufacture of footwear. *See* **Leatheropolis** in Dictionary.

**Churi-mengreskey gav** [Cutlers' town] Sheffield, a city long associated with the manufacture of cutlery. *See* **Steel Capital of England** in Dictionary.

**Coro-mengreskey tem** [Potters' country] Staffordshire, a county in which the Potteries is an area famous for the manufacture of ceramics, including Wedgwood, Spode, and Minton. *See* **Creative County** and **Potteries** in Dictionary.

**Cosht-killimengreskey tem** [Cudgel players' country] Cornwall, a county traditionally noted for its sport of cudgel-play.

**Curo-mengreskey gav** [Boxers' town] Nottingham, a city noted for its boxing contests.

**Dinnelo tem** [Fools' country] Suffolk, a county whose inhabitants have long had a reputation for naivety. *See* **Silly Suffolk** in Dictionary.

**Giv-engreskey tem** [Farmers' country] Buckinghamshire, a county noted for its agricultural produce. (*Giv-engro* is literally "wheat fellow.")

**Gry-engreskey gav** [Horsedealers' town] Horncastle, a Lincolnshire town where a famous horse fair was long held, as described by Borrow in *The Romany Rye* (1857).

**Guyi-mengreskey tem** [Pudding-eaters' country] Yorkshire, a county whose Yorkshire pudding, a baked batter pudding, is still traditionally eaten with roast beef.

**Hindity-mengreskey tem** [Dirty fellows' country] Ireland, a land whose inhabitants, especially country folk, are still sometimes popularly regarded as crude or boorish.

**Jinney-mengreskey gav** [Sharpers' town] Manchester, a city formerly famous for the knowledge and cunning of its inhabitants.

**Juggal-engreskey gav** [Dog-fanciers' town] Dudley, a town once noted for its dog racing. (Romany *juggal*, "dog," is probably related to English "jackal.")

**Juvalo-mengreskey tem** [Lousy fellows' country] Scotland, described in terms of its people, at one time popularly regarded as verminous. *See* **Louseland** in Dictionary.

**Kaulo gav** [The black town] Birmingham, a

city formerly noted for its heavy industries. *See* **Black Country** in Appendix 1, p. 269.

**Levin-engreskey tem** [Hop country] Kent, a county still famous for its hop fields.

**Lil-engreskey gav** [Book fellows' town] Oxford, a famous university city.

**Matchen-eskey gav** [Fish town] Yarmouth, a noted fishing port on the North Sea coast.

**Mi-develeskey gav** [My God's town] Canterbury, a city whose cathedral is the mother church of the Anglican Communion. (Romany *devel*, "god," is related to Celtic *deva*, "goddess." *See* **Deva** in Dictionary.)

**Mi-krauliskey gav** [My King's town] London, England's capital, and the site of the British monarch's residence, Buckingham Palace.

**Nashi-mescro gav** [Racers' town] Newmarket, a town with a famous racecourse. *See* **Headquarters of the English Turf** in Dictionary.

**Pappin-eskey tem** [Duck country] Lincolnshire, a county noted for its fens and marshes. *See* **Aviary of England** in Dictionary.

**Paub-pawnugo tem** [Apple-water country] Herefordshire, a county famous for its cider ("apple water"). *See* **Cider Country** in Dictionary.

**Porrum-engreskey tem** [Leek-eaters' country] Wales, seen in terms of its symbolic plant. *See* **Land of the Leek** in Dictionary.

**Pov-engreskey tem** [Potato country] Norfolk, a county still noted for its potatoes.

**Rashayeskey gav** [Clergyman's town] Ely, a cathedral city not far from Cambridge. (Romany *rashi*, "clergyman," is related to Hindu *rishi*, "holy," as in the title *maharishi*, "great sage.")

**Rokr-engreskey gav** [Talking fellows' town] Norwich, a city noted for its lawyers.

**Shammin-engreskey gav** [Chairmakers' town] Windsor, home of the Windsor chair, a distinctive type of wooden dining chair with a semicircular back.

**Tudlo tem** [Milk country] Cheshire, a county famous for its cheese.

**Weshen-eskey gav** [Forest town] Epping, a town in Epping Forest, Essex, which still survives in places.

**Weshen-juggal-slommo-mengreskey tem** [Fox-hunting fellows' country] Leicestershire, a county famous for its hunts, such as the Cottesmore and the Quorn. (*Weshen-jugall* is literally "dog of the wood," i.e. "fox"; *slommo* is from *slom*, "to follow.")

**Wongareskey gav** [Coal town] Newcastle, a city formerly famous for its coal mines and as a port for shipping coal.

**Wusto-mengreskey tem** [Wrestlers' country] Devonshire, a county where wrestling was long a traditional sport.

## *Alphabetical Index to Above Places*

# Appendix 4: Renamed Countries

*The following countries have been renamed since 1900. A date after the original or earlier name is that of the country's adoption of that name. The date after the present name is that of the year of renaming. Plus signs (+) linking the names of original countries mean that those countries joined to form a new country. Plus signs linking the names of present countries mean that these countries devolved from an earlier country. Thus, Bohemia and Slovakia Moravia combined in 1918 to form Czechoslovakia, from which in turn the Czech Republic, and devolved in the years stated. The notation "(and originally)" means that the present country has reverted to its original name. Thus, Cambodia was known by this name before it became the Khmer Republic in 1970. It will be seen that many of the renamings are of countries in Africa, where a "wind of change" blew in the second half of the 20th century.*

Afars and Issas *see* French Somaliland

Basutoland (1822) Lesotho (1966)

Bechuanaland (1885) Botswana (1966)

Belgian Congo (1908) Congo (1960); Zaïre (1971); Democratic Republic of the Congo (1997)

Belorussia (1919) Belarus (1991)

Bohemia + Moravia Czechoslovakia (1918); Czech Republic (1993) + Slovakia (1993)

British Central Africa (1893) Nyasaland (1907); Malawi (1966)

British Guiana (1831) Guyana (1966)

British Honduras (1840) Belize (1971)

Burma Myanmar (1989)

Central African Empire *see* Ubangi-Shari-Chad

Ceylon Sri Lanka (1972)

Congo *see* Belgian Congo

Czechoslovakia *see* Bohemia

Dahomey (1894) Benin (1975)

East Pakistan (1947) Bangladesh (1971)

Ellice Islands (1819) Tuvalu (1976)

Fernando Po (1494) + Rio Muni (1885) Spanish Guinea (1926); Equatorial Guinea (1963)

Formosa (1590) Taiwan (1895)

French Somaliland (1885) Afars and Issas (1967); Djibouti (1977)

French Sudan (1920) Sudanese Republic (1958); Mali (1960)

German East Africa (1891) Tanganyika (1920); (+ Zanzibar) Tanzania (1964)

German Southwest Africa (1885) South-West Africa (1915); Namibia (1968)

Gilbert Islands (1788) Kiribati (1977)

Gold Coast Ghana (1957)

Kampuchea *see* Khmer Republic

Khmer Republic (1970) Kampuchea (1976); Cambodia (1989) (and originally)

Korea North Korea + South Korea (1948)

Malagasy Republic (1960) Madagascar (1975) (and originally)

Moldavia Moldova (1990)

Moravia *see* Bohemia

New Hebrides (1774) Vanuatu (1980)

North Vietnam (1954) (+ South Vietnam) Vietnam (1975) (and originally)

North Yemen (1962) (+ South Yemen) Yemen (1990)

Northern Rhodesia (1911) Zambia (1964)

Nyasaland *see* British Central Africa

Persia Iran (1935)

Porto Rico Puerto Rico (1935)

Portuguese East Africa (1891) Mozambique (1975) (and originally)

Portuguese Guinea (1879) Guinea-Bissau (1973)

Portuguese West Africa (1589) Angola (1914)

Rio Muni *see* Fernando Po

Ruanda Ruanda-Urundi (1916); Rwanda (1962) + Burundi (1962) (and originally)

Siam Thailand (1938)

South Vietnam (1954) (+ North Vietnam) Vietnam (1975) (and originally)

South Yemen (1967) (+ North Yemen) Yemen (1990)

South-West Africa *see* German Southwest Africa

Southern Rhodesia (1900)    Rhodesia (1964); Zimbabwe (1980)

Soviet Union (1922)    Russia (1991) (and originally)

Spanish Guinea *see* Fernando Po

Spanish Sahara (1884)    Western Sahara (1976)

Tanganyika *see* German East Africa

Ubangi-Shari-Chad (1906)    Central African Republic (1958); Central African Empire (1976); Central African Republic (1979)

Upper Volta (1947)    Burkina Faso (1984)

Urundi *see* Ruanda

USSR *see* Soviet Union

Yugoslavia (1918)    Croatia (1991) + Slovenia (1991) + Macedonia (1991) + Bosnia-Hercegovina (1992) + Serbia (2006) + Montenegro (2006)

Zaïre *see* Belgian Congo

Zanzibar *see* German East Africa

# Appendix 5: Roman Names of Towns and Cities in Europe

*The list below is supplied partly for historical interest and partly for contemporary reference, since some of the names live on in a secondary context, as in literature or commerce. As such they can qualify for entry in the dictionary, as **Augusta**, **Deva**, **Eblana**, or **Lutetia**. (By definition, the listing includes only towns and cities, not countries and provinces. European names such as **Caledonia**, **Cambria** and **Lusitania** will even so be found in the dictionary.)*

Abbatis Villa   Abbeville, France
Abellinum   Avelino, Italy
Acunum Acusio   Montélimar, France
Aedua   Autun, France
Aeminium   Coimbra, Portugal
Agedincum   Sens, France
Agrigentum   Agrigento, Italy
Alba Pompeia   Alba, Italy
Albania   Aubagne, France
Albiga   Albi, France
Alburgum   Aalborg, Denmark
Aletrium   Alatri, Italy
Ambacia   Amboise, France
Ambianum   Amiens, France
Ameria   Amelia, Italy
Andematunnum   Langres, France
Anicium   Le Puy, France
Anneciacum   Annecy, France
Antipolis   Antibes, France
Antiquaria   Antequera, Spain
Antunnacum   Andernach, Germany
Apuania   Carrara, Italy
Apulum   Alba Iulia, Italy
Aquae   Acqui Terme, Italy
Aquae Arnemetiae   Buxton, England
Aquae Augustae   Dax, France
Aquae Calidae   Bath, England
Aquae Flaviae   Chaves, Portugal
Aquae Grani   Aachen, Germany
Aquae Gratianae   Aix-les-Bains, France
Aquae Mortuae   Aigues Mortes, France
Aquae Panoniae   Baden, Germany
Aquae Sextiae   Aix-en-Provence, France
Aquae Sulis   Bath, England

Aquae Tarbellicae   Dax, France
Arausio   Orange, France
Arcobriga   Arcos de la Frontera, Spain
Arelas   Arles, France
Argentorate   Strasbourg, France
Ariminum   Rimini, Italy
Arretium   Arezzo, Italy
Artesium   Artois, France
Asculum Picenum   Ascoli Piceno, Italy
Asisium   Assisi, Italy
Asta Colonia   Asti, Italy
Asta Pompeia   Asti, Italy
Asturias   Oviedo, Spain
Asturica Augusta   Astorga, Spain
Athenae   Athens, Greece
Augusta   London, England
Augusta Auscorum   Auch, France
Augusta Pretoria   Aosta, Italy
Augusta Suessionum   Soissons, France
Augusta Taurinorum   Turin, Italy
Augusta Treverorum   Trier, Germany
Augusta Vangionum   Worms, Germany
Augusta Vindelicorum   Augsburg, Germany
Augustobona Tricassium   Troyes, France
Augustodunum   Autun, France
Augustodurum   Bayeux, France
Augustonemetum   Clermont (now Clermont-Ferrand), France
Augustoritum   Lemovicensium   Limoges, France
Aurelia Aquensis   Baden-Baden, Germany
Aurelianum   Orléans, France
Autesiodorum   Auxerre, France
Autricum   Chartres, France

Avaricum   Bourges, France
Baeterrae   Béziers, France
Barium   Bari, Italy
Bauzanum   Bolzano, Italy
Belli Quadrum   Beaucaire, France
Bellovacum   Beauvais
Beneventum   Benevento, Italy
Bergomum   Bergamo, Italy
Bigorra   Tarbes, France
Blesae   Blois, France
Bononia   (1) Bologna, Italy; (2) Boulogne, France; (3) Vidin, Bulgaria
Borbetomagus   Worms, Germany
Bracara Augusta   Braga, Portugal
Brigantium   (1) Bregenz, Austria; (2) Briançon, France
Briovera   St.-Lô, France
Briva Curretia   Brive-la-Gaillarde, France
Briva Isarae   Pontoise, France
Brixia   Brescia, Italy
Brundisium   Brindisi, Italy
Burdigala   Bordeaux, France
Butuntum   Bitonto, Italy
Cabillonum   Chalon-sur-Saône, France
Cadurcum   Cahors, France
Caesarobriga   Talavera de la Reina, Spain
Caesarodunum   Tours, France
Caesaromagus   (1) Beauvais, France; (2) Chelmsford, England
Caesena   Cesena, Italy
Camberiacum   Chambéry, France
Cameracum   Cambrai, France
Camulodunum   Colchester, England
Canusium   Canosa di Puglia, Italy
Caralis   Cagliari, Italy
Carpentorate   Carpentras, France
Casinum   Cassino, Italy
Castra Albiensium   Castres, France
[Castra Legionis   Caerleon, Wales]
Castra Regina   Regensburg, Germany
Centum Cellae   Civitavecchia, Italy
Cephaloedium   Cefalù, Italy
Cetobriga   Setúbal, Portugal
Cistercium   Cîteaux, France
Civitas Altae Ripae   Brzeg, Poland
Civitas Carnutum   Chartres, France
Civitas Eburovicum   Évreux, France
Civitas nemetum   Speyer, Germany
Clarium   Chiari, Italy
Clippiacum   Clichy, France
Clunia   Feldkirch, Austria
Clusium   Chiusi, Italy
Colonia Agrippina   Cologne, Germany
Colonia Julia Fanestris   Fano, Italy
Comactium   Comacchio, Italy
Compendium   Compiègne, France

Compludo   León, Spain
Complutum   Alcalá de Henares, Spain
Compniacum   Cognac, France
Comum   Como, Italy
Concangis   Chester-le-Street, England
Condate   (1) Northwich, England; (2) Rennes, Frances
Condivicum   Nantes, France
Consentia   Cosenza, Italy
Constantia   Coutances, France
Constantiana   Constantsa, Romania
Corduba   Córdoba, Spain
Coriallum   Cherbourg, France
Corinium Dobunnorum   Cirencester, England
Corinthia   Corinth, Italy
Coriovalium   Heerlen, Netherlands
Crotona   Crotone, Italy
Curia Rhaetorum   Chur, Switzerland
Danum   Doncaster, England
Dertosa   Tortosa, Spain
Derventio   Malton, England
Desiderii Fanum   St.-Dizier, France
Deva   Chester, England
Dianium   Denia, Spain
Domus Dei   Domodossola, Italy
Drepanum   Trapani, Italy
Duacum   Douai, France
Dubris   Dover, England
Durnomagus   Dormagen, Germany
Durnovaria   Dorchester, England
Durobrivae   Rochester, England
Durocasses   Dreux, France
Durocobrivis   Dunstable, England
Durocortorum   Reims, France
Duroliponte   Cambridge, England
Durostorum   Silistra, Bulgaria
Durovernum Cantiacorum   Canterbury, England
Dyrrachium   Durrës, Albania
Eblana   Dublin, Ireland
Eburacum   York, England
Eburodunum   Yverdon, Switzerland
Elimberum   Auch, France
Emerita Augusta   Mérida, Spain
Epidamnus   Durrës, Albania
Eporedia   Ivrea, Italy
Eugubium   Gubbio, Italy
Faesulae   Fiesole, Italy
Fanum Fortunae   Fano, Italy
Faventia   Faenza, Italy
Felicitas Julia   Lisbon, Portugal
Felsina   Bologna, Italy
Feltria   Feltre, Italy
Fidentia   Fidenza, Italy
Firmum Picenum   Fermo, Italy
Fiscanum   Fécamp, France

Formiae   Formia, Italy
Forum Julii   Fréjus, France
Fossa Claudia   Chioggia, Italy
Fulginium   Foligno, Italy
Genua   Genoa, Italy
Gerunda   Girona, Spain
Gesoriacum   Boulogne, France
Glevum   Gloucester, England
Gobannium   Abergavenny, Wales
Gratianopolis   Grenoble, France
Helmantica   Salamanca, Spain
Hipponium   Vibo Valentia,Italy
Histonium   Vasto, Italy
Hydruntum   Otranto, Italy
Iculisma   Angoulême, France
Igabrum   Cabra, Spain
Illiturgis   Andújar, Spain
Interamna Nahars   Termi, Italy
Isca   Caerleon, Wales
Isca Dumnoniorum   Exeter, England
Isca Silurum   Caerleon, Wales
Juliomagus   Angers, France
Juvavum   Salzburg, Austria
Lacobriga   Lagos, Portugal
Lactodurum   Towcester, England
Lapurdum   Bayonne, France
Laudunum. Laon, France
Laudus   St.-Lô, France
Lemovices   Limoges, France
Lentia   Linz, Austria
Lentium   Lens, France
Lilybaeum   Marsala, Italy
Limonum   Poitiers, France
Lindum Colonia   Lincoln, England
Lingones   Langres, France
Lipsia   Leipzig, Germany
Londinium   London, England
Longovicium   Lanchester, England
Lucentum   Alicante, Spain
Lugdunum   Lyon, France
Luguvalium   Carlisle, England
Lupatia   Alta Mura, Italy
Lutetia Parisiorum   Paris, France
Maleventum   Benevento, Italy
Mamucium   Manchester, England
Marcodurum   Düren, Germany
Maritima Avaticorum   Martigues, France
Massilia   Marseille, France
Matisco Aeduorum   Mâcon, France
Mediolanum   (1) Milan, Italy; (2) Whitchurch, England
Mediolanum Santonum   Saintes, France
Melodunum   Melun, France
Menevia   St. David's, Wales
Mogontiacum   Mainz, Germany
Montilium Adhemari   Montélimar, France

Moridunum   Carmarthen, Wales
Mutina   Modena, Italy
Mylae   Milazzo, Italy
Namnetes   Nantes, France
Narbo Martius   Narbonne, France
Neapolis   Naples, Italy
Nebrissa   Lebrija, Spain
Nemausus   Nîmes, France
Nemetacum Atrebatum   Arras, France
Nemetocenna   Arras, France
Nemetodurum   Nanterre, France
Neretum   Nardò, Italy
Netum   Noto, Italy
Nicaea   Nice, France
Nidum   Neath, Wales
Nova Civitas   Neustadt an der Weinstrasse, Germany
Novaesium   Neuss, Germany
Novaria   Novara, Italy
Noviodunum   Nevers, France
Noviodunum   Nyon, Switzerland
Noviomagus   (1) Chichester, England; (2) Lisieux, France; (3) Nijmegen, Netherlands; (4) Noyon, France
Novus Portus   Dover, England
Odessus   Varna, Bulgaria
Olisipo   Lisbon, Portugal
Opitergium   Oderzo, Italy
Oppidum Ubiorum   Cologne, Germany
Orolaunum   Arlon, Belgium
Palantia   Palencia, Spain
Panormus   Palermo, Italy
Patavium   Padua, Italy
Patrae   Patras, Greece
Pax Augusta   Badajos
Pietas Julia   Pula, Croatia
Pinciacum   Poissy, France
Pistoria   Pistoia, Italy
Placentia   Piacenza, Italy
Pompaelo   Pamplona, Spain
Pons Aelii   Necastle upon Tyne,England
Pons Vetus   Pontevedra, Spain
Pontisarae   Pontoise, France
Portus Ardaoni   Portchester, England
Portus Magnus   Almería, Spain
Potentia   Potenza, Italy
Puteoli   Pozzuoli, Italy
Ratae Coritanorum   Leicester, England
Reginum   Regensburg, Germany
Regium Lepidum   Reggio nell'Emilia, Italy
Remi   Reims, France
Rhegium   Reggio di Calabria, Italy
Ricomagus   Riom, France
Riduna   Alderney, UK
Roma   Rome, Italy
Roscianum   Rossano, Italy

Rotomagus   Rouen, France
Rupella   La Rochelle, France
Sabaria   Szombathely, Hungary
Saguntum   Sagunto, Spain
Salernum   Salerno, Italy
Salinae   (1) Droitwich, England; (2) Middlewich, England
Salmantica   Salamanca, Spain
Saluciae   Saluzzo, Italy
Samarobriva   Amiens, France
Sedunum   Sion, Switzerland
Segedunum   Wallsend, England
Segodunum   Rodez, France
Segontium   Caernarvon, Wales
Senones   Sens, France
Serdica   Sofia, Bulgaria
Setabis   Játiva, Spain
Singidunum   Belgrade, Serbia
Sorviodunum   Salisbury, England
Spalatum   Split, Croatia
Sparnacum   Épernay, France
Spoletium   Spoleto, Italy
Surrentum   Sorrento, Italy
Talabriga   Talavera de la Reina, Spain
Tarraco   Tarragona, Spain

Tarvisium   Treviso, Italy
Taurasia   Turin, Italy
Telo Martius   Toulon, France
Ticinum   Pavia, Italy
Toletum   Toledo, Spain
Tolosa   Toulouse, France
Trajani Portus   Civitavecchia, Italy
Tridentum   Trento, Italy
Tullum Leucorum   Toul, France
Turoni   Tours, France
Ugernum   Beaucaire, France
Unci   Almería, Spain
Urbinum Hortense   Urbino, Italy
Valentia   Valencia, Spain
Vapincum   Gap, France
Venetia   Venice, Italy
Venta Belgarum   Winchester, England
Verulamium   St Albans, England
Vesontio   Besançon, France
Vesulum   Vesoul, France
Vesuna   Périgueux, France
Vibiscum   Vevey, Switzerland
Vicentia   Vicenza, Italy
Vindobona   Vienna, Austria
Virodunum   Verdun, France

# Appendix 6: English County Names

There can be uncertainty regarding the use of the element "-shire" in English county names. The following is a list of current [and former] English county names:

| | | | |
|---|---|---|---|
| [Avon] | Devon | Kent | Shropshire |
| Bedfordshire | Dorset | Lancashire | Somerset |
| Berkshire | Durham | Leicestershire | Staffordshire |
| Buckinghamshire | Essex | Lincolnshire | Suffolk |
| Cambridgeshire | Gloucestershire | [Middlesex] | Surrey |
| Cheshire | Hampshire | Norfolk | Sussex |
| [Cleveland] | Herefordshire | Northamptonshire | Warwickshire |
| Cornwall | Hertfordshire | Northumberland | [Westmorland] |
| [Cumberland] | [Humberside] | Nottinghamshire | Wiltshire |
| Cumbria | Huntingdonshire | Oxfordshire | Worcestershire |
| Derbyshire | Isle of Wight | Rutland | Yorkshire |

In matters of local government, one must now distinguish between counties, unitary authorities, and districts. As at 2005:

(1) Berkshire exists only as West Berkshire, with unitary authority (not county) status.

(2) Gloucestershire is a county, but South Gloucestershire is a unitary authority.

(3) Herefordshire has unitary authority (not county) status.

(4) Huntingdonshire has district (not county) status.

(5) Lincolnshire is a county, but North East Lincolnshire and North Lincolnshire are unitary authorities.

(6) Rutland has unitary authority (not county) status.

(7) Somerset is a county, but North Somerset and (the cumbersomely named) Bath and North East Somerset are unitary authorities.

(8) Sussex is divided into the two counties of East Sussex and West Sussex.

(9) Yorkshire, England's largest county, was historically divided into the three Ridings (literally "thirdings") of North Yorkshire, West Yorkshire, and East Yorkshire. It is now represented by the county of North Yorkshire and the two unitary authorities of York City and the East Riding of Yorkshire.

(10) The three "new" counties of Avon, Cleveland, and Humberside, formed in 1974, were abolished in 1996 and replaced by unitary authorities.

The 44 county names listed above can be divided into three groups:

(A) Those that *never* add "-shire,"
(B) Those that *always* have "-shire,"
(C) Those that *sometimes* add "-shire."

(A) The counties below *never* add(ed) "-shire." (*See* **Shires** in Appendix 1, p. 269, for more.)

| | |
|---|---|
| [Avon] | Kent |
| [Cleveland] | Middlesex |
| Cornwall | Norfolk |
| [Cumberland] | Northumberland |
| Cumbria | Suffolk |
| Durham | Surrey |
| Essex | Sussex |
| [Humberside] | [Westmorland] |
| Isle of Wight | |

(B) The counties below *always* have "-shire," mainly for distinction from the town or city after which they are named. Thus, Bedfordshire is named for Bedford, Buckinghamshire for Buckingham, Derbyshire for Derby, etc. An exception may be made when county status is denoted in some other way, as "the County of Buckingham," or where the counties are shown as such on a map. But this alternate designation is not common where the eponymous town or city name does not exactly match that of the county. Thus, Cheshire is named for Chester, Hampshire for Southampton (formerly known as Hampton), Lancashire for Lancaster, Shropshire for Shrewsbury, Wiltshire for Wilton, etc. The only "-shire" county not to be named for a town is Berkshire. The final "-s" in abbreviated forms of these county names, such as **Beds, Berks, Bucks, Lincs, Notts, Wilts** (see all these in Dictionary), represents the first letter of "-shire." Such forms usually comprise the first syllable of the full name followed by "-s," so that "Notts" represents "Nott(ingham)s(hire)." There are exceptions, however, notably for Hampshire as **Hants**, Northamptonshire as **Northants**, Oxfordshire as **Oxon**, and Shropshire as **Salop** (although "Shrops" is also found).

| | |
|---|---|
| Bedfordshire | Leicestershire |
| Berkshire | Lincolnshire |
| Buckinghamshire | Northamptonshire |
| Cheshire | Nottinghamshire |
| Derbyshire | Oxfordshire |
| Gloucestershire | Shropshire |
| Hampshire | Staffordshire |
| Herefordshire | Warwickshire |
| Hertfordshire | Wiltshire |
| Huntingdonshire | Worcestershire |
| Lancashire | Yorkshire |

(C) The counties below are *sometimes* found with "-shire," mainly in historical, official, or traditional contexts. Devonshire is a case in point. The Duke of Devonshire is always titled thus, and Devonshire cream is the regular name of a type of clotted cream. But "Drake he was a Devon man" (Henry Newbolt) and *cp.* **Glorious Devon** in Dictionary. Rutland usually takes "-shire" only as a hunting county, in the **Shires** (see in Appendix 1, p. 269).

Devon(shire)
Dorset(shire)
Rutland(shire)
Somerset(shire)

Devonshire — Devon to the Romantics — is one of the best known English counties [Theodora Benson and Betty Askwith, *Muddling Through, or Britain in a Nutshell*, 1936].

# Appendix 7: Astronomical Names

*Many astronomical objects such as stars and planets have nicknames or alternate names just as terrestrial places do. Below is a selection of such names for these "heavenly bodies." (The names of the Sun and Moon are capitalized when considered astronomically, but lower case when treated generally, often in a literary context.)*

**Apollo** *Sun*. The name of the Greek god of the sun is frequently found as a poetic personification. *See also* **Helios**; **Hyperion**.

Bright-hair'd Apollo!— thou who ever art
A blessing to the world — whose mighty heart
Forever pours out love, and light, and life
[Michael Clarke, "The Story of Aeneas," 1898].

**Beetlejuice** *Betelgeuse*. A humorous corruption of the name of the star Alpha Orionis, popularized by the 1988 US movie so titled. The name seems to have originated in the late 1930s among British aircrews.

**Big Blue Marble, the** *Earth*. A nickname referring to the appearance of the planet as viewed from a spacecraft. The name was the title of a US children's TV series shown weekly from 1974.

**Big Dipper, the** *(prominent part of) Ursa Major*. The popular, mainly American, name of the seven brightest stars in the constellation Ursa Major, which resemble the outline of a dipper (a ladle with a long handle). *Cp.* **Plough**.

**Big Red Sun**. The nickname came into prominence during the Gulf War of 1991, in which the glare and heat of the Sun was a force to be reckoned with.

**Blaze Star, the** *T Coronae Borealis*. The name is popularly given to the brightest known recurrent nova, which was visible to the naked eye when flaring up in 1866 and 1946.

**Charles's Wain** *(prominent part of) Ursa Major*. A former popular name for the seven brightest stars in the constellation Ursa Major, which resemble a cart or chariot. Charles is Charlemagne. The adoption of his particular name appears to have come about because the name of the nearby star Arcturus, which actually means "bear guard," was taken to be a form of the name Arturus (Arthur), and the English king

Arthur and Christian emperor Charlemagne are associated in legend. *Cp.* **Big Dipper**.

(1) Those bright starres
Which English Shepheards, Charles his waine,
do name;
But more this Ile is Charles, his waine,
Since Charles her royall wagoner became [John Davies, *Poems*, c.1626].
(2) And we danced about the may-pole and in the hazel copse,
Till Charles's Wain came out above the tall white chimney-tops [Alfred, Lord Tennyson, "New Year's Eve," 1832].

**Cynthia** *Moon*. A poetic name adopted from classical mythology, in which Cynthia is an epithet of **Diana**, from Mt. Cynthus on the island of Delos, her birthplace. *See also* **Selene**.

(1) Upon that night (a peasant's is the tale)
A Serf that cross'd the intervening vale,
When Cynthia's light almost gave way to morn,
And nearly veil'd in mist her waning horn [Lord Byron, *Lara*, 1814].
(2) O Cynthia, ten-times bright and fair!
From thy blue throne, now filling all the air,
Glance but one little beam of temper'd light
Into my bosom [John Keats, *Endymion*, 1818].

**Demon Star, the** *Algol*. The star Beta Persei is popularly so known as a translation of its Arabic name, meaning "the demon" (from the word that gave English *ghoul*). The Arabic name itself arose because the star lies in the head of Medusa, the Gorgon, in the constellation Perseus.

**Diana** *Moon*. A poetic name adopted from Roman mythology, in which Diana is a goddess of the moon.

(1) Pale fac'd Dian maketh haste to hide
Her borrow'd glory in some neighb'ring cloud
[James Shirley, *Andromana, or The Merchant's Wife*, 1660].
(2) While, on the other hand, meek Dian's crest
Floats through the azure air — an island of the

blest! [Lord Byron, *Childe Harold's Pilgrimage*, 1818].

**Dipper** *see* **Big Dipper**

**Dog Star, the** *Sirius*. The brightest star in the sky, Alpha Ursae Majoris, is so popularly known for its location in the constellation Canis Major ("Greater Dog"). The name gave "dog days" as a term for the hottest period of the year, as the star rises almost with the Sun. Hence its mention in Spenser's lines quoted below (with his gloss to explain the passage).

The rampant Lyon hunts he fast, with Dogge of noysome breath,
  Whose balefull barking brings in hast pyne, plagues, and dreery death [Edmund Spenser, *The Shepheardes Calender*, "July," 1579].
  (Thys is poetically spoken, as if the Sunne did hunt a Lion with one Dogge. The meaning whereof is, that in Iuly the sonne is in [the constellation] Leo. At which tyme the Dogge starre, which is called Syrius or Canicula reigneth, with immoderate heate causing Pestilence, drougth, and many diseases.)

**Evening Star, the** *(1) Mercury; (2) Venus*. The poetic name can apply to either planet when appearing in the western sky after sunset. *Cp.* **Morning Star**. (The ancient Greeks thought Venus was two separate stars, calling it Hesperus when it appeared in the evening, and Phosphorus when they saw it in the morning. Mercury, similarly, was called Hermes as an evening star and Apollo as a morning one.)

Disporting, till the amorous bird of night
  Sung spousal, and bid haste the Evening-star
  On his hill-top to light the bridal lamp [John Milton, *Paradise Lost*, 1674].

**Gaia** *Earth*. The planet Earth has been so labeled as a living entity within the Solar System. The name is that of Gaea (Ge), the Greek goddess or personification of Earth, and was adopted in this altered spelling by the British scientist James Lovelock for his so-called Gaia hypothesis, elaborated in the 1970s, as a theory that the Earth functions as a single organism, a giant cell.

When I first introduced Gaia, I had vague hopes that it might be denounced from the pulpit and thus made acceptable to my scientific colleagues. As it was, Gaia was embraced by the theologians and by a wide range of New Age writers and thinkers but denounced by biologists [James Lovelock, "Gaia Takes Flight," *Earthwatch*, September/October 1992].

**Great Bear, the** *Ursa Major*. A translation of the Latin name of the third-largest constellation. *Cp.* **Little Bear**.

**Guardians of the Pole, the** *Kochab and Pherkad*. A popular name for the two stars Beta and Gamma Ursae Minoris that lie in the bowl of the **Little Dipper** and that thus seem to be guarding the **Pole Star**.

**Helios** *Sun*. A poetic personalization of the Sun, from the Greek word for it. In Greek mythology, Helios is the equivalent of the Roman **Sol**. (In the quote below, Eos is the goddess of the dawn.)

Helios is doomed to labour every day;
  And rest there never is for him
  Or for his horses, when rose-fingered Eos
  Leaves Ocean and to heaven ascends [Mimnermus, *Nanno*, 1st c. BC, quoted in Thomas Keightley, *Classical Mythology*, rev. and ed. by Leonhard Schmitz, 1902].

**Hyperion** *Sun*. In Greek mythology, Hyperion was the son of Uranus and Gaea (*see* **Gaia**), and father of **Helios** and **Selene**. As such, he is also equated with Helios himself, so personifies the Sun. His name occurs in literature, as in the quotes below. (In astronomical nomenclature, Hyperion is one of the 18 satellites of Saturn.)

(1) Even from Hyperion's rising in the east
  Until his very downfall in the sea [William Shakespeare, *Titus Andronicus*, 1594].
  (2) When the might
  Of Hyperion from his noon-tide throne
  Unbends their [i.e. the winds'] languid pinions [Mark Akenside, "Hymn to the Naiads," 1758].

**Kids, the** *Zeta and Eta Aurigae*. The popular name for the two stars takes them to represent two young goats, offspring of the bright star Capella (Alpha Aurigae), "she-goat." The name directly translates the Latin name for the pair, *Haedi*, from *haedus*, "young goat."

(1) Considering it grew toward the end of Autumne, and the starre named the Kids were risen [Philemon Holland, *The Roman Historie*, 1609].
  (2) Tempt not the winds forewarned of dangers nigh,
  When the Kids glitter in the western sky [Callimachus, *Anthologia*, 240 BC, quoted in Richard Hinckley Allen, *Star-Names and Their Meanings*, 1899].

**Little Bear, the** *Ursa Minor*. A translation of the Latin name of the small constellation. *Cp.* **Great Bear**.

**Little Dipper, the** *(prominent part of) Ursa Minor*. The popular, mainly American, name of the seven brightest stars in the constellation Ursa Minor, which have a shape similar to that of the **Big Dipper** or **Plough** in Ursa Major.

You all know the Dipper? Yes, it is in the Great Bear. The Little Dipper is in Ursa Minor [*Lowell* (Massachusetts) *Offering*, 1842].

**Lucifer** *Venus*. A poetic name for the planet as a **Morning Star**, the name being Latin for "bearer of light." The name can be compared to the biblical epithet "day star" for Christ, as in 1 Peter 1:19 ("A light that shineth in a dark place, until the day dawn, and the day star arise in your hearts"), translating Greek *Phosphoros* (*see* **Evening Star**), an exact equivalent of the Latin name.

> The stars with deep amaze
> Stand fixed in steadfast gaze,
> Bending one way their precious influence,
> And will not take their flight,
> For all the morning light,
> Or Lucifer that often warned them thence [John Milton, "On the Morning of Christ's Nativity," 1645].

**Luna** *Moon*. A poetic name adopted from Roman mythology, in which Luna (whose name is Latin for "moon") is a goddess of the moon. Her Greek equivalent is **Selene**.

> (1) *Dull*: What is Dictynna?
> *Holofernes*: A title to Phœbe, to Luna, to the moon [William Shakespeare, *Love's Labour's Lost*, 1598].
> (2) Back, with the conscious thrill of shame
> Which Luna felt, that summer night,
> Flash through her pure immortal frame,
> When she forsook the starry height
> To hang over Endymion's sleep [Matthew Arnold, "Isolation," 1857].

**Milky Way, the** *Galaxy*. A traditional name for the galaxy (star system) containing the Solar System. The name translates Latin *via lactea*, describing the appearance of the band of faint stars as a "milky way." The word "galaxy" shares the reference in its derivation from Greek *gala*, "milk."

> Methought I lay
> Watching the zenith, where the milky way
> Among the stars in virgin splendour pours [John Keats, *Endymion*, 1818].

**Morning Star, the** *(1) Mercury; (2) Venus*. The poetic name is normally applied to the planet Venus, when visible in the east before sunrise, but can sometimes apply similarly to Mercury. The name is also a biblical epithet for Christ, as in Revelation 22:16 ("I am the root and offspring of David, and the bright and morning star"), where it translates Greek *hō astēr hō prōinos* ("the star in the morning"). *Cp*. **Evening Star; Lucifer**.

> (1) As bright as doth the morning starre appeare
> Out of the East, with flaming locks bedight [i.e. arrayed],
> To tell that dawning day is drawing neare,
> And to the world does bring long wished light [Edmund Spenser, *The Faerie Queene*, 1590].
> (2) Now the bright morning-star, day's harbinger,
> Comes dancing from the east, and leads with her
> The flowery May [John Milton, "Song on May Morning," 1630].
> (3) Hast thou a charm to stay the morning-star
> In his steep course? [S.T. Coleridge, "Hymn before Sunrise, in the Vale of Chamouni," 1809].

**Mother Earth** *Earth*. A name for the earth (as world rather than planet) regarded as the mother of its inhabitants and productions. The name to some extent evolved from that of Terra Mater, the Roman mother goddess of the earth, corresponding to the Greek Ge (*see* **Gaia**). In recent times the title has become associated with mystic or New Age beliefs, and has all along evoked earth (soil) seen as a source of birth and growth and ultimately as a place of death and burial.

> (1) To My Mother: And To Earth, My Mother, Whom I Love [Michael Fairless (Margaret Fairless Barber), dedication, *The Roadmender*, 1902].
> (2) Before the Romans foisted their Straight Lines upon us, these [British] isles undulated with all that was the wonder of our Mother Earth [Julian Cope, *The Modern Antiquarian*, 1998].

**Northern Cross, the** *(prominent part of) Cygnus*. The name is popularly applied to the shape formed by the main stars of the constellation Cygnus. The top of the cross is marked by Deneb, and its foot by Albireo. The name is sometimes applied to the whole constellation, which is seen in the northern sky. *Cp*. **Southern Cross**.

**North Star** *see* **Pole Star**

**Old Sol** *Sun*. An affectionate name for the Sun, based on the classical **Sol**.

> Warm up to old Sol in latest Imax film [*Solarmax*] [Headline, *Post-Intelligencer* (Seattle), December 29, 2000].

**Oliver** *Moon*. A former personalization of the Moon, said to derive either from the name of Oliver Cromwell, leader of the Parliamentary forces during the English Civil War (1642–51), or from the letter "O" referring to its shape.

> "There's a moon out." "The better for us to pick 'em off, Dan," I returned, laughing at him.
> "What — Oliver? damn Oliver!" said Zacchary.
> "Let's push forward and come to quarters" [*New Review*, July 7, 1895].

**Phoebe** *Moon*. A poetic name adopted from classical mythology, in which Phoebe is another name of **Diana** as a goddess of the moon. (In astronomical nomenclature, Phoebe is the outermost satellite of Saturn.)

> To-morrow night, when Phœbe doth behold
> Her silver visage in the wat'ry glass,
> Decking with liquid pearl the bladed grass [William Shakespeare, *A Midsummer Night's Dream*, 1600].

**Phoebus** *Sun*. A poetic personification adopted from classical mythology, in which Phoebus is the Greek god of the sun, the equivalent of the Roman **Sol**. *See also* **Apollo**.

> (1) Hark! hark! the lark at heaven's gate sings,
> And Phoebus 'gins arise [William Shakespeare, *Cymbeline*, c.1609].

(2) Phœbus or Sol, or golden-hair'd Apollo,
Cynthian or Pythian, if thou dost follow
The fleeing night, oh, hear
Our hymn to thee, and willingly draw near!
[Michael Clarke, "The Story of Aeneas," 1898].

**Planet Earth** *Earth*. A byname for Earth as viewed in the context of the universe.

(1) Here men from the planet Earth first set foot upon the Moon, July 1969 AD. We came in peace for all mankind [Text of plaque left on Moon by Buzz Aldrin and Neil Armstrong, first astronauts there, July 20, 1969].

(2) I have never been keen on the "men are from Mars, women are from Venus" thesis ... For a start, you would hope that both hail from Planet Earth [Tim Hames in *The Times*, September 5, 2005].

**Plough, the** *(prominent part of) Ursa Major.* The popular, mainly British name (and spelling) of the seven brightest stars in the constellation Ursa Major, which form the shape of an old horse-drawn plow. *Cp.* **Big Dipper.**

**Pointers, the** *Dubhe and Merak.* A common designation for the two stars Alpha and Beta Ursae Majoris, which point toward the **Pole Star.**

**Pole Star, the** *Polaris.* A common name for the star in the constellation Ursa Minor, from its position near the north celestial pole. It is also known as the North (or Northern) Star.

**Pup, the** *Sirius B.* A popular name for the white-dwarf companion of Sirius, the **Dog Star.**

**Red Planet, the** *Mars.* The planet is popularly so known for its ruddy hue, caused by regions of reddish dust. (This strong red color, the color of blood, led to its being named for the Roman god of war.)

(1) *Mars.* The Red Planet salutes you. But you are a slow lot [*Punch*, January 4, 1873].

(2) The two Viking landers and their orbiters have spent much of the 15 months since the arrival on Mars snapping pictures of the Red Planet [*Time*, October 17, 1977].

(3) This summer, Nasa launched the *Mars Reconnaissance Orbiter* to make the trip to the Red Planet while the journey is shorter than usual [*The Times*, October 26, 2005].

**Selene** *Moon.* A poetic name adopted from Greek mythology, in which Selene (whose name is Greek for "moon") is a goddess of the moon. Her Roman equivalent is **Luna.**

Then, methinks, thou wouldst murmur, like thine own Simaetha, the love-lorn witch, "Farewell, Selene, bright and fair; farewell, ye other stars, that follow the wheels of the quiet Night" [Andrew Lang, *Letters to Dead Authors*, "To Theocritus," 1886].

**Seven Sisters, the** *Pleiades.* The star cluster in the constellation Taurus is popularly so named because at one time seven of its component stars could be seen with the unaided eye on a clear night. (Today six can be seen.) The stars are named after the Pleiads, the daughters of Atlas in classical mythology.

**Seven Stars, the** *Pleiades.* An alternate name for the **Seven Sisters.**

(1) Seek him that maketh the seven stars and Orion [Amos 5:8].

(2) *Fool*: The reason why the seven stars are no more than seven is a pretty reason.
*Lear*: Because they are not eight?
*Fool*: Yes, indeed: thou wouldst make a good fool [William Shakespeare, *King Lear*, 1608].

**Sol** *Sun.* A poetic personalization of the Sun, from the Latin word for it. In Roman mythology, Sol is the equivalent of the Greek god **Helios.** *See also* **Apollo; Phoebus.**

(1) And therefore is the glorious planet Sol
In noble eminence enthron'd and spher'd [William Shakespeare, *Troilus and Cressida*, 1609].

(2) Sol through white curtains shot a tim'rous ray,
And oped those eyes that must eclipse the day [Alexander Pope, *The Rape of the Lock*, 1714].

**Southern Cross, the** *Crux.* A popular name for the constellation, translating its Latin name and placing it in the southern sky. Its four brightest stars, Alpha, Beta, Gamma, and Delta Crucis, form a distinctive cross shape. (The fifth brightest, Eta, somewhat spoils the symmetry of the constellation.) *Cp.* **Northern Cross.**

**Spaceship Earth** *Earth.* A name representing the planet Earth and its inhabitants as a spaceship with its passengers, who depend for survival on its limited resources. The sobriquet was popularized by the author and work cited in quote (1) below.

(1) We have not been seeing our Spaceship Earth as an integrally-designed machine which to be persistently successful must be comprehended and serviced in total [R. Buckminster Fuller, *Operating Manual for Spaceship Earth*, 1969].

(2) What may happen between now and then is that the world will stop thinking in terms of superpowers and more in terms of Spaceship Earth [*Newsweek*, January 1, 1973].

**Third Rock from the Sun, the** *Earth.* A name for the third planet from the Sun, familiar as the title of a TV sci-fi series from 1996.

**Titan** *Sun.* In Greek mythology Titan, a descendant of Uranus and Gaea (*see* **Gaia**), was equated with **Hyperion,** the sun god, and in poetry thus also personifies the Sun.

Let Titan rise as early as he dare,
I'll through and through you! [William Shakespeare, *Troilus and Cressida*, 1609].

# Bibliography

*The list below represents the somewhat eclectic selection of titles that were used in preparing material for the present book. Some were consulted for examples of nicknames; others provided appropriate quotations.*

*Special mention should be made of the Kane and Alexander compilation, giving many hundreds of names in the United States, including 99 for New York City, from "America's Tourist Resort" to "The World's Most Exiting [sic] All Year Round Vacation Center." But only eight of these are glossed, and no explanation is provided for Big Apple or Empire City, for example. Colloquial or "folksy" forms are mostly absent, moreover, so that there is no Bama for Alabama and no Bal City or Balt (or Big B) for Baltimore, Maryland. The fact that there are around 360 examples of places named "Gateway" (to somewhere), and 284 dubbed "Home" (of someone or something), on the other hand, exemplifies the predominantly self-promotional or commercial nature of United States alternate names. The last entry in the book is "Wonderful Wyoming," which, while agreeably alliterative, is typical of the majority of names listed. (This is not to belittle the value of the work, but to show its distinctiveness from the present dictionary. Its chief value is in depicting the mostly conservative and "worthy" nature of American bynames.)*

*Where only part of a book's content is relevant to the subject, an indication is given in square brackets of the pertinent portion, as for the Fowler and Quinion titles.*

Aurousseau, Marcel. *The Rendering of Geographical Names*. London: Hutchinson University Library, 1957.

Ayto, John. *The Oxford Dictionary of Slang*. Oxford: Oxford University Press, 1998.

Ayto, John, and Ian Crofton, comps. *Brewer's Britain and Ireland*. London: Weidenfeld & Nicolson, 2005.

Booth, David, and David Perrott. *The Shell Book of the Islands of Britain*. London: Guideway, 1981.

Branford, Jean. *A Dictionary of South African English*. 3d ed. Cape Town: Oxford University Press, 1987.

Brewer, E. Cobham. *The Reader's Handbook*. London: Chatto & Windus, 1882.

Chapman, Robert L., ed. *New Dictionary of American Slang*. New York: Harper & Row, 1986.

Cohen, Saul B., ed. *The Columbia Gazetteer of the World*. New York: Columbia University Press, 1998. 3 vols.

*The Compact Oxford English Dictionary*. 2d ed. Oxford: Clarendon Press, 1991.

Cowan, Robert. *The Dictionary of Urbanism*. Tisbury: Streetwise Press, 2005.

Davidson, George, ed. *Roget's Thesaurus of English Words and Phrases*. London: Penguin Books, 2002

Davis, J. Madison, and A. Daniel Frankforter. *The Shakespeare Name Dictionary*. New York: Garland Publishing, 1995.

Delahunty, Andrew. *Oxford Dictionary of Nicknames*. Oxford: Oxford University Press, 2003.

Dickson, Paul. *What's in a Name?* Springfield, MA: Merriam-Webster, 1996.

Dodd, Philip, and Ben Donald. *The Book of Cities*. London: Pavilion Books, 2004.

Drabble, Margaret, ed. *The Oxford Companion to English Literature*. 6th ed. Oxford: Oxford University Press, 2000.

Fowler, H.W. *A Dictionary of Modern English Usage*. Oxford: Oxford University Press, 1926 [for article "Sobriquets," pp. 546–8].

Freedman, David Noel, ed.-in-chief. *Eerdman's Dictionary of the Bible*. Grand Rapids, MI/Cambridge, UK: Wm. B. Eerdmans, 2000.

Giles, Herbert A. *A Glossary of Reference on Subjects Connected with the Far East*. 3d ed. London: Curzon Press/Totowa, NJ: Rowman & Littlefield, 1974 [1900].

Green, Jonathon. *Cassell's Dictionary of Slang*. 2d ed. London: Weidenfeld & Nicolson, 2005.

Grose, Francis. *Dictionary of the Vulgar Tongue*. London: Bibliophile Books, 1984 [1811].

Hadfield, John, ed. *The Shell Book of English Villages*. London: Michael Joseph, 1980.

Hadfield, John, ed. *The New Shell Guide to England*. London: Book Club Associates, 1981.

Hargrave, Basil. *Origins and Meanings of Popular Phrases & Names*. London: T. Werner Laurie, 1925.

*Harrap "Pardon My French!" Pocket Slang Dictionary: English-French/French-English*. Edinburgh: Harrap, 1998.

Hendrickson, Robert. *The Facts on File Encyclopedia of Word and Phrase Origins.* 3d ed. New York: Facts on File, 2004.

Hogg, Garry. *The Shell Book of Exploring Britain.* London: John Baker, 1971.

Hook, J.N. *All Those Wonderful Names.* New York: John Wiley & Sons, 1991.

Hyamson, Albert M. *A Dictionary of English Phrases.* Detroit: Gale Research, 1970.

Jackson, Kenneth T., ed. *The Encyclopedia of New York City.* New Haven, CT: Yale University Press, 1995.

Johnson, S. *Where Is It?* Exeter: A. Wheaton & Co., 1948.

Jolly, Rick. *Jackspeak.* Torpoint: Palamanando Publishing, 2000.

Kane, Joseph Nathan, and Gerard L. Alexander. *Nicknames and Sobriquets of U.S. Cities, States, and Counties.* 3d ed. Lanham, MD: Scarecrow Press, 1979.

Killanin, Lord, and Michael V. Duignan. *The Shell Guide to Ireland.* London: Macmillan, 1989.

Latham, Edward. *A Dictionary of Names, Nicknames, and Surnames of Persons, Places, and Things.* London: George Routledge & Sons, 1904.

Leier, Manfred, pub. and ed. *100 Most Beautiful Cities of the World.* Hamburg: Rebo, 2004.

Lewin, Esther, and Albert E. Lewin. *The Thesaurus of Slang.* New York: Facts on File, 1994.

Macnie, Donald Lamond, and Moray McLaren, eds. *The New Shell Guide to Scotland.* London: Ebury Press/George Rainbird, 1977.

Marks, Georgette A., and Charles B. Johnson. *Harrap's Slang Dictionary: English-French/French-English.* Rev.and ed. by Jane Pratt. London: Harrap, 1984.

*Merriam-Webster's Geographical Dictionary.* 3d ed. Springfield, MA: Merriam-Webster, 1998.

Nash, Jay Robert. *Dictionary of Crime.* London: Headline, 1992.

Nelson, Derek. *Off the Map: The Curious Histories of Place-Names.* New York: Kodansha America, 1997.

*The New Encyclopædia Britannica.* 15th ed. Chicago: Encyclopædia Britannica, 2002.*

Newton, Norman. *The Shell Guide to the Islands of Britain.* Newton Abbot: David & Charles, 1992.

Orkin, Mark M. *Speaking Canadian English.* Toronto: General Publishing, 1970

Ousby, Ian. *Blue Guide Literary Britain and Ireland.* 2d ed. London: A & C Black, 1990.

Partridge, Eric. *A Dictionary of the Underworld, British and American.* New York: Bonanza Books, 1949.

Partridge, Eric. *A Dictionary of Slang and Unconventional English.* Ed. by Paul Beale. 8th ed. London: Routledge, 1984.

*Philip's Astronomy Encyclopedia.* Rev. ed. London: Philip's, 2002.

Pickering, David. *The Cassell Dictionary of Abbreviations.* London: Cassell, 1996.

Quinion, Michael. *Port Out, Starboard Home.* London: Penguin Books, 2004 [for articles on Big Apple, Dixie, Windy City].

*Reader's Digest Guide to Places of the World.* 2nd ed. London: Reader's Digest, 1995.**

*Reader's Digest Illustrated Guide to Britain's Coast.* London: Reader's Digest, 1996.**

*Reader's Digest Illustrated Guide to Ireland.* London: Reader's Digest, 2003.**

Ridpath, Ian, ed. *A Dictionary of Astronomy.* Oxford: Oxford University Press, 1997.

Robinson, Adrian, and Roy Millward. *The Shell Book of the British Coast.* Newton Abbot: David & Charles, 1983.

Shadbolt, Maurice, ed. *The Shell Guide to New Zealand.* London: Michael Joseph, 1969.

Shankle, George E. *State Names, Flags, Seals, Songs, Birds, Flowers and Other Symbols.* New York: H.H. Wilson Co., 1938.

Share, Bernard. *Naming Names: Who, What, Where in Irish Nomenclature.* Dublin: Gill & Macmillan, 2001.

Sharp, Harold S. *Handbook of Geographical Nicknames.* Lanham, MD: Scarecrow Press, 1980.

Shearer, Benjamin F., and Barbara S. Shearer. *State Names, Seals, Flags and Symbols.* Westport, CT: Greenwood Press, 1994.

Smith, Benjamin E., ed. *The Century Cyclopedia of Names.* London: The Times, 1904.

Smith, Eric. *A Dictionary of Classical Reference in English Poetry.* Cambridge: D.S. Brewer, 1984.

Smith, W.G. *The Oxford Dictionary of English Proverbs.* 3d ed. Revised by F.P. Wilson, with an introduction by Joanna Wilson. Oxford: Oxford University Press, 1970.

Speaight, George, ed. *The New Shell Guide to Britain.* London: Guild Publishing, 1985.

Tomakhin, G.D. *Amerika cherez amerikanizmy* (America through Americanisms). Moscow: Vysshaya shkola, 1982.

Urdang, Laurence. *A Dictionary of Names and Nicknames.* Rev. ed. Oxford: Oxford University Press, 1991.

Vaughan-Thomas, Wynford, and Alun Llewellyn. *The Shell Guide to Wales.* London: Michael Joseph, 1969.

Wagner, Leopold. *Names: And Their Meaning.* London: T. Fisher Unwin, 1892.

Wagner, Leopold. *More About Names.* London: T. Fisher Unwin, 1893.

Wheeler, William A. *A Dictionary of the Noted Names of Fiction.* London: George Bell & Sons, 1892.

*Where's Where: A Descriptive Gazetteer.* London: Eyre Methuen, 1974.

Weinreb, Ben, and Christopher Hibbert, eds. *The London Encyclopaedia.* Rev. ed. London: Macmillan, 1993.

Yapp, Peter, ed. *The Travellers' Dictionary of Quotation.* London: Routledge, 1988.

Young, Edward, ed. *The Shell Guide to France.* London: Michael Joseph, 1983.

*Quotes from this edition have the short title *Britannica*, with volume and page numbers. Quotes from earlier editions are identified as *Encyclopædia Britannica* with publication year.

**Quotes from these sources have titles abbreviated respectively as *RD Places of the World*, *RD Britain's Coast*, and *RD Ireland*.

# Index

*This Index gives the real names of places entered in the Dictionary (but not the Appendices). The geographical abbreviations used in the Index are prefaced below. In general, any place in a country is located by its country, as Cape Town SAF in South Africa, and every country is located by its continent, as Côte d'Ivoire AFR in Africa. Some of the island territories, especially when remote from their parent country, are located by ocean, as Easter Island PAC in the Pacific. Precise locations are given in the Dictionary entries.*

AFG Afghanistan
AFR Africa
ALB Albania
ALG Algeria
ANT Antarctica
ARC Arctic
ARG Argentina
ASI Asia
ATL Atlantic Ocean
AUS Australia
AUT Austria
AZE Azerbaijan
BAN Bangladesh
BEL Belgium
BEN Benin
BEZ Belize
BHU Bhutan
BOL Bolivia
BOS Bosnia-Hercegovina
BOT Botswana
BRA Brazil
BRU Brunei
BUF Burkina Faso
BUL Bulgaria
CAM Cambodia
CAN Canada
CEM Central America
CHA Channel Islands
CHI Chile
CHN China
CIV Côte d'Ivoire
COL Colombia
COM Comoros
CRO Croatia
CUB Cuba
CZR Czech Republic
DEN Denmark
DOM Dominican Republic
ECU Ecuador
EGY Egypt

ENG England
EQG Equatorial Guinea
ERI Eritrea
ETH Ethiopia
EUR Europe
FIN Finland
FRA France
GEO Georgia
GER Germany
GHA Ghana
GRE Greece
GUA Guatemala
GUI Guinea
HAI Haiti
HON Honduras
HUN Hungary
INA Indonesia
IND India
IRE Ireland
IRN Iran
IRQ Iraq
ISR Israel
ITA Italy
JAM Jamaica
JAP Japan
JOR Jordan
KEN Kenya
KIR Kiribati
LEB Lebanon
LIB Libya
MAC Macedonia
MAD Madagascar
MAL Mali
MAS Malaysia
MAU Mauritania
MEX Mexico
MIC Micronesia
MLT Malta
MNT Montenegro
MON Monaco

MOR Morocco
MOZ Mozambique
MWI Malawi
MYA Myanmar
NAM North America
NEP Nepal
NET Netherlands
NIC Nicaragua
NIG Nigeria
NIR Northern Ireland
NMB Namibia
NOR Norway
NZL New Zealand
OMA Oman
PAC Pacific Ocean
PAK Pakistan
PAL Palestine
PAN Panama
PER Peru
PHI Philippines
PNG Papua New Guinea
POL Poland
POR Portugal
ROM Romania
RUS Russia
SAF South Africa
SAM South America
SAR Saudi Arabia
SCO Scotland
SEN Senegal
SER Serbia
SEY Seychelles
SKO South Korea
SLO Slovakia
SOL Solomon Islands
SOM Somalia
SPA Spain
SRI Sri Lanka
SUD Sudan
SWE Sweden

SWI Switzerland
SYR Syria
TAI Taiwan
TAJ Tajikistan
TAN Tanzania
THA Thailand
TRI Trinidad and Tobago

TUN Tunisia
TUR Turkey
UAE United Arab Emirates
UKR Ukraine
URU Uruguay
USA United States of America
VEN Venezuela

VIE Vietnam
WAL Wales
WBK West Bank
WIN West Indies
YEM Yemen
ZIM Zimbabwe

Aachen GER: (1) Aix-la-Chapelle; (2) Rome of the West; (3) Seat of Royalty; (4) Watering Place of Kings
Aarhus DEN: World's Smallest Big City
Aba NIG: Taiwan of Nigeria
Abbeville FRA: Maiden Town
Abbeville USA: Birthplace of the Confederacy
Aberchirder SCO: Foggieloan
Aberdeen SCO: (1) Brave Toun; (2) City of Bon Accord; (3) Flower of Scotland; (4) Furry Boots City; (5) Granite City; (6) Silver City; (7) Silver City by the Sea
Abergavenny WAL: Gateway to Wales
Aberystwyth WAL: (1) Aber; (2) Biarritz of Wales; (3) Brighton of Wales
Abidjan CIV: (1) Manhattan of West Africa; (2) New York of the Tropics; (3) Paris of West Africa; (4) Pearl of the Lagoon
Abomey BEN: Royal City
Abingdon ENG: Oldest Inhabited Town in England
Abu Dhabi UAE: Garden City of the Gulf
Acapulco MEX: (1) Pearl of the Pacific; (2) Queen of the Mexican Riviera
Achicourt FRA: Agincourt
Acoma USA: Sky City
Acton ENG: W3
Addis Abeba ETH: Addis
Adelaide AUS: (1) City of Churches; (2) Farinaceous City; (3) Holy City; (4) Twenty-Minute City
Adrian USA: Maple City
Adriatic Sea EUR: Adria
Aegean Sea EUR/ASI: Archipelago
Aflenz Kurort AUT: Davos of Styria
Africa AFR: (1) Afric; (2) Bongo Bongo Land; (3) Dark Continent; (4) Wild Continent
Agde FRA: Black Town
Agny FRA: Agony

Ailsa Craig SCO: Paddy's Milestone
Aix-en-Provence FRA: City of a Thousand Fountains
Ajaccio FRA: Emperor's Cradle
Akron USA: Rubber City
Alabama USA: (1) Alabamy; (2) Bama; (3) Camellia State; (4) Cotton State; (5) Heart of Dixie; (6) Lizard State; (7) Yellowhammer State
Alaska USA: (1) Eskimo Pie Land; (2) Frozen Wilderness; (3) Great Land; (4) Land of the Midnight Sun; (5) Last Frontier; (6) Mainland State; (7) Russian America; (8) Seward's Folly; (9) Sourdough State; (10) Switzerland of America; (11) Uncle Sam's Attic; (12) Uncle Sam's Icebox; (13) Up Over
Albany USA: (1) Edinburgh of America; (2) Smallbany
Albuquerque USA: (1) Big A; (2) Kirk
Alcatraz USA: Rock
Aldershot ENG: (1) Home of the British Army; (2) Shot
Alentejo POR: Granary of Portugal
Aleutian Islands USA: Chain
Alexandra SAF: (1) Dark City; (2) Gomora
Alexandria EGY: (1) Alex; (2) Mother of Books
Algiers ALG: Argier
Alice Springs AUS: Alice
Allahabad IND: Holy City
Allentown USA: Mack City
Alma USA: Spinach Capital of the World
Alnwick ENG: Windsor of the North
Alps EUR: Holy Land of Mountain Adventure
Altoona USA: Mountain City
Amarillo USA: (1) Big A; (2) Cactus City
Amazon River SAM: (1) King of Waters; (2) Sweet Sea
Ambato ECU: Garden of Ecuador

Amesbury ENG: Almesbury
Amman JOR: City of Waters
Amsterdam NET: (1) 'Dam; (2) Diamond City; (3) Gay Capital of Europe; (4) Triple X; (5) Venice of the North
Anaconda USA: Copperopolis
Anadarko USA: Indian Capital of the Nation
Anchorage USA: (1) Chicago of the North; (2) Iceberg; (3) Los Anchorage
Andalusia SPA: (1) Garden of Spain; (2) Gold Purse of Spain; (3) Granary of Spain
Andersonstown NIR: Andytown
Andes SAM: Treasury of Peru
Angers FRA: (1) Black City; (2) City of Flowers; (3) Gateway to the Loire Valley
Angkor CAM: City of Gods
Anglesey WAL: (1) Anglesea; (2) Mona; (3) Mother of Wales
Annapolis USA: (1) Athens of America; (2) Crabtown; (3) Paris of America
Annapurna NEP: Sanctuary of the Gods
Anshan CHN: Capital of Steel
Anstruther SCO: (1) Anster; (2) Auld Ainster
Antakya TUR: Queen of the East
Antarctica ANT: (1) Blue Continent; (2) Frozen Continent; (3) White Continent
Antwerp BEL: Manhattan of the Middle Ages
Apennines ITA: Backbone of Italy
Apidanus GRE: Father of Rivers
Apulia ITA: (1) Granary of Italy; (2) Heel of Italy; (3) Kingdom of Drought and Stone
Arabia ASI: Araby
Aran Islands IRE: Next Parish to America
Araucania CHI: Grainery of Chile
Arbor Low ENG: Stonehenge of the North
Arbroath SCO: Aberbrothock
Arcadia GRE: Arcady

Basingstoke ENG: (1) Amazingstoke; (2) Dallas of South
England

Bastille, La FRA: Bastaga

Bath ENG: (1) Akemanchester;
(2) Bath; (3) City of Beauty;
(4) Queen City of the West

Bathurst AUS: (1) Plain City of
the Queans; (2) Queen City
of the Plains

Baton Rouge USA: BR Town

Battersea ENG: (1) South
Chelsea; (2) Swone One

Battignoles, les FRA: Badingues

Beauce FRA: Granary of France

Beaumaris WAL: Little London
beyond Wales

Beddgelert WAL: Gem of Welsh
Villages

Bedfordshire ENG: Beds

Bedford-Stuyvesant USA: Bed-
Stuy

Beijing CHN: (1) Celestial City;
(2) Forbidden City; (3) Peking

Beirut LEB: (1) Little Paris; (2)
Paris of the Middle East

Belarus EUR: White Russia

Belchertown USA: Burp

Belfast NIR: (1) Athens of Ireland; (2) Athens of the North;
(3) Irish Liverpool; (4) Linenopolis; (5) Northern Athens;
(6) Redbrick City; (7) Reindeerland

Belgium EUR: (1) Belgia; (2)
Biljam; (3) Cockpit of
Europe; (4) Crossroads of
Europe; (5) Garden of
Europe; (6) Noble Belgium

Belgravia ENG: (1) Asia Minor;
(2) Mesopotamia; (3) New
Jerusalem

Belize CEM: Land of the Free

Belzoni USA: Catfish Capital of
the World

Ben Loyal SCO: Queen of the
Scottish Peaks

Ben Nevis SCO: Monarch of
British Mountains

Berat ALB: Town of a Thousand
Eyes

Bergen NOR: (1) Brummagem;
(2) Gateway to the Fjords

Bering Sea RUSS/USA: Smoky
Sea

Berkeley USA: (1) Berzerkeley;
(2) People's Republic of
Berkeley

Berkshire ENG: (1) Berks; (2)
Royal Berkshire

Berlin GER: (1) Athens on the
Spree; (2) Big City; (3) City

of Intelligence; (4) Elektropolis; (5) Neulin

Bermondsey ENG: Berm-on-Sea

Bermuda ATL: (1) Bermoothes;
(2) Happy Island

Berwick-upon-Tweed ENG:
Second Alexandria

Bethlehem USA: (1) Steel City;
(2) Steeltown

Bethlehem WBK: (1) Bedlam;
(2) City of David

Beverly Hills USA: (1) BH; (2)
City of the Stars; (3)
Poshopolis

Bhutan ASI: Land of the Dragon

Big Bend USA: Irish City

Bijapur IND: Palmyra of the
Deccan

Bilbao SPA: Hole

Billericay ENG: Billy Ricky

Binghamton USA: Carrousel
Capital of the World

Bioko EQG: (1) Fernando Po;
(2) Madeira of the Gulf of
Guinea

Birkenhead ENG: One-Eyed
City

Birmingham ENG: (1) Big Heart
of England; (2) Brum; (3)
Capital of the Midlands; (4)
City of a Thousand Trades;
(5) City of Dreadful Knights;
(6) City of Entertainment; (7)
City on Seven Hills; (8)
Hardware Village; (9) Heart
of England; (10) Midland
Metropolis; (11) Second City;
(12) Second City of the
Empire; (13) Toyshop of
Europe; (14) Venice of the
North; (15) Workshop of the
World

Birmingham USA: (1) Bombingham; (2) Magic City; (3)
Pittsburgh of the South

Birr IRE: Navel of Ireland

Biscay, Bay of FRA/SPA: Bay

Blackpool ENG: Las Vegas of
the North

Black Sea EUR/ASI: (1) Euxine
Sea; (2) Pontic Sea

Blackwater River IRE: Irish
Rhine

Blaenau Ffestiniog WAL: Slate
Capital of Wales

Blekinge SWE: Garden of Sweden

Bletchley ENG: Fun City

Blindheim GER: Blenheim

Bloemfontein SAF: Bloem

Blois FRA: City of Kings

Bloomsbury ENG: WC1

Bob Marshall Wilderness Complex USA: Bob

Bodrum TUR: (1) Halicarnassus;
(2) St. Tropez of Turkey

Bogotá COL: (1) Athens of
America; (2) Athens of South
America

Boise USA: (1) Big Potato; (2)
Spud Town

Bolivia SAM: Switzerland of
South America

Bologna ITA: (1) Fat City; (2)
Red Bologna

Bondi AUS: County Bondi

Bootle ENG: Brutal Bootle

Bophuthatswana SAF: Bop

Borroloola AUS: Loo

Bosporus TUR: Bosphorus

Boston ENG: St. Botolph's
Town

Boston USA: (1) America's Liter-
ary Emporium; (2) America's
Walking City; (3) Athens of
America; (4) Bean Town; (5)
Bitches' Heaven; (6) Bristol of
America; (7) City of Kind
Hearts; (8) City of Notions;
(9) Cradle of Liberty; (10)
Highbrowville; (11) Hub; (12)
Modern Athens; (13) Pump-
kinshire; (14) Puritan City;
(15) Trimountain City

Botany Bay AUS: Bay

Boulogne FRA: Bolong

Bourke AUS: Gateway to the
Outback

Bournemouth ENG: (1) Bo-Mo;
(2) Britain's Coolest City; (3)
City of Pines; (4) English
Naples; (5) Queen of the
South Coast

Bourton-on-the-Water ENG:
Venice of the Cotswolds

Boys Town USA: City of Little
Men

Bradford ENG: Bradders

Brahmaputra River BAN:
Mighty Brahmaputra

Brasília BRA: (1) City of the
Future; (2) Moon's Backside

Braunschweig GER: Brunswick

Brazil SAM: Fleuron of the
Americas

Breathitt County USA: Bloody
Breathitt

Breconshire WAL: (1) Breakneckshire; (2) Brecknockshire

Breezewood USA: Motel City

Bremen GER: Rome of the North

Brewarrina AUS: Bree

Briançon FRA: Highest Town in
Europe

Bridgwater ENG: (1) Bilgewater; (2) Home of the Carnival

Bridlington ENG: Brid

Brighton ENG: (1) Belle of the South Coast; (2) City by the Sea; (3) Doctor Brighton; (4) Gay Capital of Britain; (5) Jerusalem-on-Sea; (6) London-by-the-Sea; (7) London-on-Sea; (8) London-super-Mare; (9) Queen of Watering Places

Brighton Beach USA: Little Odessa

Brisbane AUS: (1) Banana City; (2) Bris; (3) BrisVegas; (4) Brizzie

Bristol ENG: (1) Brizzie; (2) Treacle Town

Bristol Channel ENG/WAL: Severn Sea

Britain EUR: (1) Albion; (2) Britannia; (3) British Lion; (4) Britsville; (5) Cold Country; (6) Cool Britannia; (7) 51st State; (8) Fogland; (9) Gem of the Ocean; (10) Great Nation; (11) Home; (12) Home for Lost Frogs; (13) Isle of Honey; (14) John Bull; (15) Land of Hope and Glory; (16) Limeyland; (17) Mainland; (18) Mistress of the Seas; (19) Motherland; (20) Mother of Colonies; (21) Nation of Shopkeepers; (22) Old Country; (23) Old Dart; (24) Pomgolia; (25) Pommyland; (26) Sceptred Isle; (27) Sea-Girt Isle; (28) Tight Little Island; (29) Workshop of the World (*see also* England; United Kingdom)

British Columbia CAN: BC

British Empire: (1) Greater Britain; (2) Weary Titan

British Isles EUR: (1) Hibernian Archipelago; (2) These Islands

British Virgin Islands WIN: BVIs

Brittany FRA: (1) Armorica; (2) Little Britain

Brixton ENG: Greasepaint Avenue

Brno CZR: Austrian Leeds

Broadway ENG: Show Village of England

Broek NET: Cleanest City in the World

Broken Hill AUS: Silver City

Brooklyn USA: (1) City of Churches; (2) City of Homes;

(3) Crookland; (4) Dormitory of New York

Brooklyn Heights USA: Nation's First Commuter Suburb

Broughty Ferry SCO: Ferry

Bruce Peninsula CAN: Bruce

Bruges BEL: (1) Beautiful Bruges; (2) Jewel of Flanders; (3) Venice of the North

Brunei ASI: Shellfare State

Brussels BEL: (1) Boring Brussels; (2) Brothels; (3) Bru-Bru Land; (4) Little Paris; (5) Paris of the Belgians

Buchan SCO: Cold Shoulder of Scotland

Bucharest ROM: (1) Little Paris; (2) Paris of Eastern Europe; (3) Paris of the Balkans; (4) Paris of the East

Buckinghamshire ENG: (1) Beechy Bucks; (2) Bucks

Buda HUN: Key of Christendom

Budapest HUN: (1) Bangkok of Europe; (2) Most Beautiful City in Europe; (3) Paris of the East; (4) Queen of the Danube

Budva MNT: St. Tropez of the Adriatic

Buenos Aires ARG: (1) BA; (2) Baires; (3) Bs.As.; (4) Head of Goliath; (5) Paris of the South

Buffalo USA: (1) Buffer; (2) Miami of the North; (3) Queen City of the Lakes

Bulawayo ZIM: City of Kings

Bundaberg AUS: Bundie

Burbure FRA: Burberry

Burford ENG: Gateway to the Cotswolds

Burghead SCO: Broch

Burgundy FRA: Somerset with Vines

Burketown AUS: Barramundi Capital of Queensland

Burlington USA: Queen City of Vermont

Burslem ENG: Mother of the Potteries

Bury St Edmunds ENG: (1) Bury; (2) Cradle of the Law; (3) Montpellier of England; (4) St Edmundsbury

Butte USA: (1) Big Butte; (2) Brass; (3) Richest Hill on Earth

Buxton ENG: Bitter Buxton

Cadbury ENG: Camelot

Cádiz SPA: (1) Cadiz the Joyous; (2) Cales

Caerleon WAL: (1) Camelot; (2) City of Legions

Caernarfon WAL: Carnarvon

Cairo EGY: (1) City of Victory; (2) Mother of the World; (3) Old Home Town

Cairo USA: Little Egypt

Calabria ITA: Toe of Italy

Calgary CAN: Cow Town

California USA: (1) Bear Flag Republic; (2) Cal; (3) Cali; (4) Californ-i-ay; (5) Coast of Dreams; (6) El Dorado State; (7) Eureka State; (8) Golden State; (9) Grape State; (10) Land of Gold; (11) Land of the Golden Hills; (12) Land of the Sky; (13) Out-Yonder State; (14) Shakyside; (15) Sierra State; (16) Sunshine State; (17) Wine State

California, Gulf of USA: Vermilion Sea

Camagüey CUB: Texas of Cuba

Camberwell ENG: Bonkersville

Cambodia ASI: Kampuchea

Cambridge ENG: (1) Camcreek; (2) Cantab; (3) City of Perspiring Dreams; (4) Granta; (5) Other Place; (6) Silicon Fen

Cambridge NZL: Town of Trees

Cambridgeshire ENG: Cambs

Camden AUS: Birthplace of the Nation's Wealth

Camden Town ENG: NW1

Camelford ENG: Camelot

Campania ITA: Garden of Italy

Campbell River CAN: Salmon Capital of the World

Camp David USA: Shangri La

Cam River ENG: Granta

Canaan PAL: (1) Land of the Covenant; (2) Promised Land

Canada NAM: (1) Big Country; (2) Big Moose; (3) Canady; (4) Dominion; (5) Great Lone Land; (6) Great Weird North; (7) Great White North; (8) Land of the Little Sticks; (9) New France; (10) Our Lady of the Snows

Canary Islands ATL: (1) Fortunate Isles; (2) Hesperides

Canberra AUS: (1) Bush Capital; (2) Cluster of Suburbs in Search of a City

Canton USA: Fame Town

Cape Horn CHI: Cape Stiff

Cape May USA: President's Playground

Cape of Good Hope SAF: (1)